THE ROUTLEDGE INTERNATIONAL HANDBOOK OF YOUNG CHILDREN'S THINKING AND UNDERSTANDING

This ground-breaking handbook provides a much-needed, contemporary and authoritative reference text on young children's thinking. The different perspectives represented in the 39 chapters contribute to a vibrant picture of young children, their ways of thinking and their efforts at understanding, constructing and navigating the world.

The Routledge International Handbook of Young Children's Thinking and Understanding brings together commissioned pieces by a range of hand-picked influential, international authors from a variety of disciplines who share a high public profile for their specific developments in the theories of children's thinking, learning and understanding.

The handbook is organised into four complementary parts:

- How can we think about young children's thinking? Concepts and contexts
- Knowing about the brain and knowing about the mind
- Making sense of the world
- Documenting and developing children's thinking.

Supported throughout with relevant research and case studies, this handbook is an international insight into the many ways there are to understand children and childhood paired with the knowledge that young children have a strong, vital and creative ability to think and to understand, and to create and contend with the world around them.

Sue Robson is Principal Lecturer and Subject Leader for Early Childhood Studies at Froebel College, University of Roehampton, UK.

Suzanne Flannery Quinn is Senior Lecturer in Early Childhood Studies at Froebel College, University of Roehampton, UK.

The Routledge International Handbook Series

The Routledge International Handbook of the Arts and Education
Edited by Mike Fleming, John Toole and Loira Bresler

The Routledge International Handbook of English, Language and Literacy Teaching
Edited by Dominic Wyse, Richard Andrews and James Hoffman

The Routledge International Handbook of the Sociology of Education
Edited by Michael W. Apple, Stephen J. Ball and Luis Armand Gandin

The Routledge International Handbook of Higher Education
Edited by Malcolm Tight, Ka Ho Mok, Jeroen Huisman and Christopher C. Morpew

The Routledge International Companion to Multicultural Education
Edited by James A. Banks

The Routledge International Handbook of Creative Learning
Edited by Julian Sefton Green, Pat Thomson, Ken Jones and Liora Bresler

The Routledge International Handbook of Critical Education
Edited by Michael W. Apple, Wayne Au, and Luis Armando Gandin

The Routledge International Handbook of Lifelong Learning
Edited by Peter Jarvis

The Routledge International Handbook of Early Childhood Education
Edited by Tony Bertram, John Bennett, Philip Gammage and Christine Pascal

The Routledge International Handbook of Lifelong Learning
Edited by Peter Jarvis

The Routledge International Handbook of Teacher and School Development
Edited by Christopher Day

THE ROUTLEDGE INTERNATIONAL HANDBOOK OF YOUNG CHILDREN'S THINKING AND UNDERSTANDING

*Edited by Sue Robson and
Suzanne Flannery Quinn*

Routledge
Taylor & Francis Group

LONDON AND NEW YORK

KH

First published 2015
by Routledge
2 Park Square, Milton Park, Abingdon, Oxon OX14 4RN

and by Routledge
711 Third Avenue, New York, NY 10017

Routledge is an imprint of the Taylor & Francis Group, an informa business

© 2015 S. Robson and S. Flannery Quinn

British Library Cataloguing in Publication Data
A catalogue record for this book is available from the British Library

Library of Congress Cataloging-in-Publication Data
A catalog record for this book has been requested

ISBN: 978-0-415-81642-7 (hbk)
ISBN: 978-1-315-74604-3 (ebk)

Typeset in Bembo
by Cenveo Publisher Services

Printed and bound in the United States of America by
Edwards Brothers Malloy on sustainably sourced paper

9/30/15

CONTENTS

Contents

Contents

Contents

Contents

FIGURES AND TABLES

Figures

Tables

CONTRIBUTORS

Editors

Sue Robson is Principal Lecturer and Subject Leader for Early Childhood Studies at Froebel College, University of Roehampton, London, England. Her teaching and research interests are centred on young children's thinking, and include her work on the Froebel Research Fellowship project, 'The Voice of the Child: Ownership and Autonomy in Early Learning' (2002–15), and her doctoral study of young children's self-regulation and metacognition. She is interested particularly in young children's perspectives, and the development of innovative methodological approaches to support this. Sue has also conducted research on pedagogy in higher education, and is a National Teaching Fellow in England. Sue has published widely in journals and contributed to a number of books. She is the author of *Developing Thinking and Understanding in Young Children* (Routledge, 2012, 2nd edn) and co-author of *Young Children's Creative Thinking* (Sage, 2012) with Hiroko Fumoto, Sue Greenfield and David Hargreaves. Sue is currently conducting research on young children's well-being, in the 2013–2015 phase of the Froebel Research Fellowship project, and can be contacted on s.robson@roehampton.ac.uk.

Suzanne Flannery Quinn is Senior Lecturer in Early Childhood Studies at Froebel College, University of Roehampton, London, England. Suzanne's teaching and research projects are related to understanding sociocultural aspects of young children's experiences, particularly those that can be considered in relation to pedagogic practices of early years practitioners. Suzanne's interest in human memory is related to the temporal, spatial and social aspects of human collaborative thinking and valuing, and the tools of art, culture and communication that are used to support this kind of thinking with children. Current projects include the study of photography and pedagogical documentation techniques in early years education and teacher training, and the use of pedagogic documentation as a democratic space for thinking and remembering. Suzanne can be contacted on Suzanne.Quinn@roehampton.ac.uk.

Contributors

Cath Arnold is a parent of three children and currently grandparent of four children. She has worked with young children in private and public sector settings for the last 37 years. More recently, she has been working with adults, many of whom have been studying for an MA in Integrated Provision for Children and Families in the Early Years at the Pen Green Research Base in Corby, Northamptonshire, in England. Cath qualified as an early years teacher in 1992, gained a Masters degree in education in 1997 and a PhD in 2007. Her enduring interest has been and still is in how children learn, and most of her research has been concerned with understanding how young children learn. She has written three books on child development and learning and several articles and chapters.

Rehana Asani is a graduate student of the University of Cambridge in Psychology and Education. She has worked as a research associate at the Institute of Education, London, with Professor Iram Siraj. She has an MSc from the University of Oxford in Child Development and Education where she worked under the supervision of Professor Kathy Sylva. Rehana has also completed the Graduate Basis for Chartered Membership for the British Psychology Society (BPS).

Milda Brèdikytè is a senior researcher and lecturer at the Lithuanian University of Educational Sciences, Vilnius. She teaches courses on child development and narrative learning in play and Vygotskian theory of cultural development in childhood. She is the senior researcher in the Research Laboratory of Play (LUES) and the coordinator of research activities in the research project 'Development of Self-regulation in Play'. She worked at Kajaani University Consortium, University of Oulu, Finland, from 2002 to 2010. She has been responsible for the organisation of university courses and research activities at the research laboratory on children's play (Play Lab 'Silmu') since 2002. Her research interests include cultural development, the impact of creative activities on child development, and the role of imagination in play.

John T. Bruer has been president of the James S. McDonnell Foundation in St Louis, USA, since 1986. The Foundation's major programme interests have been in cognitive neuroscience and applications of cognitive science to education and rehabilitation. He is the author of *Schools for Thought: A Science of Learning in the Classroom* (MIT Press, 1993) and *The Myth of Birth to Three* (Free Press, 1999). His academic training was in the philosophy of science. Bruer is an Adjunct Professor of Philosophy at Washington University, St Louis, Missouri.

Jeremy I. M. Carpendale is Professor of Developmental Psychology in the Psychology Department at Simon Fraser University in British Columbia, Canada. His work focuses on the nature and development of thinking about social and moral matters and the role of language and social interaction in such development. He is author, with Charlie Lewis, of *How Children Develop Social Understanding* (Blackwell,

2006), and editor of several books including the *Cambridge Companion to Piaget* (Cambridge University Press, 2009).

Guy Claxton is Emeritus Professor of the Learning Sciences at the Centre for Real-World Learning, University of Winchester, England, and Visiting Professor of Education at King's College London. His research focus is on learnable intelligence: what it is, why it matters, and how to grow it. He is the author of many books including *Wise Up: The Challenge of Lifelong Learning* (Bloomsbury, 1999), *Hare Brain Tortoise Mind* (Fourth Estate, 1997), *The Wayward Mind* (Little, Brown, 2005), *Building Learning Power* (TLO, 2002), *What's the Point of School?* (Oneworld, 2008) and, with others, *The Learning Powered School* (TLO, 2011). With Bill Lucas he is author of *The Creative Thinking Plan* (Prentice Hall, 2007), *New Kinds of Smart: How the Science of Learnable Intelligence is Changing Education* (Open University Press, 2010), and *Expansive Education: Teaching Learners for the Real World* (Open University Press, 2013). His practical Building Learning Power approach to creating learning cultures in schools has influenced youngsters' lives throughout the UK as well as in, for example, Ireland, Poland, Switzerland, Dubai, Thailand, Argentina, Brazil, Australia and New Zealand. Guy has an MA in Natural Sciences from Cambridge and a DPhil in Cognitive Science from Oxford. He is a Fellow of the British Psychological Society and the Royal Society of Arts, and an Academician of the Academy of the Social Sciences.

Jennifer M. Clegg is a PhD student at the University of Texas at Austin. She graduated from Emory University in 2011 with a BA in Psychology and Linguistics and a minor in Italian language. Jennifer's research interests include cognitive development, cross-cultural models of early childhood education, and the development of pro-social behaviour.

Douglas H. Clements is the Kennedy Endowed Chair in Early Childhood Learning and Professor at the University of Denver, Colorado, USA. Doug has published over 125 refereed research studies, 18 books, 80 chapters, and 300 additional publications on the learning and teaching of early mathematics; computer applications; creating, using and evaluating research-based curricula; and taking interventions to scale, mostly with colleague and wife Julie Sarama. He served on the US President's National Mathematics Advisory Panel, the Common Core State Standards committee, and the National Research Council's Committee on early mathematics, and is co-author of each of their reports. See http://du.academia.edu/DouglasClements and http://www.researchgate.net/profile/Douglas_Clements/

Andrew Coates is a part-time lecturer at the University of Warwick, England, where he supervises research dissertations for students on the BA (Hons) degree in Early Childhood Education Studies. He is a practising artist and a member of the Royal Birmingham Society of Artists (RBSA), sometime Head of Art and Director of the Performing and Visual Arts course at Westhill College, Birmingham, and adviser for the visual arts at the School of Continuing Studies at the University of Birmingham.

Together with Elizabeth Coates he has been involved since September 2003 in an action research project which focuses upon young children, aged between 3 and 7 years, talking and drawing together. The data collected has resulted in a number of publications, conference papers and exhibitions, and work at present is examining the nature of young children's scribbling. Recent one-person exhibitions include in 2008, 'A Response to Primitivism – Particularly in Relation to the Drawings of Young Children' at the Alexandra Gallery, University of Cumbria, Lancaster, and in 2007, 'Children Also Have Artistic Ability and There is Wisdom in Their Having It (Paul Klee, 1912): An Exhibition of Constructions and Constructed Collages Informed by the Drawings of Young Children', at the Royal Birmingham Society of Artists Gallery, Birmingham, England.

Elizabeth Coates was an associate professor and Director of the Early Childhood Studies undergraduate programme at the University of Warwick, England. Since her retirement in 2013 she has been teaching part-time at the university on courses that include child development, education, and early years' policy and practice. During her time at Warwick she organised and directed five triennial international early years conferences and was founding editor of the *International Journal of Early Years Education*. Her background as an early years teacher has been a strong influence and, with Andrew Coates, she is involved in a longitudinal action research project focusing on young children (3 to 7 years) talking and drawing together. This has resulted in a number of conference papers and publications which include, among others, 'The Subjects and Meanings of Young Children's Drawings' in Dorothy Faulkner and Elizabeth Coates (eds) (2011) *Exploring Children's Creative Narratives* (Routledge, 2011).

Penny Coltman gained extensive experience working in both pre-school and Key Stage One settings in Essex, England. She now lectures in early mathematics and science in the University of Cambridge Faculty of Education. Penny has worked with several major publishers on an extensive range of curriculum materials. Her research interests include the development of mathematical metalanguage in young children, and self-regulation in relation to the early years, including the extent to which encouraging classroom talk can support self-regulated learning. Penny shares the role of coordinator of the East Anglian regional Cambridge Primary Review Trust Network.

Chelsea A. Cornelius is a doctoral candidate in the Department of Psychology at the University of Texas at Austin, where she received her BA in Psychology in 2006. Her research interests lie in the area of supernatural reasoning. During her time in graduate school, she has pursued studies on children's belief in a just world, the development of the use of luck as an explanatory concept, and individual differences in tolerance of uncertainty.

Anna Craft was, until her untimely death in August 2014, Professor of Education at Exeter University and the Open University researching creativity, the arts and learning futures. *Possibility Thinking* is one of several studies which Anna directed. It explores the heart of creativity, particularly, although not exclusively, with young children; to this she added concerns for how childhood is changing, and she explored the ends to which creativity is put, developing the notion of 'wise creativity'. She was Principal Investigator at the Open University and Exeter University respectively for two studies funded by the European Union, 'C2Learn' and 'CREAT-IT', each exploring how Possibility Thinking can fuel empowered childhoods. She was Principal Investigator at the Open University of a further European project, 'Creative Little Scientists' (completed March 2014), researching creativity in early science and mathematics. Anna wrote and edited over 20 books, the most recent being *Creativity and Education Futures* (Trentham Books, 2011). She was founding co-editor of the journal *Thinking Skills and Creativity*, and founding co-convenor of *British Educational Research Association Special Interest Group, Creativity in Education*. Alongside her university appointments she was Research Director of the Cambridge Primary Review Trust.

Stephanie M. Curenton, is an author, professor, and researcher, at Rutgers University, USA. She has published textbooks for teachers and practitioners that focus on cultural competence in classroom instruction and family engagement. She has also published numerous research articles about the social, cognitive, language and literacy development of low-income, ethnically and language diverse children. She serves as the associate editor for *Early Childhood Research Quarterly*, and was a former associate and guest editor of *Early Education and Development*. Her research has been funded by the US Department of Health and Human Services, the Office of Program Research and Evaluation, the National Academy of Science, Ford Predoctoral Fellowship, American Education Research Association, and the Foundation for Child Development. She received a national fellowship from the Society for Research on Child Development/American Association for the Advancement of Science Policy Fellowship that enabled her to work as a research policy fellow in the Office of Child Care in the Administration for Children and Families. She has served on the governing board of the National Association for the Education of Young Children (NAEYC). She earned her PhD in Developmental and Community Psychology from the University of Virginia.

Dario Cvencek is a research scientist at the University of Washington Institute for Learning & Brain Sciences, USA. His research focuses on the developmental origins of social cognition and its links to education. In his work, Dr Cvencek addresses stereotypes, attitudes, intergroup relations and school readiness from a developmental perspective using implicit and explicit measures with preschool (and older) children.

Keryn Davis is a senior researcher at CORE Education in Christchurch, New Zealand. She has been a teacher, professional development facilitator, teacher educator, writer and consultant. Her interests include collaborative practitioner research and change, assessment, and supporting children's working theories. Keryn has worked collaboratively with practitioners, early childhood and primary school advisors and academics promoting cross-sector relationships and understandings for the past 15 years. Her email is keryn.davis@core-ed.ac.nz.

Sheila Degotardi is a senior lecturer in early childhood at the Institute of Early Childhood, Macquarie University, Australia. Her research falls into two connecting themes: the first is an interest in infant-toddler pedagogy, curriculum and development, and the second involves exploring the quality and implications of interpersonal relationships and relatedness in early childhood settings. With Emma Pearson, Sheila is co-author of *The Relationship Worlds of Infants and Toddlers: Multiple Perspectives from Early Years Theory and Practice* (Open University Press, 2014).

Jonathan Delafield-Butt is a lecturer in Early Years at the University of Strathclyde, Scotland. His work examines the origins of conscious experience and the embodied and emotional foundations of psychological development for learning and health. He began work with a PhD in the neurobiology of brain development at the University of Edinburgh before extending to psychobiological development of perception and movement, especially in social interaction in infancy, at Edinburgh and Copenhagen Universities. Philosophical implications have been developed at Harvard University and at the Institute for Advanced Studies in the Humanities at Edinburgh University. He trained in psychoanalytic psychotherapy at the Scottish Institute for Human Relations and is a member of the World Association for Infant Mental Health.

Darlene DeMarie is an associate professor of Educational Psychology and the Fulbright Faculty Advisor at the University of South Florida. She has been conducting autophotography research internationally since the late 1990s. Additional research interests and publications are in the area of children's memory strategies and the relation between children's working memory and their academic achievement. From 2007 to 2009 she was a Fulbright Scholar for lecturing/research in South Africa. During that time, she co-created the University of Limpopo's Child Development Centre for children aged from 2 to 6.

Carl Gabbard is Professor and Director of Motor Development Studies in the Motor Neuroscience Division, Department of Health & Kinesiology at Texas A&M University. He is a Fellow in the National Academy of Kinesiology and his primary research interest is the planning of motor actions in children.

Nicole Gardner-Neblett, PhD, is an Investigator at the FPG Child Development Institute and Research Assistant Professor in the Department of Psychology at the University of North Carolina at Chapel Hill. Dr Gardner-Neblett's work at FPG focuses on investigating factors that promote children's language and communication development. This focus includes examining the design and implementation of professional development programmes for teachers on promoting young children's language and communication development. She led the creation of *More Than Baby Talk*, a guide for early childhood professionals on key practices to promote language and communication skills among infants and toddlers. In addition, Dr Gardner-Neblett studies the oral narrative skills of African American children in relation to children's reading development. Before joining FPG, Gardner-Neblett worked as a Society for Research in Child Development Policy Fellow at the US Department of Health and Human Services in the Office of the Assistant Secretary for Planning and Evaluation, where she designed and monitored research and evaluation projects aimed at promoting child well-being. Dr Gardner-Neblett holds a PhD and MA in Developmental Psychology from the University of Michigan and a ScB in Psychology from Brown University.

Pentti Hakkarainen is Professor (Emeritus) at the University of Oulu, Finland, and Professor of Psychology at the Lithuanian University of Educational Sciences, Vilnius. He is head of the Research Laboratory of Play (LUES) and the scientific leader of the research project 'Development of Self-regulation in Play'. He reads courses on qualitative research methods and cultural historical psychology for MA students. Since 1997 he has been Professor of Early Education at Kajaani University Consortium, University of Oulu. He has taught early education, developmental teaching and research methodology. He runs the research programme, 'Meaningful learning in narrative environments' and an experimental programme of school transition. He is the editor of the *Journal of Russian and East European Psychology*. His research interests include creative, developmental teaching and learning in preschools, schools and higher education, narrative learning and development in play and virtual environments.

Joanna Haynes is Associate Professor in Education Studies at Plymouth University, England. She is author of *Children as Philosophers* (Routledge, 2002, 2008), which has been translated into several languages. She is co-author, with Karin Murris, of *Picturebooks, Pedagogy and Philosophy* (Routledge, 2012). Joanna has been involved in writing, presenting, teaching and leading courses in the field of philosophy with children since 1994. Her main research interests are in the ethics of classroom interaction and in critical and transformative pedagogies.

Maria Hjalmarsson is Senior Lecturer in Educational Work at Karlstad University, Sweden. She is a former leisure-time pedagogue and her research focuses on the tasks and work of teachers. Recent publications deal with aspects of governance and voluntariness for children in leisure-time centres as well as how male primary school teachers view and relate to other people's expectations of them as teachers.

Beatriz Ilari is Assistant Professor of Music Education at USC (University of Southern California) Thornton School of Music. Prior to her appointment at USC, she served as Associate Professor of Music Education at the Federal University of Paraná in Brazil (2003–10). Her main research interests lie in the intersection between music, childhood, cognition and culture. She is currently a research fellow at USC's Brain and Creativity Institute, and a co-investigator on the Advancing Interdisciplinary Research in Singing initiative (AIRS).

Vickii B. Jenvey has worked at the University of Melbourne and most recently as a senior research fellow at Monash University in Melbourne, Australia. She has published widely and received grants for research on children's play, nutrition and aspects of social and cognitive development of typically developing children and children with disabilities. Some of her recent publications discuss the nature of poverty and its multiple affects on children's growth and development and family functioning.

Alina Konradt has an educational background in child development and linguistics, and commences her PhD programme this year at University College London, UK. Alina's research interests lie within children's bilingual syntactic representation with a particular focus on the processes that underlie mapping of conceptual information onto syntactic structure during early language production. Alina's current project aims to examine the effects of bilingual acquisition on the mechanisms that govern these processes at the discourse-syntax interface. Alina is also involved in child language data collection for the Slavic Languages Corpora in collaboration with St Petersburg Institute for Linguistic Studies, Russian Academy of Sciences.

Shirley Larkin is a senior lecturer in the Graduate School of Education, University of Exeter, England. She has a background in English Literature and Psychology. Since 1999 she has researched metacognition in young children. She worked with Philip Adey and Michael Shayer on the metacognitive aspects of their Cognitive Acceleration programmes before moving to Exeter where she has researched metacognition and learning to write and metacognition in primary Religious Education classes. She is the author of *Metacognition in Young Children* (Routledge, 2010) and has written a number of book chapters and journal articles on developing metacognition across the primary curriculum.

Cristine H. Legare is an associate professor in the Department of Psychology at the University of Texas at Austin. Her training and research reflect her commitment to interdisciplinary approaches to research on learning and reasoning in childhood. She studies the intersection of several topics in the field of cognitive development, including causal learning, the development of scientific reasoning, and science education.

Rosemary Lever began her interest in children's early language development as part of Dr Carole Peterson's research lab at Memorial University in Newfoundland. She then continued her research during her Masters thesis under the supervision of Monique Sénéchal at Carleton University, Ottawa, Canada. Her thesis and ensuing research included an intervention study designed to enhance the storytelling of children at risk of academic difficulties. She is now part of a research team at Simon Fraser University conducting a five-year scientific evaluation of a province-wide prevention programme in British Columbia involving at-risk new mothers and children.

Charlie Lewis is Professor of Family and Developmental Psychology at Lancaster University in the UK. He has written or edited 15 books and scores of papers and book chapters. His work on family relationships examines the roles of parents (particularly fathers but also other family members) in children's development.

Increasingly his research has focused upon how young children, and latterly infants, develop fundamental skills, including number, a control over their actions and an understanding of the social world.

Triin Liin works as a lecturer in Cognitive and School Psychology at the Department of Psychology at the University of Tartu, Estonia. She is the current head of the department as well as the manager of the Psychology Masters programme. She has worked both as a school psychologist and career counsellor and is the current head of the Estonian school-psychologist qualification committee. Her main research topics involve school psychology, cognitive development and concept formation.

Annica Löfdahl is Professor in Educational Work at Karlstad University, Sweden. She is a former preschool teacher and her research focuses are preschool, children's play and peer culture as well as changing teacher professionalism in neo-liberal times. Recent publications deal with diversity in preschool, peer culture and play, teachers' work and performativity in Early Childhood Education.

Jenna McLain is a first-year doctoral student in Educational Psychology at the University of South Florida. She is developing research interests in the areas of social and emotional development and early childhood. Previous research experiences included involvement with Head Start and the development of social and emotional interventions.

Danielle L. Mead is a doctoral student of applied developmental psychology at George Mason University in Fairfax, Virginia, USA. Her research examines the nature and function of private speech, including crib speech, and its relation to self-regulation and play. Her interests also include narrative storytelling, bilingual language development, and kindergarten retention. She is an instructor at George Mason University, the managing editor for the journal *Early Childhood Research Quarterly*, and an ad hoc reviewer. For more information, please email dmead@gmu.edu.

Andrew N. Meltzoff is the Co-Director of the University of Washington Institute for Learning & Brain Sciences and holds the Job and Gertrud Tamaki Endowed Chair. His work addresses the development of social cognition in children, and the links between developmental science, education and neuroscience. Dr Meltzoff is a Fellow of the American Academy of Arts & Sciences, the American Association for the Advancement of Science, the Norwegian Academy of Science and Letters, and is a recipient of a MERIT Award from the National Institute of Health for outstanding research. His email is Meltzoff@uw.edu.

Laura Mockensturm is a second-year undergraduate student at the University of South Florida where she is working towards a double major in Statistics and Psychology as well as a minor in Educational Foundations and Research. In addition to the undergraduate research that she began as a freshman, Laura is also involved in USF's Honors College.

Emma Newton is a clinical psychologist specialising in developmental clinical psychology. Presently she is a senior clinician working with children, adolescents and families within the public mental health service in Melbourne, Australia. She has conducted research with preschool children and adolescents examining factors such as play, theory of mind, emotion recognition and temperament and the associations with social functioning and mental health problems.

Courtenay Frazier Norbury is a professor in the Psychology Department at Royal Holloway, University of London. She worked as a speech-language therapist before completing her DPhil in Experimental Psychology at Oxford University. Her research centres on the nature of language impairment in developmental disorders, most notably specific language impairment and autism spectrum disorder. She leads the Surrey Communication and Language in Education Study (SCALES), the first UK population study of risk for language impairment at school entry, funded by the Wellcome Trust.

Sally Peters is an associate professor at the University of Waikato, Hamilton, New Zealand, and an associate director of the university's Early Years Research Centre. Sally has a background in early years education and a particular interest in young children's learning and development. This broad interest includes several main research threads, including transitions, working theories and key competencies. Sally has been involved in a range of research projects, all of which involved working collaboratively with teachers.

Deborah Pino-Pasternak is a lecturer at the School of Education, Murdoch University in Western Australia. Her research focuses on the development of self-regulatory skills in young children and how those are affected by interactions with significant adults such as parents and teachers.

Ingrid Pramling Samuelsson is Professor of Early Childhood Education at the Department of Education, Communication and Learning at the University of Gothenburg, Sweden. She has a UNESCO Chair in ECE and Sustainable Development and for two periods (2008–13) was the world president of OMEP (Organisation Mondiale pour l'Èducation Préscolaire). Her main research field is young children's learning and curriculum questions in early years education. Her email is ingrid. pramling@ped.gu.se.

Niklas Pramling is Professor of Education at the Department of Education, Communication and Learning at the University of Gothenburg, Sweden. He is a member of LinCS (the Linnaeus Centre for Research on Learning, Interaction and Mediated Communication in Contemporary Society), a Swedish national centre of excellence for research on learning and new technologies, funded by the Swedish Research Council. His research is focused on teacher-child communication and children's learning in the arts. His email is niklas.pramling@ped.gu.se.

Kimberly Raymond is a doctoral candidate in the Department of Child and Family Studies at Syracuse University, USA. Her research interests include the area of child social withdrawal, as well as the influence of social, emotional and cognitive development on child social functioning and peer interactions.

Rachel Razza is an assistant professor in the Department of Child and Family Studies at Syracuse University, USA. The primary focus of her scholarly work is children's self-regulation. Specifically, her research explores associations among different facets of self-regulation, contextual predictors of self-regulation, and implications of various self-regulatory skills for children's school readiness and later school success. She is particularly interested in specifying these pathways among disadvantaged children, as these children are at heightened risk for self-regulatory deficits. In addition, her recent work examines mindfulness-based practice (e.g. breathing, yoga) as an intervention strategy to enhance self-regulation among young children.

Kathy Ring is a senior lecturer in Early Years Education at York St John University, England. Kathy has worked extensively with local authorities and early years practitioners developing young children's use of drawing as a tool for meaning making. With Angela Anning she co-authored *Making Sense of Children's Drawings* (Oxford University Press, 2003), translated into several languages, and she contributed to *Mark Making Matters* (DCSF, 2008). Her current research focus is on how practitioners create opportunities for skill development across the multi-modality of children's engagement with their worlds.

Rosemary Roberts works to support the development of resilient wellbeing through companionable learning. She has worked in nursery, primary and higher education, and in the voluntary sector; and was a founder director of Parents Early Education Partnership (PEEP) in the UK, working with Sure Start programmes in disadvantaged areas. She holds a postgraduate diploma from the Tavistock Clinic UK in Psychoanalytic Observational Studies, and a PhD for which she researched well-being development from birth to three in the home. In 2011 to 2012 she worked on various early years projects in Australia. She has written two books: *Self Esteem and Early Learning* (Sage, 3rd edn 2006) and *Wellbeing from Birth* (Sage, 2010).

Sue Rogers is Professor of Early Years Education at the Institute of Education, London. Her research interests include play, curriculum and pedagogy in early childhood, young children's perspectives and child–adult interaction. She has published widely in the field of early childhood education, including three books: *Inside Role Play in Early Childhood Education: Researching Children's Perspectives* (Routledge, 2008, with Julie Evans), an edited collection on play pedagogy entitled *Rethinking Play and Pedagogy: Concepts, Contexts and Cultures* (Routledge, 2011) and *Adult Roles in the Early Years* (Open University Press, 2012, with Janet Rose).

Roger Säljö is Professor of Psychology of Education at the University of Gothenburg, Sweden. He specialises in research on learning, interaction and human development in a sociocultural perspective. Much of his work is related to issues of how people learn to use cultural tools and how we acquire competences and skills that are foundational to learning in a socially and technologically complex society. In recent years, he has worked extensively with issues that concern how digital technologies transform human learning practices inside and outside formal schooling. He is Director of the Linnaeus Centre for Research on Learning, Interaction and Mediated Communication in Contemporary Society (LinCS), a national centre of excellence funded by the Swedish Research Council.

Julie Sarama is Kennedy Endowed Chair in Innovative Learning Technologies and Professor at the University of Denver, Colorado, USA. She has taught high school mathematics and computer science, gifted, and early mathematics. She directs six projects funded by the National Science Foundation and the Institute of Education Sciences and has authored over 50 refereed articles, four books, 30 chapters and 20 computer programs, many with husband and colleague Doug Clements. Her research interests include children's development of mathematical concepts and competencies, implementation and scale-up of educational interventions, professional development models' influence on student learning, and implementation and effects of software environments. See http://portfolio.du.edu/jsarama.

Monique Sénéchal is a Professor of Psychology at Carleton University, Ottawa, Canada, and director of the Child Language and Literacy Research Laboratory. Along with colleagues and students, she studies how children learn vocabulary and early literacy from naturally occurring events in their homes. She also examines how children learn to read and spell in different languages, with particular interest in the French language. The nature of her research depends on the questions asked: exploratory questions are addressed with descriptive studies; component skills questions as well as interrelation questions are examined with correlational designs; and more causal questions are typically answered with intervention studies.

Iram Siraj is Professor of Education at the Institute of Education, University of London and the University of Wollongong, Faculty of Social Science, in Australia. Iram's recent research projects have included leading on the Evaluation of the Foundation Phase across Wales and she is a principal investigator of the major DfE 17-year study on Effective Pre-school, Primary and Secondary Education (EPPSE 3-16, 1997–2014) and of the influential Researching Effective Pedagogy in the Early Years project (REPEY). She has always been particularly interested in undertaking research that investigates disadvantage and to give children and families from these backgrounds an equal start. She is a specialist early years advisor to governments and ministers in the UK and overseas and has advised UNESCO, World Bank and UNICEF. She is currently specialist advisor to the House of Commons Select Committee on Education and undertaking reviews for the Welsh and Scottish governments. Her most recent publications include co-author of *Effective Teachers in*

Primary Schools: Key Research on Pedagogy and Children's Learning (forthcoming 2015); *Social Class and Educational Inequality: The Impact of Parents and Schools* (Cambridge University Press, 2014, with A. Mayo); *Effective and Caring Leadership in the Early Years* (Sage, 2014, with E. Hallet); *Major Work International Reader: Early Childhood Education* (4 vols, Sage, 2012, with A. Mayo).

Alison Sparks is a research associate in the Psychology Department at Amherst College. Dr Sparks received her doctorate in developmental psychology from Clark University and is also a certified speech language pathologist. Her research explores the social origins of early language and literacy learning in children from diverse cultural and linguistic backgrounds. Dr Sparks has conducted research with families from diverse ethnic backgrounds in the United States and in Latin America, using parent–child storytelling and shared book reading as a context for understanding children's early cognitive-linguistic development.

Christine Stephen is a research fellow in the School of Education, University of Stirling, Scotland. The focus of her research and writing is children's learning in the early years and the ways in which this is supported in preschool settings and at home. She has co-directed three Economic and Social Research Council-funded projects which have examined young children's learning with technologies at home and in preschool and led a number of studies examining the experiences of children as they move from preschool to Primary 1. Her interest in pedagogy includes studying the challenges of learning in Gaelic-immersion preschool settings and the learning opportunities offered to children younger than three years old.

Colleen Stevenson is an associate professor of Psychology at Muskingum University, Ohio, USA. She also is the Faculty Administrator for the Muskingum University Center for Child Development. Her research interests include metacognitive and language development in early childhood.

Colwyn Trevarthen is Professor (Emeritus) of Child Psychology and Psychobiology at the University of Edinburgh, Scotland. He has studied development of the brain and body, and infant and child communication, learning and emotional health, especially infants' motives for creative play and shared learning, as well as the effects of disorders of development and stressful early childhood. Recently, with musician Stephen Malloch, he has written on how rhythms and expressions of Communicative Musicality in movement share emotions, build relationships, and help learning of language and other cultural skills.

Cecilia Wallerstedt is an associate professor in Education at the University of Gothenburg, Sweden. She has a PhD in research on arts education from the Academy of Music and Drama at the University of Gothenburg. She is a member of the Swedish national centre of excellence for research on learning and new technologies (LinCS), funded by the Swedish Research Council. She currently conducts her postdoctoral research on how new technologies transform music learning inside and outside school. She has worked in several research projects on children's learning in the arts (music, dance and poetry). Her email is cecilia.wallerstedt@gu.se.

David Whitebread is a senior lecturer in the Faculty of Education, University of Cambridge. He is a developmental psychologist and early years education specialist (having previously taught children in the 4 to 8 age range for 12 years). His research interests are concerned with children's development and implications for early years and primary education. He is currently directing research projects investigating the role of play in children's development of metacognition and self-regulation and their impact upon children's learning. His publications include *Teaching and Learning in the Early Years* (3rd edn, Routledge, 2008) and *Developmental Psychology and Early Childhood Education* (Sage, 2012).

Adam Winsler is Professor of Applied Developmental Psychology at George Mason University in Fairfax, Virginia, USA. His research, represented in over 80 publications, examines private speech (self-talk) and its role in behavioural self-regulation and executive function among typically developing children as well as children with ADHD or autism. He also studies early childhood programmes, school readiness, kindergarten retention and bilingual language development among low-income, ethnically diverse, immigrant children. He is author of the popular book, *Scaffolding Children's Learning: Vygotsky and Early Childhood Education* (Berk & Winsler, 1995). His latest book (Cambridge University Press, 2009) is entitled *Private Speech, Executive Functioning, and the Development of Verbal Self-regulation*. He is editor-in-chief of the journal *Early Childhood Research Quarterly* (ECRQ), served previously as associate editor of *Early Education and Development*, is on the editorial board for *Early Education and Development* and *Social Development*, and he is a regular ad hoc reviewer for many other journals. For more information see http://winslerlab.gmu.edu or email awinsler@gmu.edu.

Elizabeth Wood is Professor of Education at the University of Sheffield, England, and Director for Research in the School of Education. She specialises in early childhood and primary education, and has conducted research into teachers' professional knowledge and beliefs; progression and continuity; gender and underachievement; play and pedagogy; children's choices during free play; critical perspectives on early childhood policy and practice. Elizabeth has an international reputation for her research on play and pedagogy. Her research with Dr Dylan Yamada-Rice explores the ways in which children blend traditional and digital forms of play. Their project, funded by the Arts and Humanities Research Council, focuses on Videogames and Play for Hospitalised Children, and brings together hospital play specialists, videogames developers, artists and academics to explore the potential for supporting children's freely chosen play in hospital and recovery spaces.

Jacqueline D. Woolley is a Professor of Psychology at the University of Texas at Austin. She received her BS in Psychology from Carnegie Mellon University and her PhD in Developmental Psychology from the University of Michigan. She is a Fellow of the Association for Psychological Science and serves on the editorial boards of the *Journal of Cognitive Development* and the *Journal of Cognition and Culture*. Dr Woolley's research addresses how children assign reality status when they encounter novel information. She investigates the effects of three broad classes of factors: (1) characteristics of the individual *child* that may affect judgements regarding reality status, (2) characteristics of the *stimulus* that may affect judgements about reality status, and (3) effects of the *environment* or social setting on children's decisions.

ACKNOWLEDGEMENTS

This book would not have been possible without the committed contributions of many people. First, we wish to wholeheartedly thank the authors of all of the chapters. Their enthusiastic and positive responses to our invitations to contribute a chapter confirmed for us the potential value of a volume such as this. Throughout the process of writing, they have been supportive and encouraging. The result is a collection from academics and professionals who are leaders in their fields, and we are enormously proud that they all said 'yes'. For all, our invitation placed more pressure on already overcrowded workloads, and for many of them it was at times a considerable personal and professional challenge, and we are very grateful to every one of them. We particularly wish to acknowledge a huge debt to Anna Craft, who was determined to contribute her chapter whilst undergoing treatment for the cancer which unfortunately took her life in August 2014. She will be greatly missed, by family, friends and colleagues. We also wish to acknowledge the valuable contribution of a number of colleagues who acted as reviewers for individual chapters. They are: Sigrid Brogaard-Clausen, Darlene DeMarie, Hiroko Fumoto, Sue Gifford, Sofia Guimarães, Sally Howe, Samantha King, Maria Kambouri, Lucy Parker, Jessica Pitt, Helen Tovey and Carrie Winstanley. Finally, but by no means least important, we both wish to thank our families. Sue's grateful appreciation, love and thanks to Ken, Charlotte and Isabella for their support and encouragement can never be expressed enough. Suzanne is grateful for the support of her family: Suzanne, Charles, Ian, Shannon, Nathan, and Siobhan – especially for the months of conversations we have all enjoyed about thinking and remembering.

INTRODUCTION

The opportunity to look closely at young children's thinking and understanding is a sheer pleasure and a privilege. This handbook brings together researchers, theorists and practitioners from around the world, in an effort to represent some facets of that pleasure, and to provide a picture of current ideas and understandings. The handbook reflects the multi-disciplinary, multi-professional nature of work with and for young children. Authors here span (and cross) many disciplines and fields of study. All of them have their own histories, traditions and conventions, reflected in different ways of writing and talking about young children, and often different views about how young children's thinking develops and can be supported. The chapters collected here also represent a variety of different ways of thinking about thinking, reflecting the different interests and disciplines of the contributing authors. Some chapters report on research, others focus on reviews of extant literature, or engage in more theoretical analysis. In addition, the extent to which authors relate their ideas to how adults might support young children's thinking varies. What each chapter has in common is a focus on young people, from birth onwards, to about eight years of age, the period of life generally seen as 'early childhood'.

While there are some very distinct and different traditions represented here, there are also some important similarities that characterise the book as a whole, and these constitute a number of principal themes that run throughout the handbook. These include a view of children as both competent and skilful, a belief in the integrity of childhood as a time in its own right, and a sociocultural perspective on thinking that emphasises its development and display in social contexts.

First, and most importantly, is a view of young children as competent and skilful, with sophisticated capabilities as thinkers: 'rich in potential, strong, powerful, competent' (Malaguzzi, 1993: 10). While such a perspective may have its strongest roots in the sociology of childhood movement, much research (including that documented in this book) reflects a range of disciplinary perspectives that consider even the very youngest children as capable constructors and creators of and within the world around them. This world involves an interconnected ecology of social relations as well as a terrain of objects (both natural and human-made) and ideas which are manipulated and used by all those, children and adults, who inhabit and navigate it together. Given the variability of the terrain, and the complexity of thinking as a tool for both construction and navigation of the world, this text intentionally incorporates multiple disciplinary and cross-disciplinary perspectives, which are characteristic of the field of early childhood studies. Authors here present often different ways of thinking about children's thinking and understanding, but each begins with the conviction, characteristic of the field as a whole, that young children have a strong, vital and creative ability to think and to understand, and to create and contend with the world around them.

Second, the work documented here reflects a view of the integrity of early childhood, as a time with its own rights and needs, rather than as merely a time of preparation for later life. Under the aegis of 'a positive agenda for rights in early childhood', the United Nations asserts that 'children, including the very youngest children, (should) be respected as persons in their own right' (United Nations, 2005: Section 5), and seen as social actors from the beginning of life. This rights-based perspective is based on the ethical stance that children are people who are young, and that being a young person is accorded with a sense of respect and understanding of youth. Such a perspective views children as neither objects of amusement, nor as (potential) social capital. The authors here put forward ideas about children's thinking and understanding that foreground a respect for the experiences and abilities of young people who are creating and navigating the world now.

At the same time, we are mindful of Kalliala's (2014) injunction that the idea of the child as 'competent social actor' should not be elevated to an 'ideal', if all it does is lead us to replace an old paradigm of the child as a 'fragile novice' (Sommer, 1999, cited in Kalliala, 2014: 4) with a new one, that of the child as resilient and *un*needful. This leads us to the third theme: that is, that children's development, and thus their thinking and understanding, occur within social contexts, in which all protagonists (children and adults) are interdependent, and dependent upon one another. This has a number of consequences. First, that much thinking, by both adults and children, is collective. Littleton and Mercer (2013) describe the process of thinking creatively and productively together as 'interthinking', which occurs, for Rogoff, in a process of 'guided participation in social activity with companions who support and stretch children's understanding of and skill in using the tools of a culture' (Rogoff, 1990: vii).

Such ideas owe much to the sociocultural perspective outlined first by Vygotsky (1978) and built upon by many writers and researchers since. A second consequence is that different social and cultural contexts will engender different and diverse ways of developing, dependent upon what is needed and valued (and thought about) within those contexts. As Hedegaard (2009) suggests, young children will be interacting with multiple cultural and social groups, experiencing continuously evolving cultural practices. A third consequence concerns the roles of adults, and the integral part they play in recognising, supporting and enabling children's thinking in these varied contexts.

In collating this handbook, we have tried to organise all the chapters into a meaning-ful whole. Each chapter, of course, has its own merits, and can be read independently of any other. However, influenced by Bruner's (1991) view of narrative as a sense-making act, we have attempted to create a series of narratives in the four parts here, with, we hope, chapters following one another in a way that enhances both under-standing and enjoyment. Our choices are, though, our own, influenced by our own individual and collective thinking, and ways of making sense. They also changed often as the book progressed, and new chapters arrived, and each reader will create their own 'combinatorial flexibility' (Bruner *et al.*, 1976), taking ideas and information from chapters and putting them together in many different ways.

The handbook is organised in four complementary parts. In Part I, 'How can we think about young children's thinking? Concepts and contexts', the emphasis is on ideas and theories that we believe are fundamental to an understanding of the field. Reflecting the sociocultural theme of the handbook as a whole, chapters here look at children as social beings from birth onwards, and consider how they construct and negotiate the world as thinking beings with the tools of theorising, creativity, play, talking, questioning and wondering. This part also provides an opportunity to look afresh at some of the principal theorists, including Piaget and Vygotsky, and their continuing influence on theory, research and practice in the twenty-first century.

In Part II, 'Knowing about the brain and knowing about the mind', the emphasis is on both what babies and young children know about their own and others' minds, as well as what adults know about them. Current interest in young children's knowl-edge about the mind is reflected in very lively research agendas in all aspects. Carlson (2011), for example, identifies a five-fold increase in journal articles about executive function in childhood over the past ten years. With this heightened interest, we are keenly aware of the caution that is needed as we explore children's thinking. This section of the handbook includes contemporary thinking on a range of intercon-nected ideas that help us to gain a broader awareness of what is (possibly) happening when young people are thinking. The authors here recognise different ways of thinking, and take critical stances on issues which, in some instances, have become fragile discourses, such as 'school readiness' and the idea of 'critical periods'.

In Part III, 'Making sense of the world', authors focus on young children's efforts to make sense of their worlds, both in general, through the development of concepts and 'working theories' (Ministry of Education, New Zealand, 1996), and in some particular contexts, including astronomy, music and mathematics, technology, mark-making and narrative. Building on ideas first encountered in Part I, chapters here attest to the vital importance of play, particularly pretend play, and narrative of all kinds in supporting and extending young children's thinking.

The final part of the handbook, 'Documenting and developing children's think-ing', considers some of the different ways in which we may potentially observe and document young children's thinking and understanding, and on the roles of adults and more experienced peers in their support and development. Throughout the handbook, the importance of hearing young children's own voices, and their thoughts about their experiences, has been emphasised. This theme, along with a number of others that run throughout the book, is returned to here. Authors provide crucial reminders of the agency and capability of young children, the significance of play and narrative, and of the interrelationships between children's cognitive, social and emotional lives.

The different perspectives represented in the 39 chapters here contribute to a vibrant picture of young children, their ways of thinking and their efforts at understanding, constructing, and navigating their worlds. As befits an International Handbook such as this, authors come from around the world. We have tried to honour these different traditions and ways of writing about their work. Accordingly, the reader will find chapters that are structured very differently, as well as written in both 'English' and 'American' English. These multiple diversities contribute to the richness of the book. There are many ways to understand children and childhood (Dahlberg *et al.*, 2007): we hope that the chapters here contribute to such understanding in readers.

References

Bruner, J. (1991) The narrative construction of reality, *Critical Inquiry*, 18(1), 1–21.

Bruner, J. S., Jolly, A. and Sylva, K. (1976) *Play: Its Role in Development and Evolution.* Harmondsworth, Penguin.

Carlson, S. M. (2011) Editorial: Introduction to the special issue: Executive function, *Journal of Experimental Child Psychology*, 108, 411–13.

Dahlberg, G., Moss, P. and Pence, A. (2007) *Beyond Quality in Early Childhood Education and Care,* 2nd edn. London: Routledge.

Hedegaard, M. (2009) Children's development from a cultural-historical approach: Children's activity in everyday local settings as foundation for their development, *Mind, Culture and Activity*, 16, 64–81.

Kalliala, M. (2014) Toddlers as both more and less competent social actors in Finnish day care centres, *Early Years*, 34(1), 4–17.

Littleton, K. and Mercer, N. (2013) *Interthinking: Putting Talk to Work.* Abingdon, Oxon: Routledge.

Malaguzzi, L. (1993) For an education based on relationships. *Young Children*, 49(1), 9–13.

Ministry of Education, New Zealand (1996) *Te Whāriki: He whāriki mā tauranga mōngā mokopuna o Aotearoa. Early Childhood Curriculum.* Wellington, New Zealand: Learning Media.

Rogoff, B. (1990) *Apprenticeship in Thinking: Cognitive Development in Social Context.* New York: Oxford University Press.

United Nations Committee on the Rights of the Child (2005) *General Comment No. 7.* Available at: www.unicef-irc.org/portfolios/general_comments/GC7.Rev.1_en.doc.html (accessed 15/01/2006).

Vygotsky, L. S. (1978) *Mind in Society.* Cambridge, MA: Harvard University Press.

PART I

How can we think about young children's thinking? Concepts and contexts

1

THE INFANT'S CREATIVE VITALITY, IN PROJECTS OF SELF-DISCOVERY AND SHARED MEANING

How they anticipate school, and make it fruitful

Colwyn Trevarthen and Jonathan Delafield-Butt

Introduction

This chapter presents the child as a creature born with the spirit of an inquisitive and creative human being, seeking understanding of what to do with body and mind in a world of invented possibilities. He or she is intuitively sociable, seeking affectionate relations with companions who are willing to share the pleasure and adventure of doing and knowing with 'human sense'. Recent research traces signs of the child's impulses and feelings from before birth, and follows their efforts to master experience through stages of self-creating in enjoyable and hopeful companionship. Sensitive timing of rhythms in action and playful invention show age-related advances of creative vitality as the body and brain grow. Much of shared meaning is understood and played with before a child can benefit from school instruction in a prescribed curriculum of the proper ways to use elaborate symbolic conventions. We begin with the theory of James Mark Baldwin, who observed that infants and young children are instinctive experimenters, repeating experience by imitating their own as well as others' actions, accommodating to the resources of the shared world and assimilating new experiences as learned ideas for action. We develop a theory of the child's contribution to cultural learning that may be used to guide practice in early education and care of children in their families and communities and in artificially planned and technically structured modern worlds of bewildering diversity.

3

Cycles in moving and learning of the human spirit

In 1894 Baldwin published his seminal thesis on psychological development of the infant. He studied the motor development of children to discover the origin of intelligence, and his attention was attracted to the repetition of actions, most obvious at first in limb movements of the young infant, but true of all the infant's actions, including looking movements of the head and eyes, touching with the hands, and vocalising. He termed this tendency for moving and sensing to repeat itself the 'circular reaction':

> the self-repeating or 'circular' reaction … is seen to be fundamental and to remain the same, as far as structure is concerned, for all motor activity whatever: the only difference between higher and lower function being, that in the higher, certain accumulated adaptations have in time so come to overlie the original reaction, that the conscious state which accompanies it seems to differ *per se* from the crude imitative consciousness in which it had its beginning.
>
> (Baldwin, 1894, p. 23)

Baldwin claimed that the tendency for an action to be repeated expresses an invariant principle of organisation within human psychological development, which persists in behaviours at every degree of complexity. Baldwin's circular reactions were the forerunner of Jean Piaget's sensorimotor and cognitive 'schemas' (Piaget, 1962). Both conceived the developing mind as generated in embodied movement. Higher mental functions emerge as abstractions from earlier sensorimotor experience, and are therefore structured by the same principles. Repetition observed in early motor action in infancy, develops into repetition in complex and abstract cognitive thought process in later childhood and adult life. The invariant feature is the tendency for an act, in real movement or in thought, to repeat itself, and for the plan of successfully accomplished acts to be retained and developed through further repetition with variation.

The idea has become a core principle of preschool education theory, originating from the understanding of early childhood gained by the revolutionary educators Comenius, Pestalozzi and Froebel (Athey, 1990; Bruce, 2012). But attention only to object use is insufficient to understand the way a young child learns meanings in human company (Donaldson, 1978). A young child's action is to be understood in the context of innate capacities for signalling intentions, feelings and experiences to communicate about a shared world, first with parents and family, and then with assistance from companions and teachers in an expanding community (Whalley *et al.*, 2007). The circular reactions of intelligence must be expectant of experiences in relationships, with different degrees of intimacy and reliability.

Baldwin was aware that social collaboration in the making of shared meaning needs circular reactions between the intentions of individuals. He observed the growth of the young child's self-awareness in engagement with other persons, and their readiness to learn from individuals by attending to the different purposes of their actions. He saw that the principles of repetition in action – 'accommodation' to new circumstances in awareness enabling creative novelty, and 'assimilation' of successful experience to guide further actions – also regulate and elaborate social habits. He was as interested in changing sociological theory as in advancing developmental psychology in a science of the 'child and the race'. These ideas influenced George Herbert Mead's sociological theory of the development of a social 'Me' (Mead, 1934) and Jerome Bruner's psychological theory of development within 'the culture of education' (Bruner, 1996). We are built from the start to be attuned social creatures seeking engagement with initiatives and knowledge of other humans. That is how all our cultural habits and achievements are made (Trevarthen and Delafield-Butt, 2013; Trevarthen *et al.*, 2014).

The innate rhythms of experience in the time of action

The existence of a 'motor image' formed in the mind, one that anticipates and organises bio-mechanical effects of moving, in the body and in engagement with objects, was firmly established in the 1920s by a young Russian neurophysiologist, Nikolai Bernstein (1967), who used examination of film to accurately trace the regulation of forces in the moving body of a tool-user, a runner, or a child learning to walk. He analysed how the many motor components of any body action are assembled by the dynamic *motor image* formed in the brain into a coherent, intended movement, which is highly efficient, wasting almost no energy. Bernstein noted that well-done movements are always rhythmic, smoothing out the irregular inertial forces they master through planned steps of time. This power of the brain to integrate its activities in coherent rhythmic patterns is recognised in the philosophy of phenomenology, which admits that motility and consciousness express the brain-generated 'subjective' time of intentional doing and thinking (Merleau-Ponty, 1962; Goodrich, 2010). We share an inborn sense of time, and this makes shared doing and thinking or shared meaning possible (Trevarthen and Delafield-Butt, 2013).

The developmental psychobiology of sensorimotor learning

Two lines of research in the last four decades have brought new evidence confirming the generative power of human motives and their timing in self-discovery, and in regulation of relationships.

Careful attention with the aid of film and video recording technology to the capacities and needs of newborns, including those born up to three months before term, has brought to light an intelligence that is expressive in human ways and highly sensitive to the pulse and qualities of human expression, and their tendency to compose narrations (Trevarthen, 2011a). Developments of sensorimotor intelligence in the first three months lead the infant to be a skilled performer in a 'musicality' of companionship with a willing partner (Malloch, 1999; Malloch and Trevarthen, 2009). In every human community babies three to four months old begin to enjoy participating in the rituals of traditional action games or baby songs

(Trevarthen, 1999, 2006, 2008; Gratier and Trevarthen, 2008; Ekerdal and Merker, 2009) (see Figure 1.4).

Newborn infants less than a week old respond to the expressions of other persons and use the imitated actions to establish a dialogue of purposes and experiences (Nagy, 2011). However, in spite of controlled studies by Maratos, Meltzoff, Heimann and others that prove the infants can imitate, this is a highly controversial area of research, because the findings contradict long-held beliefs and rational arguments that an infant can have no intentional self that is conscious of an outside reality for weeks or months after birth, and no ability to perceive the actions of another person as like those of a self (Kugiumtzakis and Trevarthen, 2014).

Detailed study of videos of interactions with full-term and premature infants in the first days after birth shows a baby can focus attention and imitate movements of head, eyes, and mouth, with parts of their own body they cannot see, and even try to imitate simple sequences of vocal utterances (Figure 1.1). Emese Nagy with Peter Molnár (2004) made an important modification of the testing procedure by waiting for a few seconds after the newborn infant has imitated her, which evokes a repetition of the imitated act by the baby as a 'provocation' for a response from the adult. Concurrent recording of heart rate changes showed that while 'imitation' is associated with effort signalled by heartbeat acceleration, 'provocation' is accompanied by a slowing of the heart, indicative of focused attention for a response.

Imitations of a newborn infant are the product of nine months of development in brain and body. Research tracing the first stages of the conception of a human being reveals a time-regulated process of collaboration between living elements (Delafield-Butt and Trevarthen, 2013).

The human foetus at eight weeks has distinctive body form with adaptations of hands, hearing organs, eyes, mouth and vocal organs that show anticipation of a life in conversation (Trevarthen, 2001). At this stage the subcortical brain, that will be the integrator of intrinsic motives for sensory-motor functions of the whole, and for emotional appraisal of objects of action is forming in close relation to the systems that regulate hormonal functions of the vital self:

> The first integrative pathways of the brain are in the core of the brain stem and midbrain, and the earliest whole body movements, though undifferentiated in their goals, are coherent and rhythmic in time. When sensory input develops, there is evidence, not just of reflex *response* to stimuli, but of the *intrinsic generation of prospective control* of more individuated actions, before the neocortex is functional. In the third trimester of gestation, when the cerebral neocortex is beginning formation of functional networks, movements show guidance by touch, by taste and by responses to the sounds of the mother's voice, with learning.
>
> *(Delafield-Butt and Trevarthen, 2013, p. 205)*

The origin of the mental life of a child is identified at this time, at 50 days' gestational age, as the integrated neuromotor system enacts the first spontaneous circular reactions of the organism (Delafield-Butt and Gangopadhyay, 2013). Movies made

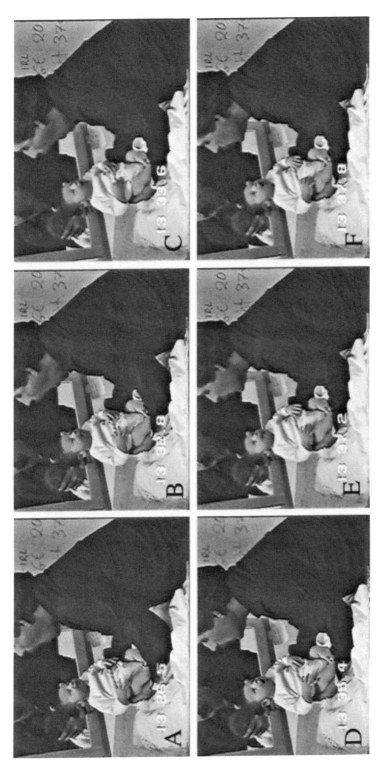

Figure 1.1 A cycle of imitations of Mouth Opening with a female infant 20 minutes after birth. Recorded at a maternity hospital in Herakleion, Crete in 1983 by Giannis Kugiumutzakis for his PhD research at the University of Uppsala (Kugiumutzakis and Trevarthen, 2014). A (0 sec.) The researcher presents a wide open mouth for the first time to the attentive infant, focusing on his mouth, and with slightly closed eyes and pursed mouth. B (6.3 sec.) The researcher opens his mouth for the first time to the attentive infant, focusing on his mouth with evident interest. The right hand moves up. C (11.1 sec.) The researcher opens his mouth for the fourth time. The neonate continues to observe his mouth with evident interest. The right hand moves right hand closes. D (12.9 sec.) The researcher opens his mouth for the fifth time. The neonate imitates him once, synchronously while watching his mouth. The The infant is still looking at his eyes. F (15.3 sec.) The infant imitates a second time, looking up at the researcher's eyes as he waits. E (14.7 sec.) Both pause, waiting. The infant is still looking at his eyes. F (15.3 sec.) The infant makes a third large imitation while looking at the researcher's mouth.

7

by ultrasound, which enable sight of the foetus alive in the mother's body and the measurement of activities, confirm that from mid-gestation limb movements of the foetus are purposefully guided, anticipating sensory feedback, and experimenting with it. These self-regulating movements not only show differences of vitality that identify different foetuses as more or less animated personalities, even in 'identical' twins (Piontelli, 2010). They also reveal a special sensibility for the presence of an 'other', reaching and touching with special care towards a twin. Facial expressions show that the foetuses have emotions of pleasure in appreciation of 'good' tastes or physical sensations, and of anxiety or disgust for 'bad' experiences. Hearing develops in the last months and the mother's distinctive voice is recognised by the newborn to identify her as a preferred partner. This helps the baby learn her face in the first days.

New brain science of shared intentions

Perceiving the intentions in others' actions is now shown to be mediated directly by neural resonance, or 'mirroring' (Gallese *et al.*, 1996), but the process is not an automatic reflection: it requires persons to receive and take up one another's purposes. It demonstrates reciprocal inter-subjective and sympathetic engagement with mutual accommodation of actions and emotions (Ammaniti and Gallese, 2014). This is how experiences of the world can be assimilated into a common 'human sense' of meanings (Donaldson, 1978). Mutual learning by accommodation, and the playful assimilation of rhythmic game routines, are enacted in facial expressions and vocal utterances, and in the 'vitality dynamics' or 'musicality' of repetitive actions of the whole body (Malloch and Trevarthen, 2009; Stern, 2010; Trevarthen and Delafield-Butt, 2013).

Humberto Maturana has called the spontaneous need of a human organism to move in creative, expectant ways that express ideas of being in the world 'languaging' (Maturana *et al.*, 1995). The reactions of a newborn to affectionate and playful attentions of a companion indicate that there is a specific readiness for languaging in movements that have the power to 'make sense' for others, without words. We can see this in a picture of a newborn engaging with attentive others with the emphasised expressions in attitude and gestures of an orator, or critic (Figure 1.2). The cerebral hemispheres develop complementary ways of taking care of inner life functions with the help of maternal care, and seeking adventures in discovery of the resources of an external world (Trevarthen, 2001; Trevarthen *et al.*, 2006). This is shown by the ways a newborn baby's hands move. Commonly the right hand projects outward 'declarative' gestures while the left is more directed to the body.

Emergence of learning in companionship

Infants are born at a fragile stage of life when the body is adapting to a new world and brain is growing rapidly (Nagy, 2011). They need support, protection and nourishment and are adapted to stimulate a mother's care. A mother who is

Figure 1.2 A 4-day-old girl intently regards her grandmother, who is speaking to her, using an expressive body, with an attentive mouth and asymmetric hand gestures, 'languaging'.

emotionally depressed, anxious and inattentive to her infant will have difficulty holding her baby's attention, and the baby may be avoidant and even become depressed as well. Crucial help can come from others who offer care, and the baby will respond (Narvaez *et al.*, 2012). We know that the quality of early care matters for future self-confidence and learning, and the infant has ways of expression that reinforces an affectionate personal relationship. In 'bonds' of mutual trust with favoured companions, shared repertoires of expressive tricks and exchanges of feeling are discovered that nourish the infant's vitality and imagination (Stern, 1995, 2000; Trevarthen, 2009, 2012a, 2013a).

The intensity of interest and the delicacy of response of young babies to persons who speak to them reinforces an affectionate personal relationship, which has great importance in the baby's wellbeing and mental development. In the 'bond' that develops between them, infant and favourite companion cultivate this shared repertoire of expressive tricks and exchanges of feeling.

Microanalysis of ordinary face-to-face play between parents and young babies confirms a precise *timing* in the way they address one another and reply. The infant stimulates an adult to use a gentle and questioning *infant directed speech*, 'motherese' or 'baby talk', that has a regular beat and characteristic expressions of mood in its changing intonation, rhythm, and in the accompaniment of movements of head, eyebrows, eyes, and hands. The infant listens and watches the affectionate and playful display intently, and then makes a reply – on the beat, with a smile, and with head and body movements, cooing, hand movements, and lip-and-tongue movements of *pre-speech*. The attempts at vocal expression are synchronised with delicate hand gestures, as in adult conversation. In collaboration with the parent, infants make rudimentary 'utterances' that form *phrases* of two or three seconds, and that are organised in *narratives* of expressed excitement with characteristic phases of 'introduction', 'development', 'climax', and 'resolution', typically lasting around 30 seconds. The enjoyment parent and child have in extended 'protoconversations' demonstrates a state of 'primary intersubjectivity' or dynamic interpersonal awareness that allows mutual regulation of feelings and motives (Trevarthen and Delafield-Butt, 2013) (Figure 1.3).

Analysis of vocal exchanges in protoconversation by acoustic techniques shows that the timing, rhythms, pitch modulations and quality of sound expressions constitute a 'communicative musicality' (Malloch, 1999; Malloch and Trevarthen, 2009), and tests of young infants' preferences and capacities to discriminate sounds show that they hear musical melodies, harmonies, rhythms, and accents, in both vocal and instrumental sound. These sensibilities are particularly adapted to hear the melody of emotions and states of animation in the human voice, especially the mother's.

How games with mother lead to sharing of tasks, tools and words, artefacts of a 'proto-habitus'

In 1974, Penelope Hubley, in PhD research at Edinburgh University, made an observation that led to new understanding of how shared understanding of using and naming objects begins. She was studying films of communication between an infant girl, Tracy, and her mother from three weeks after birth (Trevarthen and Hubley, 1978). She observed a first protoconversation at four weeks, and paid particular attention to the development of play from three months when the baby began to use her hands for grasping and manipulating objects. After five months games developed as her mother teased Tracy's interests in entertaining ways. The teasing became reciprocated, Tracy acting in provocative uncompliant ways for fun. This is how infants get to know minds better (Reddy, 2008). They played 'person-person' games with one another's movements, of face, hands and voice, then after seven months games were played with objects that the mother moved to attract Tracy's interest and participation. Tracy practised 'secondary circular reactions', shaking and banging objects she was holding, and she watched when her mother joined the rhythmic game with her expressions. The object, or its use by Tracy to 'move' her mother, became a mediator in shared interest and action, animated by Tracy's clear expressions of pleasure, puzzlement, etc.

As Tracy's two-handed play developed, the games with her mother became more elaborate and protracted. Then, at 40 weeks, for the first time Tracy acknowledged her mother's initiative in a new way, seeking to understand what new intention was offered. They began to share intentions in a task in what we called 'secondary

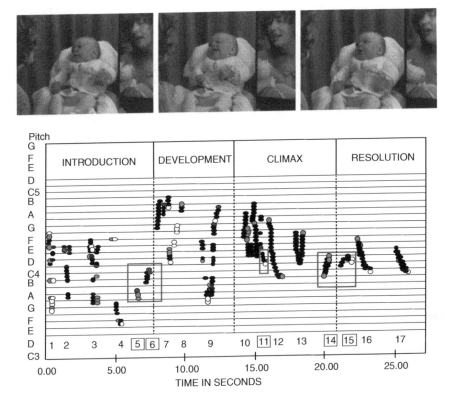

Figure 1.3 Proto conversations with a 6-week-old, showing mutual attention between infant and mother, the pitch plot of the narrative showing how the voices move in the octave above middle C (C4), and the verbal utterances of the mother. The infant's vocalisations are enclosed in boxes (Malloch and Trevarthen, 2009; Trevarthen and Delafield-Butt, 2013).

intersubjectivity', person-person-object cooperation, and Tracy's new willingness to become a partner greatly changed how her mother communicated. As they efficiently 'worked' in joint tasks, performing complimentary steps, her mother's 'directives' by speech and gesture took over from playful 'reactive' imitations of sounds and actions.

Hubley followed this with a study of five girls, making films at two-week intervals when the infants were 34 to 54 weeks of age (Hubley and Trevarthen, 1979). All subjects changed in their willingness to follow directives of their mothers from 46 weeks and by the end of their first year were learning new purposeful acts from their mothers' example, including some words. They were mastering Michael Halliday's 'proto-language' of gesture and vocalisation (Halliday, 1979). We identified the infant as the motivator of the important development in companionship:

> Our work leads us to suggest that at the end of the first year our subjects had become pupils by some positive genesis of an adaptive function essential to being human. They could then gain understanding not only through their own activity, but also from another person by imitating, and even more power-fully by the more complex tactics of cooperation that provoke assistance and instruction.
>
> *(Hubley and Trevarthen, 1979, p. 74)*

The chart of changing motives for shared experience through infancy, and how toddlers make meaning in their world

Research on the development of communication with infants, which was recorded in three multi-disciplinary volumes in the 1970s (Schaffer, 1977; Lock, 1978; Bullowa, 1979), revealed stages by which innate capacities for action-with-aware-ness and communication are elaborated, from the subtle two-way imitations of expressions by newborns with mother and father to the acquisition of speech. We defined age-related changes in infants' motives for learning by their own efforts and in communication with familiar companions and we found strong relationships between the ages of change and developments in the body and brain (Trevarthen, 2001; Trevarthen and Aitken, 2003). The most conspicuous changes were the development of protoconversations at two months (Figure 1.3), a period when the narratives of rhythmic action games and baby songs were enjoyed in months four to eight (Figure 1.4), and the change to cooperative use of objects and significant actions at nine months.

After the 18 months of infancy, the body becomes very mobile and the toddler seeks wider social relations. Creativity within the experience of the repetitive act, discovering how, in communication, each repeated act is a newly created expres-sion and will carry with it some degree of creative novelty or playfulness, is par-ticularly strong in exuberant activities of young children, before school, and remains so for exceptionally creative adults (Bruce, 2001; Bateson and Martin, 2013; Trevarthen, 2014). In play, repetition in the interpersonal dialogic cycle promotes the generation of understanding and the creation of new meanings with sociocul-tural value, and these become part of an endlessly inventive tradition of storytelling (Bruner, 1990). Each new expression offered in exchange contains within it refer-ence to the utterance that came before it, from the other person. Next it may be assimilated with all the associations, motivations, playful novelty, and intentional aspirations of the listener or watcher, who will reply by speaking or by doing a responsive action. Thus dialogue creates new meaning.

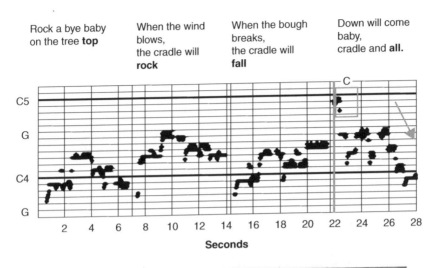

| Rock a bye baby on the tree **top** | When the wind blows, the cradle will **rock** | When the bough breaks, the cradle will **fall** | Down will come baby, cradle and **all.** |

Clappa, clappa handies
Mommy's at the **well,**
Daddy's away to Hamilton
To buy wee Emma a **bell.**

Round and round the gar-den
Ran the ted-dy **bear,**
One step. two step,
And a tickly un-der **there.**

Figure 1.4 English baby songs show the universal structure, with groups of four lines, making verses each of which is a narrative that lasts around 25 to 30 seconds. The rhythm is 'iambic' with alternating accented and unaccented syllables, and commonly there is rhyming of words at the ends of the lines. The infants attend and react in time with the song. Many songs are accompanied by ritual body games, and in 'Clappa-clappa-handies', and 'Round-and-round-the-garden' shown. 'Rock-a-bye baby' is a lullaby, sung slowly. The lines make up a four-part narrative (Trevarthen and Delafield-Butt, 2013).

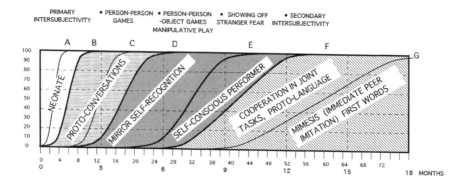

Key developmental changes		
	Behaviour and motor activities	**Communication**
A (3):	Regulations of sleep, feeding and breathing. Innate 'pre-reaching'.	Imitation of expressions. Smiles to voice.
B (5):	Pre-reaching declines. Swipes and grabs.	Fixates eyes with smiling. Proto-conversations. Mouth and tongue imitations. Distressed by 'still-face' test.
C (12):	Smooth visual tracking, with strong head support. Reaching and catching.	'Person-person' games, mirror recognition.
D (16):	Interest in surroundings increases. Accurate reach and grasp. Binocular stereopsis. Manipulative play with objects.	Imitation of clapping and pointing. 'Person-person-object' games.
E (32):	Babbling. Persistent manipulation, rhythmic banging of objects. Crawling and sitting, pulling up to stand.	Playful, self-aware imitating. Showing off. 'Stranger fear'.
F (42):	Combines objects, 'executive thinking'. Categorises experiences. Walking.	Declarations with 'joint attention'. Protolanguage. Clowning.
G (60):	Self-feeding with hand.	Mimesis of purposeful actions, uses 'tools' and cultural learning. Imitates first words.

Figure 1.5 Age-related changes in the abilities of infants that prepare the way for language and learning of culturally significant skills.

Two artists, a poet and a musician, praised the powers of sociable invention by young children. Both became investigative psychologists. The Russian poet and cultural activist Kornei Chukovsky, who became the most famous children's poet in Russia, had discovered, when he listened to young children playing where he was writing, that between two and five years children are 'linguistic geniuses', inventive and sensitive to the poetic resources of their talk in play (Chukovsky, 1968). Professor of

Musicology Jon-Roar Bjørkvold, in his *The Muse Within* (1996), similarly reports discovering the inventiveness of 'children's musical culture' when he studied material he had collected in Russia, the United States and Norway.

Baldwin's principle of psychological development as circular repetition reminds us that creative novelty is present in every new act, and the rhythms, feelings, and interests in engagement with the world are adapted to be shared between persons. Successful and rewarding experiences are repeated with playful variation. Appreciation of the child's contribution to the discovery of meaning by collaboration with companions in imitation supports a more generous, more creative, more enjoyable, and more fruitful, practice of education at all later stages (Whitehead, 1929; Malaguzzi, 1993; Bruner, 1996; Hurst, 1997; Donaldson, 1992; Rogoff, 2003; Trevarthen, 2011b, 2012b, 2013a, b). This practice must be more than childcare by staff occupied with protecting babies and toddlers while mothers are at work. It needs specially trained teachers who appreciate the changing abilities of young children for active learning in rich environments that favour creative collaboration with companions of all ages, who know that children respond to exploration with the natural world, who involve parents in their children's learning, and who do not impose formal primary school instruction too early. Life-readiness is already rich before school-readiness is required.

References

Ammaniti, M. and Gallese, V. (eds) (2014) *The Birth of Intersubjectivity Psychodynamics, Neurobiology, and the Self*. New York: Norton.

Athey, C. (1990) *Extending Thought in Young Children: A Parent-Teacher Partnership*. London: Paul Chapman.

Baldwin, J. M. (1894). *Mental Development of the Child and the Race*. New York: Macmillan.

Bateson, P. and Martin, P. (2013) *Play, Playfulness, Creativity and Innovation*. Cambridge: Cambridge University Press.

Bernstein, N. (1967) *Coordination and Regulation of Movements*. New York: Pergamon.

Bjørkvold, J.-R. (1992) *The Muse Within: Creativity and Communication, Song and Play from Childhood through Maturity*. New York: Harper Collins.

Bruce, T. (2001) *Learning Through Play: Babies, Toddlers and the Foundation Years*. London: Hodder and Stoughton.

Bruce, T. (2012) *Early Childhood Practice: Froebel Today*. London: Sage.

Bruner, J. S. (1990) *Acts of Meaning*. Cambridge, MA: Harvard University Press.

Bruner, J. S. (1996) *The Culture of Education*. Cambridge, MA: Harvard University Press.

Bullowa, M. (ed.) (1979) *Before Speech: The Beginning of Human Communication*. London: Cambridge University Press.

Chukovsky, K. (1968) *From Two to Five*. Berkeley and Los Angeles: University of California Press.

Delafield-Butt, J. and Gangopadhyay, N. (2013) Sensorimotor intentionality: The origins of intentionality in prospective agent action. *Developmental Review, 33*(4), 399–425.

Delafield-Butt, J. and Trevarthen, C. (2013) Theories of the development of human communication. In P. Cobley and P. J. Schultz (eds) *Theories and Models of Communication: Handbook of Communication Science*, Vol. 1, pp. 199–221. Berlin: De Gruyter Mouton.

Donaldson, M. (1978) *Children's Minds*. Glasgow: Fontana/Collins.

Donaldson, M. (1992) *Human Minds: An Exploration*. London: Allen Lane/Penguin.

Eckerdal, P. and Merker, B. (2009) 'Music' and the 'action song' in infant development: An interpretation. In S. Malloch and C. Trevarthen (eds) *Communicative Musicality: Exploring the Basis
of Human Companionship* (pp. 241–62). Oxford: Oxford University Press.

Gallese, V., Fadiga, L., Fogassi, L. and Rizzolatti, G. (1996) Action recognition in the premo-
tor cortex. *Brain, 119*, 593–609.

Goodrich, B. G. (2010) We do, therefore we think: Time, motility, and consciousness. *Reviews
in the Neurosciences, 21*(5), 331–61.

Gratier, M. and Trevarthen, C. (2008) Musical narrative and motives for culture in mother–
infant vocal interaction. *Journal of Consciousness Studies, 15*(10–11), 122–58.

Halliday, M. A. K. (1979) One child's protolanguage. In M. Bullowa (ed.), *Before Speech: The
Beginning of Human Communication* (pp. 171–90). London: Cambridge University Press.

Hubley, P. and Trevarthen, C. (1979) Sharing a task in infancy. In I. Uzgiris (ed.) *Social
Interaction During Infancy: New Directions for Child Development, 4* (pp. 57–80). San Francisco:
Jossey-Bass.

Hurst, V. (1997) *Planning for Early Learning: Educating Young Children*, 2nd edn. London: Paul
Chapman.

Kugiumutzakis, G. and Trevarthen, C. (2014) Neonatal imitation. In J. Wright (ed.) *The
International Encyclopedia of the Social and Behavioral Sciences*, 2nd edn. Oxford: Elsevier.

Lock, A. (ed.) (1978) *Action, Gesture and Symbol: The Emergence of Language*, London: Academic
Press.

Malaguzzi, L. (1993) History, ideas and basic philosophy. In C. Edwards, L. Gandini and
G. Forman (eds) *The Hundred Languages of Children* (pp. 41–89). Norwood, NJ: Ablex.

Malloch, S. (1999) Mother and infants and communicative musicality. *Rhythms, Musical Narrative,
and the Origins of Human Communication. Musicae Scientiae*, Special Issue, 1999–2000, 29–57.
Liège, Belgium: European Society for the Cognitive Sciences of Music.

Malloch, S. and Trevarthen, C. (eds) (2009) *Communicative Musicality: Exploring the Basis of
Human Companionship*. Oxford: Oxford University Press.

Maturana, H., Mpodozis, J. and Letelier, J. C. (1995) Brain, language and the origin of human
mental functions. *Biological Research, 28*: 15–26.

Mead, G. H. (1934) *Mind, Self, and Society*. Chicago: Chicago University Press.

Merleau-Ponty, M. (1962) *Phenomenology of Perception* (trans. C. Smith). London: Routledge
and Kegan Paul (original in French, 1945).

Nagy, E. (2011) The newborn infant: A missing stage in developmental psychology. *Infant and
Child Development, 20*, 3–19.

Nagy, E. and Molnár, P. (2004) *Homo imitans* or *Homo provocans*? The phenomenon of neonatal
initiation. *Infant Behavior and Development, 27*, 57–63.

Narvaez, D., Panksepp, J., Schore, A. and Gleason, T. (eds) (2013) *Evolution, Early Experience and
Human Development: From Research to Practice and Policy*. New York: Oxford University
Press.

Piaget, J. (1962) *Play, Dreams and Imitation in Childhood*. London: Routledge and Kegan Paul.

Piontelli, A. (2010) *Development of Normal Fetal Movements: The First 25 Weeks of Gestation*.
Vienna and New York: Springer-Verlag.

Reddy, V. (2008) *How Infants Know Minds*. Cambridge, MA: Harvard University Press.

Rogoff, B. (2003) *The Cultural Nature of Human Development*. Oxford: Oxford University Press.

Schaffer, H. R. (ed.) (1977) *Studies of Mother–Infant Interaction: The Loch Lomond Symposium*.
London: Academic Press.

Stern, D. N. (1995) *The Motherhood Constellation: A Unified View of Parent-infant Psychotherapy*.
New York: Basic Books.

Stern, D. N. (2000) *The Interpersonal World of the Infant: A View from Psychoanalysis and
Development Psychology*, 2nd edn. New York: Basic Books.

Stern, D. N. (2010) *Forms of Vitality: Exploring Dynamic Experience in Psychology, the Arts,
Psychotherapy and Development*. Oxford: Oxford University Press.

Trevarthen, C. (1999) Musicality and the intrinsic motive pulse: Evidence from human psychobiology and infant communication. *Rhythms, Musical Narrative, and the Origins of Human Communication, Musicae Scientiae*, Special Issue, 1999–2000, 157–213. Liège, Belgium: European Society for the Cognitive Sciences of Music.

Trevarthen, C. (2001) The neurobiology of early communication: Intersubjective regulations in human brain development. In A. F. Kalverboer and A. Gramsbergen (eds) *Handbook on Brain and Behavior in Human Development* (pp. 841–82). Dordrecht, The Netherlands: Kluwer.

Trevarthen, C. (2006) First things first: Infants make good use of the sympathetic rhythm of imitation, without reason or language. *Journal of Child Psychotherapy, 31*(1), 91–113.

Trevarthen, C. (2008) The musical art of infant conversation: Narrating in the time of sympathetic experience, without rational interpretation, before words. *Musicae Scientiae*, Special Issue, 11–37.

Trevarthen, C. (2009) The functions of emotion in infancy: The regulation and communication of rhythm, sympathy, and meaning in human development. In D. Fosha, D. J. Siegel and M. F. Solomon (eds) *The Healing Power of Emotion: Affective Neuroscience, Development, and Clinical Practice* (pp. 55–85). New York: Norton.

Trevarthen, C. (2011a) What is it like to be a person who knows nothing? Defining the active intersubjective mind of a newborn human being. *Infant and Child Development*, Special Issue, *20*(1), 119–35.

Trevarthen, C. (2011b) What young children give to their learning, making education work to sustain a community and its culture. *European Early Childhood Education Research Journal*, Special Issue, 'Birth to Three', *19*(2), 173–93.

Trevarthen, C. (2012a) Embodied human intersubjectivity: imaginative agency, to share meaning. *Cognitive Semiotics, 4*(1), 'The Intersubjectivity of Embodiment', 6–56.

Trevarthen, C. (2012b) Finding a place with meaning in a busy human world: How does the story begin, and who helps? *European Early Childhood Education Research Journal, 20*(3), 303–12.

Trevarthen, C. (2013a) Born for art, and the joyful companionship of fiction. In D. Narvaez, J. Panksepp, A. Schore, T. Gleason (eds) *Human Nature, Early Experience and the Environment of Evolutionary Adaptedness* (pp. 202–18). New York: Oxford University Press.

Trevarthen, C. (2013b) Artful learning makes sense. *Early Education, British Association for Early Childhood Education, 90th Anniversary of Early Education*, Article 1.

Trevarthen, C. (2014) The imaginative and cultural purposes of human play: Joy in movement bringing companionship to practical tasks and meaning to social practice. In J. E. Johnson and S. Eberle (eds) *The Handbook of the Study of Play*. Lanham, MD: Rowman and Littlefield (in press).

Trevarthen, C. and Aitken, K. J. (2003) Regulation of brain development and age-related changes in infants' motives: The developmental function of 'regressive' periods. In M. Heimann (ed.) *Regression Periods in Human Infancy* (pp. 107–84). Mahwah, NJ: Erlbaum.

Trevarthen, C. and Delafield-Butt, J. (2013) Biology of shared experience and language development: Regulations for the inter-subjective life of narratives. In M. Legerstee, D. Haley and M. Bornstein (eds) *The Infant Mind: Origins of the Social Brain* (pp. 167–99). New York: Guilford Press.

Trevarthen, C. and Hubley, P. (1978) Secondary intersubjectivity: Confidence, confiding and acts of meaning in the first year. In A. Lock (ed.) *Action, Gesture and Symbol: The Emergence of Language* (pp. 183–229). London: Academic Press.

Trevarthen, C., Aitken, K. J., Vandekerckhove, M., Delafield-Butt, J. and Nagy, E. (2006) Collaborative regulations of vitality in early childhood: Stress in intimate relationships and postnatal psychopathology. In D. Cicchetti and D. J. Cohen (eds) *Developmental Psychopathology, Vol. 2, Developmental Neuroscience*, 2nd edn (pp. 65–126). New York: Wiley.

Trevarthen, C., Gratier, M. and Osborne, N. (2014) The human nature of culture and education. *Wiley Interdisciplinary Reviews: Cognitive Science* (in press).

Whalley, M. and the Pen Green Centre Team (2007) *Involving Parents in their Children's Education*, 2nd edn. London: Paul Chapman.

Whitehead, A. N. (1929) *The Aims of Education and Other Essays*. New York: Macmillan.

2

'I WONDER WHY OUR DOG HAS BEEN SO NAUGHTY?'

Thinking differently from the perspective of play

Elizabeth Wood

Introduction

The aim of this chapter is to contrast two strands of research on young children's thinking and understanding. The first strand focuses on the forms of thinking that are considered valuable in the context of 'educational play', that is, play that is planned to support children's learning and development in relation to curriculum goals. The second, and more substantial, focus is on the forms of thinking that children have to master in order to be in a state of play, that is, to act in and on the world from the perspective that 'this is play'. Although these two strands have points of intersection, a critical distinction is that children's thinking in play is not directed towards accomplishing or demonstrating adults' purposes or curriculum goals, but is shaped by the 'what if' and 'as if' qualities that mark the essence, spirit and flow of their play.

This distinction between 'educational' and freely chosen play creates some of the tensions that exist regarding the ways in which play is constructed and enacted in early childhood settings. This is because the discourses of quality and effectiveness that circulate in national and international contexts tend to value the outcomes that are inscribed in policy frameworks and are expressed as curriculum-based knowledge or learning standards. Although it is frequently claimed that play is the natural, spontaneous and optimal way of learning for young children, the developmental and educational discourse has focused on proving the purposes that play serves for social, physical, cognitive and behavioural outcomes. In contrast, the purpose of this chapter is to argue that play enables children to think and act differently from the perspective of play. Freely chosen play, humour and playfulness enable children to demonstrate metacognitive and metacommunicative skills, but the spontaneous application of those skills is directed towards their intrinsically motivated activities and purposes.

The title of this chapter comes from an episode of play recorded by Cook (2003) in a nine-month study of four children, aged 4–5 years (two boys and two girls) in a Foundation Stage class in England. Alice, Lucy and Richard are playing in the role-play area, designed around the theme of 'Hogwarts' – the school for wizards in the Harry Potter stories by J.K. Rowling. They have access to a range of resources that reflect this theme (wands, books of spells, and 'magic potions' – bottles of coloured water), as well as the everyday home corner resources, such as kitchen equipment. One child is the dog 'in his kennel' and two more boys join them as dogs. SG denotes Small Group, Cb denotes boy, and Cg girl.

> Alice: *He's in his kennel ... Hey Lucy, he's going to come out. Hey, come on dog, wake up.*
> Alice assigns roles: *You're Hermione and I'm Hermione's mum, and Richard is Hermione's dad.*
> *I wonder why our dog has been so naughty.*
> (To two boys) *You two play about and eat sweets as bones. I need a doll.*

The boys play in role, hiding bones in the washing machine. Then Richard decides to join them as a dog, not as the dad, which gives rise to some renegotiation of roles:

> Lucy: *Richard's turned into a dog.*
> Alice–Lucy: *But he can't.*
> Richard–Alice and Lucy: *I'm a doggy.*
> Alice–SG: *No, turn him back to Hermione's dad, we want somebody to marry.*
> Lucy–Cbs: *Marry me marry me. Abracadabra. Make Richard turn into a boy.*

The girls chase Richard around the role-play area, with Alice again in control:

> Alice–Lucy: *Hey Lucy, there's a big surprise for you. These wands will turn Richard into a grown up ... I've got off his doggy hair.*
> Richard–Alice: *I've put on real hair.*
> Alice–SG: *He's standing up like a real person.*

The girls are getting really excited now and speak in much louder voices:

> Lucy–Alice: *The spells aren't working.*
> Alice–Lucy: *I know, magic drink.*
> They pick up bottles of coloured water and pretend to mix a drink.

Alice is a skilled player who likes to get everyone organised, and knows the routines for developing the momentum of the play. Alice's invitation, 'I wonder why our dog has been so naughty', enables her co-players to step into the flow of this episode, as she assigns the roles and events that will guide the action. Richard resists Alice's invitation to be Hermione's dad, which then provokes invocations of imagined power through spells, potions and incantations as she attempts to manage ambiguities and sustain the internal logic of the play.

Although the variability and unpredictability of young children's play provide a significant challenge to identifying and analysing their thinking, this episode is an invitation to consider the complexities of play, and to conceptualise the distinctive characteristics of playful thinking and communication. The first section outlines the benefits and problems with 'educational play'. The second section explores the nature of children's thinking from the perspective of play. Three themes are explored in relation to international research evidence, namely metacognition, theory of mind, and the use of tools, signs and symbols.

Educational play

Contemporary research continues to be devoted to proving, or at least demonstrating, the role and purposes of play for young children's learning and development. Claims are made for the all-round contribution that play makes to their physical, emotional, cognitive and social development, with cognitive neuroscience adding further support for its role in brain development and imagination (Brown, 2009; Oates *et al.*, 2012). This research has been instrumental in justifying play within different pedagogical approaches and curriculum frameworks, as well as in training programmes for the early childhood workforce (Saracho, 2012; Zhu and Zhang, 2008). Detailed attention has been given to the forms of thinking and understanding (such as creativity, problem-solving, metacognition) that are evident in children's play, and to subject-specific knowledge, notably in language and communication, literacy, mathematics and science (Smith, 2010).

Within the 'play as education' discourse, play can be used to accomplish specific learning objectives within early childhood curricula, and generic developmental goals. This discourse has a long history, and has drawn on an eclectic range of theories (Ross, 2013), which have been interpreted selectively and in different ways (Wood, 2013). Vygotsky's theories (1978) have been particularly influential in this discourse from two perspectives. First, Vygotsky's work has been interpreted pedagogically as supporting educative interactions between the learner and the 'more knowledgeable other' who is able to lead learners (and particularly young children) ahead of their development. Second, Vygotsky argued for the subject disciplines (such as literacy, numeracy, technology) as distinctive cultural ways of thinking, and of organising knowledge, skills and concepts. Enculturation into disciplined forms of knowledge provides children with the tools for learning, thinking, enquiring, making sense and constructing knowledge. Emergent literacy and numeracy, for example, are seen as important indicators of children's cognitive development, as they progressively master signs and symbol systems. Play is a leading activity – that is, a developmental process, and a necessary transition from 'informal' to 'formal' learning which is characterised by the acquisition of scientific concepts (Fleer, 2010; Towsey and Macdonald,

2009). From the perspective of educational play, how this transition is accomplished, and at what ages, varies according to different pedagogical approaches; the combination of adult- and child-initiated play (Gupta, 2009; Saracho, 2012; Wallerstedt and Pramling, 2012); and the extent to which the early childhood curriculum is framed around subject (content) knowledge, or generic developmental goals such as socialisation, communication, and emotional well-being.

In spite of a substantial international research base, play remains problematic in relation to pedagogy and practice (Bodrova, 2008; Wood, 2013). Within academically oriented pre-schools, the focus tends to be on preparing children for the formal routines, approaches to learning and ways of thinking that lay the foundations for later success in school. The research evidence remains inconclusive about what play leads to in terms of more disciplined and mature forms of thinking and understanding, and claims that children progressively learn abstract concepts through discovery, play and experiential learning are not substantiated (Aubrey and Durmaz, 2012; Smith, 2010). Young children do not learn to read, write and calculate as a result of spontaneous play activities, but play can provide opportunities for them to act competently as readers, writers, mathematicians, artists, designers, technologists, and to use and apply their knowledge in contexts that are purposeful, authentic and meaningful. Because of its variability and spontaneity, tracing causal relationships between play and learning remains problematic (Wallerstedt and Pramling, 2012). However, it is the constellation of activities within and around play that appear to be influential (Sutton-Smith, 2001), particularly in children's social relationships, friendship patterns and symbolic activities.

Different approaches to early childhood education are outcomes of particular socio-cultural and political contexts, and the forms of thinking that are valued reflect wider values and beliefs about what early childhood education is for, the position of children in societies, and what knowledge and skills are considered vital to the workplaces of the future. Accordingly, the different pedagogical approaches that are evident in international policy frameworks have implications for the forms of thinking and understanding that are typically valued and promoted. For example, dispositions such as independence, autonomy, self-motivation, self-regulation and resilience continue to be identified as desirable characteristics of children's learning in many early childhood policy frameworks (Wood, 2013). Self-regulation of behaviour is also a desirable goal, because 'good' behaviour is equated with the ability to learn (paying attention, sitting still, following classroom routines). These dispositions are likely to lead to the thinking skills that are also valued in formal education, notably the meta-level cognitive skills, which include planning, information-processing, problem-solving, evaluating, deliberate selection of strategies and skills to accomplish tasks or goals, and the ability to reflect on thought and action in ways that drive further learning. Positive dispositions for learning, metacognitive abilities and the achievement of defined outcomes are all considered to be indicators of the quality and effectiveness of pre-school education. This is another point of vulnerability, because interpreting play from the perspective of defined curriculum goals privileges educational 'effectiveness' and reduces complexity. When children are in a state of play, their thinking is both playful and playfully directed towards their goals and purposes. Therefore, alignment with an 'educational' agenda becomes problematic unless practitioners are highly skilled in understanding play. So what are the alternative ways of interpreting play from a more complex position?

The complexity of play

There are distinctive forms of thinking and understanding that children have to master in order to be in a state of play, that is, to act in and on the world from the perspective that 'this is play'. Play activities provide opportunities for children to use and apply their knowledge and skills, and to demonstrate imaginative, humorous and playful forms of thinking through multi-modal interactions, symbolic activity, and behaviours. Their mastery of these forms of thinking and understanding is tuned to the service of different forms of play. Successful engagement in play requires a suspension of belief, and the ability to imagine, or see things differently from the perspective that 'this is play'. Invention, imagination and pretence have their own cognitive characteristics, which mean that children at play utilise qualitatively different forms of thinking and understanding. Knowledge about the rules, rituals and practices embedded in different forms of play include learning how to gain entry, take on a role, develop momentum, collaborate, and leave the play. As the 'Hogwarts' episode indicates, participation can be dynamic, with subtle shifts, negotiations, and compromises as children manage to sustain the play, and their positions within the narrative.

Crucial to the development of play is the ability to make thinking visible and audible, through a range of communicative practices and semiotic devices. The success of play relies on the alignment of perspectives, and ongoing adjustments to those perspectives, for example through negotiating roles, developing the action, explaining the sequence of events, justifying actions, and making symbolic transformations (one thing stands for another). Joint attention, inter-subjective attunement, and out-loud thinking are all cognitive characteristics that determine the flow and success of the play, but at the same time place high cognitive demands on the players.

The 'Hogwarts' episode that opens this chapter demonstrates the importance of these cognitive characteristics, specifically how children need to align their thinking, knowledge, intentions, and understanding in play activities. Several intersecting themes have been evident in previous episodes: robbers and burglars stealing goods and money; firefighters being involved in rescue and recovery, accidents and dying; naughty dogs, monsters and sharks, and some competition between groups of boys and girls for space and control of the play (Wood and Cook, 2009). The children appear to be bringing different themes and perspectives to the play, and Alice's efforts are directed towards inter-subjective attunement, This relies on the collective memorisation of play themes, and mixing in everyday knowledges, to support the processes of planning, managing and developing the play. Central to the complexity of play are children's metacognitive and metacommunicative competences, their social competence, and the development of theory of mind abilities.

Metacognition and metacommunication in play

Whitebread (2010) argues that there is compelling evidence for the significance of playful activities for children's emotional well-being, their language development and their development of metacognitive and self-regulatory abilities, and that these developmental processes underpin academic achievement, creativity and problem-solving. Children's play and self-initiated activities are significant for their progress from other- to self-regulation, a process that is supported by talking about their activities (with peers and adults), developing strategies to regulate their own (and others') behaviour and developing awareness of their thinking and learning. 'Out-loud' thinking is integral to the complex and dynamic nature of play activities: children verbalise and make visible the shifts of direction, control and power, as they negotiate their own identities and positions. Through these processes, children express their identities, reveal how they exercise choice and agency, and how they develop relationships with others. The research of Whitebread and colleagues (Whitebread, 2010; Whitebread and O'Sullivan, 2012) and Robson (2010) indicates that these processes are evident in children's play activities. Developed by Whitebread and colleagues, the Cambridge Independent Learning Framework (CIndLe) has evolved over several projects, and proposes three main areas of cognitive self-regulation:

- *Metacognitive knowledge*: the individual's knowledge about personal, task and strategy variables affecting the cognitive performance.
- *Metacognitive regulation*: the cognitive processes that take place during activities, including planning, monitoring, control and evaluation.
- *Emotional and motivational regulation*: the ways in which learners monitor and control emotions and motivational states during tasks.

In a study of self-regulation and metacognition in young children's play, Robson (2010) used qualitative methods of videotaping episodes of children's play and audio-taping discussions of the children's post-hoc Reflective Dialogues about those episodes. Robson's study involved 12 children aged from 3.10 to 4.10 years, and the Reflective Dialogues took place between the children and their key person about the videotaped play activities (2010). The study found extensive evidence of metacognitive and self-regulatory behaviour in their activities and in the Reflective Dialogues, across similar categories to the CIndLe projects. A key issue in Robson's study is that the success of play activities (especially role play and pretence) relies on children's abilities to share their thinking in order to plan, manage and sustain the play, and, over time, to develop the complexity and challenge that is documented in ethnographic research (Alcock, 2010; Edmiston, 2008; Moore, 2010; Broadhead and Burt, 2012). However, thinking is not always 'visible' through verbal utterances or interactions, because much communication is embodied through gestures, signals and actions. As Robson (2010) argues, the opportunity for children to engage in reflective dialogues makes visible what is implicit, or understood by the players. Robson's study exemplifies contemporary shifts towards involving children as research participants in documenting and narrating their play lives, rather than relying on rating scales and measures that reflect adults' categorisations of play skills and characteristics.

Focusing specifically on social pretend play, Whitebread and O'Sullivan (2012) review research that explores the role of metacommunication in supporting children's developing ability to control their own cognition and behaviour, and for developing strategies which support other-regulation and co-regulation. This review incorporates verbal and non-verbal forms of metacommunication: children's meanings and intentions are visual and embodied because actions, gestures and words are used to convey pretence (mental representations) and action. Whitebread and O'Sullivan propose that more complex forms of social pretend play place greater demands on children to co-ordinate their roles with other players and jointly plan and maintain their play (2012). These demands are evident when children assert and express themselves in ways that are qualitatively different from non-play situations, and involve skills that are associated with developing a theory of mind.

Research by Newton and Jenvey (2011) examined the links between the development of *theory of mind* (ToM) and play to the development of socially competent behaviour in children, notably the ability to understand the moods, emotions, intentions and perspectives of other people. The study used a mixed methods approach combining a range of ToM tests, interviews and rating scales with parents, and observations of children at play in classroom settings. The study highlighted the importance of social interaction during play in relation to social competence, and showed that children who engaged in more solitary than social play had poorer social skills and presented more behaviour problems. This is a complex area of research, but if we accept the point made by Whitebread and O'Sullivan (2012), that social pretend play places quite complex demands on young children, then developing ToM abilities would seem integral to their successful engagement and participation. Talking about their thinking and imagination, explaining roles, and determining sequences of action and interaction contribute to the internal logic as children 'make sense' and construct meaning in their play. Central to these processes is the support provided by cultural tools, and how these are used in the context of play.

Tools, signs and symbols in play

From a Vygotskian perspective, development is a gradual process of entry into human cultures through various means, including the mastery of language, tools and symbols, of interactions with people and with the surrounding culture (1978). However, the processes of 'entry into' and 'mastery of' are not one-way (that is, from adult to child, or expert to novice) but mediational, because these tools are used by individuals to drive their own learning and development and to influence how they act in and on the surrounding culture. As play becomes the leading activity in early childhood, children use cultural tools to enable them to analyse situations independently, to organise their own learning activity, to lead interactions with people (peers and adults), and to create or invent their own cultural practices. In play, specific (often imaginary) meanings are attached to signs and symbols and children have to pay close attention to the dynamic interactions in which those meanings are conveyed. Symbolic activities are multi-modal and embodied through gestures, facial expression, gaze, movement, voice change, all of which are evident in the 'Hogwarts' episode.

The signs and symbols that children use in their play serve particular functions and convey meanings that may be created at a meta-level. In the case of the 'Hogwarts' episode, the function and purposes of everyday resources were transformed and communicated. Alice's instruction 'You two play about and eat sweets as bones' signifies that the 'sweets' in the role play area were now transformed into bones for the dogs. A second symbolic transformation, turning Richard from a dog into a boy, required the use of magic potions which signified Alice's access to imagined power. This episode supports the claim by Whitebread and O'Sullivan (2012) that social pretend play activities place quite high demands on children's social, cognitive and emotional capabilities.

The 'meta' qualities of children's play are also expressed in multi-modal ways. Building on Hall's study of children's drawings (2010) Wood and Hall (2011) examined the role of drawings as spaces for intellectual play in which children were playing at drawing, playing in drawings and playing with drawings. The role of drawings in play was enhanced where they took on the metacommunicative status of symbolic tools and artefacts that mediate collaborative activities. By playing at, in and with their drawings children revealed the complex imaginative and meditational processes that underpin playful transformations of their social and cultural worlds, in which concepts of power, agency and identity are embedded. Play and drawing are mutually constitutive practices in which children draw on imagination and material culture to represent their everyday and imagined worlds.

Tools and symbols also enable children to manage the many ambiguities and paradoxes of play. As they learn how to play by the rules, and learn how to subvert or change the rules for different purposes, play provides the means by which children think differently about the meaning and purposes of rules within the framework of approved behaviours and institutional order, and how they can manage resistance. They also have to learn the complex skills of negotiating the rules within play events, and situating themselves accordingly. From the perspective 'this is play' it becomes possible to think, act and behave in ways that appear to disrupt institutional order but make sense and meaning in the context of the play. For example, in a small-scale study of children aged 3–4 in a pre-school setting, Wood (2014) documents a range of devices that children use for creating imagined power, such as taking on adult and superhero roles, using magic spells, potions and incantations. The process of making their own rules in play and disrupting institutional rules often involves issues of power, identity, status which can be played out through different subjectivities. Thus play becomes a space of relationality, aesthetics and fluidity as children constantly adjust their perspectives and meanings over time. These adjustments take place 'in the moment', and, as demonstrated by Alice and her co-players, communicative activity is both playful and serious as they take up their positions and act out their roles. Being able to think differently from the perspective of play therefore involves multiple layers of complexity, and fluid orchestration of thinking, feeling, and performing. The distinctive qualities of play therefore support distinctive ways of thinking.

Porous borders – play as a liminal space

It would be erroneous to emphasise 'mind' as the driver for children's play motivations and abilities. Drawing on Vygotskian theories, Holzman (2009) argues that play creates unity of affect and cognition, of mind and personality, which enables children to become contributing members of communities, culture and society. Much of children's activity is refracted through their emotional experience and not only via the executive skills that characterise metacognition and metacommunication. Furthermore, play creates emotional 'hyperventilation' because of the exaggeration of emotional states such as fear, bravery, sorrow, excitement, happiness. The liminality of play means that children occupy a threshold or space in which the 'what if' and 'as if' qualities of play determine their performance and actions. The borders of play are porous: imagination is the pivot between reality and unreality, sense and nonsense, seriousness and playfulness, risk and safety. Temporal porosity includes movement between past-present-future, and spatial porosity includes the transformation of physical space and artefacts into imagined spaces and places. These may be delineated by boundaries, buildings, natural features of the landscape, and by children's creativity and imagination (Moore, 2010). In playful meaning-making practices, children transform meanings and use these in different ways and for different purposes, but always from the perspective that 'this is play'.

Play is transformative and consummatory

Henricks (2010) argues that the qualities of play are transformative and consummatory, both of which enable children to think differently from the perspective of play. For Henricks, play activities are transformative because they represent the efforts of people to assert themselves against the elements of the world, to alter those elements, and in doing so learn about the nature of reality and about their own powers to operate in those settings. Playful forms of thinking include transforming their relationship to themselves and to the people around them, and constructing their identities (and different ways of understanding those identities). Play involves pushing boundaries, for example through deep play, adventurous play, edge work, dizzy play, and risky play. The 'boundaries' may by temporal, physical, social, personal or institutional, for example breaking or challenging rules that are imposed by adults.

Play is consummatory because, as Henricks argues, the players operate inside the boundaries of space and time that mark the play occasion; they are preoccupied with the quality of their experience, and the goals that lie within the event, and they are fulfilled or completed within the boundaries of the event (Henricks, 2010). Returning to the tensions between 'educational' and free play, in pre-school settings young children are expected to exercise levels of agency, control, autonomy and independence that are not typical (or allowed) in other areas of their lives, which again places certain demands on their thinking and actions, such as solving problems, managing behaviour and regulating emotions. Here we have a significant paradox of play: pre-school and school settings are major sites for the socialisation of children, where 'everyday life … is tightly regulated by rules, routines and pre-defined activities in time and place, and by adults'/practitioners' authority' (Markström, 2010, p. 305). So, play is expected to accomplish some of the socialisation work of early childhood, but within spaces that are arguably more high-risk. The risk comes from the uncertainties of what will happen (or indeed whether anything will happen), which depends on establishing inter-subjectivity and alignment, and the extent to which children can manage the ambiguities of play.

Play is deeply connected to the different cultural repertoires that children bring from their homes and communities, including popular culture, TV and film characters, and everyday family events (Hedges, 2011; Marsh and Bishop, 2014). These influences are evident in their own play cultures, and the different ways in which they represent their knowledge and experiences. Children do things in play that they have not been taught explicitly by adults, and thereby learn what knowledge, skills and dispositions are relevant to managing and sustaining play. Play enables children to use and apply everyday knowledge in multi-modal and multi-dimensional ways, and it is here that they reveal the emerging connections, threads or assemblages that characterise development in their thinking and understanding. Drawing on Vygotskian theories to connect working theories, popular culture and funds of knowledge, Hedges (2011, 2014) has documented children's interests as a foundation for curriculum and pedagogy. Working theories occur in children's thinking and sense-making as they attempt to make connections between areas of experience, knowledge and understanding, and may subsequently form the links between everyday and scientific knowledge. As children create their own collective repertoires of knowledge and action, based on the development of themes over time, play offers different ways of constructing and performing identities, and positioning themselves in relation to different discourses and expectations. This requires that children develop the skills of self-understanding as well as metacognition, and the ways in which identities are understood as relational and not just individual.

Conclusions

Although the dominant educational discourse about the value of play has its own place, the challenge for research is to sustain a more complex understanding of the meanings that play holds for children. Ethnographic and interpretive methodologies have proved particularly effective for studying play and providing a means of understanding children's explanations for their thinking and actions. These methodological orientations allow detailed documentation of the creative ways in which children manipulate the tools and symbols of their cultures, and think creatively and imaginatively with these tools.

From the perspective of educational play, the question still remains whether play and self-initiated activities can or should enable children to learn generic thinking skills, or whether subject-specific skills should be taught intentionally through adult-led activities. It is typically the role of teachers to make thinking visible through pedagogical routines and practices, and as a means of checking that children have acquired the forms of knowledge and understanding that are validated in specific domains and curriculum frameworks. This is not to dichotomise or reinforce play/not play, or play/work boundaries, because imagination and pretence are the currencies of children's play lives, supported by their funds of knowledge. Children have the capacity to internalise knowledge and events that are of importance to them, and to represent their thinking in play activities, through fragments and working theories that may gradually connect to more coherent frameworks. A key distinction is that the forms of thinking and understanding that are evident in children's play activities may have profound significance for their development, but not in ways that align neatly or temporally with educational constructions of 'progress' and 'achievement'. Playful forms of thinking are shaped by the imaginative potential that enables (indeed requires) children to think differently from the perspective that 'this is play'. Therefore it can be argued that play is a domain in its own right in that children need specific play knowledge of how to perform roles, tasks and identities from those unique perspectives. Children's motivations to play are focused on becoming a more skilled player, developing play repertoires, and engaging in more complex forms of play. The ability to think differently from the perspective of play remains an important dimension of human development beyond childhood.

References

Alcock, S. (2010) Young children's playfully complex communication: Distributed imagination. *European Early Childhood Education Research Journal*, *18*(2), 215–28. doi: 10.1080/13502931003784404.

Aubrey, C. and Durmaz, D. (2012) Policy-to-practice contexts for early childhood mathematics in England. *International Journal of Early Years Education*, *20*(1), 59–77. http://dx.doi.org/10.1080/09669760.2012.664475.

Bodrova, E. (2008) Make-believe play versus academic skills: A Vygotskian approach to today's dilemma of early childhood education. *European Early Childhood Education Research Journal*, *16*(3), 357–69.

Broadhead, P. and Burt, A. (2012) *Understanding Young Children's Learning Through Play: Building Playful Pedagogies*. Abingdon: Routledge.

Brown, S. (2009) *Play: How it Shapes the Brain, Opens the Imagination, and Invigorates the Soul*. New York: Avery.

Cook, J. S. (2003) Progression and continuity in role play in the Foundation Stage. Unpublished MEd thesis, University of Exeter, UK.

Edmiston, B. (2008) *Forming Ethical Identities in Early Childhood Play*. Abingdon: Routledge.

Fleer, M. (2010) *Early Learning and Development: Cultural-historical Concepts in Play*. Cambridge: Cambridge University Press.

Gupta, A. (2009) Vygotskian perspectives on using dramatic play to enhance children's development and balance creativity with structure in the early childhood classroom. *Early Child Development and Care*, *179*(8), 1041–54.

Hall, E. (2010) The communicative potential of young children's drawings. Unpublished PhD thesis, University of Exeter, UK.

Hedges, H. (2011) Rethinking SpongeBob and Ninja Turtles: Popular culture as funds of knowledge for curriculum co-construction. *Australasian Journal of Early Childhood*, *36*(1), 25–9.

Hedges, H. (2014) Young children's 'working theories': Building and connecting understandings. *Journal of Early Childhood Research*, *12*, 35–49.

Henricks, T. S. (2010) Play as ascending meaning revisited: Four types of assertive play. In E. E. Nwokah (ed.) *Play as Engagement and Communication*, Play and Culture Studies, Vol. *10* (pp. 189–216). Lanham, MD: University Press of America.

Holzman, L. (2009) *Vygotsky at Work and Play*. East Sussex: Routledge.

Markström, A. (2010) Talking about children's resistance to the institutional order and teachers in preschool. *Journal of Early Childhood Research*, 8(3), 303–14.

Marsh, J. and Bishop, J. (2014) *Play, Media and Commercial Culture from the 1950s to the Present Day*. Milton Keynes. McGrawHill/Open University Press.

Moore, D. (2010) 'Only children can make secret places': Children's secret business of place. Unpublished MEd thesis, Monash University, Victoria, Australia.

Newton, E. and Jenvey, V. (2011) Play and theory of mind: Associations with social competence in young children. *Early Child Development and Care*, 181(6), 761–73.

Oates, J., Karmiloff-Smith, A. and Taylor, M. H. (2012) *Developing Brains, Early Childhood in Focus*, 7. Milton Keynes: Open University Press (wwbernardvanleer.org).

Robson, S. (2010) Self-regulation and metacognition in young children's self-initiated play and reflective dialogue. *International Journal of Early Years Education*, 18(3), 221–41.

Ross, D. (2013) Ambiguity and possibility: Cognitive and educational grounds for play. *International Journal of Play*, 2(1), 22–31.

Saracho, O. (2012) *An Integrated Play-based Curriculum for Young Children*. New York: Routledge.

Smith, P. K. (2010). *Children and Play*. Chichester: Wiley-Blackwell.

Sutton-Smith, B. (2001). *The Ambiguity of Play*, 2nd edn. Cambridge, MA: Harvard University Press.

Towsey, P. M. and Macdonald, C. A. (2009) Wolves in sheep's clothing and other Vygotskian constructs. *Mind, Culture, and Activity*, 16(3), 234–62. doi: 10.1080/10749030802596306.

Vygotsky, L. S. (1978) *Mind in Society* (trans. and ed. M. Cole, V. John-Steiner, S. Scribner and E. Souberman). Cambridge, MA: Harvard University Press.

Wallerstedt, C. and Pramling, N. (2012) Learning to play in a goal-directed practice. *Early Years: An International Journal of Research and Development*, 32(1), 5–15. doi.org/10.1080/0957514 6.2011.593028.

Whitebread, D. (2010) Play, metacognition and self-regulation. In P. Broadhead, J. Howard and E. Wood (eds) *Play and Learning in the Early Years: From Research to Practice* (pp. 161–76). London: Sage.

Whitebread, D. and O'Sullivan, L. (2012) Preschool children's social pretend play: Supporting the development of metacommunication, metacognition and self-regulation. *International Journal of Play*, 1(2), 197–213.

Wood, E. (2013) *Play, Learning and the Early Childhood Curriculum*, 3rd edn. London: Sage.

Wood, E. (2014) Free choice and free play in early childhood education: Troubling the discourse. *International Journal of Early Years Education*, 22:1, 4–18. doi: 10.1080/09669760.2013.830562.

Wood, E. and Cook, J. (2009) Gendered discourses and practices in role play activities: A case study of young children in the English Foundation Stage. *Educational and Child Psychology*, 26(2), 19–30.

Wood, E. and Hall, E. (2011) Drawings as spaces for intellectual play. *International Journal of Early Years Education*, 19(3–4), 267–81. doi: 10.1080/09669760.2011.642253.

Zhu, J. and Zhang, J. (2008) Contemporary trends and developments in early childhood education in China. *Early Years*, 28(2), 173–82.

3

HOW PLAY CREATES THE ZONE OF PROXIMAL DEVELOPMENT

Pentti Hakkarainen and Milda Brėdikytė

> In play children develop and master the structures of their own thinking. They lay the foundations of the inner forms of basic human notions. Play provides the channel of expression of children's emotional experiences and releases their spiritual potential.
>
> *(Brėdikytė, 2011, p. 203)*

Introduction

In this chapter we describe the problems that may arise in the interpretation of the Zone of Proximal Development (ZPD) particularly concerning children's play activity. We then give our interpretation of the term and provide examples of critical episodes of children's play. We conclude the chapter with a discussion and implications for practice.

Our supposition is that Vygotsky had as a goal the development of a comprehensive framework which could unite the idea of the ZPD in different contexts (e.g. play, learning and work). But he wrote about the ZPD in only two concrete contexts, play and learning (Hakkarainen and Brėdikytė 2008). His goal is clearly stated in the text:

> The relationship of play to development should be compared with that of teaching-learning to development. Changes of needs and consciousness of a more general kind lie behind the play.
>
> *(Vygotsky, 1933/1966, p. 70)*

It seems to us that Vygotsky was referring to two different units of analysis of development in two contexts of the ZPD. In problem-solving he was writing about new mental functions. In our opinion, 'more general kind of changes' in a play context

31

refers to changes of psychological systems consisting of several functions. Vygotsky described the ZPD in the context of play:

> Play is the source of development and creates the zone of proximal development. Action in the imaginary sphere, in an imagined situation, the creation of voluntary intentions and the formation of real-life plans and volitional motives – all appear in play and makes it the highest level of preschool development.
>
> *(Vygotsky, 1977, p. 96)*

Chaiklin (2003) reminds us that an essential key to an understanding of the Vygotskian concept of the ZPD is an understanding of what he meant by 'development': Chaiklin's conclusion from the reading of Vygotsky's texts on child development was that the activity of the child does not reveal development directly, but it is the system of psychological functions carried out in realizing the actions that underlies development.

ZPD and developmental transitions during the play age

If we follow Chaiklin's reading, we should ask how the system of higher mental functions develops during the 'play age', between Vygotsky's two crisis periods[1] – the crisis of three years and the crisis at seven. The only analysis of the relation between play and development Vygotsky focused on is in pretend play, which is possible after the crisis at three and fades after the crisis at seven. The criterion for this choice is separation of the sense field[2] and visual field from each other (Vygotsky, 1977). Vygotsky uses the same criterion in separating stages in play development in general. His classification is: infant – clean field (no play); early childhood – merger of visual and sense fields (Ernstspiel); preschooler – separation of the external sense field and the visual field (pretend play); school child – development of internal independent sense field coordinated with the external (athletic play); adolescent – 'Ernstspiel' develops in consciousness (Vygotsky, 2005, p. 92).

The creation of imaginary situations, in which the 'realization of unrealizable tendencies and desires' is possible, is the central structural element of pretend play in Vygotsky's approach. He argues that an imaginary situation is the main characteristic of play. The creation of the imaginary situation is based on the separation of visual and sense fields. Imagination is the neo-formation of the crisis of the third year and makes illusory realization of desires possible. Vygotsky defined children's play as imagination in actions (adolescents' imagination is play without actions!). He emphasized that play is the realization of wishes – not isolated ones, but generalized affects. This means that the child does not understand his own motives. He plays, but is not aware of the motives of his play. A paradox of play for Vygotsky is connected with the rules and joy of play. Acting on immediate impulses is usually the route to maximum pleasure and subjugation to the rules eliminates the joy of action. But play rules[3] and actions bring a change. Vygotsky (2005, p. 91) claims that 'play gives the child a new form of desire, that is, teaches him to want, relating the desire to the fictional ego' (i.e. to his role in play and its rules). In play Vygotsky found Spinoza's ideal of will and freedom. His conclusion was the paradox: the child subjugates himself to the rules of his role and in spite of that gets maximum pleasure out of play.

Vygotsky writes about the 'main genetic contradiction' of play and describes it as follows:

> An action replaces another action as a thing replaces another thing. How does the child transform one thing into another, one action into another? Through movement in the sense field not connected to visual, real things, which subordinates to itself all the real things and real actions. This movement in the sense field is the main thing in play: on the one hand it is movement in an abstract field (the field of sense arises earlier than voluntary operations with meanings), but the method of movement in the sense field is situational, concrete (i.e. not logical, but effective movement). The development of the sense field, but with movement taking place in it as if it were real, is the main genetic contradiction of play.
>
> *(Vygotsky, 2005, p. 97)*

The developmental results of make-believe play are something different from the correct solving of a problem, or imitation of adult mental functions. Make-believe play requires child initiative and creativity, which is needed in a range of practical life situations, and not only in specific problem-solving situations. Zuckerman (2007) emphasized the role of adult help as different from that originally proposed in the definition of the ZPD. For her, the adult is not just a person who helps the child to solve problems, but the most important factor in adult help is the support for children's initiative. This radical proposal introduces non-linearity to the old concept of ZPD and opens up the possibility of children's creativity because children's initiatives may lead to unexpected results of make-believe play or problem solving.

Zuckerman (2007) denied a linear model of development describing movement from point A to point B, and instead proposed a multidimensional model of possible development (Figure 3.1). In this model children make choices between alternative lines of development and adults may support or not support children's choices. The change of ZPD depends more on the type of adult help (interaction) than the content of tasks jointly solved.

Vygotsky states that 'from the point of view of development, play is not the predominant form of activity, but is, in a certain sense, the leading source of development in preschool years' (Vygotsky, 1977, p. 76). Vygotsky (2005) proposed two transitions of play during the 'play age': (1) from Ernstplay (object play) to pretend play, which can be seen as differentiation of visual and external sense fields, and (2) from pretend play to athletic play (having in mind all types of games with explicit rules) when the internal independent sense field is coordinated with the external visual field.

Vygotsky's brief sketch does not reveal the direct relation of these play transitions to the crisis periods. The main problem in transitions from one age to another in Vygotsky's analysis is the changes between the main line of development and the

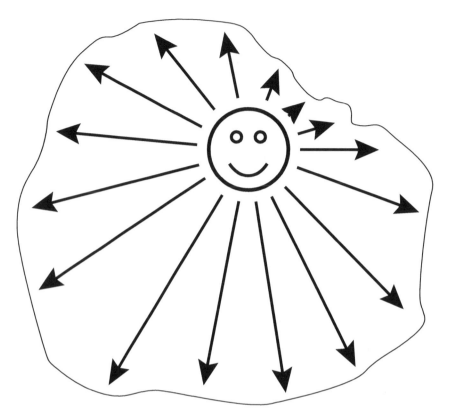

Figure 3.1 Multidimensional model of ZPD proposed by Zuckerman (2007, p. 53).

sidelines of development. In other words, at transition the main line of development from a previous age becomes a sideline, and a new main line of development arises. This is the problem of the dynamics of the appearance of psychological functions. Vygotsky tried to explain this by emphasizing the relationship between the child's personality and the social environment. This relation was called 'the social situation of development', which is specific for each age of the child (Vygotsky, 1998). A classic example is the crisis of the third year. The child thinks that he is 'big' already and does not accept any more help from adults because 'big boys' manage independently. His social environment should accept this and demonstrate the proper relationship towards 'independent big boys'.

Unfortunately the general theoretical concept of the 'social situation of development' does not show the developmental impact of play. Critical questions at the beginning of the play age are why children start to play and can we explain play development on the basis of differentiation of visual and sense fields? An answer to the first question should be found from the analysis of the crisis of the third year. What is the new psychological formation of this crisis? Vygotsky refers to a new type of motivation, which arises when mutual social relations between the child's personality and people around the child are reorganized. The child's relation to joint activity becomes less important and he gives precedence to relations with the people who are inviting him to joint activity. The child starts to motivate his actions not by referring to the situation, but to his relations with other people.

Vygotsky (1998) argues that the essence of all crises is the change of *perezhivanie* (emotionally living through). The substance of *perezhivanie* is different at each crisis, as is the content of the social situation of development. Vygotsky suggests that the crisis at 7 years (today the crisis often starts at 5–6 years) brings three main qualitative changes: (1) disappearance of the child's immediacy, (2) appearance of intelligent (rational) emotions, and (3) the change of generalizations. But what are new psychological formations resulting in mature pretend role-play?

We can deduce the following essential qualitative changes by juxtaposing Vygotsky's sketch of the main developmental line of play and epochs (crisis periods) of psychological age:

- The crisis of the third year produces the child's orientation to human relations, and role-play offers an appropriate and safe space for experimenting and field-testing experiences of these relations.
- A mature form of social pretend role-play develops the creative imagination and symbolic function, but at the same time reveals the limitations of acting in imaginary situations. Advanced play creates the need for real mastery of the environment.
- The mode of *perezhivanie* and the main line of development are changed at crisis periods. New needs and new motivational structures are born, and future developmental steps require a new social situation of development.

The ideal and real subject of the ZPD in play

Vygotsky's definition of the ZPD in play refers to the development of psychological characteristics (worldview, own will, motivation), which can be associated with personality traits. We interpret these traits as results of the whole play age, i.e. new functions of preschool age. There are several mechanisms supporting subject development in make-believe play.

Vygotsky noted the difference between real and ideal forms (of behavior). El'konin (2005) continued his work. Simplified we can say that culture is the world of ideal objects (images, patterns, ideas, symbols, signs, etc.) and actions. The world in front of the child is not only concrete, but is a world of ideas, understandings, and human deeds. An illustrative example might be a child going on all fours and adults around him going on two legs. Going on all fours (crawling) is the real form of the child and walking is the higher, ideal form. In other words, ideal forms exist at the same time as the real form of the child's behavior. Ideal forms invite the child to adopt walking as no adults go on all fours any more.

The first point Vygotsky (2005) paid attention to in his analysis was rule-dominated forms of play – make-believe play (hidden rules) and rule-play (open rules). In these forms the relation between the visual field (what is seen) and the sense field (idea, thought) is interesting. In make-believe play children operate with real objects, but they do not use them according to their normal use. Children's pretend actions are not the result of visual errors, but are made on purpose. Ideas direct actions, not objects. The same happens with roles and positions. Children adopt make-believe roles and act as if other persons (or imaginary beings) are following the hidden rules of the role.

A child in role is aware of the fact that the role is an 'as if' role. In other words, there is a tension between the real subject and the ideal 'as if' subject. The tension between real and ideal may be the reason behind Vygotsky's argument that the child can create his ZPD in play situations without the help of others.

Cases of creating joint ZPDs in play

The authors of this chapter had a unique opportunity to construct an experimental play laboratory at a remote teacher education unit in Finland, between 2002 and 2008. Children came to our laboratory on a voluntary basis and some of them spent one to three years there, one day per week during semesters. Creative activities for children were organized as a part of the obligatory university courses for the students of early childhood and primary education (future kindergarten and elementary school teachers).

There were several goals in our play laboratory: one of them was to provide courses on play and child development, to develop research abilities in our students and to carry out our own research projects exploring different aspects of child development through play. More specifically, the main purpose of our research activities was to examine how shared play activity creates the zones of proximal development of children and adults.

Our hypothesis was that all types and forms of play are not equally effective in promoting general child development and the ZPD. We believe that play promotes child development only if the child moves from elementary to mature forms of joint play. Children's play starts from object-oriented actions, then moves to short everyday life episodes. Later children move to role-oriented play. In parallel they become involved in construction play and simple games with rules. At the end of the preschool age, play activity is developed in a group of children through the construction of the plot; roles became secondary, subordinate to it. Children develop complex plots based not only on everyday life experiences but also on favorite tales, stories, TV programs, etc.

The students' role was not only to observe children's play, but also to intervene, actively play, and to construct play together. For the students this is a complicated task. The students have to be inside the activity, to act only when needed and do only what is really needed. The students' main task is to support the development of joint play activity. Besides that the students have to give appropriate individual support to participating children.

The main task of the adults is to find a common idea for play that satisfies every participant and to construct a play narrative that will motivate children to participate. Why is it important that children play together? We believe that play skills are acquired only from play interactions through active participation.

In our play interventions, joint creativity and dialogic improvisation is the central focus. We aim at more mature forms of play and children's play initiatives.

The following excerpts demonstrate three aspects of the development of children's joint play.

Beginning play participation

Three children and three students participate in a long-lasting role-play. They are sailors sailing in a ship. Robbers attack the ship in a port and now they are chasing them. Two children and students are in role. Urho, a 5-year-old boy, is participating as himself. Quite unexpectedly, Urho comes up with a spontaneous solution and takes on the role of a tracker dog. He has never before taken on a role and has previously been more of an observer of other children playing than an active participant. In the middle of the activity when everybody is searching for the robbers, Urho drops down on all fours and starts sniffing the carpet like a dog. 'Do you smell robber?' asks the Captain (a student in role). 'Yes, I do,' answers Urho also in role. Everybody appreciates the idea and agrees to include the dog. Urho becomes an active player in the group.

In this episode the child became comfortable taking on a role, which, from his point of view, was necessary in order to perform a successful search operation. Nobody told him to do so; we might say that play events required a dog and Urho performed a necessary action.

It is important to mention that this was the seventh time that Urho had participated in a joint play session with students and children. In fact, he came to play during the first play session but did not join in the play activity. He spent quite a lot of time sitting on the slide in the middle of a play 'ship' just observing play, sometimes making comments. Students invited him to join the play but he refused every time with a shy smile. Yet, he was physically already in the play ship as the slide was a part of ship construction. It is possible that the theme and dangerous events interested him a lot as he had participated in six play sessions before he finally became an active participant in the activity. Such persistence allows us to speculate that he became emotionally involved in the play once he took on the tracker dog's role.

Dramatic collision of story line (princess play)

Two 5-year-old girls are princesses and two students are their maids of honor. Little princesses have a picnic in the garden and return to the castle, celebrate birthdays, dance and so on. At the same time three boys aged 4–5 are playing knights and from time to time come to see the princesses, but there is no play interaction with the girls. Spontaneously one student dresses as a prince and comes to visit the party in the castle. At the moment when he is about to enter the castle, a big and angry bear (an adult in a mask) attacks him. The prince is shouting for help. The princesses are excited, but do not come to help the prince. Paula, a young 3-year-old, hears the noise and comes running from the other room. In a glance she realizes what is happening, takes a plastic sword and with a broad movement 'kills' the bear. Her movement of killing is very expressive and symbolical; the bear 'falls dead' at once. In fact the girl does not touch the bear with a sword but it is clear that she is very much aware of the frame 'this is play'. Everybody bursts into a loud shout: 'hurray!' and praises a young and brave prince (a tiny 3-year-old girl).

In general, the young girl is not on the level of constructing dramatic play events when playing by herself and in this episode she also performed a play action but the action was crucial to move the activity forward. This example demonstrates how the play structure is 'guiding' participants. They follow the structure of the activity and perform the required steps, which are above their individual abilities. Here we can speak about the ZPD in play. In this episode adults (a student and a teacher) created a dramatic event, which required creative steps from the players: it was clear for all participants (children and adults) that somebody should help the prince and the small girl was courageous enough to perform the action.

The adults were participating in this play together with children. When princess play became boring the adults made an intervention: a 'bear' attacked the prince. The student's aim was to move play events further. Usually, when adults are not involved in play, children themselves take such steps. If this does not happen, play stops and children move to other activities. They might come back to the same play theme again and again until they manage to move it forward.

Understanding the essence of structure in play

At the end of the day three girls are involved in a short play episode (eight minutes). The activity takes place in a big meeting room on the couch. Three girls are trying to play together. No adults are supervising them; one adult is filming. At the beginning Liisa (3.10) is sitting on the couch, and Lucy (6.2) on the floor.

Lucy has a transformer Little Red Riding Hood puppet[4] and Liisa has a 'Flower Princess' puppet with a long red skirt under which there is a stick. Noora (3.5) has a stick puppet 'bear' in her hand and tries to join the play using it as a role character.

Liisa's puppet lies on the couch; Lucy is just turning her puppet from grand-mother to Little Red Riding Hood. Liisa tries to get the transformer puppet, but Lucy does not give it to her, shouting that she is Little Red Riding Hood. Liisa disagrees, shouting that she is the real one in spite of the fact that Lucy has the real Red Riding Hood puppet! She suggests that Lucy could be a 'Red man'. But Lucy does not agree. The girls begin to compare their puppets. When Lucy does not succeed in getting the role she wants, she moves aside. Lucy seems disappointed and not interested in playing any more. With the 'bear' in her hand, Noora tries to get into the play. When Lucy moves aside, Liisa and Noora follow her, showing that they still want to play together.

After a few minutes Lucy transforms her puppet into grandmother and proposes a journey to England on the ship. When Lucy transforms her puppet into grandmother the joint play starts.

Often such role conflicts stop the play and children leave for other activities. Most conflicts arise from a 'central' role, which several participants want to have. When Lucy introduced 'grandmother' to the joint play it was possible to integrate Noora's 'bear' to joint play. The physical positions of the girls and emerging plot made sense when 'grandmother' rushed between the growling 'bear' and Little Red Riding Hood, and shouted, 'Bear, stop immediately intimidating my granddaughter!' Lucy thus demonstrated her relation (protection) towards Little Red Riding Hood.

It seems that the wish to play together is stronger than the ambition to play a particular role. The turning point in this situation is Lucy's decision to take grandmother's role. This is how children, by trial and error, begin to realize that in order to move the play forward there have to be mutually interrelated roles. Proper play is about events and relationships between the characters. The next step is finding a common theme and building a story line through constant negotiations.

Discussion: creation of the ZPD is a reciprocal process

Using all three examples we would like to move to some more general ideas about how the zone of proximal development is created.

In the first episode the *play events provoked* the child, Urho, to take a role and to act above his usual behavior in play. Of course, those play events were constructed by all participants together. Nevertheless, the students' role and the strategy they used in this particular case is very important. The students tried indirectly and directly to invite him to play. Every time in their reports they described how his behavior changed, what comments he made about play and they were sure that sooner or later he would start playing. At the same time they were very surprised when Urho joined the play as a tracker dog but not as a policeman. 'Most children want to be policemen,' they commented. We think that Urho made a very clever decision, because a policeman cannot smell the pirates, only a dog can!

Without the *adults constructing dramatic collision* between the bear and the prince in the second episode it is probable that the play would have stopped and the young girl Paula would have had no opportunity to carry out an action that saved the play and moved it forward. At the same time she made a significant step in her own development, because her action was part of a play activity that was above her individual abilities. We might say that she was acting in the zone of her proximal development.

In the third play episode Lucy would not have performed her creative step and started joint play without two young girls – Noora and Liisa – 'pushing' her all the time.

Here we can also refer to El'konin (1999), who said that 'human relations' and 'social roles' are the main purposes of role-play. We might say that role-play allows children to experiment and to test their personal attitudes and 'adjust' them to their experiences. In Urho's case, policemen are chasing pirates and the dog helps to track them down. In Paula's case we can see that she performed the role of a hero – the saver. Probably she was not very conscious of the role but she is already aware that some brave people are the savers of those who are in trouble.

Taking roles and constructing play narratives together children can explore different aspects of human relations trying to understand 'the universal meanings of human activity', as El'konin (1999) put it.

In all the examples we have tried to reveal how the players create and develop their play spontaneously and collaboratively improvising, as Sawyer (1997) describes. Play activity develops through creative steps carried out by individual players but those steps are possible only in concrete play activity and because of very concrete play situation. They are collective products of play activity and at the same time the vehicles through which the activity develops. As a result, developing activity develops the participants. So the creation of the ZPD is a reciprocal process: participants start developing play activity and the evolving activity demands that participants act in the zones of their proximal development.

We think that individual children and their ideas cause the development of the activity. In fact all participants (even the most passive and shy) are important. When children start playing, the activity itself creates tension and demands creative steps from the players. We claim that this might be the situation which Vygotsky (1977, p. 96) refers to when he describes play as 'creat[ing] the zone of proximal development' of the child. The players are demanding creative steps from each other because otherwise the activity may fall apart! When a decisive step is finally made and the whole play activity moves forward all the participants witness the creative step and the ownership of it is also collective.

Another very important feature of play is that it has many levels. Because of this feature of play, the players participating in the same activity, each develops on their own level. Collaborative make-believe play is enormously spacious; it can accommodate all possible experiences of the young child and provide the space to explore those experiences and enact them with other children. When we observe children playing we can follow the visible events, the external narrative. In fact, each individual child participating in the same play activity constructs her own version of the play narrative. Often children incorporate their own play themes into a larger play. When we observe children's play for a longer time we realize that there are many different levels of play and many small themes in one big play activity.

A good example could be a group of children of different ages playing being in a restaurant. A 5-year-old girl as a 'mother' came to the restaurant with a 'child' and a 'dog' – two 4-year-old girls. 'Mother' asked for the menu. The 'owner' of the restaurant, a 6-year-old girl, took a piece of paper and with the help of two other children wrote the names of the dishes. It took some time before they wrote 'pizza', 'apple juice', 'water' and brought the menu to the 'mother'. The 'mother' started 'reading' the menu and ordering. At that time the 'child' and the 'dog' went to play in the 'yard'. When the food was ready, they returned to eat.

This is an example of how play provides a space for the different needs of the children. For a while the 'mother' and the 'owner' of the restaurant were busy writing and reading the menu, while the younger girls developed their own play narrative. Older children often become involved in activities of real learning, exploration or work. They often need to write a letter, to make 'tickets' or 'money', to build and to make their play props. Advanced forms of play often 'move' children to real learning and exploration. This is the moment when adult help is needed.

Our observations and research findings prove that advanced play does not appear in the classroom 'naturally': it requires efforts from children and adults. At this stage of development of role and narrative play, direct adult guidance is almost impossible, but the role of the adult is very important.

Adult guidance and help in play should proceed in two main directions: (1) to develop joint activity of children, and (2) to support individual children participating in the activity. Adult help may be needed to keep children in the play frame (inexperienced children constantly 'fall out' of it), or to highlight children's ideas and use them for play construction. Adults should support the whole structure of play when it is starting to fall apart. In practice this means that they have to help individual children to participate in the activity but they also have to take an active role and move the activity one step forward when it is needed. We believe that the direct impact of the adult on development or learning is a fiction. An adult should create the experiences through the activities (not just separate tasks), participation in which would demand the child to act on their highest level, which in turn, sooner or later, will move their development.

Shared play activity is always an 'unknown' situation for the participants (children) but even more so for the adult. Supporting higher forms of play is a very challenging task for the teacher. We might say that this situation creates the ZPD for the adult. Adults can prepare and support the development, but not 'produce' it. They meet the challenge of their own ZPD in interventions because each child is a new unique individual person demanding specific interaction.

Notes

1 Vygotsky separated from early childhood crisis periods of development e.g. crisis of birth, first, third and seventh year. Needs, motives and dynamics of development changes at crisis he supposed. He wrote: 'The essence of every crisis is a reconstruction of the internal experience, a reconstruction that is rooted in the change of the basic factor that determinates the relation of the child to the environment, specifically, in the change in needs and motives that control the behavior of the child' (Vygotsky, 1998: 296).
2 In the translations into English usually 'the meaning-field' is used, but we think the Russian term 'smyslovoe pole' has a broader meaning: it means a broader field of meanings and ideas, including personal and cultural meanings.
3 Play rules refer to approved ways of constructing a role, not to more strict rules of adult life. These rules are often negotiated among children
4 It is a puppet [Red Riding Hood] that has several characters [a grandmother and a wolf] under her dress, and can be transformed into each of the characters.

References

Brėdikytė, M. (2011) *The Zones of Proximal Development in Children's Play*. Finland, Oulu: University of Oulu. Available at: http://herkules.oulu.fi/isbn9789514296147/isbn9789514296147.pdf.
Chaiklin, S. (2003) The zone of proximal development in Vygotsky's analysis of learning and instruction. In A. Kozulin, B. Gindis, V. Ageyev and S. Miller (eds) *Vygotsky's Educational Theory in Cultural Context* (pp. 39–64). New York: Cambridge University Press.

Hakkarainen, P. and Brėdikytė, M. (2008) The zone of proximal development in play and learning. *Cultural-Historical Psychology*, *4*(4), 2–11.

El'konin, D. B. (1999) Toward the problem of stages in the mental development of children. *Journal of Russian and East European Psychology*, *37*(6), 11–30.

El'konin, D. B. (2005) Psychology of play (I, II). *Journal of Russian and East European Psychology*, *43*(1 & 2).

Sawyer, R. K. (1997) *Pretend Play as Improvisation: Conversation in the Preschool Classroom.* Mahwah, NJ: Erlbaum.

Vygotsky, L. S. (1933/1966) Igra i ee rol' v psikhiceskom razvitii rebenka [Play and its role in the mental development of the child]. *Voprosy psikhologii*, No. *6*, 62–76.

Vygotsky, L. S. (1977) Play and its role in the mental development of the child. In M. Cole (ed.) *Soviet Developmental Psychology* (pp. 76–99). White Plains, NY: M.E. Sharpe.

Vygotsky, L. S. (1998) *The Collected Works*, ed. R. Rieber, Vol. *5*. New York: Plenum Press.

Vygotsky, L. S. (2005) Appendix: From the notes of L. S. Vygotsky for lectures on the psychology of preschool children. *Journal of Russian and East European Psychology*, *43*(2), 90–7.

Zuckerman, G. A. (2007) Child–adult interaction that creates a zone of proximal development. *Journal of Russian and East European Psychology*, *45*(3), 43–69.

4

DEVELOPING IMPLICIT SOCIAL COGNITION IN EARLY CHILDHOOD

Methods, phenomena, prospects

Dario Cvencek and Andrew N. Meltzoff

Overview

Social cognition concerns young children's knowledge of themselves, other people and the groups to which they belong. This type of knowledge can operate at a conscious and deliberate level (explicit knowledge) and also at an unconscious and non-verbal level (implicit knowledge). Implicit social cognition can exert a powerful influence on children's behavior. Social psychologists have studied implicit social cognition in adults, but implicit cognition has only recently become a focus of study in children. Implicit measures permit assessment of spontaneous aspects of children's thinking which may not always be captured accurately by conventional verbal reports. Children may not be able to verbalize or explain what they know or feel. They may also distort their true beliefs or attitudes to experimenters based on 'social desirability' of what they think the adult wants to hear. In such cases, measures of implicit social cognition can provide a valuable, even unique, window into children's thinking. This chapter describes the newly emerging field of implicit social cognition from preschool through elementary school. A special emphasis is placed on discoveries concerning young children's thinking and understanding of themselves and their social groups in the domains of gender and race.

Why study children's implicit understanding?

Social psychology as well as cognitive science studies with adults distinguish between deliberate, controlled, and conscious processes and more automatic and unconscious cognitive ones. These are captured by two types of measures: *explicit* and *implicit* measures (e.g. Greenwald and Banaji, 1995; Jacoby, 1991). In explicit measures, participants are often asked to provide verbal self-reports of their reactions and are aware of what is being assessed. In implicit measures, there is no self-report and participants are not necessarily informed about what is being assessed. When socially sensitive domains are measured in adults, such as racial stereotypes, implicit measures have often been shown to be *more* predictive of actual behavior than explicit measures.

In developmental science, experimental techniques designed to measure implicit social cognition are just emerging. Some relevant measures tap children's verbal responses indirectly, without requiring much introspection on the child's part. For example, one task involves showing children pictures of ambiguous situations and asking them to interpret these situations (Killen *et al.*, 2008) – which is sometimes referred to as an 'indirect' measurement technique. However, a stronger case for an implicit measure is one that bypasses verbal responses entirely. In one such case the child is simply given social items and characteristics and instructed to sort which go together most naturally (for example, the social items 'man' vs 'woman' and the characteristics of 'rough' vs 'gentle'). Children and adults find certain pairings to be more natural or 'congruent', and they group them with more facility than the opposite pairings. Such categorization tasks constitute an implicit measure of social cognition, one that the child may not be able to explain, but nonetheless can be measured.

The Implicit Association Test (IAT) is a widely used implicit measure in adult social psychology (Greenwald *et al.*, 1998). The adult IAT is an easy-to-administer sorting task that measures the strength of association among two pairs of categories. People generally find it easier (they are faster) to give the same response to items if they are associated in memory than if they are not. The IAT permits assessment of both *beliefs* (cognitive, non-valenced associations about groups) and *feelings* (affective, valenced associations about groups) without verbal report.

Young children's implicit understanding: conceptual distinctions

Beliefs and feelings are two facets of psychology that are important to investigate in childhood social cognition. Beliefs concern cognitive non-valenced mental representations – for example, the belief that 'math is for boys' is a *stereotype* and the belief that 'I am a boy' is part of a *self-concept*. In contrast, when affective or valenced feelings about a person or group are involved this is said to reflect an *attitude*. The feeling that item (or group) A is more likeable or nice, and item (or group) B is less likeable or mean are attitudes toward these social groups.

Beliefs and attitudes about groups (and about the self) are among the most important constructs in social psychology (Greenwald *et al.*, 2002). Although stereotypes, self-concepts, and attitudes can be studied using verbal reports in children, such approaches have often been stymied when probing the youngest children – due to children's inability to introspect about their beliefs/feelings or due to 'social desirability' distortions or both. Therefore, researchers have begun to explore the feasibility of investigating these fundamental aspects of the child's developing mind using implicit measures. In particular, the adult IAT procedure has been adapted for use with young children. It is often administered in conjunction with conventional tests using verbal introspective reports, and the relation between implicit and explicit measures is a topic of growing interest.

How to study children's implicit understanding: measuring implicit gender self-concept

Child-friendly versions of the IAT task have been created (Baron and Banaji, 2006; Cvencek *et al.*, 2011b). The Preschool IAT (PSIAT) is an adaptation of the IAT for children that we have developed in our laboratory and successfully used with children as young as 4.5 years of age. The PSIAT is suitable for children who do not read, because it includes: (a) the simultaneous presentation of visual and auditory stimuli, (b) detailed, color-coded visual reminders for children, and (c) a shorter protocol than that used with adults and older children (for methodological details see Cvencek *et al.*, 2011a). This experimental technique is useful for examining a range of stereotypes, self-concepts, and attitudes in preschoolers.

As an example of the utility and power of the child-friendly IAT, we can consider the child's self-identification regarding their own gender – whether they are a boy or a girl. Previous research has established that such gender self-concepts (the self-labeling of oneself as a boy or girl) are clearly and easily measurable using explicit measures by 3–4 years of age, if not younger (e.g., Leaper, in press; Martin and Ruble, 2010; Ruble and Martin, 1998). We recently demonstrated the validity and value of measuring gender self-concepts using a child-friendly IAT procedure.

Figure 4.1 provides a schematic overview of the Child IAT procedure that can be used to study young children's implicit social cognition. At the beginning of the procedure, the children are first told that they will 'play a game on a computer'. Children are then told that they will see and hear words during the game and will have to press a button to 'let the computer know which word it is'. During a gender

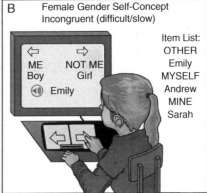

Figure 4.1   A schematic overview of the Child IAT technique for studying children's implicit social cognition. From Cvencek *et al.* (2011b), p. 769. Copyright © 2011 Society for Research in Child Development, Inc. Adapted with permission.

self-concept IAT, in one task, *me* words and *girl* names share a response key, with *not-me* words and *boy* names sharing the other response key (Figure 4.1, Task A). For girls with a strong own-gender identification, this would be an easy, 'congruent' task because it fits their own gender self-concept *(me = girl)*. In the other task, two of the response assignments are reversed, such that *me* and *boy* share one key while *not-me* and *girl* share the other key (Figure 4.1, Task B). For girls who identify strongly with their gender, this would be an 'incongruent' task and therefore more difficult. Girls with a strong own-gender self-concept *(me = girl)* should respond faster to the congruent task (Task A) than the incongruent task (Task B).

In our laboratory this Child IAT measure of gender self-concept was administered in five studies of boys and girls as young as 5 years old. Figure 4.2 plots the gender self-concept results for the studies. Data for the Studies 1–2 were collected with elementary school samples in the U.S. and Singapore; data for Studies 3–5 were collected with preschoolers in the US (see figure caption for details). In all five studies, the implicit measure of gender self-concepts showed, as expected, that girls significantly paired *me = girl* more strongly than boys do, with boys showing the *me = boy* pattern. These gender self-concept findings are consistent with previous research using explicit measures (see Ruble and Martin, 1998, for a review). These results are also useful because they establish that, even at the youngest preschool ages tested, the

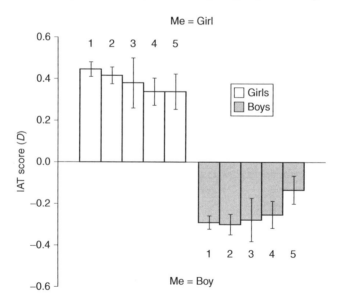

Figure 4.2 Implicit measurement techniques provide a continuous measure with sensitivity to individual differences in *stronger* or *weaker* identifications with own-gender. All participants were in preschool or elementary school. Data are plotted separately for each study, as indicated by the number (1, 2, 3, 4, and 5) above/below each bar. Study 1 = Cvencek *et al.* (2011b). Study 2 = Cvencek *et al.* (2014b). Studies 3–5 = Cvencek *et al.* (2014a). *N*s of 222, 155, 39, 96, and 60 are associated with Studies 1, 2, 3, 4, and 5 respectively. Error bars = *SE*s.

children have an understanding of their gender identity at an implicit level and this understanding can be measured and yields robust results while bypassing verbal report. The validity of our measuring instrument has been established (see Cvencek *et al.*, 2011b and Cvencek *et al.*, 2011a for more details).

The Child IAT and PSIAT methods go beyond the simple dichotomous classification of children into those who do/do not self-identify with their own-gender – which are often the dependent measures used in explicit measurement systems. The implicit measurement techniques are useful beyond this because they provide a continuous measure with a rational zero point, good internal consistency, and a sensitivity to individual differences in *stronger* or *weaker* identifications with own-gender on an interval scale (see Figure 4.2; and Cvencek *et al.*, 2011a for details). The ability to capture the strength or weakness of the social identification – and not merely its presence and absence – will be increasingly useful for predictions in longitudinal studies.

In-group preferences

At a young age, children's developing identity is shaped, in part, by their sense of self in relation to others: children feel a strong sense of relationship with the groups to which they belong ('in-groups'). In-groups are social categories that are related to the self and serve as one of the primary organizers of social knowledge. In development, in-groups emerge fairly early: children's recognition that others are 'like me' (Meltzoff, 2007, 2013) quickly translates to a *preference* or *liking* for the in-group members. How early such in-group preferences are formed and how early they begin to influence observable behavior is an emerging topic of the social cognition research in childhood.

Children's gender in-group preferences were measured using the PSIAT. In a study with 4.5-year-olds, Cvencek *et al.* (2011a) found that both girls and boys exhibited significant 'in-group' preferences, with girls holding that *girls* = *good* and boys that *boys* = *good*. Figure 4.3 displays the scores for the PSIAT gender attitude measure of 4.5-year-old girls and boys. The majority of the girls' scores is in the *girls* = *good* direction, and the majority of the boys' scores is in the *boys* = *good* direction. Crucially, the PSIAT in-group preference measure (a) correlated significantly with an explicit self-report measure of in-group preference and (b) predicted variance in parents' reports of their children's gendered play activities beyond that predicted by the explicit measure.

Both boys and girls demonstrated a preference for their own in-group, but it is also interesting that this in-group effect was more pronounced in girls than it was in boys (Figure 4.3B). Why would 4.5-year-old girls have stronger own-gender preference than 4.5-year-old boys (a result also found in adults)? One source could be more frequent interactions with maternal than paternal caregivers: positive attitudes towards one's *mother* may generalize to positive attitudes toward all females (i.e. *female* = *good*). For girls, the influence of this positive attitude towards one's mother works in the same direction as their in-group preference, and the two influences may combine, thus resulting in stronger own-gender preferences for girls than for boys. For boys, the

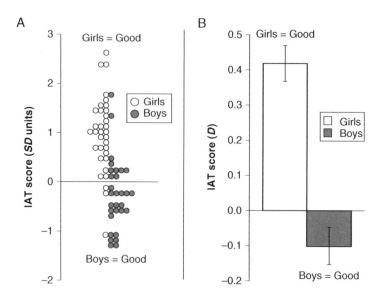

Figure 4.3 At a very young age, children already have a strong implicit sense of preference for the groups to which they belong ('in-groups'). The data plotted are from 4.5-year-old children. Individual scores (A) and mean scores (B) for the PSIAT measure of gender attitudes are plotted in standard deviation [*SD*] and IAT score [*D*] units, respectively. *N* = 64. (Panel (A) adapted and corrected from Cvencek *et al.* (2011a); the original figure had a few values for the boys mis-plotted; the original statistical tests were correct.). Error bars = *SEs*.

two influences work in the *opposite* directions. Another hypothesis about the source of the stronger own-gender preferences in girls may be diffuse negative perception of males: greater tendencies towards 'rough-and-tumble' play behaviors in boys are documented even during preschool years (e.g. Pellegrini, 1987). Young children of both genders may develop feelings that boys in general are the more rowdy and 'trouble-making' gender, contributing to the observed pattern of results.

The origins of STEM stereotypes in children

Research has examined how gender stereotypes influence participation and achievement in science, technology, engineering, and math (STEM) disciplines. In North America, England, and other cultures there is a widespread *stereotype* among adults that math is a male domain. Such gender stereotypes may have pernicious developmental consequences – playing a role in undermining young girls' mathematical performance and curtailing their aspirations about the future. Recent research has investigated *when* these stereotypes develop in elementary school children and *how* they influence children's emerging self-concepts, their interest in math, and their math achievement.

In one study with elementary-school children, participants completed Child IAT measures of gender self-concept, math–gender stereotype and math self-concept

(Cvencek *et al.*, 2011b). Elementary school years were chosen, because during this time girls' grades in mathematics are higher than boys' and they are not significantly behind boys on standardized test scores. Remarkably, the children demonstrated the cultural stereotype that 'math is for boys' as early as Grade 2. These findings suggest that the math–gender stereotype is acquired early and prior to ages at which there are actual differences in math achievement. These societally held stereotypes, once assimilated by the child, may have a detrimental effect on children's emerging math identities.

Other research using different implicit methods further corroborates that implicit math–gender stereotypes can be detected among: (a) 5-year-old Asian-American girls using a memory recall paradigm (Ambady *et al.*, 2001), (b) 7-year-old Caucasian-American girls using a picture-sorting and drawing task (Steele, 2003), and (c) 9-year-old German girls using a Child IAT (Steffens *et al.*, 2010). When the Child IAT methods were extended to adolescent girls in the Steffens *et al.*'s German sample, implicit math–gender stereotypes were predictive of math self-concepts and enrollment preferences in math classes above and beyond explicit math–gender stereotypes. This suggests that implicit gender stereotypes may be an important contributing factor to several different math-related outcomes for female students.

The impact of math–gender stereotypes on children's actual math achievement has been a topic of interest for those interested in connecting social cognition to school success. Research on *stereotype threat* (Steele, 1997) has provided convincing evidence for the impact of gender stereotypes on girls' math achievement (e.g. Aronson and Good, 2003). The underlying assumption of the stereotype threat model is that female students enter the testing situation with a concern that their poor performance will confirm a widely held stereotype about the poor mathematical ability of females. As a result, they experience 'stereotype threat', which then disrupts their performance on a math achievement test. Such detrimental effects of math–gender stereotypes have also been demonstrated with Asian-American girls as young as 5 years of age (Ambady *et al.*, 2001) and Italian girls as young as 6 years of age (Galdi *et al.*, 2014).

Cross-cultural studies have begun to investigate whether children's implicit self-concepts are similarly shaped by the prevailing cultural stereotypes. Singaporean children excel in math (OECD, 2011), but very little is known about their math stereotypes. In a recent study, Singaporean elementary school children (7–11 years old) completed Child IAT measures of gender self-concept, math–gender stereotype, and math self-concept, as well as a standardized math achievement test (Cvencek *et al.*, 2014b). The students demonstrated stereotypes about the math ability of girls, despite the fact that there were no gender differences in actual math achievement when the same children were given a standardized math test. In addition, Singaporean children's math–gender stereotypes increased as a function of age. Although the youngest Singaporean children did not show significant evidence of the stereotype (whereas American children did), the older Singaporean children began to demonstrate the stereotype, perhaps suggesting that that math–gender stereotypes reach Singaporean children through print and electronic media and the worldwide web as they become older (see Cvencek *et al.*, 2014b for a further discussion of cross-cultural effects).

Race attitudes and stereotypes

Race is another early emerging and important aspect of social categorization that features prominently in children's thinking. Do in-group preferences about race form as early and in the same fashion as the in-group preferences about gender? Using the Child IAT, Dunham and colleagues examined the development of implicit race attitudes in children aged 6–10. The results showed that at 6 years of age children already have positive race attitudes towards their own in-group. This effect was particularly pronounced when that in-group was contrasted with a minority out-group or the out-group was low in social status (Dunham *et al.*, 2006; Newheiser and Olson, 2012; Rutland *et al.*, 2005).

Children also hold stereotypical beliefs regarding race. One widespread cultural stereotype about race purports that Asian students are the 'model minority' who excel in math. A recent study explored the degree to which elementary and middle-school students hold racial stereotypes about who can be good at math (Cvencek *et al.*, in press). The Child IAT measure of math–race stereotype revealed that children associated *Asian* = *math* at the implicit level. Statistical analyses further suggest a developmental change in implicit math–race stereotypes – these stereotypes were significantly stronger in adolescence than in elementary school. The explicit measures in this study also assessed whether children were *aware* of the stereotype that Asians are good at math (cultural knowledge), and also whether they *endorsed* this particular stereotype (personal belief). Results showed that children were aware of and also endorsed the racial stereotype that 'Asians are good at math'. Interestingly, the Child IAT appeared to be more strongly related to the general awareness of cultural stereotypes than the personal endorsement of them. It seems likely, based on these findings and others, that children first recognize and register the cultural stereotypes and then are increasingly likely to take them on as their personal beliefs. We argue that cultural stereotypes are internalized and influence children's developing self-concepts (Cvencek *et al.*, 2011b).

Affective-cognitive consistency: how children organize their social knowledge

Stereotypes and attitudes do not exist in isolation. They are situated within a larger network of self-related concepts, beliefs, and evaluations. In adults, these cognitive networks tend to organize themselves to become mutually consistent or balanced (e.g. Greenwald *et al.*, 2002; Heider, 1946). These notions from social psychology about cognitive balance or consistency have recently been applied to young children. This research explores the degree to which children's cultural stereotypes and their self-concepts are in balance. It is predicted, for example, that a boy who associates *self* with *male* (gender self-concept), and also associates *math* with *male* (cultural stereotype), should be prone to develop the additional connection of *self* with *math* (math self-concept).

Recent research suggests that principles of cognitive consistency operate in elementary school children in the U.S. (Cvencek *et al.*, 2011b). More recently and for theoretical reasons, principles of cognitive consistency were also tested in East Asian cultures. These cultures are considered to be 'collectivist' in their interpersonal orientation (Brewer and Chen, 2007), meaning that they are not as individualistic or focused on the self as most Western cultures. Therefore, it was of considerable interest for developmental theory to find that even in collectivist cultures, children's social cognition during elementary school years is already organized according to the principles of cognitive consistency (Cvencek *et al.*, 2014b). We have hypothesized that the pressure to bring one's beliefs and attitudes into balance with each other and to be internally consistent may be a culturally universal mechanism or pressure that motivates psychological change in children's social-cognitive development. Thus the push towards cognitive balance may be a key mechanism of change in children's social-cognitive development.

Future directions

The construct of self-esteem is one of the most central constructs in social psychology, and it is thought to underlie a range of psychological and behavioral reactions in people. Interest in self-esteem can be traced at least back to William James's (1890) theorizing about self-feeling and self-love in his book *Principles of Psychology*. Developmental scientists have since sought techniques for exploring the origins, causes, and developmental changes in self-esteem. Yet, as important a construct as this is, developmental scientists have been unsuccessful in getting at it in young children.

Harter (2006) has done some of the best and most influential work on the development of self-esteem in children. According to her, young children (ages 3–7) can evaluate themselves in terms of *particular* cognitive abilities, but show no measurable evidence of *integrating* the domain-specific self-evaluations into a higher-order, overall evaluation of themselves, or global self-esteem.

The fact that young children cannot verbally formulate a global evaluation of themselves does not, however, dictate that they lack general self-esteem (*me = good*). We took up the challenge of testing for the existence of self-esteem at ages younger than Harter had shown it (Cvencek *et al.*, 2014a). The results from this ongoing work suggest that self-esteem is already strong in children as young as 5 years of age when tested with PSIAT techniques. Future studies will explore whether this early self-positivity may serve as a foundation for and interact with the formation of in-group biases that develop based on in-group membership characteristics.

The newly emerging ways of measuring implicit self-esteem have implications for educational theory and practice. Feelings of self-esteem may be connected to school readiness and educational success. Children commonly experience 'corrections' and failure in school contexts, since few of them consistently score 100 per cent on all tests. It would be desirable to assess self-esteem and problem-solving persistence in an integrative study of very young children. The availability of the self-concept PSIAT will also make it possible to conduct studies with preschoolers to explore the emergence of academic self-concepts (e.g. children's identification with math or reading) and how well they predict young children's subsequent educational achievement.

Conclusion

The study of implicit social cognition and inter-group relations in young children unites social, developmental, and cognitive psychology with education and informs an interdisciplinary 'science of learning' (Meltzoff *et al.*, 2009; Olson and Dweck, 2008). Future studies will profit from comparing implicit, unconscious measurement tools with verbal, deliberate measures in the same children both cross-sectionally and longitudinally – an effort that promises to advance our knowledge about the mechanisms, developmental timeline, and personal experiences surrounding young children's development. Although the formal, experimental study of implicit social cognition is relatively new, its usefulness and promise has already been shown by producing results in multiple domains of inter-group relations (gender, race), across diverse age groups (preschool, elementary school and beyond), and cross-culturally in different countries (U.S., Singapore, Japan, Italy, Germany).

References

Ambady, N., Shih, M., Kim, A. and Pittinsky, T. L. (2001) Stereotype susceptibility in children: Effects of identity activation on quantitative performance. *Psychological Science, 12,* 385–90.

Aronson, J. and Good, C. (2003) The development and consequences of stereotype vulnerability in adolescents. In F. Pajares and T. Urdan (eds) *Adolescence and Education, Vol. 2: Academic Motivation of Adolescents* (pp. 299–330). Greenwich, CT: Information Age Publishing.

Baron, A. S. and Banaji, M. R. (2006) The development of implicit attitudes: Evidence of race evaluations from ages 6 and 10 and adulthood. *Psychological Science, 17,* 53–8.

Brewer, M. B. and Chen, Y. (2007) Where (who) are collectives in collectivism? Toward conceptual clarification of individualism and collectivism. *Psychological Review, 114,* 133–51.

Cvencek, D., Greenwald, A. G. and Meltzoff, A. N. (2011a) Measuring implicit attitudes of 4-year-olds: The Preschool Implicit Association Test. *Journal of Experimental Child Psychology, 109,* 187–200.

Cvencek, D., Meltzoff, A. N. and Greenwald, A. G. (2011b) Math–gender stereotypes in elementary school children. *Child Development, 82,* 766–79.

Cvencek, D., Greenwald, A. G. and Meltzoff, A. N. (2014a) *New implicit measures for preschool children confirm self-esteem's identity maintenance function.* Manuscript submitted for publication.

Cvencek, D., Meltzoff, A. N. and Kapur, M. (2014b) Cognitive consistency and math–gender stereotypes in Singaporean children. *Journal of Experimental Child Psychology, 117,* 73–91.

Cvencek, D., Nasir, N. S., O'Connor, K. M., Wischnia, S. and Meltzoff, A. N. (in press) The Development of Math–race Stereotypes: 'They say Chinese people are the best at math'. *Journal of Research on Adolescence.* Retrieved from http://onlinelibrary.wiley.com/enhanced/doi/10.1111/jora.12151/.

Dunham, Y., Baron, A. S. and Banaji, M. R. (2006) From American city to Japanese village: A cross-cultural investigation of implicit race attitudes. *Child Development, 77,* 1268–81.

Galdi, S., Cadinu, M. and Tomasetto, C. (2014) The roots of stereotype threat: When automatic associations disrupt girls' math performance. *Child Development, 85,* 250–63.

Greenwald, A. G. and Banaji, M. R. (1995) Implicit social cognition: Attitudes, self-esteem, and stereotypes. *Psychological Review, 102,* 4–27.

Greenwald, A. G., McGhee, D. E. and Schwartz, J. L. K. (1998) Measuring individual differences in implicit cognition: The Implicit Association Test. *Journal of Personality and Social Psychology, 74*, 1464–80.

Greenwald, A. G., Banaji, M. R., Rudman, L. A., Farnham, S. D., Nosek, B. A. and Mellott, D. S. (2002) A unified theory of implicit attitudes, stereotypes, self-esteem, and self-concept. *Psychological Review, 109*, 3–25.

Harter, S. (2006). Developmental and individual difference perspectives on self-esteem. In D. K. Mroczek and T. D. Little (eds) *Handbook of Personality Development* (pp. 311–34). Mahwah, NJ: Erlbaum.

Heider, F. (1946) Attitudes and cognitive organization. *The Journal of Psychology, 21*, 107–12.

Jacoby, L. L. (1991) A process dissociation framework: Separating automatic from intentional uses of memory. *Journal of Memory and Language, 30*, 513–41.

James, W. (1890) *The Principles of Psychology*. New York: Holt.

Killen, M., McGlothlin, H. and Henning, A. (2008) Explicit judgments and implicit bias: A developmental perspective. In S. R. Levy and M. Killen (eds) *Intergroup Attitudes and Relations in Childhood Through Adulthood* (pp. 126–45). Oxford, England: Oxford University Press.

Leaper, C. (in press) Gender and social-cognitive development. In R. M. Lerner (series ed.), L. S. Liben and U. Muller (volume eds) *Handbook of Child Psychology and Developmental Science* (7th ed), Vol. 2 (pp. 806–53). New York, NY: Wiley.

Martin, C. and Ruble, D. N. (2010) Patterns of gender development. *Annual Review of Psychology, 61*, pp. 353–81.

Meltzoff, A. N. (2007) 'Like me': A foundation for social cognition. *Developmental Science, 10*, 126–34.

Meltzoff, A. N. (2013) Origins of social cognition: Bidirectional self-other mapping and the "Like-Me" hypothesis. In M. R. Banaji and S. A. Gelman (eds) *Navigating the Social World: What Infants, Children, and Other Species Can Teach Us* (pp. 139–44). New York, NY: Oxford University Press.

Meltzoff, A. N., Kuhl, P.K., Movellan, J. and Sejnowski, T. J. (2009) Foundations for a new science of learning. *Science, 325*, 284–8.

Newheiser, A. K., and Olson, K. R. (2012) White and Black American children's implicit intergroup bias. *Journal of Experimental Social Psychology, 48*, 264–70.

OECD (Organisation for Economic Co-operation and Development) (2011) *Lessons from PISA for the United States: Strong Performers and Successful Reformers in Education* Paris, France: OECD.

Olson, K. R. and Dweck, C. S. (2008) A blueprint for social cognitive development. *Perspectives on Psychological Science, 3*, 193–202.

Pellegrini, A. D. (1987) Rough-and-tumble play: Developmental and educational significance. *Educational Psychologist, 22*, 23–43.

Ruble, D. N. and Martin, C. L. (1998) Gender development. In N. Eisenberg (ed.) *Handbook of Child Psychology: Social, Emotional, and Personality Development*, Vol. 3 (pp. 933–1016). New York: Wiley.

Rutland, A., Cameron, L., Milne, A. and McGeorge, P. (2005) Social norms and self-presentation: Children's implicit and explicit intergroup attitudes. *Child Development, 76*, 451–66.

Steele, C. M. (1997) A threat in the air: How stereotypes shape intellectual identity and performance. *American Psychologist, 52*, 613–29.

Steele, J. (2003) Children's gender stereotypes about math: The role of stereotype stratification. *Journal of Applied Social Psychology, 33*, 2587–606.

Steffens, M. C., Jelenec, P. and Noack, P. (2010) On the leaky math pipeline: Comparing implicit math–gender stereotypes and math withdrawal in female and male children and adolescents. *Journal of Educational Psychology, 102*, 947–63.

5

THE ORGANISATION OF MEMORY AND THOUGHT

Where the boundaries of now meet the boundaries of me

Suzanne Flannery Quinn

Introduction

This chapter is a brief introduction to memory as a temporal and self-referential construct that is presumed to have a structure. In this chapter I outline the premises upon which memory rests in relation to young children's thinking and provide an overview of theory and research related to a range of ideas about the structure of memory.

Memory is a construct that is specifically related to a component of the thought process involving information from previous experience (or thought about that experience). The activity of remembering involves recall of information that has been taken in by the sensory register, has been stored, and therefore is available for use by the person who is remembering.

Researchers within the field have developed models of memory that have posited theoretical distinctions between different types of memory related to the duration and use of the memory, such as short-term memory, long-term memory, and working memory (see Alloway et al., 2006; Baddeley, 1986, 2000; Baddeley and Hitch, 1974). Further distinctions are made between the memory of personal events (called episodic memory), the memory of general knowledge (called semantic memory), and the memory of specific skills and movements (called procedural memory) (see Tulving, 1983, 2002; Renoult et al., 2012; Picard et al., 2012). There are also distinctions made within research related to the differing processes that might be involved in remembering, that may be contingent upon different forms of sensory input; for example, visual-spatial, auditory/verbal, or tactile information may require differing processing strategies (see Alloway et al., 2006).

Other issues of interest to researchers of memory include the amount of experience an individual has with the ideas that are remembered, as well as the impetus for the remembering: for example, what causes or facilitates remembering, and whether it is explicit (effortful) or implicit (seemingly automatic). An understanding of all aspects of memory requires a theoretical understanding of how memory operates both for individuals but also for people who relate to one another, such as parents and children, siblings, friends, and even communities. Remembering is something that people are thought to do on their own, but also together, in the process of collective (or joint) remembering.

The study of memory is relevant to a range of disciplines including, and not limited to, psychology, education, philosophy, the humanities, and health sciences. Memory studies has also grown to become a discipline in itself, with its own subdivisions (Roediger and Wertsch, 2008). The breadth of perspectives on the topic of memory presents a unique challenge to a person who wants to know more about it, because there are diverse ways of thinking and talking about memory, and, as with any aspect of human thinking, there will always be more to know about it.

Remembering is a capacity that humans have across the lifespan, and is a skill that is thought to develop and change over time (Bauer, 1997; Bjorklund and Douglas, 1997; Courage and Howe, 2004; Schneider and Pressley, 1997; Strange and Hayne, 2013). Memory capacities and skills are variable from person to person, and memory is subject to disability via injury and disease. The study of children's memory is of interest to people who work with children, but is also of interest to those with a broader interest in the development of thinking for people of all ages.

With this in mind, I begin with a few provisional premises upon which the concept of memory in relation to young children's thinking is built. I outline these premises to preface some of the very basic questions and issues that connect memory and young children's thinking in a range of theory and research specific to young people's cognition. These premises involve the child's emerging sense of time (called the boundaries of now) and their emerging sense of self (called the boundaries of me). These premises are inspired by an understanding of human phenomenological experience as a Physical Transcendent Presence (Stables, 2008, 2012) that involves personal vantage points of selves as experienced within time, each of which has boundaries. I use these ideas to suggest that a development of memory occurs within a lived space where a young person's boundaries of 'now' meet their (biologically and socially) constructed boundaries of their 'me'.

The boundaries of now

Perhaps the most important premise is that memory is a temporal construct in relation to a thought process. That is, it exists in time (Kontopodis, 2009). The notion of memory and remembering requires that we accept and employ the basic language of time as a way to describe the ordering of human experiences (as past, present, or future). Using memory, as a component of a thought process, implies that information from the thinker's past experiences (which could have occurred as recently as a few moments or a lifetime in the past) can be, and has been, stored for later use, and can be recalled, and thought about, by the thinker in a time that is relative to the past. The moment of recall is always now, but memories are thoughts about the past, which have been stored for future use. Because of this characteristic, memory is often described as mental time-travel (Suddendorf and Corballis, 1997; Tulving, 2002). Therefore, memory is contingent upon boundaries of 'now'. If we did not have a concept of successive time, or a boundary around now, then memories would not exist.

The boundaries of me

Another important premise of memory is related to the relationship between the people who are remembering, what is important to be remembered, and how this is communicated. Memory, as a temporal construct involved in thought, rests on the idea that the information that is used in thought has initially come from a range of sensory input to an individual (a person who knows themselves as 'me'), but that sensory input itself, and the ideas related to the meaning of the input, are mediated collectively by others. For young children, this is most often their immediate family (for examples see Fivush et al., 2008; Fivush and Nelson, 2006; Harris et al., 2008; Horn, 1984; Kulkofsky, 2011; Ornstein et al., 2004; Ratner, 1984; Reese et al., 1993; Rogoff et al., 1993; Salmon et al., 2008).

The premise of a mediated memory suggests that no object or idea comes into the cognitive range of a person without the action of another person, even if another person is not co-present. For example, even though I am alone right now, the ideas I am writing about are those first presented by others, in a language we share, which is a form of mediation. Therefore, cognitively, I am not alone. I might also suggest that none of us are ever alone, in our thinking. Thought and memory is dependent upon a permeable boundary of 'me'. This is possibly a fragile proposition, from some philosophical viewpoints, but it is one I will posit here, because it is particularly relevant in the study of memory in relation to young children's thinking. For even the youngest newborn infant finds themselves constantly in a world full of objects and ideas that they are brought into cognitive contact with because of others. Only a newborn left naked in the forest would be in the world alone, and would have a slim chance at survival, and she or he still would have been placed in that situation by another. Further, young people are thought to be in a developing state of understanding the boundaries of their 'me' in time (Cunningham et al., 2013; Salmon et al., 2008). According to this line of reasoning, thinking (and its constituent memory), while they are processes that occur biologically within an individual, are never a solitary endeavour. Memory, therefore, is contingent upon the mediated boundaries of the thinker's 'me' in relation to others.

The premise of structure

Finally, the last important premise of memory that I will posit to help us to understand the concerns of theorists, researchers, and practitioners is that memories are structured or organised. It is this idea that we can take as a point of departure, for how memories are organised is at the heart of inquiry and a matter of key debate in theory and research related to memory. Most researchers believe that memory is a constructive process that is highly dependent upon a person's biological architecture, their ability to encode and retrieve thoughts, their current and past experiences, as well as culturally mediated values for what is important to be remembered. I will briefly address each of these proposed structural attributes of memory related to thought in what follows, but for a fuller account of the range of issues and debates specific to young children's memory development you may wish to consult Bauer and Fivush (2013).

How do we organise our thoughts as memories?

The answers to questions about how memory is organised are many and varied, and depend on the theoretical and disciplinary background of the researchers. All of the research that addresses the organising principles of thought and memory can be placed in relation to their conceptualisations of the child's emerging boundaries of now (time) and me (self). Neuroscientists, for example, generally work within narrow boundaries of time and self, and are concerned with specific biological structures within the central nervous system. Experimental psychologists are concerned with the measurable behavioural processes of encoding and storage, and in some cases, the role of experience in the development of memory in relation to thought. Their generalisations can be thought of as loosening the conceptual constraints of time and self. Researchers who work within a socio-cultural paradigm (who might be from a variety of disciplines) stretch the boundaries of time and self even further to consider the culturally mediated aspects of human memory, which might extend beyond the lifetime of the thinker, and locate thinking beyond the boundaries of self, as it is always mediated by others.

Organisation within our biological architecture

It seems logical that thought and memory occur somewhere within the central nervous system, intuitively, in the brain. Neuroscientists aim to study the functions of the neural system, and many studies are devoted to the specific study of memory. Through neuro-imaging data, researchers have examined the potential location of networks within the brain that are related to remembering. Interestingly, some have suggested that there is a link between the pathways for remembering and imagining, two components of the thought process that might not have been otherwise conceptually linked (Addis *et al.*, 2007; Atance and O'Neill, 2001; Hassabis *et al.*, 2007; Schacter *et al.*, 2007; Spreng *et al.*, 2009). Neuroscience suggests that thoughts and memories are organised for retrieval within the central nervous system. However, scientists have not been able to pinpoint the location of a specific 'thought' or 'memory' within this system; they merely have been able to create images of what happens within the system when we think, remember, and imagine.

Clearly, thought and memory involve the brain, but as processes that use information from sensory input, they also involve other parts of the body, in complex interactions (via language, movement, logic, and culture) in relation to our sense of self, our understanding of others (Fivush and Nelson, 2006), and within a physical and social environment that surrounds us. All these aspects may serve as frameworks for organising thought. However, they are variable, because humans may have varying capacities related to the senses, and because there are a variety of cultural influences on language, movements, and logic, and also varying abilities and dispositions that each person has with regard to the understanding of self and other. As a component of a broader thinking process, memory is not thought to be a unitary trait or function, but a set of (hypothetical) systems, that many believe are composed of differing rules of operation, regardless of the 'location' of the process within the central nervous system (Bartlett, 1932; Bauer, 1997, Courage and Cowan, 2009; Hudson and Fivush, 1990; Kuhn, 2000; Renninger, 1990; Tulving, 1983, 2002).

Encoding and retrieval of thoughts

The origins of organised thoughts in the form of memory in infancy is of particular interest because of the peculiar phenomenon of infant 'amnesia', which is the inability of most adults to recall events from their early years (prior to the age of 3 or 4). Infant amnesia is a mystery. As Rovee-Collier and Gerhardstein (1997) explain, this amnesia had been hypothesised to be because of differences in the abilities of young children to encode and store memories long term. Yet research has found that children can recall events from their childhood, even if adults cannot (Boyer *et al.*, 1994). That is, young children (as young as 9 months) have been found to recall specific novel events and sequences for up to 24 hours. Yet most adults cannot recall events from the time period during which they were infants. The length of time in which children can recall is found to increase with age, which has challenged the assumptions of some of the traditional perspectives on memory (Bauer, 1997). However, Bauer explains that children may need to be shown how to remember over longer retention intervals, because if they are not, then the early memories may become inaccessible over time and into adulthood.

Bauer and others have wondered why some memories that were once accessible become inaccessible. Two explanations might be: the immaturity of the neural architecture in young children; and/or the lack of a means by which early memories later can be made available for verbal expression. This is a puzzle that still raises questions for researchers, and highlights the varieties of concerns, theories, and disciplinary approaches in the fields of study concerned with how and why young children remember.

More recently, Gross *et al.* (2013) explain that the amnesia associated with early memories can refer to information that is forgotten over time, as well as situations in which information has not been encoded, or registered (and presumably not well organised) in the memory successfully. Their research of children aged 2–5 and their recall of the birth of their sibling was compared to similar data collected from adults by Davis *et al.* (2008). They found a similarity between adult and child recollections of the birth of a sibling to be related to the age of the person at the time of the birth of the sibling. This suggests that the differences in recollections are a function of age, and perhaps differences in encoding at the time the event took place, rather than due to forgetting.

An alternative explanation is that the differences in memory are due to differences in retrieval rather than encoding. For example, Boyer *et al*'s (1994) experimental study of 3-year-old children's memory of a novel play event (making make-believe spaghetti out of modelling clay) that had occurred when they were 20 months old found no strong evidence for verbal or behavioural recall of the event after a long delay. However, older children could sequence the event more accurately (after a long delay) than younger children (after a short delay) and only marginally better than children who were the same age, but in the control group. Boyer *et al.* (1994) suggest that a possible explanation for this is that older children may have a better understanding of how memory works, and what it means to remember, which may underlie an understanding of what to do when they were asked to re-enact the task that they were meant to remember. Another possibility for differences in older children's ability to remember is that they have better retrieval strategies, or a better understanding of how their memory works, and their capacity for remembering (DeMarie and Ferron, 2003; Roebers, 2013).

Current and past experiences

Researchers have highlighted the influence of a person's knowledge base, background knowledge, and experience on the functional capacity of their memory (Bjorklund and Douglas, 1997; Farrar and Goodman, 1990; Kuhn, 2000; Schneider and Pressley, 1997). Chi's (1978) studies of the memory span of children who were experts at chess compared to adults who were not experts at chess is often cited by researchers interested in the role of experience in relation to memory. Findings from this well-known study were that the child experts had a greater memory span than the non-expert adults. However, this capacity for memory was not sustained when digits were used as stimuli rather than chess pieces. Bjorklund and Douglas (1997) explain that this is generally interpreted as a change in a person's functional capacity over time and in relation to what is being remembered, rather than a change in a person's actual capacity for remembering. In essence, it is easier to remember things about which you have developed a knowledge base. Kuhn (2000) explains that the chessboard studies also reveal that memory capacity cannot be identified in domain-general terms. Others have suggested that while knowledge can be correlated with memory, it is not necessarily causally related (DeMarie-Dreblow, 1991; Muir-Broaddus *et al.*, 1995).

Knowledge has an impact on all types of memory, and that advantage is not always mediated by the use of specific strategies. Bjorklund and Douglas (1997) note that a typical pattern of development of memory involves children using but not benefiting from the use of strategies. They firmly state that 'more differences in memory performance can be attributed to differences in knowledge base than any other factor' (p. 220). This is a viewpoint that is held by many researchers who view knowledge and familiarity as an asset in the process of remembering (Bauer and Mandler, 1990; Ratner *et al.*, 1990), and has clear implications for the importance of meaningful first-hand experiences for young people. This viewpoint would suggest that provision of meaningful activities that afford children the opportunities to touch and experience materials and to subsequently question and talk about ideas is beneficial with regard to the development of memory and recall.

Culturally mediated values for what is important to be remembered

Socio-cultural perspectives on memory acknowledge that memory and thinking is a socially meaningful process that involves collective memory, and as such alludes to remembering as an activity that occurs in sharing often via discussion among people (Rogoff and Mistry, 1990; Fivush and Nelson, 2006). In these discussions, a signal is sent about what is valued, and hence what is important to be remembered. For children, their primary partners in early conversations are their caregivers, usually their parents. Research in this area has been concerned with the cognitive demands that these conversations place on children. Ratner's research demonstrated that 'mothers who required their children to use their memories most often, then, had children who continued to be best able to produce information from long-term memory a year later' (Ratner, 1984, p. 2185).

Because memory within a socio-cultural paradigm is thought of as being related to understanding of self in relation to others, a key aspect of memory is autobiographical, and directly related to the child's emerging sense of the boundaries of 'me' (as I have described previously). This has led to questions about the kinds of processes that may underlie children's emerging autobiographical understanding. A socio-cultural approach to the study of memory helps to address these questions. Socio-cultural perspectives represent a different focus on memory processes than those offered by pure neuroscience. Rather than a focus on biological processes, research and theory in a socio-cultural tradition seeks a socially and contextually oriented understanding of cognitive development as embedded within a larger socio-historical context, with the appropriate unit of analysis as the interaction between children and adults, rather than the individual person (Boyer, 2009). A socio-cultural perspective can help us to understand how culture is communicated through intimate relationships, how these relationships signal what is valued within culture, and what is useful and meaningful to be remembered by the young person in culture.

Hudson's (1990) research suggested that an interactive learning model is most appropriate to describe how very young children's autobiographical memories are constructed. She explains that what is learned in the conversations that the child has with another (the mother in the case of her observations and experiments) helps to form a narrative structure of memories, and further aids the child in how to search memories for details. This is distinguished from a rote memorisation approach to memory. Hudson found that 'how mothers talked about the past was more important than the specific content of what they mentioned. Children whose mothers used an elaborative style were better able to answer information requests about more remote events and profited more from prior conversations when remembering events with an experimenter' (1990, p. 190).

Research within this paradigm has examined mother–child conversations of present events as well as reminiscing of past events, and has continued to find an association between children's developing memory skills and mothers who have used an 'elaborative' conversational style when their children were young (Ornstein *et al.*, 2004, p. 378). Ornstein's experimental study of mothers and children aged 2.5 years found that the manner in which mothers conversed with their children affected what their children were able to recall. When mothers ask questions about an ongoing event such as 'what', 'where', or 'why', they alert the child to aspects of the situation that are personally and culturally important. If the mother's questioning is followed by the child's further verbal elaboration, then the child's representation of the situation or event may be enriched.

It is thought that mother–child conversations offer a unique context in which the mother, who knows the child's experiences and preferences, can 'take advantage of the child's interests, and positive evaluations of the child's contributions can serve to encourage joint discussion' (Ornstein *et al.*, 2004, p. 386). This process of intimate and responsive conversation helps children to make sense of situations, and calls their attention to what is culturally relevant. Although their research primarily addressed elaborative talk during ongoing situations, they note that it clearly indicates that there is evidence that memory is facilitated by elaborative joint discussions between caregivers and children.

Current research on children's cognitive development places emphasis on the importance of warm family relationships and intimate discussions and reminiscences between parents and their young children. Our current understanding of how children grow to understand themselves in relation to others begins with the intimacy of the parent–child relationship. Robust findings within the socio-cultural paradigm of memory studies have indicated that parental conversations alert children to relevant cultural information and events or ideas that may be important to 'remember' (Fivush and Nelson, 2006; Fivush *et al.*, 2008; Harris *et al.*, 2008; Horn, 1984; Kulkofsky, 2011; Ornstein *et al.*, 2004; Reese *et al.*, 1993; Rogoff *et al.*, 1993; Ratner, 1984, Salmon *et al.*, 2008).

The benefits of recognising the social nature of early thinking in relation to learning are firmly established in current thinking about young children, as exemplified by concepts such as Sustained Shared Thinking (Siraj-Blatchford, 2009), scaffolding (Wood *et al.*, 1976), interthinking (Mercer, 2000, p. 141), and Vygotsky's (1978) 'zone of proximal development' (Rogoff *et al.*, 1993), all of which highlight the importance of interactions mediated by cultural understandings.

Conversations about the past are essential in a person's construction of mind. They offer a unique challenge for young people, because the topic of the conversation is not something that is physically present. This activity goes a step beyond inter-subjectivity, in which the child and a partner are focused on present activities or objects. It could be said that these conversations help children to establish the boundaries of now (time) and me (self).

References

Addis, D. R., Wong, A. T. and Schacter, D. L. (2007) Remembering the past and imagining the future: Common and distinct neural substrates during event construction and elaboration. *Neuropsychologia*, 45, 1363–77.

Atance, C. M. and O'Neill, D. K. (2001) Episodic future thinking. *Trends in Cognitive Sciences*, 5, 533–9.

Alloway, T. P., Pickering, S. J. and Gathercole, S. E. (2006) Verbal and visuospatial short-term and working memory in children: Are they separable? *Child Development*, 77(6), 1698–716.

Baddeley, A. D. (1986) *Working Memory*. Oxford, UK: Clarendon.

Baddeley, A. D. (2000) The episodic buffer: A new component of working memory? *Trends in Cognitive Science*, 4, 417–23.

Baddeley, A. D. and Hitch, G. (1974) Working memory. In G. Bower (ed.) *The Psychology of Learning and Motivation*, Vol. 8 (pp. 47–90). New York: Academic Press.

Bartlett, F. C. (1932) *Remembering: A Study in Experimental and Social Psychology*. New York: Cambridge University Press.

Bauer, P. J. (1997) Development of memory in early childhood. In N. Cowan and C. Hulme (eds) *The Development of Memory in Childhood* (pp. 83–111). Hove, East Sussex: Psychology Press.

Bauer, P. J. and Fivush, R. (eds) (2013) *The Wiley Handbook on the Development of Children's Memory*, Volume I/II. West Sussex: Wiley.

Bauer, P. J. and Mandler, J. M. (1990) Remembering what happened next: Very young children's recall of event sequences. In R. Fivush and J. A. Hudson (eds) *Knowing and Remembering in Young Children* (pp. 9–29). Cambridge: Cambridge University Press.

Bjorklund, D. E. and Douglas, R. N. (1997) The development of memory strategies. In N. Cowan and C. Hulme (eds) *The Development of Memory in Childhood* (pp. 201–46). Hove, East Sussex: Psychology Press.

Boyer, M. E., Barron, K. L. and Farrar, M. J. (1994) Three-year-olds remember a novel event from 20 months: Evidence for long-term memory in children? *Memory*, 2(4), 417–45. http://dx.doi.org/10.1080/09658219408258957.

Boyer, P. (2009) What are memories for? Functions of recall in cognition and culture. In P. Boyer and J. V. Wertsch (eds) *Memory in Mind and Culture* (pp. 3–28). New York: Cambridge University Press.

Chi, M. T. H. (1978) Knowledge structures and memory development. In R. Siegler (ed.) *Children's Thinking: What Develops?* (pp. 73–96). Hillsdale, NJ: Erlbaum.

Courage, M. L. and Cowan, N. (2009) *The Development of Memory in Infancy and Childhood*. East Sussex: Psychology Press.

Courage, M. L. and Howe, M. L. (2004) Advances in early memory development research: Insights about the dark side of the moon. *Developmental Review*, 24, 6–32.

Cunningham, S. J., Brebner, J. L., Quinn, F. and Turk, D. J. (2013) The self-reference effect on memory in early childhood. *Child Development*. doi: 10.1111/cdev.12144.

Davis, N., Gross, J. and Hayne, H. (2008) Defining the boundary of childhood amnesia. *Memory*, 16, 465–74. doi: 10.1080/09658210802077082.

DeMarie, D. and Ferron, J. (2003) Capacity, strategies, and metamemory: Tests of a three-factor model of memory development. *Journal of Experimental Child Psychology*, 84, 167–93.

DeMarie-Dreblow, D. (1991) Relation between knowledge and memory: A reminder that correlation does not imply causation. *Child Development*, 62, 484–98.

Farrar, M. J. and Goodman, G. S. (1990) Developmental differences in the relation between scripts and episodic memory: Do they exist? In R. Fivush and J. A. Hudson (eds) *Knowing and Remembering in Young Children* (pp. 30–64). Cambridge: Cambridge University Press.

Fivush, R. and Nelson, K. (2006) Parent–child reminiscing locates the self in the past. *British Journal of Developmental Psychology*, 24, 235–51.

Fivush, R., McDermott Sales, J. and Bohanek, J. G. (2008) Meaning making in mothers' and children's narratives of emotional events. *Memory*, 16(6), 579–94.

Gross, J., Jack, F., Davis, N. and Hayne, H. (2013) Do children recall the birth of a younger sibling? Implications for the study of childhood amnesia. *Memory*, 21(3), 336–46. http://dx.doi.org/10.1080/09658211.2012.726628.

Harris, C. B., Paterson, H. M. and Kemp, R. I. (2008) Collaborative recall and collective memory: What happens when we remember together? *Memory, 16*(3), 213–30. http://dx.doi.org/10.1080/09658210701811862.

Hassabis, D., Kumaran, D. and Maguire, E. A. (2007) Using imagination to understand the neural basis of episodic memory. *Journal of Neuroscience, 27,* 14365–74.

Horn, H. (1984) Memory demands and the development of young children's memory. *Child Development, 55*(6), 2173–91.

Hudson, J. A. (1990) The emergence of autobiographical memory in mother-child conversation. In R. Fivush and J. A. Hudson (eds) *Knowing and Remembering in Young Children* (pp. 166–96). Cambridge: Cambridge University Press.

Hudson, J. A. and Fivush, R. (1990) Introduction: What young children remember and why. In R. Fivush and J. A. Hudson (eds) *Knowing and Remembering in Young Children* (pp. 1–8). Cambridge: Cambridge University Press.

Kontopodis, M. (2009) Editorial: Time. Matter. Multiplicity. *Memory Studies, 2*(5), 5–10.

Kuhn (2000) Does memory development belong on an endangered topics list? *Child Development, 71*(1), 21–5.

Kulkofsky, S. (2011) Characteristics of functional joint reminiscence in early childhood. *Memory, 19*(1), 45–55.

Mercer, N. (2000) *Words and Minds: How We Use Language to Think Together.* London: Routledge.

Muir-Broaddus, J., Rorer, R., Braden, T. and George, C. (1995) The effects of a knowledge base manipulation on individual differences in processing speed and recall. *Contemporary Educational Psychology, 20,* 403–9.

Ornstein, P. A., Haden, C. A. and Hedrick, A. M. (2004) Learning to remember: Social-communicative exchanges and the development of children's memory skills. *Developmental Review, 24,* 374–95.

Picard, L., Cousin, S., Guillery-Girard, B., Eustache, F. and Piolino, P. (2012) How do the different components of episodic memory develop? Role of executive functions and short-term feature-binding activities. *Child Development, 83*(3), 1037–50.

Ratner, H. H. (1984) Memory demands and the development of young children's memory. *Child Development, 55*(6), 2173–91.

Ratner, H. H., Smith, B. S. and Padgett, R. J. (1990) Children's organisation of events and event memories. In R. Fivush and J. A. Hudson (eds) *Knowing and Remembering in Young Children* (pp. 66–93). Cambridge: Cambridge University Press.

Reese, E., Haden, C. A. and Fivush, R. (1993) Mother-child conversations about the past: Relationships of style and memory over time. *Cognitive Development, 8,* 403–30.

Renninger, K. A. (1990) Children's play interests, representation, and activity. In R. Fivush and J. A. Hudson (eds) *Knowing and Remembering in Young Children* (pp. 127–65). Cambridge: Cambridge University Press.

Renoult, L., Davidson, P. S. R., Palombo, D. J., Moscovitch, M. and Levine, B. (2012) Personal semantics: At the crossroads of semantic and episodic memory. *Trends in Cognitive Sciences, 16*(11), 550–8.

Roebers, C. M. (2013) Children's deliberate memory development: The contribution of strategies and metacognitive processes. In P. J. Bauer and R. Fivush (eds) *The Wiley Handbook on the Development of Children's Memory,* Volume I/II (pp. 865–94). doi: 10.1002/9781118597705.

Roediger III, H. L. and Wertsch, J. V. (2008) Creating a new discipline of memory studies. *Memory Studies, 1*(1), 9–22. doi: 10.1177/1750698007083884.

Rogoff, B. and Mistry, J. (1990) The social and functional context of children's remembering. In R. Fivush and J. A. Hudson (eds) *Knowing and Remembering in Young Children* (pp. 197–222). Cambridge: Cambridge University Press.

Rogoff, B., Mistry, J., Goncu, A. and Mosier, C. (1993) Guided participation in cultural activity by toddlers and caregivers. *Monographs of the Society for Research in Child Development, 58* (7, Serial No. 236).

Rovee-Collier, C. and Gerhardstein, P. (1997) The development of infant memory. In N. Cowan and C. Hulme (eds) *The Development of Memory in Childhood*. Hove, East Sussex: Psychology Press.

Salmon, K., Champion, F., Pipe, M., Mewton, L. and McDonald, S. (2008) The child in time: The influence of parent-child discussion about a future experience on how it is remembered. *Memory*, *16*(5), 485–99.

Schacter, D. L., Addis, D. R. and Buckner, R. L. (2007) Remembering the past to imagine the future: The prospective brain. *Nature Reviews Neuroscience*, *8*, 657–61. doi: 10.1038/nrn2213.

Schneider, W. and Pressley, M. (1997) *Memory Development Between 2 and 20*, 2nd edn. New York: Erlbaum.

Siraj-Blatchford, I. (2009) Conceptualising progression in the pedagogy of play and sustained shared thinking in early childhood education: A Vygotskian perspective. *Educational & Child Psychology*, *26*(2), 72–89.

Spreng, R. N., Mar, M. A. and Kim, A. I. S. (2009) The common neural basis of autobiographical memory, prospection, navigation, theory of mind, and the default mode: A quantitative meta-analysis. *Journal of Cognitive Neuroscience*, *21*, 489–510. doi: 10.1162/jocn.2008.21029.

Stables, A. (2008) *Childhood and the Philosophy of Education: An Anti-Aristotlean Perspective*. London: Continuum.

Stables, A. (2012) *Be(com)ing Human: Semiosis and the Myth of Reason*. Rotterdam: Sense.

Strange, D. and Hayne, H. (2013) The devil is in the detail: Children's recollection of details about their prior experiences. *Memory*, *21*(4), 431–43. http://dx.doi.org/10.1080/09658211.2012.732722.

Suddendorf, T. and Corballis, M. C. (1997) Mental time travel and the evolution of the human mind. *Genetic, Social and General Psychology Monographs*, *123*, 133–67.

Tulving, E. (1983) *Elements of Episodic Memory*. Oxford: Oxford University Press.

Tulving, E. (2002) Episodic memory: From mind to brain. *Annual Review of Psychology*, *53*, 1–25.

Vygotsky, L. (1978) *Mind and Society: The Development of Higher Mental Process*. Cambridge, MA: Harvard University Press.

Wood, D., Bruner, J. and Ross, G. (1976) The role of tutoring in problem solving. *Journal of Child Psychology and Psychiatry*, *17*(2), 89–100.

6

THE DEVELOPMENT OF CHILDREN'S CAUSAL EXPLANATIONS

Cristine H. Legare and Jennifer M. Clegg

Introduction

A fundamental task for all humans is explaining why things happen. Research on conceptual development indicates that even children as young as 3 years of age can use knowledge of cause and effect relationships to make predictions (Shultz, 1982), engage in efficacious interventions (Kushnir and Gopnik, 2007; Schulz and Gopnik, 2004), and provide explanations for phenomena in the world (Legare *et al.*, 2009; Wellman *et al.*, 1997). Not only do young children frequently seek explanations by asking questions (Callanan and Oakes, 1992; Chouinard, 2007; Hickling and Wellman, 2001), they also construct their own explanations (Legare, 2012; Legare and Gelman, 2014; Legare *et al.*, 2010).

However, other research (e.g. concerning children's metacognition) has shown that young children are surprisingly poor at assessing their own understanding and that this ability develops dramatically across development. Indeed, both adults and children overestimate the detail and depth of their explanatory knowledge (Mills and Keil, 2004; Wilson and Keil, 1998). Taken together, these two sets of findings produce something of a paradox in the literature on children's causal reasoning. On the one hand, children are active explanation-seekers and readily seek out and provide causal explanations. On the other hand, they seem to be poor at assessing their own causal knowledge and often think they understand things when they do not. What then motivates children to ask questions and generate explanations if the result of this process is often children concluding that they understand something when they do not? More specifically, what kinds of events do children feel most compelled to explain?

Children readily make use of covariation information, statistical regularities, and causal relationships in order to understand causal outcomes, frequently from very limited available input (Gopnik *et al.*, 2001; Schulz and Gopnik, 2004; Kushnir and

Gopnik, 2007). If children have a cognitive model of the world based on a framework of anticipatory causal regularities, they would be well equipped to rapidly form expectations contingent upon prior beliefs or knowledge. Given a predisposition to forecast causal regularities, children may anticipate that *outcomes will continue to occur as expected* and find consistent outcomes especially worthy of explanation. Constructing explanations for events that are consistent with children's prior knowledge and experience may indeed be an important function of children's own explanations. For example, explaining consistent outcomes may provide children with an important opportunity to deepen their understanding of causal phenomena by allowing them to generate causal mechanisms.

Another intriguing possibility is that explanation is motivated by discovery (Legare, 2014; Sobel and Legare, 2014). That is, young children might especially value, seek, and provide explanations for events that are inconsistent with their current expectations. According to this possibility, because children readily form expectations for causal regularities based on prior knowledge (even when sparse), children may be highly motivated to attend to irregular or discordant information. Information that is inconsistent with how they expect things to happen could be especially informative and noteworthy because it indicates that their prior knowledge about a causal relationship or outcome was incomplete or inaccurate. Therefore, children may be vigilantly attentive to and more likely to attempt to explain disconfirmatory outcomes. If this were the case, engaging in explanation would allow children the opportunity to accommodate and reconcile inconsistent information in the context of prior beliefs. Forming explanations for inconsistent outcomes may provide children with the opportunity to generate new hypotheses regarding events that seem to disconfirm their prior knowledge (Legare *et al.*, 2010; Legare, 2012, 2014).

Before addressing the question of how these two competing hypotheses about the function of children's explanations have been tested, we present an overview of the developmental literature on causal explanatory reasoning, followed by a discussion of the role of contrastive outcomes in shaping causal explanation, and an overview of the kinds of events that provoke or trigger causal explanation.

The development of causal reasoning: the role of explanation

The development of causal reasoning has been an important topic in developmental psychology since Piaget (1929), and children's causal reasoning has received renewed attention in more recent years (Gopnik and Schulz, 2007), especially from those characterizing children's knowledge in terms of naïve theories (Carey, 1985; Gopnik and Meltzoff, 1997; Gopnik and Wellman, 1994; Keil, 1989; Wellman and Gelman, 1998). A substantial amount of developmental research has demonstrated that young children understand many general causal principles (Bullock *et al.*, 1982; Kushnir and Gopnik, 2005; Schulz and Gopnik, 2004; Shultz, 1982) and possess rich causal knowledge (Wellman and Gelman, 1998). However, less is known about how causal reasoning develops and the role explanation plays in this process.

A central function of causal reasoning is to provide explanations for phenomena in the world. Causal explanations play a central role in both everyday reasoning

(Gopnik, 2000; Hickling and Wellman, 2001; Hilton, 1988; Keil, 2006; Keil and Wilson, 2000; Sloman, 2005) and scientific theories (Hempel, 1965; Pitt, 1988; Salmon, 1984, 1989; Strevens, 2006; Trout, 2002, 2007; Woodward, 2003). Additionally, prominent theories of conceptual development (Carey, 1985; Keil, 1995, 2003) and category learning (Murphy, 2002; Murphy and Allopenna, 1994) assign a central role to causal-explanatory understanding, claiming that explanation is central to the nature and development of naïve theories (Wellman, 1990) and concepts (Murphy and Medin, 1985). Indeed, the explanatory component of children's developing knowledge structures may be especially crucial. Children's causal explanations both demonstrate their understandings of the world and, like their questions (Chouinard, 2007), may constitute a mechanism for advancing causal learning and the acquisition of knowledge (Amsterlaw and Wellman, 2006; Bartsch and Wellman, 1989; Callanan and Oakes, 1992; Gopnik and Meltzoff, 1997; Siegler, 1995; Wellman, 2011).

Causal explanation is a goal-directed human activity. It depends on what is relevant or important to the person constructing an explanation. A desire to understand may underlie the motivation to construct an explanation (Gopnik, 1996). According to Gopnik (1996, 2000), the phenomenology or experience of explanation is an essential component of the task of explanation. One possibility is that a drive to explain evolved because, generally speaking, it aids in learning and contributes to an increasingly accurate understanding of the causal structure of the world around us. There is mounting evidence that a strong interest in constructing explanations may indeed be especially beneficial for learning in childhood (Legare and Lombrozo, 2014; Walker *et al.*, 2013).

Emerging developmental research has demonstrated a greater focus on the development of explanation. To the extent that explicit 'why' questions and 'because' answers can be used as prototypical indices of explanatory reasoning, developmental research indicates that both explanations and requests for explanation are widespread even in very young children (Frazier *et al.*, 2009; Keil, 2006; Keil and Wilson, 2000). Research examining preschoolers' everyday conversations with their caregivers has demonstrated that causal explanations increase in frequency with age but are common even at 2–3 years of age (Callanan and Oakes, 1992; Crowley *et al.*, 2001; Wellman *et al.*, 1997). Furthermore, causal explanations most typically serve an epistemic function; that is, they provide an interpretation for a current or past event, and do not serve an exclusively social-regulatory function (Hickling and Wellman, 2001). Given the proliferation of explanatory activity young children engage in, what triggers or motivates children to generate causal explanations?

Contrastive outcomes, counterfactuals, and causation

To investigate the kinds of events children are most compelled to explain, we turn now to a discussion of when children's explanations involve invoking a contrastive or counterfactual case, as opposed to focusing exclusively on the event-to-be-explained. Counterfactual thinking entails mentally comparing the observed case with alternative cases, and this process may direct attention to and provoke interest in inconsistent outcomes. When observing an event, children build a representation of the event that they use to interpret, explain, and predict its outcomes. Causal judgments often involve a contrast between a perceived sequence and a counterfactual case (Hilton and Slugoski, 1986), and developmental research indicates that preschool children use counterfactual thinking in causal reasoning (Harris *et al.*, 1996). That is, in order to identify a new outcome children often notice contrastive outcomes and identify the conditions that are causally responsible for differences between the outcomes. Contrary to the Humean account of causal learning, Mackie (1974) argues that our beliefs about causality are not based exclusively on repeated observations but also on an interpretation of what is observed and what might have been observed instead.

Although research using contrastive outcomes with children is limited (but see Harris *et al.*, 1996), research on infant cognition relies heavily on the use of contrastive outcome tasks as a way to prime and assess infants' expectations. Infant cognition research provides support for the hypothesis that inconsistent or problematic outcomes are compelling from a very early age (Wang *et al.*, 2004). Violation-of-expectation (VOE) tasks have been widely used to assess infants' understanding of physical (Baillargeon, 2002) and psychological (Onishi *et al.*, 2007) phenomena, based on the assumption that infants: (a) have expectations, (b) are surprised when these expectations are violated, and (c) index surprise by showing greater attention as determined by increased looking time. In a typical VOE experiment, infants watch two test events, one consistent with the expectation examined in the experiment (expected event) and one inconsistent (unexpected event). In order to introduce potentially unfamiliar test stimuli or establish specific expectations, prior to the test trials, infants usually view habituation or familiarization trials. With appropriate controls, evidence that infants look reliably longer at the unexpected than at the expected event is taken to indicate that they possess the expectation under investigation, detect the violation in the expected event, and are surprised by this violation (Wang *et al.*, 2004).

However, it is difficult to tell whether these responses (typically measured as heightened attention or arousal) from infants are truly demonstrating surprise, or even expectation-violation. Moreover with infants, one cannot tell for sure if they are actively exploring or genuinely seeking more information. For example, there is no good evidence that longer looking time corresponds to other measures of emotional state (Haith and Benson, 1997; Haith, 1998; Wang *et al.*, 2004). Although claims about explanatory phenomenology and expectation violation have been amply made in the infancy literature, there is still a big gap between the behaviors that can be measured (such as looking time) and the phenomenon of theoretical interest (for present purposes, whether an event is in need of explanation). Therefore, examining explanatory reasoning with older children may provide us with more concrete insights into the development of causal reasoning.

Children's causal explanations do more than demonstrate their understandings of the world through verbal articulation: they may also constitute a mechanism for advancing causal learning and the acquisition of knowledge (Legare, 2012, 2014; Lombrozo, 2006). Moreover, because children are actively engaged in developing causal knowledge structures, constructing explanations may engage their emerging curiosity and understanding. Additionally, prototypical indices of explanatory reasoning such as 'why' questions and 'because' answers indicate that both explanations and requests for explanation are widespread even in 2-year-olds (Frazier *et al.*, 2009; Keil, 2006; Keil and Wilson, 2000).

Explanatory triggers

Because young children have so much to learn, they have much to explain. How do children navigate the task of causal learning and what motivates children to construct causal explanations? We propose that explanatory biases play an important role in guiding children's causal explanations. Children make use of causal-explanatory understanding to explain *consistent events* (when events unfold as anticipated based on prior knowledge) but also to recognize and attempt to explain *inconsistent events* (when something unusual or discordant with prior knowledge happens). Accordingly, children's explanations may serve at least two distinct functions. One possibility is that explanation serves as a mechanism for confirming children's prior knowledge. Children are early in the process of developing explanatory knowledge and are faced with the considerable task of navigating an infinite number of outcomes and events that could potentially warrant explanation. Therefore, consolidating and confirming their explanations for events consistent with prior knowledge and experience may be especially attractive and beneficial.

Another possibility is that because children anticipate regularity or consistency with prior beliefs, they may therefore find *outcomes inconsistent with prior knowledge* especially worthy of explanation. For example, children may expect an object to continue to function or a person to continue to behave in a manner consistent with prior experience. Alternative functioning or anomalous behavior would therefore be inconsistent outcomes.

We propose that (a) events inconsistent with prior knowledge are especially powerful triggers for explanatory reasoning and (b) events consistent with prior knowledge are less likely to motivate children to construct explanations. Although the idea that inconsistent, problematic, or surprising outcomes play an important role in causal reasoning appears across multiple literatures – philosophy of science (Hempel, 1965), social psychology (Hilton, 1995), educational research (Chi *et al.*, 1989), and infancy research (Baillargeon, 2002) – there is remarkably little empirical research on what motivates causal explanations in children and how this can inform the developmental trajectory of causal explanation.

How might these alternative possibilities be tested? Imagine that a child sees two equivalent events, one in accord with prior knowledge and the other not. If explanation is largely confirmatory, children should simply explain what they already have an explanation for. If explanation is instead responsive to discordant or anomalous information, children should explain the event that falls outside their prior knowledge or expectations. This is the scenario Legare and colleagues used as an experimental paradigm to examine these competing hypotheses about the function of children's explanations (Legare and Gelman, 2014; Legare *et al.*, 2010; Legare, 2012). Moreover, they examined the nature of children's explanations, specifically whether children provided explanations primarily in terms of surface features and past histories, or whether they offered explanations focused on less-obvious properties.

To address these issues experimentally, Legare and colleagues designed a task with a set of novel 'light boxes' – electronic devices that glowed bright when activated (Legare *et al.*, 2010). The activation and deactivation of the boxes were experimenter-controlled, but appeared to be caused by objects placed on the surface of each box (materials were modeled after those used in Gopnik and Sobel, 2000; Gopnik *et al.*, 2001). These materials were used to teach children about different categories of objects, where within each category items were both perceptually identical and shared common causal properties. Objects were labeled according to their causal properties: 'starters' were objects that activated the light box when placed on top of it, 'stoppers' were objects that deactivated the light box when placed on top of it, and 'do-nothings' were objects that could neither activate nor deactivate the light box. After training, children were presented with scenarios in which a new object that looked like one type (for example, it looked like a 'starter') actually behaved like another type (behaved like a 'do-nothing'; inconsistent event). This was paired with an object that looked and behaved like those previously seen (looked like a 'do-nothing' and behaved like a 'do-nothing'; consistent event). Upon viewing such paired outcomes, children were asked a non-specific explanatory question ambiguously referring to either (visible) outcomes: 'Why did that happen?'

An important feature of the design of this study was experimentally differentiating the kinds of events that children find noteworthy and therefore feel compelled to explain. The events that led to greater interest and attention, and most importantly, increased explanation, were examined. If the role of explanations for children is confirmatory, children should have been interested in and provided explanations for the consistent event in this pair. If inconsistency plays a special role in motivating children to construct explanations, they would then be specifically interested in and provide hypotheses and explanations for the inconsistent event. The results indicated that children were most likely to first explain an inconsistent rather than a consistent event (Legare *et al.*, 2010).

A second objective of the study was to examine the types of explanations children generated. Children could have referred to a variety of features in their explanations – surface appearances, underlying causal properties and past histories, or category membership. Even children as young as 3 years of age can categorize objects in terms of novel, non-obvious properties (Jaswal and Markman, 2007; Graham *et al.*, 2004; Gelman and Coley, 1990; Gelman and Markman, 1986, 1987), apply names to objects with the same functional properties (Kemler-Nelson, 1995), and categorize and name objects based on novel causal properties (Gopnik and Sobel, 2000), overriding perceptual appearances. If information about an object's underlying causal properties or function is central to how children categorize and reason about objects, information about function and underlying causal properties should be found in children's causal explanations. The results of Legare *et al.* (2010) demonstrate that the content of children's explanations for inconsistent outcomes was more likely to refer to internal causal properties, include information about causal function, and override perceptual appearances than consistent outcomes. The findings suggest that inconsistent events motivate children to construct more sophisticated explanations and provide evidence consistent with the proposal that children's causal explanations function in the service of discovery.

Concluding summary

A growing body of research supports the proposal that children's explanations provide unique insight into the development of causal reasoning. Research examining explanatory biases has demonstrated that inconsistency with prior knowledge motivates children to construct explanations (Legare *et al.*, 2010), guides discovery-oriented behavior, and constrains the early developing capacity to reason scientifically (Legare, 2012, 2014).

References

Amsterlaw, J., and Wellman, H. (2006) Theories of mind in transition: A microgenetic study of the development of false belief understanding. *Journal of Cognition and Development*, 7, 139–72.

Baillargeon, R. (2002) The acquisition of physical knowledge in infancy: A summary in eight lessons. In U. Goswami (ed.) *Blackwell Handbook of Childhood Cognitive Development* (pp. 47–83). Oxford: Blackwell.

Bartsch, K. and Wellman, H. (1989) Young children's attribution of action to beliefs and desires. *Child Development*, *60*, 946–64.

Bonawitz, E., Lim, S. and Schulz, L. (2007) Weighing the evidence: Children's theories of balance affect play. *Proceedings of the Twenty-Ninth Annual Conference of the Cognitive Science Society*. Nashville, Tennessee.

Bullock, M., Gelman, R. and Baillargeon, R. (1982) The development of causal reasoning. In W. J. Friedman (ed.) *The Developmental Psychology of Time* (pp. 209–54). New York: Academic Press.

Callanan, M. and Oakes, L. (1992) Preschoolers' questions and parents' explanations: Causal thinking in everyday activity. *Cognitive Development*, 7, 213–33.

Carey, S. (1985) *Conceptual Change in Childhood*. Cambridge, MA: MIT Press.

Chi, M., Bassok, M., Lewis, M., Reimann, P. and Glaser, R. (1989) Self-explanations: How students study and use examples in learning to solve problems. *Cognitive Science*, *13*, 145–82.

Chouinard, M. (2007) Children's questions: A mechanism for cognitive development. *Monographs of the Society for Research in Child Development*, *72*, 1–112.

Crowley, K., Callanan, M. A., Jipson, J., Galco, J., Topping, K. and Shrager, J. (2001) Shared scientific thinking in everyday parent-child activity. *Science Education*, *85*(6), 712–32.

Frazier, B. N., Gelman, S. A. and Wellman, H. M. (2009) Preschoolers' search for explanatory information within adult–child conversation. *Child development*, *80*(6), 1592–611.

Gelman, S. A. and Coley, J. (1990) The importance of knowing a dodo is a bird: Categories and inferences in 2-year-old children. *Developmental Psychology*, *26*, 796–804.

Gelman, S. A. and Markman, E. (1986) Categories and induction in young children. *Cognition*, *23*, 183–209.

Gelman, S. A., and Markman, E. (1987) Young children's inductions from natural kinds: The role of categories and appearances. *Child Development*, *58*, 1532–41.

Gopnik, A. (1996) The scientist as child. *Philosophy of Science*, *63*, 485–514.

Gopnik, A. (2000) Explanation as orgasm and the drive for causal knowledge: The function, evolution, and phenomenology of the theory formation system. In F. Keil and R. Wilson (eds) *Explanation and Cognition* (pp. 299–323). Cambridge, MA: MIT Press.

Gopnik, A. and Meltzoff, A. (1997) *Words, Thoughts, and Theories*. Cambridge, MA: MIT Press.

Gopnik, A. and Schulz, L. (2007) *Causal Learning; Psychology, Philosophy and Ccomputation*. New York: Oxford University Press.

Gopnik, A. and Sobel, D. (2000) Detecting blickets: How young children use information about novel causal powers in categorization and induction. *Child Development, 71*, 1205–22.

Gopnik, A., and Wellman, H. (1994) The theory theory. In L. Hirschfeld and S. A. Gelman (eds) *Mapping the Mind: Domain Specificity in Cognition and Culture* (pp. 257–93). New York: Cambridge University Press.

Gopnik, A., Sobel, D., Schulz, L. and Glymour, C. (2001) Causal learning mechanisms in very young children: Two-, three-, and four-year-olds infer causal relations from patterns of variation and covariation. *Developmental Psychology, 37*, 620–9.

Graham, S. A., Kilbreath, C. S. and Welder, A. N. (2004) Thirteen-month-olds rely on shared labels and shape similarity for inductive inferences. *Child Development, 75*, 409–27.

Haith, M. M. (1998) Who put the cog in infant cognition: Is rich interpretation too costly? *Infant Behavior and Development, 21*, 167–79.

Haith, M. and Benson, J. (1997) Infant cognition. In D. Kuhn and R. Siegler (eds) *Handbook of Child Psychology*, 5th edn, *Vol. 2: Cognition, Perception, and Language Development*. New York: Wiley.

Harris, P., German, T. and Mills, P. (1996) Children's use of counterfactual thinking in causal reasoning. *Cognition, 61*, 233–59.

Hempel, C. (1965) *Aspects of Scientific Explanation*. New York: Free Press.

Hickling, A. and Wellman, H. (2001) The emergence of children's causal explanations and theories: Evidence from everyday conversation. *Developmental Psychology, 37*, 668–83.

Hilton, D. (1988) Images of science and commonsense explanation. In D. Hilton (ed.) *Contemporary Science and Natural Explanation: Commonsense Conceptions of Causality* (pp. 1–8). New York: New York University Press.

Hilton, D. (1995) Logic and language in causal explanation. In D. Sperber, D. Premack and A. J. Premack (eds) *Causal Cognition: A Multidisciplinary Debate* (pp. 495–529). Oxford: Clarendon Press.

Hilton, D. and Slugoski, B. (1986) Knowledge-based causal attribution: The abnormal conditions focus model. *Psychological Review, 93*, 75–88.

Jaswal, V. K. and Markman, E. M. (2007) Looks aren't everything: 24-month-olds' willingness to accept unexpected labels. *Journal of Cognition and Development, 8*, 93–111.

Keil, F. C. (1989) *Concepts, Kinds, and Cognitive Development*. Cambridge, MA: MIT Press.

Keil, F. C. (1995) The growth of causal understandings of natural kinds. In D. Sperber, D. Premack and A. Premack (eds) *Causal Cognition: A Multidisciplinary Debate* (pp. 234–62). Oxford: Oxford University Press.

Keil, F. C. (2003) Folkscience: Coarse interpretations of a complex reality. *Trends in Cognitive Science, 7*(8), 368–73.

Keil, F. C. (2006) Explanation and understanding. *Annual Review of Psychology, 57*, 227–54.

Keil, F. C. and Wilson, R. (2000) The shadows and shallows of explanation. In F. Keil and R. Wilson (eds) *Explanation and Cognition* (pp. 87–114). Cambridge, MA: MIT Press.

Kemler-Nelson, D. (1995) Principle-based inferences in young children's categorization: Revisiting the impact of function on the naming of artifacts. *Cognitive Development, 10*, 347–80.

Kushnir, T., and Gopnik, A. (2005) Young children infer causal strength from probabilities and interventions. *Psychological Science, 16*, 678–83.

Kushnir, T. and Gopnik, A. (2007) Conditional probability versus spatial contiguity in causal learning: Preschoolers use new contingency evidence to overcome prior spatial assumptions. *Developmental Psychology, 43*, 186–96.

Legare, C. H. (2012) Exploring explanation: Explaining inconsistent evidence informs exploratory, hypothesis-testing behavior in young children. *Child Development, 83*(1), 173–85.

Legare, C. H. (2014) The contributions of explanation and exploration to children's scientific reasoning. *Child Development Perspectives*, *8*, 101–6.

Legare, C. H. and Gelman, S. A. (2014) Examining explanatory biases in young children's biological reasoning. *Journal of Cognition and Development*, *15*, 287–303.

Legare, C. H. and Lombrozo, T. (2014) The selective benefits of explanation on learning in early childhood. *Journal of Experimental Child Psychology*, 126, 198–212.

Legare, C. H., Wellman, H. M. and Gelman, S. A. (2009) Evidence for an explanation advantage in naïve biological reasoning. *Cognitive Psychology*, *58*(2), 177–94.

Legare, C. H., Gelman, S. A. and Wellman, H. M. (2010) Inconsistency with prior knowledge triggers children's causal explanatory reasoning. *Child Development*, *81*(3), 929–44.

Lombrozo, T. (2006) The structure and function of explanations. *Trends in Cognitive Science*, 10, 464–70.

Mackie, J. L. (1974) *The Cement of the Universe: A Study of Causation*. London: Oxford University Press.

Mills, C. and Keil, F. (2004) Knowing the limits of one's understanding: The development of an awareness of an illusion of explanatory depth. *Journal of Experimental Child Psychology*, *87*, 1–32.

Murphy, G. L. (2002) *The Big Book of Concepts*. MIT Press.

Murphy, G. L. and Allopenna, P. D. (1994) The locus of knowledge effects in concept learning. *Journal of Experimental Psychology: Learning, Memory, Cognition*, *20*, 904–19.

Murphy, G. and Medin, D. (1985) The role of theory in conceptual coherence. *Psychological Review*, *92*, 289–316.

Onishi, K., Baillargeon, R. and Leslie, A. (2007) 15-month-old infants detect violations in pretend scenarios. *Acta Psychologica*, *124*, 106–28.

Piaget, J. (1929) *The Child's Conception of the World*. New York: Harcourt, Brace Jovanovich.

Pitt, J. (1988) *Theories of Explanation*. New York: Oxford University Press.

Salmon, W. (1984) *Scientific Explanation and the Causal Structure of the World*. Princeton: Princeton University Press.

Salmon, W. (1989) *Four Decades of Scientific Explanation*. Minneapolis: University of Minnesota Press.

Schulz, L. and Gopnik, A. (2004) Causal learning across domains. *Developmental Psychology*, *40*, 162–76.

Shultz, T. R. (1982) Rules of causal attribution. *Monographs of the Society for Research in Child Development*, *47*, 1–51.

Siegler, R. (1995) How does change occur: A microgenetic study of number conservation. *Cognitive Psychology*, *28*, 225–73.

Sloman, S. A. (2005) *Causal Models: How We Think About the World and its Alternatives*. New York: Oxford University Press.

Sobel, D. M. and Legare, C. H. (2014) Causal learning in children. *WIREs Cognitive Science*. doi: 10.1002/wcs.1291.

Strevens, M. (2006) Scientific explanation. In D. M. Borchert (ed.) *Encyclopedia of Philosophy*. Macmillan.

Trout, J. D. (2002) Scientific explanation and the sense of understanding. *Philosophy of Science*, *69*: 212–33.

Trout, J. D. (2007) The psychology of scientific explanation. *Philosophy Compass*, *2/3*, 564–91.

Walker, C., Lombrozo, T., Legare, C. H. and Gopnik, A. (2014) Explaining prompts children to privilege inductively rich properties. *Cognition*, *133*, 343–57.

Wang, S., Baillargeon, R. and Brueckner, L. (2004) Young infants' reasoning about hidden objects: Evidence from violation-of-expectation tasks with test trials only. *Cognition*, *93*, 167–98.

Wellman, H. M. (1990) *The Child's Theory of Mind*. Cambridge, MA: MIT Press.

Wellman, H. M. (2011) Reinvigorating explanations for the study of early cognitive development. *Child Development Perspectives*, 5(1), 33–8.

Wellman, H. M. and Gelman, S. A. (1998) Knowledge acquisition in foundational domains. In D. Kuhn and R. Siegler (eds) *Handbook of Child Psychology*, 5th edn, *Vol. 2: Cognition, Perception, and Language Development* (pp. 523–73). New York: Wiley.

Wellman, H., Hickling, A. and Schult, C. (1997) Young children's psychological, physical, and biological explanations. In H. M. Wellman and K. Inagaki (eds) *The Emergence of Core Domains of Thought: Reasoning About Physical, Psychological and Biological Phenomena*. San Francisco: Jossey-Bass.

Wilson, R., and Keil, F. (1998) The shadows and shallows of explanation. *Minds and Machines*, 8(1) Special issue: *Cognition and Explanation* (pp. 137–59).

Woodward, J. (2003) *Making Things Happen: A Theory of Causal Explanation*. Oxford: Oxford University Press.

7

DEVELOPMENT OF THE USE OF AGENTS AS EXPLANATIONS FOR EVENTS

Chelsea A. Cornelius and Jacqueline D. Woolley

Introduction

Humans often go to great lengths to determine the causal structure of the world. One of the things that most concerns us is the behavior of other people; we want to know why people do what they do, and what causes particular things to happen to particular people. Thus a critical concept that must be acquired is that of an agent, or an entity that performs intentional, goal-directed behaviors. The concept of agency affords us a host of causal explanations for the behavior of other people. If we are asked to explain why someone is doing X, a concept of agency allows us to explain the behavior with a mental state, such as 'because she desires Y' or 'because he believes Z'. In these everyday instances, a mental state is considered the antecedent cause for the person's behavior.

Much research has focused on the development of children's causal explanations of others' behavior (for a review see Wellman, 2011). In the example above, appeal to an agent's mental state is fairly straightforward in part because (1) the unit of explanation is small (i.e. a single behavior of only one person is involved) and (2) the person whose behavior we are explaining is visible and hence readily available. Yet a large amount of our explanatory reasoning is also devoted to understanding what causes things to happen to people – ourselves and others. There has been much less empirical attention to this realm of causal reasoning. In this chapter we will argue that we do not limit intentional explanations to just these straightforward cases of agents' visible behavior; rather we overextend this sort of explanation in accounting for a wide range of events, even when no agent is physically present. Just as we appeal to an agent's intention to explain its behavior, so we also appeal to an agent's intention to explain the events we experience.

The purpose of this chapter is to explain why humans detect agency and infer intentionality so readily, with a specific focus on why we rely on our knowledge of intentional agents to explain the seemingly purposeful events of our lives. The first section reviews the general function of explanation and provides evidence that even very young children utilize causal explanations. The second section describes how characteristics of the event and characteristics of the individual contribute to the perception of an event as extraordinary and in need of an explanation. The third section reviews the literature on the development of the agent concept and children's theory of mind. The fourth section reveals why we appeal to agents as explanations for events. In the final section, we discuss how children come to learn which agents are culturally acceptable as explanatory constructs.

The function and development of explanation

In her oft-cited chapter, Gopnik (2000) eloquently defines explanation and its role in detecting the causal structure of the world. According to Gopnik, explanation is the distinctive phenomenological mark of the 'theory formation system'; an evolved system that drives us to form theories or 'causal maps'. These maps are abstract representations that allow us to navigate an otherwise unpredictable world. While it may seem intuitive that we form theories to be able to explain, the evolutionary perspective is that we experience explanation as pleasurable and satisfying to ensure that we continue to form theories.

Gopnik (2000) maintains that there are two components to the phenomenology of explanation: what it feels like to search for explanation, dubbed the 'hmm', and what it feels like to find the explanation, or the 'a-ha'. Thus, not all of explanation is a pleasurable process. The state of uncertainty, in which we lack an explanation, can be characterized by arousal that motivates us to reach the satisfying state of explanation.

It could be argued that even infants experience the phenomenological 'hmm' of explanation, as measured in violation-of-expectation paradigms. Here, researchers present infants with both possible events and events that violate physical laws or social rules. From the amount of time that infants spend looking at these events, researchers make inferences about which types of events infants find surprising and worthy of explanation. For example, infants as young as 3.5 months will look reliably longer at an event that violates their expectations about a physical object, such as when the object seemingly disappears (Aguiar and Baillargeon, 2002). It is inferred that the increased looking time reflects an attempt to understand or make sense of the phenomenon – a search for explanation.

Children's use of explanation develops considerably over the preschool years. Hickling and Wellman (2001) found that by the time children reach the age of 2, they seek and provide verbal explanations in their everyday conversation. When preschoolers are seeking an explanation, they are more likely to agree or ask a follow-up question if they are provided with an explanation, whereas they are more likely to provide their own explanation or repeat their original question if a non-explanatory response is provided (Frazier et al., 2009). Moreover, children are especially motivated to seek explanations for events that are inconsistent with their prior knowledge (Legare et al., 2010), and this explanatory process can facilitate children's hypothesis testing behavior (Legare, 2012).

Results such as these highlight the role of explanation in the formation and revision of theories and provide evidence for the argument that explanation is a mechanism for children's causal learning (Wellman, 2011). The next section aims to address more specifically the characteristics of events that individuals deem inconsistent with their theories.

Events that elicit explanation

Events that are consistent with our naïve theories – physical, psychological, and biological – do not require much explanatory effort. These events, what we might call ordinary events, elicit natural explanations derived from our theories. Developmentally, as we gain experience and acquire more evidence for our theories about the world, we become familiar with a greater number of explanations, as well as which types of explanations are appropriate for which events (Hickling and Wellman, 2001; Pepitone and Saffioti, 1997; Woolley *et al.*, 2011).

However, sometimes we experience an extraordinary event that is difficult to explain. One reason why an event may be perceived as extraordinary is because the event is novel to us, and its rarity alone might suffice to make it extraordinary. In this case, we have no theory with which to explain the event. For example, a child who experiences a hailstorm for the first time is likely to find this event extraordinary given that he or she has no theory to explain why ice is falling from the sky. Indeed, Zusne and Jones (1989) propose that inadequate experience with the natural world is one condition that leads to insufficient information about the cause of an event. Given individual differences in experience and perceptions of what constitutes ordinary, individuals will vary in their judgment of what constitutes an extraordinary, seemingly unexplainable event.

A second reason why an event may be deemed extraordinary is because the event defies the laws that make up our personal repertoire of ordinary explanations. In this case, the event contradicts at least one of our current theories. For example, someone who has a theory that explains how snow forms may consider a hailstorm extraordinary given his or her expectations that cold weather is necessary for frozen precipitation. However, a meteorologist, who has expert knowledge about how the atmosphere causes particular weather events, will not consider an ordinary hailstorm difficult to explain; rather this event will be easily explained given the expert's extensive theory of meteorology. Thus, to the extent that individuals differ in the contents of their theories, they will also vary in their subjective judgment of what constitutes an extraordinary event.

Another reason why an event might not be easily explained pertains to the specific causal question being asked. Often it is not just the physical basis of an event that we are trying to explain, rather we are seeking the meaning of the event's occurrence, especially if the event is personally relevant. That is, we want to explain 'why' and not just 'how'. For example, when a hailstorm causes my flight to be delayed, which results in me missing my grandfather's funeral, I am not looking for an explanation of how the storm formed or how the plane was limited in its ability to withstand bad weather: rather I am seeking an explanation for why the storm had to form at that location and at that time, preventing me from making a very important trip. Someone else might easily answer the question of 'Why did she miss the funeral?' with explanations pertaining to the storm causing the flight's delay, whereas such explanations would be unlikely to provide me with the ultimate meaning I desire. In this case, others would be offering proximate causes, whereas I would be looking for an ultimate explanation. Thus, to the extent that individuals vary in the level of meaning they are aiming to obtain with their explanations, they will also vary in the degree to which they perceive events as difficult to explain.

The level of explanation one seeks may affect the type of explanation provided, with ultimate explanations being more likely to refer to abstract or non-material concepts. In one study, Pepitone and Saffioti (1997) presented adults with events that were designed to be difficult to explain, that is, the outcome was unexpected and seemed to 'just happen'. For example, one vignette described a woman who was diagnosed with a terminal illness but subsequently learned that her disease had suddenly gone away on its own. Results revealed that adults appeal to a host of non-material explanations (e.g. fate, luck, justice, God) to account for why these events occur. It is noteworthy that the participants were asked to explain 'why' the events happened and not 'how'. Perhaps the phrasing of the question led participants to believe that the experimenter was asking for an ultimate explanation pertaining to meaning and not just a proximate explanation pertaining to physical causality.

A similar study (Woolley *et al.*, 2011) conducted with adults and children aged 8 to 12 found that older children and adults provided non-material explanations significantly more often than younger children, whereas the youngest children were more likely to provide physical or psychological explanations. One possibility for these age differences is that younger children were interpreting the question, 'Why did that happen?' as 'How did that happen?' and hence appealed to a physical cause. However, it could also be argued that incorporating non-material concepts such as luck, justice, and God into one's explanatory framework requires some degree of socialization and experience. We will further address this topic in the final section of the chapter.

The more experience we gain, the more we can refine our explanatory theories. Events need an explanation when they are perceived as anomalous or outside the explanatory power of the theories we have available to us. However, if explanations afford us a sense of predictability, why would we appeal to other agents (and their invisible and ever changing mental states) as explanations for events? Before explaining why an appeal to agents is satisfying, it is first necessary to discuss the development of the agent concept. When do we acquire a concept of agents and a theory with which to explain their behavior?

Development of the agent concept

Some researchers maintain that evolution has equipped humans with cognitive mechanisms designed to detect agents (Barrett, 2004; Carey, 2009; Gergely and Csibra, 2003; Guthrie, 2002), and recent theoretical and empirical research has sought to determine the function of this agency detection. For example, Guthrie (2002) maintains that perceptual uncertainty may trigger our evolved propensity to discover hidden agents and may even result in an overestimation of agency. According to error management theory (Haselton and Buss, 2000), cognitive mechanisms are likely to evolve if there is a difference in potential costs to survival between false positives and false negatives. For example, detecting an agent that is not truly present (i.e. a false positive) is far less costly to survival than failing to detect an agent that is truly present (i.e. a false negative).

Indeed, agency detection is so robust that some developmental psychologists maintain that infants have innate knowledge about agents, and that this knowledge includes inferences about goal-directed behavior (Carey, 2009). For example, looking-time studies suggest that infants as young as 6 months attribute goal-directed behavior even to something as simple as animated geometric shapes (Csibra *et al.*, 1999). Woodward (1998) has demonstrated that infants are capable of discriminating among objects that perform similar actions, such that only actions performed by a particular object are represented as goal-directed. For example, 6-month-olds inferred as goal-directed the action of a hand moving across the stage and grasping one of two objects, whereas the same inferences were not made for a stick with a glove at the end of it nor for an arm that flopped down on the object with the hand backwards.

Other research suggests that infants are capable of inferring goal-directed behavior even in the absence of an agent. In one study (Saxe *et al.*, 2005), infants aged 10–12 months were familiarized to either a puppet moving around a display or a bean bag sitting still and were then habituated to an event in which the object (either the puppet or the bean bag) flew across the display area. Afterwards, infants observed a hand appear on one of two sides of the display. Results indicated that infants looked longer when the hand appeared on the opposite side of the display from which the bean bag had emerged; however, there was no difference in looking time between the two sides of the display in the puppet condition, suggesting that infants were surprised by the possibility that a seemingly inert beanbag could be capable of goal-directed behavior. Thus, even when there is no agent present but an event is perceived as goal-directed, an agent will be assumed to be the cause of the event.

During the second year of life, this early ability to represent another agent's goal-directed behavior expands to include representations of other agents' mental states, such as desires, even if the desires differ from those of the child (Repacholi and Gopnik, 1997). By the age of 3, children can reason explicitly about others' intentions and beliefs (Wellman and Bartsch, 1988), and by the time they are 4, children can reason about how others' false beliefs may motivate particular behaviors (Wellman *et al.*, 2001). Thus, by the time children begin school, they not only have a coherent agent concept but also a representational theory of mind that allows them to attribute a host of mental states to other agents and consider those mental states when reasoning about the behavior of other agents.

While our theory of mind may have evolved primarily to explain the behavior of other people, we often use it to explain events that are perceived as the consequences or effects of an agent's behavior. Barrett (2004) argues that our agency detection devices are extremely sensitive, leading him to propose that humans have evolved a 'hyperactive agency detection device' (HADD) that not only identifies traces of agency in the form of seemingly goal-directed behavior, but that also identifies *events* as the result of agency. Barrett explains that 'when we attend to an event that has no obvious mechanistic or biological cause, HADD springs into action. HADD searches for any present people or animals that might have caused the event. It also tries to determine if the event might accomplish some goal' (2000, p. 34). The ability to reason about the motivations of others' behavior is necessary to explain events as the result of an agent's intentional behavior. This is especially true for those events in which the responsible agent is not present and hence cannot be detected in the strict sense. In these cases, we can employ our theory of mind and appeal to an unseen agent's intention as the cause for the event. Along these lines, Bering (2002) has proposed an 'existential theory of mind', which finds meaning in autobiographical experiences by interpreting them as the communicative intent of some nondescript agent. Thus, our drive to seek meaning and determine the causal structure of our world capitalizes on our knowledge of agents in order to provide a causal explanation for otherwise inexplicable events.

Why are agents good explanations for events?

One explanation for the use of agents as explanations for extraordinary events draws on research with adults on effectance motivation. Waytz and colleagues define effectance motivation as 'the motivation to attain control, predictability, and understanding, and to reduce uncertainty, unpredictability, and randomness' (2010, p. 424). According to these authors, effectance motivation is one factor that explains our anthropomorphic tendencies, that is, our attribution of humanlike characteristics, including intention, to non-human entities (Epley *et al.*, 2007). When we encounter an unpredictable object, one that does not act in accordance to our expectations, we rely on our self-knowledge to reason about the object, and treating it as humanlike satisfies our motivation to be effective social agents who have control over our environment. Research on anthropomorphism among adults supports the hypothesis that perceived unpredictability increases effectance motivation, and as a result, anthropomorphism (Waytz *et al.*, 2010).

Researchers have also demonstrated a relation between perceived lack of control and attributions of agency. For example, college students who did not experience personal control over balls being used to solve a puzzle were more likely to attribute agency to the balls, as captured by their talking to the balls and describing them in terms usually reserved for animate entities (Barrett and Johnson, 2003). Other research suggests that anxiety associated with randomness and perceived lack of control may facilitate belief in supernatural agents. For example, Kay *et al.* (2010) had adult participants ingest a herbal supplement and told half of the participants that a common side effect of the pill was mild anxiety or arousal. In reality, everyone was given a placebo pill. Participants then completed a priming task that entailed either unscrambling words that pertained to randomness or unscrambling negative words. Finally, participants were asked to rate the extent to which they agreed with various statements designed to measure belief in supernatural sources of control (e.g. God or other non-human entities). Results revealed a significant interaction, such that participants who were primed to think of randomness and were told nothing about the side effect of the pill were most likely to believe in supernatural sources of control. There was no effect of the randomness prime for those participants who were told that the pill could cause arousal, suggesting that any anxiety participants experienced as a result of thinking about randomness was attributed to the pill's alleged side effect. These results highlight not only the disquiet we experience from randomness but also the tendency to appeal to agents as a source of control when alternative explanations are not readily available.

Because randomness is typically associated with a lack of order, when we do detect patterns or ordered outcomes, we often assume that an agent capable of intentional behavior produced them. Even very young children have expectations regarding the strong positive correlation between agents and patterns. Newman and colleagues (2010) had children aged 3 to 6 listen to vignettes that included either an agent or an inanimate force as the cause of an event, and children selected which of two pictures best depicted that focal event. For example, children heard a story about a little boy who left his room and went outside to play. Half the children were told that while the boy was outside, his sister went into his room and changed his things; the other half of children were told that while the boy was outside, the wind blew through a window and changed his things. All children were presented with two pictures, one depicting an ordered array and the other depicting a disordered array (e.g. blocks arranged in a line versus blocks in a pile). Finally, children were asked to select which picture looked most like how the sister (or wind) had changed the boy's things. Results indicated that children of all ages believed that the person was significantly more likely than the inanimate force to create the ordered outcome. While children did select the disordered outcome for the agent some of the time (38 per cent of responses), they rarely chose the ordered outcome for the inanimate force (12 per cent of responses). A similar study using computer animations and looking-time measures extended these findings to children as young as 12 months, indicating that, from the first year of life, the presence of an agent creates expectations about outcomes, specifically that agents produce ordered outcomes.

In preschool-aged children, the tendency to verbally appeal to order and intentionality when explaining events appears to be quite pervasive. This type of reasoning is so prevalent among children that they have been said to possess a 'promiscuous teleology' (Kelemen, 1999a). Kelemen (1999b) demonstrated that children often agree that natural objects (e.g. pointy rocks) are made for a particular reason (e.g. so that animals won't sit on them), and that natural events (e.g. speciation) are the result of intentional causality (e.g. because they needed more nature in the country) (Kelemen and DiYanni, 2005). Recent research by Banerjee and Bloom (2013) suggests that young children will also reason teleologically about life events. For example, after hearing about Monica, who lost her favorite teddy bear, most of the children aged 5 to 7 agreed with both teleological explanations (e.g. it happened in order to make Monica learn to be more careful) and non-teleological explanations (e.g. it happened because Monica left her bear on the bus); whereas half of the older children, aged 8 to 10, preferred only the non-teleological explanation. While these examples of teleological explanations do not make reference to specific agents, they serve to demonstrate how appeals to order and intention (both of which are usually associated with agents) can function as satisfying explanations for otherwise difficult-to-explain events.

In this section, we have illustrated how events that elicit lack of control and perceptions of disorder motivate us to seek an explanation that will help us regain predictability and order. A sense of order can be achieved by attributing events to some purpose or the intentional behavior of an agent. Until now, we have not discussed the types of agents to which people might appeal in the service of explanation. Examples of these agents will be provided in the next section, followed by a discussion of how children's use of agents as explanations develops with age.

Development of the use of agents as explanations

As discussed previously, our causal explanatory frameworks are challenged by extraordinary events, or events that appear to violate our theories of natural causation. In order to explain such events, we often appeal to extraordinary agents, because their special powers seem necessary to bring about such events. An extraordinary agent can be defined as an agent that is inconsistent with our theory of ordinary agents. More specifically, it is an animate being that can behave in ways that are deemed impossible for ordinary agents. Similar to individual differences in perceptions of extraordinary events, individuals may also differ in their judgments of agents as extraordinary.

But how are extraordinary agents conceptualized? We argue that both children and adults often reason about the behavior of extraordinary agents with the same theory of mind used to reason about the behavior of ordinary agents, namely as behavior that is motivated by desires, beliefs, and intentions. Research by Barrett and Keil (1996) supports the idea that our representations of supernatural agents may be constrained by our concept of ordinary agents. They found that participants tended to anthropomorphize God in a story processing task, despite endorsing explicit theological beliefs about the ways in which God differs from humans.

While gods may be the most obvious example of intentional agents being used to explain extraordinary events, research indicates that different cultures believe in a variety of supernatural agents that are capable of affecting our lives. For example, a 2009 Harris poll of 2,303 American adults indicated that 72 per cent believe in angels, 60 per cent believe in the devil, and 42 per cent believe in ghosts. Western Amazonian cultures that practice ayahuasca shamanism believe in a variety of spirits, including those of the forest and river that can alter their physical appearance and inflict disease in humans (Thomas and Humphrey, 1994). Many cultures maintain beliefs that deceased relatives directly affect the lives of those still alive (Morris, 1987).

Another example of agents being used to explain extraordinary events can be found in beliefs about bewitchment. Ivey and Myers (2008) documented bewitchment beliefs in indigenous South African communities and found that adults will often appeal to the ill intentions of other people (i.e. witches) in order to find a meaningful explanation for their misfortune. Legare and Gelman (2008) found that both children and adults in Sesotho-speaking South African communities endorse bewitchment as an explanation for illness. In one of their studies, participants listened to vignettes that described a person who was diagnosed with AIDS and then rated the extent to which they agreed with a variety of explanations, such as 'Lerato has been bewitched by a neighbor who is jealous of her' and 'Lerato used a razor with someone else's sick blood on it.' Results indicated that all participants agreed with bewitchment explanations to some extent; however, children preferred biological explanations to bewitchment explanations, whereas adults considered these two types of explanations as equally effective.

Interestingly, it seems that adults in many cultures are more prone than children to endorse the intentions of supernatural agents when searching for meaningful explanatory concepts (Legare and Gelman, 2008; Mead, 1932; Woolley *et al.*, 2011). Research by Bering and Parker (2006) suggests that a certain level of cognitive maturity is necessary for having a concept of a communicative invisible being. These findings are in contrast to the traditional view among cognitive developmental psychologists that children become increasingly logical in their reasoning, as indicated by their increasing use of mechanistic and scientific explanations. For example, Piaget (1929) demonstrated that children in the pre-operational and concrete operational stages of development were more likely to endorse animistic explanations for natural phenomena than formal operational children. Although young children may be more prone to animistic and teleological explanations, it is possible that this mode of thinking never really disappears; rather it is suppressed with age. For instance, research with adults suggests that teleological reasoning may be the default explanatory mode, especially for those with poor inhibitory control or little scientific knowledge (Keleman and Rosset, 2009).

Moreover, with age also comes increased experience using culturally accepted explanations, including supernatural ones, and perhaps socialization explains the findings that adults are more likely than children to invoke supernatural agents as explanations. If socialization is the process by which children acquire particular supernatural agents as explanatory concepts, then testimony is likely to be an important factor (Harris *et al.*, 2006). In their discussion of children's evaluation of testimony, Bergstrom *et al.* (2006) discuss the role of children's intuitive ontologies in the acquisition and evaluation of cultural information. Specifically, they propose that the degree of fit between culturally specific input and children's ontological expectations will affect the extent to which children monitor the source of novel cultural information. For example, the notion of bodiless ancestral spirits may violate children's assumptions about agents as both physical and mental beings. Accordingly, children are likely to pay closer attention to the source and quality of testimony when encountering such explanations than when hearing explanations that are consistent with their theories. Research on children's use of testimony indicates that children do in fact monitor the familiarity (Corriveau and Harris, 2009), credibility (Jaswal and Malone, 2007) and previous accuracy of informants (Koenig *et al.*, 2004).

Thus, despite a universal ability to detect agents and reason about the motivations of their behavior, cultures differ in the particular agents believed to be responsible for real-world events, and socialization may be one mechanism that facilitates the transmission of information pertaining to culturally specific supernatural agents.

Conclusion

In this chapter, we aimed to explain the prevalence of causal explanations that entail agency. We highlighted how the process of explanation aids in theory formation, helping us better understand and predict our environment. We also argued that when we encounter personally relevant, extraordinary events, our knowledge of intentional agents helps provide us with a sense of meaning and order.

Belief in supernatural causal agents is a culturally universal phenomenon, suggesting that humans in all cultures share cognitive mechanisms that facilitate agency detection. Future research should investigate the ways in which our agentive explanations are similar and whether there are similarities in the types of events for which most cultures appeal to supernatural agents as explanations. Another interesting research endeavor would be to explore the possibility that certain non-material causal explanations may be conceptualized as intentional agents. For example, the common personification of luck (e.g. 'Lady Luck') suggests that our notion of luck may be blended with our agent concept. Similarly, people might also conceive of karma as an agent-like force with goal-directed behavior, keeping track of our deeds and ensuring that people get what they deserve.

Given the cultural variation in belief in particular supernatural agents, it is also important to further investigate the effects of socialization on the use of supernatural agents as explanations for extraordinary events. How do parents, education, and cultural practices interact to produce this cultural variation? It is our hope that the fundamental human drive to explain our world will result in research that sheds light on these important questions.

References

Aguiar, A. and Baillargeon, R. (2002) Developments in young infants' reasoning about occluded objects. *Cognitive Psychology, 45*, 267–336.

Banerjee, K. and Bloom, P. (2013) *'Everything happens for a reason': Developmental Origins of Teleological Reasoning About Life Events*. Poster presented at the biennial meeting of the Society for Research in Child Development, Seattle, WA.

Barrett, J. L. (2004) *Why Would Anyone Believe in God?* Walnut Creek, CA: AltaMira.

Barrett, J. L. and Johnson, A. H. (2003) The role of control in attributing intentional agency to inanimate objects. *Journal of Cognition and Culture, 3*, 208–17.

Barrett, J. L. and Keil, F. C. (1996) Conceptualizing a non-natural entity: Anthropomorphism in god concepts. *Cognitive Psychology, 31*, 219–47.

Bergstrom, B., Moehlmann, B. and Boyer, P. (2006) Extending the testimony problem: Evaluating the truth, scope, and source of cultural information. *Child Development, 77*, 531–8.

Bering, J. M. (2002) The existential theory of mind. *Review of General Psychology, 6*, 3–24.

Bering, J. M. and Parker, B. D. (2006) Children's attributions of intentions to an invisible agent. *Developmental Psychology, 42*(2), 253–62.

Carey, S. (2009) *The Origin of Concepts*. New York: Oxford University Press.

Csibra, G., Gergely, G., Koos, O. and Brockbank, M. (1999) Goal attribution without agency cues: The perception of 'pure reason' in infancy. *Cognition, 72*, 237–67.

Corriveau, K. and Harris, P. L. (2009) Choosing your informant: Weighing familiarity and recent accuracy. *Developmental Science, 12*, 426–37.

Epley, N., Waytz, A. and Cacioppo, J. T. (2007) On seeing human: A three-factor theory of anthropomorphism. *Psychological Review, 114,* 864–86.

Frazier, B. N., Gelman, S. A. and Wellman, H. M. (2009) Preschoolers' search for explanatory information within adult–child conversation. *Child Development, 80,* 1592–611.

Gergely, G., and Csibra, G. (2003) Teleological reasoning in infancy: The naïve theory of rational action. *Trends in Cognitive Sciences, 7,* 287–92.

Gopnik, A. (2000) Explanation as orgasm and the drive for causal knowledge: The function, evolution, and phenomenology of the theory formation system. In F. C. Keil and R. A. Wilson (eds) *Explanation and Cognition* (pp. 299–323). Cambridge, MA: MIT Press.

Guthrie, S. (2002) Animal animism: Evolutionary roots of religious cognition. In I. Pyysiainen and V. Anttonen (eds) *Current Approaches in the Cognitive Science of Religion* (pp. 38–67). London: Continuum.

Harris, P. L., Pasquini, E. S., Duke, S., Asscher, J. J. and Pons, F. (2006) Germs and angels: The role of testimony in young children's ontology. *Developmental Science, 9,* 76–96.

Haselton, M. G. and Buss, D. M. (2000) Error management theory: A new perspective on biases in cross-sex mind reading. *Journal of Personality and Social Psychology, 78*(1), 81–91.

Hickling, A. K. and Wellman, H. M. (2001) The emergence of children's causal explanations and theories: Evidence from everyday conversation. *Developmental Psychology, 37*(5), 668–83.

Ivey, G. and Myers, T. (2008) The psychology of bewitchment (Part I): A phenomenological study of the experience of bewitchment. *South African Journal of Psychology, 38,* 54–74.

Jaswal, V. K. and Malone, L. S. (2007) Turning believers into skeptics: 3-year-olds' sensitivity to cues to speaker credibility. *Journal of Cognition and Development, 8,* 263–83.

Kay, A. C., Moscovitch, D. A. and Laurin, K. (2010) Randomness, attributions of arousal, and belief in God. *Psychological Science, 21,* 216–18.

Kelemen, D. (1999a) The scope of teleological thinking in preschool children. *Cognition, 70,* 241–72.

Kelemen, D. (1999b) Why are rocks pointy? Children's preference for teleological explanations of the natural world. *Developmental Psychology, 35,* 1440–52.

Kelemen, D. and DiYanni, C. (2005) Intuitions about origins: Purpose and intelligent design in children's reasoning about nature. *Journal of Cognition and Development, 6,* 3–31.

Kelemen, D. and Rosset, E. (2009) The human function compunction: Teleological explanation in adults. *Cognition, 111,* 138–43.

Koenig, M. A., Clément, F. and Harris, P. L. (2004) Trust in testimony: Children's use of true and false statements. *Psychological Science, 15,* 694–8.

Legare, C. H. (2012) Exploring explanation: Explaining inconsistent evidence informs exploratory, hypothesis-testing behavior in young children. *Child Development, 83,* 173–85.

Legare, C. H. and Gelman, S. A. (2008) Bewitchment, biology, or both: The co-existence of natural and supernatural explanatory frameworks across development. *Cognitive Science, 32,* 607–42.

Legare, C. H., Gelman, S. A. and Wellman, H. M. (2010) Inconsistency with prior knowledge triggers children's causal explanatory reasoning. *Child Development, 81,* 929–44.

Mead, M. (1932) An investigation of the thought of primitive children, with special reference to animism. *The Journal of the Royal Anthropological Institute of Great Britain and Ireland, 62*: 173–90.

Morris, B. (1987) *Anthropological Studies of Religion: An Introductory Text.* Cambridge University Press.

Newman, G. E., Keil, F. C., Kuhlmeier, V. A. and Wynn, K. (2010) Early understandings of the link between agents and order. *Proceedings of the National Academy of Sciences, 107,* 17140–5.

Pepitone, A., and Saffioti, L. (1997) The selectivity of nonmaterial beliefs in interpreting life events. *European Journal of Social Psychology, 27,* 23–35.

Piaget, J. (1929) *The Child's Conception of the World.* London: Routledge and Kegan Paul.

Repacholi, B. M. and Gopnik, A. (1997) Early reasoning about desires: Evidence from 14 and 18-month-olds. *Developmental Psychology, 33,* 12–21.

Saxe, R., Tenebaum, J. and Carey, S. (2005) Secret agents: 10 and 12-month-olds infer an unseen cause as the motion of an inanimate object. *Psychological Science, 16,* 995–1001.

Thomas, N. and Humphrey, C. (eds) (1994) *Shamanism, History and the State.* University of Michigan Press.

Waytz, A., Carey, M. K., Epley, N., Monteleone, G., Gao, J. and Cacioppo, J. T. (2010) Making sense by making sentient: Effectance motivation increases anthropomorphism. *Journal of Personality and Social Psychology, 99,* 410–35.

Wellman, H. M. (2011) Reinvigorating explanations for the study of early cognitive development. *Child Development Perspectives, 5,* 33–8.

Wellman, H. M. and Bartsch, K. (1988) Young children's reasoning about beliefs. *Cognition, 30,* 239–77.

Wellman, H. M., Cross, D. and Watson, J. (2001) Meta-analysis of theory-of-mind development: The truth about false belief. *Child Development, 72,* 655–84.

Woodward, A. L. (1998) Infants selectively encode the goal object of an actor's reach. *Cognition, 69,* 1–34.

Woolley, J. D., Cornelius, C. A. and Lacy, W. (2011) Developmental changes in the use of supernatural explanations for unusual events. *Journal of Cognition and Culture, 11,* 311–37.

Zusne, L. and Jones, W. H. (eds) (1989) *Anomalistic Psychology: A Study of Magical Thinking.* Hillsdale, NJ: Routledge.

8

THE CLINICAL INTERVIEW

The child as a partner in conversations versus the child as an object of research

Niklas Pramling and Roger Säljö

Introduction

In this chapter we re-examine some elements of the 'méthode clinique', the approach to interviewing children that Piaget developed as a cornerstone of his scientific project. We will scrutinize some of the excerpts presented in one of his most famous books, *The Child's Conception of the World* (originally published in 1926). Our ambition is to show that if the interviews are read as instances of communication between two parties, rather than as expressions of the child's thinking only, a different account of children's capacities for reasoning may emerge.

Jean Piaget (1896–1980) is one of the most influential developmental psychologists of all time, and through his contributions he has shaped scholarly and public views of children (Beilin, 1992). Based on his dissatisfaction with standardized testing as a mode of assessing child development, he suggested that the focus of research should be redirected from the study of static products of thinking to the analysis of the processes by means of which children construe the world they live in. This conviction may be seen as one of the first attempts to introduce into research what we now refer to as a child perspective on activities and on the world more generally. To pave the way for such inquiries, Piaget developed his 'clinical method'.

In her historical analysis, Mayer (2005) traces the origin of this method to a combination of elements of three traditions that shaped Piaget's thinking: naturalistic observation, psychometrics, and psychiatric clinical examination. In spite of its later fame, the clinical method is presented in some detail in only two of Piaget's books: by Claparède in his foreword to Piaget's first book, *The Language and Thought of the Child* (originally published in 1923), and by Piaget himself in the first chapter of *The Child's Conception of the World* (CCW). Claparède begins his foreword to the former book stating that the 'importance of this remarkable work deserves to be doubly emphasized, for its novelty consists both in the results obtained and in the method by which they have been reached' (1926, p. ix). He further argues:

> This clinical method [...], which is also an art, the art of questioning, does not confine itself to superficial observation, but aims at capturing what is hidden behind the immediate appearance of things. [...] It does not give up the struggle when the child gives incomprehensible or contradictory answers, but only follows closer in chase of the ever-receding thought, drives it from cover, pursues and tracks it down till it can seize it, dissect it and lay bare the secret of its composition.
>
> *(Claparède, 1926, p. xiv)*

Arguing from the premise that *what* we know through research cannot be separated from *how* we know, we will start by looking at how Piaget himself presented the method on which he based his claims about child development. We will then reconsider some excerpts from his work, looking at the transcripts as records of communication in order to suggest an alternative account of what children attempt to achieve in such interviews.

Piaget's clinical method

In the first chapter of CCW, Piaget presents his method in detail over 30 pages. He defines the problem of his investigations as (a) 'What conceptions of the world does the child naturally form at the different stages of its development?', and (b) what is 'the child's notion of *reality*?' (p. 1). Contrasting CCW with his earlier work, including *The Language and Thought of the Child*, Piaget points to the distinction between studying the form and the content of children's thinking: 'There the problem was an analysis of the form and functioning of child though; here [in CCW] it is an analysis of its content' (1951, p. 2). Thus, Piaget introduces the clinical method as an approach for investigating the 'content' of the child's thinking. The clinical method is contrasted to two traditional methods for studying child development: tests and observations. Critiquing these methods – tests for falsifying 'the natural mental inclination of the subject' (p. 3), and 'pure observation' for being 'inadequate for distinguishing belief from romancing' (p. 7) – Piaget argues that the clinical method avoids the pitfalls of these dominant approaches. It is also interesting to note that he argues that the mastery of this method is 'the fruit of at least one or two full years' training' (p. 2).

When interpreting the material generated through the clinical method, Piaget warns against seeing everything children say as if it 'lies on the same psychological level', 'as revealing equally the child's mentality' (p. 25); being all 'pure gold' or all 'dross' (p. 9). Rather, the strength of the clinical method is precisely its capacity to 'separate the wheat from the tares and to keep every answer in its mental context' (p. 9). Context here is referred to as 'mental context', and there is no discussion of conversational context or how interactional features may be important to consider when analysing what children say. It is the latter issue that we will pursue in what follows.

Two additional distinctions made by Piaget are informative when attempting to understand how he construed children's thinking and what we gain access to through the clinical method. First, he suggests that 'an attempt must be made to strip the answers of their verbal element' (p. 27). Thus, we have to consider that '[w]hen the child is questioned he translates his thought into words, but these words are necessarily inadequate' (p. 27). Making a distinction between thoughts as something independent of, or more basic than, language (the verbal element of words) is a notion that later has been severely criticized by many including Wittgenstein (1953) and Vygotsky (1987). The other distinction that Piaget makes interpreting children's answers is 'that of distinguishing from among the results of the examination the part to be regarded as the child's original contribution and that due to previous adult influences' (p. 28). Taking the perspective that '[t]he history of the child's intellectual development is largely the history of the progressive socialisation of its individual thought … it follows that throughout the whole course of the child's development, the contents of its thought fall into two categories: one due to adult influence and the other to the child's original reactions' (p. 28). How to 'show whether a particular conviction has been simply borrowed by the child from adults by passive imitation, or whether it is in part the product of the child's mental structure' (p. 32) is an important task where the clinical interview is thought to show its strength. This argumentation testifies to Piaget's grounding in a cognitivist tradition, where the object of inquiry is something that is more 'real' (the functioning of the child's own mental apparatus) than what the child has appropriated through interactions with significant others. Many present-day theorists of development would take issue with this position (e.g. Edwards, 1997; Wertsch, 1985).

As a scientific text, CCW is interesting in the sense that it presents rich empirical data in the form of transcripts of the clinical interviews. Piaget claims that the investigation was based on more than 600 observations/interviews. Exactly how the interviews have been transcribed is not explicated. Writing that the cases studied cannot be summarized, since that 'would be to misrepresent them', Piaget argues that 'all the words quoted are exactly as they were spoken' (p. 39). Considering that the interviews took place in French, the translator has added an interesting claim: 'French-speaking children generally have a wider vocabulary than English children of the same age, and where on account of an unnatural ring in the English equivalent, any modification has been made, the French phrase is inserted in brackets' (p. 39). How to study and interpret children's conceptions is thus discussed at great length, but exactly how the data have been transformed into text was not commented upon.

Communication as joint meaning-making

In the following, we will critically re-analyse excerpts from CCW, building on theoretical development in the field of communication studies, particularly insights from traditions emphasizing communication as a joint meaning-making practice. To very briefly summarize this field of study as it is relevant for our objective, we will point to some important assumptions of recent, more dialogically oriented, theories of communication (Linell, 1998).

First, communication cannot be understood in terms of a pipeline or conduit metaphor (Reddy, 1993), i.e. as a matter of one person sending information to his/her interlocutor to receive in ready-made form. Rather, communication is at heart a joint endeavour (Aronsson and Hundeide, 2002); what is meant by what is said cannot be judged by considering the contributions of one interlocutor only. Speakers' utterances are responsive to what has been said previously at the same time as they provide background to the responses of the others. This makes it difficult, even impossible, to analytically separate, in isolation, the sense made by one speaker from utterances by their interlocutor(s). Second, communication always implies adopting a perspective. The interlocutor who initiates a conversation frames (Goffman, 1974) the conversation as a particular kind of talk where some contributions are relevant and others are not. In the case of research interviews, the interviewer is inviting and directing the conversation. Third, the relation between what is said and what is meant is always a negotiated issue. For instance, sometimes speakers tend to use different kinds of meta-markers (Goatly, 1997; Pramling, 2006) to clarify the tension between what they *say* and what they *mean*. We will use these three insights as guiding principles when reconsidering some of Piaget's excerpts.

Negotiating the meaning of words

One of the concepts that Piaget investigates in CCW is the notion of thought. Consider the following excerpt, in which a child (Ratt) is asked, 'Where does thought come from?' (p. 44; the child's utterances are *italicized*):

> RATT (8; 10) told us, as we saw, that there is nothing in the head, when we think. 'Can one see the voice? – *No.* – Can one feel it? – *Yes.* – Have words got strength? – *Yes.* – Tell me a word which has strength? – *The wind.* – Why has the word 'wind' got strength? – *Because it goes quickly.* – Is it the word or the wind which goes quickly? – *The wind.* – Tell me a word which has strength. – *When you give something a kick.* – Is that a word? – *No.* – Tell me a word which has strength – … – What do you think with? – *With the mouth.* – What is inside the head when you think? – *Nothing.* – What does the voice do? – *It speaks.* – You know what words are? – *When you speak.* – Where is the word "house"? – *In the mouth.* – Is it in the head? – *No.*'
>
> *(Piaget, 1951, p. 45)*

According to Piaget, this excerpt illustrates when a child has not 'distinguished words from the things named', and that 'Ratt was unable to understand that it is things and not words that have strength' (p. 45). If we look at this excerpt as a communicative encounter between two parties, we note that when initially faced with a rather ambiguous question, 'Have words got strength?', the child says 'yes'. However, when asked in terms of the distinction, 'Is it the word or the wind which goes quickly?', he clarifies that it is the wind and not the word which 'has strength'. Thus, it seems problematic using these data to claim that the child is unable to make a distinction between 'words' and 'things named'.

Furthermore, and even more interesting, whether or not words have strength is a rather tricky question; in everyday life we may speak about 'strong words' or the 'strength of words', words that are powerful in terms of what they communicate or in terms of how they are expressed.[1] Hence, metaphorically speaking, there is no problem to argue that words have strength without being considered unable to distinguish 'words from things named'.

Another interesting example of where a realist interpretation of the progression of a conversation would differ from a more dialogical one is the following, where the issue is one of the ontological nature of a 'name'.

> FERT (7) [---] 'Then where is the name of the sun? – *It isn't anywhere.* – Where would it be if it had a place? – *It's we who know it.* – Where is the name when we think of it? – *In the sun, when we think of the sun.* – But where is the name when we think of it? – *In the sun.* – Where is the thought when we think? – *It's what we think.* – Where is what we think? – *It doesn't matter what* (he confuses the object and the thought). – What do we think with? – *When we remember.... With the memory.* – Where is the memory? – ... – In the feet? – *No.* – Where? – ... – In the head? ... – *Yes* (very hesitating). – And where are names? When you think of the name of the sun, where is the name of the sun? – *It's we who know it.* – Yes, but where is it? – *It isn't anywhere.* – Is it in the head? – *No.* – Why not? – *Because it's we who are thinking* (fresh confusion between object and thought: the moment we think of the sun, it is no longer in our head).'
>
> *(Piaget, 1951, p. 74)*

'The interest of this quotation', Piaget argues, 'is in Fert's determined resistance to our increasingly pressing suggestions and his final confession of a realism that is still as strong as ever: for us to think of the sun means that the name of the sun must be "in the sun"' (p. 74). It may be noted that the child initially answers the question, 'Where is the name of the sun' with, 'It isn't anywhere.' Where a name 'is', again, is a rather ambiguous question that the child has to struggle with: what is the background against which one asks where a name is? Is it when thought about or when spoken about? In response to the child's contribution, Piaget shifts from an 'as-is' mode to an 'as-if' one, asking, 'Where would it be if it had a place?' The child responds that 'It's we who know it.' Through the interviewer's persistence, the child eventually says that the word is 'in the sun, when we think of the sun'. But asked again, shortly after, he reiterates that 'It's we who know it' and 'It isn't anywhere.' Thus, an alternative interpretation of this sequence is that the child, through the pressure exerted by the interviewer, temporarily concedes to saying that the name is 'in the sun'. But when returning to the matter, he seems to come back to his original position of considering it as something we 'know' but which 'isn't anywhere'.

In this excerpt there is also an important qualifying marker in transcript; the child answers 'yes (very hesitating)'. Such transcription comments are rare, and in this case, nothing is made of it in the analysis when making claims about the child's understanding. Piaget comments that the child 'confuses the object and the thought', but in our interpretation of this sequence, what happens may equally well be seen as an indicator that the interviewer and the child are not coordinated in perspectives, and that the child struggles to accommodate and keep the conversation going.

The following are two additional examples of children said to be unable to distinguish between internal and external, and thought and matter:

KENN (7 ½): [---] 'When you dream of school, where is the dream? – *At school, because it's as if you were at school.* – Is the dream really at school or is it only as if it were at school? – *It is at school.* – Really and truly? – *No.* – Is it at school or in your mouth? – *In my mouth.* – You said it was far away. Is that true or not true? – *It's far away.'*

ZIMM (8; 1) contrary to Kenn does not believe the dream to be at school but places it in front of his eyes. When he dreams of school, Zimm says: '*I think I'm there.* – When you dream, is the dream at school or inside you? – *In my room?'*

(Piaget, 1951, p. 114)

Piaget argues:

Naturally, Kenn does not suppose that the dream actually takes the dreamer 'to school'; he simply believes that the image of the school, the image seen in the dream, is 'at school', just as children of his age think that, when they speak, the name of the sun is 'in the sun'. However, for the majority of children in the second stage [of developing the ability to distinguish between thought and object in Piaget's model, our comment], the dream is close to them, usually 30 cms in front of their eyes.

(Piaget, 1951, p. 114)

When asked where the dream of school 'is', Kenn responds that 'At school, because it's as if you were at school.' He thus spontaneously uses the marker 'as if' to qualify his assertion. When asked again, whether it is in fact so, or only 'as if', he changes his response, but then changes back again. To ask someone the same questions (even if somewhat rephrased) could in itself be seen as a form of meta-comment making clear that the initial response was not what was expected. In response to such a retake of a question, people tend to change their response. Note also how the child says 'it's as if *you* were at school' (our italics), while the interviewer follows up by asking whether '*it*', that is, '*the dream*' (our italics), is really, or only 'as if', at school. Asked whether saying that the dream is far away is 'true or not true', the child is unlikely to respond that it is untrue; doing so would imply that he had not been truthful in his previous reasoning. There really is no other position for him to take than to confirm that what he has said is true. But it is difficult to clarify on the basis of this piece of conversational data the nature of his understanding of dreams.

In contrast to Piaget's interpretation, in our reading, the other child, Zimm, offers a mode of reasoning that is similar to Kenn's by saying that 'I think I'm there.' Saying that he thinks so could be read as the child providing a qualifying marker, clarifying that he is uncertain (what is asked of him). This is also indicated by his hesistant, 'In my room?'

Consider also the following example of a child being asked about dreams:

> GRAND (8): 'You know what it is to dream? – *Once I saw a man who frightened me in the day and I dreamed of it at night.* – Where does a dream come from? Where is it made? – *In the head.* – Where is the dream while you are dreaming? – ... – In the head or outside? – *It seems (!) as if it's outside.*' Grand thus seems to regard the external nature of the dream as an illusion. But we then asked: 'Where is the dream? – *Neither outside nor inside.* – Where then? – *In the room.* – Where? – *All round me.* – Far or quite near? – *Quite near, when my brother dreams he shivers.*'
>
> *(Piaget, 1951, p. 116)*

'Since the dream made Grand's brother shiver,' Piaget argues, 'it must be something, immaterial perhaps, but external' (p. 116). 'These last cases,' – of which we have quoted Grand – 'in which the child reasons and seeks, evidently show that it is not simply through lack of verbal capacity that children of the second stage say the dream is in the room. They clearly distinguish "being" from "seeming". They doubt the external nature of the dream yet without it they can find no explanation of how one can "see something"; "you can't see what is inside the head!"' (p. 116). In this excerpt, the child's 'as-if' reasoning is marked out in the transcript through the introduction of the exclamation mark after 'seems'.

Discussion and conclusions

Investigating communication with children – including, as we do here when re-analysing excerpts presented by Piaget – it is evident that children (as do adults) qualify their own speech, by using meta-markers such as 'as if' and mental state verbs as 'it seems' or 'I think'. Such meta-markers are intended to make the conversation partner aware of the stance that the speaker takes to his own claims. But speakers may also use non-verbal markers, such as gesturing, gaze and tone of voice, to communicate how they consider that their utterances should be taken. While some of the excerpts presented by Piaget contain markers of the former kind (but it is not clear how systematic transcripts are in this respect), there is no indication of the non-verbal markers. The development of communication studies has led to a demand for higher precision when transcribing – and recording – conversations. We must therefore ask how the children's contributions would have appeared had transcription conventions of today been used. Still, already in the presented excerpts meta-markers are so frequent as to force us to conclude that the relationship between what children *say* and *mean* in asymmetric social situations is complex.

Read in terms of the communicative perspective that we have proposed, what the children do in the interviews is to a large extent to contribute to ongoing discourse. In so doing, they align with the premises of the conversation, and the terms in which the interviewer asks the questions. Using meta-markers (Goatly, 1997), the children qualify their utterances, making clear that they speak in a tentative way about things that are difficult to know about and explain. In this way, the children meta-communicate that they attempt to make themselves understood, and they fulfill the obligations as conversation partners by accommodating to the framing introduced by the interviewer. Reading the interviews as unfolding interactive achievements, rather than as windows into the child's mind, it is difficult, even impossible, to consider what the child says without contextualizing it in a dialogue of a particular kind. In some cases, the communicative frame established by the interviewer is rather peculiar. For example, asking the child where the thought is when you think transforms an activity (thinking) into an object. These kinds of questions imply a 'things ontology' (Shotter, 1993; Säljö, 2002), according to which phenomena exist through being located in a physical space or container (e.g. in the head of the individual). Communicating about activities such as thinking in such reified terms presumes a particular communicative perspective. When children encounter such talk, part of their communicative competence is the ability to identify and align with the communicative premises. This is a radically different reading from one which interprets what the child says as showing what he or she really believes to be the case. What children say in interviews is not unrelated to what they think, but what they say in interviews is collaboratively achieved and contains many tensions, between, for example, saying and meaning, believing and thinking, and claiming and suggesting.

In a sense, there is a paradox in Piaget's account of development. On the one hand, and as we mentioned in the introduction, he was critical to the work he initially conducted in Binet's tradition, arguing that measuring intelligence as a product does not inform us about children's development, and that it is therefore necessary to study the processes whereby children arrive at their answers. That is, it is necessary to make the child's perspective visible. On the other hand, and as seen in his interpretations of the interview data, he tended to make claims about children's thinking as if it existed as such for the researcher to 'seize it, dissect it and lay bare the secret of its composition' (as Claparède, 1926, p. xiv, put it), rather than as contributions to evolving accounts in a situation with specific communicative demands. How to interpret what children say and mean is not only an analytical issue, it is also an ethical one. Research attempting to adopt a child perspective cannot study reasoning as if the child acts in a vacuum; seeking to adapt to adult initiatives and qualifying what one says through various kinds of meta-communicative markers are significant constituents of advanced forms of thinking. Furthermore, these are abilities that children must develop to handle the complexities of interaction and meaning-making.

Note

1 In the French original, the third utterance of the interviewer in this excerpt is 'ça a de la force les mots?', the fourth utterance is 'Dis-moi un mot qui a de la force?', and the fifth question is 'Pourquoi il a de la force le mot "vent"?' In these questions, it is the interviewer who introduces the possibility that 'words have strength'.

References

Aronsson, K. and Hundeide, K. (2002) Relational rationality and children's interview responses. *Human Development*, *45*, 174–86.

Beilin, H. (1992) Piaget's enduring contribution to developmental psychology. *Developmental Psychology*, *28*(2), 191–204.

Claparède, E. (1926) Preface. In J. Piaget, *The Language and Thought of the Child* (trans. M. Warden, pp. ix–xvii). New York: Harcourt, Brace (original work published 1923).

Edwards, D. (1997) *Discourse and Cognition*. London: Sage.

Goatly, A. (1997) *The Language of Metaphors*. London: Routledge.

Goffman, E. (1974) *Frame Analysis: An Essay on the Organization of Experience*. New York: Harper and Row.

Linell, P. (1998) *Approaching Dialogue: Talk, Interaction and Contexts in Dialogical Perspectives*. Amsterdam: John Benjamins.

Mayer, S. J. (2005) The early evolution of Jean Piaget's clinical method. *History of Psychology*, *8*(4), 362–82.

Piaget, J. (1926) *The Language and Thought of the Child* (trans. M. Warden). New York: Harcourt, Brace (original work published 1923).

Piaget, J. (1951) *The Child's Conception of the World* (trans. J. Tomlinson and A. Tomlinson). Savage, MD: Littlefield Adams (original work published 1926).

Pramling, N. (2006) 'The clouds are alive because they fly in the air as if they were birds': A re-analysis of what children say and mean in clinical interviews in the work of Jean Piaget. *European Journal of Psychology of Education*, *21*(4), 453–66.

Reddy, M. J. (1993) The conduit metaphor: A case of frame conflict in our language about language. In A. Ortony (ed.) *Metaphor and thought*, 2nd edn (pp. 164–201). New York: Cambridge University Press.

Säljö, R. (2002) My brain's running slow today – the preference for 'things ontologies' in research and everyday discourse on human thinking. *Studies in Philosophy and Education*, *21*(4–5), 389–405.

Shotter, J. (1993) *Conversational Realities: The Construction of Life Through Language*. Newbury Park: Sage.

Vygotsky, L. S. (1987) *The Collected Works of L. S. Vygotsky*, Vol. 1: *Problems of General Psychology*, including the volume *Thinking and Speech* (ed. R. W. Rieber and A. S. Carton, trans. N. Minick). New York: Plenum.

Wertsch, J. V. (1985) *Vygotsky and the Social Formation of Mind*. Cambridge, MA: Harvard University Press.

Wittgenstein, L. (1953) *Philosophische Untersuchungen/Philosophical investigations* (trans. G. E. M. Anscombe). Oxford: Basil Blackwell.

9

YOUNG CHILDREN'S NARRATIVE ABILITIES

Links to syntax comprehension and reading

Monique Sénéchal and Rosemary Lever

Author note: We sincerely thank Melissa Malette for her invaluable help with the meta-analysis.

Introduction

In trying to make sense of the world around them, young children take in and organize complex events. Children's storytelling can reflect their understanding of these complex events. In this chapter, we examine two aspects of children's storytelling abilities. First, we examine whether children's syntactic knowledge would help explain individual differences in their narrative abilities. Second, we examine whether individual differences in young children's narrative skills would be an excellent predictor of future reading skills. In both sections, special attention is given to whether the findings apply to two distinct genres of storytelling, namely, telling stories about pretend events and telling stories about real events.

The theoretical view adopted herein is that narrated stories comprise two distinct but interrelated components: coherence and cohesion (for a thorough review, see Hickman, 2004). Coherence refers to the hierarchical integration of complex events whereas cohesion refers to the use of linguistic devices that connect statements and parts of statements. Coherence, also called the macro-structure of narratives, is synonymous with story grammars in fictional narratives (i.e. stories about pretend events) and event schemas in autobiographical narratives (i.e. stories about personal events). Cohesion, also called the micro-structure of narratives, encompasses similar language dimensions across the two story genres – dimensions such as the richness of the vocabulary used, the use of connectives (e.g. *and then*), and the mean length of children's utterances. The joint analysis of coherence, a cognitive component, and cohesion, a linguistic component, is necessary for a comprehensive understanding of narrative development.

Individual differences in children's narratives: the role of syntax

Much of the research on individual differences in narrative acquisition has focused on parent–child interaction as the source of development. This has certainly been the case for research on autobiographical storytelling, embedded in a theoretical framework of meaning-making and the social construction of memories (Nelson, 2007; Peterson, 1994). That is, researchers have focused on the conversational styles of families and cultures to describe the varied experiences children have with joint narrative construction of past events (Fivush and Fromhoff, 1988; Noel *et al.*, 2008; Reese and Fivush, 1993). Research on fictional storytelling has focused on parent–child interactions during shared book reading events. Although the frequency of shared reading is not linked to narrative production (Sénéchal *et al.*, 2008), there is some evidence that individual differences in children's fictional narratives might be due to the quality of shared reading interactions. Two intervention studies have found that reading storybooks in a dialogic manner improved aspects of children's narrative coherence (Lever and Sénéchal, 2011; Zevenbergen *et al.*, 2003).

In addition to parent–child interactions, children's oral language also seems to be a source of individual differences in narrative skills. One hypothesized source of individual differences is children's understanding of syntax. Bishop and Donlan (2005) suggested that syntax knowledge might lead to a greater understanding of cause and effect. They proposed that children's ability to encode representations of events, a skill necessary to produce a logical plot sequence, might be constrained by their ability to understand and use complex syntax. That is, as children begin to talk more about physical causality and temporal relationships through complex sentences, it might be expected that their understanding of these dependent relations might increase. For example, the sentence *The mother took the dog while father played with the boy and girl* implies a simultaneous temporal relation between the event of the mother taking the dog and the father playing with the children. Therefore, the comprehension of complex sentences might be a requirement to produce sequential story plots.

A parallel argument has been made previously about children's understanding of mental language and theory of mind (De Villiers and De Villiers, 2000; Lohmann and Tomasello, 2003). Children's understanding of syntactic complements are thought to allow children to frame concepts about thoughts and beliefs in their minds. For instance, in the example, *Sara thought that the cookie was in the jar*, the idea that the cookie may not be in the jar can only be understood if one can understand the complement *that the cookie was in the jar* in conjunction with the noun-verb phrase, *Sara thought*. Although this argument is based on understanding complements and not dependent clauses, it is the idea that comprehension of complex syntax can lead to a greater understanding of mental concepts that is of importance.

The research conducted on the role of syntax in narrative development has focused on atypically developing children's fictional narratives (Bishop and Donlan, 2005; Botting *et al.*, 2001; Reilly *et al.*, 2004). Although the findings obtained lend support to the theory that children with poor syntax skills may not encode the causal relations of event sequences as well as children who have achieved a higher level of syntax acquisition, the question remains as to whether similar support would be found in a sample of typically developing children. Moreover, the extant research has focused on children's telling fictional narratives; the question also remains as to whether similar support would be found for autobiographical narratives.

In the research we present here, we tested whether syntactic knowledge was a source of individual differences in the narrative production of typically developing children. To test the role of syntactic knowledge on narrative production, we used data from Sénéchal *et al.* (2008). Children's stories were analyzed for coherence (i.e. story grammars) and cohesion (i.e. language elements) to assess whether both dimensions were similarly linked to syntactic knowledge. If syntax comprehension facilitates causal understanding, then it should hold a strong relation to cohesion and coherence. Whether similar patterns of relations would be found for both fictional and autobiographical narratives was also explored.

Method

A total of 104 English-speaking 4-year-old children participated in this study. On average, the children (55 per cent girls) were 4.7 years of age (ranging from 4.1 to 5.2 years). Children participated in two testing sessions that were less than one week apart, with each lasting approximately 30 minutes.

The detailed description of materials is in Sénéchal *et al.* (2008). In this study, children's fictional storytelling was measured with a standardized test (the Edmonton Narrative Norms Instrument, Schneider *et al.*, 2002) for which children are asked to tell from wordless picture-books two stories: a one-episode and a three-episode story. In addition, children were asked to tell an autobiographical story about a birthday party that happened recently in their lives (Purcell-Gates, 1988). The story could be about one of their own, a friend's, or a fictional birthday party if they were unable to remember a recent birthday party. All but two children provided real narratives of their last birthday parties.

Resulting fictional and autobiographical stories were transcribed from audiotapes and analyzed for story coherence (i.e. number of story grammar units such as *initiating event*, *attempt*, and *outcome*) and story cohesion (i.e. micro-structure linguistic elements). These linguistic cohesion elements included mean-length utterance (MLU, i.e. the number of morphemes per sentence) and the use of connectives (i.e. number of different connectives such as *and*, *then*, *but*, *now*, *so*, *because*, *or*). The linguistic cohesion measures were obtained using the Child Language Analysis (CLAN) program available from the Child Language Data Exchange System (CHILDES, MacWhinney, 2000).

Measures of syntactic knowledge included two subtests of the *Test for Auditory Comprehension of Language – 3* (TACL-3, Carrow-Woolfolk, 1999). Children's comprehension of syntactically complex sentences was measured with the Elaborated Phrases and Sentences Subtest (test-retest reliability = .88; *Standardized Test Mean* = 10 and *Study Mean* = 11.5, *SD* = 2.6). This subtest measures children's understanding of syntactically complex phrase and sentence constructions. Children's comprehension of sentences that include morphologically complex words was assessed with the

Grammatical Morphemes subtest (test-retest reliability = .86; *Study Mean* = 12.0, *SD* = 2.1).

Control variables included vocabulary, non-verbal intelligence, and parent literacy. Both receptive and expressive vocabularies were measured. Children's receptive vocabulary was measured with the Vocabulary subtest of the TACL-3 (test-retest reliability = .96; *Study Mean* = 12.3, *SD* = 2.7). Children's expressive vocabulary was assessed using the Expressive Vocabulary Test (EVT, Williams, 1997; mean split-half reliability = .91; *Standardized Test Mean* = 100 and *Study Mean* = 110.2, *SD* = 12.8). Children's non-verbal intelligence was assessed using the Animal Pegs subtest of the Wechsler Preschool and Primary Scale of Intelligence – Revised (WPPSI-R, Wechsler, 1989; test-retest stability = .66; *Standardized Test Mean* = 10 and *Study Mean* = 11.9, *SD* = 2.5). *Parent literacy* was measured indirectly by asking parents to complete the Adult's Book Author Checklist (alpha = .95, Sénéchal *et al.*, 1996; Stanovich and West, 1989). This checklist assesses parents' recognition of adult book authors (*Study Mean %* = 40.9, *SD* = 22.6). *Parent education* was also a control variable (*Study Mean years of post-secondary education* = 3.0, *SD* = 2.0 with 17 per cent of the parents not completing high school).

Whenever multiple measures of the same construct were used, we created composite variables by averaging z-scores obtained from raw scores for the standardized measures of language. Thus, syntactic knowledge included the understanding of morphologically complex sentences as well as syntactically complex phrases and sentences, whereas vocabulary included the receptive and expressive vocabulary measures. Also, the two fictional narratives were averaged to create a single variable, and all subsequent analyses are conducted on this composite variable.

Results and discussion

Examination of the correlation patterns among variables revealed three key findings. First, measures of coherence and cohesion were interrelated for both fictional (*r*s ranging from .26 to .67, *p*s < .05) and autobiographical narratives (*r*s ranging from .26 to .78, *p*s < .05), providing support for the model of narrative dimensions used in the present research. Second, the fictional and autobiographical narratives were not correlated (*r*s ranging from .03 to .16, *p*s > .05) with one exception: story grammars in fictional narratives and connectives in autobiographical stories were correlated (*r* = .21, *p* < .05). This general lack of association between fictional and autobiographical storytelling raises the possibility that these are distinct abilities – a possibility that has yet to be tested in the research literature. Third, and as predicted, syntactic knowledge was related to the structure (*r* = .47, *p* < .05) and MLU-morphemes (*r* = .30, *p* < .05) in children's fictional narratives, although it was not statistically significantly associated with the number of different connectives (*r* = .15, *p* > .05). Third, and contrary to expectation, autobiographical narrative components were not correlated with syntactic knowledge (*r*s ranging from −.02 to .07), or the key control variables of child vocabulary, parent education and literacy (*r*s ranging from −.12 to .14).

There are at least two possible explanations for these findings. A more theoretical explanation might be that autobiographical narratives require less in-depth knowledge of causal and temporal relations than do fictional stories. In accord with this possibility, autobiographical stories rely on recall of already encoded events whereas fictional stories require the activation of more abstract knowledge necessary to create a story. A more methodological explanation might be that the recall of a birthday is too scripted in children's minds and does not allow one to capture the full range of individual differences in autobiographical storytelling. In the present research, autobiographical narratives were not analyzed further because they were not associated with syntactic knowledge.

To test the prediction that children's syntactic knowledge would be a key component to children's production of fictional narratives, we conducted a series of fixed-order hierarchical regressions. The variables entered first in the equation were controls such as parent education and literacy, as well as child IQ. These variables were followed by child vocabulary as a general measure of language, and finally, the last variable entered was the measure of syntactic knowledge. The results of these very stringent tests are in Table 9.1. The findings for narrative coherence, indexed by story grammars, were as expected: after controlling for parent education and literacy as well as child non-verbal intelligence, child vocabulary knowledge accounted for a significant 12 per cent of variance, and syntactic knowledge explained an additional 6 per cent of unique variance in narrative structure. A similar pattern of significance was found for children's story cohesion, indexed by MLU (morphemes); whereby vocabulary explained a significant 4 per cent of variance, and syntactic knowledge, entered last, accounted for an additional and significant 4 per cent.

The analyses for narrative coherence (i.e. story grammars) and cohesion (i.e. MLU) reported in Table 9.1 are interesting, but also raise the possibility that the association between child syntactic knowledge and narrative structure might be due to their respective association with narrative MLU-morphemes. To test against this possibility, the association between syntactic knowledge and narrative structure was examined after controlling for narrative MLU. As indicated in model 2 in Table 9.1, syntactic knowledge still explained a significant 4 per cent of unique variance in narrative structure even when narrative MLU is entered in the equation. Although correlational in nature, the results of these very stringent analyses lend strong support to the notion that syntactic knowledge plays a key role in young children's production of well-structured fictional narratives.

In the present study, we tested and confirmed that children's understanding of syntax explained unique variance in 4-year-olds' production of fictional narratives. The results are consistent with the idea that syntactic knowledge helps children produce more structurally complex fictional narratives. The obtained findings with typically developing children extend previous research with children experiencing language difficulties (Bishop and Donlan, 2005; Botting *et al.*, 2001; Reilly *et al.*, 2001). Theoretically, the comprehension of syntax might be required for the production of complex sentences necessary to produce cohesive fictional stories. Experience with syntactically complex sentences might also be necessary to

Table 9.1 Fixed-order Hierarchical Regression Analyses Predicting Individual Differences in Story Grammar and MLU in Children's Fictional Narratives

Outcome Predictor order	R^2	ΔR^2	ΔF	Beta	r
Story grammar: model 1					
Parent education level	.04	.04	4.54*	.10	.21*
Parent literacy	.08	.03	3.56†	.05	.25*
Child non-verbal intelligence	.09	.01	1.52	–.01	.15
Child vocabulary	.21	.12	14.57**	.20††	.43**
Child syntactic knowledge	.27	.06	8.03**	.32**	.47**
MLU					
Parent education level	.01	.01	< 1.00	.01	.08
Parent literacy	.02	.02	1.54	.05	.15
Child non-verbal intelligence	.02	.00	< 1.00	–.04	.05
Child vocabulary	.06	.04	3.83*	.07	.23*
Child syntactic knowledge	.10	.04	3.94*	.25*	.30**
Story grammar: Model 2					
Parent education level	.04	.04	4.54*	.09	.21*
Parent literacy	.08	.03	3.56†	.04	.25*
Child non-verbal intelligence	.09	.01	1.52	.00	.15
Child vocabulary	.21	.12	14.57**	.18	.43**
Child book MLU	.32	.11	15.82**	.31**	.43**
Child syntactic knowledge	.36	.03	5.02*	.24*	.47**

††p < .09; †p < .06; *p < .05; **p < .01

understand cause and effect – an understanding essential for the production of coherent fictional stories.

Notwithstanding their consistency with this theoretical framework, our findings are correlational in nature and the measures were collected concurrently. Despite our very stringent analyses, longitudinal research is warranted to confirm the direction of the relations found.

Early narrative skills as a predictor of eventual reading skills

In this section, we conducted a meta-analysis to assess whether individual differences in narrative skills would predict children's eventual success in reading. Given that we were not able to find intervention research aimed at showing that specific causal role, we examined the longitudinal correlational literature. We omitted the studies for which narrative skills and reading were measured concurrently because concurrent correlations do not provide any information about the direction of the relation between narrative and reading skills. The remainder of this section includes a succinct overview of the methodology used followed by an interpretative description of the results (the complete methodology can be obtained from the first author).

The database of studies used for this meta-analysis was determined in four steps conducted from January to July 2013: (a) a search of electronic databases, that yielded 528 potential reports, using keywords describing narrative skills (30 keywords), reading skills (33 keywords), grade level (3 keywords), and the keyword *longitudinal*; (b) a search of review articles that yielded an additional 23 potential reports; (c) a search of the reference sections of articles found in steps (a) and (b) (two additional potential reports found); and (d) contacting 20 experts in the field of children's narratives for relevant published and unpublished articles or data, and this yielded 16 potential reports. From these potential reports, those kept for the meta-analysis met the following criteria: (a) studies were longitudinal (15 per cent of studies excluded for this reason); (b) studies testing the hypothesis that oral narrative ability is related to later reading performance (53 per cent of studies excluded); and (c) studies reporting correlations or the necessary statistics permitting to calculate the correlations or had sample sizes larger than 30 (6 per cent of studies excluded). A total of 12 studies were included in the meta-analysis. One of these articles (Reese *et al.*, 2010) included findings for two independent samples, and consequently, the findings for one sample were labeled Study 1 and for the other Study 2. As a result, the meta-analysis consisted of 13 independent samples. In all of these studies, children told or retold fictional narratives. None of the studies that met our criteria included autobiographical stories. For the studies selected, three types of characteristics were coded, namely, the characteristics of the narratives, participants, and studies (see Table 9.2).

The studies included were synthesized using standard meta-analytic procedures such as adjusting correlations for sample sizes prior to calculating the mean correlation for a class of studies (Shadish and Haddock, 1994). Meta-analytic procedures allow one to assess the degree of variability across studies. The obtained correlation coefficients between narrative skills and reading are presented in Table 9.3. Whenever available, we also report the correlation between the two components of narrative skills (i.e. coherence and cohesion) and different types of reading outcomes (i.e. reading comprehension, word reading). For the three studies that included a third testing time, the correlations reported were those for the test time where the age of the children were comparable to the remaining studies. Hence, we used the second test time for Adlof *et al.* (2010) and the third test time for Roth *et al.* (2002) and Tabors *et al.* (2001; itself a follow-up of Snow *et al.*, 1995).

These 13 studies, described in Table 9.2, represent a total of 1,738 children. The first question we asked was whether a statistically significant relation existed between early narrative skills and later reading skills broadly defined and there was. The mean correlation was moderate at .37 (95 per cent CIs .27, .43) and statistically significant ($z = 9.21$, $p < .01$). The homogeneity statistic, however, was significantly different from zero ($Q = 49.04$, $p < .01$), indicating that there was considerable variability across studies, and therefore findings should be interpreted with caution.

Table 9.2 Narrative, participant, and study characteristics for each of the 13 studies

| | Characteristics | | | | | | | | | |
| | Narrative | | Participant | | | | Study | | | |
Narration task / Study author(s)	Type	Prompts	Age 1	Age 2	Child	SES	N	Duration (y; m)	Reading measure	Country
Child tells a story										
Cabell and others (2011)	2	No	4; 4	5; 8	2	1	330	1; 4	1	USA
Griffin and others (2004)	3	No	5; 0	8; 0	1	2	32	3; 0	1	USA
O'Neill and others (2004)	2	No	3; 1	6; 2	1	2	48	2; 3	3	CA
Ragnarsdottir and Birgisdottir (2012)	2	No	6; 6	8; 6	1	–	133	2; 0	3	ICE
Tabors and others (2001)	2	No	5; 0	9; 0	2	1	69	1; 0	2	USA
Van Kraayenoord and Paris (1996)	2	No	5; 10	7; 10	1	–	62	2; 0	3	AU
Child retells a story										
Adlof and others (2010)	1	Yes	5; 0	7; 0[a]	3	–	433	8; 0	1	USA
Bishop and Adams (1990)[b]	1	Yes	4; 6	8; 6	3	–	77	4; 0	3	UK
Catts and others (1999)	1	Yes	7; 11	9; 11	3	–	604	2; 0	1	USA
Reese and others Study 1 (2010)	1	Yes	6; 0	7; 0	3	3	61	1; 0	2	NZ
Reese and others Study 2 (2010)	1	Yes	7; 0	8; 0	3	3	39	1; 0	2	NZ

Continued

Table 9.2 Narrative, participant, and study characteristics for each of the 13 studies **(Continued)**

	Characteristics									
	Narrative		Participant				Study			
Narration task										
Study author(s)	Type	Prompts	Age 1	Age 2	Child	SES	N	Duration (y; m)	Reading measure	Country
Roth and others (2002)	4	No	5;6	8;6	1	3	66	2;0	3	USA
Westerveld and others (2012)	1	Yes	4;0	6;0	1	3	92	2;0	3	NZ

Note: A dash indicates missing information.

[a]The ages reported are inferred from the typical age of children in kindergarten and grade 2 in the United States.

[b]Bishop and Adams (1990) is the only study that asked the children to retell a story with the help of a book.

Narrative type: 1 = Experimenter (E) reads storybook; 2 = Wordless picture book; 3 = E gives child play animals and introduces a conflict; 4= E asks child to tell favourite fictional story.

Prompts: Indicates whether the experiment give the child verbal prompts during narration.

Age 1 or 2: age in years and months at time 1 or time 2.

Child: 1 = typically developing; 2 = at risk because low SES; 3 = mixed.

SES: 1 = low; 2 = middle; 3 = mixed. *N* = Sample size at post-test.

Reading measure: 1= reading comprehension; 2 = word reading (e.g. decoding, reading fluency); 3 = combination.

Country: USA = United States; ICE = Iceland; CA = Canada; AU = Australia; NZ = New Zealand; UK = England.

Table 9.3 Overall correlation coefficients for each of the 13 studies and as a function of reading measure and narrative component

Narration task	Overall	Reading comprehension			Word reading	
Study author(s)		Cohesion	Coherence	Combination	Cohesion	Coherence
Child tells a story						
Cabell and others (2011)	.10	.10				
Griffin and others (2004)	.28	.30	.25			
Ragnarsdottir and Birgisdottir (2012)	.17	.14	.25*		.14	.14
O'Neill and others (2004)	.08	.00	.13		.03	.16
Tabors and others (2001)	.47*			.47*		
Van Kraayenoord (1996)	.45*		.43*			.47*
Child retells a story						
Adlof and others (2010)	.32*		.32*			
Catts and others (1999)	.48*		.48*			
Bishop and Adams (1990)	.56*	.50*	.64*		.50*	.61*
Reese and others Study 1 (2010)	.18					.18
Reese and others Study 2 (2010)	.34*					.34*
Roth and others (2002)	.03		.07			−.02
Westerveld and others (2012)	.26	.16	.41*		.10	.38*

Note: No studies reported correlations between word reading and a combined narrative score.
*p ≤ .05 one tail

Attempts at understanding the observed variability by contrasting studies along their characteristics failed (e.g. children told or retold a story; children typically developing or not). That is, the smaller sets of studies were still more variable than would be expected by chance. Although we did not succeed at explaining this variability, we did get a better understanding of the set of studies. For instance, one analysis revealed that the set of seven studies ($N = 1283$) where children retold stories showed a moderately strong association between narrative and reading skills ($r = .40$, CIs = .31, .48, $z = 9.70$, $p < .01$), although there was considerable variability within the set ($Q = 24.96$, $p < .001$). In contrast, the six studies ($N = 455$) where children told stories yielded a weak association between narrative skills and reading that was not statistically significantly different from zero ($r = .21$, CIs = −.07, .50, $z = 1.50$,

$p < .001$, $Q = 10.59$, $p > .05$). Within this latter set, however, the four studies that assessed the relation between story coherence and reading comprehension yielded a statistically significant correlation ($r = .27$, CIs $= -.02, .51$, $z = 2.21$, $p < .05$, $Q = 2.31$, $p > .05$, N $= 252$). This seemingly stronger link found between stories retold and reading outcomes is difficult to interpret because, in all but one of these studies (see Table 9.2) additional support in the form of prompts was given to children during narration (e.g. 'Tell me more', 'What happened next?'). Moreover, most of these studies included in their sample children at risk of reading difficulties as well as typically developing children.

In sum, there is limited evidence showing that children's ability to tell or retell fictional stories is a longitudinal predictor of eventual success in reading – although much work is needed to understand the nature of this association. Also, there is a lack of studies examining a possible longitudinal link between young children's auto-biographical storytelling and eventual reading success. At present, one cannot make evidence-based claims about the relation between autobiographical storytelling and eventual success in reading.

Conclusion

In this chapter, we examined children's understanding of complex events as revealed in their storytelling about real and fictional events. Our main focus was on individual differences. In the first part of the chapter, we were concerned with skills that might explain individual differences in children's storytelling. In the second part, we examined whether storytelling itself would predict children's reading abilities. The findings obtained provide guidance for future research. First, we found that children's comprehension of syntactically complex sentences was robustly associated with their production of fictional narratives. These preliminary findings obtained from concurrent assessments of children skills would require replication in longitudinal research to ascertain whether syntactic comprehension is a prerequisite to the production of coherent and cohesive stories. Second, we found some evidence that young children who produced more coherent and cohesive fictional stories tended to be better readers later on. At the same time, we found great variability in findings across the studies surveyed. Hence, prudence is needed when making claims about the role of narrative abilities in the development of reading. In fact, we have yet to determine whether there is a causal longitudinal relation between fictional storytelling and reading. Third, the findings obtained for fictional storytelling did not generalize to autobiographical storytelling. That is, syntactic knowledge did not predict autobiographical storytelling, nor did we find any studies examining whether autobiographical storytelling was predictive of children's reading ability. Therefore, the questions of whether autobiographical and fictional storytelling rely on a general storytelling ability and whether autobiographical storytelling is linked to reading ability need to be addressed in order to provide accurate and helpful research-based evidence to educators.

References

★ indicates studies included in the meta-analysis.

★Adlof, S. M., Catts, H. W. and Lee, J. (2010) Kindergarten predictors of second versus eighth grade reading comprehension impairments. *Journal of Learning Disabilities, 43*, 332–45.

★Bishop, D. V. M. and Adams, C. (1990) A prospective study of the relationship between specific language impairment, phonological disorders and reading retardation. *Journal of Child Psychology and Psychiatry, 31*, 1027–50.

Bishop, D. V. M. and Donlan, C. (2005) The role of syntax in encoding and recall of pictorial narratives: Evidence from Specific Language Impairment. *British Journal of Developmental Psychology, 23*, 25–46.

Botting, N., Faragher, B., Smikin, Z., Knox, E. and Conti-Ramsden, G. (2001) Predicting pathways of Specific Language Impairment: What differentiates good and poor outcome? *Journal of Child Psychology and Psychiatry, 42*, 1013–20.

★Cabell, S. Q., Justice, L. M., Piasta, S. B., Curenton, S. M., Wiggins, A., Turbull, K. and Petscher, Y. (2011) Children's narrative ability and reading comprehension. Unpublished raw data.

Carrow-Woolfolk, E. (1999) *Test for Auditory Comprehension of Language*, 3rd edn. Austin, TX: PRO-ED.

Catts, H. W., Fey, M. E., Zhang, X. and Tomblin, J. B. (1999) Language basis of reading and reading disabilities: Evidence from a longitudinal investigation. *Scientific Studies of Reading, 3*, 331–61.

De Villiers, J. G., and De Villiers, P. A. (2000) Linguistic determinism and the understanding of false beliefs. In P. Mitchell and K. J. Riggs (eds) *Children's Reasoning and the Mind* (pp. 191–228). Hove, Sussex: Psychology Press.

Fivush, R., and Fromhoff, F. A. (1988) Style and structure in mother–child conversations about the past. *Discourse Processes, 11*, 337–55.

★Griffin, T., Hemphill, L., Camp, L. and Wolf, D. (2004) Oral discourse in the preschool years and later literacy skills. *First Language, 24*, 123–47.

Hickman, M. (2004) Coherence, cohesion, and context: some comparative perspectives in narrative development. In S. Stromqvist and L. Verhoeven (eds) *Relating Events in Narrative*, Vol. 2: *Typological and Contextual Perspectives* (pp. 281–306). Mahwah, NJ: Erlbaum.

Lever, R. and Sénéchal, M. (2011) Discussing stories: Using a dialogic reading intervention to improve oral narrative skills. *Journal of Experimental Child Psychology, 108*, 1–24. doi: 10.1016/j.jecp.2010.07.002.

Lohmann, H. and Tomasello, M. (2003) The role of language in the development of false belief understanding: A training study. *Child Development, 74*, 1130–44.

MacWhinney, B. (2000) *The CHILDES Project: Tools for Analyzing Talk*, 3rd edn. Mahwah, NJ: Erlbaum.

Noel, M., Peterson, C. and Jesso, B. (2008) The relationship of parenting stress and child temperament to language development among economically disadvantaged preschoolers. *Journal of Child Language, 35*, 823–43.

Nelson, K. (2007) *Young Minds in Social Worlds: Experience, Meaning and Memory*. Cambridge, MA: Harvard University Press.

★O'Neill, D. K., Pearce, M. J. and Pick, J. L. (2004) Preschool children's narratives and performance on the Peabody Individualized Achievement Test – Revised: evidence of a relation between early narrative and later mathematical ability. *First Language, 24*, 149–83.

Peterson, C. (1994) Narrative skills and social class. *Canadian Journal of Education, 19*: 251–69.

Purcell-Gates, V. (1988) Lexical and syntactic knowledge of written narrative held by well-read-to kindergartners and second graders. *Research in the Teaching of English, 22*, 128–60.

★Ragnarsdóttir, H., and Birgisdóttir, F. (2012) Do narrative skills in 1st grade contribute independently to the variance in reading skills in 3rd grade? A longitudinal study of Icelandic children. Poster session presented at the meeting of International Conference

NIL 2012 *Narrative, Intervention and Literacy: Development of Oral Narratives, Intervention Procedures and Reading Comprehension*, Paris, France.

Reilly, J., Losh, M., Bellugi, U. and Wulfeck, B. (2004) Frog, where are you? Narratives in children with Specific Language Impairment, early focal brain injury, and Williams syndrome. *Brain and Language, 88*, 229–47.

Reese, E., and Fivush, R. (1993) Parental styles of talking about the past. *Developmental Psychology, 29*, 596–606.

*Reese. E., Suggate, S., Long, J. and Schaughency, E. (2010) Children's oral narrative and reading skills in the first 3 years of reading instruction. *Reading and Writing, 23*, 627–44.

*Roth, F. P., Speece, D. L. and Cooper, D. H. (2002) A longitudinal analysis of the connection between oral language and early reading. *Journal of Educational Research, 95*, 259–72.

Sénéchal, M., LeFevre, J., Hudson, E. and Lawson, E. P. (1996) Knowledge of storybooks as predictor of young children's vocabulary. *Journal of Educational Psychology, 88*, 520–36.

Sénéchal, M., Pagan, S., Lever, R. and Ouellette, G. (2008) Relations among the frequency of shared reading and 4-year-old children's vocabulary, morphological and syntax comprehension and narrative skills. *Early Education and Development*. Special Issue: *Parent–child Interaction and Early Literacy Development, 19*, 27–44.

Schneider, P., Dubé, R. V. and Hayward, D. (2002) *The Edmonton Narrative Norms Instrument.* Edmonton: AB.

Schneider, P., Hayward, D. and Dubé, R. V. (2006) Storytelling from pictures using the Edmonton Narrative Norms Instrument. *Journal of Speech-Language Pathology and Audiology, 30*, 224–38.

Shadish, W. R. and Haddock, C. K. (1994) Combining estimates of effect size. In H. Cooper and L. V. Hedges (eds) *The Handbook of Research Synthesis* (pp. 261–81). New York: Russell Sage Foundation.

Snow, C. E., Tabors, P. O., Nicholson, P. A. and Kurland, B. F. (1995) SHELL: Oral language and early literacy skills in kindergarten and first-grade children. *Journal of Research in Childhood Education, 10*, 37–48.

Stanovich, K. E. and West, R. F. (1989) Exposure to print and orthographic processing. *Reading Research Quarterly, 24*, 402–33.

Stein, N. L. and Glenn, C. G. (1979) An analysis of story comprehension in elementary school children. In R. O. Freedle (ed.) *New Directions in Discourse Processing* (pp. 53–120). Norwood, NJ: Ablex.

*Tabors, P. O., Snow, C. E. and Dickinson, D. K. (2001) Homes and schools together: Supporting language and literacy development. In D. K. Dickinson and P. O. Tabors (eds) *Beginning Literacy with Language: Young Children Learning at Home and School* (pp. 313–34). Baltimore, MD: Paul H. Brookes.

*Van Kraayenoord, C. E. and Paris, S. G. (1996) Story construction from a picture book: An assessment activity for young learners. *Early Child Research Quarterly, 11*, 41–61.

Wechsler, D. (1989) *Wechsler Preschool and Primary Scale of Intelligence – Revised*. San Antonio, TX: Psychological Corporation.

*Westerveld, M.F., van Bysterveldt, A.K., Boyd, L. and Gillon, G. T. (2013) Oral narrative ability of New Zealand kindergarten children and reading skills two years later. Manuscript in preparation.

Williams, K. T. (1997) *Expressive Vocabulary Test*. Circle Pines, MN: American Guidance Service.

Zevenbergen, A., Whitehurst, G. and Zevenbergen, J. (2003) Effects of a shared-reading intervention on the inclusion of evaluative devices in narratives of children from low-income families. *Applied Development Psychology, 24*, 1–15.

10

CROSS-LANGUAGE SYNTACTIC PRIMING IN BILINGUAL CHILDREN

Alina Konradt

Introduction

This chapter offers an overview of syntactic priming, an experimental research methodology utilized to assess early grammatical knowledge as well as to explore cognitive processes that define its growth and development. The reviewed priming studies address the presence of abstract syntactic understanding early in life as well as examining implicit learning mechanisms in young children. Following the results from cross-linguistic and bilingual studies, the question of whether priming is a purely structural phenomenon is raised, suggesting a role of discourse pragmatic factors in eliciting priming effects.

Despite a popular claim that thought is autonomous from the constraints of language (Pinker, 2010), the question posed in this chapter is very much underpinned by an opposing view. First expressed by Vygotsky (1934), it suggests that language functions as a cognitive tool which aids understanding, speculation, planning and reflection in young children, and that language and thought form an atomic unit, and therefore, must be researched as such. It has also been argued that compared to their monolingual peers, young bilinguals have advantage in a number of cognitive outcomes, such as working memory, attention control, metalinguistic awareness, executive functioning and abstract representation skills (Adesope *et al.*, 2010; Bialystok, 1999).

Within the broad spectrum of language acquisition research (Foster-Cohen, 2009; Lust, 2006; Slobin, 2014), the domain of syntactic development, or the process of achieving mastery in the comprehension and production of sentence structures, is of major interest in the study of language and continues to be vigorously debated (Chen, 2010; Chien and Wexler, 1990; Fisher, 2002; Radford, 2000; Mehler *et al.*, 2008; Marcus *et al.*, 1999; Szendrői, 2003; Tomasello, 2000; Van Hout *et al.*, 2009). Understanding the processes that govern the emergence of children's grammar, and syntax in particular, can potentially provide answers to such fundamental questions of human development as the innateness of linguistic knowledge or the existence of the Universal Grammar that defines acquisition of all human languages (Gathercole and Hoff, 2009).

More often than not, young children's language production leads to incorrect assumptions not only about their linguistic competence, but also about the ways they think of and perceive the world (one such assumption being children's egocentricity, another being the inability to successfully pass false-belief tasks by children under the age of 4). However, examining early syntax through careful input manipulation could shed light on the question of how age-related cognitive and computational constraints could affect language production and comprehension, adjusting views on the development of children's thinking (Guasti, 2002; Grodzinsky and Reinhart, 1993).

One of the most valuable ways to explore syntactic understanding is through examining syntactic priming effects. Syntactic or structural priming (the terms are used interchangeably) is a natural language phenomenon whereby a speaker is inclined to utilize recently experienced sentence structures in her own speech (Vasilyeva *et al.*, 2006). Syntactic priming effects (or a significant increase in the production of specific structures after subsequent exposure to them) have been recorded in spontaneous speech of adults as well as occurring in conversations between children and their caregivers (Pickering and Branigan, 1999; Pickering and Ferreira, 2008).

The term also describes an innovative, primarily experimental methodology, which is based on this tendency (Bock, 1986). The most common strategy employed by psycholinguists in priming research with children includes young participants and an experimenter taking turns in describing a set of images. While the experimenter's sentences are scripted and follow a chosen grammatical structure (prime), the children's responses are examined for the presence of the primed structure (Vasilyeva *et al.*, 2012). Despite the fact that children appear to demonstrate priming effects in their speech, the question of whether the effects are purely structural (whereby only the syntactic form repetition is involved) or whether they incorporate other psychological, cognitive and pragmatic factors, is still open (Vasilyeva and Waterfall, 2012).

Regarding the approach to priming as a purely structural phenomenon, studying priming effects in children's speech could potentially resolve a longstanding theoretical problem: is abstract syntactic knowledge present from the onset of language or is children's sentence production driven mainly by the lexically based patterns known to them through frequent exposure? If the effects are found in young children consistently, a claim that they possess abstract syntactic understanding, which permits them to use particular sentence constructions productively, could potentially be made. Furthermore, as priming effects have been shown to last over days and even weeks, priming research has the potential to tackle the issue of implicit learning and investigate the mechanisms which underline it, thus informing the language curriculum at school and early years settings (Vasilyeva *et al.*, 2006).

Cross-language priming research involving young bilingual children is limited. Yet, conducting priming tasks with bilingual children could present crucial evidence for the account that priming is more than just a structural repetition, but is driven by particular ways of thinking about the described event, and is triggered by the discourse function of the primed structure (Vasilyeva *et al.*, 2010). Cross-language priming tasks involve hearing the primes in one language of a bilingual child, while the target sentences produced by her are in the other. If hearing a prime structure in one language activates a specific pragmatic function, it would stimulate the child to think about newly encountered events in a certain way and to focus on that function during the production of the target description in the other language. Thus, provided that the languages of the bilingual utilize different structures to encode pragmatically similar meanings, we would expect the child's utterances to preserve the discourse function of the prime rather than its syntactic form.

Such priming research could also contribute to achieving a deeper understanding of interaction between the languages of a young bilingual (or cross-linguistic stimulation) during the acquisition stage, which is critical for developing and improving bilingual education practices (Genesee, 2006; Kidd, 2012; Vasilyeva *et al.*, 2010). Bilingual education, it must be emphasised, has become an essential part of provision for young children, as bilingualism itself is no longer just a linguistic advantage, but a vital aspect of life for the majority of the world's population (Baker, 2011; García, 2011; Bruce *et al.*, 2010).

Bilingual acquisition

Language acquisition research is largely concerned with the poverty of stimulus problem, which holds that quality, amount and form of language input does not equal uptake (Foster-Cohen, 2009). The issue is closely related to the nature versus nurture argument, the most prominent dichotomy still present in human development research. Among many, two theories of language acquisition stand out: the experience-based perspective and the nativist account, where the former places emphasis on input, imitation and experience, and the latter on the child's innate biological predisposition for acquiring language, which is not determined by input (Chomsky, 1965; Crain and Thornton, 2008).

Despite much disagreement about the process of language acquisition and its origins, linguists accept that typical language development occurs in more or less universal stages across all languages: speech-babbling begins at the age of 6 to 10 months followed by appearance of recognizable words at around 11 to 16 months; word-combinations emerge sometime before 2 years of age, while the mastery of most complex grammatical structures is achieved around the age of 10 to 12 years (Clark, 2009). These stages, however, bear only an approximate connection to the age, as each child's linguistic growth is individual and varies substantially. The focus of this chapter, bilingual first language acquisition or simultaneous bilingualism, whereby a child is exposed to both of her languages from birth, can be thought of as following a stage-based process similar to that of monolingual, allowing for varying degrees of language proficiency and code-switching competence (Duarte, 2009; Genesee and Nicoladis, 2007).

Widely accepted until recently, the unitary-system hypothesis (USH) states that simultaneous acquisition of two languages occurs within a single linguistic system, which is gradually separated when relative language fluency is achieved (Leopold, 1970). However, researchers have lately argued that the systems are autonomous from the start of acquisition (Paradis *et al.*, 2011). For example, Wapole (2000) analysed morphological, phonological, lexical and syntactic development of two young bilinguals and found much fewer instances of mixing words between languages in the children's early speech samples than in the later ones. Moreover, these children displayed no confusion on the level of sentence production despite distinct syntactic differences in the languages spoken by them. These findings, Wapole (2000) believes, contradict USH.

There is currently an agreement that typically both languages of a simultaneous bilingual develop just as each of these languages progresses during monolingual language acquisition and lead to the same level of grammatical competence (Meisel, 2006). However, the emerging grammars of a bilingual alter and stimulate one another, and such cross-language interferences make a considerable impact on the linguistic development of the child and therefore must not be underestimated (McGregor, 2009).

Early syntax and syntactic priming

Syntactic development, specifically the emergence of syntactic abstractness, has caused controversy among child language specialists. Syntactic abstractness, a capacity that young children do not possess, some researchers claim (Tomasello, 2000), could be defined as a speaker's ability to use sentence structures productively rather than repeating previously heard word–clusters. Tomasello (2000) states that children under the age of 3 years tend to use lexically based patterns heard in adults' speech, adopting 'social, imitative learning' strategies, rather than creating novel utterances with familiar words (Tomasello, 2000, p. 238). Relying mainly on the evidence from experiments that demonstrated young children's virtual inability to use novel (nonce) verbs creatively, Tomasello concludes that abstract syntactic understanding is practically absent in children under 3, after which it steadily increases. Fisher (2002), however, notes that adults also exercise caution when utilizing words unknown to them and often restrict their use to the utterances heard before, highlighting that the child's language therefore should not be expected to be free of those constraints. Thus, the question concerned with the presence of syntactic abstractness in young children remains to be answered. Attempts to resolve the issue, however, come from psycholinguistic research, which employs priming.

Priming as methodology

Syntactic priming is 'a speaker's tendency to produce a syntactic structure encountered in the recent discourse, as opposed to an alternate structure' (McDonough and Mackey, 2008, p. 31). The exposure to a particular sentence construction increases the speaker's capacity to mentally access it, subsequently leading to improved comprehension and more frequent use of this construction (Vasilyeva *et al.*, 2012). Syntactic priming, an experimental methodology based on this phenomenon, is applied within the field of developmental psychology, psycholinguistics and language acquisition. A priming task usually involves an experimenter and a participant taking turns to describe images: the experimenter's image descriptions containing a chosen sentence structure are followed by the participant's descriptions (targets), which are then checked for the primed structure repetition (Vasilyeva *et al.*, 2012).

Initially, priming was developed as a tool for examining syntactic representation in English-speaking adults (Bock, 1986; Pickering and Ferreira, 2008). The methodology has since been used in research with mature bilingual speakers to investigate a possibility of shared syntactic systems in bilingual language production (Desmet and Declercq, 2006; Loebell and Bock, 2003). Moreover, this paradigm has become particularly useful for assessing the role of input in language acquisition and determining the emergence of abstract syntactic knowledge in English-speaking children (Gerard *et al.*, 2010; Huttenlocher *et al.*, 2004; Messenger *et al.*, 2011; Rowland *et al.*, 2012; Thatcher *et al.*, 2008; Thothathiri and Snedeker, 2008). Furthermore, investigations made into lasting effects of priming in young children have led some researchers to suggest that grammatical structures could be learnt implicitly through priming (Chang *et al.*, 2006; Kidd, 2012; Savage *et al.*, 2006; Vasilyeva *et al.*, 2006). More recently, syntactic priming has emerged as one of the most fascinating approaches to cross-linguistic research with bilingual children (Fitzpatrick, 2011; Vasilyeva *et al.*, 2010).

Assessing early syntactic abstractness through priming

Shimpi *et al.* (2007) employed the priming paradigm to assess syntactic abstractness in children aged 3 and 4. After being exposed to double-object datives (such as 'the girl gave her friend a book') and passives (such as 'the puppy was licked by the kitten'), the young children significantly increased the production of the primed structures respectively. Shimpi and colleagues (2007) argue for the presence of abstract syntactic knowledge: the children's use of the dative and passive structures with words different to the ones used by the experimenter was activated by hearing dative and passive primes. In contrast, Savage *et al.* (2003) found priming effect in 6-year-olds, but not in children aged 3 and 4.

However, the study of Huttenlocher *et al.* (2004) provides support for early abstract syntactic understanding in 4-year-olds. The researchers examined the production of the passive voice by children aged 4 and 5 in three different priming conditions: (1) taking turns with an experimenter to describe pictures, which included children repeating the experimenter's sentence prior to producing their own picture description; (2) without that repetition; (3) producing ten picture descriptions after hearing a block of ten experimenter's descriptions. Priming effect was reported in all three conditions, thus supporting the early syntactic abstractness account. In addition, while Huttenlocher *et al.* (2004) did not find that participants' prime-repeats significantly impact on priming effect, Bencini and Valian (2008) report that passive prime repeating in fact promoted production of passive targets by 3-year-olds in their study. This does not deny young children the ability to abstractly manipulate sentence structures, but might point at a change in syntactic processing between the ages of 3 and 4.

More evidence supporting the emergence of syntactic abstractness in children aged 3 to 4 comes from the study of Messenger *et al.* (2011), who investigated the production of full passives (i.e. 'the dog was washed by the girl') by adults and 3- to 4-year-olds after the exposure to short passives ('the dog was washed') and active structures ('the girl washed the dog'). Messenger and colleagues (2011) highlight that both children and adults produced more full passives after hearing short passives than after hearing actives. In addition, the priming effect was stronger in children than in adults, which, authors suggest, reveals that less proficient language users are more susceptible to priming.

Rowland *et al.* (2012) also report a higher proportion of responses containing a primed structure during the sentence production in children aged 3 and 4 compared to children aged 5 to 6 and adults. This could be either because less-skilled speakers 'know fewer structures, so there is less competition between structures to convey meaning' or because 'they have only weakly represented structures, which are more susceptible to change' (Rowland *et al.*, 2012, pp. 58, 51). Whatever the reason for such results, they once more support the early abstract syntax hypothesis. However, Gerard *et al.* (2010), analysing child language corpus data, found that priming effect increased with age. Consequently, further investigations into this issue and the priming method execution are needed in order to establish the reasons for such varying results.

Priming and implicit learning

Thothathiri and Snedeker (2008) employed a preferential looking technique (an eye-tracking method) that allowed them to assess comprehension abilities in children aged 3 to 4 during a task with double-object dative and prepositional-object dative (i.e. 'the girl gave a book to her friend') primes. The procedure elicited priming effect pointing at young children's capacity for abstract syntactic generalization. More importantly, the experimental procedure was designed so that there was at least a three-sentence-long conversational gap between a prime and a target, yet the priming effect was still significant. Although this study did not aim to investigate the persistence of priming effect in time, its methodology unintentionally raised a possibility that the priming process could trigger implicit learning mechanisms. If, based on the sources reviewed above, we accept the hypothesis that suggests that young children possess abstract syntactic abilities early in life, it would also be of a great significance for educational practice to explore how these abilities could facilitate implicit learning through priming. Some evidence in support of the priming-as-implicit-learning account is presented below.

Kidd (2012) states that despite the popularity of the poverty of stimulus argument (Chomsky, 1980) within modern linguistics, the evidence from both experimental and naturalistic studies indicates a considerable impact of grammatical structures input frequency on acquisition of these structures by young children. In Kidd's study

(2012) 100 children aged 4 to 6 performed a general language level test, an explicit and implicit learning measurement test and a priming task. Data analysis demonstrated correlations between children's implicit learning performance and their ability to maintain a long-lasting priming effect, which, Kidd (2012) suggests, points at a unified mechanism that governs implicit learning abilities and susceptibility to priming. Furthermore, structural priming was investigated for its potential ability to evoke implicit learning by Savage *et al.* (2006), who found that the passive structure priming effect lasted for at least a week, and in a presence of repeated reinforcement could also evolve into learning. The authors note that involving children in dialogues where the frequency of a particular sentence structure is increased could benefit its acquisition.

Similar conclusions were drawn by Vasilyeva *et al.* (2006), who administered priming tasks within a naturalistic context. In their study children aged 4 to 5 were divided into two groups, both of which listened to the same set of stories over the course of two consecutive weeks during their circle time. The stories contained only active structures when narrated to the first group and a high proportion of passives when narrated to the second. The pre- and post-experiment comprehension and production test results revealed that the concentrated exposure to passives during the storytelling sessions positively affected children's usage frequency and understanding of this structure. Considering that there was an interval of at least a day between the intervention and the post-experiment assessment, these findings suggest preservation of priming effect, which provides critical evidence in support of the priming-as-implicit-learning account (Vasilyeva *et al.*, 2006). In addition, limited knowledge of passives was demonstrated by all 72 participants during pre-intervention assessments, and by the active-condition group in post-intervention tests. The authors suggest that incorporating narratives with less familiar sentence structures such as passives into children's daily activities could advance their general school performance through facilitating the growth of syntactic competence (Vasilyeva *et al.*, 2006).

Cross-linguistic priming and the shared-syntax account

With the implicit-learning-through-priming hypothesis in mind, it is essential to examine bilingual children's cross-linguistic stimulation (the influence of a grammatical structure found in one of the child's languages on a parallel structure existing in the other language), as it could establish whether the mastery of certain syntactic forms in one language affects the acquisition of similar forms in the other. The research discussed below investigated bilingual processing tapping into the crucial issue of cross-linguistic stimulation.

Although it is hypothesized that the bilingual speaker's languages are autonomous systems, the mechanism of bilingual processing is still in question, as it is unclear to which extent the languages are being processed independently. Desmet and Declercq (2006) successfully elicited production of several structures in English through exposing mature Dutch-English bilinguals to the corresponding constructions in Dutch. Similar results were obtained by Schoonbaert *et al.* (2007), who examined the delivery of dative structures by Dutch-English bilingual adults and found the occurrence of cross-linguistic priming in both Dutch-to-English and English-to-Dutch conditions, concluding that 'bilinguals employ a single lexical-syntactic system' (p. 167). Furthermore, Weber and Indefrey (2009) tested this model through the use of neuro-imaging experiments, which demonstrated repetition suppression effects during a cross-language comprehension priming task performed by German-English adult bilinguals. The above supports the shared-syntax model of bilingual processing, as do the results of the study conducted by Loebell and Bock (2003), who used syntactic priming tasks with German-English bilinguals and found cross-linguistic priming effects in instances when English and German had similar sentence structures.

There has been a very limited number of priming studies addressing children's bilingual language processing. Fitzpatrick (2011) utilized syntactic priming techniques with three Spanish-English bilingual children to identify grammatical structures suitable for measuring children's linguistic development typicality. However, only one study explored priming effects in young bilinguals cross-linguistically. Vasilyeva *et al.* (2010) conducted their research with bilingual Spanish-English children (mean age 5.11) whose levels of English and Spanish were equally advanced. This passive priming task was administered bidirectionally: the experimenter described their images in English while children described their pictures in Spanish and the other way around. Vasilyeva and colleagues (2010) note that passives are constructed similarly in these languages, and that although their use in English and Spanish is infrequent, typically monolingual Spanish and English children aged 5 to 6 have a good understanding of this structure. However, the analysis of the participants' responses questioned the age of acquisition of passives by bilingual children as this structure appeared challenging for the children tested. More importantly, the research findings also highlighted asymmetry of a priming effect: the children produced a high number of passives in English following Spanish passive primes (Spanish-to-English condition), but no passive structures under English-to-Spanish condition. According to Vasilyeva *et al.* (2010) these results could be a consequence of less frequent spontaneous occurrences of passives in Spanish compared to English and availability of Spanish passive-alternatives (sentence structures which emphasize the patient of an action), which are practically absent in English.

Similarly, a possible influence of language-specific factors on priming effect was highlighted in a Russian-English comparative project by Vasilyeva and Waterfall (2012). In this study three groups of monolingual participants were primed with the passive structure: English children (mean age 5.11), Russian children (mean age 5.10) and Russian-speaking adults. Significant effect of priming condition was found only in English-speaking children. However, all Russian participants produced a high number of passive-alternatives under passive priming condition. The authors propose that what got primed in the experiment with Russian participants was not just a structure independent of meaning, but a discourse function, a particular way of perceiving, interpreting and thinking about a given event or situation. In this case, the passive primes triggered the production of targets containing the alternative forms that emphasized the patient in Russian, which are more frequent in spontaneous speech than canonical passives. The above suggests that both form (sentence structure) and function (pragmatic meaning) should be incorporated into any priming data analysis.

A viewpoint that balances the shared-syntax and implicit-learning-through-priming accounts allows us to hypothesize that learning a structure in one language of a bilingual child could potentially be supported by the child's acquisition of this structure in the other language (and vice versa). Further research is needed to contribute to the growing body of research concerned with young bilinguals' cross-linguistic stimulation through testing this hypothesis. Such research has the potential to inform bilingual education practice through providing a theoretical foundation for creating dialogical strategies that foster bilingual children's syntactic development. This in turn could enhance general communication skills in young bilinguals and advance their overall academic achievement (Savage *et al.*, 2006; Vasilyeva *et al.*, 2006).

Conclusion

The awareness of the ways children acquire syntactic rules certainly has a conceivable impact on the strategies employed to support the growth of language proficiency at home, early years settings and school (Vasilyeva *et al.*, 2006). As discussed, priming is not only an innovative methodology used to assess early syntactic representation, but also a phenomenon which, as some researchers argue, appears to activate implicit learning mechanisms (Kidd, 2012; Savage *et al.*, 2006). As the literature suggests, priming effects in monolingual children aged 3 years and older exist within the boundaries of one language. If future research is able to demonstrate that the priming effect also occurs cross-linguistically (between the languages of a bilingual), it could be hypothesized that supporting the acquisition of a particular sentence structure in one language of a bilingual child might lead to enhancing the use of a similar structure in another. Consequently, introducing strategies designed around priming phenomena to a mixed monolingual and bilingual classroom might be able to benefit both groups equally.

Moreover, selecting the passive voice as the experiment's target structure could have a considerable value for educational practice in general. Although the passive voice appears sparsely in everyday speech of both adults and children, in many languages (including English, Russian and Spanish) this form is frequently used in schoolbooks and is expected to be utilized by school children in assignments (Vasilyeva *et al.*, 2006). In such cases, the mastery of the passive structure is essential for school achievement. Establishing that the effects of priming extend to implicit learning, followed by developing activities that enhance children's capacity to use passives in a flexible and versatile way could benefit general academic progress of young learners.

References

Adesope, O., Lavin, T., Thompson, T. and Ungerleider, C. (2010) A systematic review and meta-analysis of the cognitive correlates of bilingualism. *Review of Educational Research*, *80*(2), 207–45.

Baker, C. (2011) *Foundations of Bilingual Education and Bilingualism*, 5th edn. Toronto: Multilingual Matters.

Bencini, G. and Valian, V. (2008) Abstract sentence representations in 3-year-olds: Evidence from language production and comprehension. *Journal of Memory and Language*, *59*(1), 97–113.

Bock, K. (1986) Syntactic persistence in language production. *Cognitive Psychology*, *18*(3), 355–87.

Bruce, T., Meggitt, C. and Grenier, J. (2010) Talk, talk. *Nursery World*, *110*(4240), 18–19.

Bialystok, E. (1999) Cognitive complexity and attentional control in the bilingual mind. *Child Development*, *70*(3), 636–44.

Chang, F., Dell, G. and Bock, K. (2006) Becoming syntactic. *Psychological Review*, *113*(2), 234–72.

Chen, A. (2010) Is there really an asymmetry in the acquisition of the focus-to-accentuation mapping? *Lingua*, *120*(8), 1926–39.

Chien, Y. C. and Wexler, K. (1990) Children's knowledge of locality conditions in binding as evidence for the modularity of syntax and pragmatics. *Language Acquisition*, *1*(3), 225–95.

Chomsky, N. (1965) *Aspects of the Theory of Syntax*. Cambridge, MA: MIT Press.

Chomsky, N. (1980) *Rules and Representations*. New York: Columbia University Press.

Clark, E. (2009) *First Language Acquisition*, 2nd edn. Cambridge: Cambridge University Press.

Crain, S. and Thornton, R. (2008) *Language Acquisition*. Available at: www.ling.mq.edu.au/clas/child_meg/images/Pomona.pdf (accessed 20/01/13).

Culicover, P. (2009) *Natural Language Syntax*. Oxford: Oxford University Press.

Desmet, T. and Declercq, M. (2006) Cross-linguistic priming of syntactic hierarchical configuration information. *Journal of Memory and Language*, *54*(4), 610–32.

Duarte, J. (2009) *Bilingual Language Proficiency: A Comparative Study*. Hamburg: Waxmann.

Fisher, C. (2002) The role of abstract syntactic knowledge in language acquisition: A reply to Tomasello (2000). *Cognition*, *82*(3), 259–78.

Fitzpatrick, K. (2011) *Morphosyntactic Priming in Bilingual Children*. Masters Thesis, University of Texas at Austin. Texas Digital Library (accessed 09/09/2012).

Foster-Cohen, S. (2009) *Language Acquisition*. Chippenham: Palgrave Macmillan.

García, O. (2011) *Bilingual Education in the 21st Century: A Global Perspective*. Chichester: John Wiley.

Gathercole, V. C. M. and Hoff, E. (2009) Input and the acquisition of language: Three questions. In E. Hoff and M. Shatz (eds) *Blackwell Handbook of Language Development* (pp. 107–27). John Wiley.

Genesee, F. (2006) Bilingual first language acquisition in perspective. In P. McCardle and E. Hoff (eds) *Childhood Bilingualism: Research on Infancy through School Age*. Clevedon, Buffalo, Toronto: Multilingual Matters.

Genesee, F. and Nicoladis, E. (2007) Bilingual acquisition. In E. Hoff and M. Shatz (eds.) *Handbook of Language Development*, Oxford: Blackwell Publishing.

Gerard, J., Keller, F. and Palpanas, T. (2010) Corpus evidence for age effects on priming in child language. In *Proceedings of Cognitive Science Society*. Available at: http://csjarchive.cogsci.rpi.edu/proceedings/2010/papers/0036/paper0036.pdf (accessed 17/12/12).

Grodzinsky, Y. and Reinhart, T. (1993) The innateness of binding and coreference. *Linguistic Inquiry*, *24*(1), 69–101.

Guasti, M. (2002) *Language Acquisition: The Growth of Grammar*. Cambridge, MA: MIT Press

Huttenlocher, J., Vasilyeva, M. and Shimpi, P. (2004) Syntactic priming in young children. *Journal of Memory and Language*, *50*(2), 182–95.

Kidd, E. (2012) Implicit statistical learning is directly associated with the acquisition of syntax. *Developmental Psychology*, *48*(1), 171–84.

Leopold, W. (1970/1939–1949) *Speech Development of a Bilingual Child: A Linguist's Record*. New York: AMS Press.

Loebell, H. and Bock, K. (2003) Structural priming across languages. *Linguistics*, *41*(5), 791–824.

Lust, B. (2006) *Child Language*. Cambridge: Cambridge University Press.

McDonough, K. and Mackey, A. (2008) Syntactic priming and ESL question development. *Studies in Second Language Acquisition, 30*(1), 31–47.

McGregor, W. (2009) *Linguistics: An Introduction.* London: Continuum.

Marcus, G. F., Vijayan, S., Rao, S. B. and Vishton, P. M. (1999) Rule learning by seven-month-old infants. *Science, 283*(5398), 77–80.

Mehler, J., Endress, A., Gervain, J. and Nespor, M. (2008) From perception to grammar. Early language development: Bridging brain and behaviour. *Trends in Language Acquisition Research (TiLAR), 5*, 191–213.

Meisel, U. (2006) The bilingual child. In T. Bhatia and W. Ritchie (eds) *The Handbook of Bilingualism.* Oxford: Blackwell.

Messenger, K., Branigan, H. and McLean, J. (2011) Evidence for (shared) abstract structure underlying children's short and full passives. *Cognition, 121*(2), 268–74.

Paradis, J., Genesee, F. and Crago, M. (2011) *Dual Language Development and Disorders: A Handbook on Bilingualism and Second Language Learning.* Baltimore: Brookes Publishing Company.

Pickering, J. and Branigan, H. (1999) Syntactic priming in language production. *Trends in Cognitive Sciences, 3*(4), 136–41.

Pickering J. and Ferreira, S. (2008) Structural priming: A critical review. *Psychological Bulletin, 134*(3), 427–59.

Pinker, S. (2010) *The Language Instinct: How the Mind Creates Language.* London: Penguin.

Radford, A. (2000) *Children in Search of Perfection: Towards a Minimalist Model of Acquisition.* Department of Language and Linguistics, University of Essex.

Rowland, C., Chang, F., Ambridge, B., Pine, J. and Lieven, E. (2012) The development of abstract syntax: Evidence from structural priming and the lexical boost. *Cognition, 125*(1), 49–63.

Savage, C., Lieven, E., Theakston, A. and Tomasello, M. (2003) Testing the abstractness of children's linguistic representations: Lexical and structural priming of syntactic constructions in young children. *Developmental Science, 6*(5), 557–67.

Savage, C., Lieven, E., Theakston, A. and Tomasello, M. (2006) Structural priming as implicit learning in language acquisition: The persistence of lexical and structural priming in 4-year-olds. *Language Learning and Development, 2*(1), 27–49.

Shimpi, P., Gamez, P., Huttenlocher, J. and Vasilyeva, M. (2007) Syntactic priming in 3- and 4-year-old children: Evidence for abstract representations of transitive and dative forms. *Developmental Psychology, 43*(6), 1334–6.

Schoonbaert, S., Hartsuiker, R. and Pickering, M. (2007) The representation of lexical and syntactic information in bilinguals: Evidence from syntactic priming. *Journal of Memory and Language, 56*(2), 153–71.

Slobin, D. (ed.) (2014) *The Cross-Linguistic Study of Language Acquisition*, Vol. 5. New York: Psychology Press.

Szendrői, K. (2003) Acquisition evidence for an interface theory of focus. *Proceedings of Generative Approaches to Language Acquisition, 2*, 457–68.

Thatcher, K., Branigan, H., McLean, J. and Sorace, A. (2008) Children's early acquisition of the passive: Evidence from syntactic priming, *Proceedings of the 2007 Child Language Seminar.* Available at: www.reading.ac.uk/web/FILES/cls/CLS_Proceedings2.pdf#page=188 (accessed 10/12/12).

Thothathiri, M. and Snedeker, J. (2008) Syntactic priming during language comprehension in three- and four-year-old children. *Journal of Memory and Language, 58*(2), 188–213.

Tomasello, M. (2000) Do young children have adult syntactic competence? *Cognition, 74*(3), 209–53.

Van Hout, A., Harrigan, K. and De Villiers, J. (2009) Comprehension and production of definite and indefinite noun phrases in English preschoolers. *Proceedings of the 3rd Conference on Generative Approaches to Language Acquisition North America (GALANA 2008)*, Cascadilla Proceedings Project, Somerville (pp. 76–87).

Vasilyeva, M. and Waterfall, H. (2012) Beyond syntactic priming: Evidence for activation of alternative syntactic structures. *Journal of Child Language, 39*(2), 258–83.

Vasilyeva, M., Huttenlocher, J. and Waterfall, H. (2006) Effects of language intervention on syntactic skill levels in preschoolers. *Developmental Psychology, 42*(1), 164–74.

Vasilyeva, M., Waterfall, H., Gamez, P., Gomez, L., Bowers, E. and Shimpi, P. (2010) Cross-linguistic syntactic priming in bilingual children. *Journal of Child Language, 37*(5), 1047–64.

Vasilyeva, M., Waterfall, H. and Gomez, L. (2012) Using priming procedures with children. In E. Hoff (ed.) *Research Methods in Child Language: A Practical Guide*. London: Wiley-Blackwell.

Vygotsky, L. (1934) *Thought and Speech*. Moscow: Poligraphkniga.

Wapole, C. (2000) The bilingual child: One system or two? In E. Clark (ed.) *The Proceedings of the Thirtieth Annual Child Language Research Forum* (pp. 187–94). Stanford: Center for the Study of Language and Information.

Weber, K. and Indefrey, P. (2009) Syntactic priming in German-English bilinguals during sentence comprehension. *NeuroImage, 46*(4), 1164–72.

PART II

Knowing about the brain and knowing about the mind

11

THE DEVELOPMENT OF CHILDREN'S UNDERSTANDING OF SOCIAL INTERACTION

Jeremy I. M. Carpendale and Charlie Lewis

Introduction

Children come to be able to reflect on the past and contemplate the future, as well as to understand their complex social worlds. The development of these abilities begins in infancy with early forms of communication and increasing skill in coordinating action with others as babies master routine activities. This continues through childhood with learning a language that allows children to talk about and then to reflect on human activity in psychological terms. A number of theories have been proposed to account for the development of these skills. During the last three decades theories of children's thinking about social matters have been predominantly cognitivist in the perspective they assume. There has been considerable debate among three main theories – i.e. theory theory, innate modules, and simulation theory – but criticism from outside this group has been neglected. We will review criticism of particular theories, as well as describe the common starting preconceptions they are based on, making them more similar than it might appear. These preconceptions set up the problem in the same way, which smuggles in the possible solutions. Thus, the critical evaluation of such theories must also examine the worldview on which they are based. A number of alternative accounts have recently been proposed (e.g. De Jaegher *et al.*, 2010) and they converge with a longer tradition (e.g. Mead, 1934; Newson, 1974; Piaget, 1995; Vygotsky, 1986). We outline one of these based on a constructivist or relational worldview. Rather than taking the individual mind as given, from this alternative perspective the goal is to explain the emergence of mind within social processes.

Any theory of human development is steeped in sets of preconceptions regarding knowledge, meaning and mind. The far-reaching implications of these assumptions are taken for granted and rarely discussed or critiqued. These preconceptions are not derived from empirical studies but are used in interpreting research. An adequate approach must ensure that theories are built on sound foundations by examining the preconceptions on which they are built (e.g. Jopling, 1993; Overton, 2010). We first briefly introduce current approaches to explaining human thinking about social matters, and then review criticism of these accounts before outlining an alternative approach.

Theories of thinking

An example of an approach to theorizing about cognition is Gopnik and Wellman's (2012, p. 1087) claim that 'the fundamental idea of cognitive science is that the brain is a kind of computer designed by evolution to perform particular cognitive functions'. They link this to their view of cognitive development as a process of theory formation with their claim that 'even newborn infants may have innate intuitive theories and those theories are subject to revision even in infancy itself' (i.e. it is 'theories all the way down' – p. 1087). To begin with, it is not clear how applying a theory can be described as computation, or how computers could revise the theories that their computation is based on. This approach, however, is an example of a way of viewing children's thinking that is consistent with Onishi and Baillargeon's (2005, p. 257) claim 'that children are born with an abstract computational system that guides their interpretation of others' behavior'.

Although the computational view of the mind has been a common way of thinking, it has also been extensively criticized and is no longer the dominant approach in cognitive science (Hutto and Myin, 2013). To begin with, many writers are not clear about exactly what they mean when they claim that infants have innate knowledge, but the most common assumption seems to be that it is 'specified by our genetic program' (e.g. Pinker, 1997). This claim, however, no longer fits with what is currently known about genetics (e.g. Meaney, 2010) and neuroscience (Mareschal, *et al.*, 2007; Westermann *et al.*, 2007). Genes are an essential part of development, but they are not master molecules that control development. Instead, they are one of the many essential levels of bi-directionally interacting factors that result in typical outcomes (e.g. Griffiths and Tabery, 2013; Gottlieb, 2007). Genes are inert molecules so they cannot turn themselves on and off; their expression is influenced by their micro and macro environments (e.g. Meaney, 2010; van IJzendoorn *et al.*, 2011), and it is a long way from genes to knowledge (Fisher, 2006).

Even if genes did carry 'information' in the way claimed, it has been argued that there are simply not enough of them to pre-specify the incredible interconnectivity of the human brain that, presumably, innate knowledge would require. Furthermore, humans have about the same number of genes as mice, and no one has claimed that mice have something like the innate knowledge or the full panoply of genetically determined modules claimed for humans (Mareschal *et al.*, 2007). Instead, neuroconstructivists convincingly argue that neural interconnectivity is shaped by experience (Mareschal *et al.*, 2007). In order to take biology seriously, what is needed is an account of the multiple levels of bi-directionally interacting factors from cell to society, molecules to minds, through which social and biological levels mutually construct each other.

The idea that children's understanding of the social world develops through a process of theory formation (e.g. Gopnik and Wellman, 2012) is vulnerable to Fodor's (1975, 1980) criticism that the notion of learning as hypothesis formation and testing is problematic because it already presupposes knowledge in order to form the hypotheses. An alternative approach is simulation theory (e.g. Tomasello *et al.*, 2005), according to which infants experience their own intentional action, which they then apply to others. Because they see others as 'like me' they reason by analogy about others from their own experience. This, however, already assumes a mind and a self–other distinction to begin with as well as an ability to reflect on one's experience (Carpendale *et al.*, 2013a; Carpendale and Lewis, in press; Wittgenstein, 2009). This same view of the mind is also assumed in accounts of how language is related to children's social understanding. That is, to assume that when children hear mental state words they map these onto their own inner experience, must presuppose a Cartesian-inspired view of the mind (for discussion see Carpendale and Lewis, 2004).

The computational view of the mind is based on the assumption that thinking consists of manipulating symbols that are about the world. The problem is that these symbols must be related to the world; they must be meaningful rather than arbitrary. This is known as the symbol-grounding problem, the problem of how to get meaning into the system (e.g. Heil, 1981). This approach is based on the computer as a metaphor, but with a computer meaning is attributed to symbols by the operator of the computer. Having a person, or homunculus, in the system, however, is not a viable option for a model of the mind (Kenny, 1991). One claim is that meaning is based on a causal connection to the world (Perner, 1991). But a camera records information through a causal connection with the world, yet it does not acquire knowledge in the way that a person does. This approach skates over the problem of how children develop knowledge because the meaning of the word *information* differs when referring to a camera recording information compared to a child learning about the world (Müller *et al.*, 1998).

In addition to this critical evaluation of the particular claims of the three theories (for further critique see Carpendale and Lewis, 2004, 2006, 2010), there are further problems that apply to all of them. In spite of disagreements between each, they all share the same starting assumptions, and thus they can each be evaluated in terms of this set of preconceptions on which they are based. They assume a private inner mind as given to begin with, which means that children learning about their social world are, from this perspective, faced only with other bodies and must infer mental states and minds, which is known as 'the problem of other minds'. This way of setting up the problem already brings with it the possible solutions: (1) to make inferences about others and form theories about other minds based on the movements of bodies, (2) to be born with such a theory, or (3) to introspect on one's own mind and reason by analogy about others. This is, of course, painted with broad strokes and there are many versions of these positions and ways in which they can be combined. Instead, we suggest an alternative approach that avoids the problems noted and explains the mind as emerging in social processes. Explaining meaning is a crucial requirement of a complete account of thinking because human thinking is based on a system of meaning.

Taking interaction seriously: interactive emergence

Theorists taking dualist or split approaches do, of course, acknowledge interaction. For Pinker (1997) this acknowledgement is a minor comment, pages after his bold claim that thinking is based on evolved genetically determined modules. Although most theorists acknowledge interaction, there are markedly different ways of conceiving of it. The recognition of interaction is the thread that we feel necessarily results in moving to quite a different approach. Upon close examination it becomes clear that it is not easy to separate clearly the many biological and social levels (e.g. Griffiths and Tabery, 2013; Gottlieb, 2007; Spencer *et al.*, 2009).

When an aspect of child development is described as emerging, a possible response is to claim that the potential must pre-exist. In one sense, this is just a truism – it did happen, so it could have happened, and therefore the potential was there. But in another sense this move smuggles in, in a Trojan Horse fashion, an assumption about *how* it happens. That is, the complexity already pre-exists somewhere in this 'potential'. This way of thinking has ancient roots. One version of this idea was called 'preformationism' – the idea that the complexity of a person was already there like a small person already in the sperm or the egg and it just gets bigger. This version no longer has serious supporters, but the idea of complexity pre-existing re-emerges in more sophisticated versions in terms of pre-existing information encoded in the genome: that is, the idea of a 'genetic blueprint' or 'genetic program' (Griffiths and Tabery, 2013; Lickliter and Honeycutt, 2009, see also Bickhard, 2006).

The problem of explaining emergence, however, cannot be put off indefinitely. The phenomena of interest for developmentalists such as meaning, mind and morality did not always exist, and, therefore, development must be explained. An alternative to the dualist approach that complexity must pre-exist in one or the other level is interactive emergence, according to which complexity does not pre-exist but instead emerges through bi-directional interaction among multiple factors. A helpful analogy in illustrating interactive emergence is ecological succession in which the outcome of a mature forest, for example, is the result of interaction among the various plant species and the physical conditions (Lewontin, 2001). This results in regularity in outcome that is due to the multiple interactions among the species as well as the physical nature of the environment, but the outcome did not pre-exist. This way of thinking is needed in order to understand interactive emergence in human development, and this requires being aware of the whole developmental system in which humans develop (Hendriks-Jansen, 1996).

A constructivist account of the development of children's thinking

As an alternative to the dualist and individualistic accounts we have critiqued above, we propose a relational constructivist approach to the development of thinking, which begins from a different starting point. Instead of beginning with the individual mind as presupposed and not explained, in this approach the starting point is the social process, and communication of increasing complexity emerges within this process, and then language and mind (e.g. Mead, 1934). From this perspective, knowledge is constructive rather than representational (this is not Gopnik and Wellman's 2012 version of 'constructivism'). Infants learn about the interactive potential of the world; they learn what they can do with the world and how it responds. They learn to anticipate the outcome of their actions (e.g. Bickhard, 2001; Piaget, 1972). This is a practical or sensorimotor intelligence that applies to the physical world as well as the social world, which responds differently. Infants construct knowledge of objects and causes, and they also learn about others' actions and how others respond to their actions, and in this process they develop skills in interacting with other people (e.g. Bibok *et al.*, 2008).

From the perspective of explaining the mind as emerging within social interaction, the problem is, how does the social process begin? There is a spectrum of biological characteristics of infants and parents that play roles in this process. For example, human infants are born early and relatively helpless (e.g. Portmann, 1990), guaranteeing a social environment because they must be cared for to survive. The characteristics and sensitivities of the organism result in the environment experienced (e.g. Lewontin, 2001; von Uexküll, 1934). There are many ways in which infants are well suited to eliciting the social process. For example, infants are born with a sensitivity to eyes (Farroni *et al.*, 2004), and this may be facilitated by the fact that human eyes are unusual because the dark iris is surrounded by white sclera, making it easy to notice eye movements (Kobayashi and Kohshima, 1997). Furthermore, infants' initial focal length means that it is likely that their caregivers' faces will be a significant part of their environment (Hendriks-Jansen, 1996). Their tendency to look at eyes could elicit a response from caregivers because it may be taken as an expression of interest from the infant. These are just examples of some characteristics that result in the human developmental system, the social and emotional cradle in which infants develop. Note that some of these characteristics may be considered biological, yet they result in the social and emotional environment in which infants develop. This system is due to the interactions between the infant's characteristics, caregivers' interactional styles, their culturally influenced beliefs and practices as well as factors such as their level of stress. Such factors constantly change as the infant develops further abilities (e.g. Lickliter and Honeycutt, 2009; Jablonka and Lamb, 2007; Lewontin, 2001).

Both the infant and the caregiver contribute to the developmental system in which the baby develops. Characteristics of the infant such as her or his emotional reactivity, for example, could influence the typical social process and result in difficulties in social understanding (Shanker, 2004). Problems with relations can also be due to the way adults respond to the infant, as shown in the extensive research on attachment. In extreme cases, such as Romanian orphanages, severe social deprivation can result in autism-like symptoms (for reviews see Carpendale and Lewis, 2006, 2010, in press).

Somewhat different trajectories may emerge in different dyads, and idiosyncratic communicative gestures may develop. Similar problems, such as moving around, may be faced by all infants but their solutions may differ. For example, many learn how to crawl before walking, but others figure out how to scoot around on their bottoms quite efficiently. Similarly, making requests is a problem infants face, but the particular gestures they develop to achieve this social act may differ.

As infants master further social skills they become able to elicit more complex interactions. The development of smiling is an example. Smiling emerges in interaction with parents (e.g. Jones, 2008; Messinger and Fogel, 2007), and then this ability makes new forms of interaction possible because infants can elicit interaction with smiling. For example, when faced with mothers who have been asked to hold a still face and not respond to their babies for one minute, those infants who have experienced contingent interaction with their mothers tend to use smiling as a social bid in attempts to get the usually enjoyable interaction going again (Mcquaid *et al.*, 2009). This social process is saturated with emotion. Enjoyment of sharing attention and responding to each other emerges in the social and emotional cradle that is the human developmental system and also maintains this system.

Early social skills have been grouped together with the concept of *joint visual attention*, but this combines diverse skills such as pointing, which involves conveying meaning, and gaze following, which may not, at least in the same sense. We suggest that a more useful way of thinking about early social and communicative development is in terms of *joint action* such as learning routines like walking and holding hands, feeding, greeting, and sharing. Such routines are the foundations on which shared understanding is based. Some of these patterns of activity are based on natural reactions such as reaching towards desired objects, which may lead to the development of requests as infants learn how others respond to their actions. Others may be cultural and conventional, such as waving as a gesture used in greetings or farewells. Some social acts may be common across cultures but the way they are accomplished may differ. Directing attention is often achieved in many cultures with an extended index finger, but some cultures use other actions to accomplish this social act (Wilkins, 2003).

Communication develops through several different forms. For example, an infant's crying can be meaningful to caregivers because it indicates that the infant is not comfortable for some reason. It functions to communicate even if the young infant is not yet attempting to do so, just as an adult turning red with embarrassment communicates this fact unintentionally. Similarly, a reach towards a caregiver or an object is a manifestation of the infant's interest and desire, and thus is meaningful to caregivers, even if the infant is not yet aware of this and is not attempting to communicate. The caregiver may respond and the infant can gradually learn the meaning that her action has for others. As the infant learns to anticipate how others typically respond to her action this response becomes a gesture used to communicate (e.g. Mead, 1934). For example, an extended arm and opening and closing of the hand can mean that the infant wants something (Carpendale and Carpendale, 2010). Then the word *want* can be used as well as the gesture and can later replace the gesture. Thus, from this perspective, language has its roots in such routines (Canfield, 2007). The child can then learn how to use the word to refer to others' desires or even to request permission (Budwig, 2002).

The use of pointing may develop in a similar way through the extended index finger first being an infant's means for exploring close-by objects and then becoming linked to the child's attention and orientation to the world. Caregivers may respond to this manifestation of interest, and as children learn the meaning the action has for others it can become a gesture (e.g. Carpendale and Carpendale, 2010; Mead, 1934). Using pointing gestures is linked to a practical understanding of what others have or have not seen, and these routines can form the foundation for children's use of words like *see* and *look*. These are early words that are linked to more complex words like *know* and *think*. Once infants master pointing gestures they can then start to use words like *look* and *see* with the gesture, and such words can replace the gesture (Canfield, 2007). Language is an extension of patterns of interaction (Canfield, 2007). This is a view of language as based on activity, routines in which child and adult share a history of interaction and know what is coming up next. These routines are contexts in which the child and adult understand each other and thus meaning is conveyed. This system of meaning, which originates in social activity, can then be mastered by children as a way of thinking about events that are not right in front of them. It is a way for individuals to distance themselves from immediate reactions to the world and to be able to consider alternative ways of responding. This is the basis for intelligent action.

This approach to the emergence of communication and meaning is grounded in human activity. It also is linked to a critique of approaches focusing on individual mental processes as a sufficient explanation. For these reasons, relational constructivist approaches such as Mead (e.g. 1934) and Wittgenstein (2009) can be misunderstood and labeled as 'behaviorism'. Behaviorism, however, just like mentalism, also begins with a split between mental states and behavior. The difference is only in what is focused on. That is, they both begin from the same dualist or split worldview. The preconception on which such theories are built is a view of the mental states as separate from and as causing physical movement. This is not an empirical finding based on research. Rather, it is a framework assumption through which research is interpreted. Within this worldview there are only the two options of mentalism or behaviorism. In contrast, a relational constructivist or developmental systems approach does not begin with this split. Instead, human activity is the starting point, which is saturated with intentions, desires and beliefs. People do things intentionally to achieve the goals they desire. This activity can be described either in terms of physical movements or mental states. But this split is from the observer's perspective. Infants are just engaged with others in routine shared activities. So, it is not that infants either understand others in terms of mere 'surface' behavior, or underlying mental states (e.g. Perner and Ruffman, 2005). Instead they learn how to coordinate their actions with others, and they later learn how to talk about such activity in terms of mental states, and to think about their social world. Then they achieve the experience of having a mind as adults do, but this is a developmental outcome and it cannot be assumed as a starting point.

Conclusion

Human forms of thinking are based on a system of meaning, and we have argued that meaning is necessarily social not individual. Therefore, thinking cannot be individual and children cannot be born with this system. Instead thinking and mind must develop within social relations. We have outlined a post-cognitivist approach to the development of children's thinking, according to which communication and language emerge within interaction, and then children can use language as a form of thinking. This approach can be extended to further aspects of social understanding such as morality (see Carpendale *et al.*, 2013b).

References

Bibok, M. B., Carpendale, J. I. M. and Lewis, C. (2008) Social knowledge as social skill: An action based view of social understanding. In U. Müller, J. I. M. Carpendale, N. Budwig and B. Sokol (eds) *Social Life and Social Knowledge: Toward a Process Account of Development* (pp. 145–69). New York: Taylor and Francis.

Bickhard, M. H. (2001) Why children don't have to solve the frame problems: Cognitive representations are not encodings. *Developmental Review, 21,* 224–62.

Bickhard, M. H. (2006) Developmental normativity and normative development. In L. Smith and J. Vonèche (eds) *Norms in Human Development* (pp. 57–76). Cambridge: Cambridge University Press.

Budwig, N. (2002) A developmental-functionalist approach to mental state talk. In E. Amsel and J. P. Byrnes (eds) *Language, Literacy, and Cognitive Development: The Development and Consequences of Symbolic Communication* (pp. 59–86). Mahwah, NJ: Erlbaum.

Canfield, J. V. (2007) *Becoming Human: The Development of Language, Self, and Self-consciousness.* New York: Palgrave Macmillan.

Carpendale, J. I. M. and Carpendale, A. B. (2010) The development of pointing: From personal directedness to interpersonal direction. *Human Development, 53,* 110–126.

Carpendale, J. I. M. and Lewis, C. (2004) Constructing an understanding of mind: The development of children's social understanding within social interaction. *Behavioral and Brain Sciences, 27,* 79–96.

Carpendale, J. I. M. and Lewis, C. (2006) *How Children Develop Social Understanding.* Oxford: Blackwell.

Carpendale, J. I. M. and Lewis, C. (2010) The development of social understanding: A relational perspective. In W. F. Overton (ed.) *Handbook of Life-span Development,* Vol. 1: *Cognition, Biology, and Methods Across the Lifespan* (pp. 548–627). Hoboken, NJ: Wiley.

Carpendale, J. I. M. and Lewis, C. (in press) The development of social understanding. In L. Liben and U. Müller (eds) *The Handbook of Child Psychology and Developmental Science,* 7th edn, Vol. 2: *Cognitive Processes.* Wiley Blackwell.

Carpendale, J. I. M., Atwood, S. and Kettner, V. (2013a) Meaning and mind from the perspective of dualist versus relational worldviews: Implications for the development of pointing gestures. *Human Development, 56,* 381–400.

Carpendale, J. I. M., Hammond, S. I. and Atwood, S. (2013b) A relational developmental systems approach to moral development. In R. M. Lerner and J. B. Benson (eds) *Advances in Child Development and Behavior,* Vol. *45: Embodiment and Epigenesis: Theoretical and Methodological Issues in Understanding the Role of Biology within the Relational Developmental System* (pp. 105–33).

De Jaegher, H., Di Palolo, E. and Gallagher, S. (2010) Can social interaction constitute social cognition? *Trends in Cognitive Sciences, 14,* 441–7.

Farroni, T., Massaccesi, S., Pividori, D. and Johnson, M. H. (2004) Gaze following in newborns. *Infancy, 5,* 39–60.

Fisher, S. E. (2006) Tangled webs: tracing the connections between genes and cognition. *Cognition, 101,* 270–97.

Fodor, J. A. (1975) *The Language of Thought.* New York: Thomas Y. Crowell.

Fodor, J. A. (1980) On the impossibility of acquiring 'more powerful' structures. In M. Piattelli-Palmarini (ed.) *Language and Learning: The Debate between Jean Piaget and Noam Chomsky* (pp. 142–62). Cambridge: Harvard University Press.

Goldberg, B. (1991) Mechanism and meaning. In J. Hyman (ed.) *Investigating Psychology: Sciences of the Mind after Wittgenstein* (pp. 48–66). New York: Routledge.

Gopnik, A. and Wellman, H. M. (2012) Reconstructing constructivism: Causal models, Bayesian learning mechanisms, and the theory theory. *Psychological Bulletin, 136.*

Gottlieb, G. (2007) Probablistic epigenesis. *Developmental Science, 10,* 1–11.

Greenberg, G. and Partridge, T. (2010) Biology, evolution, and psychological development. In W. F. Overton (ed.) *The Handbook of Life-span Development,* Vol. *1: Cognition, Biology, and Methods across the Lifespan* (pp. 115–48). Hoboken, NJ: Wiley.

Griffiths, P. E. and Tabery, J. (2013) Developmental systems theory: What does it explain, and how does it explain it? In R. M. Lerner and J. B. Benson (eds) *Advances in Child Development and Behavior,* Vol. *44: Embodiment and Epigenesis: Theoretical and Methodological Issues in Understanding the Role of Biology within the Relational Developmental System* (pp. 65–94).

Heil, J. (1981) Does cognitive psychology rest on a mistake? *Mind, 90,* 321–42.

Hendriks-Jansen, H. (1996) *Catching Ourselves in the Act.* Cambridge, MA: MIT Press.

Hutto, D. D. and Myin, E. (2013) *Radicalizing Enactivism: Basic Minds Without Content.* Cambridge, MA: MIT Press.

Jablonka, E. and Lamb, M. (2007) Precis of: Evolution in four dimensions. *Behavioral and Brain Sciences, 30,* 378–92.

Jones, S. (2008) Nature and nurture in the development of social smiling. *Philosophical Psychology, 21,* 349–57.

Jopling, D. (1993) Cognitive science, other minds, and the philosophy of dialogue. In U. Neisser (ed.) *The Perceived Self* (pp. 290–309). Cambridge, MA: MIT Press.

Kenny, A. (1991) The homunculus fallacy. In J. Hyman (ed.) *Investigating Psychology: Sciences of the Mind after Wittgenstein* (pp. 155–65). London: Routledge (original work published 1971).

Kobayashi, H. and Kohshima, S. (1997) Unique morphology of the human eye. *Nature, 387,* 767–8.

Lewontin, R. C. (2001) Gene, organism and environment. In S. Oyama, P. E. Griffiths and R. D. Gray (eds) *Cycles of Contingency: Developmental Systems and Evolution* (pp. 55–66). Cambridge, MA: MIT Press (original work published 1983).

Lickliter, R. and Honeycutt, H. (2009) Rethinking epigenesis and evolution in light of developmental science. In M. Blumberg, J. Freeman and S. Robinson (eds) *Developmental and Comparative Neuroscience: Epigenetics, Evolution, and Behavior.* Oxford University Press.

Mameli, M. and Bateson, P. (2006) Innateness and the sciences. *Biology and Philosophy, 21,* 155–88.

Mareschal, D., Johnson, M. H., Sirois, S., Spratling, M. W., Thomas, M. S. C. and Westermann, G. (2007) *Neuroconstructivism: How the Brain Constructs Cognition,* Vol. *1.* New York: Oxford University Press.

Mcquaid, N., Bibok, M. and Carpendale, J. I. M. (2009) Relationship between maternal contingent responsiveness and infant social expectation. *Infancy, 14,* 390–401.

Mead, G. H. (1934) *Mind, Self and Society.* Chicago: University of Chicago Press.

Meaney, M. J. (2010) Epigenetics and the biological definition of gene x environment interactions. *Child Development, 81,* 41–79.

Messinger, D. and Fogel, A. (2007) The interactive development of social smiling. In R. Kail (ed.) *Advances in Child Development and Behavior, 35,* 327–66. Oxford: Elsevier.

Müller, U., Sokol, B. and Overton, W. F. (1998) Reframing a constructivist model of the development of mental representations: The role of higher-order operations. *Developmental Review, 18,* 155–201.

Newson, J. (1974) Towards a theory of infant understanding. *Bulletin of the British Psychological Society, 27,* 251–7.

Onishi, K. H. and Baillargeon, R. (2005) Do 15-month-old infants understand false beliefs? *Science, 308,* 255–8.

Overton, W. F. (2010) Life-span development: Concepts and issues. In W. F. Overton (ed.) *The Handbook of Life-span Development,* Vol. *1: Cognition, Biology, and Methods Across the Lifespan* (pp. 1–58). Hoboken, NJ: Wiley.

Perner, J. (1991) *Understanding the Representational Mind*. Cambridge, MA: MIT Press.

Perner, J. and Ruffman, T. (2005) Infants' insight in the mind: How deep? *Science*, *308*, 214–16.

Piaget, J. (1972) *Psychology and Epistemology: Towards a Theory of Knowledge* (trans. A. Rosin). New York: Penguin (original work published 1970).

Piaget, J. (1995) *Sociological Studies*. London: Routledge (original work published 1977).

Pinker, S. (1997) *How the Mind Works*. New York: W. W. Norton.

Portmann, A. (1990) *A Zoologist Looks at Humankind*. New York: Columbia University Press (original work published 1944).

Shanker, S. G. (2004) Autism and the dynamic developmental model of emotions. *Philosophy, Psychiatry and Psychology*, *11*, 219–33.

Spencer, J. P., Blumberg, M. S., McMurray, B., Robinson, S. R., Samuelson, L. K. and Tomblin, J. B. (2009) Short arms and talking eggs: Why we should no longer abide the nativist-empiricist debate. *Child Development Perspectives*, *3*, 79–87.

Tomasello, M., Carpenter, M., Call, J., Behne, T. and Moll, H. (2005) Understanding and sharing intentions: The origins of cultural cognition. *Behavioral and Brain Sciences*, *28*, 675–735.

van IJzendoorn, M. H., Bakermans-Kranenburg, M. J. and Ebstein, R. P. (2011) Methylation matters in child development: Toward developmental behavioral epigenetics. *Child Development Perspectives*, *5*, 305–10.

von Uexküll, J. (1934) A stroll through the worlds of animals and men: A picture book of invisible worlds. In C. H. Schiller (ed.) *Instinctive Behavior: The Development of a Modern Concept* (pp. 5–80). New York: International Press.

Vygotsky, L. (1986) *Thought and Language*. Cambridge: MIT Press (original work published 1934).

West, M. J. and King, A. P. (1987) Settling nature and nurture into an ontogenetic niche. *Developmental Psychobiology*, *20*, 549–62.

Westermann, G., Mareschal, D., Johnson, M. H., Sirois, S., Spratling, M. W. and Thomas, M. S. C. (2007) Neuroconstructivism. *Developmental Science*, *10*, 75–83.

Wilkins, D. (2003) Why pointing with the index finger is not a universal (in sociocultural and semiotic terms). In S. Kita (ed.) *Pointing: Where Language, Culture, and Cognition Meet* (pp. 171–215). Mahwah, NJ: Erlbaum.

Wittgenstein, L. (2009) *Philosophical Investigations*, 4th edn. Oxford: Blackwell (original work published 1953).

12

EXECUTIVE FUNCTIONS AND SCHOOL READINESS

Identifying multiple pathways for school success

Rachel Razza and Kimberly Raymond

Introduction

Executive functions (EF) refer to a suite of higher-order cognitive skills, including working memory, inhibitory control, and mental flexibility, that underlie goal-directed behavior (Garon *et al.*, 2008; Welsh *et al.*, 1991). Collectively, these inter-related processes support children's ability to monitor and control thought and action. For example, EF allows children to remember and reflect on rules, think before they act, and remain focused on an activity while avoiding distractions. Thus, it is not surprising that EF is considered a key aspect of self-regulation, as these skills are inherent to adaptive behavior (Blair and Ursache, 2011; Diamond, 2013). Indeed, a growing body of research supports EF as a predictor of both academic achievement and socioemotional competence across childhood. Interestingly, some evidence suggests that inhibitory control may play a predominant role in these links during the preschool period (Espy *et al.*, 2004), as it predicts many aspects of young children's development. This chapter reviews the critical role of EF for children's school readiness as well as for their future school success. In addition, it provides an overview of successful interventions targeting early EF and identifies promising strategies for the future.

Executive functions: dimensions and development

In general, executive functions (EF) reflect top-down mental processes that aid in the volitional control of thought and action. Specifically, these interrelated cognitive skills allow individuals to override more prepotent or automatic responses, thereby facilitating planning and goal-directed behavior (Diamond, 2013; Blair and Ursache, 2011). Although the terminology may differ across researchers, there is a general consensus that EF consists of three core components: working memory, inhibitory control, and cognitive flexibility (Best and Miller, 2010; Garon *et al.*, 2008; Miyake *et al.*, 2000). Working memory refers to the ability to temporarily hold and manipulate information in the mind (Baddeley, 2000). Put simply, working memory allows children to actively store and update information while they simultaneously engage in other relevant activities (Alloway *et al.*, 2004). For example, this critical skill underlies the ability to follow directions, recall a sequence of events in a story, and perform mental operations such as multiplying numbers together without writing them down (Gathercole *et al.*, 2006; Jarrold and Towse, 2006). Inhibitory control is defined as the ability to withhold or suppress a dominant response in favor of a subdominant response (Nigg, 2000; Rothbart and Posner, 1985). In particular, this skill allows children to resist distractions and control impulsive behaviors, thereby facilitating selective attention and self-control, respectively (Diamond, 2013). Cognitive flexibility (also referred to as set-shifting) involves the ability to shift one's thinking or focus of attention in response to the changing demands of the environment (Garon *et al.*, 2008). This skill allows children to take new perspectives, classify objects across multiple dimensions (such as color and shape), and generate creative solutions to problems (Diamond, 2013).

Although working memory, inhibitory control, and cognitive flexibility represent distinct facets of EF, each with its own unique function and developmental course, an integrative model of EF suggests that these three components work together to guide goal-directed behavior (Best *et al.*, 2009; Diamond, 2013; Garon *et al.*, 2008). In fact, it is debatable whether these components are even divisible before age 5, as empirical evidence suggests that EF skills are best represented by a single construct during the preschool years (Wiebe *et al.*, 2008, 2011; Willoughby *et al.*, 2010). EF processes share a common origin in the brain, the prefrontal cortex (PFC), which exerts cognitive control by successfully coordinating information across different systems (Miller and Cohen, 2001). The PFC follows a protracted course of development, which includes rapid development between the ages of 3 and 5 years (Diamond, 2006; Garon *et al.*, 2008), followed by significant improvement and differentiation across the school-age years (Best *et al.*, 2009; Lee *et al.*, 2013). Yet not all children improve at the same rate. Individual differences in early EF have become an increasingly popular area of research, as they serve as a key marker for self-regulatory functioning and are associated with children's functioning across multiple domains of development (Blair and Diamond, 2008). Given the plasticity of the PFC during early childhood, EF skills also represent an important target for interventions targeting school readiness and success, particularly among disadvantaged children (Buckner *et al.*, 2009; Blair and Diamond, 2008; Raver, 2012).

The importance of EF for academic achievement

The cognitive processes that constitute EF are thought to directly facilitate the acquisition of knowledge by allowing children to monitor their thinking, focus their attention, and flexibly apply strategies while problem solving (Blair and Diamond, 2008). Such skills are essential for learning, as they allow children to build core knowledge and engage in higher-order thinking and planning. For example, working memory aids in the memorization of numbers and mathematical solutions (Geary, 1993) and in the encoding of letters and words (Siegel and Ryan, 1989), which reflect critical academic tasks that lay the foundation for more advanced arithmetic and reading. Moreover, inhibitory control and cognitive flexibility are implicated in the problem-solving process, as suppressing irrelevant information and alternating between strategies are essential skills for arithmetic (Bull and Scerif, 1999; Oberle and Schonert-Reichl, 2013), written expression (Altemeier *et al.*, 2006; Hooper *et al.*, 2002), and reasoning (Handley *et al.*, 2004; Richland and Burchinal, 2013; van der Sluis *et al.*, 2007).

There is substantial evidence to indicate that EF skills are fundamental to children's academic achievement beginning in early childhood and continuing through adolescence. In particular, preschool EF is consistently supported as a unique predictor of children's school readiness; early EFs are associated with both math and literacy skills in kindergarten, independent of general cognitive ability (Blair and Razza, 2007; Fitzpatrick and Pagani, 2012; McClelland *et al.*, 2007). Moreover, EF at school entry has significant implications for children's math and reading trajectories across childhood for children both with and without specific learning disabilities (see Best *et al.*, 2009, for review). It should be noted that similar associations have been replicated by studies using data from large, nationally representative samples in the United States (ages 5 to 17 years; Best *et al.*, 2011), as well as with samples representing children from different countries including Great Britain (Bull and Scerif, 2001; Gathercole *et al.*, 2004), New Zealand (Clark *et al.*, 2010), and China (Lan *et al.*, 2011). In fact, results from a recent cross-cultural study support links between EF and academic achievement for children ages 6 to 11 spanning four diverse countries: Sweden, Spain, Iran, and China (Thorell *et al.*, 2012). Thus, while there are some discernible differences between cultures, overall, the literature suggests that the association between EF and academic achievement is universal.

Domain generality versus specificity for reading and math achievement

Given that EF has important implications for both math and reading, it is considered a domain-general skill that can enhance academic performance (Blair, 2002; Bull *et al.*, 2008). In recent years, however, researchers have been increasingly interested in the specificity of the associations between EF and academic achievement. In particular, studies have examined whether the associations differ across domains (i.e. math vs reading) or within a domain (i.e. simple vs complex tasks), and whether these patterns differ by age or facet of EF (see Müller *et al.*, 2008, for review). Unfortunately, no single study has accounted for all of these factors simultaneously and variations across samples, EF dimensions, and achievement measures have resulted in divergent findings.

For example, using a nationally representative sample, Best *et al.* (2009) found that the strength of the correlation between global EF and academic achievement was similar for overall math and reading across childhood and adolescence. This domain-general pattern is consistent with work by St Clair-Thompson and Gathercole (2006), who found that working memory and inhibitory control made independent contributions to both math and reading achievement among children aged 11 and 12 (with stronger associations reported for working memory across both domains). Similarly, both working memory and inhibitory control have been implicated in reading (Chiappe *et al.*, 2000) and math deficits (Passolunghi and Siegel, 2001). Mental flexibility has also been linked concurrently and longitudinally with both early math and literacy (Coldren, 2013; George and Greenfield, 2005), and identified as a predictor of reasoning development in adolescence (Richland and Burchinal, 2013). Collectively, these studies support broad implications of EF with respect to children's academic achievement, as these skills had significant effects across both the math and reading domains.

Other studies examining independent facets of EF, however, suggest specificity across academic domains. Specifically, Sabol and Pianta (2012) found that working memory at 54 months was related to fifth grade math achievement, but not reading achievement; independent effects of inhibitory control were not supported for either domain and mental flexibility was not investigated. This pattern is consistent with previous research supporting working memory as the predominant predictor of mathematics, over and above the other EF skills (Bull and Scerif, 2001; Toll *et al.*, 2011), and with literature indicating that working memory is a more robust predictor of future math achievement than reading achievement (Gathercole *et al.*, 2004; Savage *et al.*, 2007). However, it also contradicts studies highlighting the important role of inhibitory control in reading (Protopapas *et al.*, 2007; Roebers *et al.*, 2011) and writing (Altemeier *et al.*, 2006). Thus, while there is evidence of domain specificity in the link between EF and achievement, additional research is needed to determine how such patterns can be reconciled with domain-general trends.

Explanations for domain specificity in the link between EF and achievement

One source of discrepancy may be intra-domain variability, as research suggests that EF may be more closely linked to particular skills over others within the same academic domain. For example, complex EF (a composite reflecting working memory, inhibitory control, and mental flexibility) was more strongly correlated with children's performance on mathematical word problems than with their calculation skills (Best *et al.*, 2011). The authors speculated that the former problem-solving tasks might be more reliant on strategy implementation and monitoring which involve multiple components of EF, while the latter tasks may rely more on working memory. Indeed, different facets of EF have been uniquely associated with different aspects of performance within both the math and reading domains. For example, mental flexibility (i.e. efficiency in shifting) accounted for the most variance in children's (aged 6–10 years) accuracy on mathematical tests, while their speed was best accounted for by inhibitory control (Ellefson *et al.*, 2006). Differential associations are also found within the reading/writing domain, as inhibition accounted for unique variance in children's ability to take notes while reading, while verbal fluency was the strongest predictor of children's ability to use notes to write a report across both third and fifth grade (Altemeier *et al.*, 2006). Thus, it is possible that domain specificity reflects differences in the complexity of skills across tasks rather than inherent differences across academic domains.

Our understanding of domain specificity is further complicated by differences across models of early EF. For example, some research suggests that the concurrent association between EF and emergent math achievement is best represented by a single latent EF factor during preschool (Bull *et al.*, 2011), and that independent links between the three facets of EF (i.e. working memory, inhibitory control, and shifting) and math performance first emerge during early elementary school (Bull and Scherif, 2001). Other studies, however, find that all three facets of EF account for unique variability in early mathematic achievement during preschool (Clark *et al.*, 2010; Clark *et al.*, 2013).

Moreover, it is possible that there are age-related developmental trends with respect to domain specificity. For example, while working memory emerged as the dominant EF facet associated with math performance during the primary grades (Bull and Scerif, 2001; Toll *et al.*, 2011), research highlights inhibitory control as the predominant predictor of early math abilities during preschool (Blair and Razza, 2007; Espy *et al.*, 2004) and kindergarten (Brock *et al.*, 2009). This trend is consistent with previous research indicating that preschoolers are more challenged by inhibitory demands than working memory demands, while the opposite is true for older children and adults (Davidson *et al.*, 2006). It is possible that different facets of EF are emphasized when children are first learning basic concepts versus when they are solving more advanced problems. For example, there is evidence that children's behavioral regulation (i.e. inhibitory control, working memory, and attention focusing), predicted gains across both early math and reading skills during preschool (McClelland *et al.*, 2007), but only predicted gains in math over the kindergarten year (Ponitz *et al.*, 2009). Ponitz and colleagues (2009) speculated that the narrowing effect of behavioral regulation could be a result of the cognitive processes for reading becoming more automatic for literacy than for math over time. Such an explanation is consistent with the idea that early literacy tasks become increasingly difficult with respect to content, while early math tasks also place increasing demands on children's regulatory functioning, particularly working memory (Blair and Razza, 2007; Espy *et al.*, 2004).

Implications of EF for adaptive classroom behaviors

Finally, in addition to directly influencing math and reading achievement, EF skills also manifest themselves in adaptive classroom behaviors that are more global indicators of children's academic trajectories. For example, there is evidence that children's global EF in the fall of kindergarten predicted their spring levels of classroom behavioral regulation (e.g. following directions, concentrates while working, completes complex tasks in an organized way) (Ponitz *et al.*, 2009). Moreover, inhibitory control was associated with teacher-reported on-task behaviors (e.g. working hard, staying on task, staying focused) among Head Start preschoolers (Blair and Peters, 2003) and predicted learning-related behaviors and engagement among kindergarteners (Brock *et al.*, 2009). Specifically, the association between EF and academic achievement may be partially mediated by learning-related behavior (Turner *et al.*, 2013). A concern, however, is whether EF is conceptually distinct from learning-related behaviors or whether it is simply the behavioral manifestation of EF skills.

The importance of EF for socioemotional competence

Research suggests that EF also has implications for children's social development (e.g. Kochanska *et al.*, 1997; Kopp, 1982; Schultz *et al.*, 2001). Recent conceptual models have placed EF in a central role in relation to both the promotion of social competence as well as the avoidance of behavior problems (Beauchamp and Anderson, 2010; Eisenberg *et al.*, 2000; Olson *et al.*, 2005; Yeates *et al.*, 2007). While comprising cognitive skills, EF also reflects an outward behavioral feature that includes problem solving, planning, and organization skills (Brocki and Bohlin, 2004; Gioia *et al.*, 2000). Such skills are important for social interactions, as children who demonstrate organizational skills and flexible behavior are viewed as more competent play partners (Diamantopoulou *et al.*, 2007). In contrast, uninhibited and impulsive behaviors serve as indices of EF dysfunction that underlie a range of behavioral disorders (Eslinger, 1996).

Social competency is conceptualized as the ability to adapt to one's social environment, to be effective and achieve personal goals in one's interaction with others (Ciairano *et al.*, 2007; Green and Rechis, 2006; Rose-Krasnor, 1997; Rubin and Rose-Krasnor, 1992). Such competency has important implications for children's social relationships and later life adjustment (Ashiabi, 2007; Wentzel and Asher, 1995). Children who struggle with EF skills may find everyday social tasks, such as sharing and taking turns, picking up on subtle social cues and staying attentive in class, to be particularly challenging. Furthermore, behaviors that are considered adaptive in one social situation may be ineffective in another. For example, a competitive playground game would require different social behaviors than a classroom group project. Children must be able to recognize the change in context and modify their behaviors accordingly. However, it is not only important for socially competent children to recognize contextual variation. Perhaps if adults were also more mindful of children's EF, they would refrain from placing them into situations beyond their current EF skills.

In order for children to be effective social agents, they must possess the cognitive skills necessary to regulate behaviors and emotions and also to adjust goals to varying environmental contexts (Hughes, 1998; Hughes *et al.*, 1998; Razza and Blair, 2009). Thus, the successful navigation of social interactions and the maintenance of peer relationships depend upon the proper development of EF skills (Bellanti and Bierman, 2000; Semrud-Clikeman and Hynd, 1990).

EF and social skills

Previous studies examining the facilitative role executive functions play in children's social behavior have found links to positive socioemotional outcomes. For example, EF skills have been consistently linked to children's theory of mind skills (i.e. the ability to attribute and understand the mental states of others) (Carlson *et al.*, 2004a; Carlson and Moses, 2001; Carlson *et al.*, 2002; Carlson *et al.*, 2004b; Hughes, 1998; Hughes and Ensor, 2007; Nilsen and Graham, 2009). This ability to think about the intentions of others, and thereby utilize the information to guide actions in social situations, is a crucial cognitive skill related to successful social outcomes (Hughes *et al.*, 2006; Hughes and Leekam, 2004). The ability to manage emotions (as well as behaviors) in accordance with societal expectations is also an essential component of social competence and has been shown to play an important role in school adjustment during preschool and kindergarten, particularly as learning environments become more structured and socially demanding (Liew *et al.*, 2004; Olson *et al.*, 2005; Denham *et al.*, 2003; Pianta *et al.*, 1995; Rimm-Kaufman *et al.*, 2005). Cognitive processes, such as those which comprise EF, also support the ability to regulate emotion; the process of monitoring, evaluating and modifying emotional reactions in a manner that is socially acceptable (Kopp, 1982, 1989; Kopp and Neufeld, 2003; Carlson and Wang, 2007). Children who enter the school system with poor EFs may be at increased risk of failing to regulate emotions with socially acceptable strategies that aid in the development and engagement of prosocial relationships. Thus, these early difficulties with social interaction place children at increased risk for a range of long-term negative outcomes, including academic failure, peer rejection, and delinquent behavior (Caspi and Moffitt, 1995; Coie and Dodge, 1998).

EF and problem behaviors

Research has also revealed the presence of EF deficits in relation to poor socioemotional functioning among children, particularly with regard to externalizing and internalizing behaviors. The link between EF and externalizing behavior, specifically, is robust and long term, holding across diverse assessments, multiple informants and age. Studies have shown that young children with such aggressive behaviors exhibit inadequate control of attention and impulses (Moffit, 2003; Belsky *et al.*, 2007; Riggs *et al.*, 2003; Eisenberg *et al.*, 1997; Olson *et al.*, 2005), impaired working memory (Speltz *et al.*, 1999), deficits in planning and inhibitory control (Hughes *et al.*, 2000) and inhibition of prepotent responses (Hughes, 1998). Although less studied, EF deficits have also been linked to teacher ratings of emotional symptoms and internalizing behaviors (e.g. anxiety/depression) in older children (Hughes and Ensor, 2010).

Specificity in the link between EF and socioemotional competence

In addition to the aforementioned general links, recent studies have revealed more specific links, as each of the three individualized facets of EF have important implications for children's socioemotional competence. Inhibitory control is vital to successful cooperative interactions with others, as it allows children to inhibit inappropriate or aggressive behaviors in order to behave collaboratively in their social interactions (Riggs *et al.*, 2003). Indeed, while high levels of inhibitory control have been associated with more cooperative behaviors among dyads of school-aged children (Ciairano *et al.*, 2007; Giannotta *et al.*, 2011), poor inhibitory control has resulted in more negative exchanges with peers (Balaraman, 2003). Cognitive flexibility allows children to think about social situations in different ways and find more effective methods to interact in cooperation rather than competition. Studies show that children with proficient cognitive flexibility have more cooperative interactions with peers than children with lower levels of flexibility (Bonino and Cattelino, 1999; Ciairano *et al.*, 2006). Finally, working memory promotes the understanding of social cues and the ability to use those cues to respond to the demands of social situations, while deficits are thought to significantly disrupt an individual's social decoding ability. Evidence supports the involvement of working memory in social interactions (Phillips *et al.*, 2007) and social problems in young children (Alloway *et al.*, 2005).

EF as a critical target for intervention

Given the great importance of EF for children's school readiness and success, these skills have become an increasingly popular target for intervention. The promotion of EF among at-risk children is of particular interest, as these children typically have lower EF skills (Blair *et al.*, 2011; Evans and English, 2002; Raver *et al.*, 2011), but also demonstrate the greatest gains (Flook *et al.*, 2010; Tominey and McClelland, 2011). Moreover, EFs are strongly implicated in the higher incidence of cognitive and social-emotional deficits within at-risk samples (Blair *et al.*, 2011; Evans and English, 2002; Raver, 2004). For example, EFs account for over 30 per cent of the variance in math and reading test scores among low-income fifth graders (Waber *et al.*, 2006). There is also evidence that EF mediates and moderates the effect of intervention programs targeting social-emotional learning (Riggs *et al.*, 2006b; Bierman *et al.*, 2008). Thus, strengthening children's EF has been viewed as a promising strategy for leveling the playing field for those at risk of early academic deficits and behavioral problems (Diamond, 2012; Raver, 2012).

Interventions targeting EF

Although diverse in nature, existing interventions can be broadly classified into the following three categories: direct-skills training, school curricula, and physical activity (for reviews, see Diamond, 2012; Diamond and Lee, 2011). Direct-skills training typically takes place in a lab and many involve computerized games that increasingly challenge EF skills. For example, CogMed is a commercialized computer program that targets preschoolers' working memory (Bergman Nutley *et al.*, 2011; Thorell *et al.*, 2009). There is also evidence that a short-term (i.e. five-day) computerized executive attention training (Rueda *et al.*, 2005) increased reasoning among preschoolers. Efforts to directly promote early EF via repeated practice and training on standard EF tasks (Dowsett and Livesey, 2000; Röthlisberger *et al.*, 2012) or using classroom-based self-regulation tasks (Tominey and McClelland, 2011) have also been successful with young children. While these programs offer exciting possibilities, additional research is needed, as it is presently unclear whether these trainings improve only the specific EF skill or measure targeted, or whether they have more general effects for children's EF functioning.

Classroom-based efforts to enhance EF include both stand-alone comprehensive curricula and interventions that were created to supplement existing curricula. An example of the former is the *Tools of the Mind* program (Bodrova and Leong, 2007), a packaged curriculum that targets self-regulation via teacher-directed exercises designed to support children's social pretend play. *Tools of the Mind* has been shown to increase inhibitory control and attention flexibility among at-risk preschoolers (Diamond *et al.*, 2007). Likewise, add-on interventions that coach teachers on behavior management strategies (e.g. The Chicago Readiness Project; Raver *et al.*, 2011) or focus on social-emotional learning (e.g. The Head Start REDI project; Bierman *et al.*, 2008) within Head Start preschools and elementary schools (e.g. PATHS; Riggs *et al.*, 2006a) have been successful in promoting attention, inhibitory control, and mental flexibility. Finally, martial arts and mindfulness practices, which typically combine physical activity with mental focusing, offer promise as effective strategies for enhancing EF (see Zelazo and Lyons, 2012, for review). For example, children who received tae-kwon-do training outperformed control children on measures of working memory and inhibitory control (Lakes and Hoyt, 2004). Similarly, mindfulness-based interventions have effectively promoted teacher- and parent-reported EF (Flook *et al.*, 2010) and attention (Napoli *et al.*, 2005) among elementary school children.

Trends in intervention and suggestions for future research

Despite differences in implementation and effectiveness, there are general principles that pertain to EF interventions. These trends, which were thoughtfully summarized by Diamond (2012) and colleagues (Diamond and Lee, 2011), highlight the importance of progressive challenge and repeated practice for increasing EF skills and underscore the greater benefit of training for children with poorer EFs. Another important pattern discussed focuses on transfer effects, as some trainings are good at increasing the specific EF skill they target, but the benefits do not generalize to other unpracticed EFs. For example, the benefits of a computer-based training targeting working memory did not extend to mental flexibility, and vice versa (Bergman Nutley *et al.*, 2011). In contrast, approaches that address EF more globally, such as school curricula (Raver *et al.*, 2011) and martial arts (Lakes and Hoyt, 2004) are associated with wider transfer effects. Thus, while there is evidence that EF can be trained, there are still questions regarding whether different methods work for different skills. Perhaps direct skills trainings are particularly useful for working memory and mental flexibility (Mackey *et al.*, 2011; Thorell *et al.*, 2009), while curricula and physical activity may be more helpful for targeting inhibitory control (Lakes and Hoyt, 2004; Riggs *et al.*, 2006b).

Moreover, future research needs to examine the long-term effects of EF training and determine the impact of increased EF on children's later academic achievement and behavioral competence. While the results of studies examining the effect of improved working memory on academic outcomes are promising (e.g. Holmes *et al.*, 2009; Holmes and Gathercole, 2013), long-term follow-up is needed. Furthermore, others argue that the association between EF and academic achievement during preschool is spurious (Willoughby *et al.*, 2012). Finally, identifying the neural systems underlying improvements in EF (Berkman *et al.*, 2012) and documenting the changes in psychophysiology that result from EF trainings (Blair *et al.*, 2011) is of utmost importance for informing future interventions. Indeed, there is a need to understand both the potential and limitations of such intervention strategies (see Kray and Ferdinand, 2013).

Conclusion

In sum, EF is a complex construct comprising of interrelated skills that support the intentional control of thought and action. While the components of EF are controversial, particularly among young children, the literature supports the importance of the three key skills: working memory, inhibitory control, and cognitive flexibility. Indeed, there is a great deal of evidence that these EF skills are important for children's success in academic areas and are related to their socioemotional functioning. Existing research indicates that EF may be improved via different types of intervention or training. Future studies are needed to discover whether there are long-term effects of intervention or training and to investigate the actual neural systems that underlie these improvements.

References

Alloway, T. P., Gathercole, S. E., Willis, C. and Adams, A. M. (2004) A structural analysis of working memory and related cognitive skills in young children. *Journal of Experimental Child Pyschology*, 87, 85–106.

Alloway, T. P., Gathercole, S. E., Adams, A. M., Willis, C., Eaglen, R. and Lamont, E. (2005) Working memory and other cognitive skills as predictors of progress towards early learning goals at school entry. *British Journal of Developmental Psychology*, 23, 417–26.

Altemeier, L., Jones, J., Abbott, R. D. and Berninger, V. W. (2006) Executive functions in becoming writing readers and reading writers: Note taking and report writing in third and fifth graders. *Developmental Neuropsychology*, 29, 161–73.

Ashiabi, G. S. (2007) Play in the preschool classroom: Its socioemotional significance and the teacher's role in play. *Early Childhood Education Journal*, 35, 199–207.

Baddeley, A. D. (2000) The episodic buffer: A new component of working memory? *Trends in Cognitive Sciences*, 4, 417–22.

Baddeley, A. D. (2007) *Working Memory, Thought and Action.* Oxford: Oxford University Press.

Balaraman, G. R. (2003) Children's self-regulation and peer interaction at 36 and 54 months: Concurrent and longitudinal relations. Paper presented at the Biennial Meeting of the Society for Research in Child Development, Tampa, Florida (April).

Beauchamp, M H. and Anderson, V. (2010) SOCIAL: An integrative framework for the development of social skills. *Psychological Bulletin, 136*, 39–64.

Bellanti, C. J. and Bierman, K. L. (2000) Disentangling the impact of low cognitive ability and inattention on social behavior and peer relationships. Conduct Problems Prevention Research Group. *Journal of Clinical Child Psychology, 29*(1), 66–75.

Belsky, J., Vandell, D., Burchinal, M., Clarke-Stewart, K. A., McCartney, K., Owen, M. and NICHD Early Child Care Research Network (2007) Are there long-term effects of early child care? *Child Development, 78*, 681–701.

Bergman Nutley, S., Söderqvist, S., Bryde, S., Thorell, L. B., Humphreys, K. and Klingberg, T. (2011) Gains in fluid intelligence after training non-verbal reasoning in 4-year-old children: A controlled, randomized study. *Developmental Science, 14*(3), 591–601.

Berkman, E. T., Graham, A. M. and Fisher, P. A. (2012) Training self-control: A domain-general translational neuroscience approach. *Child Development Perspectives, 6*(4), 374–84.

Best, J. R. and Miller, P. H. (2010) A developmental perspective on executive function. *Child Development, 81*(6), 1641–660.

Best, J. R., Miller, P. H and Jones, L. L. (2009) Executive functions after age 5: Changes and correlates. *Developmental Review, 29*, 180–200.

Best, J. R., Miller, P. H. and Naglieri, J. A. (2011) Relations between executive function and academic achievement from ages 5 to 17 in a large, representative national sample. *Learning and Individual Differences, 21*, 327–36.

Bierman, K. L., Nix, R. L., Greenberg, M. T., Blair, C. and Domitrovich, C. E. (2008) Executive functions and school readiness intervention: Impact, moderation and mediation in the Head Start REDI program. *Development and Psychopathology, 20*, 821–43.

Blair, C. (2002) School readiness as propensity for engagement: Integrating cognition and emotion in a neurobiological conceptualization of child functioning at school entry. *American Psychologist, 57*(2), 111–27.

Blair, C. and Diamond, A. (2008) Special issue on biological processes in prevention and intervention: the promotion of self-regulation as a means of preventing school failure. *Development and Psychopathology, 20*, 899–911.

Blair, C. and Peters, R. (2003) Physiological and neurocognitive correlates of adaptive behavior in preschool among children in Head Start. *Developmental Neuropsychology, 24*, 479–97.

Blair, C. and Razza, R. P. (2007) Relating effortful control, executive function, and false belief understanding to emerging math and literacy ability in kindergarten. *Child Development, 78*(2), 647–63.

Blair, C. and Ursache, A. (2011) A bidirectional theory of executive functions and self-regulation. In R. Baumeister and K. Vohs (eds) *Handbook of Self-regulation*, 2nd edn (pp. 300–20). New York: Guilford.

Blair, C., Granger, D., Willoughby, M., Mills-Koonce, R., Cox, M., Greenberg, M.T., Kivlighan, K., Fortunato, C. and the FLP Investigators (2011) Salivary cortisol mediates effects of poverty and parenting on executive functions in early childhood. *Child Development, 82*, 1970–84.

Bodrova, E. and Leong, D. J. (2007) *Tools of the Mind: The Vygotskian Approach to Early Childhood Education*, 2nd edn. Upper Saddle River, NJ: Pearson Education/Merrill.

Bonino, S. and Cattelino, E. (1999) The relationship between cognitive abilities and social abilities in childhood: A research on flexibility in thinking and cooperation with peers. *International Journal of Behavioral Development, 23*, 19–36.

Brock, L. L., Rimm-Kaufman, S., Nathanson, L. and Grimm, K. J. (2009) The contributions of 'hot' and 'cool' executive function to children's academic achievement, learning-related behaviors, and engagement in kindergarten. *Early Childhood Research Quarterly, 24*, 337–49.

Brocki, K. C. and Bohlin, G. (2004) Executive functions in children aged 6 to 13: A dimensional and developmental study. *Developmental Neuropsychology, 26*, 571–93.

Buckner, J., Mezzacappa, E. and Beardslee, W. (2009) Self-regulation and its relations to adaptive functioning in low-income youths. *America Journal of Orthopsychiatry, 79*(1), 19–30.

Bull, R. and Scerif, G. (2001) Executive functioning as a predictor of children's mathematics ability: Inhibition, switching, and working memory. *Developmental Neuropsychology, 19,* 273–93.

Bull, R., Espy, K. A. and Wiebe, S. A. (2008) Short-term memory, working memory, and executive functioning in preschoolers: Longitudinal predictors of mathematical achievement at age 7 years. *Developmental Neuropsychology, 33*(3), 205–28.

Bull, R., Espy, K. A., Wiebe, S. A., Sheffield, T. D. and Nelson, J. M. (2011) Using confirmatory factor analysis to understand executive control in preschool children: Sources of variation in emergent mathematical ability. *Developmental Science, 14,* 679–92.

Carlson, S. M. and Moses, L. J. (2001) Individual differences in inhibitory control and children's theory of mind. *Child Development, 72,* 1032–53.

Carlson, S. M., Moses, L. J. and Breton, C. (2002) How specific is the relation between executive function and theory of mind? Contributions of inhibitory control and working memory. *Infant and Child Development, 11,* 73–92.

Carlson, S. M., Mandell, D. J. and Williams, L. (2004a) Executive function and theory of mind: Stability and prediction from ages 2 to 3. *Developmental Psychology, 40,* 1105–22.

Carlson, S. M., Moses, L. J. and Claxton, L. J. (2004b) Individual differences in executive functioning and theory of mind: An investigation of inhibitory control and planning ability. *Journal of Experimental Child Psychology, 87,* 299–319.

Caspi, A. and Moffitt, T. E. (1995) The continuity of maladaptive behavior: From description to explanation in the study of antisocial behavior. *Developmental Psychopathology* (pp. 472–511). New York: Wiley.

Chiappe, P., Hasher, L. and Siegel, L. S. (2000) Working memory, inhibitory control, and reading disability. *Memory and Cognition, 28,* 8–17.

Ciairano, S., Bonino, S. and Renato, M. (2006) Cognitive flexibility and social competence from childhood to early adolescence. *Cognition, Brain, and Behavior, 10*(3), 343–66.

Ciairano, S., Visu-Petra, L. and Settanni, M. (2007) Executive inhibitory control and cooperative behavior during early school years: a follow-up study. *Journal of Abnormal Child Psychology, 35,* 335–45.

Clark, C. A. C., Pritchard, V. E. and Woodward, L. J. (2010) Preschool executive functioning abilities predict early mathematics achievement. *Developmental Psychology, 46,* 1176–91.

Clark, C. A. C., Sheffield, T. D., Wiebe, S. A. and Espy, K. A. (2013) Longitudinal associations between executive control and developing mathematical competence in preschool boys and girls. *Child Development, 84,* 662–77.

Coie, J. D. and Dodge, K. A. (1998) Aggression and antisocial behavior. In W. Damon and N. Eisenberg (eds) *Handbook of Child Psychology: Social, Emotional and Personality Development* (pp. 779–862). New York: Wiley.

Coldren, J. T. (2013) Cognitive control predicts academic achievement in kindergarten children. *Mind, Brain, and Education, 7,* 40–8.

Davidson, M. C., Amso, D., Cruess Anderson, L. and Diamond, A. (2006) Development of cognitive control and executive functions from 4 to 13 years: Evidence from manipulations of memory, inhibition and task switching. *Neuropsychologia, 44,* 2037–78.

Denham, S. A., Blair, K. A., DeMulder, E., Levitas, J., Sawyer, K., Auerbach-Major, S. *et al.* (2003) Preschool emotional competence: Pathways to social competence? *Child Development, 74,* 238–56. doi: 10.1111/1467-8624.00533.

Diamond, A. (2006) The early development of executive functions. In E. Bialystok and F. Craik (eds) *Lifespan Cognition: Mechanisms of Change* (pp. 70–95). New York: Oxford University Press.

Diamond, A. (2012) Activities and programs that improve children's executive functions. *Current Directions in Psychological Science, 21,* 335–41.

Diamond, A. (2013) Executive functions. *Annual Review of Psychology, 64,* 135–68.

Diamond, A., Barnett, W. S., Thomas, J. and Munro, S. (2007) Preschool program improves cognitive control. *Science, 318*(5855), 1387–8.

Diamond, A. and Lee, K. (2011) Interventions shown to aid executive function development in children 4 to 12 years old. *Science, 333*, 959–64.

Diamantopoulou, S., Rydell, A.-M., Thorell, L. B. and Bohlin (2007) Impact of executive functioning and symptoms of Attention Deficit Hyperactivity Disorder on children's peer relations and school performance. *Developmental Neuropsychology, 32*, 521–42.

Dowsett, S. and Livesey, D. J. (2000) The development of inhibitory control in pre-school children: Effects of 'executive skills' training. *Developmental Psychobiology, 36*(2), 161–74.

Eisenberg, N., Guthrie, I. K., Fabes, R. A., Reiser, M., Murphy, B. C., Holmgren, R., *et al.* (1997) The relations of regulation and emotionality to resiliency and competent social functioning in elementary school children. *Child Development, 68*, 295–311.

Eisenberg, N., Guthrie, I. K., Fabes, R. A., Shephard, S., Losoya, S., Murphy, B. C., *et al.* (2000) Prediction of elementary school children's externalizing problem behaviors from attentional and behavioral regulation and negative emotionality. *Child Development, 71*, 1367–82.

Ellefson, M. R., Johnstone, E. L., Blagrove, E. L. and Chater, N. (2006) Can developmental changes in switch costs be explained by age alone? Poster presented at the 28th annual meeting of the Cognitive Science Society, Vancouver, BC, Canada. Published in R. Sun (ed.) *The Proceedings of the 28th Annual Conference of the Cognitive Science Society* (p. 2476). Mahwah, NJ: Erlbaum.

Eslinger, P. J. (1996) Conceptualizing, describing, and measuring components of executive function. In G. R. Lyon and N. A. Krasnegor (eds) *Attention, Memory, and Executive Function* (pp. 367–95). Baltimore: Paul H. Brookes.

Espy, K. A., McDiarmid, M. D., Cwik, M. F., Stalets, M. M., Hamby, A. and Senn, T. E. (2004) The contribution of executive functions to emergent mathematic skills in preschool children. *Developmental Neuropsychology, 26*, 465–86.

Evans, G. W. and English, K. (2002) The environment of poverty: Multiple stressor exposure, psychophysiological stress, and socioemotional adjustment. *Child Development, 73*, 1238–48.

Fitzpatrick, C. and Pagani, L. S. (2012) Toddler working memory skills predict kindergarten school readiness. *Intelligence, 40*(2), 205–12.

Flook, L., Smalley, S. L., Kitil, M. J., Galla, B. M., Kaiser-Greenland, S., Locke, J., *et al.* (2010) Effects of mindful awareness practices on executive functions in elementary school children. *Journal of Applied School Psychology, 26*, 70–95.

Garon, N., Bryson, S. E. and Smith, I. M. (2008) Executive function in preschoolers: A review using an integrative framework. *Psychological Bulletin, 134*(1), 31–60.

Gathercole, S. E., Pickering, S. J., Knight, C. and Stegmann, Z. (2004) Working memory skills and educational attainment: Evidence from national curriculum assessments at 7 and 14 years of age. *Applied Cognitive Psychology, 18*, 1–16.

Gathercole, S. E., Lamont, E. and Alloway, T. P. (2006) Working memory in the classroom. In S. Pickering (ed.) *Working Memory and Education*, pp. 219–40. Elsevier Press.

Geary, D. C. (1993) Mathematical disabilities: Cognitive, neuropsychological, and genetic components. *Psychological Bulletin, 114*, 345–62.

George, J. and Greenfield, D. B. (2005) Examination of a structured problem-solving flexibility task for assessing approaches to learning in young children: Relation to teacher ratings and children's achievement. *Applied Developmental Psychology, 26*(1), 69–84.

Gianootta, F., Burk, W. J. and Ciairano, S. (2011) The role of inhibitory control in children's cooperative behaviors during a structured puzzle task. *Journal of Experimental Child Psychology, 110*, 287–98.

Gioia, G. A., Isquith, P. K., Guy, S. C. and Kenworthy, L. (2000) Behavior rating inventory of executive function. *Child Neuropsychology, 6*, 235–8.

Green, V. A. and Rechis, R. (2006) Children's cooperative and competitive interactions in limited resource situations: A literature review. *Applied Developmental Psychology, 27*, 42–59.

Handley, S. J., Capon, A., Beveridge, M., Dennis, I. and Evans, S. T. (2004) Working memory, inhibitory control and the development of children's reasoning. *Thinking and Reasoning, 10*(2), 175–95.

Holmes, J. and Gathercole, S. E. (2013) Taking working memory training from the laboratory into schools. *Educational Psychology*.

Holmes, J., Gathercole, S. E. and Dunning, D. (2009) Adaptive training leads to sustained enhancement of poor working memory in children. *Developmental Science, 12*, F9–F15.

Hooper, S. R., Swartz, C. W., Wakely, M. B., de Kruif, R. E. and Montgomery, J. W. (2002) Executive functions in elementary school children with and without problems in written expression. *Journal of Learning Disabilities, 35*, 57–68.

Hughes, C. (1998) Executive function in preschoolers: Links with theory of mind and verbal ability. *British Journal of Developmental Psychology, 16*, 233–53.

Hughes, C. and Ensor, R. (2007) Executive function and theory of mind: predictive relations from ages 2 to 4. *Developmental Psychology, 43L*, 1447–59.

Hughes, C. and Leekam, S. (2004) What are the links between theory of mind and social relations? Review, reflections and new directions for studies of typical and atypical development. *Social Development, 13*(4), 590–619.

Hughes, C., Dunn, J. and White, A. (1998) Trick or treat? Patterns of cognitive performance and executive function among 'hard to manage' preschoolers. *Journal of Child Psychology and Psychiatry, 39*, 981–94.

Hughes, C., White, A., Sharpen, J. and Dunn, J. (2000) Antisocial, angry, and unsympathetic: 'Hard-to-manage' preschoolers' peer problems and possible cognitive influences. *Journal of Child Psychology and Psychiatry, 41*, 169–79.

Hughes, C., Fujisawa, K. K., Ensor, R., Lecce, S. and Marfleet, R. (2006) Cooperation and conversations about the mind: A study of individual differences in 2-year-olds and their siblings. *British Journal of Developmental Psychology, 24*(1), 53–72.

Jarrold, C. and Towse, J. N. (2006) Individual differences in working memory. *Neuroscience, 139*, 39–50.

Kochanska, G., Murray, K. and Coy, K. (1997) Inhibitory control as a contributor to conscience in childhood: From toddler to early school age. *Child Development, 68*, 263–77.

Kopp, C. (1982) The antecedents of self-regulation: A developmental perspective. *Developmental Psychology, 18*, 199–214.

Kopp, C. (1989) Regulation of distress and negative emotions: A developmental view. *Developmental Psychology, 25*, 343–54.

Kopp, C. B. and Neufeld, S. J. (2003) Emotional development during infancy. In R. J. Davidson, K. Scherer and H. H. Goldsmith (eds) *Handbook of Affective Sciences* (pp. 347–74). New York: Oxford University Press.

Kray, J. and Ferdinand, N. K. (2013) How to improve cognitive control in development during childhood: Potentials and limits of cognitive interventions. *Child Development Perspectives, 7*(2), 121–5.

Lakes, K. D. and Hoyt, W. T. (2004) Promoting self-regulation through school-based martial arts training. *Applied Developmental Psychology, 25*, 283–302.

Lan, X., Legare, C. H., Ponitz, C. C., Li, S. and Morrison, F. J. (2011) Investigating the links between the subcomponents of executive function and academic achievement: A cross-cultural analysis of Chinese and American preschoolers. *Journal of Experimental Child Psychology, 108*, 677–92.

Lee, K., Bull, R. and Ho, R. M. H. (2013) Developmental changes in executive functioning. *Child Development.* doi: 10.1111/cdev.12096.

Liew, J., Eisenberg, N. and Reiser, M. (2004) Preschoolers' effortful control and negative emotionality, immediate reactions to disappointment, and quality of social functioning. *Journal of Experimental Child Psychology, 89*, 298–319. doi: 10.1016/j.jecp.2004.06.004.

Mackey, A. P., Hill, S. S., Stone, S. I. and Bunge, S. A. (2011) Dissociable effects of reasoning and speed training in children. *Developmental Science, 14*, 582–90.

McClelland, M. M., Cameron, C. E., Connor, C. M., Farris, C. L., Jewkes, A. M. and Morrison, F. J. (2007) Links between behavioral regulation and preschoolers' literacy, vocabulary, and math skills. *Developmental Psychology, 43*, 947–59.

Miller, E. K. and Cohen, J. D. (2001) An integrative theory of prefrontal cortex function. *Annual Review of Neuroscience, 24*, 167–202.

Miyake, A., Friedman, N. P., Emerson, M. J., Witzki, A. H., Howerter, A. and Wager, T. D. (2000) The unity and diversity of executive functions and their contributions to complex 'frontal lobe' tasks: A latent variable analysis. *Cognitive Psychology, 41*, 49–100.

Moffitt, T. E. (1993) Adolescence-limited and life-course persistent antisocial behaviour: A developmental taxonomy. *Psychological Review, 100*, 674–701.

Müller, U., Lieberman, D., Frye, D. and Zelazo, P. D. (2008) Executive function, school readiness, and school achievement. In S. K. Thurman and C. A. Fiorello (eds) *Applied Cognitive Research in K-3 Classrooms* (pp. 41–84). New York: Routledge.

Napoli, M., Krech, P. K. and Holley, L. C. (2005) Mindfulness training for elementary school students: The Attention Academy. *Journal of Applied School Psychology, 21*, 99–125.

Nilsen, E. and Graham, S. (2009) The relations between children's communicative perspective taking and executive functioning. *Cognitive Psychology, 58*, 220–49.

Nigg, J. T. (2000) On inhibition/disinhibition in developmental psychopathology: Views from cognitive and personality psychology and a working inhibition hypothesis. *Psychological Bulletin, 126*, 220–46.

Oberle, E. and Schonert-Reichl, K. A. (2013) Relations among peer acceptance, inhibitory control, and math achievement in early adolescence. *Journal of Applied Developmental Psychology, 34*(1), 45–51.

Olson, S. L., Sameroff, A. J., Kerr, D. C. R., Lopez, N. L. and Wellman, H. M. (2005) Developmental foundations of externalizing problems in young children: The role of effortful control. *Development and Psychopathology, 17*(1), 25–45.

Passolunghi, M. C. and Siegel, L. S. (2001) Short-term memory, working memory, and inhibitory control in children with difficulties in arithmetic problem solving. *Journal of Experimental Child Psychology, 80*, 44–57.

Pianta, R. C., Steinberg, M. and Rollins, K. B. (1995) The first two years of school: Teacher–child relationships and reflections in children's classroom adjustment. *Development and Psychopathology, 7*, 295–312. doi: 10.1017/S0954579400006519.

Phillips, L. H., Tunstall, M. and Channon, S. (2007) Exploring the role of working memory in dynamic social cue decoding using dual task methodology. *Journal of Nonverbal Behavior, 31*, 137–52. doi: 10.1007/s10919-007-0026-6.

Ponitz, C. C., McClelland, M. M., Matthews, J. S. and Morrison, F. J. (2009) A structured observation of behavioral self-regulation and its contribution to kindergarten outcomes. *Developmental Psychology, 45*, 605–19.

Protopapas, A., Archonti, A. and Skaloumbakas, C. (2007) Reading ability is negatively related to Stroop interference. *Cognitive Psychology, 54*, 251–82.

Raver, C. C. (2004) Placing emotional self-regulation in sociocultural and socioeconomic contexts. *Child Development, 75*, 346–53.

Raver, C. C. (2012) Low-income children's self-regulation in the classroom: Scientific inquiry for social change. *American Psychologist, 67*(8), 681–9. doi: 10.1037/a0030085.

Raver, C. C., Jones, S. M., Li-Grining, C. P., Zhai, F., Bub, K. and Pressler, E. (2011) CSRP's impact on low-income preschoolers' pre-academic skills: Self-regulation and teacher-student relationships as two mediating mechanisms. *Child Development, 82*(1), 362–78.

Razza, R. A. and Blair, C. (2009) Associations among false-belief understanding, executive function, and social competence: A longitudinal analysis. *Journal of Applied Developmental Psychology, 30*, 332–43.

Richland, L. E. and Burchinal, M. R. (2013) Early executive function predicts reasoning development. *Psychological Science, 24*, 87–92.

Riggs, N. R., Blair, C. B. and Greenberg, M. T. (2003) Concurrent and 2-year longitudinal relations between executive function and the behavior of 1st and 2nd grade children. *Child Neuropsychology*, *9*, 267–76.

Riggs, N. R., Greenberg, M. T., Kusche, C. A. and Pentz, M. A. (2006a) The mediational role of neurocognition in the behavioral outcomes of a social-emotional prevention program in elementary school students: Effects of the PATHS Curriculum. *Prevention Science*, *7*, 91–102.

Riggs, N. R., Jahromi, L. B., Razza, R. P., Dillworth-Bart, J. E. and Mueller, U. (2006b) Executive function and the promotion of social-emotional competence. *Journal of Applied Developmental Psychology*, *27*, 300–9.

Rimm-Kaufman, S. E., LaParo, K. M., Downer, J. T. and Pianta, R. C. (2005) The contribution of classroom setting and quality of instruction to children's behavior in the kindergarten classroom. *Elementary School Journal*, *105*, 377–94. doi: 10.1086/429948.

Roebers, C. M., Rothlisberger, M., Cimeli, P., Michel, E. and Neuenschwander, R. (2011) School enrolment and executive functioning: A longitudinal perspective on developmental changes, the influence of learning context, and the prediction of pre-academic skills. *European Journal of Developmental Psychology*, *8*, 526–40.

Rose-Krasnor, L. (1997) The nature of social competence: A theoretical review. *Social Development*, *6*, 111–35.

Rothbart, M. K. and Posner, M. (1985) Temperament and the development of self-regulation. In L. C. Hartlage and C. F. Telzrow (eds) *The Neuropsychology of Individual Differences: A Developmental Perspective* (pp. 93–123). New York: Plenum.

Röthlisberger, M., Neuenschwander, R., Cimeli, P., Michel, E. and Roebers, C. M. (2012) Improving executive functions in 5- and 6-year-olds: Evaluation of a small group intervention in prekindergarten and kindergarten children. *Infant and Child Development*, *21*, 411–29.

Rubin, K. H. and Rose-Krasnor, L. (1992) Interpersonal problem-solving. In V. B. Van Hassett and M. Hersen (eds) *Handbook of Social Development* (pp. 283–323). NY: Plenum.

Rueda, M. R., Rothbart, M. K., McCandliss, B. D. and Posner, P. (2005) Training, maturation, and genetic influences on the development of executive attention. *Proceedings of the National Academy of Sciences*, *102*, 14931–6.

Sabol, T. J. and Pianta, R. C. (2012) Patterns of school readiness forecast achievement and socioemotional development at the end of elementary school. *Child Development*, *83*, 282–99.

Savage, R., Lavers, N. and Pillay, V. (2007) Working memory and reading difficulties: What we know and what we don't know about the relationship. *Educational Psychology Review*, *19*, 185–221.

Schultz, D., Izard, C. E., Ackerman, B. P. and Youngstrom, E. A. (2001) Emotion knowledge in economically-disadvantaged children: Self-regulatory antecedents and relations to social maladjustment. *Development and Psychopathology*, *13*, 53–67.

Semrud-Clikeman, M. and Hynd, G. W. (1990) Right hemispheric dysfunction in nonverbal learning disabilities: Social, academic, and adaptive functioning in adults and children. *Psychological Bulletin*, *107*, 196–209.

Siegel, L. S. and Ryan, E. B. (1989) The development of working memory in normally achieving and subtypes of learning disabled children. *Child Development*, *60*, 973–80.

Speltz, M. L., DeKylen, M., Calderon, R., Greenberg, M. T. and Fisher, P. A. (1999) Neuropsychological characteristics and test behaviors of boys with early onset conduct problems. *Journal of Abnormal Psychology*, *108*, 315–25.

St Clair-Thompson, H. L. and Gathercole, S. E. (2006) Executive functions and achievements in school: shifting, updating, inhibition, and working memory. *Quarterly Journal of Experiemental Psychology*, *59*, 745–59.

Thorell, L. B., Lindqvist, S., Bergman Nutley, S., Bohlin, G. and Klingberg, T. (2009) Training and transfer effects of executive functions in preschool children. *Developmental Science*, *12*(1), 106–13.

Thorell, L. B., Veleiro, A., Siu, A. F. and Mohammadi, H. (2012) Examining the relation between ratings of executive functioning and academic achievement: Findings from a cross-cultural study. *Child Neuropsychology*. doi: 10.1080/09297049.2012.727792.

Toll, S. W. M., Van der Ven, S. H. G., Kroesbergen, E. H. and Van Luit, J. E. H. (2011) Executive functions as predictors of math learning disabilities. *Journal of Learning Disabilities*, *44*, 521–32.

Tominey, S. L. and McClelland, M. M. (2011) Red light, purple light: Findings from a randomized trial using circle time games to improve behavioral self-regulation in preschool. *Early Education and Development*, *22*(3), 489–519.

Turner, K., Fuhs, M. W., Farran, D., Norvell, J. and Newman, K. M. (2013) Adaptive classroom behaviors mediate effects of executive function skills on academic achievement in prekindergarten. Paper presented at the biennial meeting of the Society for Research in Child Development, Seattle, WA (April).

van der Sluis, S., de Jong, P. F. and van der Leij, A. (2007) Executive functioning in children, and its relations with reasoning, reading, and arithmetic. *Intelligence*, *35*, 427–49.

Waber, D. P., Gerber, E. B., Turcios, V. Y., Wagner, E. R. and Forbes, P. W. (2006) Executive functions and performance on high-stakes testing in children from urban schools. *Developmental Neuropsychology*, *29*(3), 459–77.

Welsh, M. C., Pennington, B. F. and Groisser, D. B. (1991) A normative-developmental study of executive function: A window of prefrontal function in children. *Developmental Neuropsychology*, 7, 131–49.

Wentzel, K. R. and Asher, S. R. (1995) The academic lives of neglected, rejected, popular, and controversial children. *Child Development*, *66*, 754–63.

Wiebe, S. A., Espy, K. A. and Charak, D. (2008) Using confirmatory factor analysis to understand executive control in preschool children: I. Latent structure. *Developmental Psychology*, *44*, 575–87.

Wiebe, S. A., Sheffield, T. D., Nelson, J. M., Clark, C. A. C., Chevalier, N. and Espy, K. A. (2011) The structure of executive function in 3-year-old children. *Journal of Experimental Child Psychology*, *108*, 436–52.

Willoughby, M., Blair, C., Wirth, R. J., Greenberg, M. and the FLP Investigators (2010) The measurement of executive function at age 3: Psychometric properties and criterion validity of a new battery of tasks. *Psychological Assessment*, *22*, 306–17.

Willoughby, M. T., Kupersmidt, J. B. and Voegler-Lee, M. E. (2012) Is preschool executive function causally related to academic achievement? *Child Neuropsychology*, *18*(1), 79–91.

White, J. L., Moffitt, T. E., Caspi, A., Jeglum Bartusch, D., Needles, D. J. and Stouthamer-Loeber, M. (1994) Measuring impulsivity and examining its relationship to delinquency. *Journal of Abnormal Psychology*, *103*, 192–205.

Yeates, K. O., Bigler, E. D., Dennis, M., Gerhardt, C. A., Rubin, K. H., Stancin, T., Taylor, H. G. and Vannatta, K. (2007) Social outcomes in childhood brain disorder: A heuristic integration of social neuroscience and developmental psychology. *Psychological Bulletin*, *133*, 535–56.

Zelazo, P. D. and Lyons, K. E. (2012) The potential benefits of mindfulness training in early childhood: a developmental social cognitive neuroscience perspective. *Child Development Perspectives*, *6*(2), 154–60.

13

CHILDREN'S PRIVATE SPEECH

Danielle L. Mead and Adam Winsler

Introduction

Children often talk to themselves as they go about their daily activities – while problem solving or working on an academic task, during solitary imaginative play, during sport activity, or before falling asleep. Private speech is defined as overt speech that is not directed to another person (Winsler, 2009). Researchers from a variety of different theoretical perspectives have examined the important role that private speech plays in the development of children's thinking, problem solving, motivation, self-regulation, and executive functioning (Winsler, 2009). In this chapter, we will first discuss different theoretical perspectives on children's private speech and then summarize research findings with respect to developmental trajectories of such speech, the content and multiple functions and types of self-talk, as well as relations between private speech and task performance and executive functioning. Finally, we will conclude with potential applications of private speech research, namely, for classrooms and for children with problems of self-regulation.

Perspectives on private speech

In 1923, Piaget published *The Language and Thought of the Child* (Piaget, 1962), in which he observed young children talking to themselves in classrooms. He considered this type of 'egocentric speech' as merely indicating cognitive immaturity and evidence of poor social speech not appropriately addressed to others. Consistent with his notion of cognitive development being primary and language and other domains being secondary, Piaget saw no special function or role for private speech in child development. Lev Vygotsky, in *Thought and Language* (Vygotsky, 1962, originally published 1934), however, proposed that private speech stems from social speech, emerging from the guiding nature of children's parent–child interactions. The dialogic, back-and-forth nature of private speech is similar to the speech between parents and children, which supports Vygotsky's view that private speech has social origins (Fernyhough, 2009). Vygotsky theorized that language begins as a means of communication with others, but then becomes overt communication with the self to guide one's behavior and thinking before such speech is internalized to form silent, inner verbal thought. The mind, therefore, becomes verbally mediated through private speech and a new, uniquely human, level of cognitive and behavioral self-regulation is formed. Luria (1961), continuing in the Vygotskian tradition, extended our understanding of how language in the form of private speech is linked with motor control and helps children exhibit self-control, and how such links between speech and action might be represented in the functional and anatomical organization of the brain.

More recently, Zelazo and his colleagues have formulated Cognitive Complexity and Control theory (CCC-r; Zelazo and Frye, 1998; Zelazo and Jacques, 1996; Zelazo *et al.*, 2003), which attempts to understand age-related changes in the complexity of children's reasoning and self-reflection. More specifically, developmental changes in executive function can be explained by the increased complexity of the rules that children follow while solving problems, and self-directed speech is used to maintain the rules in focus (Müller *et al.*, 2009; Zelazo and Frye, 1998). Children need to plan ahead to achieve goals, and since many plans correspond to if-then rules (i.e. 'if it is a blue one, it goes over here'), using self-directed speech can help distance themselves from interference and distractions from the environment and help attend to and carry out the rules to complete a task successfully (Müller *et al.*, 2009; Zelazo and Frye, 1998). For example, a commonly used measure of executive functioning in children is the Dimensional Change Card Sorting task, which requires children to sort cards according to one dimension (e.g. color, number, shape), but then the correct sorting rule switches. When children are instructed to use verbal strategies (e.g. labeling) during such executive functioning tasks, performance improves compared to when not instructed to use verbal strategies (Agina *et al.*, 2011; Diamond *et al.*, 2002; Jacques and Zelazo, 2001; Kirkham *et al.*, 2003; Müller *et al.*, 2004, 2008). Children have also been observed to use private speech spontaneously (rather than being told to) on similar executive functioning tasks, with such speech being positively related to performance (Fernyhough and Fradley, 2005; Winsler *et al.*, 2003).

Cognitive psychologists, within the information processing theoretical perspective, have examined the role of speech in working memory, one aspect of executive functioning, by positing that a phonological loop is critical for working memory (Baddeley, 2000; Baddeley and Hitch, 1974). The phonological loop holds and rehearses limited amounts of verbal and auditory information, which helps individuals store and manipulate the information required for complex tasks. A task-switching paradigm with or without articulatory suppression is often used for research in this area. In this paradigm, it is presumed that verbal mediation in the form of rehearsal (saying the relevant dimension in one's head) is needed for successful task performance, and individuals are instructed to either overtly or covertly say either the relevant dimension for the task (e.g. saying 'color' when the task is matching items by color), or something irrelevant (e.g. saying 'color' when the task is matching by shape, or saying something else altogether like the alphabet). In the articulatory suppression condition when the individual is not allowed to say the relevant dimension to themselves, performance on such tasks is greatly impaired, as found in studies using adults (Baddeley *et al.*, 2001; Bryck and Mayr, 2005; Emerson and Miyake, 2003; Goschke, 2000) and children (Blaye and Chevalier, 2011; Kray *et al.*, 2008; Lidstone *et al.*, 2010). Kray *et al.* (2008) examined age-related effects by including four age groups: younger children (aged 7–9), older children (aged 11–13), younger adults (aged 20–27), and older adults (66–77). By asking participants to say the label used in the task (for example, saying 'color' when the task is to identify if a picture of an animal is in black-and-white or in color), performance improved compared to when the participants were told to use an overt task-irrelevant three-word sequence, and this was most pronounced for the younger children. However, the reduction in the error rate when participants were allowed to use task-relevant labels was greatest for the younger children, meaning that asking children to use speech to guide their behavior improved performance, especially for those who did not spontaneously do so in the practice sessions. Lidstone and colleagues (2010) examined the effects of articulatory suppression on school-age children with the Tower of London task (Shallice, 1982). The children alternated between two conditions: articulatory suppression (i.e. repeating the word 'Monday') or control (i.e. tapping the foot during the task). Performance in the articulatory suppression condition was impaired compared to the foot-tapping condition, and children's spontaneous private speech use increased as the difficulty level of the task also increased (Lidstone *et al.*, 2010).

Still another subdiscipline of psychology – namely sports psychology – using still another theoretical perspective – namely cognitive behaviorism (Beck, 1976) and social cognitive theory (Bandura, 1989) – examines the 'self-talk' that child and adult athletes use (or more usually, report using) when engaged in their sport (for a review, see Hatzigeorgiadis *et al.*, 2011; Hardy, 2006; Tod *et al.*, 2011). The things that athletes say to themselves, either overtly or inside their head, are usually classified into two categories related to their primary presumed function – either motivational/emotional regulation (i.e. 'You can do this,' 'Calm down') or instructional ('Keep your eye on the ball' and 'A little higher'). Athletes who use more positive self-talk and self-praise have been shown to perform better than athletes who talk to themselves in a negative way, such as self-criticism (Hardy, 2006; Moran, 1996; Theodorakis *et al.*, 2000).

Developmental trajectories

Vygotsky (1986/1934) originally found an inverted U-shape pattern over time in terms of the frequency of overt private speech observed in children, peaking during the preschool years and declining during the early years of elementary school. During the decline of overt private speech, there is an increase in the amount of muttering or whispers, reflecting the hypothesized internalization toward inner verbal thought. More recent cross-sectional and longitudinal research has confirmed this pattern. Winsler and Nagleiri (2003) included a large, diverse, and representative sample across a wide age range, and used the same, standardized task for all participants. Almost half of those aged 4–5 engaged in private speech during a planning task, but only 10 per cent of the 17-year-olds talked to themselves, while on the other hand, one-third of the older children reported using inner speech with very few younger children reporting such use. The use of whispers and mutterings peaked for the 9-year-olds and then declined (Winsler and Naglieri, 2003). A handful of longitudinal studies (Montero *et al.*, 2001; San Martin *et al.*, 2011; Winsler *et al.*, 2000a, 2003) have also confirmed this pattern with some also showing stability of individual differences in speech use across tasks and time. For example, Winsler and colleagues (2003) observed private speech in a group of preschool children and observed them again six months later. The authors found that there was an increase in the proportion of task-relevant private speech over time, and the children used fewer words per private speech utterance as they got older. It is important to note that although one sees age-related trends in the frequency of private speech when averaging across many tasks and task difficulties, older children (and adults) will often resort to using overt private speech as a tool when engaged in particularly challenging problem solving tasks (Alarcón-Rubio *et al.*, 2013; Winsler, 2009). Finally, there is also a microgenetic developmental trajectory in private speech use within individuals over time as they master a particular multi-trial task over a short period of time (Winsler, 2009). Microgenetic studies have shown a relation between speech and task-performance, in that as children exhibit more competence during the task or tasks, they use less overt private speech and more muttering over time (Berk and Spuhl, 1995; Duncan and Pratt, 1997).

Diverse contexts, functions, and types of private speech

Private speech researchers over the years have documented a variety of different functions of private speech; however, most have focused on young children talking to themselves during cognitive problem-solving activities, with the particular goal of understanding the self-regulatory function of such speech and relations between private speech and task performance (Beaudichon, 1999; Behrend *et al.*, 1989; Berk, 1999; Chiu and Alexander, 2000; Fernyhough and Russell, 1997; Frauenglass and Diaz, 1999; Furrow, 1984; Goudena, 1999; Krafft and Berk, 1998; Murray, 1999; for a review, see Winsler, 2009). Children often give themselves commands ('Put this here'), ask themselves questions ('Where is the square?') or describe relevant features of the task ('I need a blue one') or their current activity ('I put that there') during such tasks. These types/functions of speech occur more frequently in children's private than their social speech (Furrow, 1984). Private speech is more likely to occur during moments of task difficulty when children encounter an obstacle (Diaz, 1992; Duncan and Pratt, 1997; Behrend *et al.*, 1992), and such speech has been found to be positively related to children's concurrent (Duncan and Pratt, 1997; Fernyhough and Fradley, 2005; Winsler *et al.*, 2000b) or future (Atencio, 2004) performance. The relationship between private speech and task performance is dynamic and complex, however, and is best examined microgenetically or longitudinally because if examined at one point in time such speech occurs when the child is having difficulty (Winsler, 2009).

Similar to researchers in sport psychology discussed above, the role of spontaneous private speech in regulating children's motivation has also been explored (Atencio and Montero, 2009). Chiu and Alexander (2000) asked preschool children to per-form a variety of tasks while encouraging them to work independently. Their speech was classified as off-task, task-relevant and non-facilitative, cognitive, or metacogni-tive. Children's motivation to master the task and ability to work independently was positively correlated with the proportional use of metacognitive private speech. The use of private speech as a tool for emotion regulation has also been hypothesized. Children tell themselves to 'calm down' and say things like 'it's gonna be okay' in an attempt to modulate emotional responses to tasks and situations. Broderick (2001) found a relation between emotion regulation and private speech use in children aged 4 and 5; those who were reported as having good emotion regulation skills by teachers used more private speech in Head Start classrooms than children who had poorer emotion regulation skills.

Private speech use has also been related to a variety of other psychological func-tions or attributes. Daugherty *et al.* (1994) measured creativity and private speech in preschoolers and kindergarteners, and found that coping/reinforcing private speech use during a puzzle task was positively related to child creativity. Increased use of task-relevant private speech has also been linked with stronger autobiographical memory in children (Al-Namlah *et al.*, 2012), and with children's skills at referential communication with others (San Martin Martinez *et al.*, 2011).

Although most research has focused on the self-regulatory functions of private speech during problem solving, there is another very different context in which young children talk to themselves, namely in the bed or crib at nap/bedtime. Crib speech is the monologue speech of a young child shortly before he or she falls asleep (Weir, 1962). Winsler *et al.* (2006) found that 55 per cent of predominantly White, middle-class mothers interviewed reported that their child engaged in pre-sleep monologues. Given its prevalence, it is, therefore, surprising that very little is known about this special type of private speech, and what we do know is limited to a handful of single-subject case studies in which the investigators typically recorded their own toddler at home (Kuczaj, 1983; Mead *et al.*, 2013; Nelson, 1989; Weir, 1962). Children included in the case studies of crib speech are typically about two years younger (from ages 15 to 50 months) than children involved in most studies of children's private speech use during tasks.

Rather than cognitive or behavioral self-regulation, the primary function of crib speech appears to be language practice, either in the form of word play, repetition, or language modification (Kuczaj, 1983; Mead *et al.*, 2013; Nelson, 1989; Weir, 1962). Weir (1962) carefully tracked the language complexity of her son's crib speech between 28 and 30 months of age, documenting the phonology, grammar, and para-graphs of his speech, and found many episodes of language play. Kuczaj (1983) was able to examine social speech and crib speech in 14 children between the ages of 15 and 24 months, and found that language practice was more commonly found in crib speech compared to social speech. He suggested that the environment of a crib may be more conducive for practicing language, allowing the child to have an enjoyable time playing with words and sounds. Although not explicitly tested, crib speech researchers imply that perhaps certain speech forms appear first in the child's private speech before their social speech. A remarkable study of the private vocalizations of an African Grey parrot tested this and discovered that some speech forms did appear in practice form in the parrot's private speech before it appeared in a social setting (Pepperberg *et al.*, 1991). Nelson (1989) analyzed the crib speech of her daughter between the ages of 22 and 36 months, and discovered, in addition to language play, a common autobiographical memory theme in the content of the speech, including a transition from recalling past and current day events to anticipating and talking about upcoming events in the future. In the most recent case study of pre-sleep narratives with a somewhat older child, Mead *et al.* (2013) found a variety of different types of language modification and practice in a 4-year-old, including correcting oneself, practicing to count numbers or label colors, as well as experimentation with reading books. The most prominent type of self-talk exhibited by this older child during naptime, however, was fantasy dialogue and role-playing narratives involving stuffed animals, often involving singing and humming. Interestingly, crib speech was more complex (greater mean length of utterance) during utterances that were sung than were spoken. Many instances of self-guiding and emotional regulation utterances were also found (Mead *et al.*, 2013), more frequently than in studies with younger children (Nelson, 1989).

Applications

Private speech in classrooms

Because of research supporting the relation between task-relevant private speech and task performance, several investigators have recommended that teachers should encourage and allow children to use private speech in classroom situations (Berk and Winsler, 1995; Winsler, 2009; Winsler *et al.*, 2000b, 2000a; Winsler and Diaz, 1995). Indeed, naturalistic observational studies of children in early childhood classrooms show frequent and task-relevant use of private speech (Krafft and Berk, 1998; Winsler and Diaz, 1995; Winsler *et al.*, 2000a). Winsler *et al.* (2007) observed spontaneous and instructed use of private speech during a speech-action coordination task in preschool children. The researchers found that children performed better when instructed to talk to themselves during the task, that most children spontaneously used self-talk, and that one-third of the children continued to naturally use private speech even after being asked to be quiet. These findings imply that children naturally use private speech as a problem-solving tool, and asking them to be quiet puts an additional burden on them and interferes with performance. Teachers are generally aware of students talking to themselves in the classroom, but many teachers discourage children from talking to themselves in class because they (erroneously) believe that children's self-talk disturbs other children, and about half of teachers report that such speech disturbs them as teachers (Deniz, 2009; Oliver *et al.*, 2003). Obviously, if children's self-talk is very loud and confirmed to be disturbing other students, the student could be asked to speak more quietly, but generally we recommend that teachers tolerate, if not encourage, task-relevant private speech use in the classroom. Also, given that children talk to themselves when tasks are appropriately challenging (not too easy and not too difficult) as a form of self-scaffolding, teachers interested in keeping their children appropriately challenged and growing cognitively can use the appearance of self-talk as an indicator that the task in which an individual child is engaged is at the right developmental level (Berk and Winsler, 1995).

Children with problems of self-regulation

Children with attention deficit hyperactivity disorder (ADHD) struggle with behavioral self-regulation, inhibitory control, and executive functioning (Barkley, 1997; Pennington and Ozonoff, 1996; Schachar *et al.*, 2000), the very things for which private speech is thought to be useful. There is a small body of research that has examined the private speech of children with behavior problems who are at-risk for ADHD (Winsler *et al.*, 1999), and those clinically diagnosed with ADHD (Berk and Potts, 1991; Copeland, 1979; Corkum *et al.*, 2008; Kopecky *et al.*, 2005; Lawrence *et al.*, 2002; Winsler, 1998; Winsler *et al.*, 2007). Children with behavior problems and ADHD do talk to themselves in relevant ways during problem-solving tasks, similar to typically developing children, and, in fact, they are more likely to use overt private speech, and often show more speech use compared to non-diagnosed, same-age, children working on the same task and obtaining equivalent levels of performance (see Winsler, 2009 for a review). Therefore, they do not need to be taught how to talk to themselves as was presumed in early work (Meichenbaum and Goodman, 1971). However, they appear to be delayed in the internalization of private speech, as indicated by less use of partially internalized forms of speech such as whispers and inaudible muttering, increased irrelevant speech, and the absence of negative correlations between such speech use and age as is found with typical children (Berk and Potts, 1991; Winsler, 1998). Thus, those with ADHD continue to try to guide their attention and behavior with overt speech (often to the dismay of parents and teachers) when other children of the same age have moved to more internal forms of verbal mediation. Children with ADHD also elicit increased negative control by parents and teachers which inhibits opportunities for such children to effectively regulate their own behavior with the tool of speech because their behavior is more often being controlled by others (Winsler, 1998). Winsler (2009) suggests that parents and teachers should try to relinquish external control as much as possible with children with ADHD, and provide children with ADHD with more opportunities to use private speech effectively to help regulate themselves during tasks by sensitively 'scaffolding' their problem-solving activities.

Another group of children, namely those diagnosed on the autism spectrum, are also known to have particular difficulties with executive functioning (Hill, 2004; Russell, 1997). A few investigators have explored the silent, inner speech of children with autism with the task switching and articulatory suppression paradigm, finding mixed support for the notion that children with autism might not use inner speech as much because they are not as impaired compared to typical children when they are prevented from using verbal mediation via articulatory suppression (Holland and Low, 2009; Wallace *et al.*, 2009; Whitehouse *et al.*, 2006). However, very little work has examined the overt, spontaneous private speech of children with autism. Winsler and colleagues (2007) examined children and adolescents with high-functioning autism engaging in computerized executive functioning tasks, and found that they used comparable amounts of task-relevant private speech as control children and children with ADHD, and that they showed better performance on the task when they used private speech than when they were silent. This finding indicates that verbal children with high-functioning autism do utilize private speech in relevant ways and that it appears to improve their performance on challenging tasks. Interestingly, the children with autism were less likely to use partially internalized forms of private speech, which suggests that, similar to children with ADHD, autistic children may be delayed in the internalization of private speech.

Finally, LaRocque and Winsler (2012) with the same sample of children with ASD, ADHD, and controls as Winsler *et al.* (2007), subsequently examined private speech use and the quality of parent–child scaffolding during the classic (non-computerized) Tower of London task, first done collaboratively with their parent and then done individually. In contrast to what the same children with autism showed during the computerized tasks in Winsler *et al.* (2007), the ASD children were less likely to use private speech than the control groups after the collaborative social interaction with their parent. Further, the parent–child scaffolding that children with ASD received was of marginally poorer quality (but not characterized by increased negative control as found among ADHD children) than that received by control children. For all groups, individual child performance improved when parents talked less in the dyad session and when children talked more in the dyad session. This finding, combined with associations between child speech in the dyad and child performance in the individual session, indicate that we should encourage children with ASD to talk during joint activities because it likely improves their private speech use and performance later on when completing similar tasks alone.

Conclusions

Private speech research has allowed us to tap into the thoughts and self-regulatory processes of children and provides an opportunity to explore the internalization of the social nature of communication with others to communication with the self. There are a number of important areas for future research in this area, however. First, we need more research on private speech use in children from more diverse cultural and linguistic backgrounds since most research has been conducted on relatively white, middle-class, North American children. Although private speech is seen as a universal tool children use for thinking, we need research with other languages, especially from cultures where children might be less encouraged to speak. Another important area for research is children's awareness of private speech. Manfra (2009) found that although most children regularly use private speech during challenging tasks, not all preschoolers are aware that they are talking out loud, and that such awareness increases after the child's fourth birthday and may be related to child speech use and performance. With the large number of cross-sectional designs in private speech research, future efforts should also be made to conduct more longitudinal and microgenetic studies to examine individual patterns and speech trajectories over time. There is also a need for more attention to children's private speech in other, non-problem-solving contexts, such as pre-sleep monologues and private speech use during solitary, imaginary play. Finally, while there are established links with private speech and executive function and task performance, there is still a need for research on the best ways to help children with executive functioning deficits use their private speech effectively for self-regulation.

References

Agina, A. M., Kommers, P. A. M. and Steehouder, M. F. (2011) The effect of the external regulator's absence on children's speech use, manifested self-regulation, and task performance during learning tasks. *Computers in Human Behavior, 27,* 1118–28.

Alarcón-Rubio, D., Sánchez-Medina, J. A. and Winsler, A. (2013) Private speech in illiterate adults: cognitive functions, task difficulty, and literacy. *Journal of Adult Development.* doi: 10.1007/s10804-013-9161-y.

Al-Namlah, A. S., Meins, E. and Fernyhough, C. (2012) Self-regulatory private speech relates to children's recall and organization of autobiographical memories. *Early Childhood Research Quarterly, 27,* 441–46.

Atencio, D. J. (2004) The emerging volitional self: A dynamic assessment of the mediating role of social and private dialogue in the development of self-direction and task motivation. *Dissertation Abstracts International Section A: Humanities and Social Sciences,* Vol. *64*(9–A), 3186.

Atencio, D. J. and Montero, I. (2009) Private speech and motivation: The role of language in a sociocultural account of motivational processes. In A. Winsler, C. Fernyhough and I. Montero (eds) *Private Speech, Executive Functioning, and the Development of Verbal Self-regulation* (pp. 201–23). New York, NY: Cambridge University Press.

Baddeley, A. (1986) *Working Memory*. New York, NY: Oxford University Press.

Baddeley, A. D. (2000) The episodic buffer: A new component of working memory? *Trends in Cognitive Science, 4*(11), 417–23.

Baddeley, A. D. and Hitch, G. J. L. (1974) Working memory. In G. A. Bower (ed.) *The Psychology of Learning and Motivation: Advances in Research and Theory,* Vol. *8* (pp. 47–89). New York: Academic Press.

Baddeley, A. D., Chincotta, D. and Adlam, A. (2001) Working memory and the control of action: evidence for task switching. *Journal of Experimental Psychology: General, 130,* 641–57.

Bandura, A. (1989) Social cognitive theory. In R. Vasta (ed.) *Annals of Child Development, Vol. 6: Six Theories of Child Development* (pp. 1–60). Greenwich, CT: JAI Press.

Barkley, R. A. (1997) Behavioral inhibition, sustained attention, and executive functioning: Constructing a unifying theory of ADHD. *Psychological Bulletin, 121,* 65–94.

Beaudichon, J. (1999) Nature and instrumental function of private speech in problem solving situations. In P. Lloyd and C. Fernyhough (eds) *Lev Vygotsky: Critical Assessments: Thought and Language,* Vol. *2* (pp. 230–47). Florence, KY: Taylor and Francis/Routledge.

Beck, A. T. (1976) *Cognitive Therapy and the Emotional Disorders*. Oxford, UK: International Universities Press.

Behrend, D. A., Rosengren, K. S. and Perlmutter, M. (1989) A new look at children's private speech: The effects of age, task difficulty, and parent presence. *International Journal of Behavioral Development, 12,* 305–20.

Behrend, D. A., Rosengren, K. S. and Perlmutter, M. (1992) The relation between private speech and parental interactive style. In R. M. Diaz and L. E. Berk (eds) *Private Speech: From Social Interaction to Self-regulation* (pp. 85–100). Hillsdale, NJ: Erlbaum.

Berk, L. E. (1999) Children's private speech: An overview of theory and the status of research. In P. Lloyd and C. Fernyhough (eds) *Lev Vygotsky: Critical Assessments: Thought and Language,* Vol. *2* (pp. 33–70). Florence, KY: Taylor and Francis/Routledge.

Berk, L. E. and Garvin, R. A. (1984) Development of private speech among low-income Appalachian children. *Developmental Psychology, 20,* 271–86.

Berk, L. E. and Potts, M. K. (1991) Development and functional significance of private speech among attention-deficit hyperactivity disordered and normal boys. *Journal of Abnormal Child Psychology, 19*, 357–77.

Berk, L. E. and Spuhl, S. T. (1995) Maternal interaction, private speech, and task performance in preschool children. *Early Childhood Research Quarterly, 10*, 145–69.

Berk, L. E. and Winsler, A. (1995) *Scaffolding Children's Learning: Vygotsky and Early Childhood Education.* Washington, DC: National Association for the Education of Young Children.

Blaye, A., and Chevalier, N. (2011) The role of goal representation in preschoolers' flexibility and inhibition. *Journal of Experimental Child Psychology, 108*(3), 469–83. doi: 10.1016/j.jecp.2010.09.006

Broderick, N. Y. (2001) An investigation of the relationship between private speech and emotion regulation in preschool-age children. *Dissertation Abstracts International: Section B: The Sciences and Engineering,* Vol. *61*(11-B), June: 6125.

Bryck, R. L. and Mayr, U. (2005) On the role of verbalization during task set selection: Switching or serial order control? *Memory and Cognition, 33*(4), 611–23.

Camp, B. W., Blom, G. E., Herbert, F. and van Doorninck, W. J. (1977) 'Think Aloud': A program for developing self-control in young aggressive boys. *Journal of Abnormal Child Psychology, 5*, 157–69.

Chiu, S. and Alexander, P. A. (2000) The motivational function of preschoolers' private speech. *Discourse Processes, 30*, 133–52.

Copeland, A. P. (1979) Types of private speech produced by hyperactive and nonhyperactive boys. *Journal of Abnormal Child Psychology, 7*, 169–77.

Corkum, P., Humphries, K., Mullane, J. C. and Theriault, F. (2008) Private speech in children with ADHD and their typically developing peers during problem-solving and inhibition tasks. *Contemporary Educational Psychology, 33*(1), 97–115. doi: 10.1016/j.cedpsych.2006.12.003.

Daugherty, M. and White, C. S. (2008) Relationships among private speech and creativity in Head Start and low-socioeconomic status preschool children. *Gifted Child Quarterly, 52*(1), 30–9. doi: 10.1177/0016986207311059.

Daugherty, M., White, C. S. and Manning, B. H. (1994) Relationships among private speech and creativity measurements of young children. *Gifted Child Quarterly, 38*(1), 21–6. doi: 10.1177/001698629403800103.

Deniz, C. B. (2009) Early childhood teachers' awareness, beliefs, and practices toward children's private speech. In A. Winsler, C. Fernyhough and I. Montero (eds) *Private Speech, Executive Functioning, and the Development of Verbal Self-regulation* (pp. 236–46). New York: Cambridge University Press.

Diamond, A., Kirkham, N. and Amso, D. (2002) Conditions under which young children can hold two rules in mind and inhibit a prepotent response. *Developmental Psychology, 38*: 352–62.

Diaz, R. M. (1992) Methodological concerns in the study of private speech. In R. M. Diaz and L. E. Berk (eds) *Private Speech: From Social Interaction to Self Regulation* (pp. 55–81). Hillsdale, NJ: Erlbaum.

Duncan, R. M. and Pratt, M. W. (1997) Microgenetic change in the quantity and quality of preschoolers' private speech. *International Journal of Behavioral Development, 20*, 367–83.

Emerson, M. J. and Miyake, A. (2003) The role of inner speech in task switching: A dual-task investigation. *Journal of Memory and Language, 48*, 148–68.

Fernyhough, C. (2009) Dialogic thinking. In A. Winsler, C. Fernyhough and I. Montero (eds) *Private Speech, Executive Functioning, and the Development of Verbal Self-regulation* (pp. 42–52). New York: Cambridge University Press.

Fernyhough, C. and Fradley, E. (2005) Private speech on an executive task: Relations with task difficulty and task performance. *Cognitive Development, 20*, 103–20.

Fernyhough, C. and Russell, J. (1997) Distinguishing one's own voice from those of others: A function for private speech? *International Journal of Behavioral Development, 20*(4), 651–65.

Frauenglass, M. H. and Diaz, R. M. (1985) Self-regulatory functions of children's private speech: A critical analysis of recent challenges to Vygotsky's theory. *Developmental Psychology, 21,* 357–64.

Furrow, D. (1984) Social and private speech at two years. *Child Development, 55*(2), 355–62. doi: 10.2307/1129948.

Goschke, T. (2000) Intentional reconfiguration and involuntary persistence in task set switching. In S. Monsell and J. Driver (eds) *Control of Cognitive Processes: Attention and Performance XVIII* (pp. 331–55). Cambridge, MA: MIT Press.

Goudena, P. P. (1999) The social nature of private speech of preschoolers during problem solving. In P. Lloyd and C. Fernyhough (eds) *Lev Vygotsky: Critical Assessments: Thought and Language,*Vol. 2 (pp. 321–39). Florence, KY: Taylor and Francis/Routledge.

Hatzigeorgiadis, A., Zourbanos, N., Galanis, E. and Theodorakis, Y. (2011) Self-talk and sports performance: A meta-analysis. *Perspectives on Psychological Science, 6*(4), 348–56. doi: 10.1177/1745691611413136.

Hardy, J. (2006) Speaking clearly: A critical review of the self-talk literature. *Psychology of Sport and Exercise, 7,* 81–97.

Hill, E. L. (2004) Executive dysfunction in autism. *Trends in Cognitive Sciences, 8,* 26–32.

Holland, L. and Low, J. (2009) Do children with autism use inner speech and visuospatial resources for the service of executive control? Evidence from suppression in dual tasks. *British Journal of Developmental Psychology, 28*(2), 369–91. doi: 10.1348/026151009X424088.

Jacques, S., and Zelazo, P. D. (2001) The Flexible Item Selection Task (FIST): A measure of executive function in preschoolers. *Developmental Neuropsychology, 20,* 573–91.

Kendall, P. C. (1977) On the efficacious use of verbal self-instructional procedures with children. *Cognitive Therapy and Research, 1,* 331–41.

Kirkham, N. Z., Cruess, L. and Diamond, A. (2003) Helping children apply their knowledge to their behavior on a dimension-switching task. *Developmental Science, 6,* 449–67.

Kopecky, H., Chang, H. T. and Klorman, R. (2005) Performance and private speech of children with attention-deficit/hyperactivity disorder while taking the Tower of Hanoi Test: Effects of depth of search, diagnostic subtype, and Methylphenidate. *Journal of Abnormal Child Psychology, 33,* 625–38.

Krafft, K. C. and Berk, L. E. (1998) Private speech in two preschools: Significance of open-ended activities and make-believe play for verbal self-regulation. *Early Childhood Research Quarterly, 13,* 637–58.

Kray, J., Eber, J. and Karbach, J. (2008) Verbal self-instructions in task switching: A compensatory tool for action-control deficits in childhood and old age? *Developmental Science, 11*(2), 223–36. doi: 10.1111/j.1467-7687.2008.00673.x.

Kuczaj, S. A. (1983) *Crib Speech and Language Play.* New York: Springer-Verlag.

LaRocque, R. and Winsler, A. (2012) Parent–child interaction, scaffolding, and private speech among children with ADHD or high functioning autism. Unpublished masters thesis. Department of Psychology, George Mason University, Fairfax, VA.

Lawrence, V., Houghton, S., Tannock, R., Douglas, G., Durkin, K. and Whiting, K. (2002) ADHD outside the laboratory: Boys' executive function performance on tasks in videogame play and on a visit to the zoo. *Journal of Abnormal Child Psychology, 30,* 447–62.

Lidstone, J. S. M., Meins, E. and Fernyhough, C. (2010) The roles of private speech and inner speech in planning during middle childhood: evidence from a dual task paradigm. *Journal of Experimental Child Psychology, 107*(4), 438–51. doi: 10.1016/j.jecp.2010.06.002.

Luria, A. R. (1961) *The Role of Speech in the Regulation of Normal and Abnormal Behavior* (ed. J. Tizard). New York: Liveright.

Manfra, L. (2009) Preschool children's awareness and theory of speech. In A. Winsler, C. Fernyhough, and I. Montero (eds) *Private Speech, Executive Functioning, and the Development of Verbal Self-regulation* (pp. 134–42). New York: Cambridge University Press.

Mead, D. L., LaRocque, R., Lindgren, E. and Winsler, A. (2013) Change over time in the type and functions of crib speech around the fourth birthday. Poster presented at the Society for Research in Child Development biennial meeting. Seattle, WA (April).

Meichenbaum, D. H. and Goodman, J. (1971) Training impulsive children to talk to themselves: A means of developing self-control. *Journal of Abnormal Psychology, 77*, 115–26.

Montero, I., de Dios, M. J. and Huertas, J. A. (2001) El desarrollo de la motivacion en el contexto escolar: Un estudio a través del habla privada [The development of motivation in school contexts: A study through private speech]. *Estudios de Psicología, 22*, 305–18.

Moran, P. A. (1996) *The Psychology of Concentration in Sport Performance*. East Sussex, UK: Psychology Press.

Müller, U., Jacques, S., Brocki, K. and Zelazo, P. D. (2009) The executive functions of language in preschool children. In A. Winsler, C. Fernyhough, and I. Montero (eds) *Private Speech, Executive Functioning, and the Development of Verbal Self-regulation* (pp. 53–68). New York: Cambridge University Press.

Müller, U., Zelazo, P. D., Hood, S., Leone, T. and Rohrer, L. (2004) Interference control in a new rule use task: Age-related changes, labeling, and attention. *Child Development, 75*, 1594–609.

Müller, U., Zelazo, P. D., Lurye, L. E. and Liebermann, D. P. (2008) The effect of labeling on preschool children's performance in the Dimensional Change Card Sort Task. *Cognitive Development, 23*(3), 395–408. doi:10.1016/j.cogdev.2008.06.001.

Murray, J. D. (1999) Spontaneous private speech and performance on a delayed match-to-sample task. In P. Lloyd and C. Fernyhough (eds) *Lev Vygotsky: Critical Assessments: Thought and Language*, Vol. 2 (pp. 248–64). Florence, KY: Taylor and Francis/Routledge.

Nelson, K. (1989) *Narratives from the Crib*. Cambridge, MA: Harvard University Press.

Oliver, J. A., Edmiaston, R. and Fitzgerald, L. (2003). Regular and special education teachers' beliefs regarding the role of private speech in children's learning. Symposium paper. *Awareness, attitudes, and beliefs concerning children's private speech: Perspectives from children, parents, and teachers*. Biennial meeting of the Society for Research in Child Development, Tampa, FL (April).

Pennington, B. F. and Ozonoff, S. (1996) Executive dysfunctions and developmental psycho-pathologies. *Journal of Child Psychology and Psychiatry, 37*, 51–87.

Pepperberg, I. M., Brese, K. J. and Harris, B. J. (1991) Solitary sound play during acquisition of English vocalizations by an African Grey parrot (Psittacus erithacus): Possible parallels with children's monologue speech. *Applied Psycholinguistics, 12*(2), 151–78. doi: 10.1017/S0142716400009127.

Piaget, J. (1962) *The Language and Thought of the Child* (trans. M. Gabain). Cleveland, OH: Meridian (original work published 1923).

Russell, J. (ed.) (1997) *Autism as an Executive Disorder*. New York: Oxford University Press.

San Martín Martínez, C., Boada i Calbet, H. and Feigenbaum, P. (2011) Private and inner speech and the regulation of social speech communication. *Cognitive Development, 26*(3), 214–29. doi: 10.1016/j.cogdev.2011.05.001.

Schachar, R., Mota, V. L., Logan, G. D., Tannock, R. and Klim, P. (2000) Confirmation of an inhibitory control deficit in attention-deficit/hyperactivity disorder. *Journal of Abnormal Child Psychology, 28*, 227–35.

Shallice, T. (1982) Specific impairments in planning. *Philosophical Transactions of the Royal Society of London, B298*: 199–209.

Theodorakis, Y., Weinberg, R., Natsis, P., Douma, I. and Kazakas, P. (2000) The effects of motivational versus instructional self-talk on improving motor performance. *Sport Psychologist, 14*, 253–71.

Tod, D., Hardy, J. and Oliver, E. (2011) Effects of self-talk: A systematic review. *Journal of Sport and Exercise Psychology, 33*(5), 666–87.

Vygotsky, L. S. (1962) *Thought and Language* (ed. and trans. E. Hanfmann and G. Vakar). Cambridge, MA: MIT Press (original work published 1934).

Wallace, G. L., Silvers, J. A., Martin, A. and Kenworthy, L. E. (2009) Brief report: Further evidence for inner speech deficits in autism spectrum disorders. *Journal of Autism and Developmental Disorders, 39*(12). doi: 10.1007/s10803-009-0802-8.

Weir, R. H. (1962) *Language in the Crib*. The Hague, Netherlands: Mouton.

Whitehouse, A. J., Maybery, M. T. and Durkin, K. (2006) Inner speech impairments in autism. *Journal of Child Psychology and Psychiatry and Allied Disciplines, 47*(8), 857–65. doi: 10.1111/j.1469-7610.2006.01624.x.

Winsler, A. (1998) Parent–child interaction and private speech in boys with ADHD. *Applied Developmental Science, 2,* 17–39.

Winsler, A. (2009) Still talking to ourselves after all these years: A review of current research on private speech. In A. Winsler, C. Fernyhough, and I. Montero (eds) *Private Speech, Executive Functioning, and the Development of Verbal Self-regulation* (pp. 3–41). New York: Cambridge University Press.

Winsler, A. and Diaz, R. M. (1995) Private speech in the classroom: The effects of activity type, presence of others, classroom context, and mixed-age grouping. *International Journal of Behavioral Development, 18,* 463–88.

Winsler, A. and Naglieri, J. A. (2003) Overt and covert verbal problem-solving strategies: Developmental trends in use, awareness, and relations with task performance in children age 5 to 17. *Child Development, 74,* 659–78.

Winsler, A., Diaz, R. M., McCarthy, E. M., Atencio, D. and Adams Chabay, L. (1999) Mother–child interaction, private speech, and task performance in preschool children with behavior problems. *Journal of Child Psychology and Psychiatry and Allied Disciplines, 40,* 891–904.

Winsler, A., Carlton, M. P. and Barry, M. J. (2000a) Age-related changes in preschool children's systematic use of private speech in a natural setting. *Journal of Child Language, 27,* 665–87.

Winsler, A., Diaz, R. M., Atencio, D. J., McCarthy, E. M. and Adams Chabay, L. (2000b) Verbal self-regulation over time in preschool children at-risk for attention and behavior problems. *Journal of Child Psychology and Psychiatry and Allied Disciplines, 41,* 875–86.

Winsler, A., De León, J. R., Wallace, B., Carlton, M. P. and Willson-Quayle, A. (2003) Private speech in preschool children: Developmental stability and change, across-task consistency, and relations with classroom behavior. *Journal of Child Language, 30,* 583–608.

Winsler, A., Feder, M., Way, E. and Manfra, L. (2006) Maternal beliefs concerning young children's private speech. *Infant and Child Development, 15,* 403–20.

Winsler, A., Manfra, L. and Diaz, R. M. (2007) 'Should I let them talk?' Private speech and task performance among preschool children with and without behavior problems. *Early Childhood Research Quarterly, 22,* 215–31.

Winsler, A., Ducenne, L. and Koury, A. (2011) Singing one's way to self-regulation: The role of early music and movement curricula and private speech. *Early Education and Development, 22,* 274–304.

Zelazo, P. D., and Frye, D. (1998) Cognitive complexity and control: The development of executive function. *Current Directions in Psychological Science, 7,* 121–6.

Zelazo, P. D., and Jacques, S. (1996) Children's rule use: Representation, reflection and cognitive control. *Annals of Child Development, 12,* 119–76.

Zelazo, P. D., Müller, U., Frye, D. and Marcovitch, S. (2003) The development of executive function in early childhood. *Monographs of the Society for Research in Child Development, 68* (3, Serial No. 274).

14

THE DEVELOPMENT OF THEORY OF MIND AND ITS ROLE IN SOCIAL DEVELOPMENT IN EARLY CHILDHOOD

Vickii B. Jenvey and Emma Newton

Introduction

Early childhood (from birth to 8 years) represents a period of rapid growth in physical, cognitive, social and emotional domains of development. The rate and pattern of growth in each domain uniquely and interactively contribute to overall development. Delayed or precocious development in one domain can affect development in other domains. In the cognitive domain, the mentalising abilities that characterise *theory of mind* development influence development in the social domain during early childhood. Theory of mind capacities are especially important to how children make sense of and navigate their social environments and get along with others. This is because theory of mind abilities form the substrate of social cognition, which enables young children to reflect upon their own thoughts, feelings and intentions and communicate with others about their thoughts while at the same time being capable of understanding that others have thoughts, feelings and intentions, and that others' thoughts, feelings and intentions can differ from their own. When children can communicate with others about their own thoughts, feelings and motives and understand these mental states in others, children can adapt to and accommodate others' beliefs and expectations, be mindful of others' emotional states and anticipate certain behaviours of others. Theory of mind development has been linked to children's social development, in relation to, for example, social skills development, peer relationships and empathy development. Despite decades of research on theory of mind development in early childhood, there remain problems with how theory of mind is conceptualised, with methods used to investigate theory of mind in younger children and with delineation of the underlying processes by which theory of mind development influences social development of both typically and non-typically developing children in early childhood.

The nature and development of theory of mind

The term *theory of mind* was first used by primate researchers Premack and Woodruff (1978). These authors showed a short video to a chimpanzee. The video portrayed a caged human, who was trying to reach bananas outside the cage. After chimpanzees watched the video, they were presented with two photographs. One photo portrayed the caged human using a rod to reach the bananas outside his cage, and the other showed the person still reaching for the bananas but without the rod. The chimpanzee consistently chose the photo depicting the caged person solving the problem of how to reach the bananas (Premack and Woodruff, 1978). By consistently choosing the photo depicting the person solving the problem, the authors argued that the chimpanzees appeared to attribute intention to the person's (problem-solving) behaviour. Researchers called the intention inferred from the chimpanzees' choice of photos, *theory of mind*. According to these authors' concept of theory of mind, chimpanzees (and humans) possess mental states themselves and thus were able to impute mental states to others. This system of inferences is viewed as a *theory*, because the imputed mentalising abilities are not directly observable, and because these (mentalising capacities) can be used to make predictions about others' behaviour (Premack and Woodruff, 1978).

The nature of theory of mind

In humans, theory of mind refers to cognitive capacities that develop and enable children to understand that they themselves and others have thoughts, feelings, beliefs and intentions (Flavell, 2004). Young children's thoughts, feelings, beliefs and intentions can be inferred from their actions and statements and accompanying gestures and vocalisations, which they use to communicate to others about what they think, feel, believe or intend to do. That is, children's appraisal of others' actions, statements and accompanying gestures and vocalisations is used to consider others' thoughts, desires and intentions (Astington and Edward, 2010).

The development of theory of mind

In the earliest stages of development, infants seem biologically predisposed to develop the cognitive capacities that embody a theory of mind. Infants display a range of sensory and motor behaviours that lay the foundations for the development of theory of mind (Astington and Edward, 2010; Flavell, 2004). Between one and two months, when infants scan human faces they attend more to eyes and mouths of faces presented to them and have a visual preference for their own mother's face to other unfamiliar faces presented to them (Maurer and Salapatek, 1976). Infants learn quickly to discriminate and attend longer to human voices rather than other sounds, and pay closer attention to familiar voices compared with unfamiliar voices and sounds in their environment (Saffran *et al.*, 2006). Infants also spend more time attending to and tracking humans in motion and upright in preference to stationary or sedentary beings. There is evidence also that they begin to anticipate certain sequences of others' movements (Haith and Benson, 1998). By attending to vocal and facial cues (accompanied by later developing motor behaviours) infants take turns in, for example, peek-a-boo games. All these early infant behaviours in response to familiar people and stimuli in their environment represent the precursors to communicative skills that will be needed for future social interaction (Brooks and Meltzoff, 2005). By 18 months, infants can discriminate between expressions of positive and negative affect, evidenced by the fact that they will only offer food to an adult experimenter towards whom another adult has reacted positively rather than negatively (Repacholi and Gopnik, 1997). When presented with food from an adult towards whom they originally reacted positively, they will continue to react positively to the same adult. This suggests a nascent understanding that others will feel happy when they get what they want. By 3 years, children have vocabularies that include desire terms – 'want', 'need' – and use them correctly in context (Bartsch and Wellman, 2005). They also understand that there is a relationship among desires, emotions and behavioural outcomes (Flavell, 2004).

Between 4 and 5 years, children can demonstrate early visual perspective taking. In experiments, children can identify that another person (or doll prop), who is looking at an object from a different vantage point to their own, will have a different view of that object from their own, given different lines of sight (perspectives) of the two observers. In a social sense, around 4 to 5 years, this development in cognitive ability is manifest in children's awareness that people talk and act from their own viewpoint of how they think the world is, even when their thoughts are not compatible with the reality of the situation (Astington and Edward, 2010).

Somewhere around 5 to 8 years, young children show signs of understanding others' emotional states in that many can respond with their own (congruent) expression of distress when they witness another's distress, and will even attempt to comfort the person who is in distress (Hoffman, 2000). This marks the development of children's ability to understand others' emotional states and to react appropriately to others' attributed emotional states. Such responsive actions represent some of earliest manifestations of empathy in young children (Hoffman, 2000; Knafo *et al.*, 2008). Congruent displays of affect have been documented among children aged 5 to 8 in response to a range of emotional displays (for example, happiness, anger and fear) of others (Knafo *et al.*, 2008).

The role of language in theory of mind development

Children's understanding of others' interior lives develops and is consolidated through social interaction with others, a process that relies heavily on conversational exchange between children and others in their social environments (Astington and Baird, 2005). Developments in language also help children's representational development (Astington and Baird, 2005; Piaget, 1953), supporting the ability to self-talk and reflect verbally on conversations with others that take place in the context of social events and encounters. The contribution of language to theory of mind development is clearly enhanced by modelling, direct instruction and opportunities for conversations with parents and family members and others in home or preschool.

Pretence, play and theory-of-mind development in early childhood

Pretend play involves non-literality, and objects and actions are used by children in unintended ways. For example, a child may use a stick to depict a 'fairy wand' or a 'gun'. In pretence, children may also adopt exaggerated gestures, vocalisations and changes to their posture and gait. The effect of pretence is to project or create a non-literal context in which children may include both real and imagined themes. Pretend play can be solitary or social, and take place with or without toys and props. The frequency of pretend play peaks between 3 to 5 years during early childhood. Social pretend play that involves dyadic or group role assignment and theme setting and enactment appears to entail well-developed social capabilities, such as joint proposal, complex language usage and reaction to observed and anticipated actions of others in the play frame (Jenvey and Jenvey, 2002; Turnbull and Jenvey, 2006). It is not surprising, therefore, that pretend play in preschool children has often been linked to the development of theory of mind in young children (Lillard *et al.*, 2013). While an association between theory of mind and pretence seem plausible, empirical attempts to demonstrate an association have yielded conflicting results (Lillard *et al.*, 2013). The ability to represent an idea mentally and think about a situation from more than one perspective (i.e. meta-representation) is common to pretend play and theory of mind abilities (Lillard, 1998). During pretend play children often practise taking another's perspectives (social meta-representation) (Astington and Jenkins, 1999; Lillard, 1998). Meta-representation is also required for theory of mind, although there is debate about whether pretence assists theory of mind development or vice versa (Astington and Jenkins, 1999; Lillard, 1998), or whether pretence is associated with theory of mind development at all (Jenvey, 2013; Newton and Jenvey, 2011). Paradoxically, children can pretend as early as two years but typically they do not pass false belief tasks until 4 to 5 years (Lillard, 1998). Others argue that children do appear to understand mental representation from a young age (see, for example, Harris, 1992; Leslie, 1994) and only have difficulties passing false belief tasks because of the nature of the tasks. Perhaps younger children fail false belief tasks because of their level of language development rather than yet-to-be-developed theory of mind capacities. Still other researchers suggest that children may understand pretence as 'acting-as-if' rather than having developed the underlying mentalising abilities. This then enables very young children to participate in pretence before they acquire certain theory of mind skills (Lillard, 1998). Only when children can pass theory of mind tasks can they understand mental representations (Lillard, 1998).

It is also unclear whether type or frequency of pretend play is related to theory of mind. For example, Astington and Jenkins (1995) found that the numbers of joint proposals and role assignments during pretend play were associated with greater success in passing false belief tasks, and, in a longitudinal study, more pretend play role enactments in earlier years of development were related to performance on false belief tasks in later years of children's development (Youngblade and Dunn, 1995). On the other hand, no significant associations were found between false belief task performance and either solitary or social pretend play (Schwebel *et al.*, 1999). In another study, there was a significant association between fantasy play and combined theory of mind scores of 4-year-old children but not for 3-year-olds (Taylor and Carlson, 1997). Despite the ubiquity of other play forms such as locomotor play and exploratory play among preschoolers (Pellegrini and Smith, 1998), few studies have investigated play forms other than pretence in relation to preschoolers' theory of mind abilities.

It is likely that some of these conflicting results may be because of methodologies used in the different studies, including observations of individual children in contrived (experimental) situations and the focus on solitary pretend play, without considering other play forms or play that occurs when children interact with their peers in familiar (home, school) or unfamiliar settings. Fewer researchers have focused on the potential influence of environments (e.g. home or preschool) where play occurs, or the social compositions (alone or with other children) or play types (e.g. pretend or activity) which might affect young children's performance on theory of mind tasks (Newton and Jenvey, 2011).

In order to address many of the shortfalls in previous research, the authors completed a study in which we included observations of preschool children's (4–5 years) different forms of play (activity or pretence), social composition of play (alone or with other children) and use of props and equipment during play episodes, children's combined performance on standard theory of mind tasks (Gopnik and Astington (1988) representational change task) and children's language skills. These independent variables were then examined in relation to children's social competence and antisocial behaviours in different social settings (home and school) (rated by parents and preschool teachers, respectively on PKBS-2 (Merrell, 2002)). Although children's performance on theory of mind tasks increased with age, there was no association found between theory of mind scores and social competence. Neither was pretend nor activity play associated with social competence. These results should be considered as valid, given that all children were assessed as having normal language development for their age and sex, and children's engagement in other play types in addition to pretend play were documented. Children who played frequently with other children (social play) were more socially competent, but children who most often played alone (solitary play) were less socially competent. Thus, what was significant about play for children's developing social competence was how frequently children initiated and engaged in play with their peers. Playing with other children was associated more with social development in young children than their theory of mind development.

It is important to consider what aspects of sociable play might contribute to children's early social development, or how not playing with other children might contribute to difficulties in social behaviour. In earlier work (Jenvey and Jenvey, 2002; Turnbull and Jenvey, 2006), when shown video excerpts of children's solitary and social pretend and activity play, both adults and children described social pretend play as language practice, e.g. 'they need to talk about what/how they're going to play' (child, 5 years) and e.g. 'important for communication between the players' (adult teacher), friendship and cooperation – e.g. 'getting along with other kids' (child, 8 years), 'they need to be able to take turns and get along with others' (adult) or pretend play was only played with close friends, e.g. 'They're good friends to play like that, play those games' (child, 7 years). Such statements suggest that both children and adults believe social pretend play with others (with or without props) was an activity (a) that involved cooperation, (b) communication and (c) intimacy among the players. Perhaps forms of social pretend play may offer social contexts where developing mentalising abilities are consolidated, and may be an important precursor or adjunct to developing theory of mind skills in early childhood. Longitudinal, multi-method (observation, interviews and adult reports) research designs could begin to delineate any associations between pretend play and theory of mind development in young children.

Assessment of theory of mind in early childhood

In contemporary developmental psychology, theory of mind abilities in children are commonly determined by children's performance on so-called *first* and *second order tasks*. Standard first order tasks, known as *false belief* tasks, involve identification and articulation of another person's thoughts or beliefs about an event that has occurred (Perner and Wimmer, 1985). A classic false belief task is the unexpected contents task, the so-called *Smarties task*. Children are shown a closed Smarties™ (small, choco-late sweets, with multi-coloured coatings) box and asked what they think is inside. It is then revealed that the box contains coloured pencils. The box is closed. Before it is reopened, children are asked again what they think will be in the box (representa-tional change question) and what another child/toy, who has not seen what is really in the Smarties box, might think is inside the box (false belief question). Other first order tasks require young children to distinguish between appearance and reality (Wimmer and Perner, 1983). Most children 'pass' the Smarties test between 3 and 5 years.

All types of theory of mind tasks are correlated and it is thus argued that the vari-ous tasks all appear to be measuring the same underlying skill (Astington and Jenkins, 1995). In studies where differences were found, it has been shown that the ability to pass false belief tasks in which an understanding of representational change was assessed develops later in children (closer to 5 years). Accordingly, these tasks are often used in studies of older preschool children (5 years or older) to detect ceiling effects in theory of mind task performance (Gopnik and Astington, 1998). Results of other studies suggest that performance on false belief tasks are more predictive of emotional understanding (Slomkowski and Dunn, 1996) and thus are included more frequently in studies investigating social skill development in children.

First order theory of mind begins to develop between 3 and 5 years in typically developing children, with more reliable theory of mind performance increasing with age (e.g. Gopnik *et al.*, 1994). However, some 5-year-old children may still have difficulties with false belief understanding (Battacchi *et al.*, 1997). Although some studies show that boys and girls do not differ in their ability to pass theory-of-mind tasks (e.g. Sperling *et al.*, 2000), others have found differences in performance between the sexes (e.g. Walker, 2005).

Understanding that people can think about other people's thoughts is a more advanced form of theory of mind and is clearly important for social interaction. This understanding develops between 6 and 7 years and is incorporated into second order tasks (Perner and Wimmer, 1985). Understanding of *faux pas* (e.g. a social blunder) develops later, in middle childhood, between 9 and 11 years (Baron-Cohen *et al.*, 1999). The majority of children aged 10 to 11 perform successfully on *third order* theory-of-mind tasks, while a minority perform successfully on *fourth order* theory of mind tasks (Liddle and Nettle, 2006). There is emerging evidence to suggest that theory of mind abilities continue to develop throughout adolescence (Burnett and Blakemore, 2009). In recognition of the age-related trend in theory of mind development from infancy through adolescence, Wellman and Liu (2004) proposed a five step development of theory-of-mind understanding. In order, children master theory-of-mind concepts thus:

1   diverse desires (e.g. that other people may prefer to have different things (i.e. food preference) than what the child would like for him/herself)
2   diverse beliefs (e.g. that people can hold different opinions about a situation and both options are possibly true)
3   knowledge access (e.g. that people know things once they see them, but without seeing something they will not be aware)
4   false belief (e.g. that people can hold beliefs that are invalid)
5   hidden emotions (e.g. that people have the potential to hide their feelings by controlling their facial expressions and body language).

Progression to a higher step implies that children have mastered the preceding steps.

There is some evidence to suggest differences in the sequence of acquisition among different cultural groups. For example, Iranian and Chinese children seem to acquire the five levels in a different order to children from North American populations (Shahaeian *et al.*, 2011). A sixth step has since been added and is measured by children's performance in response to a *sarcasm task*. This sixth step was demonstrated reliably because many 9-year-old children experienced difficulties in understanding requirements to succeed on the sarcasm task (Peterson *et al.*, 2012).

Although the classical theory of mind tests, such as the false belief task and appearance-reality tasks, are still widely used in theory of mind research, debate persists among researchers about how well these much used tests actually measure metacognitive abilities, especially in young children (Flavell, 2004). Perhaps it is not the tests *per se* that are problematic but how researchers interpret the research findings (Astington and Edward, 2010).

Theory of mind and its role in the development of social competence in young children

Social skills and social competence in early childhood

Social competence is often characterised as the successful social functioning of individuals with their peers (Howes, 1987). Social skills facilitate effective social interactions and are deployed by children in response to the social demands of their environments. Social competencies allow young children to interact appropriately with others (Merrell and Caldarella, 2002). Lack of appropriate social skills acts as a barrier to successful social interaction in young children. Difficulties in social situations during early childhood are indicative of early developmental problems, such as inhibition and shyness or externalising (e.g. aggression) behaviours in early and later stages of development (Merrell and Caldarella, 2002). The ability of children to successfully interact with peers and adults in social situations and to display positive social skills assists them in coping with stressful situations, and may prevent the emergence of behavioural and emotional problems in later stages of development (Garmezy, 1991).

Theory of mind development and its association with social competence

As mentioned previously, the development of theory of mind has been linked to the development of socially competent behaviour in young children and theory of mind is often described as critical to appropriate social development in early childhood (Astington and Edward, 2010, Flavell, 2004).

Theory of mind and social competence

In earlier section of this chapter, the early, antecedent perceptual and motor, cognitive and language skills of theory of mind development were discussed. These early skills have been argued to be significant precursors to later-stage social development and suggest that human infants are biologically predisposed to adapt to their social environment. During the early years, children begin to develop early stage mental state understanding, and their language begins to reflect this understanding (Brown and Dunn, 1991). Behaviours indicative of theory of mind development in young children are associated with the development of social interaction skills (Brown and Dunn, 1991). These basic foundations prepare children for adaptation to the more structured social environment of preschool.

For many young children, preschool is the first significant social environment they experience beyond their home and family, and in which they need to respond to others' demands. Children need both to seek and attend to instructions from teachers and carers and respond to the requests of peers, e.g. for help or sharing toys or turn-taking on equipment (Anthony *et al.*, 2005). During this period, playing with other children provides young children with opportunities to acquire social skills, interaction abilities and develop friendships, all important steps for future successful interpersonal relationships (Howes, 1987; Ladd, 2006). During this preschool period, in concert with social skill development, children's cognitive abilities (thinking, remembering, reasoning and language mastery) and particularly their theory of mind abilities develop (Astington, 1993) and contribute significantly to the development of social competence (Astington and Edward, 2010).

Because of their increasing cognitive maturity, children in later stages of early childhood (6 to 8 years) understand more clearly how to initiate and maintain peer relationships and spend more time interacting with their peers (Ladd, 1999). The cognitive accomplishments of early childhood and early middle childhood (8 to 10 years) enable children to anticipate the behaviour of others, understand and respond to feelings and thoughts, and react with appropriate social behaviours and skills (Green and Rechis, 2006). Increasing development of more advanced theory of mind abilities enables children to conduct an internal dialogue, which allows them to think about other people's thoughts. For example, around 6 to 7 years old, children think about how others might feel in a given situation and anticipate how others are likely to respond. This enables children to adapt their own behaviours in response to anticipated behaviour of others (Perner and Wimmer, 1985). These skills continue to develop through middle childhood and adolescence (Baron-Cohen et al., 1999). Beginning in early childhood, such mentalising abilities characteristic of theory of mind development contribute to future social achievements of understanding, for example, the need to compromise with others, to become trustworthy, display empathy to others and help when others experience difficulty. Each of these social achievements predict stable and harmonious friendships in primary school and signify social competence, all of which are related to theory of mind development in earlier stages of development (Warnes et al., 2005).

Using observations in natural settings, Astington and Jenkins (1995) reported associations among theory of mind performance and joint proposals and explicit role assignments during social interactions among preschool-aged children. In another study, a positive association was found between false belief task performance and teacher ratings of children's social skills, when controlling for age and language ability. However, false-belief understanding was not associated with peer ratings of popularity (Watson et al., 1999).

Other studies indicate that only specific components of social skilfulness were associated with theory of mind task performance. For example, the ability to coordinate peer interactions, a component of social skill behaviour, was associated with successful performance by children on false belief tasks (Slomkowski and Dunn, 1996). Similarly, teacher ratings of 3-year-olds' social-emotional skills and behaviours were associated with false belief task performance, but only for behavioural items classified as *intentional* (i.e. those relating to an understanding of others' beliefs and feelings) (Lalonde and Chandler, 1995). *Conventional* items, incorporating children's use of social conventions and self-control, were not found to be associated with performance on false belief tasks. These results support propositions of age-related stages of theory of mind abilities (Lalonde and Chandler, 1995).

In contrast, other researchers have found no association between theory of mind task performance and social competence development. Additionally, there were no significant differences between children identified as *peer rejected* and children rated by peers to have *average* popularity and their ability to pass theory of mind tasks (see, for example, Badenes *et al.*, 2000).

There are also potential sex differences in associations between theory of mind task performance and social competence. In one study, ability to pass theory of mind tasks was associated with aggressive and disruptive behaviour in boys, but with prosocial behaviour in girls (Walker, 2005).

Studies in this area contain equivocal findings, perhaps because many studies have not used standardised measure of social skills that could assess all areas of preschool children's social skilfulness, including social cooperation, social interaction and social independence. Other studies have failed to control for language and/or verbal abilities, although both have been linked to social competence in young children (e.g. Doctoroff *et al.*, 2006) and studies of preschool-aged children have found associations between language ability and theory of mind task performance (see, for example, Astington and Jenkins, 1999; Hughes and Dunn, 1997). This has led some researchers to assert that children will not pass false belief tasks before they attain an appropriate level of language development (Jenkins and Astington, 1996).

Language ability has also contributed to outcomes of studies that have investigated associations between theory of mind and social competence. For example, in two studies examining the relationship between theory of mind and peer acceptance in preschool children, one study found theory of mind ability was related to peer acceptance, and popular children scored higher on theory of mind tasks than rejected children (Slaughter *et al.*, 2002). In the other study, when verbal ability was controlled, there was no significant relationship between theory of mind ability and children's peer status (Slaughter *et al.*, 2002). Additionally, there was no association between theory of mind ability and young children's prosocial behaviour when both age and verbal ability were controlled (Slaughter *et al.*, 2002). Findings indicate that age may also play a role, because theory of mind ability is associated with peer acceptance in children older than 5 years but not in children younger than that (Slaughter *et al.*, 2002). Despite claims that language ability may affect associations between social competence and theory of mind in children, there is some evidence of an association between theory of mind and social competence, independent of children's language development (see, for example, Watson *et al.*, 1999).

Developmental studies in this area have repeatedly utilised 'standard' theory of mind tasks, which, as reported earlier, are reliant on children's verbal capabilities (Astington and Jenkins, 1999). In future research, it will be important to examine the associations between theory of mind tasks performance and young children's social competence by utilising tests that are less reliant on children's language development and verbal skills. An example of a theory of mind test developed to minimise children's reliance on language and verbal skills to follow test instructions and answer experimenter questions is the mechanical analogue test developed by Baron-Cohen (1995) to assess theory of mind in developmentally delayed children with autism spectrum disorders. Such studies may help to better understand the proposed associations between theory of mind and social competence, without children's verbal ability differentially affecting the results.

Owing to the complex and conflicting research findings, more research is needed to determine the actual nature of associations between theory of mind and social competence in young children. Future research should include age and verbal ability controls, and be mindful of sex differences. Furthermore, choice of a valid measure of social skills and social competence and its component skills is warranted. Such additions and controls might lead to more consistent findings about the role of theory of mind in social competence development in early childhood. Furthermore, various informants (i.e. peers, parents or teachers) and contexts (i.e. home or school) could be used in future research designs to reflect the finding that children's social competencies are strongly influenced by the social context in which they are measured (Newton, 2012). As mentioned earlier in this chapter, to establish the nature and extent of mentalising abilities in the development of social competence in early childhood, longitudinal designs are needed in future studies. It is likely that a bi-directional relationship might exist between theory of mind skills and social competence. That is, while the ability to pass theory of mind tasks may be related to social skill development in early childhood, socially competent behaviours may also lead to advanced mentalising abilities that enable quite young and socially competent children to succeed on theory of mind tasks.

Theory of mind and social competence in young children with developmental delays and disorders

There are many studies of theory of mind and social development in young children with autism spectrum disorders (ASDs). For example, Perner *et al.* (1989) found that autistic children, known to have difficulties with social interaction, do not gain the ability to pass false belief tasks until approximately 13 years. Other studies have shown theory of mind deficits in children with ASDs (Buitelaar *et al.*, 1999). Others have demonstrated that children aged 3–12 years with autism develop theory of mind skills in a different sequence from their typically developing peers (Peterson *et al.*, 2012).

Difficulties with passing theory of mind problems have also been noted for young children with other behavioural and emotional difficulties. For example, theory of mind delays were found in toddlers with behavioural problems (Hughes and Ensor, 2006) and 'hard to manage' or disruptive preschool aged children (Hughes *et al.*, 1998). Children with attention deficit hyperactivity disorder (ADHD) and autism spectrum disorders have been found to have similar delays in theory of mind capacities measured by performances on first and second order tasks (Buitelaar *et al.*, 1999). Despite these findings, others report that young children 'at risk for ADHD', based on their current difficult behaviour (Perner *et al.*, 2002), and children with conduct disorder (Buitelaar, *et al.*, 1999) did not have significant difficulties.

Conclusion

There is abundant evidence that, during the period of early childhood development, most children develop theory of mind abilities in a temporally predictable sequence. Existing evidence demonstrates that, once developed, these cognitive capacities enable young children to understand and reflect upon their own thoughts, beliefs, desires, emotions and intentions and understand and attribute those mental states to others. There is evidence for biological origins of theory of mind, and these are evident in perceptual and motor precursors in early infancy. It is argued that particular early perceptual and motor behaviours in infancy enable the biologically immature infant, from the earliest stages, to adapt to certain social cues in their environments. In addition to early biological responsiveness, there is also evidence that practice, social feedback and language development, and perhaps engagement in pretend play facilitate children's theory of mind development during early childhood. Almost all leading developmental researchers propose a relationship between theory of mind development and social competence in early childhood. Conflicting results in these studies may be attributed to inconsistencies in definition, operationalisation and measurement of social development in early childhood, in addition to problems with measuring theory of mind dichotomously (pass/fail) on traditional theory of mind tasks. There is also evidence that theory of mind delays are related to delayed social development and social difficulties among children with certain developmental delays and disorders. Potential directions are suggested for future investigations of associations between theory of mind and social competence development in early childhood. Future directions need to include longitudinal research designs that include multi-method approaches to data collection and more rigorous operationalisation of concepts to be investigated.

References

Antony, L. G., Antony, B. G., Glanville, D., Naiman, D. Q., Waanders, C. and Shaffers, S. (2005) The relationship between stress, parenting behaviour and preschoolers' social competence and behavioural problems in the classroom. *Infant and Child Development*, 14, 133–54.

Astington, J. W. (1993) *The Child's Discovery of the Mind*. Cambridge, MA: Harvard University Press.

Astington, J. W. (2003) Sometimes necessary, never sufficient: False belief-understanding and social competence. In B. Repacholi and V. Slaughter (eds) *Individual Differences in Theory of Mind* (pp. 13–38). New York: Psychology Press.

Astington, J. W. and Baird, J. A. (eds) (2005) *Why Language Matters for Theory of Mind*. New York: Oxford University Press.

Astington, J. W. and Edward, J. (2010) The development of theory of mind in early childhood. In R. E. Tremblay, M. Boivin and R. deV. Peters (eds) *Encyclopedia on Early Child Development* (online). Montreal, Quebec: Centre of Excellence for Early Childhood Development and Strategic Knowledge Cluster on Early Child Development, 1–7. Available at: www.child-encyclopedia.com/documents/Astington-EdwardANGxp.pdf (accessed 23/07/13).

Astington, J. W. and Jenkins, J. M. (1995) Theory of mind and social understanding. *Cognition and Emotion*, 9(2–3), 151–65.

Astington, J. W. and Jenkins, J. M. (1999) A longitudinal study of the relation between language and theory-of-mind development. *Developmental Psychology*, 35, 1311–20.

Badenes, L. V., Estevan, R. A. C. and Bacete, F. J. G. (2000) Theory of mind and peer rejection at school. *Social Development, 9*, 271–83.

Baron-Cohen, S., O'Riordan, M., Stone, V., Jones, R. and Plaisted, K. (1999) Recognition of faux pas by normally developing children and children with Asperger syndrome or high-functioning autism. *Journal of Autism and Developmental Disorders, 29*(5), 407–18.

Bartsch, K. and Wellman, H. M. (1995) *Children Talk About the Mind*. New York: Oxford University Press.

Battacchi, M. W., Celani, G. and Bertocchi, A. (1997) The influence of personal involvement on the performance in a false belief task: A structural analysis. *International Journal of Behavioral Development, 21*(2), 313–29.

Beauchamp, M. H. and Anderson, V. (2010) SOCIAL: An integrative framework for the development of social skills. *Psychological Bulletin, 136*(1), 39–64.

Bijlstra, G., Holland, R. W. and Wigboldus, D. H. J. (2010) The social face of emotion recognition: Evaluations versus stereotypes. *Journal of Experimental Social Psychology, 46*, 657–63.

Blakemore, S.-J. (2010) The developing social brain: Implications for education. *Neuron, 65*(6), 744–47.

Bower, B. (1993) A child's theory of mind: Mental life may change radically around age 4. *Science News*, 17 July. Science Services Inc.

Brooks, R. and Meltzoff, A. (2005) The development of gaze following and its relationship to language. *Developmental Science, 8*, 535–43.

Bowler, D. M., Briskman, J., Gurvidi, N. and Fornells-Ambrojo, M. (2005) Understanding the mind or predicting signal-dependent action? Performance of children with and without autism on analogues of the false-belief task. *Journal of Cognition and Development, 6*, 259–83.

Brown, J. R. and Dunn, J. (1991) 'You can cry, mum': The social and developmental implications of talk about internal states. *British Journal of Developmental Psychology, 9*(2), 237–56.

Brüne, M. (2000) Neoteny, psychiatric disorders and the social brain: Hypotheses on heterochrony and the modularity of the mind. *Anthropology and Medicine, 7*(3), 301–18.

Brüne, M. and Brüne-Cohrs, U. (2006) Theory of mind – evolution, ontogeny, brain mechanisms and psychopathology. *Neuroscience and Biobehavioral Reviews, 30*(4), 437–55.

Buitelaar, J. K., van der Wees, M., Swaab-Barneveld, H. and Jan van der Gaag, R. (1999) Theory of mind and emotion-recognition functioning in autistic spectrum disorders and in psychiatric control and normal children. *Development and Psychopathology, 11*(1), 39–58.

Burnett, S. and Blakemore, S.-J. (2009) The development of adolescent social cognition. *Annals of the New York Academy of Science, 1167*, 51–56.

Carpenter, M., Nagell, K. and Tomasello, M. (1998) Social cognition, joint attention, and communicative competence from 9–15 months of age. *Monographs of the Society for Research in Child Development, 63*(4), Serial No. 255.

Charman, T., Ruffman, T. and Clements, W. (2002) Is there a gender difference in false belief development? *Social Development, 11*, 1–10.

Connolly, J. A. and Doyle, A. B. (1984) Relation of social fantasy play to social competence in preschoolers. *Developmental Psychology, 20*, 797–806.

Cutting, A. L. and Dunn, J. (1999) Theory of mind, emotion understanding, language, and family background: Individual differences and interrelations. *Child Development, 70*(4), 853–65.

Dack, L. A. and Astington, J. W. (2011) Deontic and epistemic reasoning in children. *Journal of Experimental Child Psychology, 110*, 94–114. doi: 10.1016/j.jecp.2011.04.003.

Doctoroff, G. L., Greer, J. A. and Arnold, D. H. (2006) The relationship between social behaviour and emergent literacy among preschool boys and girls. *Applied Developmental Psychology, 27*, 1–13.

Elliot, S. N., Barnard, J. and Gresham, F. M. (1989) Preschoolers' social behavior: Teachers' and parents' assessments. *Journal of Psychoeducational Assessment, 7*, 223–34.

Filippova, E. and Astington, J. W. (2009) Further development in social reasoning revealed in discourse irony understanding. *Child Development, 79*(1), 126–38. doi: 0009-3920/2008/7901-0009.

Flavell, J. H. (2004) Theory-of-mind development: Retrospect and prospect. *Merril-Palmer Quarterly, 50*(3), 274–90.

Fraser, M. W., Galinsky, M. J., Smokowski, P. R., Day, S. H., Terzian, M. A., Rose, R. A. *et al.* (2005) Social information-processing skills training to promote social competence and prevent aggressive behavior in the third grades. *Journal of Consulting and Clinical Psychology, 73*, 1045–55.

Frith, C. D. and Frith, U. (2007) Social cognition in humans. *Current Biology, 17*(16), 724–32.

Garmezy, N. (1991) Resiliency and vulnerability to adverse developmental outcomes associated with poverty. *American Behavioral Scientist, 34*, 416–30.

Gopnik, A. and Astington, J. W. (1988) Children's understanding of representational change and its relation to the understanding of false belief and the appearance-reality distinction. *Child Development, 59*(1), 26–37.

Gopnik, A., Slaughter, V. and Meltzoff, A. (1994) Changing your views: How understanding visual perception can lead to a new theory of the mind. In C. Lewis and P. Mitchell (eds) *Children's Early Understanding of Mind: Origins and Development* (pp. 157–81). Hove, East Sussex, UK: Erlbaum.

Green, V. A. and Rechis, R. (2006) Children's cooperative and competitive interactions in limited resource situations: A literature review. *Journal of Applied Developmental Psychology, 27*(1), 42–59.

Haith, M. M. and Benson, J. (1998) Infant cognition. In D. Kuhn and R. Siegler (eds) *Handbook of Child Psychology, Vol. 2: Cognition, Perception and Language*. New York: Wiley.

Harris, P. L. (1992) From simulation to folk psychology: The case for development. *Mind and Language, 7*(1–2), 120–44.

Harris, P. L. (2000) *The Work of the Imagination*. Oxford: Blackwell.

Hoffman, M. (2000) *Empathy and Moral Development: Implications for Caring and Justice.* Cambridge: Cambridge University Press.

Howes, C. (1987) Social competence with peers in young children: Developmental sequences. *Developmental Review, 7*, 252–72.

Hughes, C. and Dunn, J. (1997) 'Pretend you didn't know': Preschoolers' talk about mental states in pretend play. *Cognitive Development, 12*, 477–99.

Hughes, C. and Ensor, R. (2006) Behavioural problems in 2-year-olds: Links with individual differences in theory of mind, executive function and harsh parenting. *Journal of Child Psychology and Psychiatry, 47*(5), 488–97.

Hughes, C., Dunn, J. and White, A. (1998) Trick or treat? Uneven understanding of mind and emotion and executive dysfunction in 'hard-to-manage' preschoolers. *Journal of Child Psychology and Psychiatry and Allied Disciplines, 39*(7), 981–94.

Hughes, C., Deater-Deckard, K. and Cutting, A. L. (1999) 'Speak roughly to your little boy?' Sex differences in the relations between parenting and preschoolers' understanding of mind. *Social Development, 8*, 143–60.

Jenkins, J. M. and Astington, J. W. (1996) Cognitive factors and family structure associated with theory of mind development in young children. *Developmental Psychology, 32*, 70–8.

Jenkins, J. M. and Astington, J. W. (2000) Theory of mind and social behavior: Causal models tested in a longitudinal study. *Merrill-Palmer Quarterly, 46*, 203–20.

Jenvey, V. B. (2013) Play and disability. In R. E. Tremblay. M. Boivin and R. DeV. Peters (eds) *Encyclopedia on Early Childhood Development* (online). Montreal, Quebec: Centre for Excellence in Early Child Development, 1–6. Available at: www.child encyclopedia.com/document/JenveyANGxp.pdf (accessed 17/08/2013).

Jenvey, V. B. and Jenvey, H. L. (2002) Criteria used by children to categorise subtypes of play: Preliminary findings. *Social Behavior and Personality, 30*(8), 731–7.

Knafo, A., Zahn-waxler, C., Van Hulle, C., Robinson, J. and Rhee, S.-H. (2008) The developmental origins of a disposition toward empathy: Genetic and environmental contributions. *Emotion, 8*(6), 737–52.

Ladd, G. W. (1999) Peer relationships and social competence during early and middle childhood. *Annual Review of Psychology, 50*, 333–59.

Ladd, G. W. (2006) *Peer Relations and Social Competence of Children and Adolescents*. New Haven, CT: Yale University Press.

Lalonde, C. E. and Chandler, M. J. (1995) False belief understanding goes to school: On the social-emotional consequences of coming early or late to a first theory of mind. *Cognition and Emotion, 9*, 167–85.

Leslie, A. M. (1987) Pretense and representation: The origins of 'theory of mind'. *Psychological Review, 94*(4), 412–26.

Leslie, A. M. (1994) Pretending and believing: Issues in the theory of ToM. *Cognition, 50*(1–3), 211–38.

Liddle, B. and Nettle, D. (2006) Higher-order theory of mind and social competence in school-age children. *Journal of Cultural and Evolutionary Psychology, 4*(3–4), 231–46.

Lillard, A. S. (1993a) Pretend play skills and the child's theory of mind. *Child Development, 64*(2), 348–71.

Lillard, A. S. (1993b) Young children's conceptualization of pretense: Action or mental representational state? *Child Development, 64*, 372–86.

Lillard, A. S. (1998) Playing with a theory of mind. In O. N. Saracho and B. Spodek (eds) *Multiple Perspectives on Play in Early Childhood Education* (pp. 11–33). Albany, NY: State University of New York Press.

Lillard, A. S. and Flavell, J. H. (1992) Young children's understanding of different mental states. *Developmental Psychology, 28*, 626–34.

Lillard, A., Lerner, M., Hopkins, R., Dore, R., Smith, E. and Palmquist, M. (2013) The impact of pretend play on children's development: A review of evidence. *Psychological Bulletin, 139*(1), 1–34.

Maurer, D. and Salapatek, P. (1976) Developmental changes in the scanning of faces by young infants. *Child Development, 47*, 523–27.

Merrell, K. W. (1995) An investigation of the relationship between social skills and internalizing problems in early childhood: Construct validity of the preschool and kindergarten behavior scales. *Journal of Psychoeducational Assessment, 13*, 230–40.

Merrell, K. W. and Caldarella, P. (2002) *Home and Community Social Behavior Scales*. Eugene, OR: Assessment-Intervention Resources.

Newton, E. and Jenvey, V. B. (2011) Play and theory of mind: Associations with social competence in young children. *Early Child Development and Care, 181*(6), 761–73.

Newton, E. (2012) Theory of mind, emotion recognition and temperament: Associations with social functioning and mental health problems in adolescents. Unpublished D. Psych thesis, Monash University, Clayton, Victoria, Australia.

Pellegrini, A. D. and Smith, P. K. (1998) Physical activity play: The nature and function of a neglected aspect of playing. *Child Development, 69*(3), 577–98.

Perner, J. (1992) Grasping the concept of representation: Its impact on 4-year-olds' theory of mind and beyond. *Human Development, 35*, 146–55.

Perner, J. and Wimmer, H. (1985) 'John thinks that Mary thinks that …': Attribution of second-order beliefs by 5- to 10-year-old children. *Journal of Experimental Child Psychology, 39*(3), 437–71.

Perner, J., Frith, U., Leslie, A. M. and Leekam, S. R. (1989) Exploration of the autistic child's theory of mind: Knowledge, belief, and communication. *Child Development, 60*, 689–700.

Perner, J., Kain, W. and Barchfeld, P. (2002) Executive control and higher-order theory of mind in children at risk of ADHD. *Infant and Child Development, 11*, 141–58.

Peterson, C. C., Wellman, H. M. and Slaughter, V. (2012) The mind behind the message: Advancing theory-of-mind scales for typically developing children, and those with deafness, autism, or Asperger syndrome. *Child Development, 83*(2), 469–85.

Piaget, J. (1953) *The Origin of Intelligence in the Child* (trans. M. Cook). London: Routledge and Kegan Paul (original work published 1936).

Premack, D. and Woodruff, G. (1978) Does the chimpanzee have a 'theory of mind'? *Behavioral and Brain Sciences, 1*(4): 515–26.

Repacholi, B. M. and Gopnik, A. (1997) Early reasoning about desires: Evidence from 14- and 18-month olds. *Developmental Psychology, 33*, 12–21.

Saffran, J. R., Werker, J. and Werner, L. A. (2006) The infant's auditory world. In D. Kuhn and R. Siegler (eds) *Handbook of Child Psychology*, Vol. 2: *Cognition, perception and language*, 6th edn. New York, NY: Wiley.

Schwebel, D. C., Rosen, C. S. and Singer, J. L. (1999) Preschoolers' pretend play and theory of mind: The role of jointly constructed pretence. *British Journal of Developmental Psychology, 17*, 333–48.

Shahaeian, A., Peterson, C. C., Slaughter, V. and Wellman, H. M. (2011) Culture and the sequence of steps in theory of mind development. *Developmental Psychology, 47*(5), 1239–47.

Sheridan, S. M. and Walker, D. (1999) Social skills in context: Considerations for assessment, intervention, and generalization. In C. R. Reynolds and T. B. Gutkin (eds) *The Handbook of School Psychology*, 3rd edn (pp. 686–708). New York: Wiley.

Slaughter, V., Dennis, M. J. and Pritchard, M. (2002) Theory of mind and peer acceptance in preschool children. *British Journal of Developmental Psychology, 20*, 545–64.

Slomkowski, C. and Dunn, J. (1996) Young children's understanding of other people's beliefs and feelings and their connected communication with friends. *Developmental Psychology, 32*, 442–47.

Smith, P. K. (ed.) (1986) *Children's Play: Research Developments and Practical Applications*. New York: Gordon and Breach Science Publishers.

Sperling, R. A., Walls, R. T. and Hill, L. A. (2000) Early relationships among self-regulatory constructs: Theory of mind and preschool children's problem solving. *Child Study Journal, 30*, 233–52.

Symons, D., McLaughlin, E., Moore, C. and Morine, S. (1997) Integrating relationship constructs and emotional experience into false belief tasks in preschool children. *Journal of Experimental Child Psychology, 67*, 423–47.

Taylor, M. and Carlson, S. M. (1997) The relation between individual differences in fantasy and theory of mind. *Child Development, 68*, 436–55.

Turnbull, J. and Jenvey, V. B. (2006) Criteria used by adults and children to categorize subtypes of play. *Early Child Development and Care, 176*(5) 539–51.

Walker, S. (2005) Gender differences in the relationship between young children's peer-related social competence and individual differences in theory of mind. *Journal of Genetic Psychology, 166*, 297–312.

Warnes, E. D., Sheridan, S. M., Geske, J. and Warnes, W. A. (2005) A contextual approach to the assessment of social skills: Identifying meaningful behaviors for social competence. *Psychology in the Schools, 42*(2), 173–87.

Watson, A. C., Nixon, C. L., Wilson, A. and Capage, L. (1999) Social interaction skills and theory of mind in young children. *Developmental Psychology, 35*, 386–91.

Wellman, H. M., Cross, D. and Watson, J. (2001) Meta-analysis of theory-of-mind development: The truth about false belief. *Child Development, 72*, 655–84.

Wellman, H. M., Fang, F. and Peterson, C. C. (2011) Sequential progressions in a theory-of-mind scale: Longitudinal perspectives. *Child Development, 82*(3), 780–92.

Wellman, H. M. and Liu, D. (2004) Scaling of theory-of-mind tasks. *Child Development, 75*(2), 523–41.

Wimmer, H. and Perner, J. (1983) Beliefs about beliefs: Representation and constraining function of wrong beliefs in young children's understanding of deception. *Cognition, 13*, 103–28.

Youngblade, L. M. and Dunn, J. (1995) Individual differences in young children's pretend play with mother and sibling: Links to relationships and understanding of other people's feelings and beliefs. *Child Development, 66*, 1472–92.

15

MIND-MINDEDNESS

Forms, features and implications for infant-toddler pedagogy

Sheila Degotardi

Introduction

In recent years, the notion of children's 'voice' has become increasingly present in early childhood research, policy and pedagogical literature. This philosophical move is consistent with the United Nations Conventions on the Rights of the Child (United Nations, 1989) in which is enshrined children's right to express opinions and have these opinions respected and heard. Similarly, the childhood studies perspective advocates a commitment towards understanding and responding to children's perspectives in the context of experiences that are salient to them at any given time (James, 2007). In both of these approaches, children are positioned as sentient beings, with feelings, intentions and thoughts that allow them to make sense of their world and contribute towards their lived experiences in purposeful and meaningful ways (Smith, 2011).

These approaches portray a socially constructed notion of childhood in which children's experiences, learning and development are firmly located within the context of the beliefs and practices of their community members (Berthelsen and Brownlee, 2005; Smith, 2007). Yet applying principles of 'voice' and perspective to the experiences of very young children has its challenges. Most empirical evidence about how these dispositions can be recognized and fostered is derived from studies of children aged 2 years and older (e.g. Harcourt *et al.*, 2011), driven perhaps by the ability of these older children to use language to label and communicate their thoughts and intentions to others. The perspectives of infants may be more difficult to access as very young children are less able to articulate their perspectives through verbal means (Degotardi and Davis, 2008; Sumsion *et al.*, 2011). In family contexts, Bornstein (2002, p. 14) argues that one of the greatest challenges facing parents of infants is the need to 'divine what is "in the baby's head" – what infants want, what they know, how they feel'. In the context of formal early childhood education and care, the same principle arguably applies when early childhood educators endeavor to understand the perspectives of infants in their program.

In this chapter, I contend that the acknowledgement of infants' 'voice' is dependent on their caregivers' willingness and ability to go beyond observations of physical behaviors to interpret and act on infants' underlying mental states. Specifically, the construct of *mind-mindedness* is explored as a means of conceptualizing this tendency within the context of infant-toddler pedagogy. I begin with a brief overview and explanation of the construct itself and a discussion of how mind-mindedness has been conceptualized in parenting literature. I then present findings from a recent study which explored how mind-mindedness was apparent and enacted in early childhood programs for infants.

Defining mind-mindedness

The term mind-mindedness was originally coined by Elizabeth Meins, who defined it as adults' propensity to 'treat their children as individuals with minds' (Meins *et al.*, 1998, p. 20). Mind-mindedness portrays the 'image of the child' as a feeling, intentional, sentient subject, as opposed to a purely physical being. By placing the locus of control within the child, mind-mindedness has an interpretive and explanatory function: interpretive because mind-mindedness necessarily focuses on the child's perspective; and explanatory because it renders another's behavior meaningful to an extent that is not afforded by reference to external events or behavior alone. While the term 'mind-mindedness' was new at the time, Stern (1985) had previously argued that a perceptiveness of infant subjectivity constitutes 'working hypotheses about infancy ... [that] ... ultimately determine how we, as parents, respond to our own infants' (p. 4). Stern contended that mind-mindedness allows parents to respond empathetically to their infants, and others agree that this form of subjective attunement enables the establishment and maintenance of intersubjective exchanges between infants and parents (Murray, 1988; Trevarthen, 1980). Mind-mindedness therefore fits within a broader relational approach to understanding infant learning and development as it is during such exchanges that relationships are formed, meanings are shared, and infants come to develop socially and culturally specific ways of understanding themselves, others and the world (Bruner, 1990; Tomasello *et al.*, 1993).

Forms of mind-mindedness

Since its introduction, research has operationalized the construct of mind-mindedness in two main ways. The first involves inferring mind-mindedness from the ways in which mothers *talk about* their infants, on the basis that the linguistic terms used to describe and explain behaviors and to attribute character traits reveal their underlying beliefs about infant characteristics and behaviors (Olson and Kamawar, 1999; D'Andrade, 1985). For example, non-mind-minded descriptions of infants would include references to physical behaviors ('He *crawls* around the kitchen'), situational explanations ('because *there's lots of space* in there to move around') and non-psychological character traits ('He's very active'). In contrast, mind-minded descriptions would refer to mental states ('She *tries* to open the cupboard'), mentalistic explanations ('because she's *knows* that we've put the ball in there') and psychological character traits ('She's very *persistent* and *strong-minded*'). Meins and colleagues derived a measure of mind-mindedness by asking parents to provide a free description of their child and calculating the proportion of the total amount of descriptions that were psychological in nature. A variation on the description measure is found in Koren-Karie and colleagues' (2002) measure of insightfulness in which mothers viewed video-footage of their infant and provided a spoken narrative to describe the observed behaviors. The resulting measure was derived from the extent to which the narrative demonstrated an awareness and acceptance of their infants' mental experiences.

The infant-description mind-mindedness measure is thus argued to indicate an internal representation of the infant in psychological terms. Meins, though, argues that mind-mindedness is not only apparent in the ways in which adults think and, accordingly, talk *about* their infants, but also in the ways that they treat them. In particular, they claim that mind-mindedness is apparent in adult–infant interactions in the words used when they *talk to* their infant (Meins *et al.*, 2003). In this form, mind-mindedness is a linguistic, declarative trait during which adults explicitly frame actions in psychological terms. It assesses the extent to which a parent explicitly labels mental states and processes during play interactions with their child, commenting, for example, on wants, feelings, interests, perceptions, knowledge and thoughts.

Mind-mindedness in infant childcare

I now turn to the question of how these forms of mind-mindedness are evident in the thoughts and words of those working with infants in childcare contexts. To do this, I present data from a study of infant pedagogy which investigated how infant educators understood and promoted the mental lives of infants. The impetus for the study was the well-established significance of educator interpretations of children's observed behaviors and characteristics as guiding cognitions behind early childhood pedagogical practice (Hatch and Grieshaber, 2002). While the observation-interpretation process serves many purposes, it is widely acknowledged that these cognitions guide educators' actions in the classroom, comprising a psychological context that has a bearing on the learning opportunities provided to children (Olson and Bruner, 1996; Curtis and Carter, 2000)

The study used video-recording and interview methods to explore factors associated with the qualities of 24 infant educators' interactions with infants aged 9 to 20 months. Educators were visited twice. During the first visit, they were video-recorded playing with a nominated infant. On the second visit, the educators viewed extracts from this footage and were asked to describe and explain the infants' actions. In this way, we hoped to gain an insight into the ways in which mind-mindedness was apparent in their interpretations of, as well as their interactions with, this infant (for full methodological details see Degotardi and Sweller, 2012).

Mind-minded interpretations

Our measure of *mind-minded interpretations* was derived from the ways in which educators described infant behaviors and characteristics during their narratives of the video extracts. Like Meins and colleagues, we focused on their use of mental-state terms when they narrated the infants' behaviors, coding descriptions as either psychological or non-psychological. In an extension to previous mind-minded measures, we further categorized psychological descriptions according to representational content on the basis that 'treating one's child as a mental agent ... implies a further understanding that the child is capable of having representations of the world and different stances of perspectives that may be taken toward reality' (Sharp and Fonagy, 2008, p. 743). We therefore categorized as follows:

Experiential ascriptions. Infant descriptions referring to psychological attitudes or drives towards objects or events were coded as *experiential ascriptions*. These psychological states and processes exist as relatively automatic responses to external stimuli and constitute an affective or motivational force towards that stimulus (Wellman, 1990).

Representational ascriptions. Infant descriptions relating to the construction of knowledge and the holding of a subjective point of view (Perner, 1991) were coded as *representational ascriptions*.

These categories of infant descriptions used to derive the measures of mind-minded interpretations are represented in Figure 15.1.

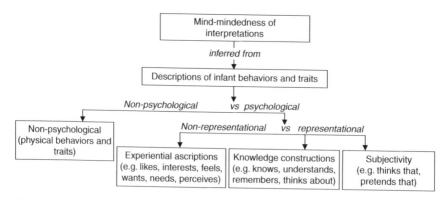

Figure 15.1 Categories of infant descriptions

Our analysis found that educators varied considerably in the proportion of mind-minded descriptions contained in their narrative, with mind-minded descriptions ranging from 25 per cent to 91 per cent of all infant descriptions. Experiential ascriptions were more common than representational ones (M = 42%, range = 21%–60%; M = 13%, range = 0%–35% respectively), but the two measures were not significantly correlated. Qualitative data illustrates how some educators tended to focus almost exclusively on experiential states and processes (Example 1), while others incorporated experiential and representational ascriptions into their narratives (Example 2).

Example 1: Suzy was a little bit, um, surprised and looking very, um, very exciting with the new toys and, ah, she liked it when the toy makes noises. She was trying to – in her mouth – trying really hard to try to put it in there. Try to put it in her mouth. Makes a noise with the toys but she liked it.

Example 2: I'm prompting David with asking him what he felt and what does it do, just to get his thinking going, so he can explore what the experience is or what the toy is. He's obviously fiddling with it and trying to figure out what's happening. I smile at David to let him know that I see what he's happy about as well. David remembers that the toy was stuck and that we couldn't open it.

Mind-minded talk

We drew our measure of mind-minded talk from research relating to adult mind-related talk to young children (e.g. Bartsch and Wellman, 1995; Ruffman *et al.*, 2002). We transcribed the talk that each educator used during their play with the infant and coded each discrete utterance according to whether or not it contained reference to a mental state or process. To retain the same conceptual categories as the mind-minded interpretations, each mental state utterance was coded as follows.

Experiential, if it contained a reference to an experiential psychological state or process, including likes, interests, emotions, desires, intentions and perceptions.

Representational, if it contained a reference to a representational state or process, including knowledge states, thinking processes and symbolic activities such as tricking and pretending. We also included utterances which contained modal verbs or adjuncts, such as 'might', 'could' or 'maybe' on the basis that such terms highlight the speakers' subjective opinions or ideas (Moore and Furrow, 1991)

Consistent with findings from parenting research, the educators varied widely in their use of mind-minded talk, with the occurrence of mind-minded utterances ranging from only 14 per cent of the utterances in a total transcript to nearly 50 per cent (M = 31.5%, SD = 9.8%). The following examples, taken from observations of different educators and infants playing with the same wind up Jack-in-a-box, illustrate how those with low levels of mind-minded talk tended to use short and repetitive utterances which focused on labeling objects and actions (Example 3) or on giving directions (Example 4).

Example 3:	**Example 4:**
Press this one	What's that?
Ready	You turn around
Ha!	Turn around this way?
Boo!	Turn this –
ready	ready?
Ready	Turn this
1, 2, 3 boo	Oh, ah,
(laughs)	put it back in,
Ready	push the teddy in,
1, 2, 3 boo	push the teddy in,
Go again	close the door.

In the mind-minded categories, experiential mental-state words were expressed in approximately 9 per cent of all utterances, while representational utterances were less frequent, with average occurrences of just 3 per cent. As with the educators' interpretations, there was no significant relationship between educators' use of experiential and representational utterances. Some educators talked a great deal about feelings and perceptions (Example 5) and desires (Example 6), yet their transcripts were largely bereft of references to representational, belief-related states and processes.

Example 5	**Example 6**
I hope it doesn't frighten you	He is stuck in there
You have to turn it now	We'll try and close him back up again
When does he pop out	You wanna have a turn this time?
Watch	You wanna have a turn?
Oh	Twirl this around
There he is again	You need to use this hand
See	If I put the box in front of you
Oh listen to that squeak	Do you want to have a turn like that

In contrast, the next example contains extracts taken from a transcript high in representational talk. The context is still the Jack-in-a-box play, but there are episodes where the educator focuses quite strongly on the infant's cognitions about the play – his expectations, thinking and learning – as well commenting on her own perspective in order to frame the play in representational, as opposed to predominantly experiential or physical terms.

Example 7

Keep turning it.
Keep going
Wow – I didn't expect that to happen
did you expect that to happen?

...

Have you figured out a different way to open it
did you figure out a different way.

...

The winder is here
but I think you found the latch that opens it.
You found an easy way to open it.

...

You might need to push teddy's head down.

Implications of mind-mindedness for infant pedagogy

At the beginning of this chapter, I identified mind-mindedness as an interpretive tendency which stems from an underlying commitment to the psychological life of the infant. The developmental significance of such belief structures can be explained with reference to Super and Harkness's (1986) concept of the *psychology of the caregiver*, which, they claim, supports and constrains the opportunities for learning that are afforded in any particular context. In the home, mind-minded parents have been found to be more sensitive, less intrusive and more able to maintain reciprocal interactions than less mind-minded parents (e.g. Meins *et al.*, 2001; Lundy, 2003). Mind-mindedness has also been positively associated with the encouragement of exploration, achievement and challenge (Bernier *et al.*, 2010; Ereky-Stevens, 2008). Given these associations, and using the video footage of the educator-infant play, we explored whether mind-mindedness was associated with the following measures that have been broadly associated with infant-toddler program quality:

Sensitivity assessed the degree to which the educator was emotionally warm and responsive to the infant's actions and intentions and, as such, would appear to embody an appreciation of, and respect for the infants' experiential states – their feelings, interests and intentions.

Stimulation assessed the degree of language and cognitive stimulation provided by the educator, including their ability to provide cognitive input, to focus and extend attention and to scaffold achievement. Stimulation would appear to embody an appreciation of the infants' representational states and processes – their thinking and knowledge construction.

We found educators with high levels of mind-mindedness in their interpretations and their talk to be significantly more sensitive and stimulating than lower-mind-minded educators (Degotardi and Sweller, 2012). Yet despite the different psychological focus of the sensitivity and stimulation measures, it was the level of *representational ascriptions* in educators' interpretations and *representational talk* in their interactions that accounted for the most variance in *both* interactions measures. Although a great deal of literature on infant-educator interactions tends to focus around fostering emotional wellbeing and catering towards infants' intrinsic motivations and interests, our findings suggest that, in a pedagogical context, an appreciation of infants' experiential mental states may not be sufficient. Instead, the kinds of high-quality interactions which not only support social-emotional development but also stimulate language and cognitive growth may be reflective of a tendency to adopt and express a *representational* understanding of infants' minds.

Teaching about the mind

To conclude, I return to my original discussion about 'voice' and perspective and its current prominence in early years pedagogy. Research has found that parental mind-mindedness, in interpretive and adult-infant talk form, is an important support for children's own developing understanding of others' thoughts, feelings and intentions (e.g. Meins *et al.*, 2003; Ereky-Stevens, 2008; Ruffman *et al.*, 2002). While there are currently no longitudinal studies in childcare centre contexts, the final example, taken from an observational study of toddler interpersonal relatedness (see Degotardi, 2014, for details) provides a clue about how educator mind-mindedness might promote a perspectival way of thinking in very young children.

Example 8

Teacher Cathy and 2½-year-old Nick are lying on their tummies looking intently at a small hole in a stone wall, watching some large ants entering and leaving the hole.

> Nick: *(pointing) That's the mum.*
> Cathy: *Do you think so?*
> Nick: *Yes (points to another ant) and that's the dad.*
> Cathy: *Mmm … I wonder where they are going?*
> Nick: *Maybe … um … I think they are going home. Their home is in there (points at the hole in the wall).*
> Cathy: *Yes, you may be right.*
> Nick: *Yes – and their kids are waiting for dinner.*
> Cathy: *You think so?*
> Nick: *Mmm –yes. They're hungry.*

Through toddlerhood, the gradual acquisition of mental-state vocabulary allows toddlers to explicitly talk about their own perspectives. Here we see Cathy using mind-minded talk to communicate her own subjective opinion and encourage Nick to express his, thus highlighting how reciprocal conversations can provide opportunities for ideas to be shared and understandings to be negotiated. What occurs is a dynamic interplay between the perspectives of educator and child which gives substance to otherwise opaque psychological states (Wenger, 1998). The result of such explicit labeling is that, in addition to the observed event, individual and shared perspectives become the topic of conversation (Degotardi, 2013).

This is not only the kind of rich conversation that has been shown to support children's developing understanding of the mind, but also illustrates the collaborative construction of learning which involves a 'reflection on one's own understandings and comparing understandings among participants in a discourse' (van Oers and Hännikäinen, 2001, p. 105). While more research is needed in this area, it may be that educator mind-mindedness underpins this relational learning process, and that the interchange and negotiation of perspectives ultimately provides very young children with opportunities to enter and learn within a community of minds (Nelson, 2007).

References

Bartsch, K. and Wellman, H. M. (1995) *Children Talk About the Mind*. New York, Oxford University Press.

Bernier, A., Carson, S. M. and Whipple, N. (2010) From external regulation to self-regulation: Early parenting precursors of young children's executive functioning. *Child Development, 81*, 326–39.

Berthelsen, D. and Brownlee, J. (2005) Respecting children's agency for learning and rights to participation in child care programs. *International Journal of Early Childhood, 37*, 49–60.

Bornstein, M. H. (2002) Parenting infants. In M. H. Bornstein (ed.) *Handbook of Parenting*, 2nd edn. Mahwah, NJ: Erlbaum.

Bruner, J. (1990) *Acts of Meaning*. Cambridge, MA: Harvard University Press.

Curtis, D. and Carter, M. (2000) *The Art of Awareness: How Observation can Transform your Teaching*. St Paul, MN: Redleaf Press.

D'Andrade, R. (1985) Character terms and cultural models. In J. W. D. Dougherty (ed.) *Directions in Cognitive Anthropology*. Urbana, IL: University of Illinois Press.

Degotardi, S. (2013) 'I think, I can': Acknowledging and promoting agency during educator-infant play. In O. F. Lillemyr, S. Dockett and B. Perry (eds) *Varied Perspectives on Play and Learning: Theory and Research on Early Years Education*. Charlotte, NC: Information Age Publishing.

Degotardi, S. (2014) 'Expressing, interpreting and exchanging perspectives during infant-toddler social interactions: The significance of acting with others in mind'. In L. Harrison and J. Sumsion (eds.) *Lived Spaces of infant-toddler education and care: Exploring diverse perspectives on theory, research, practice and policy*. New York, NY: Springer.

Degotardi, S. and Davis, B. (2008) Understanding infants: Characteristics of early childhood practitioners' interpretations of infants and their behaviours. *Early Years: An International Journal of Research and Development, 28*, 221–34.

Degotardi, S. and Sweller, N. (2012) Mind-mindedness in infant child-care: Associations with early childhood practitioner sensitivity and stimulation. *Early Childhood Research Quarterly, 27*, 253–65.

Ereky-Stevens, K. (2008) Associations between mothers' sensitivity to their infants' internal states and children's later understanding of mind and emotion. *Infant and Child Development, 17*, 527–43.

Harcourt, D., Perry, B. and Waller, T. (eds) (2011) *Researching Young Children's Perspectives: Debating the Ethics and Dilemmas of Educational Research with Children*. Oxford, UK: Routledge.

Hatch, J. A. and Grieshaber, S. (2002) Child observation and accountability in early childhood education: Perspectives from Australia and the United States. *Early Childhood Education Journal, 29*, 227–31.

James, A. (2007) Giving voice to children's voices: Practice and problems, pitfalls and potentials. *American Anthropologist, 109*(2), 261–72.

Koren-Karie, N., Oppenheim, D., Dolev, S., Sher, E. and Etzion-Carasso, A. (2002) Mothers' insightfulness regarding their infants' internal experience: Relations with maternal sensitivity and infant attachment. *Developmental Psychology, 38*, 534–42.

Lundy, B. L. (2003) Father- and mother-infant face to face interactions: Differences in mind-related comments and infant attachment? *Infant Behavior and Development, 26*, 200–12.

Meins, E., Fernyhough, C., Russell, J. and Clark-Carter, D. (1998) Security of attachment as a predictor of symbolic and mentalising abilities: A longitudinal study. *Social Development, 7*, 1–24.

Meins, E., Fernyhough, C., Fradley, E. and Tuckey, M. (2001) Rethinking maternal sensitivity: Mothers' comments on infants' mental processes predict security of attachment at 12 months. *Journal of Child Psychology and Psychiatry and Allied Disciplines, 42*, 637–48.

Meins, E., Fernyhough, C., Wainwright, R., Clark-Carter, D., Das Gupta, M., Fradley, E. and Tuckey, M. (2003) Pathways to understanding mind: Construct validity and predictive validity of maternal mind-mindedness. *Child Development, 74*, 1194–211.

Moore, C. and Furrow, D. (1991) The development of the language of belief: The expression of certainty. In D. Frye and C. Moore (eds) *Children's Theories of Mind*. Hillsdale, NJ: Erlbaum.

Murray, J. (1988) Contributions of experimental and clinical perturbations of mother–infant communication to the understandings of infant intersubjectivity. In S. Braten (ed.) *Intersubjective Communication and Emotion in Early Ontogeny*. Paris, France: Cambridge University Press.

Nelson, K. (2007) *Young Minds in Social Worlds: Experience, Meaning, and Memory*. Cambridge, MA: Harvard University Press.

Olson, D. R. and Bruner, J. S. (1996) Folk psychology and folk pedagogy. In D. R. Olson and N. Torrence (eds) *The Handbook of Education and Human Development*. Malden: Blackwell.

Olson, D. R. and Kamawar, D. (1999) The theory of ascriptions. In P. D. Zelazo, J. W. Astington and D. R. Olson (eds) *Developing Theories of Intention: Social Understanding and Self Control*. Mahwah, NJ: Erlbaum.

Perner, J. (1991) *Understanding the Representational Mind*. Cambridge, MA: MIT Press.

Ruffman, T., Slade, L. and Crowe, E. (2002) The relation between children's and mother's mental state language and theory-of-mind understanding. *Child Development, 73*, 734–51.

Sharp, C. and Fonagy, P. (2008) The parent's capacity to treat the child as a psychological agent: Constructs, measures and implications for developmental psychopathology. *Social Development, 17*, 737–54.

Smith, A. B. (2007) Children and young people's participation rights in education. *International Journal of Children's Rights, 15*, 147–64.

Smith, A. B. (2011) Respecting children's rights and agency: Theoretical insights into ethical research procedures. In D. Harcourt, B. Perry and T. Waller (eds) *Researching Young Children's Perspectives: Debating the Ethics and Dilemmas of Educational Research with Children*. London: Routledge.

Stern, D. N. (1985) *The Interpersonal World of the Infant: A View from Psychoanalysis and Developmental Psychology*. New York: Basic Books.

Sumsion, J., Harrison, L., Press, F., McLeod, S., Goodfellow, J. and Bradley, B. (2011) Researching infants' experiences of early childhood education and care. In D. Harcourt, B. Perry and T. Waller (eds) *Researching Young Children's Perspectives: Debating the Ethics and Dilemmas of Educational Research with Children*. London: Routledge.

Super, C. M. and Harkness, S. (1986) The developmental niche: A conceptualization at the interface of child and culture. *International Journal of Behavioral Development, 9*, 545–69.

Tomasello, M., Kruger, A. C. and Ratner, H. H. (1993) Cultural learning. *Behavioral and Brain Sciences, 16*, 495–552.

Trevarthen, C. (1980) The foundations of intersubjectivity: Development of interpersonal and cooperative understanding in infants. In D. R. Olson (ed.) *The Social Foundations of Language and Thought*. New York: Norton.

United Nations (1989) Convention on the Rights of the Child. Geneva: United Nations.

van Oers, B. and Hännikäinen, M. (2001) Some thoughts about togetherness: An introduction. *International Journal of Early Years Education, 9*, 101–8.

Wellman, H. M. (1990) *The Child's Theory of Mind*. Cambridge, MA: MIT Press.

Wenger, E. (1998) *Communities of Practice: Learning, Meaning, and Identity*. Cambridge, UK: Cambridge University Press.

16

METACOGNITIVE EXPERIENCES

Taking account of feelings in early years education

Shirley Larkin

Introduction

While metacognition develops with age and experience, it is opportunity and need to be metacognitive that facilitate its development. Drawing on international research, this chapter argues that the affective domain is often neglected in programmes designed to facilitate metacognitive development in children. The introductory section gives a brief outline of metacognition theory and provides evidence from empirical research to show how theory is related to educational practice. The chapter then focuses on the role of metacognitive experiences in the development of metacognition and the importance of emotional responses in learning. The final section draws on the author's own empirical research to demonstrate how metacognitive experiences might be facilitated in early years education.

The terms metacognitive experience and early years education fit uneasily together. There is plenty of work now on metacognition and self regulated learning in the early years and much of this will include reference to children's experience as a crucial factor in the development of both. However, there is little that focuses specifically on metacognitive experiences in the early years. In order to understand why this might be we need first to consider the development of the field of research that comes under the metacognition umbrella.

The foundations of metacognition lie in cognitive theories of memory (Cavanaugh and Borkowski, 1980; Hart, 1992); and in what children believe, understand and can articulate about memory and remembering, otherwise known as metamemory (Flavell and Wellman, 1977). Flavell and Brown (Brown, 1987; Flavell, 1976) extended the research on memory to include reflection on other cognitive processes, thereby creating the term 'metacognition'. The focus was often on the developmental stages from early childhood to adulthood of this ability. This was hardly surprising given Flavell's background as a Piagetian. It seemed reasonable to extend Piaget's cognitive stage development model to include children's beliefs, knowledge and understanding of their own cognitive processes. The notion of metacognition as akin to Piaget's reflective abstraction (Piaget and Inhelder, 1969) leads to the view that until children reach the level of formal operational thought they are unable to engage in metacognition. This was the consensus view of most research into metacognition until more recently when empirical studies of young children demonstrating a variety of metacognitive processes (Blair and Razza, 2007; Garrett *et al.*, 2006; Jacobs, 2004; van der Zee *et al.*, 2006) and a number of studies of non-human animals (without language) also demonstrating metacognition (Kornell *et al.*, 2007; Premack and Woodruff, 1978; Smith *et al.*, 2003) began to change this view. Theory of Mind research has shown that by the age of 4 children are able to understand that people think differently depending on the experience and knowledge they already have. My own research with children aged 5 and 6 used a constructivist theory of mind test (Carpendale and Chandler, 1996); a metamemory test; a mental rotation test (Estes, 1998) and a self as learner test to confirm that children of this age could not only articulate their understanding of their own cognitive processes but could also talk about their development as thinkers and the conditions under which they might think better (Larkin, 2010). The most sophisticated views of these 5-year-olds showed that they saw learning as an active process in which they had to engage their brain and which requires practice. They described the importance of asking questions and demonstrated their understanding of learning as a complex activity involving observing, practising, acting, talking, working things out individually, and using what they already know. They also articulated the difference between observing, remembering and learning. They spoke of remembering and forgetting as emotional experiences with forgetting often linked to sadness (Larkin, 2007).

Flavell's model of metacognition as delineated in the seminal article 'Metacognition and cognitive monitoring' (Flavell, 1979) comprises four 'classes of phenomena', described as metacognitive knowledge; metacognitive experiences; goals (or tasks); and actions (or strategies). In general, most research on metacognition in education has concentrated on the different aspects of metacognitive knowledge (person, task, strategy) including how these are facilitated and how they impact on learning or attainment or research has focused on the 'on-line' regulation of cognitive processes as outlined in an equally seminal paper (Nelson and Narens, 1992). The second of Flavell's four 'classes of phenomena' – metacognitive experiences – was in fact largely ignored in educational research until the 1990s.

However, the affective aspects of memory and learning have long been a part of the research agenda of cognitive psychologists interested in monitoring and control of cognition and memory. It is this branch of cognitive psychology which has investigated such phenomena as judgements of learning (JOL); ease of learning (EOL); feelings of confidence, familiarity and uncertainty; tip of the tongue experiences (TOT); feelings of knowing (FOK); and their determinants, cues, calibration and accuracy. For instance, experimental studies show that preschool children tend to be overconfident about the accuracy of their memory; whereas older school-age children provide more accurate predictions (Schneider and Pressley, 1997). Yet while educationalists would agree that learning is replete with emotion as well as cognition, they have been slow to investigate the affective aspect of metacognition in classroom-based studies. This may be because the adoption of metacognition theory into thinking skills interventions has often led to a skills-based approach to facilitating and developing children's metacognition in different curriculum subject areas. (For a review of thinking skills programmes see Higgins *et al.*, 2005.) In the majority of these programmes the cognitive rather than the affective domain is the focus.

Metacognitive experiences: definitions

Metacognitive experiences are defined by Flavell as 'conscious cognitive or affective experiences that accompany and pertain to any intellectual enterprise' (1979, p. 906). Flavell is clear that metacognitive experiences include both cognitive and affective states and arise from the activation of metacognitive knowledge in response to a task. There is an interactive process between the activation of metacognitive knowledge which can cause a metacognitive experience and the activation of metacognition to interpret these experiences. For example, during a task knowledge of previous similar tasks may be consciously cued in order to aid progress on the current task, or a task may cause a feeling of puzzlement which may cue metacognitive knowledge of similar incidents in order to interpret the feeling. Metacognitive experiences include feelings of confidence and puzzlement; monitoring of progress and judgements of success or failure including the feelings which accompany them. Whether conscious or not, metacognitive experiences can influence progress on a task and lead to new and better processing; to revision of existing processes or to abandonment of the tasks. From a constructivist perspective on learning just as experience and interaction with the world leads to construction of new knowledge, so these meta-level experiences focused on cognitive processes lead to the construction and revision of metacognitive knowledge. For Flavell (1979) metacognitive experiences in childhood are crucial for the development of metacognitive knowledge. However, just as children may gain inaccurate or false knowledge of the world from experience so they can develop unhelpful metacognitive knowledge of themselves as learners from the handling and resolution of metacognitive experiences.

Metacognitive experiences give rise to cognitive strategies and play a part in monitoring cognition through the interaction of metacognitive strategies, metacognitive knowledge and task goals. Metacognitive experiences are replete with emotion and highly personal as they are influenced by past and present experiences and self concept. Efklides (2001) views metacognitive experiences as influenced by three factors: (1) personal, which includes ability, self concept and personality; (2) task, which includes the nature of the task, previous experiences of similar tasks; and (3) metacognitive knowledge, which includes conscious understanding and knowledge of how person, task and strategy variables might impact on task or goal. Metacognitive experiences are seen as the implicit and explicit feelings which accompany learning and readiness to learn and which in turn influence task progression through the activation of monitoring and control processes and the activation of strategies. Efklides describes metacognitive experiences as on-line metacognition, i.e. feelings which happen in the moment, which change as the task goes on and which reoccur before, during and after a task. They can include ideas – light bulb moments; feelings of familiarity, difficulty, confidence, puzzlement; judgements and evaluations of strategies being used and predictions of success or failure. In this model metacognitive experiences are closely linked to self concept and motivation. Metacognitive experiences are both influenced by self concept and help to construct self concept through feedback (Dermitzaki and Efklides, 2001). Metacognitive experiences are seen as the interface between the person and the task (Efklides, 2006). As such they are particularly important elements in the creation of life-long and self regulated learners, yet they are often overlooked in classrooms.

Metacognitive experiences in early years

While the age at which metacognition develops in human infants has caused controversy among cognitive psychologists and educationalists, developmental psychologists have long been aware through experimental studies on infants that early signs of metacognition are in the affective rather than the cognitive domain. Studies on babies' attention-seeking behaviour have shown that as young as 6 months old children respond to the affective state of another even when the emotion is not directed at themselves (Reddy, 2001, 2003). The suggestion is that these very young children can demonstrate affective metacognition which is not yet cognitive. Esken (2012) discusses the work on children's social awareness and embarrassment which shows that by 2 years old children exhibit embarrassment indicating both an ability to view their own behaviour in relation to a social norm (Lewis, 2003) and an ability to see how others might perceive them (Lewis, 2003; Rochat, 2004). Esken (2012) goes on to suggest that there are two types of embarrassment which link to metacognitive experiences. First, the non-evaluative kind is a feeling of being uncomfortable as the centre of attention. It does not include any conscious understanding or reflection on the feeling and therefore could not be considered metacognitive. Second, the evaluative type of embarrassment includes a conceptual awareness of how others may be evaluating the behaviour and includes a self evaluation. Esken (2012) argues that the non-evaluative emotion may occur in non-human animals but the evaluative emotion involves a reflective consciousness and can be seen as an early step in the development of metacognition in children. As children experience more of the world around them they develop an ability to regulate and control their first order emotional responses in relation to emotions such as embarrassment. This self regulation and control is facilitated by inner speech. From a Vygotskian perspective it could be that the child is gradually internalizing the language of the caregiver which is directed at the regulation and control of emotions. Thus the development of metacognition can be viewed as fundamentally a social process (Wertsch, 1978). The suggestion is that metacognition develops from an inter-psychological to an intra-pyschological domain (Vygotsky, 1978).

Borkowski and Thorpe (1994) demonstrated how interaction between children and adults affects the development of cognition, metacognition and motivation. In this model of metacognition importance is placed on the development of a positive sense of self which includes an internal locus of control, self esteem, resilience and positive motivational attributions. It seems likely that the early emotional experiences of young children will impact on the regulation and control of cognition. The development of these executive functions as measured by executive function tasks appears to be closely linked to the development of theory of mind as measured by theory of mind tasks. Thus children around 4 to 5 years of age are able to pass both kinds of tests (Esken, 2012). Theory of mind involves the understanding of others and their intentions and thus the link between theory of mind and metacognition seems to be clear. However, research on pretend play has shown that this seemingly obvious link between the development of theory of mind and the development of metacognition may not be so clear cut. The two competing claims that pretend play shows evidence of theory of mind and that pretend play is behaviourist in nature requiring only that children imitate behaviour without needing to engage in meta-representational beliefs have long dominated this area of research. However, Brandl (2012) suggests that there is a middle (although difficult and complex) ground between these two extremes. This middle ground theory emphasizes the role played by metacognitive feelings. Brandl distinguishes between metacognitive judgements such as feeling of knowing, confidence judgements and feelings of uncertainty which require both the feeling and an evaluation of the feeling; and metacognitive feelings which may draw attention to an internal state without making a judgement about it. In this sense metacognitive feelings could be deemed non conceptual. Brandl argues that children gain a pleasurable sense of freedom from pretend play and that their social ability enables them to recognize the intention of others to engage in similar pleasurable activity. The argument is that by understanding the intentions of others children are able to recognize their own intentions and in turn their developing self awareness would make children more able to understand the intentions of others. Thus the metacognitive feelings of pleasure and freedom form part of a socially generated feedback loop which may account for developing metacognitive abilities. While Brandl's theory is yet to be supported by weighty empirical evidence, the argument is a convincing one especially when compared to anecdotal experiences of observing young children's ability to understand pretend from the slightest of behavioural cues. Metacognitive feelings, then, rather than theory of mind may be crucial for the development of metacognition.

Metacognitive experiences are often transitory. They are different for different people and they are sensitive to contextual cues. They can go unrecognized, be ignored, have a negative effect on progress or they can be used to help us understand more about ourselves as learners in different contexts (Efklides, 2006). While some elements of metacognition such as non-evaluative metacognition and theory of mind develop alongside cognitive development, other aspects such as the metacognitive knowledge base and the ability to regulate and control thinking need to be consciously facilitated and fostered. It is likely that recognizing and making use of our metacognitive experiences also requires some support. While learning is replete with emotional responses, little attention is paid in educational settings to how to make use of those responses and how to learn from them. The next section suggests some possibilities.

Facilitating metacognitive experiences for young children

Flavell's seminal paper on cognitive monitoring (Flavell 1979) outlined the conditions under which metacognitive experiences are most likely to occur. First, metacognitive experiences are more likely in situations that require 'highly conscious thinking'. It would be worth recording how many tasks young children are asked to do in learning situations that actually require them to consciously think about what they are doing. Second, metacognitive experiences are more likely to occur in new situations that require planning and evaluation. For some learners of all ages, such situations would give rise to very stressful metacognitive experiences which rather than developing metacognition could give rise to unhelpful metacognitive knowledge and have a debilitating effect on motivation. Clifford (1991) speaks of adventurous and cautious learners. While the former relish challenge and are resilient in the face of negative emotions, the latter seek out less challenging opportunities and find negative emotions aroused by not accomplishing goals as debilitating. Third, metacognitive experiences are more likely where decisions and actions are authentic and carry some risk. Some nursery schools foster such decision making quite well. However, as children move through the education system the content-led curriculum can constrain the opportunity to experience 'weighty and risky' decisions. The final element of Flavell's conditions under which metacognitive experiences should occur is in situations which are not highly emotionally charged and where extraneous factors are not impinging to the extent that they inhibit reflective thinking. Thus while metacognitive experiences give rise to emotions, they are most likely to occur when the external emotional climate is controlled.

Research has shown that collaborative group learning enables learners to pick up cues from the verbal and non verbal metacognitive experiences of their co-learners. The monitoring of these cues can lead to shared metacognitive experiences and to shared and co-regulation (Iiskala *et al.*, 2004; Salonen *et al.*, 2005). However, as my own research into children aged 5 and 6 collaborating on writing tasks has shown, when left unsupported these metacognitive experiences do not necessarily result in more metacognitive behaviour. I found that high levels of social cooperation, support and collaborative talk, i.e. what would look like 'good partnership work' in a classroom setting, did not always lead to metacognition. Some elements of collaborative partnerships which did give rise to metacognitive behaviour were task oriented motivation; cooperative rather than competitive interaction; attention to task instructions; degree of joint ownership of the task; periods of talk interspersed with silence and periods of writing and emotional stability or calmness (Larkin, 2009).

In order to create metacognitive experiences for young learners, adults need to deliberately structure situations that are more likely to give rise to such experiences. There are many commercially available thinking skills programmes that include some elements of metacognition. However, these have not all been empirically tested and researched. One programme designed for those aged 5–6 which is based on sound theoretical principles and which has undergone research evaluation is the *Let's Think!* programme (Adey *et al.*, 2001). *Let's Think!* is the published materials and teachers handbook from the CASE @KS1 project, and evaluation showed that overall

Let's Think! has significant effects on children's cognitive ability (Adey *et al.*, 2002). There are four basic features or pillars of any CASE programme: cognitive conflict; social construction; metacognition; bridging/transfer.

Cognitive conflict refers to presenting children with something puzzling or unexpected. This is not simply a matter of presenting difficult or challenging material. Rather it is about providing experiences that confound children's thinking; which make them reflect and think again about what they appear to know. Creating cognitive conflict is likely to lead to metacognitive experiences as children feel puzzled, experience difficulty and frustration. Many of the *Let's Think!* tasks for 5- to 6-year-olds are based on open ended questions: that is, there is no one right answer but different answers can be equally valid. This more closely resembles real world problems and while the activities may be based on schemata such as categorization and seriation they are contextualized by narrative stories. For example, one task involves children inventing a game using all the materials provided: a ball, a die and shaker and a hula hoop. The cognitive conflict comes through trying to use all of the apparatus; ensuring that all members of the group of six children are involved in the process; creating a game that is fair and reliable and managing conflicting feelings and ideas within the group. The children also have to be able to teach the game to another group, thus experiencing the role of tutor.

Social construction is described by Vygotsky (1979) as a process of semiotic mediation, which is dynamic and interactive and where knowledge is constructed through the manipulation of psychological tools, the most apparent of which is language. In the *Let's Think* tasks children create and construct knowledge together in social groups; explaining and negotiating, learning to listen and to respond appropriately; knowing when to argue a point and when to accept another's view. In order to facilitate social construction the classroom environment, including the physical layout of the classroom, the number and type of resources allocated to the group and the make-up of the group, are factors in helping or hindering collaborative work. Metacognitive experiences are created through this social construction process. Children may feel that they are being overlooked, not taken seriously, that they have little to contribute or that they are too shy or embarrassed to put forward their own ideas. In order to create constructive metacognitive experiences in collaborative group work the adult needs to observe and respond to the verbal and non verbal cues of individuals within the group.

The third pillar of CASE activities is **metacognition**. It is important that this is not seen as a simple reflection on learning at the end of an activity. Instead the fostering of metacognition through the creation of metacognitive experiences runs throughout the task from planning to evaluation. The *Let's Think!* activities meet the requirements set out by Flavell (1979) to stimulate metacognitive experiences. Making use of the metacognitive experiences that arise during these collaborative tasks requires the adult facilitator to create a learning space where failure to come up with an easy and right answer is seen as positive rather than negative; where difficulty is experienced as pleasurable rather than debilitating and where social nicety is not allowed to dominate the cognitive challenge. Young children are socialized to help, be kind to and share with others. Yet in problem solving tasks this can become an issue if children, for example, give resources to another child because this is the 'kind thing to do' rather than because this will help the group to solve the problem.

The fourth pillar of CASE refers to **bridging and transfer**, i.e. the ability to use the knowledge constructed on one specific task and transfer that to other similar tasks or to other kinds of tasks. This requires an ability to abstract general principles from specific situations and reapply them in new situations. In terms of metacognitive experiences the successful transfer of learning from one domain to another is likely to produce feelings of satisfaction and empowerment. The positive metacognitive experiences arising from successful transfer of learning are likely to lead to new thinking, to develop the metacognitive knowledge base and to enhance regulation and control of thinking.

Attribution of cause and outcome of emotions and how they might be regulated are likely to differ among a group of learners just as the strength of the emotions felt will differ (Graesser *et al.*, 2009) and it is important that teachers are able to respond to these different emotions appropriately. Many teachers do this instinctively but teacher training programmes rarely focus on how emotion and feelings might affect learning. Understanding the importance of metacognitive experiences for young children and how to facilitate them may go some way towards reinstating the importance of feelings in early years education.

References

Adey, P., Robertson, A. and Venville, G. (2001) *Let's Think! A Programme for Developing Thinking in Five and Six Year Olds*. Slough: Nfer Nelson.

Adey, P., Robertson, A. and Venville, G. (2002) Effects of a cognitive acceleration programme on Year 1 pupils. *British Journal of Educational Psychology*, 72, 1–25.

Blair, C. and Razza, R. P. (2007) Relating effortful control, executive function, and false belief understanding to emerging math and literacy ability in kindergarten. *Child Development*, 78(2), 647–63.

Borkowski, J. G. and Thorpe, P. K. (1994) Self-regulation and motivation: A life-span perspective on underachievement. In D. H. Schunk and B. J. Zimmerman (eds) *Self-Regulation of Learning and Performance: Issues and Educational Applications* (pp. 45–100). Hillsdale, NJ: Erlbaum.

Brandl, J. L. (2012) Pretend play in early childhood: the road between mentalism and behaviourism. In M. J. Beran, J. L. Brandl, J. Perner and J. Proust (eds) *Foundations of Metacognition* (pp. 146–66). Oxford: Oxford University Press.

Brown, A. L. (1987) Metacognition, executive control, self-regulation and other more mysterious mechanisms. In F. E. Weinert and R. H. Kluwe (eds) *Metacognition, Motivation and Understanding* (pp. 65–116). Hillsdale, NJ: Erlbaum.

Carpendale, J. I. and Chandler, M. J. (1996) On the distinction between false belief understanding and subscribing to an interpretive theory of mind. *Child Development*, 67, 1686–706.

Cavanaugh, J. C. and Borkowski, J. G. (1980) Searching for metamemory-memory connections: A developmental study. *Developmental Psychology*, 16, 441–53.

Clifford, M. M. (1991) Risk taking: Theoretical, empirical and educational considerations. *Educational Psychologist*, 26, 263–98.

Dermitzaki, I. and Efklides, A. (2001) Age and gender effects on students' evaluations regarding the self and task-related experiences in mathematics. In S. Volet and S. Jarvela (eds) *Motivation in Learning Contexts: Conceptual Advances and Methodological Implications* (pp. 271–93). Amsterdam: Elsevier.

Efklides, A. (2001) Metacognitive experiences in problem solving: Metacognition, motivation and self regulation. In A. Efklides, J. Kuhl and R. M. Sorrentino (eds) *Trends and Prospects in Motivation Research* (pp. 297–323). Dordrecht, The Netherlands: Kluwer.

Efklides, A. (2006) Metacognition and affect: What can metacognitive experiences tell us about the learning process? *Educational Research Review*, 3–14.

Esken, F. (2012) Early forms of metacognition in human children. In M. J. Beran, J. L. Brandl, J. Perner and J. Proust (eds) *Foundations of Metacognition* (pp. 134–45). Oxford: Oxford University Press.

Estes, D. (1998) Young children's awareness of their mental activity: The case of mental rotation. *Child Development*, 69(5), 1345–60.

Flavell, J. (1976) Metacognitive aspects of problem solving. In L. B. Resnick (ed.) *The Nature of Intelligence* (pp. 231–35). Hillsdale, NJ: Erlbaum.

Flavell, J. (1979) Metacognition and cognitive monitoring. *American Psychologist*, 34(10), 906–11.

Flavell, J. and Wellman, H. M. (1977) Metamemory. In R. V. Kail and J. W. Hagen (eds) *Perspectives on the Development of Memory and Cognition* (pp. 3–33). Hillsdale: Erlbaum.

Garrett, A. J., Mazzocco, M. M. M. and Baker, L. (2006) Development of the metacognitive skills of prediction and evaluation in children with or without math disability. *Learning Disabilities Research and Practice*, 21(2), 77–88.

Graesser, A. C., D'Mello, S. and Person, N. (2009) Meta-knowledge in tutoring. In D. J. Hacker, J. Dunlosky and A. C. Graesser (eds) *Handbook of Metacognition in Education* (pp. 361–82). New York: Routledge.

Hart, J. T. (1992) Memory and the feeling of knowing experience. In T. O. Nelson (ed.) *Metacognition: Core Readings* (pp. 133–41). Needham Heights, MA: Allyn and Bacon.

Higgins, S., Hall, E., Baumfield, V. and David Moseley (2005) *A Meta-analysis of the Impact of the Implementation of Thinking Skills Approaches on Pupils*. London: EPPI Centre, Social Science Research Unit, Institute of Education, University of London.

Iiskala, T., Vauras, M. and Lehtinen, E. (2004) Socially shared metacognition in peer learning? *Hellenic Journal of Psychology*, 1, 147–78.

Jacobs, G. M. (2004) A classroom investigation of the growth of metacognitive awareness in kindergarten children through the writing process. *Early Childhood Education Journal*, 32(1), 17–23.

Kornell, N., Son, L. K. and Terrace, H. S. (2007) Transfer of metacognitive skills and hint seeking in monkeys. *Psychological Science*, 18(1), 64–71.

Larkin, S. (2007) A phenomenological analysis of the metamemory of 5–6 year old children. *Qualitative Research in Psychology*, 4(4), 281–93.

Larkin, S. (2009) Socially mediated metacognition and learning to write. *Thinking Skills and Creativity*, 4, 149–59.

Larkin, S. (2010) *Metacognition in Young Children*. Abingdon: Routledge.

Lewis, M. (2003) The development of self-consciousness. In J. Roessler and M. Eilan (eds) *Agency and Self-awareness: Issues in Philosophy and Psychology* (pp. 275–95). Oxford: Oxford University Press.

Nelson, T. O. and Narens, L. (1992) Metamemory: A theoretical framework and new findings. In T. O. Nelson (ed.) *Metacognition Core Readings* (pp. 117–29). MA: Allyn and Bacon.

Piaget, J. and Inhelder, B. (1969) *The Psychology of the Child* (trans. H. Weaver). London: Routledge and Kegan Paul.

Premack, D. and Woodruff, G. (1978) Does the chimpanzee have a theory of mind? *Behavioural and Brain Sciences*, 1, 515–26.

Reddy, V. (2001) Infant Clowns. *Enfance*, 247–56.

Reddy, V. (2003) On being the object of attention: Implications for self–other consciousness. *Trends in Cognitive Sciences*, 7(9), 397–402.

Rochat, P. (2004) *The Infant's World*. Cambridge, MA: Harvard University Press.

Salonen, P., Vauras, M. and Efklides, A. (2005) Social interaction: What can it tell us about metacognition and co-regulation in learning? *European Psychologist*, 10, 199–205.

Schneider, W. and Pressley, M. (1997) *Memory Development Between Two and Twenty*, 2nd edn. Mahwah, NJ: Erlbaum.

Smith, J. D., Shields, W. E. and Washburn, D. A. (2003) The comparative psychology of uncertainty monitoring and metacognition. *Behavioral and Brain Sciences*, *26*(3), 317–73.

van der Zee, T., Hermans, C. and Aarnoutse, C. (2006) Primary school students' metacognitive beliefs about religious education. *Educational Research and Evaluation*, *12*(3), 271–93.

Vygotsky, L. S. (1978) *Mind in Society*. Cambridge, MA: Harvard University Press.

Wertsch, J. V. (1978) Adult–child interaction and the roots of metacognition. *Quarterly Newsletter of the Institute for Comparative Human Development*, *2*, 15–18.

17

MAKING LEARNING VISIBLE

The role of language in the development of metacognition and self-regulation in young children

*David Whitebread, Deborah Pino-Pasternak
and Penny Coltman*

Introduction

'Making Learning Visible', as will be familiar to many readers, was a phrase coined within the famous Harvard Project Zero study, which elucidated some of the pedagogical features of the Reggio Emilia approach to early childhood education (Giudici *et al.*, 2001). The theory and research discussed in the present chapter relates strongly to this analysis but draws more directly from the title of two recent highly influential books (Hattie, 2009, *Visible Learning* and 2012, *Visible Learning for Teachers*) in which an extraordinarily comprehensive meta-analysis of the international research evidence on the effectiveness of every conceivable type of teaching intervention is reported and implications for pedagogy discussed. The broad categories of the types of interventions found to be most effective, as indicated by the book titles, and relating very closely to important strands in Reggio Emilia, are those that make learning visible to students. In other words, effective teaching interventions are those that make explicit to students the processes through which they learn, and engage students in activities that oblige them to think and talk about their learning.

Within the UK, Higgins *et al.* (2011) have carried out a similar exercise on UK-based research and come to very similar conclusions. The four categories of intervention which they found to have an effect size above 0.4 (generally accepted among statisticians as an indicator of a clear and significant effect) are those supporting the quality of teacher feedback, the metacognitive and self-regulatory abilities of students and peer tutoring, together with (and this is no surprise, given the body of other evidence, e.g. Sylva and Wiltshire, 1993; Sylva *et al.*, 2004) interventions in the early years of a child's education.

The results of these analyses are highly coherent with two extensive bodies of research within developmental psychology which, until quite recently, have remained rather separate and distinct. The first of these has established the crucial role of meta-cognitive and self-regulatory abilities for learning and educational achievement, and the second, the important role of 'dialogic teaching', supporting children's oracy development and their ability to use talk to enhance their learning and understanding. What follows is a brief review of the nature of the evidence arising from these two strands of research, together with evidence establishing their close inter-connections. In the second section of this chapter we go on to review some of the new evidence emerging from an intervention study designed to combine these previously separate strands of research.

As two of the present authors have detailed elsewhere (Whitebread and Pino Pasternak, 2010), the now extensive research on metacognition and self-regulation can itself be traced back to two distinct and clear theoretical traditions within developmental psychology. These consist of the cognitive tradition, originating in the work of Piaget, which has mainly focused on the internal mental processes and capacities that comprise 'metacognition', and the socio-cultural or Vygotskian approach, which has mainly focused on the social and environmental processes which influence and support the development of metacognitive and self-regulatory abilities.

Within the first tradition, metacognition has generally been conceptualized as a combination of 'metacognitive experience', and 'metacognitive knowledge'. The former concerns our developing awareness (or 'monitoring') and control (or the construction and choice of mental 'strategies') of our own mental processes, 'online' as we perform mental tasks. The latter is the gradually accumulated knowledge and understanding about our own internal mental processes, constructed through metacognitive experience. Key findings emerging from this body of research include that these apparently rather sophisticated abilities begin to emerge in children as young as 3 years of age (Whitebread *et al.*, 2007, 2009) and that early individual differences predict educational achievement more strongly than any other early indicators, including IQ (Veenman *et al.*, 2004) and maths and reading skills (McClelland *et al.*, 2013).

Crucially, in relation to developing effective interventions, individual differences in performance on tasks have been shown to be mostly accounted for by children's relative ability or inability to use their metacognitive knowledge to inform their choice of cognitive strategies. Thus, in one of the earliest experiments which led to the recognition of the importance of metacognitive abilities (Flavell *et al.*, 1966), it was observed that 5-year-old children failed to spontaneously produce an effective strategy in a simple memory task, but, under instruction, could effectively use a verbal rehearsal strategy with a corresponding improvement in their performance. However, they still failed to produce that strategy in a subsequent, almost identical task. Consequently the children performed as poorly on the second task as they had done prior to being taught the strategy.

What appears to be underpinning this is an important difference in the trajectories of monitoring and control processes, with the former maturing relatively uniformly with age, but the latter being dependent upon experience and, possibly, the underlying efficacy of individual brain functioning. In a number of more recent studies, for example, it has emerged that high-achieving children are average for their age in their monitoring skills, but considerably advanced in their effective choice of strategies

(Eme *et al.*, 2006; Puustinen, 1998). An early study by Fabricius and Hagen (1984) gives an indication of the important role of specific experiences in the development of control strategies, and why the use of language to make the processes of learning visible might be so significant. This study explored the use of an organizational strategy in a memory task with children aged 6 and 7. In this task children were asked to remember sets of either 12 or 16 pictures which showed objects that could be put into either three or four categories (e.g. wild animals, clothing items, objects in the sky, bathroom items). Following improved performance when using a sorting strategy (i.e. placing the pictures in categories to help remember them) 61 per cent of the children attributed this to the use of the strategy, but 39 per cent thought they had recalled more because they had looked longer, used their brains more, or slowed down. While only 32 per cent of the children in the latter group transferred the use of the strategy to a second recall task, 99 per cent of those who explicitly recognized (i.e. were able to articulate) the impact of the organizational strategy they had been taught did so. As we will discuss below, some recent intervention studies have built upon this finding and shown that children's effective use of their metacognitive knowledge of strategies can be significantly enhanced by explicit discussion of strategies and why they might be helpful.

It was within the second, socio-cultural tradition that the broader term 'self-regulation' emerged, with Vygotsky originally characterizing learning originating in social contexts and being a process of the child moving from being dependent upon guidance (or 'scaffolding') from an adult or more experienced peer, or 'other-regulated', to being able to carry out a task independently and being 'self-regulated'. The focus here, then, has been on the processes by which learning is internalized and understandings and skills move from being experienced socially at what Vygotsky described as the 'inter-mental level' to being managed internally at the 'intra-mental level'. Within this body of research, the important role of interaction, communication and language in the development of metacognitive and self-regulatory abilities has been clearly established. This relationship was, of course, presaged very clearly in Vygotsky's model of development, in which social interaction and language are seen as central drivers in children's learning. As Vygotsky (1978, p. 26) expressed it: 'Children solve practical tasks with the help of their speech, as well as with their eyes and hands. The unity of perception, speech and action … constitutes the central subject matter for any analysis of the origins of uniquely human forms of behaviour.'

Evidence to support this view has directly linked early language development and the quality of social interactions with either concurrent or later emerging aspects of self-regulation. An American study of 120 toddlers in New England, for example, showed strong relationships between vocabulary size at 14, 24 and 36 months and a range of observed self-regulatory behaviours (e.g. the ability to maintain attention on tasks; the ability to adapt to changes in tasks and procedures) (Vallotton and Ayoub, 2011). Intriguingly, one possible mechanism by which language development might support self-regulation abilities arises from a body of work investigating the production by young children of 'private' or self-directed speech. It has been proposed that this type of speech might be a key mechanism by which social speech becomes internalized as inner speech or, ultimately, thought (Winsler *et al.*, 2009). Certainly, there have been studies supporting this view. Berk and Spuhl (1995), for example, in a study with 4- and 5-year-olds engaged in Lego-building tasks, demonstrated clear links between maternal interaction, the subsequent production by the children of private speech, and their level of performance.

Other studies involving the analysis of language used by children and students in social interactions within educational contexts has led to the recognition that language can support an individual child's self-regulation, but that co-regulation and socially shared regulation in peer groups can also be a powerful vehicle supporting children's regulatory processes (Volet and Vauras, 2013). A study investigating learning in primary science classrooms in Santiago, Chile, for example, showed that levels of self-regulation and performance were associated with advanced forms of 'shared' regulation during groupwork tasks (Grau and Whitebread, 2012; Whitebread and Grau Cardenas, 2012).

Alongside this work concerned with metacognition and self-regulation, the second body of work has investigated and established the important role of 'dialogic teaching', supporting children's oracy development and their ability to use talk to enhance their learning and understanding. This work has also drawn heavily on the Vygotskian, socio-cultural tradition, but has generally been concerned with direct relationships between pedagogical approaches supporting dialogue and educational outcomes. A number of different approaches and techniques have been shown to be highly effective in this regard. These include 'co-operative groupwork', involving problem-solving activities that encourage children to explain their own reasoning and enquire about the reasoning of others (Forman and Cazden, 1985; Mercer *et al.*, 1999; Tolmie *et al.*, 1993). Other techniques ask children to produce 'self-explanations' that require them to explain their reasoning, and that of their teachers (Siegler, 2002) and 'self-assessment' that requires children to make explicit judgements about their own performance and use this to make choices about the level of difficulty of new tasks (Black and Wiliam, 1998). The explicit teaching and modelling of forms of dialogue that encourage thinking (Littleton *et al.*, 2005), and 'debriefing', involve children in reflecting on difficulties encountered, their level of success, and useful approaches to the task (Leat and Lin, 2003).

These 'dialogic' approaches clearly support the development of more reflective and advanced forms of talk and discussion among children and older students, typically requiring the participants to explain their reasoning to others and to come to an agreement in relation to the solution or preferred strategy for dealing with the task at hand. In this regard, for example, Mercer (2000) developed the useful categorization of children's dialogue as 'disputational', 'cumulative' or 'exploratory'. While the first two categories involve simple arguing and adding extra ideas or information, the latter is described by Mercer (2013, p. 5) as dialogue in which 'members of a group share all relevant information and engage critically but constructively with each other's ideas. They all actively participate, ask each other questions and take each other's responses into account in seeking agreement for joint decisions. To an observer, their collective reasoning is "visible" in the talk.'

Mercer and Littleton (2007) report a series of intervention studies, encouraging children to develop 'ground rules' for talk, and showing that more exploratory talk resulted from this and was associated with improved attainment in tests of reasoning, mathematics and science. However, it is assumed in this line of research that the quality of the talk directly impacts upon children's ability to engage in abstract thought and reasoning, and, until quite recently, notions of metacognition and self-regulation were not part of the theoretical models developed.

Despite the relative separateness of these two lines of research relating, on the one hand, to children's development of metacognition and self-regulation and, on the other hand, to classroom talk and dialogue, there have been, however, some intervention studies which have effectively combined the two approaches. The earliest significant example was 'reciprocal teaching' (Palincsar and Brown, 1984), which involved students being taught something that they then subsequently taught to other classmates. These researchers were prominent among early theorists in recognizing the significance of metacognitive processes for learning. They explicitly included them in their model, arguing that the experience of being a learner and a teacher in regard to the same piece of learning would support the reflective processes required to support metacognition.

Other studies have included the provision of opportunities for children to elaborate, discuss, and assess the effectiveness of their own strategies (Brown *et al.*, 1996) and 'strategy instruction' where strategies are taught and the relation between the strategy and task success is explicitly discussed (Verschaffel *et al.*, 1999; Ornstein *et al.*, 2010). The efficacy of these latter approaches can be easily understood in relation to the evidence we discussed earlier, from such as Flavell *et al.* (1966) and Fabricius and Hagen (1984) concerning young children's failure to recognize the efficacy of strategies they had been taught and used successfully. In a review of studies of interventions in primary schools designed to support children's metacognitive and self-regulatory abilities, Dignath *et al.* (2008) showed that these were very largely successful, with impressive effect sizes. However, studies that were underpinned by a Vygotskian, social-constructivist model of learning, and consequently incorporated more opportunities for dialogue and articulation, were shown to be significantly more effective than studies based upon purely metacognitive models.

Most of this work, however, has been carried out with older children. Of the 30 studies included in the systematic review by Dignath *et al.*, only three involved children younger than third grade (i.e. 8-year-olds). This may have arisen from the common misconception, which we have discussed extensively elsewhere, that children under this age are not capable of engaging in metacognitive or self-regulatory processes (Whitebread and Basilio, 2012). In a number of more recent studies, however, the ability of younger children to benefit from interventions aimed at metacognitive and self-regulatory abilities, and the powerful consequences of doing so, has been clearly demonstrated. In the recent Ornstein studies, for example, naturally occurring differences in well-timed metacognitive discussions of memory strategies between teachers of Year 1 (i.e. with 6-year-olds) in mathematics lessons were investigated. Children in classes where there was a relatively high level of such discussions showed significant gains in attainment at the end of Year 1, and were still showing a clear advantage by Year 4.

In the second section of this chapter, we review work carried out, and some of the early analysis, from a study in which we attempted to incorporate the lessons from this combined body of research evidence. The intervention was designed for and carried out with children in UK Year 1 classrooms (i.e. aged 5 and 6). It involved teachers engaging in metacognitive discussions with the children in their classes, and supporting the children in developing the quality of their talk and discussions during collaborate problem-solving tasks. We wished to investigate the extent to which such young children could develop their metacognitive and self-regulatory abilities in a context where the processes of learning were made 'visible'.

The Children Articulating Thinking (ChAT) Project

The aim of the Children Articulating Thinking (ChAT) Project was to explore the extent to which young children's self-regulated learning (SRL) and the quality of their dialogic interactions could be enhanced by introducing specific elements of classroom pedagogy, including a framework of 'rules for talk' to be used generically in day-to-day activities and specifically in particular group work activities designed to encourage problem-solving and shared reasoning.

The project was carried out at the University of Cambridge Faculty of Education from 2008 to 2010. The study involved the development of a community of research comprising a team of faculty-based researchers, including the authors of this chapter, and teachers based in primary schools in Cambridgeshire, Hertfordshire and Essex. Six Year 1 classes were involved as 'intervention' classrooms with seven to nine target children in each class. Three 'comparison' classrooms were also studied with seven to eight children in each class. The intervention and comparison schools were matched on the basis of pupil attainment, socio-economic catchment area, and numbers of free school meals.

The design was quasi-experimental in that there was no random allocation of participants to control or experimental groups, a process rarely possible when studying children in the naturalistic setting of their schools, and took the form of a 'pre-test, intervention, post-test' model. These three phases (described below), were all video recorded by the research team:

Phase 1: Assessments were made in intervention and comparison classes of target children's metacognition and self-regulation using a teacher-reported observational scale – the ChILD observational instrument (Whitebread *et al.*, 2009) and a series of problem-solving activities embedded in the contexts of play, science and expressive arts areas of the curriculum. The children's performance on these activities was analysed in relation to their conceptual understanding, their metacognitive or self-regulatory skills, and their ability to articulate their reasoning.

Phase 2: Teachers in the intervention group carried out eight activities with three in the area of expressive arts, three in the area of science, and two that were related to the development and evaluation of 'Rules for Talk' (Dawes, 2008; Mercer and Littleton, 2007). Of these activities, four were teacher-led and four were child-led, requiring children to work independently and collaboratively, although with some teacher support. In the context of these activities children were allocated to stable three-member mixed-gender groups (talk groups) with each group comprising a range in terms of children's regulatory skills as evaluated by the ChILD instrument (one Low SRL, one Medium SRL, and one High SRL). All intervention activities were designed in collaboration with the participant teachers. Each activity was preceded and followed by discussions between the teachers and children in which the teachers introduced and modelled metacognitive and self-regulatory language and processes.

Phase 3: The target children in the intervention and control classes were all reassessed following all the same procedures as in Phase 1.

As a means of illustrating the temporal transitions in children's language-for-thinking use and regulatory activity through the intervention, a qualitative description of an exemplar case is presented below. By presenting excerpts of classroom dialogue we also show how these transitions were enabled by the classroom teacher through systematic scaffolding and use of metacognitive language.

The selected case (at group and classroom level) was chosen as an illustration of the impact of the intervention, with the participant children showing noticeable positive changes in regulatory activity after the project and with teacher-student interactions reflecting clearly the design principles of the intervention.

Emma, Omar, Abbie and their teacher Valerie

Our exemplar case focuses on the activity of Emma (High SRL), Omar (Medium SRL) and Abbie (Low SRL) throughout the intervention. Figure 17.1 shows how these children differed noticeably in their assessed self-regulatory activity in the classroom context at the start of the project. More importantly the figure shows how the children improved their regulatory profiles after the intervention with the greatest improvement evidenced by the lower SRL child.

The following sections describe how a progression of productive, exploratory talk was developed at whole-class level and how this dialogic environment translated into positive group transitions in terms of shared thinking and regulation.

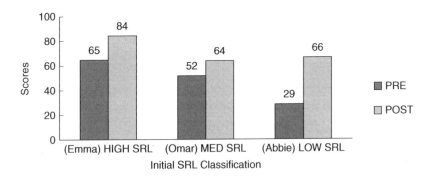

Figure 17.1 SRL improvement (ChILD Observation Instrument)

Developing a progression in the use of talk for thinking together

In the ChAT project the participant teachers laid the foundations for the study by explicitly introducing and consolidating key talk vocabulary. This language, which included words such as 'agree', 'disagree', 'take turns', 'respond', 'compromise' and 'negotiate', was gradually introduced, and systematically modelled and reinforced through whole-class discussions, role play, or the use of puppets. The following description of a segment of Valerie's first lesson illustrates how reflections about language were scaffolded in the context of whole-class discussions.

Valerie's class – Activity 1 (4 minutes into activity)
Valerie uses puppets to exemplify some talk situations experienced by two penguin characters (Pingu and Paul). She asks children to evaluate the quality of the conversation they are about to observe:
'I want you to be on the look out for things that are not going so well.' Subsequently, relevant talk vocabulary is introduced as part of the puppet interaction:
'We need to work together to find an **agreement**.'
At the end of the puppet interaction Valerie asks the children:
'What happened there?'
Child: 'At the beginning he wasn't **responding**.'
She further elaborates on what that means. Then the puppets modify their behaviour and enact productive strategies that enable the joint production of ideas. Children are then encouraged to identify these strategies:
'What did Pingu do to help?'

Situations that triggered student reflection such as the one above were combined with episodes of explicit teaching of talk vocabulary as can be observed during the second activity. This excerpt also shows how the target talk vocabulary (Respond) was reinforced in more than one lesson.

Valerie's class – Activity 2 (3 minutes into activity)
V: 'So we are going to make sure that when somebody says something to us we are going to **respond**. If I say to K Oh, you look really good in that outfit. What is it called? and K talks about something completely different like what she did over the weekend, that's **not responding**. K what would you respond to me?'
K: (pause) 'what you were saying.'
V: 'Yes, so if I say to you: What are you dressed as today? What would you say?'
K: 'I would say Scooby Doo.'
V: 'You would **respond** to my question by answering: I'm dressed as Scooby Doo.'

Having established familiarity with this vocabulary, Valerie worked towards the shared agreement of 'Rules for Talk'. This device, identified as fundamental by

Figure 17.2   Valerie using puppets to introduce key vocabulary

Mercer and Littleton in their 'Thinking Together' approach, (Dawes 2008; Mercer and Littleton 2007) involves the development of rules negotiated with the children and referred to constantly in everyday classroom interactions. These rules focus on facilitating group collaboration, the active sharing of ideas, and requiring children to give reasons for their ideas or opinions. The list of rules devised by Valerie's class included references to taking turns to speak, listening to each other, involving everyone and trying to agree. Talk in this classroom was explicitly valued. Displays about talk rules, often illustrated with photographs of the children engaged in appropriate activities, communicated key ideas to both children and parents, and teaching assistants were fully briefed about expectations and aspirations so that a cohesive approach was sustained.

Using talk and metacognitive vocabulary to explain the goal of activities and evaluate performance

In addition to using talk vocabulary as a tool for assisting children's individual and collective thinking, Valerie deliberately introduced metacognitive vocabulary when explaining activity goals. The following segment observed in Activity 2 illustrates this point. In this particular activity children were asked as groups to agree on different criteria to sort a random selection of objects. The teacher here is modelling how they might proceed with the task. Cognitive and metacognitive vocabulary used by the teacher is presented in bold.

Valerie's class – Activity 2 (11 minutes into activity)

The children sit forming a circle while Valerie places objects in the middle. She asks the children:

'Can you **describe** them using your senses?'

She discusses each object with the class, with a particular focus on materials: 'What is this made of?'

'I'm asking you to **describe** things by asking you questions?'

'Now that we have **discussed** the objects, I would like some **suggestions** as to how we could group them. **Think about it, I'll give you some thinking time.**'

'**I'd like you to sort them using the knowledge you just used.**'

Then she moves on to the learning goals of the activity:

'**Learning** to look and **think** about things, like we just did.'

'**Notice** what is the same and what is different.'

'**I'm looking to see you using all of our talk rules and coming to an agreement of what you think is the same and what you think is different.**'

'If you are **successful** today you will be able to say: I can **explain** what I have **noticed**; I can **give a reason** about what I have noticed.'

Metacognitive vocabulary was also used systematically by Valerie to encourage children's assessment of the extent to which they met the goals of an activity or the extent to which they interacted collaboratively during the group work. Examples of the questions used by Valerie are as follows:

'Now I would like to ask you what you found tricky about this activity' (Activity 5).

'Now I'm going to ask you to think about the success of this morning. If you feel you **observed** the paintings and **talked about them** and **described them** using colours, patterns, shapes and emotions please put your hands up' (Activity 6).

Emma, Omar and Abbie's group activity

As indicated in the previous sections, children in Valerie's class were exposed to constant examples of dialogic practices that encouraged shared thinking and were encouraged to develop strategies and monitor/evaluate their own use of rules for talk. In this highly enriching environment this small group made positive transitions in terms of their use of talk as well as in the extent to which all members of the group engaged in the regulation of the group activity during the target lessons. These transitions are exemplified in two excerpts, the first one observed in Activity 1 (agreeing on talk rules) and Activity 5 (ranking of objects in reference to property materials, size, and weight).

Figure 17.3   Emma, Omar and Abbie in Activity 1

Emma, Omar and Abbie – Activity 1

O: What did she say? because I didn't hear …

E: I don't know …

E: We must … sh … 'It's good to share our thoughts.'

O: It's good to share our thoughts. I think that one should be green. (Green is the colour for good ideas.)

A: Yeah. I've got green.

E: I think it's green.

O: I think it's green.

The dialogue above shows how despite the fact that there was joint attention and equivalent involvement by all group members the dialogue didn't offer explanations for the children's choices and remained repetitive in nature.

Emma, Omar and Abbie – Activity 5

E: It might squish little boxes and the little boxes might break so …

O: And the big box might not all be too heavy to maybe, the little boxes might not be too like strong to hold the big boxes. Like this would be able to hold that, wouldn't it very well?

E: (looks at the boxes O is pointing at)

A: Oh, that's heavy.

Figure 17.4 Emma, Omar and Abbie in Activity 5

E: ... that wouldn't be able to ...
O: (weighs another object) That would go there.
E: That (pointing at one object), that (pointing at another) wouldn't be able to hold that on top of it ...
O: No. So say ...
E: Have to have ... the big boxes at the bottom ...
E: Do you think so, Abbie?
O: So like that maybe (moving the bigger box closer to E),
A: Yes.
O: So that we have like that, so this at the bottom.
E: OK (grabbing a pencil ...),
O: It's still like a square.
E: OK, shall we do C at the bottom, F then, and A.

By Activity 5, we see a change emerging in the quality of dialogue. In this activity children were given a scenario in which they needed to help a removal man in doing his job. They were given a set of boxes and containers of different dimensions and weights and they were asked to find different ways of sorting the objects. As we can see here there is an effort by the group to jointly understand or express a principle that would allow them to sort the objects. Though Emma and Omar seem to dominate the discussion we see overt invitations directed to Abbie so she can join in.

Given the pre–post outcomes presented in 3.1 it is reasonable to assume that though not always an active member in the group's discussion, Abbie was clearly benefiting from the group and whole class discussions.

Valerie's example suggests that children as young as 5 are able to engage in forms of dialogue that allow them to share ideas and agree upon them. More importantly, this study as a whole shows that through the articulation of thinking and the development of a classroom culture that supports specific rules of joint participation, all children, regardless of their initial ability, are able to engage in regulatory behaviours that are directed towards the achievement of task goals and that ultimately benefit their learning. The quantitative data (to be published in subsequent papers), comparing the pre and post testing of the children in the intervention and control classrooms, reveals very large effect sizes for the intervention in relation to the children's metacognitive and self-regulatory abilities.

Conclusions

The ChAT project is one of the first to develop an intervention specifically intended to support metacognitive and self-regulatory skills in children as young as 5–6 years of age. It is also one of the first intervention studies to examine the possibility of enhancing these skills in children not by directly teaching and discussing particular learning strategies, but by supporting their ability to use talk productively in group problem solving activities, and so articulate their thinking. The evidence from the study so far seems to support the view, so eloquently first expressed by Vygotsky, that children's ability to use language to describe and reflect upon their own mental processes is fundamental to developing their metacognitive and self-regulatory processes. This area of research is attracting increasing interest among early childhood and primary school educators and researchers, along with developmental psychologists, and there is already a very valuable body of work, across this age range, examining the efficacy of practices and how they might best be realized in classrooms to best effect. A collection of work in this area has recently been published, arising from a conference, supported by the *British Journal of Educational Psychology*, held in the Faculty of Education, University of Cambridge, in June 2011 (Whitebread *et al.*, 2013). This contains reviews of research concerned with support for primary school children's self-regulation of their learning via a range of language-based interventions and practices. These include classroom processes comprising tasks, instructional practices and interpersonal interactions (Perry, 2013), peer-directed small groups (Webb *et al.*, 2013) and problem-orientated curricula (van Oers and Dobber, 2013).

This is already an exciting and rapidly developing area of research and we look forward to further insights and to their wide dissemination among the early childhood education practice and policy communities. If we seriously wish to enhance every young child's developing ability as a powerful learner, there is much to be gained, it is very clear, from making the processes of learning 'visible' to the child. In order to achieve this, various practices supporting children's use of language to help them enhance their metacognitive and self-regulatory abilities are clearly indicated.

References

Berk, L. E. and Spuhl, S. T. (1995) Maternal interaction, private speech, and task performance in preschool children. *Early Childhood Research Quarterly, 10*(2), 145–69.

Black, P. and Wiliam, D. (1998) *Inside the Black Box: Raising Standards Through Classroom Assessment*. London: Kings College School of Education.

Brown, R., Pressley, M., Van Meter, P. and Schuder, T. (1996) A quasi-experimental validation of transactional strategies instruction with low achieving second-grade readers. *Journal of Educational Psychology, 88*, 18–37.

Dawes, L. (2008) *The Essential Speaking and Listening: Talk for Learning at KS2*. London: Routledge.

Dignath, C., Buettner, G. and Langfeldt, H. P. (2008) How can primary school students learn self-regulated learning strategies most effectively? A meta-analysis on self-regulation training programs. *Educational Research Review, 3*, 101–29.

Eme, E., Puustinen, M. and Coutelet, B. (2006) Individual and developmental differences in reading monitoring: When and how do children evaluate their comprehension? *European Journal of Psychology of Education, 21*(1), 91–115.

Fabricius, W. V. and Hagen, J. W. (1984) Use of causal attributions about recall performance to assess metamemory and predict strategic memory behaviour in young children. *Developmental Psychology, 20*, 975–87.

Flavell, J. H., Beach, D. R. and Chinsky, J. M. (1966) Spontaneous verbal rehearsal in as memory task as a function of age, *Child Development, 37*, 283–99.

Forman, E. A. and Cazden, C. B. (1985) Exploring Vygotskian perspectives in education: The cognitive value of peer interaction. In J. V. Wertsch (ed.) *Culture, Communication and Cognition: Vygotskian Perspectives*. Cambridge: Cambridge University Press.

Giudici, C., Rinaldi, C. and Krechevsky, M. (2001) *Making Learning Visible: Children as Individual and Group Learners*. Project Zero, Harvard Graduate School of Education.

Grau, V. and Whitebread, D. (2012) Self and social regulation of learning during collaborative activities in the classroom: The interplay of individual and group cognition. *Learning and Instruction, 22*(6), 401–12.

Hattie, J. (2009) *Visible Learning: A Synthesis of over 800 Meta-analyses Relating to Achievement*. New York: Routledge.

Hattie, J. (2012) *Visible Learning for Teachers*. New York: Routledge.

Higgins, S., Kokotsaki, D. and Coe, R (2011) *Pupil Premium Toolkit: Summary for Schools* London: Sutton Trust. Retrieved from www.suttontrust.com/research/toolkit-of-strategies-to-improve-learning/.

Leat, D. and Lin, M. (2003) Developing a pedagogy of metacognition and transfer: Some signposts for the generation and use of knowledge and the creation of research partnerships. *British Educational Research Journal, 29*(3), 383–416.

Littleton, K., Mercer, N., Dawes, L., Wegerif, R., Rowe, D. and Sams, C. (2005) Talking and thinking together at Key Stage 1. *Early Years, 25*(2), 167–82.

McClelland, M. M., Acock, A. C., Piccinin, A., Rhea, S. A. and Stallings, M. C. (2013) Relations between preschool attention span-persistence and age 25 educational outcomes. *Early Childhood Research Quarterly, 28*(2), 314–24.

Mercer, N. (2000) *Words and Minds: How We Use Language to Think Together*. London: Routledge.

Mercer, N. (2013) Classroom talk and the development of self-regulation and metacognition. In D. Whitebread, N. Mercer, C. Howe, C. and A. Tolmie (eds) (2013) *Self-regulation and Dialogue in Primary Classrooms. British Journal of Educational Psychology Monograph Series II: Psychological Aspects of Education – Current Trends, No. 10*. Leicester: British Psychological Society.

Mercer, N. and Littleton, K. (2007) *Dialogue and the Development of Children's Thinking: A Sociocultural Approach*. London: Routledge.

Mercer, N., Wegerif, R. and Dawes, L. (1999) Children's talk and the development of reasoning in the classroom. *British Educational Research Journal, 25*(1), 95–111.

Ornstein, P. A., Grammer, J. K. and Coffman, J. L. (2010) Teachers' 'mnemonic style' and the development of skilled memory. In H. S. Waters and W. Schneider (eds) *Metacognition, Strategy Use and Instruction*. New York: Guilford Press.

Palincsar, A. S. and Brown, A. L. (1984) Reciprocal teaching of comprehension-fostering and comprehension-monitoring activities. *Cognition and Instruction*, *1*, 117–75.

Perry, N. E. (2013) Understanding classroom processes that support children's self-regulation of learning. In D. Whitebread, N. Mercer, C. Howe, C. and A. Tolmie (eds) *Self-regulation and Dialogue in Primary Classrooms. British Journal of Educational Psychology Monograph Series II: Psychological Aspects of Education – Current Trends, No. 10*. Leicester: British Psychological Society.

Puustinen, M. (1998) Help-seeking behaviour in a problem-solving situation: Development of self-regulation. *European Journal of Psychology of Education*, *23*(2), 271–82.

Siegler, R. S. (2002) Microgenetic studies of self-explanation. In N. Granott and J. Parziole (eds) *Microdevelopment: Transition Processes in Development and Learning*. Cambridge: Cambridge University Press.

Sylva, K. and Wiltshire, J. (1993) The impact of early learning on children's later development: A review prepared for the RSA inquiry 'Start Right'. *European Early Childhood Education Research Journal*, *1*, 17–40.

Sylva, K., Melhuish, E. C., Sammons, P., Siraj-Blatchford, I. and Taggart, B. (2004) *The Effective Provision of Pre-School Education (EPPE) Project: Technical Paper 12 – The Final Report: Effective Pre-School Education*. London: DfES/Institute of Education, University of London.

Tolmie, A., Howe, C., Mackenzie, M. and Greer, K. (1993) Task design as an influence on dialogue and learning: Primary school group work with object flotation. *Social Development*, *2*, 183–201.

Vallotton, C. D. and Ayoub, C. (2011) Use your words: The role of language in the development of toddlers' self-regulation. *Early Childhood Research Quarterly*, *26*(2), 169–81.

van Oers, B. and Dobber, M. (2013) Communication and regulation in a problem-oriented primary school curriculum. In D. Whitebread, N. Mercer, C. Howe, C. and A. Tolmie (eds) *Self-regulation and Dialogue in Primary Classrooms. British Journal of Educational Psychology Monograph Series II: Psychological Aspects of Education – Current Trends, No. 10*. Leicester: British Psychological Society.

Veenman, M., Wilhelm, P. and Beishuizen, J. J. (2004) The relation between intellectual and metacognitive skills from a developmental perspective. *Learning and Instruction*, *14*, 89–109.

Verschaffel, L., De Corte, E., Lasure, S., Van Vaerenbergh, G., Bogaerts, H. and Ratinckx, E. (1999) Learning to solve mathematical application problems: A design experiment with 5th graders. *Mathematical Thinking and Learning*, *1*, 195–229.

Volet, S. and Vauras, M. (eds) (2013) *Interpersonal Regulation of Learning and Motivation: Methodological Advances*. London: Routledge.

Vygotsky, L. S. (1978) *Mind in Society: The Development of Higher Psychological Processes*. Cambridge, MA: Harvard University Press.

Webb, N. M., Franke, M. L., Turrou, A. C. and Ing, M. (2013) Self-regulation and learning in peer-directed small groups. In D. Whitebread, N. Mercer, C. Howe, C. and A. Tolmie (eds) *Self-regulation and Dialogue in Primary Classrooms. British Journal of Educational Psychology Monograph Series II: Psychological Aspects of Education – Current Trends, No. 10*. Leicester: British Psychological Society.

Whitebread, D. and Basilio, M. (2012) The emergence and early development of self-regulation in young children. *Profesorado: Journal of Curriculum and Teacher Education, Monograph issue: Learn to learn. Teaching and evaluation of self-regulated learning*, *16*(1), 15–34.

Whitebread, D. and Grau Cardenas, V. (2012) Self-regulated learning and conceptual development in young children: the development of biological understanding. In A. Zohar and Y. J. Dori (eds) *Metacognition in Science Education: Trends in Current Research* (pp. 101–32). New York: Springer.

Whitebread, D. and Pino Pasternak, D. (2010) Metacognition, self-regulation and meta-knowing. In K. Littleton, C. Wood and J. Kleine Staarman (eds) *International Handbook of Psychology in Education*. Bingley, UK: Emerald.

Whitebread, D., Bingham, S., Grau, V., Pasternak, D. P. and Sangster, C. (2007) Development of metacognition and self-regulated learning in young children: Role of collaborative and peer-assisted learning. *Journal of Cognitive Education and Psychology*, 6, 433–55.

Whitebread, D., Coltman, P., Pino Pasternak, D., Sangster, C., Grau, V., Bingham, S., Almeqdad, Q. and Demetriou, D. (2009) The development of two observational tools for assessing metacognition and self-regulated learning in young children, *Metacognition and Learning*, 4(1), 63–85.

Whitebread, D., Mercer, N., Howe, C. and Tolmie, A. (eds) (2013) *Self-regulation and Dialogue in Primary Classrooms*. British Journal of Educational Psychology Monograph Series II: Psychological Aspects of Education – Current Trends, No. 10. Leicester: BPS.

Winsler, A., Fernyhough, C. and Montero, I. (2009) *Private Speech, Executive Functioning, and the Development of Verbal Self-Regulation*. Cambridge: Cambridge University Press.

18

LANGUAGE IMPAIRMENT WITHIN THE AUTISM SPECTRUM

Causes and consequences

Courtenay Frazier Norbury and Alison Sparks

Introduction

Language is a uniquely human form of communication. The building blocks of language, sets of symbols that are arbitrarily related and combine in rule governed ways, allow each of us to construct an infinite number of messages to communicate with others. Language is also an important tool for thinking and for developing self-control (Vygotsky, 1962), as language provides a mechanism for conscious reflection, negotiation and problem solving. Becoming a competent communicator requires mastering a multi-faceted and complex system, as language comprises several interacting sub-components. These include phonology, the system of sounds that combine to form words in ways that are particular to a language; semantics, the (multiple) meanings of words and how they relate to one another; and syntax, the rules for combining words into meaningful sentences. In addition to learning language structure, children must also learn the conventions that allow speakers to use language to carry out their intended goals and actions. This requires mastery of social communication and pragmatic language skills. Social communication skills are observed in dyadic exchanges and include an understanding of speaker intentions and the verbal and non-verbal cues that signal those intentions. Pragmatics refers to the ways speakers use language in context to go beyond what is explicitly stated, for example to infer new meaning or resolve ambiguities using prior knowledge and experience (Norbury, 2014). Most children acquire these skills with relative ease through interactions with peers and caregivers, but for some children, language learning and communication can be a life-long challenge.

Autism spectrum disorder (ASD) is characterized by profound deficits in social interaction and social communication, in addition to a restricted and repetitive repertoire of interests and behaviours (American Psychiatric Association, 2013). The onset and developmental course of ASD is influenced by genetic and environmental factors (Chaste and Leboyer, 2012), and has a profound impact on cognitive and social-emotional development. Language development is particularly vulnerable in ASD, though language impairment is not one of the core diagnostic criteria. Delay in the emergence of language is one of the earliest signs of autism reported by parents (Giacomo and Fombonne, 1998) and language competence is a significant predictor of educational and adaptive outcomes (Howlin, 2000; Szatmari *et al.*, 2009).

Given the social and behavioural challenges that characterize ASD, it is not surprising that language learning is often compromised. Perhaps more surprising is the very wide range of possible language outcomes, from limited expressive language (Wodka *et al.*, 2013), to verbal but with language abilities below chronological and mental age expectations (Loucas *et al.*, 2008), to fluent with grammatically complex speech indistinguishable from typically developing (TD) peers (Fein *et al.*, 2013). While the severity of social impairment may influence the developmental course of language acquisition, it is clear that social factors alone cannot explain this heterogeneity of language outcome. In this chapter, we consider whether this variation in language ability reflects distinct neurocognitive phenotypes (Tager-Flusberg and Joseph, 2003), and whether etiological risk for language impairment may be shared across neurodevelopmental disorders, particularly specific language impairment (SLI). We briefly describe the profile of language strength and weakness in two groups: those with autism and language scores within the normal range (ALN), and those with additional language impairments (ALI). Comparison of these groups has the potential to identify protective factors that may facilitate language acquisition in the face of social and behavioural challenges, as well as additional risk factors that may further compromise language acquisition in those with ALI. The extent to which these multiple risk factors are shared across clinical boundaries is considered.

Language and communication in autism: universal features

A defining feature of ASD is pronounced deficits in social communication (APA, 2013). Social communication refers to the exchange of ideas and information between two or more people and covers a multitude of skills. For example, non-verbal cues such as eye gaze, facial expression, tone of voice and body posture may be communicative in their own right or may accompany a verbal message. Understanding and use of non-verbal communication is compromised from the earliest stages in ASD, as infants and toddlers fail to orient to socially informative stimuli such as faces and eye gaze (Mundy and Crowson, 1997). Reduced communicative intent is also a feature of ASD. While many children with ASD may be able to use language or other means to make requests, they may be less likely to initiate communication for the purpose of sharing interests (for example, declarative pointing, or commenting on something in the environment), they may not use language to negotiate, refuse, persuade, joke or ask questions of others. For verbal children with ASD, difficulties with discourse management are also evident (de Villiers *et al.*, 2007; Hale and Tager-Flusberg, 2005). These difficulties may include problems maintaining a topic of conversation or providing contingent responses, poor turn-taking, and a failure to request clarification or spontaneously repair utterances. In addition, children with ASD may find it difficult to provide appropriate amounts of information to the listener, either providing too much irrelevant detail, or providing too little information such that the listener may not be able to follow the conversation. Varying communication strategies according to context may also prove challenging, for example speaking quietly in a library versus a café, or speaking more politely to the head teacher relative to one's peers. Thus, deficits in verbal and non-verbal communication for social purposes is a defining feature of ASD, even in the context of age appropriate structural language (i.e. phonology, semantics, syntax) skill.

There are also aspects of structural language development that are fairly consistent across the autism spectrum. The majority of children with ASD experience delays in reaching early language milestones such as first words and first phrases, and children with ASD are more likely than other clinical populations to experience regression of language skills (Pickles *et al.*, 2009). For most children, understanding of language is more advanced than language expression, while in ASD, this pattern is reversed (Hudry *et al.*, 2010). Children with verbal language tend to have adequate articulation skills, regardless of whether structural language skills are impaired (Kjelgaard and Tager-Flusberg, 2001), though qualitative differences in prosody are common (McCann *et al.*, 2007).

Some features of language in ASD are remarkable in that they are only rarely observed in children with other neuro-developmental disorders. Many young children with autism frequently echo, or repeat utterances immediately after they are heard (immediate echolalia) in spontaneous conversation, or heard at some recent time in the past (delayed echolalia; Prizant and Duchan, 1981). Another unique feature of autistic language is difficulty learning to deploy pronouns accurately (Lee *et al.*, 1994). While imitating an utterance some children with ASD do not reverse the pronoun *you* to *I* to make reference to oneself, a skill that reflects an understanding of role reversal imitation. It has been noted that those who outgrow the use of echolalia and go on to a more flexible use of language have better language outcomes than those who do not (Wetherby *et al.*, 2000).

Perhaps the most salient feature of language in ASD is the wide range of variation in structural language skill (Kjelgaard and Tager-Flusberg, 2001). A significant proportion of children with ASD do not achieve functional levels of language production (Hus *et al.* 2007; Wodka *et al.*, 2012). In contrast, about 50 per cent of children with non-verbal abilities within the normal range achieve age-appropriate scores on standard tests of speech, vocabulary and grammar (Kjelgaard and Tager-Flusberg, 2001; Loucas *et al.*, 2008). Still others are verbal, but their structural language skills lag behind chronological and mental age expectations, a pattern that is seen in other developmental disorders such as specific language impairment (Kjelgaard and Tager-Flusberg, 2001; Loucas *et al.*, 2008).

A landmark study by Kjelgaard and Tager-Flusberg (2001) highlighted the stark range of language profiles that exist within ASD. Children with ASD completed a wide-ranging battery of standardized language tests tapping speech, vocabulary, verbal memory and grammar. Children were grouped according to their performance on the Clinical Evaluation of Language Fundamentals (CELF: Semel *et al.*, 2003), an omnibus test of language function. The authors found that scores on the articulation test fell within the average range regardless of overall level of language ability. However, two distinct profiles of language emerged. Those children who scored within the normal range on the CELF also scored within normal limits on all other language measures, including vocabulary, grammar, and non-word repetition. However, approximately 50 per cent of these verbal children scored 2SDs or more below the mean on the CELF; these children also scored below age expectations on measures of vocabulary and non-sense word repetition, though grammar was most severely impaired. Kjelgaard and Tager-Flusberg observed that this linguistic profile closely resembled that of children with specific language impairment (SLI). Further studies reported that these groups do not differ on measures of autistic symptomatology or social ability (at least in middle childhood), questioning the extent to which variation in language can be attributed to autistic-deficits in social understanding or social engagement. Instead, Tager-Flusberg and colleagues (Tager-Flusberg and Joseph, 2003) argued that children with ALI might represent a distinct neuro-cognitive phenotype, in which autism and language impairment are co-morbid conditions. Subsequent studies have demonstrated overlap between ALI and SLI phenotypes on genetic (Bartlett *et al.*, 2014), neurobiological (De Fossé *et al.*, 2004; Hodge *et al.*, 2010) and cognitive (Norbury, 2005a) levels, using both verbal (Lindgren *et al.*, 2009) and non-verbal (Kelly *et al.*, 2013) tasks. Nevertheless, the idea that ALI represents a co-morbid condition remains controversial (Williams *et al.*, 2008; Tomblin, 2011).

Characteristics of the ALN phenotype

The most widely studied group of children with ASD are those who resemble typically developing peers in terms of language structure, but with more apparent deficits in social communication and pragmatics. However, much research has questioned whether there are qualitative differences in how these children learn and process language. For individuals with ALN, vocabulary knowledge may represent a 'peak of ability' (Mottron, 2004). However, it is important to note that this observed strength is largely based on breadth of vocabulary (quantity of words) as measured on standardized tests in which subjects name or point to a picture that best matches a single word. On the other hand, depth of vocabulary knowledge (understanding of relationships among words, and morphological and syntactic knowledge about words) may be qualitatively different from semantic knowledge of typical peers. For example, McCleery *et al.* (2010) reported a reduced neural response to incongruent word-picture pairs in toddlers with ASD, indicating a verbal semantic impairment, while Kamio and Toichi (2007) reported reduced category priming for adolescents with ASD. Henderson *et al.* (2011) used a homonym priming paradigm and revealed that adolescents with ASD (who had age appropriate language skills) demonstrated appropriate priming at short inter-stimulus intervals, but showed impairments in the selection of semantic representations at longer intervals.

Norbury *et al.* (2010) matched children with ALN to typical peers on both raw and standard scores of a receptive picture vocabulary test; however, these same children with ALN scored more than 1SD below their peers on a test of verbal definitions. Children were then asked to infer the meaning of novel words from social cues (e.g. a head turn to the target object). The children with ALN performed as well as TD peers when a cue was present, and were much better than peers at immediate naming of new objects, indicating particularly accurate phonological learning. However, whereas performance of TD children improved over time, performance of children with ALN did not. A recent study by Henderson *et al.* (2014) extended these findings and demonstrated differences between adolescent boys with ALN and their TD peers in the time course of lexical integration and specifically suggested aberrant consolidation of newly learned words. These findings suggest that the ability to follow explicit social cues in the context of good phonological discrimination and memory may allow children with ALN to acquire a large store of known words. However, reduced social understanding and atypical consolidation and integration of new information may give rise to qualitative differences in semantic processing and pragmatic language skills such as metaphor, where the ability to integrate seemingly disparate meanings in context is paramount.

Few studies have explicitly compared the syntactic skills of children with ALN to typical peers or peers with ASD and additional language impairments. Those that have report that, on structured measures of sentence production (McGregor *et al.*, 2012) and sentence comprehension (Loucas *et al.*, 2008), children with ALN do not differ in accuracy or sentence complexity from typical peers. Children with ALN also align their syntactic production to that of their interlocutors, as evidenced by robust syntactic priming (Allen *et al.*, 2011). In more naturalistic production tasks, however, it may be that children with ALN have difficulty applying their syntactic knowledge on-line. For instance, in narrative tasks, children with ALN tend to produce shorter and more grammatically simple utterances relative to peers matched on both age and language ability (King *et al.*, 2013; Norbury *et al.*, 2013).

Pragmatic language here refers to the use of language in a context. Context is particularly important because much of what we intend to communicate is not explicitly stated (requiring an inference to be made) and much of what we say is ambiguous (Wilson and Sperber, 2012). For example, many words have multiple meanings (e.g. 'bank' or 'bark') or we may use figurative expressions such as metaphors to convey a meaning that goes beyond the explicit utterance ('that man is a clown'). To recover meaning in these situations is often argued to require social cognitive understanding; in other words one must understand that a speaker intends to convey a message that is not explicit in the utterance. We would argue that recovering the appropriate intended meaning relies heavily on linguistic context (as well as general background knowledge). For instance, on hearing 'Max pedalled to school yesterday', most of us would automatically infer that Max rode his bike. Making this inference does not require accessing the speaker's mental state, but it does crucially require an understanding of the verb 'to pedal' and knowledge that pedals are things to be found on bicycles.

For many years, it was assumed that individuals with ASD, regardless of language ability, would find pragmatic language challenging, either because of the need to understand speaker intention, or because of the need to integrate information within a given context (Happé, 1999). However, recent studies have found that individuals with the ALN phenotype do not differ from TD peers on pragmatic language tasks. For instance, Norbury (2005b) investigated metaphor comprehension in children with ALN and those with ALI, aged between 8 and 15 years. Notably, these groups did not differ with respect to social communication deficit, as measured by parent report of social behaviour. Children with ALN did not differ from TD peers on the metaphor task, and achieved significantly higher scores than those with ALI. Moreover, scores on measures of structural language predicted unique variance in metaphor understanding, whereas scores on a measure of social cognition did not. Studies employing experimental measures of inferencing ability and ambiguity resolution have also found few differences between individuals with ALN and TD peers (Norbury, 2004, 2005a; Brock *et al.*, 2008; Pinjacker *et al.*, 2009). Furthermore, structural language abilities reliably predict performance on these tasks, within ASD populations (Volden *et al.*, 2009). Thus it would seem that social communication deficits may be evident in children with ALN who are indistinguishable from TD peers on measures of pragmatic language comprehension.

Pragmatic difficulties may become more evident in expressive tasks such as formulating narrative or lengthier exchanges of connected verbal discourse. For example, Norbury *et al.* (2013) examined narrative skills in children aged 6 to 15 years and found that even though children with ALN had been matched to typically developing peers on standardized measures of language structure, they scored significantly lower on measures of word count, semantic diversity, and mean length of utterance within a story retelling task. Although narrative skill improved significantly with age in the ALN group, these children were more likely to make pragmatic errors (in which erroneous information or irrelevant details were introduced) than TD peers. They were also particularly challenged in their ability to mark reference; for instance, many children failed to provide specific and consistent labels for story characters, making it difficult for the listener to ascertain who did what to whom.

Characteristics of the ALI phenotype

In contrast to children with ALN, those with ALI have demonstrable impairment in almost every facet of the language system. In verbal children with ALI, articulation skills are unimpaired (Kjelgaard and Tager-Flusberg, 2001). Nevertheless, several studies have reported deficits on tasks that tap phonological processing skills such as non-word repetition. Non-word repetition tasks require the child to repeat non-sense words of increasing length (e.g. 'hampent' versus 'blonterstaping'). There is much debate about what the task measures, but in children with SLI, it is thought to assess phonological short-term memory, a skill that is potentially important for learning new words (Gathercole, 2006; though see Melby-Lervåg *et al.*, 2012 for a challenge to this view). Numerous studies have demonstrated that performance on this task aligns with language impairment in ASD (Bishop *et al.*, 2004); those with the ALI phenotype repeat significantly fewer non-words than those with ALN (Kjelgaard and Tager-Flusberg, 2001), and at least in terms of total accuracy, performance of children with ALI is indistinguishable from children with SLI (Lindgren *et al.*, 2009).

However, many investigators have noted qualitative differences in errors on the non-word repetition task, and an attenuated effect of syllable length, leading them to conclude that apparently similar deficits may arise from different underlying cognitive impairments (Riches *et al.*, 2010; Whitehouse, *et al.*, 2008; Williams *et al.*, 2013).

For children with ALI, vocabulary scores on standard measures tend to be in the low-average range and are not dissimilar to the vocabulary scores of age-matched peers with SLI (McGregor *et al.*, 2012; Lindgren *et al.*, 2009). Measures tapping depth of semantic knowledge, such as verbal definitions and word associations, also reveal deficits in children with ALI relative to peers with ALN (McGregor *et al.*, 2012). No studies have directly compared word learning or consolidation of new words in children with ALI relative to TD peers or peers with ALN. However, the majority of studies investigating the word learning skills of children with ASD have focused on young children with pronounced language deficits. These studies demonstrate that while many children are able to follow explicit social cues, they have a particular deficit in using speaker intention to infer new word meaning (cf. Parish-Morris *et al.*, 2007). It is worth noting that most of these studies have employed a fast mapping paradigm that requires recognition of named objects. The findings of enhanced phonological learning in children with ALN reported by Norbury *et al.* (2010) strongly predicts that children with ALI, like peers with SLI, should experience additional deficits in recalling newly learned phonological forms, which may further disrupt lexical and semantic learning.

By definition, children with ALI have pronounced deficits in grammatical comprehension and production. Many investigators have focused on whether there are quantitative or qualitative differences in the grammatical skills of children with ALI relative to peers diagnosed with SLI. Some investigators have found comparable performance in the two groups (Lindgren *et al.*, 2009; McGregor *et al.*, 2012), others have found that children with SLI have more pronounced deficits in syntactic production (Riches *et al.*, 2010), while others have found that children with ALI have more severe comprehension deficits (Loucas *et al.*, 2008). Children with ALI also show reduced marking of verb tense, such as past tense (−ed) or third person singular (−s), linguistic features that have been put forward as potential clinical markers of SLI (Roberts *et al.*, 2004). However, qualitative differences in the error patterns of children with ALI and children with SLI have been noted and have caused some to question whether the same underlying deficit influences performance in both populations (Williams *et al.*, 2008). While this remains possible, we would argue that performance was affected by the same underlying causal risk factor in both groups, even though qualitative differences might still arise given that children with ALI have the additional social and cognitive deficits associated with ASD that peers with SLI do not experience. Therefore, qualitative differences in task performance should not rule out the possibility that language impairment is a co-morbid condition in ASD.

As noted earlier, successful pragmatic language skills require understanding the surrounding linguistic context to make inferences or resolve ambiguities. It is therefore not surprising that pragmatic language is highly correlated with structural language skills within the autism spectrum (Ketelaars *et al.*, 2009; Volden *et al.*, 2009). Studies that have specifically identified children with the ALI phenotype have reported significantly poorer performance relative to peers with ALN on measures of figurative language comprehension (Norbury, 2004) and ambiguity resolution (Hoy *et al.*, 2004; Norbury 2005a). Children with ALI also tend to have more difficulties with inferencing (Lucas and Norbury, under revision), though children with ALN may also find making inferences challenging in both verbal and written domains (Norbury and Bishop, 2002; Norbury and Nation, 2011). However, when inferencing is measured using implicit, on-line measures, few differences are seen between children with ASD and their peers (Saldaña and Frith, 2007).

In summary, there is now substantial evidence that there are at least two distinct phenotypes within the autism spectrum that may be distinguished on the basis of language ability. There is growing evidence that the ALI phenotype shares aetiological risk factors with more specific language impairment. However, longitudinal studies are needed to determine the stability of these language phenotypes, and whether differences in the developmental trajectories of children with ALI and SLI exist.

Language impairment is influenced by multiple factors in ASD

The evidence reviewed above suggests that impairments of structural language are not universal within ASD and the variation seen in language outcome suggests that autistic cognition alone cannot explain language impairment in ASD. Tomblin (2011) also demonstrates that linguistic vulnerabilities in autism found in grammar and non-word repetition skills are not unique to ASD or SLI, but are also features of other neuro-developmental disorders. This suggestion parallels recent genetic investigations highlighting shared aetiological risk factors, such as genetic variants of the CNTNAP2 gene, which operate across a wide range of clinical conditions and disrupt early neural development in a way that is non-optimal for language learning (Rodenas-Cuadrado *et al.*, 2014). Shared aetiological risk does not, however, imply identical language phenotypes; Tomblin (2011) notes that in addition to shared risk factors, syndrome specific risk factors and environmental factors will further shape the language development of individual children. Gene x gene interactions and gene x environment interactions will also be important in understanding the similarities and differences in language phenotypes across disorders (Bishop, 2010).

We do not wish to suggest that children with autism are not hampered by difficulties in learning language from the social context, but that a core deficit in social communication is not sufficient to explain the wide variability in language competence that is now well documented in autism. We therefore propose a multi-deficit account of language impairment within ASD, as illustrated in Figure 18.1. On this view, there are a multitude of genetic and environmental risk factors (represented by the dark and light grey circles), that confer risk for particular cognitive traits. Importantly, some of these may be syndrome specific, but many are likely to operate across neuro-developmental conditions. The particular phenotype expressed therefore results from the confluence of risk factors to which the individual is exposed. For instance, the child with atypical social development, focused interests and aberrant consolidation processes, in the absence of any phonological impairment is more likely to have an

ALN phenotype, in which structural aspects of language are acquired (though delays in language onset may be present due to social deficits), but qualitative differences in language knowledge and language use may persist. These may arise from poor social understanding and/or disrupted integration of information within the language system. In contrast, a child with poor phonological skills and perhaps impairments to implicit learning networks, but with a keen interest in making social connections and exploring environments, is more likely to have a 'specific' language impairment, in which pragmatic skills are limited primarily by poor understanding of the surrounding linguistic context. The ALI profile then arises when a combination of these risk factors is present.

There are no doubt many additional risk and protective factors (visual attention, for instance) that shape language development and disorder within ASD. Figure 18.1 also presents a top-down view of risk, but we acknowledge that the different levels (genetic, cognitive and behavioural) are likely to be interactive. Longitudinal studies that involve direct comparison of different developmental conditions, using multiple measures of risk and protective factors will further elucidate when and why language development goes awry in ASD, and will give further insights to skills that might be targeted in intervention.

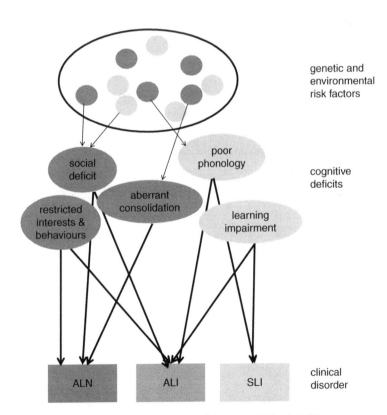

Figure 18.1 Multiple risk factors associated with language ability in ASD

Summary and conclusions

We have argued that there are distinct language phenotypes within ASD, and have provided an overview of the language profiles that exist within these phenotypes, based on available evidence. However, this is derived entirely from work on English-speaking children with ASD and there is a dearth of information available on language phenotypes in speakers of other languages. Although ASD is increasingly recognized as a global phenomenon, most of what we know about the behavioural characteristics of ASD and our cognitive theories to explain these characteristics have been developed from research that is conducted in Western societies. These cohorts reflect a minority of the world's population that may not be truly representative of the majority (Henrich *et al.*, 2010). Few studies have looked at ASD symptoms and diagnostic features across cultural/linguistic contexts (but see Freeth *et al.*, 2013), so our understanding is constrained by the cultures and languages in which the disorder has been studied and defined. There is a further need for research that examines ASD within and across cultures and languages as a way to validate and/or modify our understanding of universal features of ASD and features that will vary in differing ecological contexts (Norbury and Sparks, 2013).

References

Allen, M. L., Haywood, S., Rajendran, G. and Branigan, H. (2011) Evidence for syntactic alignment in children with autism. *Developmental Science*, *14*(3), 540–8. http://www.ncbi. nlm.nih.gov/pubmed/21477193.

American Psychiatric Association (APA) (2013) *Diagnostic and Statistical Manual of Mental Disorders*, 5th edn. Arlington, VA: American Psychiatric Publishing.

Bartlett, C. W., Hou, L., Flax, J. F., Hare, A., Cheong, S. Y., Fermano. Z., Zimmerman-Bier, B., Cartwright, C., Azaro, M. A., Buyske, S. and Brzustowicz, L. M. (2014) A genome scan for loci shared by autism spectrum disorder and language impairment. *American Journal of Psychiatry*, *171*(1), 72–81. doi: 10.1176/appi.ajp.2013.12081103.

Bishop, D. V. M. (2010) Overlaps between autism and language impairment: Phenomimicry or shared etiology? *Behavior Genetics*, *40*(5), 618–29.

Bishop, D. V. M., Maybery, M., Wong, D., Maley, A., Hill, W. and Hallmayer, J. (2004) Are phonological processing deficits part of the broad autism phenotype? *American Journal of Medical Genetics*, *128B*, 54–60.

Bloom, P. (2002) Mind reading, communication and learning the name for things. *Mind and Language*, *17*, 37–54.

Brenner, L., Turner, K. and Muller, R. (2007) Eye movement and visual search: Are there elementary abnormalities in autism? *Journal of Autism and Developmental Disorders*, *37*, 1289–309.

Brock, J., Norbury, C. F., Einav, S. and Nation, K. (2008) Eye-movements reveal context processing difficulties among children with autism and language impairments. *Cognition*, *108*, 896–904.

Chaste, P. and Leboyer, M. (2012) Autism risk factors: Genes, environment, and gene-environment interactions. *Dialogues in Clinical Neuroscience*, *14*(3), 281–92.

De Fossé, L., Hodge, S. M., Makris, N., Kennedy, D. N., Caviness, V. S. Jr, McGrath, L., Steele, S., Ziegler, D. A., Herbert, M. R., Frazier, J. A., Tager-Flusberg, H. and Harris, G. J. (2004) Language-association cortex asymmetry in autism and specific language impairment. *Annals of Neurology*, *56*(6), 757–66. doi: 10.1002/ana.20275.

de Villiers, J., Fine, J. Ginsberg, G., Vaccarella, L. and Szatmari, P. (2007) Brief report: A scale for rating conversational impairment in autism spectrum disorder. *Journal of Autism and Developmental Disorders, 37*(7), 1375–80.

Giacomo, A. D. and Fombonne, E. (1998) Parental recognition of developmental abnormalities in autism. *European Child and Adolescent Psychiatry, 7*(3), 131–6. doi: 10.1007/s007870050058.

Fein, D., Barton, M., Eigsti, I.-M., Kelley, E., Naigles, L., Schultz, R. T., Stevens, M., Orinstein, A., Rosenthal, M., Troyb, E. and Tyson, K. (2013) Optimal outcome in individuals with a history of autism. *Journal of Child Psychology and Psychiatry, and Allied Disciplines, 54*(2), 195–205. doi: 10.1111/jcpp.12037.

Freeth, M., Sheppard, E., Ramachandran, R. and Milne, E. (2013) A cross-cultural comparison of autistic traits in the UK, India and Malaysia. *Journal of Autism and Developmental Disorders, 43*, 2569–83. doi: 10.1007/s10803-013-1808-9.

Gathercole, S. E. (2006) Nonword repetition and word learning: The nature of the relationship. *Applied Psycholinguistics, 27*, 513–43.

Happé, F. (1999) Autism: Cognitive deficit or cognitive style? *Trends in Cognitive Science, 3*, 216–22.

Hale, C. M. and Tager-Flusberg, H. (2003) The influence of language on Theory of Mind. *Developmental Science, 6*, 346–59.

Henderson, L. M., Clarke, P. and Snowling, M. J. (2011) Accessing and selecting word meaning in autism spectrum disorder. *Journal of Child Psychiatry and Psychology, 52*, 964–73.

Henderson, L., Powell, A., Gaskell, G. and Norbury, C. F. (2014) Learning and consolidation of new word forms in autism spectrum disorder. *Developmental Science*.

Henrich, J., Heine, S. J. and Norenzayan, A. (2010) The weirdest people in the world? *Behavioral and Brain Sciences*, 1–75.

Hodge, S. M., Makris, N., Kennedy, D. N., Caviness, V. S. Jr, Howard, J., McGrath, L., Steele, S., Frazier, J. A., Tager-Flusberg, H. and Harris, G. J. (2010) Cerebellum, language, and cognition in autism and specific language impairment. *Journal of Autism and Developmental Disorders, 40*(3), 300–16. doi: 10.1007/s10803-009-0872-7.

Howlin, P. (2000) Outcome in adult life for more able individuals with autism or Asperger syndrome. *Autism, 4*(1), 63–83. doi: 10.1177/13623613000040010.

Hoy, J. A., Hatton, C. and Hare, D. (2004) Weak central coherence: A cross-domain phenomenon specific to autism? *Autism, 8*(3), 267–81. doi: 10.1177/1362361304045218.

Hudry, K., Leadbitter, K., Temple, K., Slonims, V., McConachie, H., Aldred, C., Howlin, P. and Charman, T. Pact Consortium (2010) Preschoolers with autism show greater impairment in receptive compared with expressive language abilities. *International Journal of Language and Communication Disorders, 45*(6), 681–90. doi: 10.3109/13682820903461493.

Hus, V., Pickles, A., Cook, E. H. Jr, Risi, S. and Lord, C. (2007) Using the autism diagnostic interview – revised to increase phenotypic homogeneity in genetic studies of autism. *Biological Psychiatry, 61*(4), 438–48. doi: 10.1016/j.biopsych.2006.08.044.

Kamio, Y. and Toichi, M. (2007) Memory illusion in high-functioning autism and Asperger's disorder. *Journal of Autism and Developmental Disorders, 37*(5), 867–76. doi: 10.1007/s10803-006-0214-y.

Ketelaars, M. P., Cuperus, J. M., Van Daal, J., Jansonius, K. and Verhoeven, L. (2009) Screening for pragmatic language impairment: the potential of the Children's Communication Checklist. *Research in Developmental Disabilities, 30*, 952–60.

Kelly, D. J., Walker, R. and Norbury, C. F. (2013) Deficits in volitional oculomotor control align with language status in autism spectrum disorders. *Developmental Science, 16*(1), 56–66.

King, D., Dockrell, J. E. and Stuart, M. (2013) Event narratives in 11–14 year olds with autistic spectrum disorder. *International Journal of Language and Communication Disorders, 48*(5), 522–33.

Kjelgaard, M. M. and Tager-Flusberg H. (2001) An investigation of language impairment in autism: implications for genetic subgroups. *Language and Cognitive Processes, 16*(2–3), 287–308.

Lee, A., Hobson, R. P. and Chiat, S. (1994) I, you, me, and autism: An experimental study. *Journal of Autism and Developmental Disorders, 24*, 155–76.

Lindgren, K. A., Folstein, S. E., Tomblin, J. B. and Tager-Flusberg, H. (2009) Language and reading abilities of children with autism spectrum disorders and specific language impairment and their first-degree relatives. *Autism Research, 2*(1), 22–38. doi: 10.1002/aur.63.

Loucas, T., Charman, T., Pickles, A., Simonoff, E., Chandler, S., Meldrum, D. and Baird, G. (2008) Autistic symptomatology and language ability in autism spectrum disorder and specific language impairment. *Journal of Child Psychology and Psychiatry, 49*(11), 1184–92. doi: 10.1111/j.1469-7610.2008.01951.x.

Lucas, R. and Norbury, C. F. (2014) Levels of text comprehension in children with Autism Spectrum Disorders (ASD): The influence of language phenotype. *Journal of Autism and Developmental Disorders*, in press.

McCann, J., Peppé, S., Gibbon, F. E., O'Hare, A. and Rutherford, M. (2007) Prosody and its relationship to language in school-aged children with high-functioning autism. *International Journal of Language and Communication Disorders, 42*(6), 682–702.

McCleery, J. P., Ceponiene, R., Burner, K. M., Townsend, J., Kinnear, M. and Schreibman, L. (2010) Neural correlates of verbal and nonverbal semantic integration in children with autism spectrum disorders. *Journal of Child Psychology and Psychiatry, 51*(3), 277–86. doi: 10.1111/j.1469-7610.2009.02157.

McGregor, K. K., Berns, A. J., Owen, A. J., Michels, S. A., Duff, D., Bahnsen, A. J. and Lloyd, M. (2012) Associations between syntax and the lexicon among children with or without ASD and language impairment. *Journal of Autism and Developmental Disorders, 42*(1), 35–47. doi: 10.1007/s10803-011-1210-4.

Melby-Lervåg, M., Lervåg, A. and Hulme, C. *et al.* (2012) Nonword-repetition ability does not appear to be a causal influence on children's vocabulary development. *Psychological Science.* doi: 10.1177/0956797612443833.

Mottron, L. (2004) Matching strategies in cognitive research with individuals with high-functioning autism: Current practices, instrument biases, and recommendations. *Journal of Autism and Developmental Disorders, 34*(1), 19–27. doi: 10.1023/B:JADD.0000018070.88380.83.

Mundy, P. and Crowson, M. (1997) Joint attention and early social communication: Implications for research on intervention with autism. *Journal of Autism and Developmental Disorders, 27*(6), 653–76. doi: 10.1023/A:1025802832021

Norbury, C. F. (2004) Factors supporting idiom comprehension in children with communication disorders. *Journal of Speech, Language and Hearing Research, 47*, 1179–93.

Norbury, C. F. (2005a) Barking up the wrong tree? Lexical ambiguity resolution in children with language impairments and autistic spectrum disorders. *Journal of Experimental Child Psychology, 90*(2), 142–71.

Norbury, C. F. (2005b) The relationship between Theory of Mind and metaphor: Evidence from children with language impairment and autistic spectrum disorder. *British Journal of Developmental Psychology, 23*, 383–99.

Norbury, C. F. (2014) Social (pragmatic) communication disorder – conceptualization, evidence and clinical implications. *Journal of Child Psychology and Psychiatry, 55*, 204–16.

Norbury, C. F. and Bishop, D. V. M. (2003) Narrative skills of children with communication impairments. *International Journal of Language and Communication Disorders, 38*, 287–313.

Norbury, C. F. and Nation, K. (2011) Understanding variability in reading comprehension in adolescents with autism spectrum disorders: Interactions with language status and decoding skill. *Scientific Studies of Reading, 15*.

Norbury, C. F. and Sparks, A. (2013) Difference or disorder? Cultural issues in understanding neurodevelopmental disorders. *Developmental Psychology, 49*, 45–58.

Norbury, C. F., Griffiths, H. and Nation, K. (2010) Sound before meaning: Word learning in children with autism spectrum disorders. *Neuropsychologia, 48*, 4012–19.

Norbury, C. F., Gemmell, T. and Paul, R. (2013) Pragmatics abilities in narrative production: A cross-disorder comparison. *Journal of Child Language*, 1–26. doi: 10.1017/S030500091300007X.

Parish-Morris, J., Hennon, E. A., Hirsh-Pasek, K., Golinkoff, R. M. and Tager-Flusberg, H. (2007) Children with autism illuminate the role of social intention in word learning. *Child Development*, 78(4), 1265–87. doi: 10.1111/j.1467-8624.2007.01065.x.

Pickles, A., Simonoff, E., Conti-Ramsden, G., Falcaro, M., Simkin, Z., Charman, T., Chandler, S., Loucas, T. and Baird, G. (2009) Loss of language in early development of autism and specific language impairment. *Journal of Child Psychology and Psychiatry*, 50(7), 843–52. doi: 10.1111/j.1469-7610.2008.02032.x.

Pijnacker, J., Hagoort, P., Buitelaar, J., Teunisse, J. P. and Geurts, B. (2009) Pragmatic inferences in high-functioning adults with autism and Asperger syndrome. *Journal of Autism and Developmental Disorders*, 39, 607–18.

Prizant, B. (1983) Language acquisition and communicative behavior in autism: Toward an understanding of the 'whole' of it. *Journal of Speech and Hearing Disorders*, 48, 296–307.

Prizant, B. and Duchan, J. (1981) The functions of immediate echolalia in autistic children. *Journal of Speech and Hearing Disorders*, 46, 241–9.

Riches, N. G., Loucas, T., Baird, G., Charman, T. and Simonoff, E. (2010) Sentence repetition in adolescents with specific language impairments and autism: An investigation of complex syntax. *International Journal of Language and Communication Disorders*, 45(1), 47–60. doi: 10.3109/13682820802647676.

Roberts, J. A., Rice, M. L. and Tager-Flusberg, H. (2004) Tense marking in children with autism. *Applied Psycholinguistics*, 25, 429–48.

Rodenas-Cuadrado, P., Ho, J. and Vernes, S. C. (2014) Shining a light on CNTNAP2: Complex functions to complex disorders. *European Journal of Human Genetics*, 22(2), 171–8. doi: 10.1038/ejhg.2013.100.

Saldaña, D. and Frith, U. (2007) Do readers with autism make bridging inferences from world knowledge? *Journal of Experimental Child Psychology*, 96(4), 310–19. doi: 10.1016/j.jecp.2006.11.002.

Semel, E., Wiig, E. H. and Secord, W. A. (2003) *Clinical Evaluation of Language Fundamentals*, 4th edn (CELF-4). Toronto: The Psychological Corporation.

Szatmari, P., Bryson, S., Duku, E., Vaccarella, L., Zwaigenbaum, L., Bennett, T. and Boyle, M. H. (2009) Similar developmental trajectories in autism and Asperger syndrome: From early childhood to adolescence. *Journal of Child Psychology and Psychiatry, and Allied Disciplines*, 50(12), 1459–67. doi: 10.1111/j.1469-7610.2009.02123.x.

Tager-Flusberg, H. and Joseph, R. M. (2003) Identifying neurocognitive phenotypes in autism. *Philosophical Transactions of the Royal Society of London. Series B: Biological Sciences*, 358, 303–14.

Tomblin, J. B. (2011) Co-morbidity of autism and SLI: Kinds, kin and complexity. *International Journal of Language and Communication Disorders*, 46(2), 127–37.

Vernes, S. C., Newbury, D. F., Abrahams, B., Winchester, L., Nicod, J., Groszer, M., Alarcon, M., Oliver, P. L., Davies, K. E., Geschwind, D. H., Monaco, A. P. and Fisher, S. E. (2008) A functional genetic link between developmental language disorders? *New England Journal of Medicine*, 359, 2337–45.

Volden, J., Coolican, J., Garon, N., White, J. and Bryson, S. (2009) Pragmatic language in autism spectrum disorder: Relationships to measures of ability and disability. *Journal of Autism and Developmental Disorders*, 39, 388–93.

Vygotsky, L. (1962) *Thought and Language*. Boston, MA: MIT Press.

Wetherby, A. M., Prizant, B. M. and Schuler, A. (2000) Understanding the nature of communication and language impairments. In A. Wetherby and B. Prizant (eds) *Autism Spectrum Disorder: A Transactional Developmental Perspective*. Baltimore, MD: Paul H. Brookes Publishing.

Whitehouse, A. J. O., Barry, J. G. and Bishop, D. V. M. (2008) Further defining the language impairment of autism: Is there a specific language impairment subtype? *Journal of Communication Disorders*, 41, 319–36.

Williams D., Botting N. and Boucher J. (2008) Language in autism and specific language impairment: Where are the links? *Psychological Bulletin*, 134(6), 944–63.

Williams, D., Payne, H. and Marshall, C. (2013) Non-word repetition impairment in autism and specific language impairment: Evidence for distinct underlying cognitive causes. *Journal of Autism and Developmental Disorders*, *43*, 404–17.

Wilson, D. and Sperber, D. (2012) *Meaning and Relevance*. Cambridge: Cambridge University Press.

Wodka, E. L., Mathy, P. and Kalb, L. (2013) Predictors of phrase and fluent speech in children with autism and severe language delay. *Pediatrics*, *131*, 1128–34. doi: 10.1542/peds.2012–2221.

19

EMBODIED COGNITION IN CHILDREN

Developing mental representations for action

Carl Gabbard

Introduction

Whereas in recent years much has been reported on the topic of embodied cognition (EC), specifics regarding the link between bodily actions and cognitive processes, and learning in children remain a mystery. In this chapter, I address one of those mysteries in the context of how bodily action influences the development of new mental representations. I will describe the basic idea of EC from different points of view with the common focus on how bodily actions influence child thinking and learning. I will also provide evidence suggesting that engaging children in activities using action simulation can be a useful tool in improving EC and thinking skills. Action simulation in the context of this chapter refers to the use of motor imagery – the mental creation (representation) of a bodily action (greater detail is provided in a subsequent section).

Embodied cognition (EC)

The consensus of opinion for EC suggests that cognitive processes, including thinking, are deeply grounded in our bodily interactions with the environment (e.g. Borghi and Cimatti, 2010; Barsalou, 2008; Bergen and Wheeler, 2010; Sadeghipour and Kopp, 2012). That is, cognitive representations and actions are inextricably linked – actions are central to the development of new representations (Boncoddo *et al.*, 2010; Rakison and Woodward, 2008). Boncoddo and colleagues, from their developmental work, state that, 'if representations are grounded in action, then during the emergence of new representations, actions should play a critical role' (p. 371). Whereas contemporary research has brought attention to the importance of EC in child learning, the general idea was discussed in the works of Piaget (1954). The renowned developmental psychologist suggested that knowledge was formed via bodily actions and those actions lead to the creation of new representations. An important point here is that in the context of this chapter, and most experts would concur, cognitive representations and *mental representations* are synonymous. Linked to the development of 'thought' and the child's ability to plan actions of any kind is recognizing *consequences* of those actions, a term frequently cited in imagery literature and given further attention in this chapter. Piaget often referred to the child's ability to *anticipate possibilities* as a major milestone in cognitive development.

One of the major propositions of this general body of work is the notion that the motor system contributes to higher-level cognitive processing. That is, processing that involves complex judgmental skills such as critical thinking and problem solving. One of the first tactics used to study EC was the classic A-not-B error paradigm (see review by Thelen *et al.*, 2001). In most of those studies, associations between attention, reaching (bodily action), and memory were explored. More recently, several innovative approaches have been used to study the connection between bodily actions and cognition in the context of, for example: language acquisition, numerical ability, and problem-solving skills (Anelli *et al.*, 2010; Boncoddo *et al.*, 2010; Bergen and Wheeler, 2010; Domahs *et al.*, 2010; Rueschemeyer *et al.*, 2010; Yu and Smith, 2012). Compared to the more contemporary dynamical systems view, earlier theorists viewed the development of object permanence as an innate endowment or one that was attained as a natural consequence of interaction with the environment during early infancy.

Mental (action) representation

The nature of mental representation is a central issue for understanding cognitive and motor development across the lifespan. Like the term EC, the concept of mental representation has been cast from several perspectives. In general, the term is used as a construct of neuro- and cognitive science involving cognitive states and processes constituted by the occurrence, transformation and storage of information-bearing structures (representations) of one kind or another (*Stanford Encyclopedia of Philosophy*, 2008). From another perspective, it is an internal cognitive construct that represents external reality. As presented here, mental simulation is a form of and key modality for the creation of mental representations (see review by Kosslyn *et al.*, 2006). Furthermore, simulation in the form of *motor imagery provides a window into the process of creating mental representations for action*; that is, it reflects an internal action representation (Jeannerod, 2001; Munzert *et al.*, 2009).

The role of simulation in EC

A key finding in this literature that underscores the primary message of interest here is the idea that *simulation* plays a significant role in EC (e.g. Bergen and Wheeler, 2010; Brouillet *et al.*, 2010; Engelen *et al.*, 2011; Garbarini and Adenzato, 2004; Hostetter and Alibali, 2008). For example, Barsalou (2008, p. 619) states, 'Grounded cognition reflects the assumption that cognition is typically grounded in multiple ways, including *simulations*, situated action, and, on occasion, bodily states.' Simulation has a role to play in the processing of language. Bergen and Wheeler (2010) explain that when processing sentences about scenes and activities, people activate perceptual and motor systems to perform mental *simulations* of what is described. Borghi and Cimatti (2010) also contend that language is a form of action and present an excellent review of the role of *simulation* in EC with their explanation of what specifically is being simulated. From their perspective, language contributes to form a unitary sense of our body and helps to reshape the way we implicitly perceive our own body. Interestingly, as noted earlier, the authors link this aspect of EC with research associated with motor cognition and simulation in the form of motor imagery (e.g. Decety and Grezes, 1999; Jeannerod, 2001). Adding to the general significance of simulated processes in information processing, Kosslyn, one of the foremost experts on the topic, declares that mental simulation underscores memory, reasoning, and learning (Kosslyn *et al.*, 2006). For example, imagery processes rely in large part on retrieved episodic information – information used to generate explicit and accessible representations in working memory. The implications for EC are that remembered events are observed through experience, and these events are used to generate new representations. A review of the literature indicates that structural and functional brain circuitries supporting episodic memory experience significant reorganization during childhood (Shing *et al.*, 2010). It certainly seems reasonable to assume that such changes affect level of EC.

The work of Boncoddo and colleagues (2010) provides an excellent example of simulation effects with children ages 3.4 to 5.7 years. The researchers asked preschoolers to solve a set of relatively simple gear-system problems. After a familiarization phase of physically turning and pushing gears, children were asked to solve problems by tracing with their fingers the directional movements of the gears (simulation). That process led most participants to discover new representations of the problems. Results indicated that the number of actions that embodied alternation information during simulation predicted later emergence of higher-order representation. The researchers concluded that their findings were consistent with the EC hypothesis suggesting that actions are central to the emergence of new representations. It seems reasonable to conclude that the ability to simulate was a key factor in solving that particular set of problems. Others, using a variety of gear-system paradigms with grade school children, have reported observations of higher-order problem solving (Dixon and Bangert, 2002; Lehrer and Schauble, 1998). Interestingly, Schwartz and Black (1996), also using a gear-system paradigm, reported that college-aged participants used imagery in the form of mental rotation ability to solve such problems.

Motor imagery (simulation)

Motor imagery is defined as an internal rehearsal or re-enactment of movements from a first-person perspective without any overt physical movement. From another perspective, motor imagery, also known as kinesthetic imagery, is an active cognitive process during which the representation of a specific action is internally reproduced in working memory without any overt motor output (Decety and Grèzes, 1999). In addition to the reasonable case that motor imagery is a reflection of action representation and motor planning, studies have found that there is a high correlation between real and simulated movements (e.g. Sharma *et al.*, 2008; Young *et al.*, 2009). For example, with studies of time to complete a series of movements via simulation and actually completing the actions (e.g. walking, hand tracing a pattern), times are not significantly different. Complementing those findings is the idea that motor control and motor simulation states are functionally equivalent (Jeannerod, 2001; Kunz *et al.*, 2009; Lorey *et al.*, 2010). Also known as 'simulation theory', this idea postulates that mental (covert) and executed (overt) actions rely on similar motor representations. Such research has drawn the interest of (for example) clinicians working to stimulate neuromuscular pathways. For example, with stroke patients, injured athletes, and those with cerebral palsy, imagery is considered an attractive means to access the motor network and restore motor function without actual overt action. Also, a relatively large body of literature indicates that sport psychologists use mental rehearsal as a means to facilitate practice and improve performance in athletes (see reviews by Munzert *et al.*, 2009 and Sharma *et al.*, 2009). Furthermore, evidence has been reported showing that motor imagery follows the basic tenets of Fitts' Law (Solodkin *et al.*, 2004; Stevens, 2005). That is, simulated movement duration, like actual movement, decreases with increasing task complexity.

One of the interesting hypothesized features of motor imagery is its role in the prediction of one's actions (e.g. Kunz *et al.*, 2009; Lorey *et al.*, 2010). Suddendorf and Moore (2011, p. 295) note, 'The ability to imagine future events is an essential part of human cognition.' Imagery allows us to generate specific predictions based upon past experience and allows us to answer 'what if' questions by making explicit and accessible the likely consequences of a specific action. One of the important aspects of an action plan is the ability to predict the outcome and consequences of intended actions. Imagining an action can serve several useful goals to that endeavor. According to Bourgeois and Coello (2009), motor representation can be viewed as a component of a predictive system, which includes a neural process that simulates through motor imagery the dynamic behavior of the body in relation to the environment. This line of reasoning presents interesting developmental issues associated with the child's cognitive understanding of environmental (perceptual) information and consequences, and one's physical capabilities.

Although there is no direct evidence that infants use motor imagery, studies do provide a rather convincing case that infants take into account situational constraints when planning and executing actions (e.g. Csibra *et al.*, 2003; Sommerville *et al.*, 2005; Willatts, 1999). These studies suggest that infants show some understanding of human actions, thus seem to have a representation of such. For example, it appears that infants understand uncompleted actions, and are able to complete perceived actions. Typical research paradigms include observations of reaching contact, forward lean, and looking time. Whereas considerable insight has been gain via such studies, the inherent limitation is determining the level of cognitive processing occurring. That is, infants cannot adequately communicate verbal judgments. Therefore, the difficulty with differentiating between cognitive and neuromotor processes in the programming of movements is compounded.

A review of the literature indicates that by 5 years of age, the ability to effectively create and use motor imagery to represent movement is present (e.g. Caeyenberghs *et al.*, 2009; Frick *et al.*, 2009; Molina *et al.*, 2008). From the work just referenced, a number of innovative tactics have been created to examine the ability of children to mentally represent action via use of motor imagery. Two of the more popular methods have been mental rotation of different hand positions and the chronometry paradigm. With the typical hand rotation task, participants are asked to judge whether a hand visually viewed in an unusual orientation is a right or left limb; reaction time is commonly recorded also. The usual strategy is to 'imagine' one's own body. Chronometry involves the comparison of simulated and actual movements. That is, the correspondence between the time-course of the participant's imagined and executed actions. This tactic follows the premise that there is a functional equivalence (relationship) between motor imagery and execution. With such studies, an array of movement tasks have been used with children, namely: walking, grasping, moving a puppet, pointing, figure drawing, and time to complete an obstacle course.

Two specific studies are worth noting that demonstrate innovation. Molina and colleagues (2008) used a chronometry paradigm with children aged 5 to 7 years to compare movement duration of actually moving (walking) a puppet to a location, and imagining executing the same action. Movement durations for actual and simulated displacements were obtained in two conditions, where either no information was provided about the weight of the puppet to be moved, or the puppet was described as being heavy. A significant correlation between actual and simulated walking durations was observed only for the 7-year-olds in the informed condition. The researchers concluded that the ability to imagine actions emerges in 7-year-olds when children are able to think about themselves in action using first-person egocentric based imagery. The researchers also noted that whereas research indicates that by 5 years children are able to use anticipatory mechanisms during goal-directed locomotion in a predictive way revealing a feed-forward control of their action (Grasso *et al.*, 1998), 5-year-olds in their study were not able to explicitly imagine themselves acting. One might also speculate that the lack of correlation related to their lack of understanding of what the word 'heavy' implied for action; therefore creating an action-language (embodied cognition) misrepresentation.

In 2009, Frick and colleagues asked children aged 5 to 9 years and adults to tilt empty glasses, filled with varied amounts of imaginary water, so that the imagined water would reach the rim. In the manual tilting condition where glasses could be tilted 'actively' with visual feedback, even 5-year-olds performed well. However, in the imagined tilting condition performance for the 5-year-olds was poor. The researchers found that in order for the 5-year-olds to use motor imagery, they had to engage self (motor), whereas the older children and adults were more reliant on visual information to solve the task. In conclusion, there was a clear age trend, indicating that bodily actions and motor feedback were particularly important in imagery performance of younger children.

Motor cognition and embodied cognition

Another term frequently mentioned with studies of motor imagery is *motor cognition*. This term commonly refers to the study of cognitive processes that drive action programming.

Motor imagery is also considered a form of motor cognition (Gabbard, 2009). Motor cognition takes into account recognizing, anticipating, predicting and production of actions. The cognitive processes involved enable us not only to react to our environment but also to anticipate the consequences of our actions. Gallese *et al.* (2009) have proposed what they refer to as the motor cognition hypothesis. This idea, much like EC, suggests that the motor system plays a pivotal role in cognitive functions. Furthermore, they suggest that the common neural mechanism shared with action and goal understanding is the mirror neuron system: a system frequently mentioned in association with mental *simulation* (imagery) of action (e.g. Filimon *et al.*, 2007; Molenberghs *et al.*, 2009; Munzert *et al.*, 2009). Mirror neurons are cortical brain cells that become active when a particular behavior is performed and when that same behavior is observed; in essence, simulation, or perhaps more correct, imitation, matches action in cognitive brain processes. Gallese and colleagues (2009) contend that a rudimentary level of the mirror neuron system is likely present at birth; a system that is flexible across time and influenced by motor experience and visuomotor learning. Although not mentioned specifically, the researchers make a strong case for embodied cognition by showing evidence that (for example) infants understand goal intentions in terms of their own motor knowledge. One of the key conclusions of their developmental treatise for a motor cognition hypothesis was that there is a motor account of the development of intentional (cognitive) understanding.

So, one might ask the question, is there a difference between motor cognition and EC? Obviously, the two are similar, but one might argue that it depends on the perspective of interest. That is, with motor cognition emphasis is typically on 'motor' behavior and what cognitive structures and processes drive it. With EC, focus is commonly on how the environment and motor system influences cognitive behaviors. In any case, both depend on the ability to simulate actions. For an excellent review of 'grounded motor cognition' in the form of gesture processing, refer to Sadeghipour and Kopp (2012).

Implications for teaching children thinking skills

The intent of this commentary was to present the argument that simulation, via use of motor imagery, has potential to provide new insights to EC. The primary rationale being that simulation, common to mental representation and EC, provides insight to the creation of cognitive constructs that underscore behavior. That is, simulation in the form of motor imagery represents the linking (reciprocal nature) of cognitive and motor representations to form a state of understanding and consequences for action. Staying with the nature of EC, that is, delineating the motor processes that drive cognition, motor imagery allows the mental exploration of movements and movement alternatives: alternatives that can be creatively linked to tap higher-cognitive processes, such as problem solving and prediction. An example of such an experiment is the one by Boncoddo *et al.* (2010), described earlier. Preschoolers solved gear movement problems by *simulating* the directional movements of the gears, a process that led to discovery of new representations. An extension of such work might consider brain imagining identifying what parts of the brain are activated during simulation of directional movements. And, from a developmental cognitive neuroscience perspective, to determine how processing changes with age and experience. Do children have more problem-solving success by imagining fine-motor as opposed to gross-motor movements, or movements that require substantial postural (cerebellar) control? Furthermore, what type of simulation are the children using – visual or motor (kinesthetic) imagery? Embodiment would seem to imply 'bodily' actions complemented by engagement of the motor system. However, the literature clearly indicates that children are capable of using both visual and motoric forms of mental simulation. With that in mind, another plausible issue worth consideration is, at what point is visual information as important as bodily actions? For example, with a hand rotation task, older children hypothetically solved the problem by using visual information, as opposed to referring (more) to their body schema (Funk *et al.*, 2005). An example is the use of bodily actions via finger counting with numerical problem solving (embodied numerosity; e.g. Crollen *et al.*, 2011; Domahs *et al.*, 2010). Of course, these examples do not account for the possibility that individuals are also simulating actions. Obviously, the questions raised here require the challenge of future innovative studies.

In summary, by studying the role of simulation in EC via imagery research, we have the potential to gain a better understanding of how children mentally represent and act on information in the environment. I have briefly argued here that this perspective has the potential for stimulating new thoughts for theories of cognitive development and embodied cognition in children.

References

Anelli, F., Nicoletti, R. and Borghi, A. M. (2010) Categorization and action: What about object consistence? *Acta Psychologica, 133*(2), 203–11.

Barsalou, L. W. (2008) Grounded cognition. *Annual Review of Psychology, 59*, 617–45.

Bergen, B. and Wheeler, K. (2010) Grammatical aspect and mental simulation. *Brain and Language, 112*(3), 150–8.

Boncoddo, R., Dixon, J. A. and Kelley, E. (2010) The emergence of novel representations from action: Evidence from preschoolers. *Developmental Science, 13*(2), 370–7.

Borghi, A. M. and Cimatti, F. (2010) Embodied cognition and beyond: Acting and sensing the body. *Neuropsychologia, 48*(3), 763–73.

Bourgeois, J. and Coello, Y. (2009) Role of inertial properties of the upper limb on the perception of the boundary of personal space. *Psychologie Française, 54*(3), 225–39.

Brouillet, T., Heurley, L., Martin, S. and Brouillet, D. (2010) The embodied cognition theory and the motor component of 'yes' and 'no' verbal responses. *Acta Psychologica, 134*(3), 310–17.

Caeyenberghs, K., Tsoupas, J., Wilson, P. H. and Smits-Engelsman, B. C. M. (2009) Motor imagery in primary school children. *Developmental Neuropsychology, 34*(1), 103–21.

Csibra, G., Bírób, S., Koósc, O. and Gergely, G. (2003) One-year-old infants use teleological representations of actions productively. *Cognitive Science, 2*(1), 111–33.

Crollen, V., Mahe, R., Collignon, O. and Seron, X. (2011) The role of vision in the development of finger-number interactions: Finger-counting and finger-montring in blind children. *Journal of Experimental Child Psychology, 109*, 525–39.

Decety, J. and Grèzes, J. (1999) Neural mechanisms subserving the perception of human actions. *Trends in Cognitive Sciences*, *3*, 172–8.

Domahs, F., Moeller, K., Huber, S., Willmes, K. and Nuerk, H. (2010) Embodied numerosity: Implicit hand-based representations influence symbolic number processing across cultures. *Cognition*, *116*, 251–66.

Dixon, J.A. and Bangert, A.S. (2002) The prehistory of discovery: precursors of representational change in solving gear system problems. *Developmental Psychology*, *38*, 918–33.

Engelen, J. A. A., Bouwmeester, S., Bruin, A. B. H. and Zwaan, R. A. (2011) Perceptual simulation in developing language comprehension. *Journal of Experimental Child Psychology*, *110*, 659–775.

Filimon, F., Nelson, J. D., Hagler, D. J. and Sereno, M. I. (2007) Human cortical representations for reaching: Mirror neurons for execution, observation, and imagery. *NeuroImage*, *37*(4), 1315–28.

Frick, A., Daum, M. M., Wilson, M. and Wilkening, F. (2009) Effects of action on children's and adults' mental imagery. *Journal of Experimental Child Psychology*, *104*, 34–51.

Funk, M., Brugger, P. and Wilkening, F. (2005) Motor processes in children's imagery: The case of mental rotation of hands. *Developmental Science*, *8* (5), 402–8.

Gabbard, C. (2009) Studying action representation in children via motor imagery. *Brain and Cognition*, *71*(3), 234–9.

Gallese, V., Rochat, M., Cossu, G. and Sinigaglia, C. (2009) Motor cognition and its role in the phylogeny and ontogeny of action understanding. *Developmental Psychology*, *45*(1), 103–13.

Garbarini, F. and Adenzato, M. (2004) At the root of embodied cognition: Cognitive science meets neurophysiology. *Brain and Cognition*, *56*(1), 100–6.

Grasso, R., Assaiante, C., Prévost, P. and Berthoz, A. (1998) Development of anticipatory orienting strategies during locomotor tasks in children. *Neuroscience and Biobehavioral Reviews*, *22*, 533–9.

Hostetter, A. B. and Alibali, M. W. (2008) Visible embodiment: Gestures as simulated action. *Psychonomic Bulletin and Review*, *15*, 495–514.

Jeannerod, M. (2001) Neural simulation of action: A unifying mechanism for motor cognition. *Neuroimage*, *14*, 103–9.

Kosslyn, S. M., Thompson, W. L. and Ganis, G. (2006) *The Case for Mental Imagery*. New York: Oxford University Press.

Kunz, B. R., Creem-Regehr, S. H. and Thompson, W.B. (2009) Evidence for motor simulation in imagined locomotion. *Journal of Experimental Psychology: Human Perception and Performance*, *35*(5), 1458–71.

Lehrer, R. and Schauble, L. (1998) Reasoning about structure and function: Children's conceptions of gears. *Journal of Research in Science Teaching*, *35*, 3–25.

Lorey, B., Pilgramm, S., Walter, B., Stark, R., Munzert, J. and Zentgraf, K. (2010) Your mind's eye: Motor imagery of pointing movements with different accuracy. *NeuroImage*, *49*(4), 3239–47.

Molenberghs, P., Cunnington, R. and Mattingley, J. B. (2009) Is the mirror neuron system involved in imitation? A short review and meta-analysis. *Neuroscience and Biobehavioral Reviews*, *33*(7), 975–80.

Molina, M., Tijus, C. and Jouen, F. (2008) The emergence of motor imagery in children. *Journal of Experimental Child Psychology*, *99*(3), 196–209.

Munzert, J., Lorey, B. and Zentgraf, K. (2009) Cognitive motor processes: The role of motor imagery in the study of motor representations. *Brain Research Reviews*, *60*(2), 306–26.

Piaget, J. (1954) *The Construction of Reality in the Child*. New York: Basic Books.

Rakison, D. H. and Woodward, A. L. (2008) New perspectives on the effects of action on perceptual and cognitive development. *Developmental Psychology*, *44*, 1209–13.

Rueschemeyer, S., Pfeiffer, C. and Bekkering, H. (2010) Body schematics: On the role of the body schema in embodied lexical-sematic representations. *Neuropsychologia*, *48*(3), 774–81.

Sadeghipour, A. and Kopp, S. (2012) Gesture processing as grounded motor cognition: Towards a computational model. *Procedia – Social and Behavioral Sciences*, *32*, 213–23.

Schwartz, D. L. and Black, J. B. (1996) Shuttling between depictive models and abstract rules: Induction and fallback. *Cognitive Science, 20,* 457–97.

Sharma, N., Jones, P. S., Carpenter, T. A. and Baron, J. (2008) Mapping the involvement of BA 4a and 4p during motor imagery. *NeuroImage, 41*(1), 92–9.

Sharma, N., Simmons, L. H., Jones, P. S., Day, D. J., Carpenter, T. A., Pomeroy, V. M., Warburton, E. A. and Baron, J. (2009) Motor imagery after subcortical stroke: A functional magnetic resonance imaging study. *Stroke, 40,* 1315–24.

Shing, Y. L., Werkle-Bergner, M., Brehmer, Y., Muller, V., Li, S. K. and Lindenberger, U. (2010) Episodic memory across the lifespan: The contributions of associative and strategic components. *Neuroscience and Biobehavioral Reviews, 34*(7), 1080–91.

Solodkin, A., Hlustik, P., Chen, E. E. and Small, S. L. (2004) Fine modulation in network activation during motor execution and motor imagery. *Cerebral Cortex, 14,* 1246–55.

Sommerville, J. A., Woodward, A. L. and Needham, A. (2005) Action experience alters 3-month-old infants' next term perception of others' actions. *Cognition, 96*(1), B1–B11.

Stanford Encyclopedia of Philosophy (2008) Mental representation. Open access on-line Encyclopedia.

Suddendorf, T. and Moore, C. (2011) Introduction to the special edition: The development of episodic foresight. *Cognition Development, 26,* 295–8.

Stevens, J. A. (2005) Interference effects demonstrate distinct roles for visual and motor imagery during the mental representation of human action. *Cognition, 95*(3), 329–50.

Thelen, E., Schöner, G., Scheier, C. and Smith, L. B. (2001) The dynamics of embodiment: A field theory of infant perseverative reaching. *Behavioral and Brain Sciences, 24*(1), 1–86.

Willatts, P. (1999) Development of means–end behavior in young infants: Pulling a support to retrieve a distant object. *Developmental Psychology, 35,* 651–67.

Young, S. J., Pratt, J and Chau. T. (2009) Misperceiving the speed-accuracy tradeoff: Imagined Movements and perceptual decisions. *Experimental Brain Research, 192*(1), 121–32.

Yu, C. and Smith, L. (2012) Embodied attention and word learning by toddlers. *Cognition, 125*(2), 244–62.

20

SENSITIVE PERIODS

John T. Bruer

Introduction

The research literature on sensitive periods is vast, complex, and, at times, contentious. In approaching this literature, minimally, one should know how the concept of sensitive periods evolved, understand what is required to establish the existence of a sensitive period, and be aware of the different types of causal mechanisms that might explain sensitive period phenomena. Even with this minimal background one can begin to weight the implications of sensitive periods for understanding children's thinking.

The evolution of the concept: critical or sensitive

Numerous reviews present the history of sensitive period research, summarizing the story of how the concept of a critical or sensitive period moved from embryology (Spemann, 1918), to animal behavior (Lorenz, 1937), to psychosocial development (Bowlby, 1953), to language learning (Penfield and Roberts, 1959; Lenneberg, 1967) and finally to developmental neurophysiology (Hubel and Wiesel, 1970). (See, for example, Colombo, 1982; Bornstein, 1987; Bruer, 2001; Lichtman and Bruer, 2001; and Michel and Tylor, 2005.)

The fundamental notion underlying critical or sensitive periods is that an organ or organism system is subject to an outside influence only during a specific time in development, the critical or sensitive period. For example in embryology, before a critical period embryonic stem cells can differentiate into many different types of cells because they are open to inter- and intra-cellular signals that influence their developmental pathway. After the critical period their developmental fate is determined. Spemann's (1918) experiments firmly established the notion of critical periods in embryonic development. Lorenz (1937) noted that the phenomenon of imprinting in geese hatchlings was analogous to critical periods in embryology.

During a limited period, which opened and closed abruptly, within a few days of hatching, the goslings would 'imprint' on the first large moving object they saw and instinctively follow that object. According to Lorenz imprinting had two distinct characteristics: it only occurred during a brief sharply delimited critical period and was irreversible. After Lorenz, scientists tended to conflate these two characteristics of imprinting and by definition critical periods effects were irreversible (Oyama, 1979). This conflated notion was appropriated into research on psychosocial development, language learning, and developmental neurophysiology, among others. Subsequent research on imprinting, as well as on other critical period phenomena, suggested that critical periods neither opened nor closed abruptly and, at least at the behavioral level, critical period effects were reversible. For this reason, the preferred term became 'sensitive period' (Bornstein 1987, Michel and Tyler 2005).

Knudson (2004) introduced a new distinction between critical and sensitive periods. Historically, sensitive periods were defined using behavioral, psychological, or neural measure. He argues that sensitive periods are fundamentally properties of neural circuits. On his view, a sensitive period is a limited period in development during which specific stimuli have unusually strong effects on a given neural circuit. Critical periods are a subclass of sensitive periods wherein the stimuli cause irreversible changes in the neural circuit. In Knudsen's view, defining sensitive periods using behavioral measures not only generates confusion, but also underestimates the prevalence and importance of sensitive periods in development. Development on this view could be viewed as a cascade of sensitive periods. However, showing effects and possibly irreversible effects at the neural level establishes a high level of proof for sensitive period phenomena. Knudsen's usage, although highly reductive and by no means universally accepted, has been found currency in the early childhood policy literature (Knudson *et al.*, 2006).

Since Spemann and Lorenz, the notion of strict critical periods has evolved into a notion of more fluid sensitive periods. Only by being aware of this conceptual evolution can one read the historical literature in such a way as to reliably integrate findings across studies that may use the terms in slightly different ways. It is safe to say that the current scientific consensus is that sensitive periods open and close gradually and are in most cases reversible, at least at the behavioral level.

Establishing the existence of a sensitive period

To show the presence of a sensitive period in a system (like the visual system) one must establish its onset, duration, and offset. This requires an intervention on the system and an outcome measure to assess the effects of the intervention. The experiment should include a control group that does not experience the intervention. Then one must expose experimental animals, as identical to one another as possible, to the same intervention at different ages. Same intervention means that not only the same treatment but also the same *duration* of treatment. A sensitive period exists if the same treatment before a certain age and after a certain age has no appreciable effect on the outcome measure, but during the sensitive period has an effect. Let us examine how three well known studies on timing of experiences during development treat the timing and duration variables: Hubel and Wiesel (1970), Johnson and Newport (1989) and the English and Romanian Adoptees Study (ERA) (Rutter *et al.*, 1998; Beckett *et al.*, 2006).

Hubel and Wiesel (1970) examined the effect of single-eye closure on the development of the cat visual system. The intervention was suturing the right eye of the kittens and (for the purposes of this discussion) the outcome measure was the percentage of binocular cells (cells driven by both eyes) responsive to stimuli as registered in neural recordings from the relevant area of visual cortex. From previous studies, Hubel and Wiesel knew that in normal adult animals and in normal 10-day-old kittens (the age at which kittens' eyes first open), around 80 per cent of recorded cells are binocular cells. They also knew that visual deprivation can cause this percentage to fall, sometimes to zero.

Hubel and Wiesel's experiment is atypical in that it systematically collected data both on age of closure and duration of closure. They described their experiment 'as plotting a set of graphs in which we varied two parameters, the onset and cessation of the deprivation' (Hubel and Wiesel, 2005, p. 405). Plotting a graph for every possible age of onset and duration of deprivation would have been impractical and unrealistic. Hubel and Wiesel chose their data points strategically. One can present their experimental results as a heat map, wherein map rows show the effect of age at closure for a given duration and columns show the effect of duration of closure at given age (Figure 20.1).

The bold cells in the map show the data points Hubel and Wiesel reported in their paper. The other cells in the map are extrapolations from reported values used here for purposes of illustration. What one should note is that there are rows in the map that contain multiple reported values. The rows show outcomes for the same the same duration of deprivation at different ages; they show sensitive period effects. Data in the columns show dose response (age of onset is constant). The row for zero days deprivation shows values for control animals. The map shows that any closure from

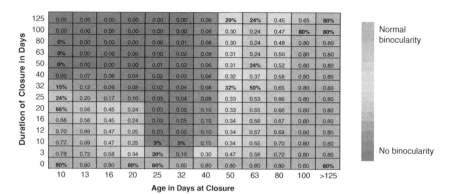

Figure 20.1   Heat map for Hubel and Wiesel (1970). The two axes are log scaled. Bold cells show the data reported in the article, with 80 per cent binocularly driven cells being the normal value. Other values are extrapolated for purposes of illustration.

day 10 through day 60 to 80 has an adverse effect on the percentage of binocular cells. Hubel and Wiesel called this the critical period. Longer duration of closure (columns) has greater effects throughout this period. Less than 10 days of closure (in their data three to six days) between 25 and 32 days of age has a profound effect on the percentage of binocular cells recorded. This they called this the sensitive period. After three months of age, closure of any duration has no effect on the percentage of binocular cells. Comparing data in rows or in columns makes sense. These comparisons support the presence of a sensitive period or dose response. Other comparisons are meaningless.

Studies of sensitive periods in second language acquisition (L2A) illustrate another way in which timing of exposure and duration of exposure are treated. Johnson and Newport (1989) examined the effects of age of exposure on English grammar (morphosyntax) acquisition in 48 adult Chinese and Korean speakers acquiring English as an L2. Their outcome measure was participants' scores on a 276-item test of English grammar. The native English control group had an average score of 269. The 'intervention' was exposure to English in an English-speaking environment. Age of onset was age of arrival in the L2 environment (AOA). They found that very early arrivals (AOA between 3 and 7 years of age) had test scores indistinguishable from native speakers' scores. However, test scores decreased significantly with AOA for older age groups, reaching a low of 210 for participants having AOAs in the 17–39 year range. They interpreted this pattern of decline as showing the existence of a sensitive period for L2A grammar acquisition that closes no later than age 16 years. The duration variable in this study is length of residence in the L2 environment (LOR). Most L2A sensitive period studies assess mature performance in the L2, performance after all learning has ceased. Researchers have established that after five to ten years in the L2 environment grammar acquisition asymptotes. Newport and Johnson report that their study participants lived in the L2 environment for at least five years and had average LOR values of around ten years. Indeed, for their total sample there was no statistically significant correlation between LOR and test scores. On average, after ten years of L2 exposure duration no longer matters. A heat map of Johnson and Newport's data would show a single row, with decreasing score values as age of onset increases. There are differences in grammar acquisition that vary by age of exposure to the L2 for learners having on average ten years exposure to the L2.

A third example is the English and Romanian Adoptees Study (ERA) (Rutter *et al.*, 2007). To be clear, the ERA investigators sometimes mention sensitive periods, but never interpret their findings as providing unequivocal evidence for the existence of sensitive periods, although sometimes the ERA findings are discussed within a sensitive period context (Zeanah *et al.*, 2011). The ERA Study assessed the long-term outcomes for 165 Romanian infants adopted into British homes in the early 1990s. These infants had experienced extreme physical and social deprivation in Romanian orphanages prior to adoption. All the Romanian infants were less than 43 months old at time of adoption. The comparison group was 52 within-UK adoptees placed before 6 months of age. ERA used a variety of outcome measures to assess the effects of deprivation and subsequent adoption on physical, cognitive, and psychosocial development.

The Romanian adoptees were grouped into three strata based on age of entry into the UK: less than 6 months, between 6 and 23 months, and between 24 and 42 months. The ERA Study has followed the adoptees into adolescence. The example here is based on data from the four-year and 11-year evaluations (Rutter *et al.*, 1998, Beckett *et al.*, 2006).

The difficulty with the ERA data is that it is impossible to separate age of exposure from duration of exposure. First, suppose ERA is a deprivation experiment, analogous to Hubel and Wiesel's. If this were the intent of the ERA study (which it is not), a heat map would show data values only on the map's diagonal (Figure 20.2A). For these data, age of deprivation equals duration of deprivation. There are no complete rows (i.e. sensitive period data) nor are there any complete columns (dose response data). One could conclude that institutional deprivation is deleterious at each age and the longer the deprivation or the older the infant at entry, the worse the outcome. Suppose instead the intervention is adoption into a UK home. This requires following the children longitudinally, as the ERA study is doing. Figure 20.2B shows the heat map for the longitudinal data available at age 11. The map's vertical axis shows the duration of adoptive experience for each age group from entry to 11 years. The horizontal axis is ambiguous, however. It is the age at entry into the UK, but it is also the duration of deprivation. One cannot separate the effects of age of deprivation from duration of

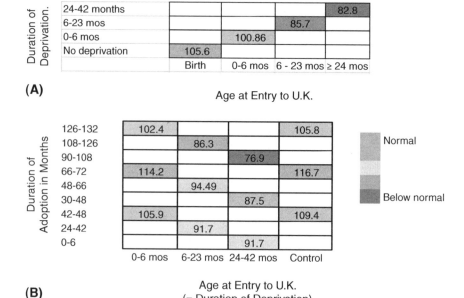

Figure 20.2 Heat map for the ERA Study Data from Rutter *et al.* (1998) and Beckett *et al.* (2006). Values in the cells are scores on a cognitive measure. Panel (A) represents data from the 1998 study assuming that deprivation is the intervention. Panel (B) represents data from the 2006 study assuming that adoption was the intervention.

deprivation in the data set. The data allow one to evaluate the dose response for a given age of adoption or duration of deprivation, but there is insufficient row data to draw any conclusions about a sensitive period.

As Rutter *et al.* (2004) state, no matter what the outcome measure used in the study, establishing the existence of sensitive periods for those outcomes would require data for various onsets of adoption among children in the same age group.

Thinking about mechanisms

Once experimental evidence has established the existence of a sensitive period, there remains a second scientific challenge of providing a causal explanation for the sensitive period phenomenon.

It is generally agreed that sensitive periods open when the underlying neural circuitry is sufficiently mature to process input and possesses mechanisms that allow the circuit to be modifiable by experience. These mechanisms include changing the shape or structure of axons and dendrites, creating or eliminating synapses, and altering the strengths of synaptic connections. Sensitive periods close when the mechanisms responsible for neural plasticity cease to operate or function with less efficiency. What kinds of mechanisms might explain diminishing neural plasticity? This is an important question because, according to Knudsen (2004), the mechanism by which a sensitive period closes has not been established for any neural circuit, even for circuits within the highly studied visual system.

A popular, naïve view posits a strictly maturational mechanism: sensitive periods close because of internal, endogenous causes. Sensitive periods are conceived as windows of opportunity that open for brief periods and then slam shut for ever, as if regulated by an internal developmental clock. However, there are alternative and well-accepted working hypotheses about the causal mechanisms underlying closure. Bateson (1979) suggested that one could think of sensitive periods as windows that open, but that never close. External stimuli and experience modify the neural circuitry until the circuitry is in 'equilibrium' with the environment and no further plastic change occurs. Experience or learning itself, that is, causes external to the organism, might close the sensitive period. If the stimuli in the environment become stable, there is nothing novel in the organism's environment to drive further plasticity (Johnson, 2005). Bateson favored a self-terminating mechanism to explain imprinting. Once an animal has imprinted, it stops attending to stimuli as possible sources of an imprinting signal and attends to different environmental features. On these alternative views, the possibility remains open that although brain plasticity diminishes the potential for further plastic change remains. Recent review of the available evidence suggests that sensitive periods are self-terminating, rather than maturationally determined (Johnson, 2005).

There are numerous examples in the sensitive period literature that invoke a self-terminating mechanism. In the area of second language learning, Kuhl and Doupe (1990), Flege (Flege *et al.*, 1995, 1999; Yeni-Komshian *et al.*, 1997), and Birdsong and Molis (2001) favor competition or interference models to explain sensitive period phenomena in second language learning. Johnson (2005) presents other non-language examples (including imprinting) of self-terminating sensitive periods.

Positing different causal mechanisms for closure of sensitive periods calls not only for different kinds of research, but also elicits different views on functional brain development. These views have different implications for child development and clinical populations. On a strictly maturational account the window of opportunity might slam shut or gradually close, but once closed the game is over. On the alternative accounts that emphasize the causal role of external stimuli and the environment, there is the possibility that even after a sensitive period appears to close, appropriate novel stimuli might still allow for functional change. Neural plasticity might decline, although not totally disappear. As Bateson (1979) argued, self-terminating accounts of sensitive period closure – acknowledging the importance of exogenous over endogenous causes – reconciles the observation that young children might be particularly susceptible to specific experiences at times during development with the observation that given appropriate experiences adult behaviors and neural circuitry can be changed, even for functions that appear to be governed by sensitive periods. Appropriate novel stimuli, even for adults, might restart plasticity and allow for recovery of function long after the sensitive period was assumed to be closed. Treatment of adult amblyopia is one area where considering non-maturational views about closure of sensitive periods has led to new insights. Setting aside the strict maturational account has led to extending the sensitive period for treating amblyopia well into adulthood (Levi, 2005). Of course, sensitive periods are numerous and various. One need not, nor should not, assume that a single type of causal mechanism explains all of them.

Implications of sensitive periods for child development and education

Of the example experiments presented above, Hubel and Wiesel's experiment is profoundly different from the other two examples. Hubel and Wiesel ran an experiment and used experiment subjects that as far as could be determined were genetically similar (from the same litter) and identical in prior experience. Sensitive period studies on humans, for the most part, are not experiments. They are observational studies. The investigator must find a natural population which by reason of their history or circumstances has been deprived of (Romanian orphans) or exposed to (L2 learners) the stimuli of interest at various ages. These are observational, not experimental studies, where sample sizes tend to be small. Furthermore, it is not a trivial task to determine whether the individuals differ only along the dimensions of age and duration of exposure to a specific experience. The ERA authors, for example, go to great lengths to address this problem of possible confounding factors. This is to say that investigating sensitive periods in humans is exceedingly difficult. Observational studies cannot provide the same strength of evidence as can experimental studies.

Despite these difficulties, investigators have made considerable progress. In vision, we know that there are numerous sensitive periods, e.g. for binocular vision, visual acuity, object processing, all with different sensitive periods for damage to the system and recovery from damage. It is a complex story, but both the scientific and clinical implications are encouraging (Maurer, 2005). In second language learning, the consensus is that there is a sensitive period for learning phonology, but no sensitive period for learning lexicon. There is disagreement about the existence of a sensitive period for learning morphosyntax. Although Johnson and Newport (1989) is very highly cited, it suffers from being on observational study on a small sample (46 subjects) of Asian language speakers. The study has been criticized on methodological grounds (Bialystok and Hakuta, 1994) and has proved difficult to replicate (Birdsong and Molis, 2001). The educational implications are not straightforward. L2A acquisition studies are studies on immersion, putting L1 speakers into an L2 environment 24 hours a day. Results from immersion studies do not generalize to classroom language learning situations, where L2 experience is limited in duration and artificial. Also one might question whether the educational goal of L2 instruction should include native phonological proficiency (Muñoz and Singleton, 2011). All would agree, however, that in learning a second language earlier is better (earlier start and longer duration).

Studies of sensitive periods for cognitive, psychological, and emotional development are exceedingly important and as we have seen with the ERA study exceedingly difficult to do. Zeanah *et al.* (2011) conclude that our ability to understand sensitive periods at the level of neural circuitry is extremely limited, severe methodological problems remain, and that apart from a few limited findings, the evidence for the existence of sensitive periods in these domains is not compelling. With respect to attachment, Thomson (2001) suggests that the attachment relation does not influence psychosocial development as one would expect of a sensitive period phenomenon.

What about the implications of sensitive periods in education or in developing children's thinking skills? We should expect that the implications are minimal to non-existent. In thinking about the implications of sensitive periods for learning, one should be mindful of Greenough *et al.*'s (1987) distinction between experience-expectant versus experience-dependent brain plasticity (Bruer, 1999; Rutter, 2002). In experience-expectant plasticity environmental stimuli are required to tune neural circuits to the environment a species inhabits. It applies to species-wide behaviors like vision, first language learning, and imprinting. Under normal conditions, where normal conditions allow for wide variation in social and cultural contexts, these stimuli are universally available. One possible mechanism for experience-expectant brain plasticity is the elimination of overabundant neural connections that occurs during developmental synaptogenesis. In contrast, experience-dependent plasticity allows animals and humans to learn about things unique to their personal or socio-cultural environment. Such plasticity is present throughout the life-span and is not subject to sensitive period constraints. Possible neural mechanism for experience-dependent plasticity might include synapse growth or change in the strength of synaptic connectivity. To the extent that formal and informal learning are experience-dependent, one should expect only limited implications of sensitive period phenomena in educational contexts or in developing children's thinking skills.

This expectation is re-enforced in recent reviews of cognition, neuroscience, and education. Discussions of sensitive periods are minimal. Although somewhat dated, *How People Learn* (Bransford *et al.*, 1999) discusses sensitive periods in a single chapter, using visual deprivation and language learning as examples. The authors tend to emphasize the importance of learning over the life-span, experience-dependent plasticity, rather than age-constrained, sensitive period phenomena. In 2012, *Cognitive Neuropsychology* devoted a special issue to children's cognitive development. Only one chapter mentioned sensitive periods. McKone *et al.* (2012) suggested that there may be critical periods in infancy for aspects of face recognition and holistic processing. In a 2012 special issue of the *British Journal for Educational Psychology*, entitled *Educational Neuroscience*, sensitive periods were mentioned in only one of the issue's ten articles. Thomas (2012) again pointed out that sensitive periods arise in work on perception, not on higher cognition, i.e. 'school' skills such as literacy, numeracy, and reasoning. Tokuhama-Espinosa's *Making Classrooms Better* (2014) synthesizes work on classroom practices from the perspective of mind, brain, and education. The book does not mention critical or sensitive periods. In *Educational Neuroscience* (Mareschal *et al.*, 2013), the terms critical or sensitive period do not occur in any of the six subject matter chapters (e.g. reading, maths). Sensitive periods are discussed, as one would expect, in the chapter on language development (Donlan and Knowland, 2013). The authors' review of behavioral research on L2A suggests to them that with appropriate instruction, a second language can be acquired at any age. In the chapter on social development (Blakemore *et al.*, 2013), the term 'sensitive period' is broadly defined as 'a time of major opportunity for teaching and learning' or a period of 'development in which the brain is particularly susceptible to certain environmental stimuli and particularly efficient at processing and assimilating new information – at learning'. These definitions arise in the context of suggesting that during adolescence there may be sensitive periods for social and emotional development.

One reason why 'sensitive period' rather than 'critical period' is the preferred usage in current policy contexts is the overgeneralization, if not abuse, of the latter term in the 1990 discussions of early childhood development (Bruer, 1999). In the wake of those discussions, Bailey (2002) provides a useful perspective on the role of timing in early childhood pedagogy. What is important, Bailey argues, is not timing experiences relative to maturational age, as is the message of sensitive periods, but rather timing experiences in a way that is appropriate to the child's developmental status, prior experience, and need or readiness to learn a particular skill or concept. Certainly neuroscience will continue to expand our understanding of development. Certainly there are variations in children's developmental status at the same age and it is reasonable to assume that there is no single, time-locked developmental path. Pedagogy must be sensitive to these variations. We also know from the cognitive literature that prior knowledge in a subject domain is a much better predictor of rate and efficiency of learning than is chronological age. Improved early childhood and educational interventions will result from attempts to match experiences to the developmental and educational level of the child. If so one should expect two things. First, experience-dependent plasticity will probably play a larger role in this effort than experience-expectant plasticity. Second, despite advances in the neurosciences, psychology and the behavioral sciences will continue to be fundamental to the enterprise.

References

Bailey, D. B. (2002) Are critical periods critical for early childhood education? The role of timing in early childhood pedagogy. *Early Childhood Research Quarterly*, 17, 281–94.

Bateson, P. (1979) How do sensitive periods arise and what are they for? *Animal Behaviour*, 27, 470–86.

Beckett, C., Maughan, B., Rutter, M., Castle, J., Colvert, E., Groothues, C., Kreppner, J., Stevens, S., O'Connor, T. G. and Sonuga-Barke, E. J. S. (2006) Do the effects of early severe deprivation on cognition persist into early adolescence? Findings from the English and Romanian Adoptees Study. *Child Development*, 77(3), 696–711.

Bialystok, E. and Hakuta, K. (1994) *In Other Words: The Science and Psychology of Second-Language Acquisition*. New York: Basic Books.

Birdsong, D. and Molis, M. (2001) On the evidence for maturational constraints in second-language acquisition. *Journal of Memory and Language*, 44: 235–49.

Blakemore, S.-J., Kadosh, K. C., Sebastian, C., Grossman, T. and Johnson, M. H. (2013) Social development. In D. Mareschal, B. Butterworth and A. Tolmie (eds) *Educational Neuroscience*. New York: Wiley-Blackwell.

Bornstein, M. H. (1987) Sensitive periods in development: Definition, existence, utility, and meaning. In M. H. Bornstein (ed.) *Sensitive Periods in Development: Interdisciplinary Perspectives* (pp. 3–110). Hillsdale, NJ: Erlbaum.

Bowlby, J. (1953) Critical phases in the development of social responses in man and other animals. In J. M. Tanner (ed.) *Prospects in Psychiatric Research: The Proceedings of the Oxford Conference of the Mental Health Fund*. Oxford, UK: Blackwell.

Bransford, J. D., Brown, A. L. and Cocking, R. R. (1999) *How People Learn: Brain, Mind, Experience, and School*. Washington, DC: National Academy Press.

Bruer, J. T. (1999) *The Myth of the First Three Years: A New Understanding of Early Brain Development and Lifelong Learning*. New York: Free Press.

Bruer, J. T. (2001) A critical and sensitive period primer. In D. B. Bailey, J. T. Bruer, F. J Symons and J. Lichtman (eds) *Critical Thinking about Critical Periods* (pp. 3–26). Baltimore, MD: Paul Brookes Publishing.

Colombo, J. (1982) The critical period concept: Research methodology and theoretical issues. *Psychological Bulletin*, 91(2), 260–75.

Donlan, C. and Knowland, V. (2013) Language development. In D. Mareschal, B. Butterworth and A. Tolmie (eds) *Educational Neuroscience*. New York: Wiley-Blackwell.

Flege, J. E., MacKay, I. A. R. and MacKay, I. (1995) Factors affecting degree of perceived foreign accent in a second language. *Journal of the Acoustical Society of America*, 97, 3125–34.

Flege, J. E., Yeni-Komshian G. H. and Liu S. (1999) Age constraints on second language learning. *Journal of Memory and Language*, 41, 78–104.

Greenough, W. T., Black, J. E. and Wallace, C. S. (1987) Experience and brain development. *Child Development*, 58(3), 539–59.

Hubel, D. H. and Wiesel, T. N. (1970) The period of susceptibility to the physiological effects of unilateral eye closure in kittens. *Journal of Physiology*, 206, 419–36.

Hubel, D. H. and Wiesel, T. N. (2005) *Brain and Visual Perception*. Oxford: Oxford University Press.

Johnson, J. S. and Newport, E. L. (1989) Critical period effects in second language learning: The influence of maturational state on the acquisition of English as a second language. *Cognitive Psychology*, 21, 60–99.

Johnson, M. H. (2005) Sensitive periods in functional brain development: Problems and prospects. *Developmental Psychobiology*, 46(3), 287–92.

Knudson, E. I. (2004) Sensitive periods in the development of the brain and behavior. *Journal of Cognitive Neuroscience*, 16(8), 1412–25.

Knudson, E. I., Heckman, J. J., Cameron, J. L. and Shonkoff, J. P. (2005) Economic, neurobiological, and behavioral perspectives on building America's future workforce. *Proceedings of the National Academy of Sciences*, 103(27), 10155–62.

Kuhl, P. and Doupe A. (1999) Birdsong and human speech. *Annual Review of Neuroscience*, 22, 567–631.

Lenneberg, E. (1967) *Biological Foundations of Language*. New York: John Wiley.

Levi, D. M. (2005) Perceptual learning in adults with amblyopia: A reevaluation of critical periods in human vision. *Developmental Psychobiology*, 46(3): 222–32.

Lichtman, J. W. (2001) Critical periods in the development of the visual system. In D. B. Bailey, J. T. Bruer, F. J Symons and J. Lichtman (eds) *Critical Thinking about Critical Periods* (pp. 3–26). Baltimore, MD: Paul Brookes Publishing.

Lorenz, K. (1937) The companion in the bird's world. *The Auk*, 64, 245–73.

Mareschal, D., Butterworth, B. and Tolmie, A. (eds) (2013) *Educational Neuroscience*. New York: Wiley-Blackwell.

Maurer, D. (2005) Introduction to the special issue on critical periods reexamined. Evidence from sensory development. *Developmental Psychobiology*, 46(3), 155.

McKone, E., Crookes, K., Jeffrey, L. and Dilks, D. D. (2012) A critical review of the development of face recognition: Experience is less important than previously believed. *Cognitive Neuropsychology*, 29(1–2), 174–212.

Michel, G. F. and Tyler, A. N. (2005) Critical period: A history of the transition from questions of when, to what, to how. *Developmental Psychobiology*, 46, 156–62.

Muñoz, C. and Singleton, D. (2011) A critical review of age-related research on L2 ultimate attainment. *Language Teaching*, 44(1), 1–35.

Oyama, S. (1979) The concept of the sensitive period. *Merrill-Palmer Quarterly*, 25(2), 83–103.

Penfield, W. and Roberts, L. (1959) *Speech and Brain Mechanisms*. Princeton, NJ; Princeton University Press.

Rutter, M. (2002) Nature, nurture, and development: From evangelism through science toward policy and practice. *Child Development*, 73(1), 1–21.

Rutter, M. and the English and Romanian Adoptees (ERA) Study Team (1998) Developmental catch-up, and deficit, following adoption after severe global early privation. *Journal of Child Psychology and Psychiatry*, 39(4), 465–76.

Rutter, M., O'Connor, T. G. and the English and Romanian Adoptees (ERA) Study Team (2007) Are there biological programming effects for psychological development? Findings from a study of Romanian adoptees. *Developmental Psychology*, 40(1): 81–94.

Spemann, H. (1918) *Embryonic Development and Induction*. New Haven, CT: Yale University Press.

Thomas, M. S. C. (2012) Brain plasticity and education. *British Journal of Educational Psychology. Monograph Series II: Psychological Aspects of Education – Current Trends No. 8 Educational Neuroscience*, pp. 142–62.

Thomson, R. A. (2001) Sensitive periods in attachment? In D. B. Bailey, J. T. Bruer, F. J. Symons and J. Lichtman (eds) *Critical Thinking about Critical Periods* (pp. 3–26). Baltimore, MD: Paul Brookes Publishing.

Tokuhama-Espinosa, T. (2014) *Making Classrooms Better: 50 Practical Applications of Mind, Brain, and Education Science*. New York: W. W. Norton.

Yeni-Komshian, G., Flege J. E. and Liu, H. (1997) Pronunciation proficiency in L1 and L2 among Korean–English bilinguals: The effect of age of arrival in the US. *Journal of the Acoustical Society of America*, 102(A): 3139.

Zeanah, C. H., Gunnar, M. R., McCall, R. B., Kreppner, J. M. and Fox, N. A. (2011) Sensitive periods. *Monographs of the Society for Research in Child Development*, 78(4), 147–62.

PART III

Making sense of the world

21

BABIES, BOYS, BOATS AND BEYOND

Children's working theories in the early years

Sally Peters and Keryn Davis

Introduction

What are some of our youngest citizens thinking about and how can we support their creative, innovative and critical thinking? This chapter reports on some of the findings of a New Zealand study looking at young children's thinking as they make sense of the world around them. It highlights the depth of ideas young children were considering and questions some assumptions about young children's thinking. The chapter also reflects on some interesting challenges for adults in supporting this aspect of children's development. We found that developing a greater understanding of these issues for our youngest children has the potential to create opportunities for meaningful dialogue about the learning of *all* children, and connects to international interest in this topic. The chapter begins with a brief overview of the project and the New Zealand educational context. The following sections draw on data to outline the rich and varied world of young children's thinking before looking more closely at the depth of some children's thinking. We conclude by reflecting on the implications for adults working with children.

Overview of the project and the New Zealand context

Our interest in children's working theories arises from the learning outcomes in the New Zealand early childhood curriculum *Te Whāriki* (Ministry of Education, 1996). Early childhood education covers the years from birth to school entry (children usually start school at age 5 years although they do not have to be at school until they are 6). The learning outcomes in *Te Whāriki* are indicative rather than definitive and each setting develops its own emphases and priorities. The document emphasises holistic, active learning in early childhood and these are broadly described as closely linked knowledge, skills, and attitudes, which:

combine together to form a child's 'working theory' and help the child develop dispositions that encourage learning. In early childhood, children are developing more elaborate and useful working theories about themselves and about the people, places, and things in their lives. These working theories contain a combination of knowledge about the world, skills and strategies, attitudes, and expectations ... As children gain greater experience, knowledge, and skills, the theories they develop become more widely applicable and have more connecting links between them.

(Ministry of Education, 1996, p. 44)

The curriculum writers drew on Claxton's (1990) view that: 'Learning at its most general is the business of improving our theories, elaborating and tuning them' (p. 23) and our basic method of learning 'involves a gradual process of editing these minitheories' (p. 66). The term working theories therefore implies fluidity and the sense of an idea that is being worked on.

However, despite the explanations within the curriculum and the long history of practice associated with *Te Whāriki* we found that children's working theories and ways to support them are generally not well understood. In contrast, the learning disposition outcome of the curriculum has received considerable research and practice attention. Our Teaching and Learning Research Initiative (TLRI) project, *Moments of Wonder, Everyday Events: How are Young Children Theorising and Making Sense of their World?*, was designed to right some of this imbalance and looked specifically at the kinds of working theories about the world children were developing, and what they were theorising about (for details of the study see Davis and Peters, 2011). We were also interested in the adult's role in supporting children's working theories and offering more opportunities for children to stretch their thinking. There is interest in these issues in many other countries. For example, the OECD (2006) Starting Strong II report noted that a challenge exists in many countries for early childhood education to focus more on the child and for educators 'to show a greater understanding of the learning strategies of young children' (p. 207).

The research discussed in this chapter was based in five Playcentre early childhood education settings. New Zealand has a diverse range of early childhood services and includes both teacher-led, (where at least 50 per cent of the adults who educate and care for children must be qualified, registered early childhood teachers) and others that are parent-led, (where parents, families or caregivers provide the education and care). Playcentres are parent-led services and began as a parent cooperative during the 1940s to support families and promote new developments in early childhood education. Playcentres are collectively supervised and managed by parents. They have a strong focus on parent education as well as children's learning (Ministry of Education, 2009; see also Stover (1998) for an overview of the Playcentre movement's history). Typically, Playcentres offer sessional programmes for mixed-age groups of children, and this was the case for the five research sites. Like teacher-led early childhood services, adults involved in Playcentre are guided by the early childhood curriculum *Te Whāriki* (Ministry of Education, 1996), but unlike most teacher-led services, Playcentres rely on the services and time of parent volunteers to manage this.

Examples of the rich and varied world of young children's thinking

Data for the project included assessments in the form of Learning Stories (see Carr, 2001; Carr and Lee, 2012), written observations, photographs, parents' written and spoken comments and observations, and video and audio recordings of interactions with children. When we analysed the data we were able to categorise some of the kinds of things children were thinking about. The following sections share examples of the data under the broad groupings of making sense of the social and physical world, and an interconnecting and overlapping theme of making sense of language.

Making sense of the social world

Within the children's developing theories about their social worlds, growing up (and 'growing down') appeared to be of particular interest to children. Many children were interested in their increased height and capabilities. For example, Barney explained:

> Me's getting bigger and bigger and bigger and then me's be Jonathan [older brother] and then me's be daddy. Then me's be an orchestra man ... Tim Tim [baby] is getting bigger and bigger. Mummy is getting tinier and tinier. She is getting tinier than Tim Tim.

The idea that adults get smaller and smaller (grow down) was found across centres. For example, when one mother said she couldn't climb on the fort because she was too big, her daughter Emme comforted her by suggesting 'You'll be able to get up here when you are little – eh?' While the theories about getting bigger related to children's observations, the explanations regarding adults growing smaller were less clear. Much earlier Carr (1997) described how her 3-year-old daughter, when required to travel in the special child's car seat in the back of the car said darkly, 'When I grow up I'll be driving the car (*pause*) and when you grow down I'll put *you* in the kiddy car seat' (p. 2). Carr suggested that theories about significant adults 'growing down' might be a way to accept with equanimity the powerlessness that goes with being a 3-year-old.

Perhaps because the Playcentres were mix-aged there was a lot of discussion among the older children about babies. For example, is moving out of nappies a signal that babyhood is past? Can babies be naughty? Within this there appeared to be over-laps with developing meanings for language, such as when Hugh initially said, 'The younger you are, the naughtier you are,' but later reflected, 'Babies can't be naughty. They start being naughty when they're one.' This seemed to be as much a working theory about the meaning of 'naughty' as it was about babies.

In another centre one girl regularly played a game with an older child where she was a 'naughty baby'. In this play she appeared to be exploring working theories about babies, and testing the boundaries to make sense of 'good' and 'bad' behaviour. Good and evil underpinned the interest another child (Ferdi) had in the book and film character, Harry Potter. However, the adults were not aware of this at first. In a number of instances we found it is easy to miss the child's central interest (Davis *et al.*, 2012; Peters and Davis, 2011); in the case of Ferdi's interest in Harry Potter, the adults tried to widen the exploration and include other children in what they saw as Ferdi's working theory focus by holding a 'wizard day' in the centre. The adults were surprised by Ferdi's lack of participation in this event but later when Eleanor (practitioner researcher) revisited his Harry Potter interest with him she noted that the ideas Ferdi was focused on in the Potter stories revolved mainly around the themes of good and evil, something the 'wizard day' had not touched on. Later Eleanor reflected, 'I wish I had just spent more time talking to him about Harry Potter and allowing myself to be genuinely interested instead of pursuing my own agenda.'

Making sense of the physical world

Other examples of working theories included children's developing ideas about the physical world. For example, 3-year-old Barney had a theory that when a piece of electrical equipment was plugged into just one of the double wall sockets, *both* of the switches needed to be turned on for the equipment to work. His mother, having observed this several times, attempted to clarify:

> M: 'So you need the top switch on, if the plug's in the top and you need the bottom switch on if the plug's in the bottom?'
> B: 'No. You need them both on. It needs to make two noises.'
> His mother commented, 'I tried to disrupt his theory but he wasn't in the zone to refine it even though I had encouraged him to experiment with switching various switches on and off. I thought this had shown flaws in his theory but he didn't accept this.'

We reflected that perhaps for Barney his theory was difficult for his mother to change because, at this time, it was successful; if both switches were in the 'on' position the equipment worked. Claxton (1990, p. 24) noted that even as adults many of our implicit theories are treated by us as reality rather than hypothesis and are 'remarkably resistant to change even in the face of good evidence,' while other theories we know to be conjectures and are willing to revise them.

Barney's view about plugs continued over several months, as did another child's (Tim's) exploration of water travel. However, while Barney's working theory was unchanged, Tim's working theories expanded and refined throughout the period. At 20 months, Tim's theories were implied by his actions more than his speech. For example:

> Today the older boys were playing in the sandpit and had made a complicated water flow system with pipes and guttering and what not. Tim was fascinated with it. He would go over and look at the water flowing into one end of the pipe

and then go round to the other end where it was coming out and lean right down to peer in and see what was happening. Then back to the start and have a good look at that and back round again.

(Observation notes)

After six months of Tim's water travel exploration his mother noted:

I left Tim in the bathroom brushing his teeth. I should have known with child number four that was a mistake. I came back and this little voice said, 'Mum the water's not going down the pipes.' I rushed into the bathroom and of course the water was indeed NOT going down the pipes. He had the plug in – the whole bathroom was under about an inch of water. Shows he's still thinking a lot about pipes though!

Tim, now age 2, began building water races and seeing balls, then coloured water and later wooden boats go down. Now his explanations were accompanied by a verbal commentary, e.g. 'It's coming, it's coming'. Many other children joined in these investigations and an eight-month focus on water led to a wide range of theorising and increasingly sophisticated thinking that progressed to complex waterways, waterwheels, seeing whether water can go up, what makes a boat float and how to make it sink. Some of these discoveries disrupted the adults' theories, such as the day one child made holes in the bottom of a cardboard 'boat'. Eleanor, one of the practitioner researchers, recalled:

Barney thought he would make a big boat out of some large cardboard boxes we had at Playcentre. He started by drilling holes in the bottom. Then he got the hammer and was ready to bash some bigger holes in it. At that point I noticed him. 'What are you doing, Barney?' 'Making a boat,' he replied. 'But what do you think will happen to your boat if you have holes in the bottom?' I asked. Rhetorical question I thought. 'It'll sink.' We decided to test it in the water trough. But do you know that boat floated? We tried to push it down but it was really difficult. If we pushed really hard we could make the water squeeze up through the little holes where we were pushing ... We were really surprised! Our theories about floating and sinking were disrupted here – the ones about the materials that float well (cardboard was not top of my list) and the ones about holes leading to sinking.

Making sense of language

While for the youngest children their ideas were implied by their actions, language played an increasing role in children's theorising. As we listened to their talk it was evident that some of the theorising related to their growing vocabularies and making sense of language. Elsewhere we have written about one child's theorising about why a see-saw is called a see-saw (Davis and Peters, 2010).

Listening to the ways children were exploring language raised questions regarding the nature of their thinking. For example, deliberations about 'Is it a boy or is it a baby?' appeared to relate to puzzling about class inclusion (whether one can be both baby and also a boy) and also about determining what the words 'baby' and 'boy' meant. In these examples the children seemed to be trying to work out if 'boy' represented a stage of development synonymous with 'child' rather than a category within the concept of baby, based on biological sex. Similarly, children were exploring ideas about place that reflected ideas about hierarchical relationships and classes and also an exploration of word meanings. In the following excerpt a child was thinking about 'Canterbury' (a region in New Zealand) and its relationship with a 'Christchurch' (a city, within that region).

> C: 'Mummy, have we ever been to Canterbury?'
> M: 'We live in Canterbury.'
> C: 'No we live in Christchurch.'
> M: 'Well Christchurch IS in Canterbury.'
> C: 'Do you mean Canterbury is in Christchurch?'
> M: 'No I mean Christchurch is in Canterbury.'
> C: 'Oh, but when we were in Australia we weren't in Canterbury were we?'
> M: 'No.'

While class inclusion is about an understanding of hierarchical relationships, we felt an intersection between conceptual understanding and making sense of language was at play for these children.

As with their working theories about the social and physical world, children's considerations of language opened up a spirit of inquiry for many adults who found their own working theories were edited and refined as much as the children's in response to some of the children's questions. These seemingly simple issues opened up rich and complex puzzling for the adults too. Once the meanings of words such as 'boy' or 'see-saw' were pondered, the history of the word and the breadth of definitions could draw adults back into the awe and wonder of the seemingly familiar in the world around them.

The surprising depth of young children's ideas

While the examples above present some of the ideas the children were thinking about in our study (and many of the associated challenges for adults), a closer look at some of the examples of children's thinking reveals the depth of some of their ideas and the ways children are developing agency through their participation in learning communities.

When mice were spotted in the worm farm at one of the Playcentres, Hugh (4 years old) took the situation very seriously. First he made a trap to catch the mice out of an egg box with sellotape in the bottom 'so their feet would stick on to it'. He baited this trap with cheese. A few days later Hugh got a piece of sequined material and proposed to use it to catch the mice in, whereupon they would take them to the far end of the field and release them. Eleanor wrote:

Seeing Hugh's sequined cloth one of the adults commented, 'Oh, that won't do,' and grabbed a transparent container and an exercise book and headed off in the direction of the worm farm. Well, I strongly questioned her theory too but dared say nothing. Off we went. After some digging and various mouse spottings, we gave up trying to catch them.

Later, when the adults were weighing up the options of how to get rid of the mice, Keryn asked Hugh (who was standing there fascinated but largely ignored by the adults) what he thought. Hugh decided to ask everyone else in the community about what they thought should be done about the mice. He created a poster to put on the door. He drew a picture of a mouse and got Eleanor to scribe for him. They wrote:

What should we do about the mouse in the worm farm?
Option 1: Keep it as a pet.
Option 2: Get rid of it ... but how?

The survey led to a number of proposals from the children, which were more empathetic to the mice than (in most cases) focused on getting rid of them. For example, 'Find some other mice and put them with the other mice so they won't be lonely' (Georgia). 'Maybe the mouse would like to come and play' (Ferdi). Eleanor's older daughter spent time at home surveying the family too, and decided it was acceptable to have more than one vote because you might agree with more than one idea. Hugh's idea to survey the community helped to grow this interesting, real-life problem into one that the whole learning community could be part of solving.

In this example Hugh's ideas were as valid as the adults' ones (which included using dogs to chase the mice as well as catching them in a plastic container). He actively resisted the adult dominated discussion of potential solutions to the problem and instead shifted the response to a more democratic one, transforming the situation into one that was more complex and sophisticated. Hugh was both experiencing agency and developing agency through positive participation in, and contribution to, the shared activity (Rainio, 2008). Although Hugh's ideas, together with the early decision by adults to follow Hugh's lead, helped ignite an interest for many of the children and adults, the investigation of the mice in the worm farm wasn't an easy one for the adults. The inquiry caused tensions and discomfort as many adults struggled with letting go of control and allowing time for the problem to be solved more slowly together with the children:

It was very interesting. There is a genuine strong desire among the adults at our centre to empower the children and give them real life opportunities for decision making but obviously not if the topic is too sensitive.

(Eleanor)

Hugh recognised and used the support of others (particularly Eleanor) to transform the activity, something Edwards and D'Arcy (2004, cited in Rainio, 2008) refer to as 'relational agency'. The five practitioner researchers in our study were trying to become better at 'growing' children's working theories by positioning the child as the professor and themselves as the student, an idea adopted from Shafer (2002), while at the same time attempting to add more breadth and complexity to the working theories. The practices the adults in our study were working on were very like the practices Martin (2004) describes as supporting agency. Practices that support agency, according to Martin, emphasise 'students' active engagement within richly furnished curricular settings with the support of teachers who encourage student risk taking and active, self-directed experimentation with the alternative possibilities available in such settings' (Martin, 2004, p. 144).

When children's ideas had been fostered in this way they sometimes exceeded everyone's expectations. In another Playcentre Sarah-Kate had been sharing a number of facts about animals with Nikki, one of the practitioner researchers. All the while Nikki listened and talked with Sarah-Kate at the same time trying to work out what she might do next to support Sarah-Kate's growing expertise. One day Nikki suggested to Sarah-Kate that she might like to make a book about her ideas. Nikki wrote down the text dictated by Sarah-Kate and Sarah-Kate illustrated it with drawings. A short time later Sarah-Kate and her mother shared a new story with Nikki, *Tuatara Expansion Lizard*. Sarah-Kate had dictated the story over the weekend and her mother had written it into a scrapbook. Sarah-Kate had spent a lot of time illustrating the story. Nikki suggested that they could publish it into a book and put it in the book case as well, which they did.

Another story, *Meerkaat Manor*, arrived from home a few weeks later and Sarah-Kate wanted to publish it into a book again. Soon Sarah-Kate telling stories and having them recorded and made into books had become a well-established practice at home and at the Playcentre. Nikki's decision to introduce authoring and illustrating books shifted Sarah-Kate's interest to a new level and provided new opportunities for her to develop and practice her creative and critical thinking. It also let others in the learning community in on her ideas. Eighteen months after her first story a devastating earthquake struck Christchurch. This was a significant event in the lives of many New Zealanders. Sarah-Kate (now recently turned 5), dictated the following story to her mother the morning after the quake:

> I got these lizards as babies. They are horned geckos. I started training them two days after they were born. I trained them to be search and rescue lizards so that they can help people stuck in the rubble and wreckage of the Christchurch quakes.
>
> I trained them how to go under bricks and rubble. They have a really sensitive tip on their tail. They feel around with their tails and if it comes in contact with someone, they bark out to get one of the teams to come and rescue the person. They draw a picture in the dust with their tail and then point with their tails to show the rescuers exactly where that person is.
>
> I have sent them out to do their job. Christchurch really needs them now. I absolutely didn't know this until they had gone out – they have had babies. They give birth to live young. I went and looked into their favourite ditch and there was a pile of babies. I am going to train these babies as well.

The females range in colour when they are young but the males are only one colour. I can tell from my research by looking at these babies that there is only one male.

This powerful story moved many adults and was later used to assist in considering how to support children's agency in the devastation and trauma following the earthquakes.

Implications for adults working with children

Although traditional Western theorising has tended to consider children's thinking as immature and illogical, the children's thinking revealed in this project's close documentation of working theory development highlighted that far from being illogical, their understandings were generally logically derived from the information they had available. Many examples showed thoughtful consideration of the world around them and the language they were making sense of. In a number of cases children's views were as valid as, (and challenged or extended) the adults' thinking. As the OECD (2006) noted, two valuable approaches in early education are a focus on agency and the child's natural learning strategies, including 'intense research on matters of interest to the child' and listening to children, which is a sign of respect for 'the child's capacity to guide his or her own learning, when supported by well-trained educators in a rich learning environment' (p. 208). When both of these were evident in the research Playcentres, and adults were authentically listening and engaging, we saw rich opportunities for thinking to be shared and developed. In New Zealand we have the framework in place for supporting these approaches with the curriculum *Te Whāriki* (Ministry of Education, 1996). However, in practice working with children in ways that respect and foster their thinking was not always easy.

Many of the children's ideas were also richly creative. Creative, innovative, and critical thinking have been described as twenty-first-century capabilities (Bolstad *et al.*, 2012; Gilbert, 2005; Ministry of Education, 2007), yet the claim has been made that we are educating our children away from creativity (Robinson and Azzam, 2009). Although not the focus of this chapter, we did see examples of adults who shifted children's complex thinking back to much 'safer water' and familiarity for the adults concerned. Hennessey and Amabile (2010) argue for greater attention to student creativity and to how teachers can support rather than hinder this learning, as creativity is 'crucial for economic, scientific, social, and artistic/cultural advancement. It is essential that we come to a far deeper understanding of how teaching techniques, teacher behaviour, and social relationships in schools affect the motivation and creativity of students' (Hennessey and Amabile, 2010, p. 585).

The emphasis in these early childhood education settings was on what the children were curious about or found interesting. Importance was put on fostering children's interests and curiosities rather than on retelling preconceived 'adult' facts or truths. Many of the children's interests emerged in seemingly unpredictable ways, and in many cases these developed over extended periods of time. Often interests were recognised retrospectively, but adults found they could sometimes 'grow' the interests of one into becoming an interest of many. The focus on interest as both the *what* and the *how* of learning stems mainly from the desire to protect and inspire the children's motivation to learn. While the link between learning outcomes and intrinsic motivation has been well established (Broussard and Garrison, 2004; Bjørnebekk *et al.*, 2011). There is still much to be learnt about how to support motivation as children progress through their education. A high focus on interest helps maintain the worthwhileness of the activity for children (Drummond, 1993). 'Worthwhileness' can be understood in terms of its meaningfulness and relevance to the children, and can measured in terms of how well the interest in an activity or a situation captured children's attention and effort, and for how long issues central to learning and teaching in both early childhood settings and schools.

Conclusion

Our findings concur with the point raised in Lucas and Claxton (2010) that some assumptions about children's minds that have traditionally underpinned education may not be as valid as once thought. As our project's title suggested, there are moments of wonder in many everyday events. Working theories are revealed when we take time to listen to and understand what children are saying or expressing through their actions. It is important to resist pedagogical practices that underestimate young children's competence and decrease their interest and motivation. Instead it is timely to reconsider pedagogy with young children and explore ways to recognise, support and stretch their thinking.

Acknowledgements

We acknowledge with thanks the funding from Teaching and Learning Research Initiative (TLRI) for the project we have drawn on in this chapter, *Moments of Wonder, Everyday Events: How are Young Children Theorising and Making Sense of their World?*, a two-year project based in five New Zealand, Playcentres. We are also very grateful to our practitioner researcher colleagues who have been central to the work of this project, and to the children and families who have allowed their experiences to be shared.

References

Bjørnebekk, G., Gjesme, T. and Ulriksen, R. (2011) Achievement motives and emotional processes in children during problem-solving: Two experimental studies of their relation to performance in different achievement goal conditions. *Motivation and Emotion, 35*(4), 351–67.

Bolstad, R., Gilbert, J., McDowall, S., Bull, A., Boyd, S. and Hipkins, R. (2012) *Supporting Future-oriented Learning and Teaching – A New Zealand Perspective.* Report to the Ministry of Education. Wellington: Ministry of Education.

Broussard, S. C. and Garrison, M. E. B. (2004) The relationship between classroom motivation and academic achievement in elementary-school-aged children. *Family and Consumer Sciences Research Journal, 33*(2), 106–20.

Carr, M. (1997) *Technological Practice in Early Childhood as a Dispositional Milieu.* Unpublished PhD thesis. University of Waikato. Hamilton, New Zealand.

Carr, M. (2001) *Assessment in Early Childhood Settings: Learning Stories.* London: Paul Chapman.

Carr, M. and Lee, W. (2012) *Learning Stories: Constructing Learner Identities in Early Education.* London: Sage.

Claxton, G. (1990) *Teaching to Learn: A Direction for Education.* London: Cassell.

Crow, S. R. (2006) What motivates a lifelong learner? *School Libraries Worldwide, 12*(1), 22–34.

Davis, K. and Peters, S. (2011) *Moments of Wonder, Everyday Events: Children's Working Theories in Action.* Teaching Learning Research Initiative Final Report. Available at: www.tlri.org.nz/moments-wonder-everyday-events-how-are-young-children-theorising-and-making-sense-their-world/.

Davis, K., Peters, S. and White, E. (2012) Growing islands of interest: nurturing the development of young children's working theories. Paper presented at *Creative Engagements: Thinking with Children* conference. Mansfield College, Oxford, UK (July).

Drummond, M. J. (1993) *Assessing Children's Learning.* London: David Fulton.

Gilbert, J. (2005) *Catching the Knowledge Wave? The Knowledge Society and the Future of Education.* Wellington, NZ: NZCER Press.

Hennessey, B. and Amabile, T. (2010) Creativity. *Annual Review of Psychology, 61,* 569–98.

Lucas, B. and Claxton, G. (2010) *New Kinds of Smart: How the Science of Learnable Intelligence is Changing Education (Expanding educational horizons).* Maidenhead, England: Open University Press.

Martin, J. (2004) Self-regulated learning, social cognitive theory, and agency. *Educational Psychologist, 39*(2), 135–45.

Ministry of Education (1996) *Te Whāriki: He whāriki mātauranga mō ngā mokopuna o Aotearoa. Early childhood curriculum.* Wellington: Learning Media.

Ministry of Education (2007) *The New Zealand Curriculum: The English-medium teaching and learning in years 1–13.* Wellington, New Zealand: Learning Media.

Ministry of Education (2009) *Types of ECE service.* Retrieved from www.minedu.govt.nz/Parents/EarlyYears/HowECEWorks/TypesOfECEService.aspx (14/11/13).

OECD (Organisation for Economic Co-operation and Development) (2006) *Starting Strong II: Early Childhood Education and Care.* Paris: OECD.

Peters, S. and Davis, K. (2011) Fostering children's working theories: Pedagogical issues and dilemmas in New Zealand. *Early Years: An International Journal of Research and Development, 31*(1), 5–17.

Rainio, A. (2008) From resistance to involvement: Examining agency and control in a play-world activity. *Mind, Culture, and Activity, 15*(2), 115–40.

Robinson, K. and Azzam, A. (2009) Why creativity now? *Educational Leadership, 67*(1), 22–6.

Shafer, A. (2002) Ordinary moments, extraordinary possibilities. In V. R. Fu, A. J. Stremmel and L. T. Hill (eds) *Teaching and Learning: Collaborative Exploration of the Reggio Emilia Approach.* Upper Saddle River, NJ: Merrill/Prentice Hall.

Stover, S. (ed.) (1998) *Good Clean Fun: New Zealand's Playcentre Movement.* Auckland: Playcentre Publications.

22

DEVELOPING AN UNDERSTANDING OF ELEMENTARY ASTRONOMY

Is the truth in the eye of the beholder?

Triin Liin

I remember rather clearly a moment from my sixth summer. It was a sunny day and I was playing outside with my friends. Somehow we started to discuss the people living on the other side of the Earth. I remember how I was sure that people living on the 'bottom' side of the Earth spend their days being upside down. I told this to my friends and we decided that it must mean that the people walk with their heads towards the Earth's surface. From that we deduced, that they must walk on their hands and spent an hour trying to do the same. After many fruitless efforts we concluded that those foreigners must be very weird indeed, because walking on your hands is hard and makes your head dizzy.

Introduction

Knowledge is information that is mentally represented and in some way structured or organized (Kikas, 2005). The amount of knowledge one person has is not constant, instead it continues to change throughout one's life. People have all kinds of knowledge that can be used to think about important matters and to solve more or less difficult problems. In broad terms that kind of knowledge can be divided into two categories: procedural knowledge, which contains knowledge of how to do something, and declarative knowledge, which is knowledge about something (Chi and Ohlsson, 2005).

Knowledge about how to swim, or ride a bike or sign documents is procedural knowledge, while knowledge that water is a liquid, that bikes are vehicles, and that signatures are important is declarative in nature. More specifically, declarative knowledge consists of concepts, principles, ideas, schemas and theories (Ohlsson, 1996).

This chapter focuses on the acquisition of declarative knowledge. In the first part the nature and origin of concepts as well as the differences between knowledge enrichment and conceptual change are discussed. It is shown that both personal experiences as well as memorized knowledge are required for the development of knowledge. The second part explains why conceptual change is often difficult for learners. It clarifies the role of inappropriate teaching methods (e.g. verbal teaching methods), and the influence of pre-existing knowledge in the emergence of inert or encapsulated knowledge as well as the construction of misconception. In the third part guidelines for supporting conceptual change via instruction are provided. The final part of the chapter further illustrates the difficulties that arise when direct experiences and scientific facts seemingly disagree by looking at one particular area of conceptual change – the development of knowledge about the Earth and gravity.

The development of concepts

Concepts can be thought of as internal aspects of a word – the instances, meanings, and generalizations that are associated with a specific term (Vygotsky, 1997). Conceptual change denotes the changes that occur in those internal aspects. These changes happen because during day-to-day living we undertake various actions, observe innumerable things, and thus the amount of knowledge based on personal experiences increases. We also hear new things from other people, read about them in books, or learn them via the internet, which in turn can influence the knowledge we already possess (Brewer *et al.*, 2000; Kikas, 2003). All these experiences create learning opportunities that lead to the acquisition of new concepts or require the reconstruction and reorganization of existing ones (Carey, 1991; Thagard, 2008). The results are long-term changes in the learners' knowledge and ways of knowledge-organization (Kikas, 2005).

Sometimes coming into contact with new information (whether by being repeatedly exposed to it or because somebody insists on the importance of that information) is enough for children to adopt this information. This process of knowledge addition is called knowledge enrichment and it usually takes place in those learning situations where the learner has no prior knowledge of the taught concepts or the new information is not in conflict with the knowledge the learner already possesses (Piaget, 2005). In those cases the process does not require much effort and the learnt information is simply added to the existing concepts or filled into the gaps of the knowledge system (Chi, 2008). Such learning can result in an increase in the amount of facts a person knows and/or in the number of connections between different concepts; representations can also become more detailed, more complex, and more generalized, and new perspectives can be adopted (Chi and Ohlsson, 2005). For example, when learning about the Earth, children can easily accept that there are other countries besides their own homeland and that those places are far away and it takes time to get to them. Most of them also find it rather easy to remember that the Earth is round (Hannust and Kikas, 2007).

At the centre of such learning is memorization of factual information, which in turn is supported by repetition, paraphrasing, and illustration. The acquisition of factual information is very important because it serves as the basis for further conceptual development while lack of it may cause the acquisition of consistent scientific concepts to fail (see Vygotsky, 1997/1934). For example, Hannust and Kikas (2007) examined how understanding of the shape of the Earth and gravity develops during learning and found that children who prior to instruction did not express any topic-related knowledge failed to learn the scientific explanations. As one of the prerequisites for knowledge development is the awareness of one's own preliminary knowledge (Vosniadou, 1996), children with higher amounts of expressed knowledge are further along the path of integrating personal experiences with verbal information and therefore benefit more from instruction than those who have not even started to think about the topic. Even if children know only a few isolated facts, those facts promote rather than disrupt the acquisition of further knowledge, which means that children with better preliminary knowledge profit more from instruction than those who have almost no pre-existing knowledge, mostly because the latter tend to become confused by the instruction and discard all of the learnt material rather easily (Hannust and Kikas, 2007; Kikas *et al.*, 2002). However, teaching does have an effect even when no topic-related preliminary knowledge is present. Vygotsky (1997) believed that all scientific concepts are based on everyday concepts but develop so that they encompass more than the immediate experiences. Therefore, if appropriate instruction methods are applied, learning will make children first conscious of their own surroundings and as a result enables them to start paying attention to their own experiences when talking about the Earth. Their answers could be described as unrelated minimal abstractions from experience that are obviously true and can therefore be used as a basis for explaining the encountered phenomena (Brown and Hammer, 2008; DiSessa, 2008).

The difficulties of conceptual change

Though knowledge of personal experiences and key facts is very important for knowledge acquisition, and thus teaching must ensure that central facts are learnt, this alone may be insufficient to ensure the acquisition of new concepts (Hannust and Kikas, 2012). In fact, by now it is evident that for children the acquisition of contemporary scientific concepts often proves to be difficult. Two different but interrelated sources of these difficulties have been acknowledged.

First, verbal teaching methods, including explanations given by parents, teachers and textbooks, are often insufficient to create understanding and therefore further undermine the process of conceptual change (e.g. Diakidoy and Kendeou, 2001; Vosniadou *et al.*, 2001). For example, sometimes the process stops when learners have memorized facts – no further effort is made to understand the connection of the learnt information with one's own experiences or with broader theories (Kikas, 1998). This may occur when the terms used in teaching are unfamiliar and teaching does not take the learner's pre-existing knowledge into account. The results of such learning are verbalisms – explanations and definitions that have been memorized without any understanding. Such knowledge is encapsulated and continues to exist alongside previously held incorrect beliefs. This means that though under some conditions learners are able to give correct answers (e.g. when the situation for reproduction is similar to the one where the information was learnt, see Tulving and Thomson, 1973), on other occasions they may be unable to generalize that knowledge and thus fail to respond accurately (Carey, 2000; Carey and Spelke, 1994; Linn, 2008). The availability of knowledge depends on the context and thus can be applied when problems are worded in one way but is unavailable when the wording is changed or when the problem is encountered outside of class. For example, it has been shown that a student who is able to apply his/her knowledge of the following formula 'force acting on an object equals mass timed acceleration, to calculate the acceleration when force and mass are given' can explain the equation by stating that the force of an object depends on its weight and movement speed (Brown and Hammer, 2008). That student uses his/her knowledge of mathematics to solve the problem but misconceptualizes it by thinking about force as a property of an object, mass as weight and acceleration as speed. Similarly in astronomy a child can answer correctly that the Earth is shaped like a ball, but at the same time can believe that some people are constantly nauseous because they are upside-down.

Furthermore, because verbalisms are reproduced flawlessly in response to the right cues, they can remain undetected for long periods of time. During all that time the information is isolated from the rest of knowledge and thus has little meaning for the child. Only when the learner discovers its connection with other pieces of information will it support the acquisition of scientific concepts.

So, it seems that very often the new concepts children encounter are not assimilated in a ready-made form. Instead, learning only starts when the learner first encounters new concepts and memorizes new information (Kikas, 2003; Vygotsky, 1997). The learnt information needs to be integrated into the learner's existing conceptual system so that it can be understood and used (Brewer *et al.*, 2000; Inagaki and Hatano, 2002; Spelke and Kinzler, 2007). And here lies the second reason why it is difficult to learn scientific concepts. All learners possess great amounts of knowledge that has been accumulated through personal experiences and is therefore intuitively perceived as correct. Such intuitive knowledge often seemingly contradicts the scientific explanations, which makes it difficult for learners to accept the counter-intuitive scientific concepts. For example, in their daily lives children see and experience the Earth as a rather flat infinite surface and because of that they may come to believe that the whole Earth is flat, like a disk, instead of adopting the spherical Earth view (Vosniadou and Brewer, 1992). Another example of conflicting beliefs would be the experience-based expectation that for movement to occur constant application of force is required, whereas according to school physics no changes in objects' movement speed or direction occur without the influence of external forces and thus bodies continue to move with constant speed in the same direction.

Such previously misconceived knowledge disrupts and inhibits the development of more consistent representations and it needs to be changed into a scientifically accurate form (Chi, 2008; Linn, 2008; Maria, 1996; Vosniadou, 1994). That kind of learning is called *conceptual change* (Carey, 1999; Chi *et al.*, 1994). It encompasses the restructuring of firmly held base beliefs about a topic, the transposition of personal experiences into a new knowledge system, changes of epistemological and ontological perspectives, and the construction of completely new concepts, which will support further knowledge acquisition (Chi, 1992; Duit *et al.*, 2008; Siegal, 2010; Vygotsky 1997). It may even require one to abandon previously held beliefs and understandings.

One reason why conceptual change fails is that learners are not conscious of their own knowledge and that makes it impossible for them to perceive the conflict between their existing beliefs and the scientific theories that should lead to reconceptualization. Even in situations where children have acquired a rather good factual knowledge base and are exposed to conflicting theories the acquisition of consistent concepts and good understanding of the topic cannot be guaranteed. Instead, it has been found that learners often just discard the conflicting information and continue to use their own 'naïve' or 'everyday' concepts that utilize only personal experiences (Chi and Ohlsson, 2005; Kikas, 2008). Hannust and Kikas (2007) describe a case of a boy whose answers indicated that though he remembered what had been taught during the lessons (specifically that because of gravity rain falls towards the surface of the Earth) he also believed at the same time that people live inside a hollow sphere. Moreover, when he had to face a string of questions about Earth and gravity he chose to discard both these explanations and described his own experiences instead.

Furthermore, the integration of knowledge may still fail even when the conflict between different parts of the concept-related material is acknowledged by the learner. There are indications that when faced with a conflict, learners sometimes construct new concepts that allow them to accommodate the learnt information while retaining the core of their experience-based beliefs (Brewer *et al.*, 2000; Vosniadou 1994). Thus the acquisition of a scientific concept has failed yet again and instead a misconception has been formed. Misconceptions, or synthetic concepts as they are sometimes called to emphasize the processes involved in their construction, are ideas and generalizations that are inconsistent with the theories of contemporary science. For example, a misconception that allows one to accept the idea of a spherical Earth alongside one's own experience of a rather flat continuous surface is the understanding that there are actually two things called the Earth – one is the round object depicted in the pictures that can be found somewhere in the outer space while the other is the place where we live (see also Hannust and Kikas, 2007; Vosniadou and Brewer, 1992). Once a misconception has been formed, the perceived conflict between the taught information and experience-based knowledge is eliminated and thus no further need for conceptual change exists (Chinn and Brewer, 1993; Maria, 1996; Smith *et al.*, 1997).

Supporting conceptual change

In order to avoid the acquisition of verbalisms or formation of misconceptions and to overcome the existing false beliefs, several requirements must be met (see also Brewer *et al.*, 2000). First, in order to perceive that a conflict requires solving, the learner has to understand the taught material. Second, the new theories and definitions have to be believable. Finally, the new concepts have to be applicable to a larger number of phenomena than the previously held ones.

Further guidelines suggest that before the introduction of new material the amount and nature of pre-existing knowledge has to be examined (see Diakidoy and Kendeou,

2001; Duit *et al.*, 2001; Howe *et al.*, 1992; Smith *et al.*, 1997; Vosniadou *et al.*, 2001). To affect conceptual change teaching must take these previously held beliefs into account (diSessa, 2008; Linn, 2008). To make learning more effective one needs to raise the learner's level of awareness about the nature of their own concepts and beliefs (Duit *et al.*, 2008; Wiser and Smith, 2008). This can be achieved by discussing the possible explanations of the observed phenomena and the sources of misconceptions and by making the shortcomings of everyday explanations explicit (Canella, 1993, Jonassen, 2008). As learners can become overloaded by too much information, enough time should be left for discussions and contemplations (Cashon and Cohen, 2004).

Children are much better off if they understand how scientific knowledge arises and they should be supported in the acquisition of such knowledge as well as be provided with opportunities to test the validity of all possible explanations (Wiser and Smith, 2008). To make sure that the learnt knowledge does not remain encapsulated, one should try to implement it in different situations and use models and analogies from different fields (DiSessa, 2008; Duit *et al.*, 2001, Linn, 2008). However, one must remember that because learners tend to overgeneralize and assume that all parts of a model can be transferred, careless use of analogies may give rise to even more misconceptions as some very distinct (but not relevant) features of the models used in instruction might increase the amount of incorrect knowledge and thus lead to the construction of synthetic ideas (Deloache and Burns, 1993; Hannust and Kikas, 2007, 2012; Kikas, 1998). For example, when a magnet is used to demonstrate the attraction between bodies, children may conclude that the Earth is also a big magnet which attracts objects with a 'magnetical' force (Hannust and Kikas, 2007; Kikas *et al.*, 2002). To avoid such misunderstandings it is important to make sure that learners know which parts of the analogy they should pay attention to and what should be discarded.

Teaching can further support conceptual development by using the same problems in different domains. For example, to teach mathematics one could use problems that usually are encountered in physics or chemistry. However, no more than one aspect (i.e. the context) should be changed at a time to make sure that learners understand what are the important aspects of the task that lead to a correct solution and what is superficial and can therefore be ignored (Marton and Pang, 2008).

Finally, a larger knowledge base makes accurate generalizations more likely. Only a sufficient amount of declarative knowledge enables one to notice the similarities between seemingly different tasks and makes it possible to apply the existing knowledge in new areas (Ohlsson, 1996). Though some topics (e.g. the topic of gravity) might indeed benefit more from model-based instruction (cf. Diakidoy and Kendeou, 2001; Hatano and Inagaki, 1991; Howe *et al.*, 1992; Smith *et al.*, 1997; Vosniadou *et al.*, 2001), both purely verbal and mode-based instruction methods can support the acquisition of scientific concepts (Kikas *et al.*, 2002).

The development of knowledge of astronomy

Similarly to knowledge development in other areas (e.g. for biology, see Inagaki and Hatano, 2008; Opfer and Siegler, 2004; for physics, see Brown and Hammer, 2008; Wiser and Smith, 2008; for math, see Vamvakoussi and Vosniadou, 2004) analyses of the acquisition of knowledge have shown that in developing understanding about the Earth, direct observations and everyday experiences do play an important role (Brewer *et al.*, 2000; Kikas, 2003). The example provided in the beginning of this chapter indicates that because things are not always what they seem, children cannot be expected to derive scientific knowledge of the world only from intuition or direct observations (e.g. Panagiotaki *et al.*, 2009).When left to their own devices learners may be unable to solve the seeming conflict between experience-based knowledge (e.g. it is uncomfortable to hang upside-down) and scientifically proven information (e.g. people can live on the other side of the Earth without any discomfort) successfully and instead construct incorrect explanations. Whether such explanations can be described as consistent models or whether there are many small pieces of information that are rather loosely related to each other has been under debate for a long time.

In the field of astronomy, the idea that in the course of development of scientific concepts children construct consistent non-scientific concepts or models as an intermediate step has been proposed by several authors (e.g. Diakidoy *et al.*, 1997; Vosniadou and Brewer, 1992; Vosniadou *et al.*, 2004, 2005; Vygotsky, 1997). Vosniadu and her colleagues argue that intuitive ideas about flatness and support may lead to the construction of several incorrect concepts (flat Earth, dual Earth, hollow sphere, and flattened sphere) that children use in a theory-like fashion while answering the questions about the Earth (Vosniadou, 1994; Vosniadou and Brewer, 1992; Vosniadou *et al.*, 2004). These representations are very resistant to instruction, which means that if new contradictory information that cannot be ignored is encountered, radical revision and reorganization of the existing conceptual system is required (Brewer *et al.*, 2000; Chi and Ohlsson, 2005; Chinn and Malhotra, 2002; Piaget, 2005/1947; Vygotsky, 1997).

However, on several occasions research has failed to confirm the claim that children's knowledge of the Earth is organized into coherent and theory-like naive mental models (e.g. Hannust and Kikas, 2007; Nobes *et al.*, 2003, 2005; Straatemeier *et al.*, 2008). Instead, it has been indicated that the majority of young children possess knowledge that consists of loosely related fragments that may or may not be accurate, and that such information is stored in individual fragments until a consistent culturally accepted theory is acquired (cf. Hannust and Kikas, 2007; Ivarsson *et al.*, 2002; Nobes *et al.*, 2003, 2005; Panagiotaki *et al.*, 2009; Schoultz *et al.*, 2001; Siegal *et al.*, 2004; Straatemeier *et al.*, 2008). In order to learn a concept, the fragmented pieces of information (some of which are based on direct experiences) associated with that concept have to be coordinated and recontextualized (DiSessa, 2008). For example, when children can use a model as an anchor during knowledge assessment, they display a rather sophisticated understanding of elementary astronomy (Panagiotaki *et al.*, 2006; Schoultz *et al.*, 2001; Siegal *et al.*, 2004).

Still, though the appearance rate of consistent non-scientific concepts is much lower than reported by Vosniadou and her colleagues (e.g. Vosniadou and Brewer, 1992; Vosniadou *et al.*, 2004), a small proportion of children have been classified as displaying consistent non-scientific concepts of the Earth even in those studies that describe children's knowledge of Earth and gravity as mostly fragmented (Hannust and Kikas, 2007, 2010, 2012; Panagiotaki *et al.*, 2006). In some of those instances the seemingly coherent sets of answers might actually be attributable to a chance combination of answers (cf. Nobes *et al.*, 2003, 2005; Straatemeier *et al.*, 2008; Vosniadou, 1994; Vosniadou and Brewer, 1992; Vosniadou *et al.*, 2004) but on other occasions lapses in instruction may be the cause. For example, Hannust and Kikas (2007) describe the case of Karel, who missed the initial lesson about gravity and as a result arrived at the understanding that there are two Earths.

Concluding summary

When conceptual development in elementary astronomy is compared to knowledge development in other areas of science certain similarities can be detected (e.g. for mathematics and simple physics see Siegler and Chen, 1998, 2002; Siegler and Svetina, 2006). It seems that most children (and actually this holds true for all learners of all ages) base their initial answers on their own experience and that while some of them react to new conflicting information with the construction of intermediate solutions (e.g. synthetic concepts), others do not use a consistent scheme for answering or adopt the scientifically accurate explanations rather easily. If instruction is to be effective for all of them, educators should concentrate on the appropriateness of their instruction methods and on making sure that learners do not acquire misconceptions during learning that resist change and impede further conceptual development.

References

Brewer, W. F., Chinn, C. A. and Samarapungavan, A. (2000) Explanation in scientists and children. In F. C. Keil and R. A. Wilson (eds) *Explanation and Cognition* (pp. 279–323). Cambridge, MA: MIT Press.

Brown, D. F. and Hammer, D. (2008) Conceptual change in physics. In S. Vosniadou (ed.) *International Handbook of Research on Conceptual Change* (pp. 127–54). New York: Routledge.

Canella, G. S. (1993) Learning through social interaction: Shared cognitive experience, negotiation strategies, and joint concept construction for young children. *Early Childhood Research Quarterly*, *8*, 427–44.

Carey, S. (1991) Knowledge acquisition: Enrichment or conceptual change? In S. Carey and R. Gelman (eds) *The Epigenesis of Mind: Essays on Biology and Cognition*. Hillsdale, NJ: Erlbaum.

Carey, S. (1999) Sources of conceptual change. In E. K. Scholnick, K. Nelson, S. A. Gelman and P. H. Miller (eds) *Conceptual Development: Piaget's Legacy* (pp. 293–326). Mahwah, NJ: Erlbaum.

Carey, S. (2000) Science education as conceptual change. *Journal of Applied Developmental Psychology*, *21*, 13–19.

Carey, S. and Spelke, E. (1994) Domain-specific knowledge and conceptual change. In L. A. Hirschfeld and S. A. Gelman (eds) *Mapping the Mind: Domain Specificity in Cognition and Culture* (pp. 169–99). New York: Cambridge University Press.

Cashon, C. H. and Cohen, L. B. (2004) Beyond U-shaped development in infants' processing of faces: An information-processing account. *Journal of Cognition and Development*, *5*, 59–80.

Chi, M. (1992) Conceptual change within and across ontological categories: Examples from learning and discovery in science. In R. Giere (ed.) *Cognitive Models of Science, Minnesota Studies in Philosophy of Science*, *15* (pp. 129–87). Minneapolis: University of Minnesota Press.

Chi, M. T. H. (2008) Three types of conceptual change: Belief revision, mental model transformation, and categorical shift. In S. Vosniadou (ed.) *International Handbook of Research on Conceptual Change* (pp. 61–82). New York: Routledge.

Chi, M. and Ohlsson, S. (2005) Complex declarative learning. In K. J. Holyoak and R. G. Morrison (eds) *Cambridge Handbook of Thinking and Reasoning* (pp. 371–99). New York: Cambridge University Press.

Chi, M.T. H, Slotta, J. D. and de Leeuw, N. (1994) From things to processes: A theory of conceptual changes for learning science concepts. *Learning and Instruction*, *4*, 27–43.

Chinn, C. A. and Brewer, W. F. (1993) The role of anomalous data in knowledge acquisition: A theoretical framework and implications for science instruction. *Review of Educational Research*, *63*, 1–49.

Chinn, C. A. and Malhotra, B. A. (2002) Children's responses to anomalous scientific data: How is conceptual change impeded? *Journal of Educational Psychology*, *94*, 327–43.

Diakidoy, I. A. N. and Kendeou, P. (2001) Facilitating conceptual change in astronomy: A comparison of the effectiveness of two instructional approaches. *Learning and Instruction*, *11*, 1–20.

Diakidoy, I. A., Vosniadou, S. and Hawks, J. D. (1997) Conceptual change in astronomy: Models of the Earth and of the day/night cycle in American-Indian children. *European Journal of Psychology of Education*, *12*, 159–84.

DiSessa, A. (2008) A bird's-eye view of the 'pieces' vs. 'coherence' controversy (from the 'pieces' side of the fence). In S. Vosniadou (ed.) *International Handbook of Research on Conceptual Change* (pp. 35–60). New York: Routledge.

Deloache, J. S. and Burns, N. M. (1993) Symbolic development in young children: Understanding models and pictures. In C. Pratt and A. F. Garton (eds) *Systems of Representation in Children: Development and Use* (pp. 91–111). New York: John Wiley.

Duit, R., Roth, W.-M., Komorek, M. and Wilbers, J. (2001) Fostering conceptual change by analogies – between Scylla and Charybdis. *Learning and Instruction*, *11*, 283–303.

Duit, R., Treagust, D. F. and Widodo, A. (2008) Teaching science for conceptual change: Theory and practice. In S. Vosniadou (ed.) *International Handbook of Research on Conceptual Change* (pp. 629–46). New York: Routledge.

Hatano, G. and Inagaki, K. (1991) Sharing cognition through collective comprehension activity. In L. B. Resnick, J. M. Levine and S. D. Teasley (eds) *Perspectives on Socially Shared Cognition* (pp. 331–48). Washington, DC: American Psychological Association.

Hannust, T. and Kikas, E. (2007) Children's knowledge of astronomy and its change in the course of learning. *Early Childhood Research Quarterly*, *22*, 89–104.

Hannust, T. and Kikas, E. (2010) Young children's acquisition of knowledge about the Earth: A longitudinal study. *Journal of Experimental Child Psychology*, *107*, 164–80.

Hannust, T. and Kikas, E. (2012) Changes in children's answers to open questions about the Earth and gravity. *Child Development Research*. Retrieved from www.hindawi.com/journals/cdr/2012/613674/ (07/07/2013).

Howe, C., Tolmie, T. and Rodgers, C. (1992) The acquisition of conceptual knowledge in science by primary school children: Group interaction and the understanding of motion down an incline. *British Journal of Developmental Psychology*, *10*, 113–30.

Inagaki, K. and Hatano, G. (2002) *Young Children's Naïve Thinking About the Biological World*. New York: Psychology Press.

Ivarsson, J., Schoultz, J. and Säljö, R. (2002) Map reading versus mind reading: Revisiting children's understanding of the shape of the Earth. In M. Limon and L. Mason (eds) *Reconsidering Conceptual Change: Issues in Theory and Practice* (pp. 77–100). Dordrecht, Netherlands: Kluwer.

Jonassen, D. (2008) Model building for conceptual change. In S. Vosniadou (ed.) *International Handbook of Research on Conceptual Change* (pp. 676–93). New York: Routledge.

Kikas, E. (1998) Pupils' explanations of seasonal changes: Age differences and the influence of teaching. *British Journal of Educational Psychology, 68*, 505–16.

Kikas, E. (2003) Constructing knowledge beyond senses: Worlds too big and small to see. In A. Toomela (ed.) *Cultural Guidance in the Development of the Human Mind* (pp. 211–27). Westport, CT and London: Ablex.

Kikas, E. (2005) Õpilase mõtlemise areng ja selle soodustamine koolis. Ots, E. (Toim.). *Üldoskused – õpilase areng ja selle soodustamine koolis* (lk 15–46). Tartu: Tartu Ülikooli Kirjastus.

Kikas, E., Hannust, T. and Kanter, H., (2002) The influence of experimental teaching on 5- and 7-year-old children's concepts of the Earth and gravity. *Journal of Baltic Science Education, 2,* 19–30.

Linn, M. C. (2008) Teaching for conceptual change: Distinguish or extinguish ideas. In S. Vosniadou (ed.) *International Handbook of Research on Conceptual Change* (pp. 694–722). New York: Routledge.

Maria, K. (1996) A case study of conceptual change in a young child. *The Elementary School Journal, 98*, 69–89.

Marton, F. and Pang, M. F., (2008) The idea of phenomenography and the pedagogy of conceptual change. In S. Vosniadou (ed.) *International Handbook of Research on Conceptual Change* (pp. 533–59). New York: Routledge.

Nobes, G., Moore, D., Martin, A., Clifford, B., Butterworth, G., Panagiotaki, G. *et al.* (2003) Children's understanding of the Earth in a multicultural community. *Developmental Science, 6*, 74–87.

Nobes, G., Martin, A. and Panagiotaki, G. (2005) The development of scientific understanding of the Earth. *British Journal of Developmental Psychology, 23*, 47–64.

Ohlsson, S. (1996) Learning from performance errors. *Psychological Review, 103*, pp. 241–62.

Opfer, J. E. and Siegler, R. S. (2004) Revisiting preschoolers' living things concept: A microgenetic analysis of conceptual change in basic biology. *Cognitive Psychology, 49*, 301–32.

Panagiotaki, G., Nobes, G. and Banerjee, R. (2006) Is the world round or flat? Children's understanding of the Earth. *European Journal of Developmental Psychology, 3*, 124–41.

Panagiotaki, G., Nobes, G. and Potton, A. (2009) Mental models and other misconceptions in children's understanding of the Earth. *Journal of Experimental Child Psychology, 104*, 52–67.

Piaget, J. (2005) *The Psychology of Intelligence* (trans. M. Piercy and D. E. Berlyne). New York: Routledge (original work published 1947).

Schoultz, J., Säljö, R. and Wyndhamn, J. (2001) Heavenly talk: Discourse, artefacts, and children's understanding of elementary astronomy. *Human Development, 44*, 103–18.

Siegal, M. (2010) *Marvelous Minds: The Discovery of What Children Know.* Oxford.

Siegal, M., Butterworth, G. and Newcombe, P. (2004) Culture and children's cosmology. *Developmental Science, 7*, 308–24.

Siegler, R. and Chen, Z. (1998) Developmental differences in rule learning: A microgenetic analysis. *Cognitive Psychology, 36*, 273–310.

Siegler, R. and Chen, Z. (2002) Development of rules and strategies: Balancing the old and new. *Journal of Experimental Child Psychology, 81*, 446–57.

Siegler, R. and Svetina, M. (2006) What leads children to adopt new strategies? A microgenetic/cross-sectional study of class inclusion. *Child Development, 77*, 997–1015.

Smith, C., Maclin, D., Grosslight, L. and Davis, H. (1997) Teaching for understanding: A study of students' preinstruction. Theories of matter and comparison of the effectiveness of two approaches to teaching about matter and density. *Cognition and Instruction, 15*, 317–93.

Spelke, E. and Kinzler, K. (2007) Core knowledge. *Developmental Science, 10*, 89–96.

Straatemeier, M., van der Maas, H. L. J. and Jansen, B. R. J. (2008) Children's knowledge of the Earth: A new methodological and statistical approach. *Journal of Experimental Child Psychology, 100*, 276–96.

Thagard, P. (2008) Conceptual change in the history of science: Life, mind, and disease. In S. Vosniadou (ed.) *International Handbook of Research on Conceptual Change* (pp. 374–87). New York: Routledge.

Tulving, E. and Thomson, D. M. (1973) Encoding specificity and retrieval processes in episodic memory. *Psychological Review, 80*, 352–73.

Vamvakoussi, X. and Vosniadou, S. (2004) Understanding the structure of the set of rational numbers: A conceptual change approach. *Learning and Instruction, 14*, 453–67.

Vosniadou, S. (1994) Capturing and modeling the process of conceptual change. *Learning and Instruction, 4*, 45–69.

Vosniadou, S. (1996) Learning environments for representational growth and cognitive flexibility. In S. Vosniadou, E. De Corte, R. Glaser and H. Mandl (eds) *International Perspectives on the Design of Technology-supported Learning Environments* (pp. 13–23). Mahwah, NJ: Erlbaum.

Vosniadou, S. and Brewer, W. F. (1992) Mental models of the Earth: A study of conceptual change in childhood. *Cognitive Psychology, 24*, 535–85.

Vosniadou, S., Ioannides, C., Dimitrakopoulou, A. and Papademetriou, E. (2001) Designing learning environments to promote conceptual change in science. *Learning and Instruction, 11*, 381–419.

Vosniadou, S., Skopeliti, I. and Ikospentaki, K. (2004) Modes of knowing and ways of reasoning in elementary astronomy. *Cognitive Development, 19*, 203–22.

Vosniadou, S., Skopeliti, I. and Ikospentaki, K. (2005) Reconsidering the role of artifacts in reasoning: Children's understanding of the globe as a model of the Earth. *Learning and Instruction, 15*, 333–51.

Vygotsky, L. (1997) *Thought and Language* (ed. A. Kozulin). Cambridge, MA: MIT Press (revised edition of 1986, original work published in 1934).

Wiser, M. and Smith, C. L. (2008) Learning and teaching about matter in Grades K–8: When should the atomic–molecular theory be introduced? In S. Vosniadou (ed.) *International Handbook of Research on Conceptual Change* (pp. 205–39). New York: Routledge.

23

SHARED UNDERSTANDING AMONG PRESCHOOLERS

Annica Löfdahl and Maria Hjalmarsson

Introduction

This chapter aims to give a brief theoretical and empirical introduction to children's shared understanding. When children come together for longer periods, as they do in preschool, it is well known that they develop shared understanding about their everyday life. Following theories on children's peer culture (Corsaro, 2005) and social representations (Moscovici, 2000) we have been able to develop a base of knowledge about how children's shared understanding is negotiated, maintained and develops. The chapter recounts results from several studies and examines how young children handle important issues of their lives, such as the meaning of being dead and buried as well as the meaning of gender divisions in society, discussed from a critical perspective on the *gender pedagogy approach* (Hermansson Hässler, 2009).

Shared thinking and understanding: peer cultures

When discussing children's thinking and understanding we take our starting point in theories emphasizing children's common activities as a ground for how thinking and understanding develops. The first theory our research is grounded on is the work of Corsaro (2005) who argues that when children spend time together over a longer period, as they do in preschool, they develop their own peer cultures. Corsaro's (2005) concept of *peer culture* is widely used in child research to describe children's perspectives and interpretations of the surrounding culture and how they deal with questions of importance for their life. Quoting Corsaro, peer culture is about 'a stable set of activities or routines, artefacts, values, and concerns that kids produce and share in interaction with each other' (2005, p. 110). Being a preschool child means that you are part of a peer culture, holding unique, shared ideas of your own social position and status as well as that of your friends. Children who share the same peer culture develop a common system of social knowledge, including information such as 'who can play with whom' and 'who is in a position to decide the play script'. The examples we present in this chapter are based on this view of peer culture, which in turn implies that interactions and dynamics between children are at the focus, rather than the individual child. Also, the examples rest on basic assumptions within a broad range of contemporary childhood studies, stressing children's competencies and children's agency (James and James, 2004).

Of particular interest when dealing with children's shared thinking and understanding is Corsaro's concept of *interpretive reproduction*. Corsaro applies the term to the innovative and creative aspects of children's participation in society. Within their peer cultures children learn to interpret and understand the surrounding culture. That is, events, norms and values that they encounter through adults' and other children's actions. It means that children 'download' and interpret and reproduce the culture that surrounds them, in the preschool, at home and in society at large, in order to make it intelligible and manageable. Children appropriate what adults say and do, not outright, but as reconstructed content in their own activities. Reproduction and production are key terms for describing how children's peer cultures are initiated and maintained, and how their actions and interactions are related to the local context and to the common history of the group. Corsaro views children as active participants in society rather than as passive novices in the way they acquire information from the adult world and use this in a creative and interpretive process. This means that each new generation seeks to create meaning from such information, in relation to their own lives and its circumstances. For children in preschool, this includes understanding their position as children relative to adults and understanding what it means to live and interact with other children at the preschool. But it is also about understanding the meanings of cultural practices and routine events inside and outside the preschool. As we interpret it, in this way interpretive reproduction offers a dynamic description of socialization which describes a more reciprocal relationship between the growing child and his or her environment than a traditional understanding, in which children passively internalize social norms and values. Corsaro emphasizes that through participation in peer culture, children are involved in cultural production as well as transformation. Children's peer cultures are thereby a context for children's changing and growing understanding of the community; hence the importance of understanding their experiences, meanings and actions, which indicate children's ability to contribute to a changed society, both here and now and in the future. This approach is in line with what has been referred to as a critical response to traditional models of children's socialisation and development. Within this tradition of new directions of child and childhood studies, an emerging body of empirical and theoretical literature has introduced concepts for describing, analysing and interpreting children as competent social agents, and childhood as a socially structured and constructed category (e.g. Burman, 2008; Dahlberg and Moss, 2005; Dahlberg *et al.*, 1999; James and James, 2004; Mayall, 2002).

Shared thinking and understanding: social representations

Language and cultural routines are important aspects of children's peer cultures: language because it is a symbolic system that encodes local, social and cultural structures, and cultural routines because of their habitual taken-for-granted character, which provide children with a secure and shared understanding of belonging to a specific social group. As such, cultural routines provide a framework for producing, displaying and interpreting a wide range of sociocultural knowledge. In this chapter we will analyse how some children participate in different cultural routines such as a (make-believe) funeral and creating a domestic area.

In companion with Corsaro's notion of interpretive reproduction, our research is also grounded on an understanding of children's shared thinking and understanding as *social representations* that might be described as specific forms of knowledge (Moscovici, 2000). In the literature on social representations, the social dimension of knowledge is emphasized as a central element. According to Flick (1998), the *social* in social representations is related to what is represented, to how these representations are constructed, and to their functions. Social representations thus concern shared rather than individual knowledge, they are constructed through social interaction rather than individual cognition, and their functions are described as 'sustaining the mutual agreement inside social groups and their dissociation from outside' (Flick, 1998, p. 52). Social representations, as we use the theory in this chapter, are seen as forms of everyday knowledge, contributing to and supporting social identity among children in the preschool group as they share their everyday lives. Social representations serve to normalize and conventionalize communication and action in a group. We might say, when using the theories together, that the social representations help to define and clarify cultural routines within the preschool peer group. What is communicated among the children when acting out cultural routines must be interpreted in the specific situation and cannot be analysed out of context without losing its meaning.

We have found two interrelated main processes in social representation theory to be most relevant in relation to studies of children's play and communication, namely anchoring and objectifying. Objectifying means transforming ideas, thoughts and actions into something more concrete, for example arranging a funeral or hanging laundry in domestic play. This process of objectifying is related to the anchoring of these ideas, thoughts and actions in everyday categories or cultural routines to make them suitable and intelligible. Moscovici suggests that 'the purpose of all representations is to make something unfamiliar, or unfamiliarity itself, familiar' (Moscovici, 2000, p. 37). This means, as we see it, that we need to understand the content in children's interactions in order to be able to understand their shared thinking and understanding. It also means, as stressed in both Corsaro's and Moscovici's theories, that it is in children's joint play situations rather than in solitary play situations that we have to search for this understanding.

Empirical examples as illustrations of children's shared thinking and understanding

In the following sections we present two empirical examples. The data come from two different ethnographic studies conducted by Löfdahl in the period 2000–05 (Löfdahl, 2007), with the common aim of focusing on how children negotiate, maintain and develop their shared understanding in play situations in preschool.

The funeral

The following example (see Löfdahl, 2005) with Maja and Karin, aged 3½ and 4 years, represents an ordinary play situation in these children's peer culture. This example, which goes on for 14 minutes, has been chosen because it embraces the complexity of shared thinking and understanding in a clear manner.

The girls' interactions and their initially different perspectives on this cultural routine of the meaning of death and funerals are the conditions for new, shared meaning and understanding to occur. The theory of social representations is used to interpret how they are objectifying and anchoring their play actions.

The two girls, Karin and Maja, are playing together in the play room; they have built a hut of blankets and pillows around an indoor slide. Initially they pretend to be friends at bedtime when they start to talk about being ill. The girls go to sleep, maintaining the theme of illness, now pretending that Karin is a princess and Maja is her mummy.

> Karin: Let's play we have been sleeping, Mummy!
> Karin: Cock-a-doodle-doo!! Morning …
> Maja: Oh, it's so light, it has to be light … the lamps.
> Karin: Yes.
> *Karin gets up and switches on the light while Maja continues to 'sleep'.*
> Maja: Yes, but then …you were awake first.
> Maja: You were awake first then.
> *Karin tries to wake her up, she shakes Maja.*
> Karin: Da dada Mummy, Wake up!!
> Maja: But I was ill.
> Karin: I was ill too, because I was soon going to die…
> Maja: Mmm …
> Karin: That's why I am in … I am in the grave.
> *Karin climbs up on the slide.*
> Maja: Mmm …
> Karin: Aren't I?
> Maja: Mmm …
> Maja: You have to die first before you can be buried.
> Karin: I was out there.
> *Karin jumps down on the floor.*
> Maja: Well, if you jump from the slide you can die.
> Karin: No, I don't want to!

When Karin defines herself as ill, about to die and then in the grave, Maja doesn't explicitly agree, she just mumbles, which means they do not share the same definition. Maja reinterprets the situation and explains that one must be dead first before one can be buried, she also suggests how Karin could enact dying and thereby make the funeral possible. At first Karin does not agree, but changes her mind as the play continues.

Karin: Then I was dead, quickly, and I was quickly …
She walks across the room where some foam plastic building blocks are transformed into her grave.
Karin: This was my grave then.
Maja: Mm …
Karin: You pushed me to my grave.
Karin: I was a princess …

Maja's responses show some hesitation; she is still not convinced. The play continues and the girls go back to sleep again. Karin now pretends to be dead and she wants Maja to notice.

Karin: Hey, Maja, you saw that I was dead.
Maja: But first I have to prepare breakfast.
Karin: But you saw I was dead!!
Karin lies down motionless. She pretends to be dead. Maja goes to the slide to prepare the breakfast.
Karin: Maja … (*Karin gets up*) … You really saw that I was dead!
Maja: Yes, I can see that now.
Karin walks around in the room.
Karin: You saw that I was out and that I was dead.
Karin pretends to die, Maja turns towards me and tells me Karin is dead.

Karin realizes the importance of being dead before she can be buried, and she is eager to convince Maja that she really is dead. As soon as they share the same representation of the play-theme, the play can continue, now with its final theme – how to arrange a funeral and the meaning of the ceremony.

Karin hides herself behind some pillows.
Karin: This was my grave!
Maja: If you bury someone who is dead, they are alive!
Maja looks for something … walks around in the room …
Maja: I need something to bury her with.
Karin: (*From inside the grave*) – Now I was alive!
Maja rushes to Karin's grave.
Maja: I have buried you now.
Karin: I'll step out this way …
Karin steps out of the grave and they pretend to move to another place. The play continues and Maja has just found a flower basket.
Maja: Look, such pretty flowers … I'm going to place them … on my grave. If Karin buries me when I am dead …

The girls now agree that one must be dead before one can be buried and their concerns are changed towards the meaning of the ceremony. Maja arranges the flowers; she intends to die and therefore asks Karin to use the flowers when she buries her. But

Karin insists that she is still dead and she goes back to her grave. Maja repeats the ceremony ...

> Maja: Now I'll bury you with these flowers, I'll put them here.
> *Maja takes the flowers out of the basket.*
> Maja: I am going to put them on you, all of them. I will take all ... I will put all the flowers down on you.
> *Karin lies still in her grave.*
> Maja: You can just wake up when you feel the flowers on your body.
> *Maja drops the flowers on Karin, slowly. Karin gets up, very slowly.*
> Maja: Now you are alive!
> Karin: I was alive and you were not dead as I was ... were you?

By repeating the funeral ceremony the girls confirm their shared understanding. They are both aware of the meaning of putting flowers in the grave, which is to revive the dead person. At the time they seem to be pleased with their new shared understanding; to use Moscovici's (2000) terms, they have 'made the unfamiliar familiar', and can continue their play with another cultural theme.

The domestic play arena: girls and boys or girls vs boys?

The data referred to in this section (see Hägglund and Löfdahl, 2010; Hjalmarsson and Löfdahl, forthcoming) are video recordings made over several days when the focus was on a group of young boys and girls, aged 3–4 years, during their everyday activities.

In order to understand the empirical example we will give a short explanation of the *gender pedagogy approach* that was applied by the teachers in the studied preschool. During the initial years of the twenty-first century, the gender pedagogy approach was set out in many Swedish preschools. In line with the Curriculum for the Swedish preschool (National Agency for School/Skolverket, 2010), the purpose was to achieve increased gender equality by challenging traditional gender patterns (Berge and Ve, 2000). The gender pedagogy concept has no equivalent in other countries where it is more common to use concepts such as feminist pedagogy or gender equality work. The gender pedagogy approach was directed at children's emotional development in widening their repertoire of features across gender boundaries; a point of view grounded in the idea from developmental psychology that girls are essentially different from boys (Hermansson Hässler, 2009). Essential aspects of the pedagogy are the need for teachers to be aware of how their own gender norms and values affect the teaching, and the careful choice of content and treatment of children with regard to gender. The approach also recognizes the need to make visible and scrutinize the teacher's ideas on feminine and masculine, and the need to acknowledge children's notions of gender and gender myths with the purpose that they will build their own future on the basis of their own will and personal interests. The gender pedagogy approach emphasizes the need to work out methods and develop working material within ordinary educational settings that support equal conditions for boys and girls to develop in various ways. All of these aspects of the approach are present in handbooks of gender pedagogy aimed at preschool teachers (Svaleryd, 2003). As we understand, gender pedagogy is to a large extent built upon notions of boys and girls as distinct characters where, very simplified and summarized, on the one hand, boys need to learn a language of emotions while on the other hand girls will be provided with courage, strength and toughness (Olofsson, 2007).

The preschool teachers included in the following example were working in accordance with the gender pedagogy approach and one of the implications of this approach was that they diffused tools and toys that were used in 'domestic' environments such as the dolls' corner and spread them out in different areas of the preschool. The stove was put in the corner containing building blocks and Lego, while the dolls' prams were placed in some of the smaller rooms. We understand their didactic agenda to be in line with one of the central aspects of the gender pedagogy approach, namely the need to make visible and develop the children's notions and gender myths with the purpose that they build their own future on the basis of their own will and personal interest.

A couple of weeks into the new semester we noted how the youngest boys had gained a superior position of power *vis-à-vis* the youngest girls, partly encouraged by the teacher who took photographs of the boys as 'angry dangerous cowboys'. We noticed how the girls were struggling to create a play environment where they could feel comfortable. They were engaged in building a home-like domestic arena where they could care for their dolls and engage in traditional household chores, washing, cooking, etc., contrary to the teachers' intentions where the dolls' corner/domestic arena was removed from the setting in order to avoid gender stereotypes.

The boys were sometimes a bit lost; one by one they did not know quite how to respond to the girls. Sometimes they were spectators, sometimes they joined the play, as a father or child.

The play situation continued with the girls hanging laundry in their newly created domestic area when the boys entered. Their pockets filled with toy tools (e.g. screwdrivers, wrenches, pliers), they seemed to have fun, laughing while pulling down the girls' laundry. The girls protested and made resistance, but the boys were more successful, pulling down all the laundry and throwing it up on the roof. When the boys were together in groups of two or three, they seemed to acquire a different position. They showed their power over the girls by breaking into their homes, destroying their laundry as they hung it out to dry, and with support from play tools they used their power by 'violating the caring values' (Hägglund and Löfdahl, 2010).

The boys continued to show their strength, supported by the use of tools. Some girls left the room to call for assistance from the teachers, leaving Stella (3) alone with the boys. The boys start to pretend to destroy the laundry and even pretended to threaten Stella with the tools, making the sound of scissors, 'clip clip'.

Stella tried to tell them she did not want this any more – 'I don't think it is funny, no! I don't want!' The boys continued to use the tools, threatening her against her face and body. Stella cried, hid her face in her hands, and continued to tell them that she did not want this. The boys continued to make fun of her, mimicking her and keeping their hands in front of their faces. Stella reiterates that she 'does not want'.

The boys left the room, joking and laughing. The male teacher gave them a reprimand by telling them they were not allowed to behave like this.

How can we interpret and understand this play situation as children's shared understanding on gender issues? Following the gender pedagogy approach, dividing boys vs girls as distinct characters we will, on the one hand, understand the boys' joint actions as boys' shared understanding of 'it is okay to destroy the domestic play arena', while the girls, on the other hand, share an understanding of how to arrange a habitual taken-for-granted cultural routine like the domestic arena. But when taking into consideration the shared norms on gender, as expressed within the didactic agenda, in these children's peer culture, we rather interpret the situation as a shared understanding among both boys *and* girls, affected by the gender pedagogy approach that the children have to relate to and deal with as an interpretive reproduction.

As we understand it, the preschool teachers had the best of intentions when trying to avoid gender stereotypes in gender role play by applying the gender pedagogy approach, but the work of gender equality did not include the children as active and competent actors. We understand the situation as a sort of clash between the preschool teacher's efforts to apply gender pedagogy, and the children's interpretations and ways of dealing with these efforts. The shared understanding on gender issues among boys *and* girls in this example is rather a strengthened consciousness on gender stereotyped roles and activities. As there were not any examples of transgendered activities in the play roles, we interpret the situation as indicating that *all* children were interpreting the cultural routine 'creating a domestic play arena' as a girlish activity and the violating actions as a boyish activity. We believe the girls' establishment of a specific homemade domestic arena, instead of one ready to make use of in the environment, to be part of their anchoring of a social representation of a cultural routine; thereby strengthening the shared understanding of gender stereotypes. In doing so the domestic arena enabled the children to normalize and conventionalize gender stereotyped actions and roles such as caring girls and violating boys.

We might understand the gender pedagogy approach as something unfamiliar to the children. They were used to having a conventional domestic play arena in their environment, and suddenly it was not available in their setting any more. The children had to come up with new social representations about the meaning of their environment to be able to make their everyday life intelligible and manageable – or to paraphrase Moscovici (2000) – the purpose of creating a new domestic arena was to make the unfamiliar gender pedagogy approach familiar. This is one situation out of many that were observed. However, drawing from this specific example, we argue that within the children's new familiar approach the children share an understanding, not of a non-gender-stereotyped mass of children but of caring girls and violating boys.

Some final words

The empirical examples shown in this chapter point to two distinct situations where children have to develop their shared understanding of the situation at hand in order to be able to continue their play or to be able to manage their everyday life in preschool. In both situations it is not something that just happens; the children are active in their efforts to understand and make the unfamiliar familiar. They act together and make use of their collective agency in order to understand the surrounding culture. According to Corsaro (2005), children appropriate the ideas from the adult world as reconstructed content in their own activities. In the empirical examples it is obvious that the children also are striving toward a shared understanding. In the funeral-play, they had to develop a shared understanding to be able to continue the play, and in the domestic arena-play they had to develop a shared understanding of what was meant within the gender pedagogy approach, built on their common history in the group. It would be meaningful to further examine what kind of shared understanding the children had developed in the absence of the gender pedagogy approach, or what kind of shared understanding of a funeral might have developed if the content of funerals had been on the didactic agenda. We will never know, of course, but we know for sure that children do develop their shared understanding regardless of teachers' didactic agendas. Though how to match children's and teachers' understandings is another project.

References

Berge, B.-M. and Ve, H. (2000) *Action Research for Gender Equity*. Buckingham: Open University Press.

Burman, E. (2008) *Deconstructing Developmental Psychology*, 2nd edn. London and New York: Routledge.

Corsaro, W. (2005) *The Sociology of Childhood*, 2nd edn. Thousand Oaks, CA: Pine Forge Press.

Dahlberg, G. and Moss, P. (2005) *Ethics and Politics in Early Childhood Education*. London: Routledge Falmer.

Dahlberg, G., Moss, P. and Pence, A. (1999) *Beyond Quality in Early Childhood Education and Care: A Postmodern Perspective*. London: Falmer Press.

Flick, U. (1998) *The Psychology of the Social*. Cambridge: Cambridge University Press.

Hägglund, S. and Löfdahl, A. (2010) Limits of care: violating caring values. Presentation at the OMEP Conference in Gothenburg (11–13 August).

Hermansson Hässler, I.-B. (2009) What is gender pedagogy? *Gender Research in Sweden. A journal from the Swedish secretariat for gender research*, No. 1, 22–3.

Hjalmarsson, M. and Löfdahl, A. (forthcoming) Confirming and resisting an underdog position: Leisure-time teachers dealing with a new practice. *European Early Childhood Education Research Journal*. Accepted for publication in 23(4), 2015.

James, A., and James, A. L. (2004) *Constructing Childhood. Theory, Policy and Social Practice*. New York: Palgrave Macmillan.

Löfdahl, A. (2005) 'The funeral': A study of children's shared meaning-making and its developmental significance. *Early Years*, 25(1), 5–16.

Löfdahl, A. (2007) *Kamratkulturer i förskolan: en lek på andras villkor* (Peer culture in preschool). Stockholm: Liber.

Mayall, B. (2002) *Towards a Sociology for Childhood*. Buckingham: Open University Press.

Moscovici, S. (2000) *Social Representations: Explorations in Social Psychology*. Cambridge: Polity Press.

Olofsson, B. (2007) *Modiga prinsessor och ömsinta killar* (Brave girls and tender boys). Lärarförbundet: Lärarförbundets förlag.

Svaleryd, K. (2003) *Genuspedagogik: en tanke- och handlingsbok för arbete med barn och unga* (Gender pedagogy: a handbook for work with children and young). Stockholm: Liber.

Swedish National Agency for Education (2010) *Curriculum for the pre-school. Lpfö 98.*

24

PRETEND PLAY AND ITS INTEGRATIVE ROLE IN YOUNG CHILDREN'S THINKING

Sue Rogers

Introduction

In a study of the origins of thinking, Hobson suggests that 'one cannot accidentally pretend' (Hobson, 2002, p. x). By this he means that the act of pretending implies some degree of intentionality on the part of the person who pretends. To deliberately 'step sideways into another reality, between the cracks of ordinary life' (Henricks, 2006, p. 1), is a reflection of a profound and uniquely human facility requiring a complex range of cognitive and social processes, particularly when enacted in the company of others. In this chapter the focus is on role-play in the context of early childhood education and through this I hope to reiterate its significance to young children, human cognition and experience more widely. By role-play, I mean here the shared pretend play between children in which they 'temporarily act out the part of someone else using pretend actions and utterances' (Harris, 2000, p. 30). This may involve taking on a role such as 'mother' or 'pirate'. Or it may mean assigning a role to a doll or other object, for example a stick becomes a horse (Vygotsky, 1978). Various terms are used in the literature to describe this type of activity – fantasy, pretend, and socio-dramatic play for example. There are inevitable overlaps between them. However, as will become clear, role adoption in children from around the age of 2 or 3 is clearly distinguishable from the early pretend play we see in toddlers in the second year of life.

The social context of role-play is highlighted because imaginative play between children of similar age is a powerful way in which they come to understand the social and material world in ways not possible in the relations between adults and children. However, to be clear I do not want to in any way set children's experiences apart from the social and cultural worlds they inhabit. Indeed, that would be a somewhat artificial exercise, since even the most casual observer of young children will note the prevalence of play themes depicting the world of adults. Teachers encourage this too in the pedagogical practice of creating 'real life' adult role-play scenarios such as shops, hospitals and pet shops. Yet, left to their own devices, children explore a wider range of themes on their own terms, gathered from stories, media, gaming, familial and social life and reassembled in complex narratives in collaboration with others. While children may incorporate elements of adult, real world scenarios into their play such as policeman and mother, the narratives are frequently led by human themes such as good versus evil, sex, death and violence and are laced with associated emotions and affects such as love, fear, desire and revulsion. At the same time, I acknowledge the 'otherness' of children (Jones, 2006), in the sense that aspects of their worlds are simply inaccessible to adults and not easily or accurately represented in research accounts. Similarly, children cannot truly access the world of adults in their play since they do not yet have the experience and understanding of what it is to be an adult policeman or mother. This might be to make a somewhat obvious point, but I do so to draw attention to the distinction between imitating adult behaviours in role and what is termed *mimesis*, a faculty which goes beyond the Platonic version of mere 'imitation' (in the sense of making a direct copy of something). By contrast, *mimesis* in role-play allows for a constructive reinterpretation of an original, which becomes a creative act in itself. Furthermore, seen in this way, the mimetic faculty we observe in role-play activity 'allows for an identification with the external world. It forges a link between the self and other. It becomes a way of empathising with the world, and it is through empathy that human beings can – if not fully understand each other – at least come ever closer to the other, through the discovery and creation of similarities' (Goldman, 1998).

In spite of a vast literature on the subject, the emergence of pretend play in the second year of life remains something of a mystery to scholars from across a wide range of disciplines and from myriad perspectives. It is argued that pretend play appears to have no obvious use in human development and for that reason is viewed by some as a frivolous and potentially threatening activity, at best an indulgence and at worst a path to delusion, loss of self-control, even anarchy (Sutton-Smith, 1997; Henricks, 2006). Harris notes the 'long intellectual tradition, uniting such diverse figures as Freud and Piaget, [which] claims that children's early fantasy life is primitive and disorganised' (2000). Others, however, argue that the emergence of pretence signals a uniquely human ability for reflective self-awareness that distinguishes humans from all other life forms and that this capacity enables us to create, innovate and engage with stories, the visual arts, music and literature (Harris and Kavanaugh, 1993). From psychoanalytic perspectives it is argued that the ability to enter into make-believe worlds offers an escape from the difficult, mundane and painful aspects of human life, which need exploration and resolution.

This chapter will describe the way in which pretend play develops across early childhood, highlighting key aspects of thinking that appear to be significant in relation to this activity. These are object permanence and mental representation, theory of mind, self-regulation and metacognition, and understanding what is real and pretend. To do this I draw on a range of empirical and conceptual studies including some of my own alongside the seminal work of Paul Harris, and the social-constructivist work of Vygotsky, which offers a compelling conceptual framework to support the case for placing role-play at the heart of early childhood education. I will locate the development of pretence and more specifically role-play in the context of pedagogy, drawing on instances from two empirical research projects conducted in classrooms over the past decade. Throughout, I will argue for the value of role-play in the development of thinking skills, drawing attention to some of the remarkable features of this uniquely human ability but acknowledge also that in spite of a vast literature on the subject, there is still little consensus on the purpose of such play, nor its contribution to development and learning. In part this is due to limitations of methodology identified in a recent systematic review led by Angeline Lillard (Lillard *et al.*, 2012), herself a distinguished researcher of pretend play in child development. Yet few would dispute its significance and prevalence in early childhood, and the evident complexity displayed in even the most mundane examples of role-play observed daily in early childhood classrooms.

There is insufficient space in this chapter to discuss in any detail the differences that surely exist between individual children in their disposition towards role-play. This includes the absence of pretend play in some children which research suggests may be an indicator of autism. I do not review the anthropological research literature on pretend play which shows differences in the nature of and the extent to which children engage in pretend play across cultures (see Goldman, 1998). There is widespread agreement that children across the world engage in play naturally and spontaneously regardless of culture, place or time (Goncu and Perone, 2005), and that it provides a powerful means through which they come to understand the complexities of the material, conceptual and social world. But while play appears to be a universal human driver (Smith, 2010), the extent to which such activities are encouraged or limited in children will be determined by specific cultural and social practices, shaped also by experiences of individual children in the home, through early attachments, relationships established with caregivers, and the nature of the communicative environment (Roulstone *et al.*, 2011).

The roots of role-play

Research evidence is unequivocal that children's development across all domains and in all cultural contexts is best supported by warm and nurturing relationships with others, and environments that foster sensory-motor, emotional and socio-linguistic experiences. In the Western tradition of early childhood education, it is argued that strong early attachment with caregivers in a communicative environment that stimulates children's language and early literacy development, relationships with others that are playful and for the most part child-led, appear to make a difference to later educational outcomes for young children. For example, these principles lie at the heart of the English Early Years Foundation Stage (DfE, 2012). When such relationships and environments are lacking, children may not be able to learn effectively and so successful entry to school is likely to be hindered and they risk playing 'catch up' for the rest of their school lives and beyond. At the same time, there is no compelling evidence to support the view that enriching environments that effectively 'hot house' and structure young children's play are beneficial to children's cognitive development in the long term (Blakemore and Frith, 2005). Rather activities that encourage self-regulation and metacognition (Whitebread, 2014), that match and extend children's current level of understanding through skilful observation and intervention on the part of adults, work best. Two key factors emerge from the literature on cognitive development, which are pertinent to the development of pretend play within early childhood education. First, the concept of *attachment*, in essence a *relational* process where a strong affectional tie develops between one person and another, appears to be critical for effective learning and healthy development (Rose and Rogers, 2012). Bowlby's original assertion that attachment ought to take place between mother and child has been broadened to include any caregiver and it is now recognised that multiple attachments can occur (Sroufe, 1995) through early childhood. Second, research which had identified critical periods for development, thus implying that in cases of developmental deprivation there is little chance of recovery, have been replaced by the notion of 'sensitive' periods which imply instead that good recovery can be made from early social and cognitive deprivation (Blakemore and Frith, 2005). These more optimistic findings afford early childhood settings and schools a significant role in helping those children most at risk to make good gains in school and hence help to close the disadvantage gap. However, this research is also clear that such gains will only be made in environments that provide for the complex learning needs of young children, built upon exploration and play, and which understand the importance of appropriate and nurturing intervention on the part of those in a caring and educative role. The roots of role-play can be seen in the earliest playful interactions between baby and caregiver, which help to build secure attachment and with it a sense of belonging, self-identity and self-efficacy (Gopnik *et al.*, 2000). Through these playful interactions and explorations babies rapidly acquire concepts about objects, places, people and self, and hence build an understanding of the world.

In the first year of life, the facility for *object permanence*, that is, understanding that something exists even when you cannot see it, is often identified as the first observable or testable evidence of a child's ability to retain and recall images or mental representations. This imaging is the basis of imagination, the building blocks of narratives or sequences of imaginings essential to even the most basic pretend play. Imagine if we couldn't think in this way. Of course, you couldn't imagine at all without this powerful capacity for remembering or for mental representation (Rogers and Evans, 2008). A second important capacity required for role-play is 'theory of mind', that is the ability to recognise and understand that others have beliefs, views and intentions that are different from your own. Theory of mind is strongly linked to the development of empathy and relies on social experiences to develop. Adopting roles, acting out the thoughts and feelings of others, and negotiating role-play plots all require that children understand perspectives and experiences different from their own. Shared pretence, then, may be a particularly significant spur for the development and consolidation of theory of mind skills (Dunn, 2004).

Typically, we see the appearance of pretence in the second year of life, and this seems to be constant across cultures even when there is significant variation between its enactment, and reception on the part of adults who observe and study it. On the surface this early pretence appears to consist mainly of imitative behaviour but as Harris (2000) argues, the cognitive processes that enable such activity to happen at all are well developed already and show a degree of sophistication in the toddler's thinking skills that it would be easy to underestimate. He provides a simple example of pretend play between an adult and a 2-year-old. To illustrate it will be helpful to present the sequence of events and a paraphrase of his analysis.

The resources used in this episode include a teddy bear, a shoe-box, a wooden brick and a piece of paper:

> *The adult makes a 'twiddling' gesture at end of box signifying turning on of the taps and asks: 'Where's the soap?'*
> The adult picks up the wooden brick and rubs Teddy's back with it.
> The 2-year-old joins in by lifting Teddy out of the box and says, 'He's all wet.'
> The 2-year-old wraps him in a piece of paper.

Within this simple everyday example of pretend play Harris asks: what cognitive processes are taking place? He explains, taken literally, we might ask if Teddy really needs a bath, what's the use of a cardboard box? Clearly the cardboard is not a suitable material for holding water. We might also ask, why rub Teddy with a wooden brick? For the pretence to work at all the child must set aside this naive literalism and to do this several key features of joint pretence need to be appreciated:

1   Either play partner can bring make-believe into a temporal public existence via a 'stipulation' e.g. twiddling gesture and 'Where's the soap?'
2   Once stipulated these make-believe entities have (imaginary and real) causal powers i.e. the tap can deliver water.
3   Once engaged in this make-believe world, play partners can suspend objective truth in favour of make-believe truth. When Teddy is lifted from the bath it is appropriate to say he is all wet even though he is objectively dry. It is not necessary to say 'we are pretending that Teddy is wet so we must dry him' as this is already understood by the players.
4   A pretend episode includes causal chains much like a narrative.

(Harris, 2000, p. 10)

According to Harris' analysis the 2-year-old is able to understand fully these elements. They engage in cognitive work just as an adult does when we interpret a pretend episode in a make-believe rather than literal mode (2000, p. 10). Even the earliest form of pretend play requires children to engage in sophisticated forms of thinking and to demonstrate social understanding as in the 'reading' of play signals within the play frame, without direct explanation from the adult. It shows also an appreciation of narrative structure, important in other forms of written and verbal communication, such as stories. All this is quite remarkable for children who may not yet have the language to articulate what is happening either in relation to objective or make-believe truth. It is significant also that Harris goes on to describe these early signs of pretend behaviours as 'the first indication of a lifelong capacity to consider alternatives to reality' (2000, p. 28), a feature of many aspects of adult life manifest in the arts, literature, social games such as flirting and joking (Simmel, 1984), and in recent decades, in virtual social and fantasy worlds through media games.

One important feature of play between children as they enter into the third year is the adoption of complementary roles, when children adopt different but related roles together. A common example of such roles is mother and baby (Harris, 2000). Such play requires children to draw on a repertoire of highly sophisticated skills, to be flexible and responsive to each other and to understand the actions and gestures displayed by the complementary role. This role reading ability can be seen in 2-year-olds but becomes especially developed in children between the ages of 3 and 5. In older children these complementary roles become ever more complex as they merge roles, for example, Roxanne (aged 4) plays at being mum in the 'space ship', merging the roles of mother and astronaut (Rogers and Evans, 2008). Roles may also shift in the course of one play episode. Keegan (aged 4) plays the monster, chasing and threatening to 'kill' the other children in his group. Then he becomes the father, protecting and rescuing his family from the monster.

Between the ages of about 3 and 5 we see children begin to adopt roles more explicitly, and not simply to act out the role of another person, character or creature, but negotiate, organise and assign roles to others during play. This means that as they play, children constantly step sideways between objective and make-believe realities. Harris refers to this as 'stage management', a feature that is not visible in the pretend play of younger children as illustrated in the 'Teddy gets wet' play. In Keegan's monster play we see elements of stage management and negotiation:

> *Keegan is making monster noises again (he is growling and speaking in a coarse voice).*
> A child asks: Can I be the master now?
> *There's lots of talking, but it is unclear as children are speaking over each other.*
> Keegan: Pretend that … pretend that … pretend that you died and that you came back up.
> Child: And when you came back up I was dead.
> Keegan (giggling): Yeah, and we said 'hello' didn't we?
> Child: Hello!
> Keegan: Yeah, and I turned you back alive.

Role-play, metacognition and the self-regulating child

It is widely agreed that pretend play is important in the development of self-regulation in young children (Whitebread and O'Sullivan, 2012; Berk, Mann and Ogan, 2006). From a sociocultural perspective the development of mind is related both to biological development and to the appropriation of cultural heritage (Wertsch, 1991; Cole, 1998); thus the nature of the individual's activity and cognitive development cannot easily be isolated from its social, historical and cultural context. In relation to self-regulation as a desirable attribute there are clearly individual and cultural distinctions between what is and is not valued and seen as desirable or acceptable in societies. For example, the extent to which we are required to self-regulate our behaviours and control impulses will not only vary between cultures but is context-dependent. There is, then, no single definition or understanding of the self-regulating child. What may be more important is that the child is able to acquire the ability to 'read' and hence distinguish between particular social situations and activities.

In a review of research on self-regulation in early childhood, Bronson identifies a wide range of perspectives on the meanings and applications of self-regulation as a desirable attribute in human social life and the marked variation between them. For example, from a behavioural perspective self-regulation is viewed mainly as learned self-control (Bronson, 2000, p. 14), largely attributable to external factors such as rewards and training. By contrast from a psychoanalytic perspective, and in the work of Freud in particular, self-regulation is viewed as a 'struggle to keep the warring forces of the personality under control and cope with their demands in the real world' (p. 12). But how does this relate to children's role-play? Vygotsky (for whom play meant role-play) also offers insight into the potential of play to support self-regulation or as he suggests 'impulse control' in young children. To contextualise this idea, Vygotsky (1978) posited that the 'imaginary situation' is characteristic of all play and not simply of what we refer to as role-play or fantasy-play activity. Further, inextricably linked to the creation of an imaginary situation and impulse control, is the presence of rules. Vygotsky wrote that 'whenever there is an imaginary situation in play, there are rules – not rules that are formulated in advance and change during the course of the game but ones that stem from an imaginary situation' (p. 95). The example he gives is of a child playing the role of mother. The child, he argues, is bound by the rules of what it means to be a mother, not purely in the sense of a particular mother, but rather within the rules of 'maternal behaviour' (p. 95). At the same time, Vygotsky argues, when children engage in games with rules (and here he gives the example of chess), they are still enacted within an imaginary situation. Thus he concludes that 'just as we are able to show … that every imaginary situation contains rules in a concealed form, [so] the reverse – that every game with rules contains an imaginary situation in a concealed form' (pp. 95–6). In terms of children's development, Vygotsky posits that the transition from play, in which rules are subservient to imagination, to games, in which the imagination is subservient to rules, outlines the evolution of children's play (p. 96). Thus the play-development relationship can be compared to the instruction-development relationship. But he suggests that play provides a much wider background for changes in needs and consciousness than is possible in instruction as he conceives it between the child and more knowledgeable other. The central point for educators is that play creates its own Zone of Proximal Development, in which the child moves forward with peers and which makes play the 'highest level of pre-school development' (p. 99). Play, then, is of central importance to the young child's development, not least because it 'continually creates demands on the child to act against immediate impulse' (p. 99). The child at play is bound by the rules of the game (whether playing 'mother' or chess). Seen in this way, play is a dialectical relationship between the child's desire to act spontaneously and by the inherent need to subordinate those desires to the rules of the game. Thus Vygotsky contends that 'the child's greatest control occurs in play' (p. 99). This is of profound importance in our understanding of role-play's contribution to children's ability to self-regulate their behaviour.

'Nothing's real, it's playing a game': understanding real and make-believe

In a series of experiments, Harris and colleagues investigated whether or not children aged 3–5 could distinguish between real and make-believe (1991). The children could understand that an object they could see was real and open to inspection by others, but an imaginary creature was not, even if it aroused fear or attachment in the child, such as in the case of an imaginary companion. Harris concluded that when children showed an emotional reaction in their play such as fear or elation, it was not because of any confusion on their part about what is real and imaginary but rather an illustration that from an early age fictional entities can arouse our emotions, even when they are clearly understood as fictions (2000, p. 65). Once again we can establish links between the early role-play witnessed in children and later forms of play in adult life such as virtual gaming, literature, participation in art forms and social play.

In an ethnographic study of children's perspectives of role-play (Rogers and Evans. 2008), 4- and 5-year-olds were asked to answer the question 'what is role play?' All children in the study appeared to distinguish easily between pretend and real. Most children referred specifically to the distinction between 'real' and 'pretend' as the following selection of response illustrates (p. 73):

> Dan: *Doesn't mean it's real, it's just pretend.*
> Lucy: Nothing's real, it's playing a game.
> Megan: Pretend play is like something that's not real.
> Alex: It means pretend play, doesn't have to be real.

Earlier studies of play (see Garvey, 1990 for example) suggest that children by the age of 2 and 3 are able to make this distinction, but may not fully understand or be able to articulate it. At 4 years old, the children in this study appeared to understand clearly the difference between real and pretend and were able to explain it. Moreover children described role-play as a *feeling*, not simply in relation to emotions, but a distinctive feeling as in an aura or ambience. Of course it was difficult for the researchers to grasp precisely what children meant although readers may well recall such a feeling from their own childhoods.

Research also demonstrates that children are driven by a strong desire to affiliate with one another, and to maintain peer interactions and relationships (Corsaro, 1985; Carpendale and Lewis, 2006; Dunn, 2004). Role-play appears to be one important way in which children seek to build relationships to the extent that friendship, and pretending with people you like, overrides the imperative to adopt a particular game. In this way social relations are foregrounded in role-play. We know also that children have a strong desire to self-generate themes in play (Rogers, 2010) and this in turn can require children to negotiate, acquiesce in the face of competing ideas and self-regulate their responses. For example, David is in the café with a group of girls who are playing at being customers and café owner, in other words within the pre-specified context of the role-play. David wants to take the play in new directions by becoming Ratman, thus he pronounces: 'I'm a robber, no I'm Robin and he takes things … no I'm Ratman, I can fly. I put my tail on that wall and I can fly up there.' However, his attempts to recruit the others to his play were thwarted. In other instances, injecting new ideas into the play, encouraging others to follow, gives momentum and energy to role play which in turn engenders sustained narratives, enacted in a complex, fast-paced and ever-changing web of happenings. In the following extract Keegan aged 5 initiates and to a large extent controls an extended episode of outdoor role-play lasting some 20 minutes.[1] His skill at driving the play and taking others with him on his imaginary journey is breathtaking in places as this brief extract illustrates:

Keegan declares: '[Child's name]'s the monster.'
Calling out to unnamed children, the target child says: 'No, no! Don't get [monster peer's name], he'll eat ya! Noooo!'
Children talk briefly, but it is unclear what they say.
Keegan: 'Yeah, but, [monster peer's name], only if we come up to you do you get us, alright? Just don't look yet.'
[…]
Keegan whispers something, makes an explosion sound, then shouts: 'Ha, ha!'
He then starts playfully saying: 'Hello! Bye-bye! Hairy, hello, hello … hello, hello, hello, hello, hello, hello …'
A child says something. Keegan then says: 'I'm on a good team. I know that you're the baddie and I'm on the good team {unclear} Quick, quick get up! Danger! If he's down here, you're not allowed down.'
Keegan calls another child's name: 'Whaaat? I'll be monster, I'll be monster.'
Keegan declares: 'You can't get up here, you can't get up here. You're not allowed to get up here.'
A child replies: 'I am.'
Keegan: 'No you're not. You're not allowed to get up here, is she?'
A child states: 'Pretend you're my {unclear}, and I'm Stephanie.'
Keegan replies: 'No, we're not playing that.'
In response, the child says: 'We're playing "my little cat".'
Somebody else calls to her: 'C'mon cat.'
Keegan starts growling like a monster.
A child declares: 'Everybody run, it's a monster. Monster!'
Keegan: 'I killed you!'
Child (in a mock angry voice): 'What have you done to my cat?'
Keegan makes monster sounds. Another child makes cat sounds.
Keegan: 'I'm not a cat. I did not say "meow".'
Keegan makes more monster sounds and crawls under the steps of the wooden climbing frame.
Running and growling: '[Other monster child's name], Kill her!'

'Only five in the role-play corner unless the teacher's looking'

So far, I have outlined aspects of children's cognitive development that appear to enable children's role-play to develop and to highlight some of the ways in which pretending changes as children progress through early childhood. I want to conclude by noting some of the challenges in providing opportunities for children to engage in role-play that is meaningful and fulfilling emotionally and socially. The ethnography of role-play reported in Rogers and Evans (2008) identified a range of strategies adopted by children in order to subvert teacher interruptions and interventions. We concluded that in order to maximise the potential of role-play to stretch children's social and imaginative capacities, a pedagogy of play would be co-constructed between adults and children, drawing on their shared concerns and interests. It would take into account the need for children to engage with open-ended props, in spaces conducive to the intensive social and physical activity, which is characteristic of role-play in this age group. I have deliberately chosen not to discuss the type of role-play that is designed to meet curriculum objectives and arranged by adults in relation to topics and themes. Even when such role-play areas are offered, children invariably transform them into contexts that have meaning to them. In the example of complex role-play led by Keegan above we see children engage in relatively free play in the outdoors, where it is possible for them to shout, scream and run as part of the play, all of which add to the thrill of the play and of being together. This type of active and highly interactive play appears to interest children most of all, but it is play from which adults are very often excluded and from which adults exclude themselves (Rogers, 2013). It simultaneously offers potential for creativity, initiative and socialisation, but also for risk and transgression, aspects that cannot be easily accommodated in the early childhood classroom. Such play, while challenging at times, compels us to see its value from the child's perspective and its contribution to children's thinking and learning beyond the prescribed curriculum and beyond childhood itself.

Note

1 Taken from Sue Waite, Julie Evans and Sue Rogers, 'Opportunities Afforded by the Outdoors for Alternative Pedagogies in the Transition between Foundation Stage and Year 1', Economic and Social Research Council Project (award number RES-000-22-3065, January 2009 to May 2011).

References

Berk, L. E., Mann, T. D. and Ogan, A. T. (2006) Make-believe play: Wellspring for development of self-regulation. In D. Singer, R. M. Golinkoff and Hirsh-Pasek (eds) *Play = Learning: How Play Motivates and Enhances Children's Cognitive and Social-emotional Growth*. New York: Oxford University Press.

Blakemore, S. and Frith, U. (2006) *The Learning Brain: Lessons for Education*. Oxford: Blackwell.

Bronson, M. (2000) *Self-Regulation in Early Childhood*. New York: Guilford Press.

Carpendale, J. and Lewis, C. (2006) *How Children Develop Social Understanding*. Oxford: Wiley-Blackwell.

Cole, M. (1998) *Cultural Psychology: A Once and Future Discipline.* Cambridge, MA: Harvard University Press.

Corsaro, W. A. (1985) *Friendship and Peer Culture in the Early Years.* Norwood, NJ: Ablex.

Dunn, J. (2004) *Children's Friendships.* Oxford: Blackwell.

Department for Education (2012) *Statutory Framework for the Early Years Foundation Stage: Setting the standards for learning, development and care for children from birth to five.* Available at: www.foundationyears.org.uk/early-years-foundation-stage-2012/orwww.education.gov. uk/aboutdfe/statutory/g00213120/eyfs-statutory-framework (accessed December 2013).

Garvey, C. (1990) *Play,* 2nd edn. London: Fontana.

Gilloch, G. (2001) Benjamin's London: Baudrillard's Venice. In N. Leach (ed.) *The Hieroglyphics of Space: Reading and Experiencing the Modern Metropolis.* London: Routledge.

Goldman, L. R. (1998) *Child's Play: Myth, Mimesis and Make-Believe: Explorations in Anthropology.* Oxford: Berg.

Goncu, A. and Perone, A. (2005) Pretend play as a life span activity. *Topoi, 24*(2), 137–47.

Gopnik, A., Meltzoff, A. and Kuhl, P. (2000) *The Scientist in the Crib: What Early Learning Tells Us About the Mind.* New York: HarperCollins.

Harris, P. (2000) *The Work of the Imagination.* Oxford: Blackwell.

Harris, P. and Kavanough, R. (1993) Young children's understanding of pretense. *Monographs of the Society for Research in Child Development, 58,* 1, Serial No. 123.

Harris, P. L., Brown, E., Marriott, C., Whittall, S. and Harmer, S. (1991) Monsters, ghosts and witches: Testing the limits of the fantasy–reality distinction in young children. *British Journal of Developmental Psychology, 9,* 105–23. doi: 10.1111/j.2044-835X.1991.tb00865.x.

Henrick, T. (2006) *Play Reconsidered: Sociological Perspectives on Human Expression.* Chicago: Illinois University Press.

Hobson, P. (2002) *The Cradle of Thought: Exploring the Origins of Thinking.* London: Macmillan.

Jones, O. (2006) True geography [ ] quickly forgotten, giving away to an adult-imagined universe. Approaching the otherness of childhood. *Children's Geographies, 6*(2), 195–212.

Lillard, A. S., Lerner, M. D., Hopkins, E. J., Dore, R. A., Smith, E. D. and Palmquist, C. M. (2013) The impact of pretend play on children's development: The state of the evidence. *Psychological Bulletin, 139*(1), 1–34.

Rogers, S. (2010) Play: A conflict of interests? In S. Rogers (ed.) *Rethinking Play and Pedagogy in Early Childhood Education: Concepts, Contexts and Cultures.* London: Routledge.

Rogers, S. (2013) The pedagogisation of play in early childhood education: A Bernsteinian perspective. In O. F. Lillemyr, S. Dockett and B. Perry (eds) *International Perspectives on Play and Learning: Theory and Research on Early Years' Education.* Information Age Publishing.

Rogers, S. and Evans, J. (2008) *Inside Role Play in Early Childhood Education: Researching Children's Perspectives.* London: Routledge.

Rose, J. and Rogers, S. (2012) *Adult Roles in the Early Years.* Maidenhead: Open University Press.

Roulstone, S., Law, J., Rush, R., Clegg, J. and Peters, T. (2011) *The Role of Language in Children's Early Educational Outcomes.* DFE Research Brief 134. Available at: www.education.gov.uk/ publications/eOrderingDownload/DFE-RB134.pdf (accessed December 2012).

Siraj-Blatchford, I. and Manni, L. (2008) Would you like to tidy up now? An analysis of adult questioning in the English Foundation Stage. *Early Years, 28*(1), 5–22.

Shore, C. (1998) Play and language: Individual differences as evidence of development and style. In D. Fromberg and D. Bergen (eds) *Play from Birth to Twelve: Contexts, Perspectives and Meanings.* New York: Garland.

Simmel, G. (1984) *On Women, Sexuality and Love.* New Haven, CT/London: Yale University Press.

Smith, P. K. (2010) *Children and Play.* Oxford: Wiley-Blackwell.

Sroufe, A. (1995) *Emotional Development.* Cambridge: Cambridge University Press.

Sutton-Smith, B. (1997) *The Ambiguity of Play.* Cambridge, MA: Harvard University Press

Vygotsky, L. (1978) *Mind in Society: The Development of Higher Psychological Processes.* Cambridge. MA: Harvard University Press.

Wertsch, J. (1991) *Voices of the Mind: A Sociocultural Approach to Mediated Action.* Cambridge, MA: Harvard University Press.

Whitebread, D. (2014) The importance of self-regulation for learning from birth. In H. Moylett (ed.) *The Characteristics of Effective Learning.* Maidenhead: Open University Press.

Whitebread, D. and O'Sullivan, L. (2012) Preschool children's social pretend play: Supporting the development of metacommunication, metacognition and self-regulation. *International Journal of Play*, *1*(2).

25

NARRATIVE THINKING

Implications for Black children's social cognition

Stephanie M. Curenton and Nicole Gardner-Neblett

Introduction

The purpose of this chapter is to explain how narrative thinking (i.e. a form of reasoning that is heavily dependent upon one's subjective memory and interpretation of events) provides the foundation for children's social cognition (i.e. their understanding of themselves and of other people's behavior and internal states). This chapter focuses on ethnic minority children across the world who share a common African ancestral cultural heritage, such as children of African American, Afro-Caribbean, Black British, or African descent. The rationale for focusing on this common ancestral heritage is that despite heterogeneity due to nationality, religion, colonization, slavery, and migration, many of the African oral narrating traditions have survived among this pan-ethnic group and continue to be passed down to future generations.

The chapter is organized into the following sections. First, we explain the theoretical rationale for how language, culture, and narrative thinking interplay. Second, we briefly explain some of the features of African language and cultural traditions. Third, we describe how culture, thinking, and oral narratives for African-ancestral ethnic minority children relate to the development of young children's social cognition. Fourth, we describe how teachers can capitalize on these traditions in order to foster children's narrative development.

Culture, language and narrative thinking

Curenton and Iruka (2013) explain that culture is defined as the social practices, beliefs, values, and behaviors that intentionally – or unintentionally – shape people's communication, interactions, and preferences. All reasoning is bound by culture because culture provides the lens through which one views the world. Hong *et al.* (2000) describe cultural knowledge as a contact lens that filters one's visual perception; however, it can also be argued that culture is a hearing aid filtering what one hears, a pair of gloves filtering what one feels, and a tongue filtering what is tasted. Culture is infused throughout everything humans do, and it is the foundation of all human thought and social interactions.

Language is the *cultural artifact* humans use to pass down cultural traditions. Language is different from other cultural artifacts because it has the ability to create and transcend the present reality, allowing people to fantasize about the future or imaginary worlds and to reminisce about the past (Bruner, 1986). Through language-based interactions children learn to internalize their culture's norms, mores, and icons because language provides the medium for *mental models* (ideas, thoughts, and other internal states) to be shared across situations and time (Astington and Perkins, 2004). Developmental theorists (see Nelson, 1996; Vygotsky, 1987) argue that children's thinking is rooted in language, and Homer (2004) explains that language slows down and stabilizes thinking.

Thinking is often equated with 'logical' reasoning (i.e. reason that can be proven accurate or inaccurate and that can be inductive or deductive based on observable evidence), but there is also another form of reasoning that is just as important: 'narrative' reasoning. Narrative reasoning, while also logical, is heavily dependent on one's subjective memory and interpretation of events and information (Bruner, 1987). Several theorists explain that people encode their culture's mental models in the form of cultural narratives, such as myths, personal stories, and fables (Bruner, 1987; Homer, 2004), and taken together these narrative mental models provide the foundation for *folk psychology*, which Churchland (1984) defines as the 'accumulated wisdom of thousands of generations' attempts to understand how humans work' (p. 59), and he explains that children learn folk psychology 'at [our] mother's knee, as we learn our language' (p. 59). Lillard (1998, 1999) believes folk psychology forms the foundation for our ability to attribute mental states to people, and she explains that there are variations across cultures in terms of people's folk psychology.

So how do children learn to use their culture's folk psychology to reason about other's behavior? We argue that people combine their culture's language traditions, particularly their narrative mental models, to help them understand behavior. Thus, we believe people use a *narrative-interpretive rationale* (see Nelson *et al.*, 1998) to reason about human behavior, and this rationale includes information about mental states, social scripts, human motivations, and one's own personal experience. Children learn to use this interpretive rationale by being exposed to the narratives within their culture. We define narratives as any spoken or written communication in which a child has the opportunity to talk about imaginary events (e.g. fictional stories or future events), past events (e.g. autobiographic stories or conversations about the past), or storybooks (e.g. during shared-readings or emergent readings).

African cultural, language, and narrative traditions

African-based oral narrating traditions

The act of oral narration, or oral storytelling, is a valued part of all African-based cultures. In West African traditions, the griot or griotte (male or female storytellers, respectively) were seen as sacred members of the community because they preserved history and educated and entertained members of the community (Champion, 2003; Hale, 1994). Even today many African-based ethnic groups use storytelling as a tool for providing instruction, entertainment, spiritual edification, and a sense of community (Bloome *et al.*, 2003; Smitherman, 2000). A modern day griot found outside of the African continent might be a preacher, singer, poet, teacher, a friend or family member in an informal group gathering, and even a child sharing a story at preschool.

These modern-day griots use many of the traditional features of African-based oral narration, and for the sake of clarity, some of these features are briefly described (for more specifics see Champion, 2003; Curenton and Lucas, 2007; Goss and Barnes, 1989; Smitherman, 2000). The African narrating tradition assumes that everyone present is actively engaged in story construction; therefore, there can, and should, be lots of interaction between the storyteller and the listener. This open interaction during storytelling creates a sense of community among the speakers and listeners. In fact, the roles of storyteller and listener can be blurred in that a listener has the right to become a co-creator of the story by interjecting and/or offering competing points of view of events or interpretations. This act of having two narrators working together to create a story is called *joint storytelling*, and it is quite common in African narrating traditions. The role of storytelling and listener blur again when the listeners interject affirmations as the storyteller is weaving the tale. These interjections convey to the speaker that the audience is listening, understanding, and agrees with what is being said. These interjections are referred to as *call-response* within the narrating tradition. Another key feature of African-based oral narrating tradition is *signifying*, which is verbal wordplay that uses irony and indirection to playfully insult a conversation partner. *Tonal semantics* are also important in that speakers use tone to convey meaning, such as speaking important words more loudly, slowly, or with a distinct accent; the use of tonal semantics highlights that in the African oral tradition *how* something is said is more important than what is said.

In addition to these features, African-based oral narrative traditions tend to be similar in terms of theme (see Banks-Wallace, 2002). These themes appear in classic African American, African, and Afro-Caribbean fables, myths, and even personal stories. One theme is *surviving against all odds*, which might be stories of a protagonist who survives insurmountable hardship. Another common theme woven throughout stories is the importance of *loving relationships and connections with family, friends, and the larger community*. A third common theme is the need to have a *strong faith in God/Spirit*. Finally, an additional theme is how *evil, injustice, or adversity can always be overcome by goodness, cunning, or perseverance*. Several African-based traditions use proverbs, folktales, and personal stories that contain these themes in order to teach moral lessons (Davies, 2008; Nsamenang and Lamb, 1994). Some examples of cultural narratives that contain these social and moral themes are *Anansi Stories*, which are trickster tales originating from West Africa and heavily adopted in Jamaica. *The People Who Could Fly* (Hamilton, 1993) is a compilation of African American folktales and *Nelson Mandela's Favorite African Folktales* (Mandela, 2002) contains many Southern African folktales. Together these African-based oral narration features and themes form the foundation for the cultural narrating traditions that shape these ethnic minority children's thinking about social situations.

Narratives and social cognition

For African-ancestral ethnic minority children, culture plays a role in their narrative production, use of internal state language, self-concept, concept of kinship ties, and social relationships. Each of these aspects of social cognition is discussed below.

Narrative production

Because storytelling is so prized among the African cultural traditions, children from these ethnic groups tend to have strong narrative skills. As early as 2 years old, children begin producing fictional stories (Sperry and Sperry, 1996) and eventually develop a wide repertoire of skills in telling narratives of different styles and structures (Bloome *et al.*, 2003; Champion, 1997, 2003). African American preschoolers create fictional narratives that are grammatically complex and contain many features of literate language (Curenton and Justice, 2004), with rich plots, themes, and internal states (Terry *et al.*, 2013). The rich narratives that African American children produce reflect strong social cognitive abilities (Curenton, 2004), which is supported by research that finds that African American children are more likely to correctly identify a character's internal state than are European American children (Curenton, 2011).

Internal state language

The use of internal state language is a fundamental tool to master when narrating because internal state language is instrumental for understanding thoughts, feelings, desires, and emotions (Bauer *et al.*, 2005; Taumoepeau and Ruffman, 2008) and creating a meaningful and interesting story. Hughes and Dunn (1998) examined the associations between preschoolers' social cognition and mental state talk using a sample of low-income children of either Caucasian or African/Caribbean descendent living in Great Britain and found that children's talk about mental states was correlated with their performance on social cognition tasks. Hicks (1991) analyzed two elementary school girls' narratives and found that a low-income African American child's narratives emphasized mental states more than her European American middle-class counterpart's narrative. In her small-scale, intensive language sampling study, Blake (1994) found that African American children in her study used internal state verbs (e.g. want, need, sleep, like, scared, and know) before their European American counterparts.

Development of self-concept

Narratives, particularly autobiographical narratives, are instrumental in shaping children's self-concept. Mother–child reminiscing (stories about the past) is an important socialization tool in regards to children's understanding of themselves in relation to others. In a rural Nso community in Cameroon, mothers talked about their children more in relation to others than did the mothers from community groups living in Berlin, Sweden, or Tallinn, and as a result when telling stories about their past these children referred to others more than themselves (Schröder *et al.*, 2013). When telling autobiographical narratives, Cameroonian children show cognitive complexity in their autobiographical narratives, and they describe themselves in relation to others (Chasiotis *et al.*, 2010). Similarly, African American preschoolers often create narratives in which they talk about themselves in relation to others (Sperry and Sperry, 1995).

Concept of kinship ties

Cameroonian mothers describe a great deal of *familialism* when creating a narrative (Chasiotis *et al.*, 2010). Familialism can be described as the sense of connection and cohesion one has to his/her family, and it is measured using the *Family Allocentric Scale* (Lay *et al.*, 1998), and includes 21 Likert-scale items (e.g. 'My own happiness depends on the happiness of my family'). In African-based culture there is a strong sense of the emotional need to be tied to the collective group, such as your kin network, family, or community, and this is instilled in children early on. For example, when West African mothers communicate with infants, they tell the infants whom they resemble, who they were named after, and what kind of adult they might become in the future (Nsamenang and Lamb, 1994). A specific example is illustrated by a Wolog Senegalese mother as she engages in a playful conversation with her infant; the mother explains the infant's relationship role within her family by referring to the infant in relation to her siblings: 'Where is Malik's sister? … Here is Umar's sister …' (Rabain-Jamin, 1994, p. 150). In essence, this type of verbal exchange is teaching the child to learn to view herself as one part of a larger family system.

Social relationships

African-based cultures socialize children to place a primary emphasis on socio-affective relationships because knowledge about emotions is seen as a key component of sociocultural knowledge (Nsamenang and Lamb, 1994). Narratives help children form the basis of emotional connections with their parents. For example, Sher-Censor *et al.* (2013) explain that mothers who tell more coherent narratives have children who view their mother as being more responsive and nurturing. Mothers are more likely to positively reinforce young infants' attempts to communicate with others than their interactions with objects (Bakeman *et al.*, 1990). This difference reflects the value placed on socio-affective relationships over learning to manipulate objects.

Social communication

Nsamenang and Lamb (1994) explain that in order to become linguistically compe-tent, children must learn to convey their own emotions (as the speaker) and recognize the emotions of those with whom they are conversing (the audience). Children learn such skills in the contexts of interactions with their families and members of their community. Instead of dyadic conversations, West African mothers try to socialize their children to engage in triadic conversations by connecting the child to other potential conversation partners and referring to these partners' speech more than her own speech during the conversation (Rabain-Jamin, 1994). Similarly, African Ameri-can children are likely to experience oral narratives as personal accounts told amid spirited group conversations (Heath, 1982). Sometimes these personal narratives are told in 'fictionalized' ways. That is, for African American children, personal narratives may in fact be 'tall tales' in which the events are exaggerated and embellished in order to enhance the dramatic effect of the story. The practice of embellishing a story for entertainment value is what English-speaking Cameroonians jokingly refer to as 'adding salt to the story' (Mills *et al.*, 2013).

How teachers can foster narrative thinking

Given the importance of narrative in promoting children's social cognition, identify-ing ways that teachers can foster children's narrative thinking has implications for children's social and academic development. Teachers have a prime opportunity to foster children's narrative thinking through their classroom interactions and instruc-tional practices. The four most important ways that teachers can foster children's skills is by: (1) modeling stories, (2) encouraging children's storytelling, (3) reading story-books, and (4) facilitating high-level conversations.

Modeling stories

As teachers tell stories, they model storytelling for children, thus giving children examples of the different elements and styles that may be included in stories. Geni-sio and Soundy (1994) suggest that early childhood teachers should use every opportunity throughout the day to tell children brief (3–5 minutes) oral stories. These stories can be generated as a response to children's questions about the teach-er's home life, family, or likes or dislikes. When telling stories, teachers can include novel vocabulary and interesting wordplay, while making the story relevant to chil-dren's lives by incorporating familiar concepts, places, events, or objects. Using exciting facial expressions and an interesting tone of voice can also make the story lively. Teachers should make sure that these stories model a clear beginning, middle, and end to the story and that stories answer the key questions of Who, What, When, Where, and Why. The teacher should encourage children's participation in the story by inviting joint storytelling by allowing children to add to the story she is creating. Oral storytelling, even with a wordless picture book, is an important feature to include in the classroom because research shows that adults create stories that are more complex in terms of social cognition, such as the use of mental states and elaboration about false beliefs, when they are telling stories as opposed to reading stories from books (Ziv *et al.*, 2013).

Encouraging children's storytelling

Story retellings. Teachers can facilitate children's skills by providing them with many opportunities to tell their own stories. By giving children opportunities to retell stories, teachers help children strengthen their understanding of stories and allow them the chance to be active participants in storytelling (Koskinen *et al.*, 1988; Morrow, 1985), and preschoolers are very capable of such a task (Price *et al.*, 2006). Teachers can also serve as models of how to retell a story by reading a text aloud and then recounting the story to children in their own words (Koskinen *et al.*, 1988). Work by Morrow (1985) shows that when children are given guidance from teachers in retelling stories and opportunities to practice retelling stories, they demonstrate greater story comprehension, have a better ability to sequence events in stories and tell stories that are more syntactically complex compared to a control group of children.

A study by Isbell and colleagues (2004) demonstrates that the benefits of story retelling on children's narrative skills go beyond storybooks and extend to oral stories children hear. Compared to a comparison group, children who listened to an adult tell stories were better at providing the setting, moral, and characters in their retelling of stories (Isbell *et al.*, 2004). Similarly, other work has found that retelling stories without the aid of picture books can result in children retelling stories that contain more compound sentences, lexical accuracy and fluency than children who use pictures to support their retelling (Masterson and Kamhi, 1991). These studies suggest that supporting children in retelling stories may assist with their understanding of story content and structure and provide opportunities to practice telling stories, thus benefiting their development of narrative thinking. When encouraging children to retell a fictional story, teachers can ask them anchoring questions that get them to focus on what happened in the beginning, middle, and end of the story.

Autobiographical stories. Allowing children the opportunity to tell stories about their personal experiences is a great way for teachers to learn more about their students and build children's narrative skills. Teachers can have children bring in photos about their home life and tell stories about it, and this strategy has been shown to be particularly effective with immigrant children (Stricklan *et al.*, 2010). Work by Boyce and colleagues (2010) shows that a similar technique has been successful with improving the narrative skills of children who were attending Migrant Head Start programs. Regardless of whether photos are used as story prompts, the ability to effectively elicit an autobiographical narrative has been shown to be successful at enhancing children's narrative skills (Reese *et al.*, 2010).

Storybook reading

Another way teachers can support children's narrative thinking is through interactive storybook reading techniques known as dialogic reading. In dialogic reading, adults give children an opportunity to practice language within the context of book reading as they provide children with feedback about their language use, praise their efforts and expand upon their verbalizations (Whitehurst *et al.*, 1988; Zevenbergen *et al.*, 2003). As teachers engage in dialogic reading strategies, they prompt children with questions and engage them in becoming storytellers, giving children the opportunity to develop a better understanding of stories. These prompts may include completion prompts (i.e. fill-in-the-blanks), recall prompts to help a child remember events in the book, open-ended questions to encourage a child to tell the story in his or her own words, 'Wh–' type questions to encourage the child to provide details about the story, or distancing prompts to help the child relate the story to his or her own life (Zevenbergen *et al.*, 2003).

Dialogic reading techniques benefit children's narrative skills in a number of ways. A study by Zevenbergen and colleagues (2003) found that children who received a dialogic reading intervention were more likely to refer to characters' internal states and make causal statements in their narratives compared to children who did not receive the intervention. Similarly, Lever and Sénéchal (2011) found that children who participated in a dialogic reading group were more likely to tell narratives that were more developed in terms of structure and context, including more mental state references and proper introduction of characters and objects than children in the comparison group. These studies suggest that by using interactive techniques during shared book reading times, teachers may help children to strengthen their narrative skills.

Facilitating high-level conversations

The final, yet most fundamental, instructional practice a teacher can do to encourage narrative skills is to create a rich, stimulating oral language environment in the classroom by creating opportunities for high-quality conversations. Throughout the school day, teachers can incorporate conversations during shared book reading, sharing time (i.e. 'show-and-share'), sociodramatic play, and science or math activities (for discussion see Curenton *et al.*, 2013). Such high-level conversations can support children's social cognitive thinking facilitating discussions of characters' internal states, and asking them to make evaluative judgments and inferences (Curenton and Zucker, 2013). Classroom conversations that are fostered by asking more Who, What, Where, When, Why, and How questions and fewer Yes/No type questions can elicit more conversation with children (Bailey and Moughamian, 2007; Peterson *et al.*, 1999). South African preschool teachers demonstrated a wide variety of questioning during their shared readings; however, they asked questions that requested information more frequently than analytic questions, and such questions are of low-level cognitive demand (Higham *et al.*, 2010). It is also common for teachers within the United States to use low-level talk (Massey *et al.*, 2008). Therefore, in order to effectively elicit conversation teachers need professional development opportunities, such as the *Conversation Compass*© instructional support strategy, that are intended to instruct teachers on how to foster cognitively stimulating conversations with ethnically and linguistically diverse children (Curenton and Zucker, 2013).

Conclusion

African-based cultures have a strong narrative tradition, and this tradition provides the framework for a culturally specific form of narrative thinking that forms the foundation of the folk psychology for millions of people of African descent now living around the world. The language and cultural traditions among this pan-ethnic group provide explanation for a variety of aspects related to social cognition, such as the development of self-concept, use of internal state language, and social communication. In order for teachers to build upon these African-based narrative traditions, they can engage in storytelling practices within their classrooms.

References

Astington, J. W. and Peskin, J. (2004) Meaning and use: Children's acquisition of the mental lexicon. In J. M. Lucariello, J. A. Hudson, R. Fivush and P. J. Bauer (eds) *The Development of the Mediated Mind: Sociocultural Context and Cognitive Development* (pp. 59–78). Mahwah, NJ: Erlbaum.

Bailey, A. L. and Moughamian, A. C. (2007) Telling stories their way: Narrative scaffolding with emergent readers and readers. *Narrative Inquiry, 17*(2), 203–29.

Bakeman, R., Adamson, L. B., Konner, M. and Barr, R. G. (1990) Kung infancy: The social context of object exploration. *Child Development, 61*, 794–809.

Banks-Wallace, J. (2002) Storytelling and analysis rooted in African American oral tradition. *Qualitative Health Research, 12*, 410–26. doi: 10.1177/104973202129119892.

Bauer, P. J., Stark, E. N., Lukowski, A. F., Rademacher, J., Van Abbema, D. L. and Ackil, J. K. (2005) Working together to make sense of the past: Mothers' and children's use of internal states language in conversations about traumatic and nontraumatic events. *Journal of Cognition and Development, 6*(4), 463–88.

Blake, I. K. (1994) Language development and socialization in young African-American children. In P. M. Greenfield and R. R. Cocking (eds) *Cross-cultural Roots of Minority Child Development* (pp. 167–95). Hillsdale, NJ: Erlbaum.

Bloome, D., Katz, L. and Champion, T. (2003) Young children's narratives and ideologies of language in classrooms. *Reading and Writing Quarterly, 19*(3), 205–23.

Boyce, L. K., Innocenti, M. S., Roggman, L. A., Norman, V. K. J. and Ortiz, E. (2010) Telling stories and making books: Evidence for an intervention to help parents in migrant Head Start families support their children's language and literacy. *Early Education and Development, 21*(3), 343–71.

Bruner, J. (1986) *Actual Minds, Possible Worlds*. Cambridge, MA: Harvard University Press.

Bruner, J. (1987) Life as narrative. *Social Research*, 11–32.

Champion, T. B. (1997) 'Tell me somethin' good': A description of narrative structures among African American children. *Linguistics and Education, 9*(3), 251–86.

Champion, T. B. (2003) *Understanding Storytelling among African American children: A Journey from African to America*. Mahwah, NJ: Erlbaum.

Churchland, P. M. (1984) *Matter and Consciousness*. Cambridge, MA: MIT Press.

Chasiotis, A., Bender, M., Kiessling, F. and Hofer, J. (2010) The emergence of the independent self: Autobiographical memory as a mediator of false belief understanding and sociocultural motive orientation in Cameroonian and German preschoolers. *Journal of Cross-Cultural Psychology, 41*(3), 368–90.

Curenton, S. M. (2004) The association between narratives and theory of mind for low-income preschoolers. *Early Education and Development, 15*, 121–45.

Curenton, S. M. (2011) Understanding the landscapes of stories: The association between preschoolers' narrative comprehension and production skills and cognitive abilities. *Early Child Development and Care, 181*(6), 791–808.

Curenton, S. M. and Iruka, I. (2013) *Cultural Competence in Early Childhood Education.* San Diego: Bridgepoint.

Curenton, S. M. and Justice, L. (2004) African American and Caucasian preschoolers' use of decontextualized language: Use of literate language features in oral narratives. *Language, Speech, and Hearing Services in the Schools, 35,* 240–53.

Curenton, S. M. and Lucas, T. M. (2007) Assessing young children's oral narrative skills: The story pyramid framework. In K. Pence (ed.) *Assessment in Emergent and Early Literacy.* San Diego: Plural.

Curenton, S. M. and Zucker, T. A. (2013) Instructional conversations in early childhood classrooms: Policy suggestions for curriculum standards and professional development. *Creative Education, 4*(7A1), 60–68.

Curenton, S. M., Justice, L. M., Zucker, T. A. and McGinty, A. S. (2013) Language and literacy curriculum and instruction. In V. Buysse and E. Peisner-Feinberg (eds) *Handbook of Response to Intervention (RTI) for Early Childhood* (pp. 237–49). Baltimore, MD: Brookes.

Davies, R. (2008) Making a difference in children's lives: The story of Nancy, a novice early years teacher in a Jamaican primary school. *International Journal of Early Years Education, 16*(1), 3–16.

Farrar, R. (1995) Praise song: Challenge. In L. Goss and C. Goss (eds) *Jump Up and Say! A Collection of Black Storytelling* (pp. 23–4). New York: Simon & Schuster.

Genisio, M. H. and Soundy, C. S. (1994) Tell me a story: Interweaving cultural and restorative strands into early storytelling experiences. *Day Care and Early Education, 22*(1), 24–31.

Goss, L. and Barnes, M. E. (1989) *Talk that Talk: An Anthology of African-American Storytelling.* NY: Simon & Schuster.

Hale, T. A. (1994) Griottes: Female voices from West Africa. *Research in African Literatures, 25*(3), 71–91.

Hamilton, V. (1993) *The People Who Could Fly: American Black Folktales.* New York: Knopf Books for Young Readers.

Heath, S. B. (1982) What no bedtime story means: Narrative skills at home and school. *Language in Society, 11,* 49–76.

Hicks, D. (1991) Kinds of narrative: Genre skills among first graders from two communities. In A. McCabe and C. Peterson (eds) *Developing Narrative Structure* (pp. 55–87). Hillsdale, NJ: Erlbaum.

Higham, S., Tönsing, K. M. and Alant, E. (2010) Teachers' interactions during storybook reading: A rural African perspective. *Early Education and Development, 21*(3), 392–411.

Homer, B. D. (2004) Literacy and the mediated mind. In J. M. Lucariello, J. A. Hudson, R. Fivush and P. J. Bauer (eds) *The Development of the Mediated Mind: Sociocultural Context and Cognitive Development* (pp. 59–78). Mahwah, NJ: Erlbaum.

Hong, Y., Morris, M. W., Chiu, C. and Benet-Martinez, V. (2000) Multicultural minds: A dynamic constructivist approach to culture and cognition. *American Psychologist, 55,* 709–20.

Hughes, C. and Dunn, J. (1998) Understanding mind and emotion: Longitudinal associations with mental-state talk between young friends. *Child Development, 34,* 1026–37.

Isbell, R., Sobol, J., Lindauer, L. and Lowrance, A. (2004) The effects of storytelling and story reading on the oral language complexity and story comprehension of young children. *Early Childhood Education Journal, 32*(3), 157–63. doi: 10.1023/B:ECEJ.0000048967.94189.a3.

Koskinen, P. S., Gambrell, L. B., Kapinus, B. A. and Heathington, B. S. (1988) Retelling: A strategy for enhancing students' reading comprehension. *The Reading Teacher, 41*(9), 892–96.

Lay, C., Fairlie, P., Jackson, S., Ricci, T., Eisenberg, J., Sato, T., *et al.* (1998) Domain-specific allocentrism–idiocentrism: A measure of family connectedness. *Journal of Cross-Cultural Psychology, 29,* 434–60.

Lever, R. and Sénéchal, M. (2011) Discussing stories: On how a dialogic reading intervention improves kindergartners' oral narrative construction. *Journal of Experimental Child Psychology, 108*(1), 1–24. doi: 10.1016/j.jecp.2010.07.002.

Lillard, A. S. (1998) Ethnopsychologies: Cultural variations in theories of mind. *Psychological Bulletin, 123,* 3–32.

Lillard, A. S. (1999) Developing a cultural theory of mind: The CIAO approach. *Current Directions in Psychological Science, 8,* 57–61.

Mandela, N. (2002) *Nelson Mandela's Favorite African Folktales.* New York: W. W. Norton.

Massey, S. L., Pence, K. L., Justice, L. M. and Bowles, R. P. (2008) Educators' use of cognitively challenging questions in economically disadvantaged preschool classroom contexts. *Early Education and Development, 19*(2), 340–60.

Masterson, J. J. and Kamhi, A. G. (1991) The effects of sampling conditions on sentence production in normal, reading-disabled, and language-learning-disabled children. *Journal of Speech and Hearing Research, 34*(3), 549–58.

Mills, M. T., Watkins, R. V. and Washington, J. A. (2013) Structural and dialectal characteristics of the fictional and personal narratives of school-age African American children. *Language, Speech, and Hearing Services in Schools, 44*(2), 211.

Morrow, L. M. (1985) Retelling stories: A strategy for improving young children's comprehension, concept of story structure, and oral language complexity. *The Elementary School Journal, 85*(5), 647–61.

Nelson, K. (1996) *Language in Cognitive Development: The Emergence of the Mediated Mind.* New York: Cambridge University Press.

Nelson, K., Plesa, D. and Hensler, S. (1998) Children's theory of mind: An experimental interpretation. *Human Development, 41*(7), 29.

Nsamenang, A. B. and Lamb, M. E. (1994) Socialization of Nso children in the Bamedana Grasslands of Northwest Cameroon. In P. M. Greenfield and R. R. Cocking (eds) *Crosscultural Roots of Minority Child Development.* Hillsdale, NJ: Erlbaum.

Peterson, C., Jesso, B. and McCabe, A. (1999) Encouraging narratives in preschoolers: An intervention study. *Journal of Child Language, 26*(1), 49–67.

Price, J. R., Roberts, J. E. and Jackson, S. C. (2006) Structural development of the fictional narrative of African American preschoolers. *Language, Speech, and Hearing Services in the Schools, 37,* 178–90.

Rabain-Jamin, J. (1994) Language and socialization of the child in African families living in France. In P. M. Greenfield and R. R. Cocking (eds) *Cross-cultural Roots of Minority Child Development* (pp. 147–66). Hillsdale, NJ: Erlbaum.

Reese, E., Leyva, D., Sparks, A. and Grolnick, W. (2010) Maternal elaborative reminiscing increases low-income children's narrative skills relative to dialogic reading. *Early Education and Development, 21*(3), 318–42.

Schröder, L., Keller, H., Kärtner, J., Kleis, A., Abels, M., Yovsi, R. D. and Papaligoura, Z. (2013) Early reminiscing in cultural contexts: Cultural models, maternal reminiscing styles, and children's memories. *Journal of Cognition and Development, 14*(1), 10–34.

Sher-Censor, E., Grey, I. and Yates, T. M. (2013) The intergenerational congruence of mothers' and preschoolers' narrative affective content and narrative coherence. *International Journal of Behavioral Development, 37*(4), 340–8.

Smitherman, G. (2000) *Talkin that Talk: Language, Culture, and Education in African America.* New York: Routledge

Sperry, L. L. and Sperry, D. E. (1995) Young children's presentations of self in conversational narratives. *New Directions for Child Development, 69,* 47–60.

Sperry, L. L. and Sperry, D. E. (1996) Early development of narrative skills. *Cognitive Development, 11,* 443–65.

Stricklan, M. J., Keat, J. B. and Marinak, B. A. (2010) Connecting worlds: Using photo narrations to connect immigrant children, preschool teachers, and immigrant families. *The School Community Journal, 20*(1), 81–102.

Taumoepeau, M. and Ruffman, T. (2008) Stepping stones to others' minds: Maternal talk relates to child mental state language and emotion understanding at 15, 24, and 33 months. *Child Development, 79*(2), 284–302.

Terry, N. P., Mills, M. T., Binghan, G. E., Mansour, S. and Marencin, N. (2013) Oral narrative performance of African American prekindergartners who speak nonmainstream American English. *Language, Speech, and Hearing Services in Schools, 44,* 291–305. doi: 10.1044/0161-1461(2013/12-0037.

Whitehurst, G. J., Falco, F. L., Lonigan, C. J., Fischel, J. E., DeBaryshe, B. D., Valdez-Menchaca, M. C. and Caulfield, M. (1988) Accelerating language development through picture book reading. *Developmental Psychology, 24*(4), 552–9. doi: 10.1037/0012-1649.24.4.552.

Vygotsky, L. S. (1987) *The Collected Works of LS Vygotsky, Volume 1: Problems of General Psychology, including the volume Thinking and Speech.* New York: Springer.

Zevenbergen, A. A., Whitehurst, G. J. and Zevenbergen, J. A. (2003) Effects of a shared-reading intervention on the inclusion of evaluative devices in narratives of children from low-income families. *Journal of Applied Developmental Psychology, 24*(1), 1–15. doi: 10.1016/S0193-3973(03)00021-2.

Ziv, M., Smadja, M. L. and Aram, D. (2013) Mothers' mental-state discourse with preschoolers during storybook reading and wordless storybook telling. *Early Childhood Research Quarterly, 28*(1), 177–86.

26

RECOGNISING 'THE SACRED SPARK OF WONDER'[1]

Scribbling and related talk as evidence of how young children's thinking may be identified

Elizabeth Coates and Andrew Coates

Introduction

Young children's scribbling is usually linked to the development of fine manipulative skills and markmaking as a precursor for writing. The research which forms the basis for this chapter explores this activity in some depth, examining the narrative which often accompanies such drawing, highlighting its value for children's cognitive and imaginative development. Far from being a purely physical activity the findings demonstrate the depth of thinking taking place as children rehearse, fantasize, plan, reason and solve problems.

John Dewey defined thinking as 'a power of following up and linking together the specific suggestions that specific things arouse'. He regarded any subject as intellectual in its ability 'to start and direct significant inquiry and reflection' (1909, p. 39). Our inquiry, carried out as part of a study of young children's drawings (see Coates and Coates, 2006, 2011), examined the thoughts of young children, working in pairs and engaged in the subject of scribbling. Their insights made it possible to begin to understand the drawings' meanings and conceptual richness. This, together with our hypothesis that children's scribbling has purpose, content and meaning, forms the basis for analysis and discussion. Throughout, therefore, we focus mainly on the role of narrative, as our findings demonstrate that the rich language accompanying young children's scribble drawings reveals a breadth of informed thinking in relation to their cultural and social environment, which goes far beyond the surface of the image itself. As Aitkin (1978) and Matthews (2003) suggest, children provide detailed commentaries about what they are doing and where they are going, supporting Gardner's (1980) contention that the 'pre-representational child' (p. 43) talks about what they would like to draw, thereby emphasising the link between the realms of drawing and language. It would seem, therefore, that observing children as they draw, and listening carefully to what they say as their pictures unfold, enables access to an imaginative and conceptual world far richer than the often held view reflected by Wood and Hall (2011, p. 269) that they are 'meaningless, abstract scribbles'.

Teachers sometimes see this earliest form of drawing, not as a form of communication, but as a form of expression, the end product of which is frequently not taken seriously (Kellogg, 1955; Kress, 1997). However, it is widely accepted that the act of scribbling, far from being random markmaking, plays an integral part in children's overall development, particularly in relation to hand–eye coordination and fine motor control, as they develop the manipulative skills needed for writing (Lindstrom, 1957; Kellogg, 1970). Equally important, but perhaps less regarded, however, is the contribution that scribbling, with its attendant talk, makes to the development of thinking, as not only does this narrative act as an accompaniment, but it can also shape and determine the way the drawing progresses. Certainly many of our narratives demonstrate the thinking process underpinning the children's drawings, showing how subject matter developed and changed direction. Cox (2005) sees this interplay of talk and drawing as a form of experimentation into diverse ways of making meaning and concept building. Such circumstances suggest that children are combining differing forms of language, the visual and the spoken, alongside the language of the imagination, translating onto paper the stories woven in their minds, or exploring the language of emotion as they seek to understand their place in the world. Egan (1999) stresses the significance of the child's developing imagination, highlighting the value of language as a means to 'stimulate visual images in the mind' (p. 89). This concept is extended by Bhroin (2007), who makes the connection between art and fantasy play, suggesting that children use the medium of drawing as a way of projecting fantasy beyond what is physically possible and into the realms of the imagination. At this point the relevance of observing the young child in action becomes more obvious since not only can a researcher note the way a scribble is built up in layers or patches (Willats, 2004), but it is also possible to follow the child's train of thought, as either the intention to draw an object is announced at the start, or an idea occurs as the drawing progresses (Lowenfeld, 1939; Luquet, 1927/2001). Jackson (1994, cited in Matthews, 1999 p.94) calls the language a child uses while drawing 'a window on consciousness' enabling the listener to achieve some understanding of the thought process underlying the representation. Without the insights provided by such utterances, any attempt at analysing the scribble drawing of a child can only be partially successful, since the level of representation inevitably falls far below the image in the child's eye.

Listening to children as they draw, while helping adults understand the thinking taking place, may also reveal the imaginative play in which the child is involved. David (1999) suggests that in play, children are testing their ideas and knowledge, a concept extended by Wood and Hall (2011) who feel that drawing is often a part of play. Our research found that children were continuing their role play while drawing, taking their storytelling to a level not possible in the physical setting (Coates

Figure 26.1   Ethan (3:11) 'There's little horses and big horses'

and Coates, 2006). Ethan's (3:11) exploration of the needs of 'little horses' and 'big horses' (Figure 26.1) is a clear example of this. The drawing took 20 minutes to complete, the detailed narrative revealing his curiosity and extensive vocabulary as well as his concept of size. This not only illustrates his ability to recognize and solve problems, but also shows how he is 'developing the conceptual framework necessary for abstract and higher order thinking' (Bhroin, 2007 p. 16). The majority of Ethan's utterances were directed at himself as he explored the nature of the environment he was drawing, although his friend, Aiden (3:8), occasionally joined in. This mixture of self-talk and social interaction enables children not only to 'improve control of actions or create adventurous thoughts' (Vygotsky cited in Trevarthen, 1995, p. 6), but also allows them to incorporate their peer's knowledge and points of view.

Ethan's horses were drawn as big or small orange oblongs all with smaller square shapes at one end – possibly heads, as this is a transition drawing moving towards the next stage of representation – suggesting that he had developed a particular schema or format to represent them (Nutbrown, 1994; Athey, 1990). His use of the same colour to denote things directly related to them conveys, perhaps, both a need to reinforce this connection as well as expressing a concept of belonging. This included 'big doors and little doors' for the horses to go through, and he made it clear that only the right sized horses could pass through their designated doors.

'And this is what I'm drawing. Some little horses … and do you know, across there is some big doors and little doors cos there's little horses and big horses … so they have to lie down and get out of the doors, but the babies, but the little horses have to but not the big ones … but not the big horses cos they're too fat … but that's a thin door for the little horses.'

He showed an understanding of the problems that might arise when the horses wanted to re-enter, by adding dots inside the door area.

'That thing at the top of the big doors is where a dot and another dot. There are dots because they can open the doors to get back in. You have to hold the dot. Just press the dot and the door opens.'

The orange horizontal lines at the centre of the page were steps for the 'little horses' to climb so they could reach their 'little doors', and he showed an informed knowledge of the relationship between horses and people as he included a 'bell to let the people come in'.

'These are steps, these are steps for the little horses to get, little steps for the little horses to get up because they have to, they have to stand on that door there and go out of that door at the top of that door and one of them has to go through that door. Those things at the top of them are these, are these kinda things of the middle. The top of the doors cos they ring, they ring their bell and they, and they, and these bells at the top of them just to have to ding dong them and the people can come through.'

These explanations were not necessarily directed at anyone, but appeared to be a form of thinking aloud as Ethan rehearsed and planned each stage of his drawing. Such talk Vygotsky terms egocentric speech, used by young children to help them understand where they have come from and where they are going to with their work (cited in Gray and MacBlain, 2012, p. 75). Ethan's utterances enabled the observer to follow his reasoning and participate in his interpretation of the horses' environment.

Our next example, completed in 14 minutes, is from Nathan, who at 6:3 is a prime example of an older child who still scribbles. His work 'I'm drawing army people' (Figure 26.2), only made visual sense in relation to an almost constant commentary which provided precise meanings and signalled his intentions, sometimes in tones of great excitement and hilarity, and accompanied by vigorous gesticulations as he warmed to his theme. Adults, particularly teachers in formal classroom situations, may often regard such behaviour as excessive, but Nathan's responses were essential to him and as Piaget suggests, to insist that he was silent as he worked would be to silence his thinking (cited in Engel, 1995). Some of his utterances were indistinct as he had a severe speech impediment and a limited vocabulary with which to express his ideas, but despite his struggle, the drawing represents a complicated fantasy reflecting his experience of both film and video games.

Figure 26.2 Nathan (6:3) 'I'm drawing army people'

Nathan started this drawing by making a line of vertical strokes in brown felt-tip pen, surmounted by red vertical dashes. His previous two drawings – the first containing recognizable diagrammatic representations of figures and trees, and the second, a house with a chimney and smoke and multicoloured dots as fireworks – placed him firmly in Lowenfeld and Brittain's (1964) Preschematic Stage of drawing development. His indignant response to the question 'Is that a fence, Nathan?' of 'Naa! Army people, I'm drawing Army people' came as a surprise as his symbolic language would seem, therefore, to have regressed. This was confirmed by the contents of the rest of the work, and the following provides the essence of Nathan's developing thinking as the drawing progressed. Much of this is related to his concept of 'goodies' and 'baddies' in warfare, their roles and their activities:

> 'These are army people, these are goodies (the brown and red vertical lines on the baseline) ... but these are the baddies (the black dots at the top of the composition, applied vigorously and accompanied by shrieks and whoops) ... The blue ones are the ones that haven't got any swords ... The blue ones, the "yucky" ones are on horses (the group of dots and multiple line overlaid circles in the middle of the composition) ... and the black ones shoot guns ... they can go rifles ... cool ... and they machine everybodies' (this last utterance was accompanied by excited repetitious noises to signify machine gunning).

At this point Nathan's account became confused as he turned his attention to the 'goodies' children, identified as the black crosses at the middle left of the composition: 'There's the goodies' children, they have things and the things have fun, and they try to give them and they've got things … and they still won't get into them.' The theme soon returned to 'goodies' and 'baddies'. The two rows of grey multiple line overlaid circles in the middle of the composition were designated as 'goodies' and the black dots were confirmed as 'baddies'. Nathan changed his mind, however, and finally designated them as 'goodies', because 'there's got to be lots of goodies, there's got to be lots of goodies. The goodies again … goodies … now there's lots of goodies.'

This example reveals how essential running commentaries are to the understanding of content. It would be impossible for such intense and fulsome narratives to be delivered on completion of the picture, since each utterance coincided with the production of specific elements.

Both Ethan's and Nathan's interaction between the non-verbal and verbal highlight their intention to portray a particular scenario, although it may be, as Shapiro (1979) suggests, that this changes when two children construct a story between them. Certainly there were a number of examples when the two children copied each other's ideas, or where the dialogue influenced the direction the drawings took, in what was essentially a sharing and extending of experiences. What is clear is that these young children had a facility with language that outstripped their representational ability, as language develops more quickly than proficiency in manipulating drawing media and making shapes. Their need to name things, therefore, and begin to tell stories and describe experiences is, as Costello (2000) states, fundamental as a requirement for learning development. The examples we gathered relating to this category provided evidence that the activity of drawing offers an outlet for children's enthusiasm for their exciting and newly developed ability to communicate with understanding. It does not matter that adults fail to recognize the subjects of the drawings, because the relationship is real to children as they share an imagined world.

Conversations were focused on either one or both of their drawings, and the seriousness with which they treated the content led to questioning and thoughtful re-evaluation. Such responses revealed the high level of learning taking place. Drawing upon each other's knowledge and expertise was a common feature and emphasized the importance of drawing's potential as a social activity as well as a solitary occupation.

This interaction of talking and drawing was evident in Megan's (4:1) work which was completed in ten minutes. Her concentration was intense and the result was multicoloured, consisting of looped continuous lines drawn at a slight angle, but closely packed so that the colours overlapped. A horizontal pink line was drawn across these going from the left-hand edge of the paper to a block of red diagonal lines. At the base of the looped lines was a patch of yellow. Throughout the session, Megan conducted a dialogue with her friend, Abigail (3:10), whose idea she said she was going to copy, 'but I'll do it a bit different'. Wood (1998) highlights the value of such dialogue as a way of offering different viewpoints, challenging ideas and causing children to rethink.

M: 'This time I'm going to copy Abby's but I'll do it a bit different.'
A: 'I'm doing a dark cave where no one is allowed in.'
M: 'I'm making a sea.'
A: 'The sea, are you making the seaside?'
M: 'Yes, and I'm going to do the sand next.'

In the end they influenced each other, but Megan's narrative showed that she named each part of her drawing as she added it.

M: 'Now I'm going to do the sand. This is the colour sand I'm doing.'
A: 'The colour sand is yellow.'
M: 'No it's not, it's a black and it's coloured a black.'
A: 'No, the sand is normally yellow.'

Although the subject matter was linked to colour throughout, the reference to black sand indicates Megan is recalling a particular experience, challenging her friend's more conventional notion. A later horizontal line in the middle of the page was named as 'a bridge'. It would seem, however, that Abigail was responsible for this element as a result of her questioning.

M: 'That's the sand, there you are and that's the sea.'
A: 'Where's the path then to walk along the bridge?'
M: 'Here it is.'
A: 'No, it takes you all the way to the sea.'
M: 'So it move ... now we make a bridge then. There you are, there's the bridge.'
A: 'Oh, the path's through there, isn't it?'

After further discussion relating to brown and pink pens, Megan added blue to her drawing, 'Well, you need blue, of course, for the sky, blue sky and what I'm going to do now is ... there you are. I'm going to put pink on now.' Both Megan and Abigail then focused on pink, making up a rhyme that illustrated not just the strength of their social interaction but also a keen sense of humour:

A: 'Pink, you said, drink'
M: 'Blinky, blinky, pink and gink'
A: 'Think and pink make a wink'
M: 'I'm going to do pink and gink'

An element of story then entered Megan's narrative as she said, 'Mine is really a cave but no one can get through.' She drew a horizontal pink line across her page saying, 'There's the cave, that's just pointing to say no one's allowed to get through.' Although this is the first time Megan made reference to a cave, she appears to be reflecting Abigail's notion of 'a dark cave where no one is allowed in' raised at the start of the drawing episode.

As Abigail announced she had finished her drawing, Megan decided she should finish as well:

'I've nearly, nearly finished. What I have to do is get a yellow, the nice colour. A really close one for this. I know how to do it. No one has seen this picture before and no one will see this picture as it's magic. In the whole world none will see it. One day you won't know this is mine, will you. How will you know it's mine, won't you?'

This dialogue revealed how the two children became involved in explanation, clarification and story telling, supporting research by Boyalzis and Albertini (2000) into the social interaction which occurs when children are drawing together. They found that learning was enhanced because of the way ideas were shared and comparisons made. Engaging with others in problem-solving and critical reflection, Bruner (1983) proposes, is fundamental to the development of higher order thinking (cited in Gray and MacBlain, 2012, p. 110).

Such development, however, is not restricted to the challenges of social interaction, for as Bruner goes on to suggest, markmaking itself is an important ingredient, and Arnheim (1956) regards the emergence of organized form in the scribbles of young children as 'one of the miracles of nature' (p. 136). Many children develop a sense of visual rightness, a visual intelligence that not only informs their placing of each element but also helps them to decide when the drawing is complete. Their deliberations, not necessarily accompanied by verbal explanations, inform juxtapositions of such as circular rhythms, zigzags and scribbled patches towards visually pleasing and dynamic compositions. These provide evidence of a clarity of intention based on criteria of appropriateness. As Lowenfeld (1954) suggests, some children's organizational sense may cause them to create a balance and rhythm within their drawing as they realize subconsciously that one area has begun to dominate. Both Alland (1983) and Matthews (2003) refer to children's aesthetic sense as instinctive, Alland suggesting that it is embedded in the child's brain, while Kellogg (1973) goes further by proposing that the brain sends a signal indicating when a drawing has reached a satisfying conclusion. This insight, although based on observing children over many years cannot be ratified, but we found 27 drawings that fell into this category. Comments such as Luke's (3:11) 'My picture is done' and Samuel's (4:8) 'I've done all the paper', suggest two possibilities, either that they had become bored with drawing or that they sensed their drawings were complete. The former is less likely, however, as both continued to make a second, indicating that they were still involved in the activity.

Samuel's drawing (Figure 26.3), which took 12 minutes to complete, appears at first glance to be a continuous blue circular line repeatedly crossing over itself as he responded to the magic of its emergence. Apart from his comment regarding completion, it was made in silence. Further scrutiny reveals upward of 12 starts or finishes, but the work's complexity makes it impossible to decipher more. Observations confirm Samuel's intense concentration, however, as he lifted his pen from the surface of the paper and with great deliberation replaced it before continuing his circular progress. The completed image is a coherent and harmonious whole, consisting of large circular rhythms that fill the whole page, and smaller concentrated ones that

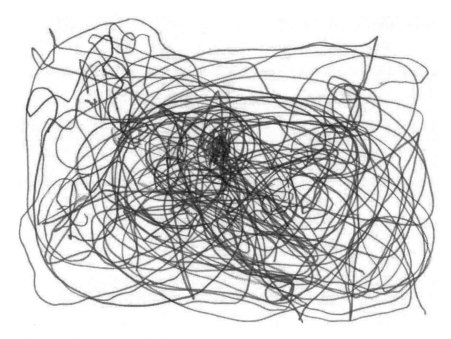

Figure 26.3 Samuel (4:8) 'I've done all the paper'

occasionally become masses as the lines coalesce. It is a source of aesthetic pleasure for both maker and observer.

Heather (4:4) (Figure 26.4) has progressed from the stage of random markmaking, when kinaesthetic activity, the enjoyment of physical movement for its own sake, was her guiding motivation (Lowenfield and Brittain, 1964), to this work, which also took 12 minutes to complete, and reflects her growing ability to make deliberate and informed judgements regarding choice of colour and the placing of elements. She is certainly exploring kinaesthetic sensations, but now her overriding concern is the careful planning of where to place each element and the ultimate achievement of a visually pleasing and cohesive composition.

Her drawing contains sufficient complexity to arrest our attention for some time. We can only speculate about much of Heather's intentions, however, as her brief, but telling utterances which reflect her need to organize the work refer mainly to choice of colour. This is what Egan (1995) called task management, as children have often been recorded as saying 'now I need …' (p. 13).

> 'I'm going to have light blue now, where's the light blue?' 'Is this purple? I thought it was the same blue as that,' she said as she pointed to the ultramarine blue pen; 'I haven't used orange, there's an orange. I need orange too'; 'I think I'll have this green now'; and in response to her friend's question, 'What green do you want?' she said, 'I don't need dark, I need light green.'

Figure 26.4   Heather (4:4) 'I don't need dark, I need light green'

It must be stressed, however, that these judgements are based on those normally reserved for describing the compositional unity of adult works of some aesthetic excellence, as children's art can only be described in relation to adult criteria because of the impossibility of achieving an insight into children's values. Fundamental to this process is an examination of the elements of design (Fry, 1909/1961) such as the arrangement of shapes and masses, rhythm, line, light and dark and colour – a complicated activity and as such, beyond the conceptual understanding of very young children. Nevertheless the careful juxtaposition of the various elements, the considered choice of colour, the variation in the drawn line, and the decisive manner in which the drawings were brought to a conclusion were impressive. A strong sense of design is evident in most of the more representational works, but it would seem that some children in the earlier stage of scribbling are also capable of making considered aesthetic judgements when drawing.

Conclusion

In conclusion, there is a tendency to denigrate scribbling to the level of markmaking rather than considering its role in the expressive and cognitive evolution of the young child. This ignores the possibilities that dialogue might offer, focusing as it does on drawing's physical manifestations. If we accept the premise, however, that the act of scribbling is relevant to the growth of hand–eye coordination and fine motor control, we cannot disregard narrative's contribution to our understanding of children's expressive and cognitive development. Our research highlights the central role that spoken language plays, and such dialogue together with the finished picture provides a rich source of information about the thinking underpinning its development and completion. It is essential, therefore, as Matthews (2003) suggests, that if adults understand the significance of scribbling, and talk intelligently to children about their work, the children's thinking, language and drawing may be extended and their awareness and confidence further developed and enriched.

Note

1 Dewey, 1909, p. 34.

References

Aitkin, J. (1978) Talk in the infant classroom. *English in Education, 12*(2), 10–14.

Alland, A. J. R. (1983) *Playing with Form – Children Draw in Six Cultures*. New York: Columbia University Press.

Arnheim, R. (1956) *Art and Visual Perception*. London: Faber and Faber.

Athey, C. (1990) *Extending Thought in Young Children*. London: Paul Chapman.

Bhroin, H. N. (2007) 'A slice of life': The interrelationships among art, play and the 'real' life of the young child. *International Journal of Education and the Arts, 8*(16). Retrieved from www.ijea.org/v8n16/ (30/05/2011).

Boyalzis, C. and Albertini, G. (2000) A naturalistic observation of children drawing: Peer collaboration processes and influences in children's art. *New Directions for Child and Adolescent Development, 90*, Winter, pp. 31–48.

Coates, E. and Coates, A. (2006) Young children talking and drawing. *International Journal of Early Years Education, 14*(3), 221–41.

Coates, E. and Coates, A. (2011) The subjects and meanings of young children's drawings. In D. Faulkner and E. Coates (eds) *Exploring Children's Creative Narratives* (pp. 86–110). London and New York: Routledge.

Costello, P. (2000) *Thinking Skills and Early Childhood Education*. London: David Fulton.

Cox, S. (2005) Intentions and meaning in young children's drawing. *Journal of Art and Design Education, 24*(2), 115–25.

David, T. (1999) Changing minds, young children learning. In T. David (ed.) *Young Children Learning* (pp. 1–12). London: Paul Chapman.

Dewey, J. (1909) *How We Think*. London: D.C. Heath.

Egan, B. A. (1995) How do children perceive the activity of drawing? Some initial observations of children in an infant school, *IDATER 95*, Loughborough University of Technology, pp. 10–14.

Egan, K. (1999) *Children's Minds, Talking Rabbits and Clockwork Oranges*. New York: Althouse Press.

Engel, S (1995) *The Stories Children Tell*. New York: W. H. Freeman.

Fry, R. (1909/1961) An essay in aesthetics. In *Vision and Design*. Harmondsworth: Penguin.

Gardner, H. (1980) *Artful Scribbles*. London: Jill Norman.

Gray, C. and MacBlain, S. (2012) *Learning Theories in Childhood*. London: Sage.

Kellogg, R. (1955) *What Children Scribble and Why*, author's edition. Later published (1959) by National Press, Palo Alto, CA.

Kellogg, R. (1970) *Analyzing Children's Art*. Palo Alto, CA: National Press.

Kellogg, R. (1973) Misunderstanding children's art. *Art Education, 26*(6), 7–9.

Kress, G. (1997) *Before Writing: Rethinking the Paths to Literacy*. London: Routledge.

Lindstrom, M. (1957) *Children's Art*. Berkeley, Los Angeles and London: University of California Press.

Lowenfeld, V. (1939) *The Nature of Creative Activity*. New York: Harcourt, Brace.

Lowenfeld, V. (1954) *Your Child and his Art – A Guide for Parents*. New York: Macmillan.

Lowenfeld, V. and Lambert Brittain, W. (1964) *Creative and Mental Growth*, 4th edn. New York: Macmillan/London: Collier-Macmillan.

Lowenfeld, V. and Lambert Brittain, W. (1987) *Creative and Mental Growth*, 8th edn. Upper Saddle River, NJ: Prentice-Hall.

Luquet, G. (1927/2001) *Children's Drawings* (trans. A. Costall). London: Free Association Books.

Matthews, J. (1999) *Helping Children to Draw and Paint in Early Childhood*. London: Hodder and Stoughton.

Matthews, J. (2003) *Drawing and Painting: Children and Visual Representation*. London: Paul Chapman Publishing.

Nutbrown, C. (1994) *Threads of Thinking*. London: Paul Chapman Publishing.

Shapiro, E. (1979) Copying and inventing: Similarities and contrasts in process and performance. In N. Smith and M. Franklin (eds) *Symbolic Functioning in Childhood* (pp. 153–63). New Jersey: Erlbaum.

Trevarthen, C. (1995) The child's need to learn a culture. *Children and Society*, *9*(1), 5–19.

Willats, J. (2004) *Making Sense of Children's Drawings*. New York: Erlbaum.

Wood, D. (1998) *How Children Think and Learn*, 2nd edn. Oxford: Blackwell.

Wood, E. and Hall, E. (2011) Drawings as spaces for intellectual play. *International Journal of Early Years Education*, *19*(3–4), 267–81.

27

MUSICAL THINKING IN THE EARLY YEARS

Beatriz Ilari

On a quiet morning, 6-month-old Cecilia turns her head towards a loudspeaker when she hears a familiar tune emanating from the media center. She moves her body up and down, signaling some recognition of the tune. Many miles away, Mitchell, an active 3-year-old, who is playing in the front yard of his nursery school, imitates the sound of a garbage truck that is driving by. A few seconds later, he is singing a modified version of the classic children's tune 'the wheels on the bus', which has now turned into 'the wheels on the truck'. As he repeats the melody, rhythmic and pitch structures gradually change, although the lyrics remain the same for the duration of the song. And not far from there, a group of preschoolers is making a wide range of body gestures as they sing a familiar song 'in their heads'. Musical thinking is in action in all three cases.

Introduction

Musical thought, as a separate form of thinking, has been the object of study of musicologists, ethnomusicologists, psychologists, neuroscientists, philosophers, and educators alike. At least two distinct yet complementary forms of musical thought (see Figure 27.1) have been outlined in the literature, namely, *thinking music* and *thinking about music* (Nettl, 1996). Thinking music, as the term suggests, involves thinking in terms of musical and sound structures such as notes, rhythmic patterns, timbres and melodies, much in the same way that composers, performers, and improvisers do (Nettl, 1996). Thinking about music relates not to musical elements *per se*, but to extramusical associations and meanings associated with musical elements and practices of different cultural groups, such as beliefs and values (Nettl, 1996). These two different forms of musical thought coexist, intersect, and are often difficult to disentangle, especially where young children are concerned. Yet, different disciplines have typically focused on one or the other. Music psychology and more recently the neurosciences, for example, have provided much information on what we know about young

318

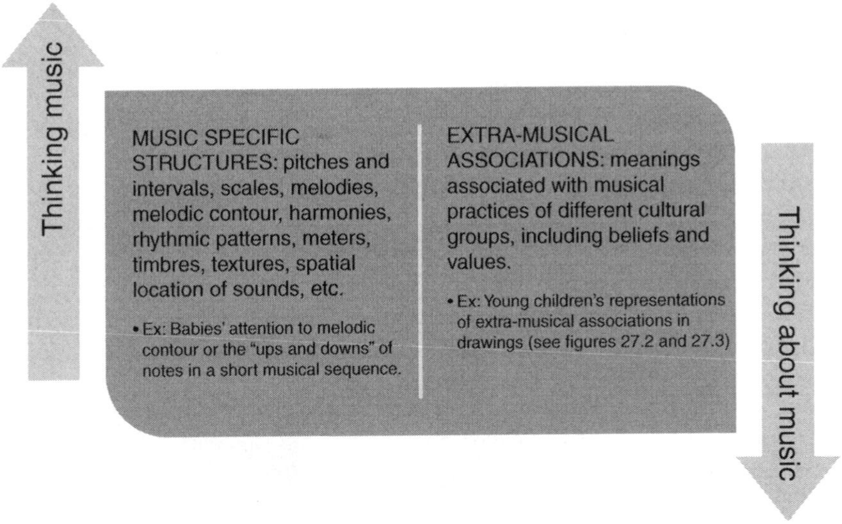

Thinking music

| MUSIC SPECIFIC STRUCTURES: pitches and intervals, scales, melodies, melodic contour, harmonies, rhythmic patterns, meters, timbres, textures, spatial location of sounds, etc.

• Ex: Babies' attention to melodic contour or the "ups and downs" of notes in a short musical sequence. | EXTRA-MUSICAL ASSOCIATIONS: meanings associated with musical practices of different cultural groups, including beliefs and values.

• Ex: Young children's representations of extra-musical associations in drawings (see figures 27.2 and 27.3) |

Thinking about music

Figure 27.1 Two categories of musical thought, adapted and expanded from Nettl (1996)

children's perception and cognition of musical elements like pitch and rhythm, or thinking music (Nettl, 1996). By contrast, early childhood education has helped us situate music within a wide array of learning contexts and their associated meanings, and disciplines such as cultural studies and ethnomusicology have contributed to our understanding of young children as social-musical actors (Young, 2013), fitting well with Nettl's (1996) concept of thinking about music. Underlying these disciplines are conceptions of children, childhood, development and, of course, musicality (Young, 2013). These, in turn, have helped to orient groups of people (researchers and practitioners), who work with young children. Important contributions from each discipline have sometimes been in conflict with one another, at times due to their underlying orientation (e.g. the 'global' versus the 'local' child), specific research methods (experimental, laboratory-based work versus more descriptive and naturalistic work), or even allegiance to particular theoretical frameworks and/or disciplines, thus becoming a political issue (for discussions see Young, 2005, 2013; Young and Ilari, 2012).

Taking an interdisciplinary perspective, this chapter discusses research on *musical thinking* – birth to 5. In order to move away from the problem of categorization of studies into specific disciplines, the chapter relies on Nettl's (1996) overarching categories of musical thought – thinking music and thinking about music – as a guiding framework. With Nettl's concepts in mind, young children's musical thought is categorized in terms of two recurrent and interconnected processes that appear in the literature: the perception and the production of music and its elements. Studies are then aggregated in relationship to certain abilities that have been identified as being eminently 'musical', such as the discrimination of sounds, responses to music and musical elements, singing and vocalizing, notating music, and exploring musical instruments.

Musical thinking as a perceptual and cognitive ability

The early years have been portrayed as an optimal time for children to experience music and develop their musical thinking in terms of specific elements such as pitch, rhythm and timbre, as well as to form musical memories (Gooding and Standley, 2011; Trainor and Corrigall, 2011). A wide range of systematic observation techniques (e.g. head turning tasks, visual habituation, electroencephalography) has been used to investigate musical perception, memory, and cognition in children under the age of 5. Contrary to previous beliefs, musical thinking is present very early in life, as demonstrated by some ingenious experiments with newborns and very young babies (e.g. Winkler *et al.*, 2009). Unsurprisingly, maturation plays an important role in shaping and fine-tuning children's musical thinking (see Trainor and Corrigall, 2011), yet it is not the only factor. Music is, after all, a social and cultural practice (Turino, 2006). Young children across the world are exposed to a wide range of musical experiences at home, in structured early childhood programs, in communities, or through the media (Young and Ilari, 2012). Coupled with maturation, motivation, cognitive, motor and social abilities, these early musical experiences are likely to shape how children think musically (e.g. Gerry *et al.*, 2010; Koelsch *et al.*, 2003; Putkinen *et al.*, 2013).

Much of what is known about young children's thinking in terms of specific musical elements and musical memory stems from research conducted with infants, where special laboratory techniques are particularly effective (Young, 2013). Likewise, researchers have examined musical thinking in preschool children aged 4 or 5, predominantly in nursery schools (Young and Ilari, 2012). There is a shortage of studies involving busy toddlers, who often become too distracted and uninterested in researcher-designed tasks, and still lack the language skills of preschoolers and older children to complete music perception and cognition tasks (Marshall and Hargreaves, 2007; Overy *et al.*, 2009; Young, 2013). Cross-sectional works tend to dominate, as longitudinal studies are still scarce (Ilari, 2002b). Furthermore, most studies have been conducted in North America and Western Europe, with only a handful originating in other parts of the world. It is important to mind these serious gaps in the literature when considering the development of musical thinking; more so, since it has been established that musical development as a whole is culturally bound and does not follow a linear pathway, but a spiral and recursive one (Bamberger, 2006).

Perceiving and responding to music and musical elements

Musical thinking begins in the womb. The auditory system is already functioning by the third trimester of pregnancy when unborn babies show changes in body movement and heart rate in response to a wide range of external sounds, including voices and music (Abrams *et al.*, 1998; Lecanuet, 1996; Parncutt, 2006). Aside from the ability to hear sounds in the womb, unborn babies appear to store some musical information in long-term memory. Traces of memory for music heard repeatedly in the womb have been reported in several studies conducted with neonates (e.g. Hepper, 1991; Wilkin, 1995), although their permanence remains elusive.

Babies come into the world not as blank states, but with some sophisticated auditory and musical abilities (Trehub, 2006), like the capacity to separate two streams of sounds or detect changes in pitch and rhythmic structures (Stefanics *et al.*, 2009; Winkler *et al.*, 2003, 2009). Also proficient in detecting contrasting rhythms, melodies, intervals, timbres, meters, textures and styles (e.g. Hannon and Johnson, 2005; Ilari and Sundara, 2009; Krumhansl and Jusczyk, 1990; Trainor *et al.*, 2002; Trainor and Zacharias, 1998; Trehub *et al.*, 1984), they are sensitive to amodal events, or, those experiences that require more than one modality, like when someone sings a song while making a happy face and clapping (Bahrick *et al.*, 2004). Additionally, young babies can perceive and respond to changes in the intensity of stimulation and affect of a caregiver, by paying attention to his or her vocal, facial and body cues (Malloch and Trevarthen, 2009; Trehub *et al.*, 2009).

Rhythm and pitch are often viewed as main dimensions of music, receiving much attention from researchers. Melodic contour is central to music perception in the early years (Trehub *et al.*, 1984). Between ages 1 and 4, children recognize familiar songs based on contour and rhythm. At around age 4 they begin to show some understanding of pitch-related concepts, like high and low (Campbell and Scott-Kassner, 1995), as well as changes in harmony, or the vertical structure of music (Corrigall and Trainor, 2010). In terms of rhythmic perception, while babies can readily detect that a rhythmic pattern has been changed (e.g. Hannon and Trehub, 2005), the ability to perceive that there is an underlying beat to a song and accurately clap along with it does not emerge until children are 2.5–3 years of age (Provasi and Bobin-Bègue, 2003), taking time to mature. By age 4, children can synchronize their clapping or drumming to the beat, even when the co-performer or soundtrack becomes faster or slower (Eerola *et al.*, 2006; Kirschner and Ilari, in press). As one would expect, both pitch and rhythmic abilities become more robust as children move towards the middle-childhood years (Gooding and Standley, 2011).

Children's thinking in terms of musical elements is not limited to tasks involving the detection of errors in sound sequences or tapping along with the music. The perception of timbre, for example, emerges very early on. Two-day-old babies recognize their mother's voices (DeCasper and Fifer, 1980), and by 6 months can tell apart the sounds of different instruments (Ilari and Polka, 2006). By contrast, the ability to perceive subtleties in musical styles, like telling the difference between a baroque and a classical piece, is arguably more difficult, and does not emerge before age 3 or so (Marshall and Hargreaves, 2007).

Importantly, the role of culture in children's perceptions of and responses to music should not be undermined. As children navigate through the early years, they tend to develop a more fine-grained ability to perceive musical structures found in the music of their culture. Enculturation effects have been found as early as in the second semester of postnatal life, when babies begin to show better discrimination skills towards scales and rhythms from their own cultural milieu (Hannon and Trainor, 2007; Hannon and Trehub, 2005; Lynch and Eilers, 1992; Soley and Hannon, 2010). Yet, when the responses of babies were compared with those of preschoolers in a test of melodic perception, the latter showed a stronger enculturation bias (Trehub *et al.*, 1997). That is, both culture and biology play a role in children's abilities to perceive and think in terms of musical elements (Nettl, 1996).

Musical thinking and children's musical productions

Another important source of evidence of musical thinking in the early years derives from studies on musical production, or the examination of young children as instrumental improvisers, singers and song makers, notators, and body movers (e.g. Barrett, 2006; Young, 2005). The repertoires that children sing, dance and improvise not only carry along with them important traces of enculturation, but also reflect the social construction and development of musical thinking (Campbell and Wiggins, 2013).

While it is probably less difficult to disentangle Nettl's (1996) musical thinking categories when examining studies on the perception of musical elements, this is arguably harder in the case of musical production. Although music perception and production are culturally bound, it is perhaps in the production of music that one can more easily trace values and beliefs of societies and groups. As Nettl (1996) contended, one of the main objects of ethnomusicological inquiry is the production of musical artifacts, in the form of songs, dances and ritual. However, the interest for children's musical productions has been particularly strong in education and music education, probably due to their applications in classrooms and other educational settings. Studies in these fields suggest that the production of musical elements and songs is directly influenced by the nature of children's engagement with the external world (Young and Ilari, 2012). Singing, playing instruments, moving and notating music may be spontaneous and child-initiated or in reaction/response to another individual (e.g. a sibling singing) or the environment (e.g. a dance movement seen on TV). Nevertheless, both forms of musical production reflect some remarkable thinking abilities of young children.

Vocal productions, invented and conventional songs

The human voice is a powerful tool in the production of sounds and musical structures, and crying is often described as the earliest vocal production that babies produce (Welch, 2006). Before babies can utter words or sentences, they communicate with their mothers or caregivers in the form of rhythmic and synchronized 'dialogs' that are musical in nature (Malloch and Trevarthen, 2009). These forms of early human communication called 'proto-conversations' are said to be at the heart of linguistic, social and musical development. Music and language overlap in early life, and the act of singing is rooted in these two forms of human communication through sounds (see Welch, 2006).

Singing is considered to be an important window into children's musical thinking. However, few studies to date have documented vocal productions prior to the age of 2, centering predominantly on preschoolers and school-aged children (Adachi and Trehub, 2012). Studies on children's singing have typically focused on two types of songs – invented and conventional – as they provide windows into some overlapping yet distinct musical and cognitive abilities (see Winner, 2006). Conventional songs are those learned in culture, like children's traditional songs, which exist in most (if not all) societies around the world. By contrast, invented songs are those created by children themselves, at their own time and pace (Barrett, 2006). Invented songs are often compared to children's drawings in the sense that both forms of expression take place in a somewhat spontaneous fashion during childhood, but tend to submerge at different times in development. In other words, most children the world over appear to invent songs in early childhood and draw in early and middle childhood, yet many abandon these practices as they develop and grow in culture.

Invented songs and conventional songs have their origins in early childhood. During the first year of life, a baby's vocal production is shaped through exposure and interaction with the acoustics of the mother's/family culture (Welch, 2006). Infants engage in vocal play early on and are responsive to expressive singing and speaking, although they are usually not able to imitate pitches (Gooding and Standley, 2011; Winner, 2006). Towards the end of the second semester of life, the vocalizations of babies become more undulated and full of continuous pitches and glissandi (e.g. vocal slides), also known as musical babble (Tafuri and Villa, 2002; Winner, 2006). Musical babble, which is also influenced by musical interactions in the home (Barrett, 2006), is often viewed as the genesis of invented and conventional songs. According to Winner (2006), during the early years, young children overcome three 'limitations' to allow most of them to sing at the level of an untrained adult by age 6. First, pitches become discrete at around 18 months. Babbled songs begin to sound somewhat closer to the sounds found in the Western musical system. Second, between ages 1.5–2.5 sung intervals become wider and more frequent, and third, melodies gradually gain rhythmic and tonal organization. Invented songs, then, emerge at around 18 months of age and tend to submerge by age 7 (Barrett, 2006).

Probably due to its relevance for education, the acquisition of conventional songs has received comparatively more attention than invented songs. Traces of familiar songs are perceived as early as in the second year of life, when children may be caught singing brief rhythmic and melodic patterns or fragments (Welch, 2006). At around age 3, children show an ability to sing in what Moog (1976) called 'pot-pourri' mode, by combining parts of a familiar tune with improvised sounds and melodies. Children in this age group also produce 'outline' songs (Hargreaves, 1996, cited in Welch, 2006), where the shape of a familiar melody is clear, although some or many individual notes may be completely out of place. These productions not only reflect children's understanding of tonal relationships, but provide compelling evidence of young children's ability to think music (Welch, 2006). Importantly, while children's abilities to sing conventional songs become more sophisticated in the course of development, the acquisition of conventional songs does not necessarily follow a linear path. As it happens with music perception, the production of song depends on a wide range of factors, including culture and individual abilities, experiences and interest (Welch, 2006).

Notating music and drawing

Researchers have also gained many insights into young children's musical thinking by examining their notations of pitch, rhythm and other musical structures (for reviews, see

Ilari, 2002a; Winner, 2006). Because babies and toddlers are still developing skills that will enable them to, for instance, hold a marker or crayon to scribble or follow verbal directions, most studies have been conducted with children older than 3 or 4. Preschool aged children show an ever-increasing understanding of musical elements through their notations of well-known songs like 'Twinkle twinkle little star' (Upitis, 1990). Yet, the task of representing music involves a great amount of personal investment on the part of preschoolers (aged 4–5), who often use what Bamberger (1982) called 'primitive enactive scribbling' in their attempts to represent a rhythmic pattern of a song. By age 5, children use abstract symbols and images to represent what they hear, be they specific musical elements or units of a musical phrase (Davidson and Scripp, 1988). As they continue to develop and grow, their notations of familiar songs become more sophisticated, with formal music training playing a major role (Ilari, 2002a; Winner, 2006).

How children move from invented notations to the conventions of western tonal music has been described through specific typologies, although most have centered on slightly older children and notations of familiar tunes (Barrett, 1997). One exception is a naturalistic inquiry in an Australian kindergarten, in which children's notations of their own songs were examined, following movement to music and exploration of sounds and instruments. Barrett (1997) found five categories associated with children's notations, namely: (1) exploration, as children attempted to make connections between sounds and symbolization; (2) pictorial representation of instruments without much evidence of connections with sounds themselves; (3) pictorial representation of instruments with some reference to sounds and musical elements; (4) symbolization of the act of producing a sound (e.g. playing an instrument) rather than the sound itself; and (5) symbolization using discrete symbols to notate their compositions. Barrett's (1997) typology is consistent with the suggestion that children's musical thinking gradually shifts with experience, becoming 'less context-bound and more concerned with musical ideas and concepts' (p. 11). That is, they gradually move from thinking about music to thinking music.

The examination of drawings to music has taken place to a lesser extent, perhaps due to young children's developing ability in this form of expression (see Winner, 2006), and to difficulties inherent in the interpretation of their products. Furthermore, asking children to freely 'draw the music that they hear' is arguably less focused than having them center on specific elements such as pitch or melody. Although early childhood educators often use this resource to enhance children's imagination and to create a relaxed environment, less has been said about their products as they relate to musical thinking. Yet the analysis of young children's drawings may also provide important hints on how they think music and think about music (see Figures 27.2 and 27.3).

Exploring and playing instruments

Musical instruments exert a fascination in young children, who are usually eager to explore them. Even if most children under the age of 5 cannot play instruments in the same level of expertise as their adult counterparts, playing instruments gives them a sense of control over their environment. Basic instruments, like small drums and

Figure 27.2   Drawing (I) of Guantamera (Cuban song) by Felipe, a 5-year-old from a kindergarten class in a Brazilian public school. In this drawing, the child represented two
musicians and a guitar, or 'what he heard' (in his own words). Here, the child was
clearly thinking music, and showed some recognition of musical instruments used
in the recording (i.e. guitar), and the number of voices/interpreters (i.e. 2 singers).

shakers, as well as different sound-makers, have been used extensively in early childhood music education programs worldwide, usually for the purposes of sound exploration and development of coordination and motor skills (Gooding and Standley,
2011). Given young children's developing sensorimotor skills, some still view their
engagement with musical instruments as mere exploration with little musical significance. Yet, others have argued that instrumental explorations in collective spaces are
way more meaningful, especially when studied as a multi-modal behavior that engages
body movement, structured play, and interpersonal interactions (Young, 2013).

   Young children's curiosity with musical instruments and sound-makers begins
quite early in life (see Gooding and Standley, 2011). This is probably a consensus, as
the practice of giving rattles and sound-makers to babies seems to exist in different
cultures across the globe. Babies, in turn, are fascinated by the sounds that they produce with these simple instruments. These experiences, however, remain unexplored,
more so since they tend to happen in difficult to reach spaces, such as the home
environment (Young, 2013). Observations of spontaneous play with musical

Figure 27.3 Drawing (II) of the same version of Guantamera (Cuban song) by Gabriel, a 5-year-old from the same class as Felipe (Figure 27.2). When he finished his drawing, the child explained that he represented two dancers holding hands. According to him, the music was 'happy' and the dancers loved each other. Here, the child appeared to be predominantly thinking about music, as evidenced by the emotional connotation attached to the song, along with a representation of gender.

instruments and sound-makers in daycares and nursery schools suggest that young children's music is more structured than previously thought. It is a form of embodied cognition that arises from the child's body, and from the characteristics of the instrument and the environment (Young, 2013). A smaller number of children under 5 also take lessons on how to play musical instruments following a more music-centered approach: that is, by being exposed to the norms and conventions of Western tonal music (e.g. Kooistra, 2012). The small number of studies conducted to date on early instrumental learning leads one to believe that such experiences have an impact on children's thinking, in and through music (Gerry *et al.*, 2010; Trainor *et al.*, 2009). Yet further research is still needed.

Concluding thoughts: towards an integrated view of musical thinking in the early years

In this chapter, I have surveyed the literature on young children's musical thinking, based on Nettl's (1996) distinction between thinking music and thinking about music, and on two interrelated processes: music perception and production. Some interesting issues emerged from this survey and are worth commenting. First, it became clear that there is a large disparity in the amount of studies concerning music perception and musical production, with the former receiving more attention than the latter. Furthermore, while most studies in music perception have been conducted in research laboratories using experimental/scientific designs, many studies in music production have been conducted in schoolyards, following a more descriptive, humanistic approach. This state of affairs not only reflects a tradition in research on human perception in general, but is also consistent with a greater interest (and funding opportunities) afforded in fields such as music psychology and the neurosciences, rather than music education (Young, 2013). Second, although movement associated to music has been highly valued in educational circles, it was remarkable to see that there were so few recent investigations on the topic. Apart from a handful of studies on rhythmic engagement and synchronization to the music in babies (Zentner and Eerola, 2010) and preschoolers (Eerola *et al.*, 2006; Kirschner and Tomasello, 2009), few recent studies have emerged, and this was particularly true for education and related fields. Third, it was interesting to see how children's musical thinking was related, to some extent, to both conceptions of development and culture dictated by different disciplines and theoretical orientations. Many humanists would probably find the concept of enculturation quite reductionist and in need of urgent revision in many psychological texts. Finally, it was clear that musical invention and creativity took on a secondary role in research, with most studies focusing on young children's perception, responses and productions of elements and music that conform to musical conventions. That is, there is a wide plethora of solid information, as well as some serious gaps that need to be urgently addressed.

Whether we interpret young children's abilities to think music and think about music as part of a process of becoming or as a separate form of thought (see Young, 2013; Young and Ilari, 2012), it is clear that young children are quite sophisticated musical thinkers. They come into the world with some remarkable abilities to perceive the subtleties in the musical world that surrounds them (Trehub, 2006), and engage with sounds and music in multiple ways as they develop and grow in culture. These multiple forms of engagement are also related to the types of experiences that are provided for them, ranging from the highly structured and formal to informal ones. Yet there is much that still needs to be uncovered. It is my hope that future research will become more interdisciplinary and integrated. By doing so, it will be possible to draw a clearer and fuller picture of musical thinking in the beginning of life. That is, it might be possible to predict how musical thinking might develop and design curricula that is consistent with the musical thinking and creative abilities of children like little Cecilia, Mitchell, and their preschool aged peers.

References

Abrams, R. M., Griffiths, S. K., Huang, X., Sain, J., Langford, G. and Gerhardt, K. J. (1998) Fetal music perception: The role of sound transmission. *Music Perception, 15*, 307–17.

Adachi, M. and Trehub, S. E. (2012) Musical lives of infants. In G. McPherson and G. Welch (eds) *The Oxford Handbook of Music Education* (pp. 229–47). New York: Oxford University Press.

Bahrick, L.E., Lickliter, R. and Flom, R. (2004) Intersensory redundancy guides the development of selective attention, perception and cognition in infancy. *Current Directions in Psychological Science*, *13*(3), 99–102.

Bamberger, J. (1982) Revisiting children's drawings of simple rhythms: A function for reflection in action. In S. Strauss and R. Stavy (eds) *U-Shaped Behavioral Growth* (pp. 191–226). New York: Academic Press.

Bamberger, J. (2006) What develops in musical development? In G. McPherson (ed.) *The Child as Musician: Musical Development from Conception to Adolescence* (pp. 690–2). Oxford: Oxford University Press.

Barrett, M. (1997) Invented notations: A view of young children's world. *Research Studies in Music Education*, *8*, 2–24.

Barrett, M. (2006) Inventing songs, inventing worlds: The 'genesis' of creative thought and activity in young children's lives. *International Journal of Early Years Education*, *14*(3), 201–20.

Campbell, P. S. and Scott-Kassner, C. (1995) *Music in Childhood*. New York: Schirmer.

Campbell, P. S. and Wiggins, T. (eds) (2013) *The Oxford Handbook of Children's Musical Cultures*. New York: Oxford University Press.

Corrigall, K. A. and Trainor, L. J. (2010) Musical enculturation in preschool children: Acquisition of key and harmonic structure. *Music Perception*, *28*(2), 195–200.

Davidson, L. and Scripp, L. (1988) Young children's musical representations: Windows on music cognition. In J. Sloboda (ed.) *Generative Processes in Music* (pp. 195–230). Oxford, England: Oxford University Press.

DeCasper, A. J. and Fifer, W. P. (1980) Of human bonding: Newborns prefer their mother's voices. *Science*, *208*, 1174–6.

Eerola, T., Luck, G. and Toiviainen, P. (2006) An investigation of preschoolers' corporeal synchronization with music. In M. Baroni, A. R. Addessi, R. Caterina and M. Costa (eds) *Proceedings of the 9th International Conference on Music Perception and Cognition* (pp. 472–6). Bologna, Italy: ICMPC-ESCOM.

Gerry, D., Faux, A. and Trainor, L. J. (2010) Effects of Kindermusik training on infants' rhythmic enculturation. *Developmental Science*, *13*, 545–51.

Gooding, L. and Standley, J. M. (2011) Musical development and learning characteristics of students: A compilation of key points from the research literature organized by age. *Update: Applications of Research in Music Education*, *30*(1), 32–45.

Hannon, E. E. and Johnson, S. P. (2005) Infants use meter to categorize rhythms and melodies: Implications for musical structure learning. *Cognitive Psychology*, *50*, 354–77.

Hannon, E. E. and Trainor, L. J. (2007) Music acquisition: Effects of enculturation and formal training on development. *Trends in Cognitive Sciences*, *11*, 466–72.

Hannon, E. E. and Trehub, S. E. (2005) Tuning in to musical rhythms: Infants learn more readily than adults. *PNAS*, *102*(35), 12639–43.

Hepper, P. G. (1991) An examination of fetal learning before and after birth. *Irish Journal of Psychology*, *12*, 95–107.

Ilari, B. (2002a) Invented representations of a song as measures of music cognition. *Update: Applications of Research in Music Education*, *20*(2), 12–16.

Ilari, B. (2002b) Music perception and cognition in the first year of life. *Early Child Development and Care*, *172*(3), 311–22.

Ilari, B. (2005) On musical parenting of young children: Musical beliefs and behaviors of mothers and infants. *Early Child Development and Care*, *175*(7–8), 647–70.

Ilari, B. and Polka, L. (2006) Music cognition in early infancy: Infants' preferences and long-term memory for Ravel. *International Journal of Music Education – Research*, *24*(1), 7–21.

Ilari, B. and Sundara, M. (2009) Musical listening preferences in early life: Infant responses to accompanied versus unaccompanied singing. *Journal of Research in Music Education*, *56*, 357–69.

Kirschner, S. and Ilari, B. (in press) Joint drumming in Brazilian and German preschool children: Cultural differences in rhythmic entrainment but no prosocial effects. *Journal of Cross-Cultural Psychology*.

Kirschner, S. and Tomasello, M. (2009) Joint drumming: Social context facilitates synchronization in preschool children. *Journal of Experimental Child Psychology*, *102*, 299–314.

Koelsch, S., Grossmann, T., Gunter, T. C., Hahne, A., Schroger, E. and Friederici, A. D. (2003) Children processing music: Electric brain responses reveal musical competence and gender differences. *Journal of Cognitive Neuroscience*, *20*, 1940–51.

Kooistra, L. (2012) Piano exploration for young children in an informal setting. *Min Ad*, *10*, 47–56.

Krumhansl, C. L. and Jusczyk, P. W. (1990) Infants' perception of phrase structure in music. *Psychological Science*, *1*, 70–3.

Lecanuet, J. P. (1996) Prenatal auditory experience. In I. Deliege and J. A. Sloboda (eds) *Musical Beginnings: Origins and Development of Musical Competence* (pp. 3–36). Oxford: Oxford University Press.

Lynch, M. P. and Eilers, R. E. (1992) A study of perceptual development for musical tuning. *Perception and Psychophysics*, *52*, 599–608.

Malloch, S. and Trevarthen, C. (2009) (eds) *Communicative Musicality*. Oxford: Oxford University Press.

Marshall, N. and Hargreaves, D. J. (2007) Musical style discrimination in the early years. *Journal of Early Childhood Research*, *5*, 32–46.

Moog, H. (1976) *The Musical Experience of the Preschool Child*. London: Schott.

Nettl, B. (1996) Ideas about music and musical thought. *Journal of Aesthetic Education*, *30*(2), 173–87.

Overy, K. and Molnar-Szakacs, I. (2009) Being together in time: Musical experience and the mirror neuron system. *Music Perception*, *26*, 489–504. doi: 10.1525/MP.2009.26.5.489.

Parncutt, R. (2006) Prenatal development. In G. McPherson (ed.) *The Child as Musician: A Handbook of Musical Development* (pp. 1–32). Oxford: Oxford University Press.

Provasi, J. and Bobin-Bègue, A. (2003) Spontaneous motor tempo and rhythmical synchronisation in 2½- and 4-year-old children. *International Journal of Behavioral Development*, *27*, 220–31.

Putkinen, V., Tervaniemi, M. and Huotilainen, M. (2013) Informal musical activities are linked to auditory discrimination and attention in 2–3-year-old children: An event-related potential study. *European Journal of Neuroscience*, *37*, 654–61.

Soley, G. and Hannon, E. E. (2010) Infants prefer the musical meter of their own culture: A cross-cultural comparison. *Developmental Psychology*, *46*, 286–92.

Stadler Elmer, S. (2011) Human singing: Towards a developmental theory. *Psychology: Music, Mind, and Brain*, *21*(1–2), 13–30.

Stefanics, G., Haden, G. P., Sziller, I., Balasz, A., Becke, A. and Winkler, I. (2009) Newborn infants process pitch intervals. *Clinical Neurophysiology*, *120*(2), 304–8. doi: 10.1016/j.clinph.2008.11.020.

Tafuri, J. and Villa, D. (2002) Musical elements in the vocalizations of infants aged 2–8 months. *British Journal of Music Education*, *19*(1), 73–88.

Trainor, L. J. and Corrigall, K. A. (2010) Music acquisition and effects of musical experience. In M. R. Jones *et al.* (eds) *Music Perception*. Springer Handbook of Auditory Research 36.

Trainor, L. J. and Heinmiller, B. M. (1998) The development of evaluative responses to music: Infants prefer to listen to consonance over dissonance. *Infant Behavior and Development*, *21*(1), 77–88.

Trainor, L. J. and Trehub, S. E. (1992) A comparison of infants' and adults' sensitivity to Western musical structure. *Journal of Experimental Psychology: Human Perception and Performance*, *18*(2), 392–402.

Trainor, L. J. and Zacharias, C. A. (1998) Infants prefer higher-pitched singing. *Infant Behavior and Development*, *21*(4), 799–806.

Trainor, L. J., Tsang, C. D. and Cheung, V. H. W. (2002) Preference for consonance in 2- and 4-month-old infants. *Music Perception*, *20*, 187–194.

Trainor, L. J., Wu, L. and Tsang, C. D. (2004) Long-term memory for music: Infants remember tempo and timbre. *Developmental Science*, *7*, 289–96.

Trainor, L. J., Shahin, A. J., Roberts, L. E. (2009) Understanding the benefits of musical training: Effects on oscillatory brain activity. *PNAS, 1169*, 133–42.

Trehub, S. E. (2006) Infants as musical connoisseurs. In G. McPherson (ed.) *The Child as Musician: A Handbook of Musical Development* (pp. 33–50). Oxford: Oxford University Press.

Trehub, S. E., Bull, D. and Thorpe, L. A. (1984) Infants' perception of melodies: The role of melodic contour. *Child Development, 55*, 821–30.

Trehub, S. E., Cohen, A. J., Thorpe, L. A. and Morrongiello, B. A. (1986) Development of the perception of musical relations: Semitone and diatonic structure. *Journal of Experimental Psychology: Human Perception and Performance, 12*, 295–301.

Trehub, S. E., Unyk, A. M., Kamenetsky, S. B., Hill, D. S., Trainor, L. J., Henderson, J. L. and Saraza, M. (1997) Mothers' and fathers' singing to infants. *Developmental Psychology, 33*, 500–7.

Trehub, S. E., Plantinga, J. and Brcic, J. (2009) Infants detect cross-modal cues to identity in speech and singing. *Annals of the New York Academy of Sciences, 1169*, 508–11.

Turino, T. (2006) *Music as Social Life*. Urbana: University of Illinois Press.

Upitis, R. (1990) Children's invented notations of familiar and unfamiliar melodies. *Psychomusicology, 9*(2), 89–106.

Welch, G. (2006) Singing and vocal development. In G. McPherson (ed.) *The Child as Musician: A Handbook of Musical Development* (pp. 311–30). Oxford: Oxford University Press.

Werner, L. A. and Vandenbos, G. R. (1993) Developmental psychoacoustics: What infants and young children hear. *Hospital and Community Psychiatry, 44*(8), 624–6.

Wilkin, P. (1995) A comparison of fetal and newborn responses to music and sound stimuli with and without daily exposure to a specific piece of music. *Bulletin of the Council for Research in Music Education, 27*, 163–69.

Winkler, I., Kushnerenko, E., Horvath, J., Ceponiene, R., Fellman, V., Huotilainen, M., Naatanen, R. and Sussman, E. (2003) Infants can organize their auditory world. *PNAS, 100*(2), 11812–15.

Winkler, I., Háden, G. P., Ladinig, O., Sziller, I. and Honing, H. (2009) Newborn infants detect the beat in music. *PNAS, 106*, 2468–71.

Winner, E. (2006) Development in the arts: Music and drawing. In R. Siegler and D. Kuhn (eds) *Handbook of Child Psychology, Vol. 2: Cognitive Language and Perceptual Development* (pp. 859–904). New York: Wiley.

Young, S. (2005) Changing tune: Reconceptualizing music with under three year olds. *International Journal of Early Years Education, 13*(3), 289–303.

Young, S. (2013) Musical childhoods. In O. N. Saracho and B. Spodek (eds) *Handbook of Research on the Education of Young Children* (pp. 250–64). New York and London: Routledge.

Young, S. and Ilari, B. (2012) Musical participation from babyhood to three: Towards a global perspective (pp. 279–95). In G. McPherson and G. Welch (eds) *Oxford Handbook of Music Education*. Oxford: Oxford University Press.

Zenter, M. and Eerola, T. (2010) Rhythmic engagement with music in infancy. *PNAS*. doi: 10.1073/pnas.100012110.

28

DEVELOPING YOUNG CHILDREN'S MATHEMATICAL THINKING AND UNDERSTANDING

Douglas H. Clements and Julie Sarama

Introduction

In contrast to the view that mathematics for very young children is developmentally inappropriate and that only simple number tasks are appropriate for the primary grades (see Balfanz, 1999; Hughes, 1986; Sun Lee and Ginsburg, 2009), research has shown that young children can think and understand mathematics content that is surprisingly broad and deep. Recent research and developmental work has suggested that *learning trajectories* can help early childhood educators respect children's developmental processes and constraints, and their potential for thinking about and understanding mathematical ideas (Bobis *et al.*, 2005; Clarke, 2008; Clements and Sarama, 2009; Sarama and Clements, 2009b; Wright, 2003). In this chapter we briefly discuss young children's natural mathematical thinking. Then, we give two concrete examples of learning trajectories, illustrating how they can be used to enhance teaching and learning.

Young children's natural mathematical thinking

It seems probable that little is gained by using any of the child's time for arithmetic before grade 2, though there are many arithmetic facts that he [sic] can learn in grade 1.

(Thorndike, 1922, p. 198)

Children have their own preschool arithmetic, which only myopic psychologists could ignore.

(Vygotsky, 1935/1978, p. 84)

For more than 100 years, views of young children's mathematics have differed widely, as these contradictory quotes from two psychologists show. Across that time, many have reported observations of children enjoying pre-mathematical activities. However, others have expressed fears of the inappropriateness of mathematics for young children, although these opinions are based on broad social theories or trends, not observation (Balfanz, 1999). The institutionalization of early childhood education often extinguished promising mathematical movements.

Consider Edward Thorndike, quoted above. He wished to emphasize health, replaced the first gift of Froebel's gifts (manipulatives, which were small spheres) with a toothbrush and the first mathematical occupation with 'sleep' (Brosterman, 1997).

Similarly, some argue children should be playing with building blocks, rather than learning mathematics. But the original inventor, Caroline Pratt (1948), created today's unit blocks to teach mathematics! She tells of children making enough room for a horse to fit inside a stable. The teacher told Diana that she could have the horse when she had made a stable for it. Diana and Elizabeth began to build a small construction, but the horse did not fit. Diana had made a large stable with a low roof. After several unsuccessful attempts to get the horse in, she removed the roof, added blocks to the walls to make the roof higher, and replaced the roof. She then tried to put into words what she had done. 'Roof too small.' The teacher gave her new words, 'high' and 'low', and she gave a new explanation to the other children. Just building with blocks, children form important ideas. Teachers such as Diana's help children explicate and further develop these intuitive ideas by discussing them, giving language to their actions.

Like Pratt, we believe that 'doing mathematics' is natural and appropriate for children of all ages – if engendered and supported well. First, to be educative (Dewey, 1938/1997), mathematical experiences should involve mathematical processes or practices such as problem-solving, reasoning, communicating, modeling, and connecting (discussion of these in depth is beyond the scope of this chapter, but the references contain many elaborations and examples). That is, every educative experience should involve helping children mathematize (De Lange, 1987; Kaartinen and Kumpulainen, 2012) their world: representing and elaborating their world mathematically – creating models of everyday situations with mathematical *objects*, such as numbers and shapes; with mathematical actions, such as counting or transforming shapes; and with *structural relationships*, such as 'one more' or 'equal length' – and using those models to solve problems. Second, to avoid being miseducative (Dewey, 1938/1997), experiences should not include inappropriate and harmful routines, such as flash cards and timed tests to promote 'memorization' of basic facts (especially before thinking strategies are well established) (Henry and Brown, 2008) or dull calendar exercises in which one child performs routine actions while others passively wait for it to be over (National Research Council, 2009, note this are miseducative for self-regulation as well as mathematics competencies). Third, to be educative, experiences should be challenging but achievable, generative of future learning, and consistent with young children's 'natural' ways of thinking and learning (Clements *et al.*, 2004; Trundley, 2008). We believe research-based *learning trajectories* are useful for ensuring that experiences are maximally educative.

Learning trajectories: paths for successful learning

Why learning trajectories?

Children generally follow certain developmental paths in learning mathematics. When teachers understand the progression of levels of thinking along these paths, and sequence and individualize activities based on them, they can build effective mathematics learning environments. Research has suggested learning trajectories are effective in this way (Clements and Sarama, in press; Sarama and Clements, 2009b). Similarly, several recent efforts have based their reports on learning trajectories (e.g. Horne and Rowley, 2001; Nes, 2009). The National Research Council report on early mathematics (2009) is subtitled, 'Learning paths toward excellence and equity'. The Early Numeracy Research Project (ENRP) in Victoria, Australia was built around using 'growth points' to inform planning and teaching (e.g. Clarke, 2008; Horne and Rowley, 2001; Perry *et al.*, 2008). The authors of the *Common Core* (CCSSO/NGA, 2010) started by writing learning trajectories for each major topic. These were used to determine what the sequence would be and were 'cut' into grade-level specific standards. Similar approaches are used in the New Zealand Numeracy Development Project, the Victorian Early Numeracy Research Project and the Count Me In Too program in New South Wales, Australia (Bobis *et al.*, 2005) as well as Mathematics Recovery (Wright, 2003).

Each learning trajectory as we define it has three parts: a goal, a developmental progression, and instructional activities (Sarama and Clements, 2009b). To develop a certain mathematical competence (the goal), children construct each level of thinking in turn (the developmental progression), aided by tasks and teaching (instructional activities) designed to build the mental actions-on-objects that enable thinking at each higher level (Clements and Sarama, in press; Sarama and Clements, 2009b).

As an initial example, take the goal of measuring length, a common goal for mathematics (e.g. MacDonald *et al.*, 2012), but one that challenges children (e.g. in the iteration of standard units, Nunes *et al.*, 2009). A typical goal is for children to learn, by the end of second grade (ages 7–8 years), to measure the length of objects using appropriate tools, relate the size of the unit to the number of units, determine how much longer one object is than another, and so forth. That is the long-range goal.

Children develop through a series of levels of thinking as they achieve that goal; that is, as they learn the ideas and skills that constitute accurate and meaningful measurement of length. At each level, children can solve a new type of problem. These levels form a *developmental progression* (cf. MacDonald and Lowrie, 2011; McDonough and Sullivan, 2011). The second column in Figure 28.1 describes several levels of thinking in the counting learning trajectory. This includes the name of each level, a description, and a brief concrete example of a behavior indicative of that level of thinking (the first, or leftmost, column is the *approximate* age at which children achieve each level of thinking. These are present-day averages and *not* the goal – with good education; children often develop these levels earlier).

The right-most column in Figure 28.1 provides examples of instructional tasks that are designed to develop each of the levels of thinking. That is, educators can use

Age	Developmental progression	Instructional tasks
3	**Length quantity recognizer** Identifies length/distance as attribute. May understand length as an absolute descriptor (e.g. all adults are tall), but not as a comparative (e.g. one person is taller than another). 'I'm tall, see?'	Teachers and other caregivers listen for and extend conversations about things that are 'long,' 'tall,' 'high,' and so forth.
4	**Length direct comparer** Physically aligns two objects to determine which is longer or if they are the same length. Stands two sticks up next to each other on a table and says, 'This one's bigger.'	In 'Compare Lengths,' teachers encourage children to compare lengths throughout the day, such as the lengths of block towers or roads, heights of furniture, and so forth. In 'As Long As My Arm,' children cut a ribbon the length of their arms and find things in the classroom that are the same length. In 'Comparisons,' children simply click on the object that is longer (or wider, etc.) In 'Line Up By Height,' children order themselves (with teacher's assistance) by height in groups of five during transitions.
5	**Indirect length comparer** Compares the length of two objects by representing them with a third object. Compares length of two objects with a piece of string. May be able to measure with a ruler, but often lacks understanding or skill (e.g. ignores starting point) Measures two objects with a ruler to check if they are the same length, but does not accurately set the 'zero point' for one of the items.	Children solve everyday tasks that require indirect comparison, such as whether a doorway is wide enough for a table to go through. Children often *cover* the objects to be compared, so that indirect comparison is actually not possible. Give them a task with objects such as felt strips so that, if they cover them with the third object such as a (wider) strip of paper (and therefore have to visually guess), they can be encouraged to then directly compare them. If they are not correct, ask them how they could have used the paper to better compare. Model laying it next to the objects if necessary. In 'Deep Sea Compare,' children move the coral to compare the lengths of two fish, then click on the longer fish.
6	**End-to-end length measurer** Lays units end-to-end. May not recognize the need for equal-length units. The ability to apply resulting measures to comparison situations develops later in this level. Lays 9 inch cubes in a line beside a book to measure how long it is.	'Length Riddles' asks questions such as, 'You write with me and I am 7 cubes long. What am I?' *Workin' on the Railroad.* In this computer activity, children lay units end to end to repair a railroad bridge.

Age	Developmental progression	Instructional tasks
		Measure with physical or drawn units. Focus on long, thin units such as toothpicks cut to 1 inch sections. Explicit emphasis should be given to the *linear nature* of the unit. That is, children should learn that when measuring with, say, centimeter cubes, it is the *length of one edge* that is the *linear* unit – not the area of a face or volume of the cube.
7	**Length unit relater and repeater** Measures by repeated use of a unit. Relates size and number of units explicitly. 'If you measure with centimeters instead of inches, you'll need more of them, because each one is smaller.' Can add up two lengths to obtain the length of a whole. 'This is 5 long and this one is 3 long, so they are 8 long together.' Iterates a single unit to measure. Uses rulers with minimal guidance. Measures a book's length accurately with a ruler.	Repeat 'Length Riddles' (see above) but provide fewer cues (e.g. only the length) and only one unit per child so they have to iterate (repeatedly 'lay down') a single unit to measure. 'Mr. Mixup's Measuring Mess' can be used at several levels, adapted for the levels before and after this one. For example, have the puppet leave gaps between units used to measure an object (for the End-to-End Length Measurer level, gaps are between multiple units, for this level, gaps would be between iterations of one unit). Other errors include overlapping units and not aligning at the starting point. 'Draw a line.' Use line-drawing activities to emphasize how you start at the 0 (zero point) and discuss how, to measure objects, you have to align the object to that point. Similarly, explicitly discuss what the intervals and the number represent, connecting these to end-to-end length measuring with physical units. 'Different Units.' Confront children with measurements using different units and discuss how many of each unit will fill a linear space. Help children make an explicit statement that the longer the unit the fewer are needed.
7-8	**Length measurer** Measures, knowing need for identical units, relationship between different units, partitions of unit, zero point on rulers, and accumulation of distance. Begins to estimate. 'I used a meter stick three times, then there was a little left over. So, I lined it up from 0 and found 14 centimeters. So, it's 3 meters, 14 centimeters in all.'	Children should be able to use a physical unit and a ruler to measure line segments and objects that require both an iteration and subdivision of the unit. In learning to subdivide units, children may fold a unit in halves, mark the fold as a half, and then continue to do so, to build fourths and eighths. Children create units of units, such as a 'footstrip' consisting traces of their feet glued to a roll of adding-machine tape. They measure in different-sized units (e.g. 15 paces or 3 footstrips each of which has five paces) and accurately relate these units. They also discuss how to deal with leftover space, to count it as a whole unit or as part of a unit.

Figure 28.1   Learning trajectory for length measurements (adapted from Clements and Sarama, in press)

these types of tasks to promote children's growth from the previous level. More complete learning trajectories provide multiple illustrations of tasks for each level (e.g. see Clements and Sarama, in press); however, keep in mind that these illustrations are simply examples – many approaches are possible and children's cultures and individual characteristics also need consideration.

Note the consistency between the standards for the grades preceding grade 2. The kindergarten standards include comparing the lengths of two objects directly (by comparing them with each other). This is Figure 28.1's 'Length direct compare' level. The first grade Common Core standards include comparing the lengths of two objects indirectly by using a third object – Figure 28.1's 'Indirect length compare' level and the ability to 'Express the length of an object as a whole number of length units, by laying multiple copies of a shorter object (the length unit) end to end; understand that the length measurement of an object is the number of same-size length units that span it with no gaps or overlaps', precisely, the 'End-to-end length measurer' level of Figure 28.1. Finally, by the end of second grade, we reach the 'Length unit relater and repeater' and 'Length measurer' levels that are consistent with the Grade 2 Common Core goals previously described.

Teaching using learning trajectories

Learning trajectories' instructional tasks might offer a 'sketch' of a curriculum – a sequence of activities. However, research suggests that they can and should offer more. They should support teachers' use of *formative assessment* – the ongoing monitoring of student learning to inform and guide instruction. Research indicates that formative assessment is an effective teaching strategy (Clarke, 2008; Clarke *et al.*, 2002; National Mathematics Advisory Panel, 2008; Shepard, 2005). However, the strategy is useless for teachers unless they can accurately assess 'where students are' in learning a mathematical topic *and* know how to support them in learning the following level of thinking. The goal of learning trajectories help define the mathematical content that teachers have to teach and so have to understand well themselves. The developmental progressions give teachers a tool to understand the levels of thinking at which their students are operating, along with the *next* level of thinking that each student should learn. Then, matched instructional tasks provide guidance as to the type of educational activity to support that learning and help explain why those activities would be particularly effective. Such knowledge helps teachers be more effective professionals. Next, we look at ways to put this all into practice.

The key to the use of formative assessment is knowing what standards or goals one is trying to reach, where the students are starting, and how to help them move from there to the goal. Notice that these three formative assessment questions align with the three components of learning trajectories, as shown in Figure 28.2.

Our second example is from the learning trajectory of early counting-based addition and subtraction. A study of textbooks in California showed the importance of teaching core concepts and meaningful strategies for arithmetic, not simply 'facts' (Henry and Brown, 2008). The learning trajectory, therefore, should include core knowledge, strategies, and skills.

Note that the following is one of two approaches to addition and subtraction involving counting-based strategies. A critical complement to these is that of conceptual subitizing and related visually and structurally based part–whole approaches (see examples in the patterns and structure curriculum, Mulligan *et al.*, 2006, and chapter 6 in both; Sarama and Clements, 2009b). Both begin in the earliest years, not represented here (see references).

Formative assessment questions	Learning trajectories' components
1. Where are you trying to go?	*The goal* – Describes the mathematical concepts, structures, and skills
2. Where are you now?	*The developmental progression* – Helps determine how the children are thinking now and on the 'next step.'
3. How can you get there?	*The instructional activities* – Provide tasks linked to each level of the developmental progression that are designed to engender the kind of thinking that will form the next level. Suggests feedback for specific errors.

Figure 28.2   Relationships between the major questions of formative assessment and the components of a learning trajectory

1 The goal. Mathematically, whole-number addition can be viewed as an extension of counting (National Research Council, 2009). The sum 7 + 5 is the whole number that results from counting up 5 numbers starting at 7; that is, 7, 8, 9, 10, 11, 12. As tedious as it would be to solve this way, the sum 194 + 746 is the number resulting from counting up 746 numbers starting at 194.

As they move through the learning trajectory, students learn to solve increasingly difficult problems. Some problems are more difficult simply because they involve larger numbers, of course. Unfortunately, such difficulties are often greater than they should be because too many curricula and teachers provide far more practice on problems with smaller digits and neglect the larger single-digit numbers (Hamann and Ashcraft, 1986). Teachers should ensure students receive more balanced experiences.

Beyond the size of the number, however, it is the *type*, or *structure* of the word problem that determines its difficulty. Type depends on the *situation* and the *unknown*. The situation can be a 'Join' problem (have 2 apples, got 4 more) or 'Separate' problem (had 2 apples, ate 1); a 'Part-part-whole' problem (3 are girls and 4 are boys – no action is suggested); or a 'Compare' problem (John has 4, Emily has 6). For each of these categories, there are three quantities that play different roles in the problem, any one of which could be the unknown. In some cases, such as the unknown parts of 'Part-part-whole' problems, there is no real difference between the roles, so this does not affect the difficulty of the problem. In others, such as the 'result unknown', 'change unknown' (had 2, got some more, now has 6), or 'start unknown' (had some, got 4 more, now has 6) of 'Join' problems, the differences in difficulty are large. 'Result unknown' problems are easy, 'change unknown' problems are moderately difficult, and 'start unknown' problems are the most difficult. This is due in large part to the increasing difficulty children have in modeling, or 'act outing', each type. In summary, a main *goal* of this addition and subtraction learning trajectory is that children learn to solve arithmetic problems of different types using counting strategies.

2 The developmental progression. A few selected levels for this component of learning trajectories are shown in the second column in Figure 28.3. Children

Age	Developmental progression	Instructional tasks
4–5	**Find Result** Finds sums for joining (you had 3 apples and get 3 more, how many do you have in all?) and part-part-whole (there are 6 girls and 5 boys on the playground, how many children were there in all?) problems *by direct modeling, counting-all, with objects.* Asked, 'You have 2 red balls and 3 blue balls. How many in all?' Counts out 2 red, then counts out 3 blue, then counts all 5. Solves take-away problems by separating with objects. Asked, 'You have 5 balls and give 2 to Tom. How many do you have left?' Counts out 5 balls, then takes away 2, and then counts remaining 3.	*Word problems.* Children solving all the above problem types using manipulatives or their fingers to represent objects. *For Separate, result unknown (take-away),* 'You have 5 balls and give 2 to Tom. How many do you have left?' Children might count out 5 balls, then take away 2, and then count the remaining 3. For *Part-part-whole, whole unknown* problems, they might solve 'You have 2 red balls and 3 blue balls. How many in all?' *Dinosaur Shop 3.* Customers at the shop asks students to combine their two orders and add the contents of two boxes of toy dinosaurs (number frames) and click a target numeral that represents the sum. *Off the Tree.* Students add two amounts of dots to identify their total number value, and then move forward a corresponding number of spaces on a game board, which is now marked with numerals.
5–6	**Counting strategies** Finds sums for joining (you had 8 apples and get 3 more…) and part-part-whole (6 girls and 5 boys…) problems with finger patterns and/or by counting on. *Counting-on.* 'How much is 4 and 3 more?' 'Fourrrr…five, six, seven [uses rhythmic or finger pattern to keep track]. Seven!' *Counting-up-to* May solve missing addend (3 + _ = 7) or compare problems by counting up; e.g. counts '4, 5, 6, 7' while putting up fingers; and then counts or recognizes the 4 fingers raised. Asked, 'You have 6 balls. How many more would you need to have 8?' says, 'Six, seven [puts up first finger], eight [puts up second finger]. Two!'	*How Many Now?* Have the children count objects as you place them in a box. Ask, 'How many are in the box now?' Add one, repeating the question, then check the children's responses by counting all the objects. Repeat, checking occasionally. When children are ready, sometimes add two, and eventually more, objects. Variations: Place coins in a coffee can. Declare that a given number of objects are in the can. Then have the children close their eyes and count on by listening as additional objects are dropped in. *Join Result Unknown* and *Part-Part-Whole, Whole Unknown.* 'How much is 4 and 3 more?' *Bright Idea.* Students are given a numeral and a frame with dots. They count on from this numeral to identify the total amount, and then move forward a corresponding number of spaces. *Easy as Pie:* Students add two numerals to find a total number, and then move forward a corresponding number of spaces on a game board.
6–7	**Deriver** Uses flexible strategies and derived combinations (e.g. '7 + 7 is 14, so 7 + 8 is 15) to solve all types of problems. Can simultaneously think of 3 numbers within a sum, and can move part of a number to another, aware of the increase in one and the decrease in another. Asked, 'What's 7 plus 8?' thinks: 7 + 8 → 7 + [7 + 1] → [7 + 7] + 1 = 14 + 1 = 15. Using BAMT (see text), thinks, 8 + 2 = 10, so separate 7 into 2 and 5, add 2 and 8 to make 10, then add 5 more, 15.	*All types* of single-digit problems. *BAMT. See text.* *Tic-Tac-Total.* Draw a tic-tac-toe board and write the numbers 1 to 10. Players take turn crossing out one of the numbers and writing it in the board. Whoever makes 15 first wins (Kamii, 1985). *21.* Play cards, where Ace is worth either 1 or 11 and 2 to 10 are worth their values. Dealer gives everyone 2 cards, including herself. On each round, each player, if sum is less than 21, can request another card, or 'hold.' If any new card makes the sum more than 21, the player is out. Continue until everyone 'holds.' The player whose sum is closest to 21 wins. Variations: Play to 15 at first.

Figure 28.3 Partial learning trajectory for addition and subtraction (emphasizing counting strategies) (adapted from Clements and Sarama, in press)

develop increasingly sophisticated counting strategies to solve increasingly difficult problem types. For example, most initially use a counting-all procedure. At the 'Find result' level, given a problem of 7 + 2, such children count out objects to form a set of 7 items, then count out 2 more items, and finally count all those and say 'nine.' Children use such counting methods to solve story situations if they understand the language in the story.

After children develop such methods, they eventually curtail them. Often independently, children as young as 4 or 5 years invent 'counting on', solving the previous problem by counting, 'Seven ... 8, 9. 9!' The elongated pronunciation may be substituting for counting the initial set one-by-one. It is *as if* they counted a set of 7 items.

Children then move to the *counting-on-from-larger* strategy, which is preferred by most children once they invent it. Problems such as 4 + 25, where the most 'counting on' work is saved by reversing the problem, often prompt children to start counting with the 25. Counting-on when increasing collections and the corresponding counting-back-from when decreasing collections are important numerical strategies for students to learn. However, they are only beginning strategies. In the case where the amount of increase is unknown, children use counting-up-to to find the unknown amount. If 6 items are increased so that there are now 9 items, children may find the amount of increase by counting and keeping track of the number of counts, as in 'Siiiix ... 7, 8, 9. 3!' And if 9 items are decreased so that 6 remain, children may count from 9 down to 6 to find the unknown decrease, as follows: 'Nine ... 8, 7, 6. 3!' However, counting backwards, especially more than two or three counts, is difficult for most children unless they have consistent instruction. Instead, children might learn *counting-up-to* the total to solve a subtraction situation. For example, 'I took away 6 from those 9, so 7, 8, 9 (raising a finger with each count) – that's 3 more left in the 9.' Students then learn to incorporate place value and other ideas.

3 The instructional tasks. As stated, instructional tasks are not the only way to guide children to achieve the levels of thinking embedded within the learning trajectories. However, those in the right-most column of Figure 28.3 are (simply) examples of the type of instructional activity that helps promote thinking at the subsequent level. Thus, teachers implement, adapt, or use them as a template to gauge the appropriateness and expected effectiveness of other lessons, including those in published curricula. Further, these tasks are often useful as problems for children to solve (via guided discovery), but teachers must make critical decisions concerning pedagogical strategies (Anthony and Walshaw, 2009), such as whether these problems might be posed in a play context (e.g. Hirsh-Pasek and Golinkoff, 2008; Lee, 2010; Sarama and Clements, 2009a; van Oers, 2003, 2010), presented as small group activities (Clarke *et al.*, 2002; Clements and Sarama, 2007, 2013; Griffin, 2004; Griffin *et al.*, 2007), or other approaches. Some principles identified by researchers include (a) that social and cultural contexts that make sense to the children (Anthony and Walshaw, 2009; Perry *et al.*, 2008), (b) that they involve thoughtful and sensitive discourse (Anderson *et al.*, 2004; Anthony and Walshaw, 2009), (c) that a careful synthesis of child-centered and teacher-guided (intentional, sequential) experiences are included, and that connections between home and school, and educators from birth through the primary years, be strong and continuous (Anthony and Walshaw, 2009; National Research Council, 2009).

In some cases, there is evidence that certain aspects of the instructional tasks are especially effective. For example, if students need extra help in learning counting on skills, there is theory and empirical work that provides specific instructional strategies. After setting up the problem situation with objects (say, 5 + 3), the teacher guides children to connect the numeral signifying the first addend to the objects in the first set (Carruthers and Worthington, 2006, describe the development of written symbols and drawings beyond the scope of this chapter). Students then learn to recognize that the last object of that set is assigned the counting word ('five'). Next, the teacher helps the children understand that the first object in the second set will always be assigned the next counting number ('six'). Students learn that they can start with the 'five' immediately and count on. These understandings and skills are reinforced with additional problems and a variety of specific, focused questions.

Besides carefully addressing necessary ideas and subskills, this instructional activity is successful because it promotes *psychological curtailment* (Clements and Burns, 2000; Krutetskii, 1976), an encapsulation process in which one mental activity gradually 'stands in for' another mental activity. Children must learn that it is not necessary to enumerate each element of the first set. The teacher explains this, then demonstrates by naming the number of that set with an elongated number word and a sweeping gesture of the hand before passing on to the second addend. El'konin and Davydov (1975) claim that such abbreviated actions are not eliminated but are transferred to the position of actions which are considered *as if* they were carried out and are thus 'implicit'. A sweeping movement gives rise to a 'mental plan' by which addition is performed, because only in this movement does the child begin to view the group as a unit. The child becomes aware of addition as distinct from counting. This construction of counting on must be based on physically present objects. Then, through introspection (considering the basis of one's own ways of acting), the object set is transformed into a symbol.

A second example of instructional activities supported by specific research evidence, found in the next level in Figure 28.3, Deriver +/-, is the Japanese approach to developing the Break-Apart-to-Make-Ten (Murata, 2004; note this is known as 'bridging through 10' in the UK and other countries, e.g. Heirdsfield, 2005; BAMT, see Murata and Fuson, 2006). The BAMT strategy actually consists of a series of instructional activities involving several interrelated learning trajectories (see Murata and Fuson, 2006; Sarama and Clements, 2009b, for descriptions). Before lessons on BAMT, children work on several related learning trajectories. They develop solid knowledge of numerals and counting (i.e. move along the counting learning trajectory). This includes the number structure for teen numbers as 10 + another number, which is more straightforward in Asian languages and Hindi than in English, Spanish, and other languages ('13' is '10 and 3' – teachers in the latter languages must be particularly attentive to this competence). They learn to solve addition and subtraction of numbers with totals less than 10, often chunking numbers into 5 (e.g. 8 as 5-plus-3) and using visual models. With these levels of thinking established, children develop several levels of thinking within the composition/decomposition developmental

The line slants between the numbers, indicating that we need to find a partner for 9 to make 10.

Four is separated into two partners, 1 and 3.

The ring shows how the numbers combine to make 10.

Ten and three are shown to add to 13.

Figure 28.4 Teaching BAMT

progression. For example, they work on 'break-apart partners' of numbers less than or equal to 10. They solve addition and subtraction problems involving teen numbers using the 10s structure (10 + 5 = 15), and addition and subtraction with three addends using 10s (e.g. 6 + 4 + 7 = 10 + 7 = 17).

Teachers then introduce problems such as 9 + 4. They first elicit, value, and discuss *child-invented strategies* and encourage children to use these strategies to solve a variety of problems. Only then do they proceed to the use of BAMT. They provide supports to connect visual and symbolic representations of quantities. In the example 9 + 4, they show 9 counters (or fingers) and 4 counters, then move 1 counter from the group of 4 to make a group of 10. Next, they highlight the 3 left in the group. Then children are reminded that the 9 and 1 made 10. Next, children see 10 counters and 3 counters and think 10-3. Last, representational drawings serve this role in a sequence such as shown in Figure 28.4.

Conclusion

Young students can learn more mathematics than many current programs provide. Learning trajectories can help teachers support their students' learning of more profound ideas in mathematics (space constraints have not allowed explorations of subitizing, early number relationships, multiplication reasoning and so forth, see Nunes *et al.*, 2009). Current research in learning trajectories points the way toward more effective and efficient, yet also more creative and enjoyable, mathematics.

References

Anderson, A., Anderson, J. and Shapiro, J. (2004) Mathematical discourse in shared storybook reading. *Journal for Research in Mathematics Education, 35*, 5–33.

Anthony, G. and Walshaw, M. (2009) Mathematics education in the early years: Building bridges. *Contemporary Issues in Early Childhood, 10*(2), 107–21.

Balfanz, R. (1999) Why do we teach young children so little mathematics? Some historical considerations. In J. V. Copley (ed.) *Mathematics in the Early Years* (pp. 3–10). Reston, VA: National Council of Teachers of Mathematics.

Bobis, J., Clarke, B. A., Clarke, D. M., Gill, T., Wright, R. J., Young-Loveridge, J. M. and Gould, P. (2005) Supporting teachers in the development of young children's mathematical thinking: Three large scale cases. *Mathematics Education Research Journal, 16*(3), 27–57. doi: 10.1007/BF03217400.

Brosterman, N. (1997) *Inventing Kindergarten.* New York: Harry N. Abrams.

Carruthers, E. and Worthington, M. (2006) *Children's Mathematics: Making Marks, Making Meaning,* 2nd edn. London: Paul Chapman.

CCSSO/NGA (2010) *Common Core State Standards for Mathematics.* Washington, DC: Council of Chief State School Officers and the National Governors Association Center for Best Practices. Retrieved from http://corestandards.org/.

Clarke, B. A. (2008) A framework of growth points as a powerful teacher development tool. In D. Tirosh and T. Wood (eds) *Tools and Processes in Mathematics Teacher Education* (pp. 235–56). Rotterdam: Sense.

Clarke, D. M., Cheeseman, J., Gervasoni, A., Gronn, D., Horne, M., McDonough, A., Montgomery, P., Roche, A., Rowley, G. and Sullivan, P. (2002) *Early Numeracy Research Project Final Report:* Department of Education, Employment and Training, the Catholic Education Office (Melbourne), and the Association of Independent Schools Victoria.

Clements, D. H. and Burns, B. A. (2000) Students' development of strategies for turn and angle measure. *Educational Studies in Mathematics, 41,* 31–45.

Clements, D. H. and Sarama, J. (2007) Effects of a preschool mathematics curriculum: Summative research on the *Building Blocks* project. *Journal for Research in Mathematics Education, 38,* 136–63.

Clements, D. H. and Sarama, J. (2009) *Learning and Teaching Early Math: The Learning Trajectories Approach.* New York: Routledge.

Clements, D. H. and Sarama, J. (2013) *Building Blocks, Volumes 1 and 2.* Columbus, OH: McGraw-Hill Education.

Clements, D. H. and Sarama, J. (in press) *Learning and Teaching Early Math: The Learning Trajectories Approach,* 2nd edn. New York: Routledge.

Clements, D. H., Sarama, J. and DiBiase, A.-M. (2004) *Engaging Young Children in Mathematics: Standards for Early Childhood Mathematics Education.* Mahwah, NJ: Erlbaum.

De Lange, J. (1987) *Mathematics, Insight, and Meaning.* Utrecht, The Netherlands.

Dewey, J. (1938/1997) *Experience and Education.* New York: Simon and Schuster.

El'konin, D. B. and Davydov, V. V. (1975) Children's capacity for learning mathematics. In L. P. Steffe (ed.) *Soviet Studies in the Psychology of Learning and Teaching Mathematics,* Vol. 7 (pp. 1–11). Chicago: University of Chicago Press.

Griffin, S. (2004) Building number sense with Number Worlds: A mathematics program for young children. *Early Childhood Research Quarterly, 19,* 173–80.

Griffin, S., Clements, D. H. and Sarama, J. (2007) *Number Worlds/Building Block: A Prevention/Intervention Program: Teacher Edition Level B.* Columbus, OH: SRA/McGraw-Hill.

Hamann, M. S. and Ashcraft, M. H. (1986) Textbook presentations of the basic addition facts. *Cognition and Instruction, 3,* 173–92.

Heirdsfield, A. (2005) One teacher's role in promoting understanding in mental computation. In H. L. Chick and J. L. Vincent (eds) *Proceedings of the 29th Conference of the International Group for the Psychology in Mathematics Education,* Vol. 3 (pp. 113–20). Melbourne, AU: PME.

Henry, V. J. and Brown, R. S. (2008) First-grade basic facts: An investigation into teaching and learning of an accelerated, high-demand memorization standard. *Journal for Research in Mathematics Education, 39,* 153–83.

Hirsh-Pasek, K. and Golinkoff, R. M. (2008) Why play = learning. In R. E. Tremblay, R. G. Barr, R. D. Peters and M. Boivin (eds) *Encyclopedia on Early Childhood Development* (pp. 1–7). Montreal, Canada: Centre of Excellence for Early Childhood Development.

Horne, M. and Rowley, G. (2001) Measuring growth in early numeracy: Creation of interval scales to monitor development. In M. Van den Heuvel-Panhuizen (ed.) *Proceedings of the 25th Conference of the International Group for the Psychology in Mathematics Education,* Vol. 3 (pp. 161–8)). Utrecht, The Netherlands: Freudenthal Institute.

Hughes, M. (1986) *Children and Number: Difficulties in Learning Mathematics*. Oxford: Basil Blackwell.

Kaartinen, S. and Kumpulainen, K. (2012) The emergence of mathematizing as a culture of participation in the early childhood classroom. *European Early Childhood Education Research Journal, 20*(2), 263–81. doi: 10.1080/1350293x.2012.681136.

Kamii, C. (1985) *Young Children Reinvent Arithmetic: Implications of Piaget's Theory*. New York: Teaching College Press.

Krutetskii, V. A. (1976) *The Psychology of Mathematical Abilities in Schoolchildren*. Chicago: University of Chicago Press.

Lee, S. (2010) Mathematical outdoor play: Toddler's experiences. In L. Sparrow, B. Kissane and C. Hurst (eds) *Shaping the Future of Mathematics Education (Proceedings of the 33rd Annual Conference of the Mathematics Education Research Group of Australasia)* (pp. 723–6). Fremantle, WA: MERGA.

MacDonald, A. and Lowrie, T. (2011) Developing measurement concepts within context: Children's representations of length. *Mathematics Education Research Journal, 23*(1), 27–42.

MacDonald, A., Davies, N., Dockett, S. and Perry, B. (2012) Early childhood mathematics education. In B. Perry, T. Lowrie, T. Logan, A. MacDonald and J. Greenlees (eds) *Research in Mathematics Education in Australasia: 2008–2011* (pp. 169–92). Rotterdam, The Netherlands: Sense.

McDonough, A. and Sullivan, P. (2011) Learning to measure length in the first three years of school. *Australasian Journal of Early Childhood, 36*(3), 27–35.

Mulligan, J., Prescott, A., Papic, M. and Mitchelmore, M. C. (2006) Improving early numeracy through a Pattern and Structure Mathematics Awareness Program (PASMAP). In P. Clarkson, A. Downtown, D. Gronn, M. Horne, A. McDonough, R. Pierce and A. Roche (eds) *Building Connections: Theory, Research and Practice (Proceedings of the 28th Annual Conference of the Mathematics Education Research Group of Australia)* (pp. 376–83). Melbourne, Australia: MERGA.

Murata, A. (2004) Paths to learning ten-structured understanding of teen sums: Addition solution methods of Japanese Grade 1 students. *Cognition and Instruction, 22*, 185–218.

Murata, A. and Fuson, K. C. (2006) Teaching as assisting individual constructive paths within an interdependent class learning zone: Japanese first graders learning to add using 10. *Journal for Research in Mathematics Education, 37*, 421–56.

National Mathematics Advisory Panel (2008) *Foundations for Success: The Final Report of the National Mathematics Advisory Panel*. Washington, DC: US Department of Education, Office of Planning, Evaluation and Policy Development.

National Research Council (2009) *Mathematics in Early Cchildhood: Learning Paths Toward Excellence and Equity*. Washington, DC: National Academy Press.

Nes, F. T. v. (2009) *Young Children's Spatial Structuring Ability and Emerging Number Sense*. Doctoral dissertation, de Universiteit Utrecht, Utrecht, the Netherlands.

Nunes, T., Bryant, P. E. and Watson, A. (2009) *Key Understandings in Mathematics*. London: Nuffield.

Perry, B., Young-Loveridge, J. M., Dockett, S. and Doig, B. (2008) The development of young children's mathematical understanding. In H. Forgasz, A. Barkatsas, A. Bishop, B. A. Clarke, S. Keast, W. T. Seah and P. Sullivan (eds) *Research in Mathematics Education in Australasia 2004–2007* (pp. 17–40). Rotterdam/Taipei: Sense.

Pratt, C. (1948) *I Learn from Children*. New York: Simon and Schuster.

Sarama, J. and Clements, D. H. (2009a) Building blocks and cognitive building blocks: Playing to know the world mathematically. *American Journal of Play, 1*, 313–37.

Sarama, J. and Clements, D. H. (2009b) *Early Childhood Mathematics Education Research: Learning Trajectories for Young Children*. New York: Routledge.

Shepard, L. A. (2005) Assessment. In L. Darling-Hammond and J. Bransford (eds) *Preparing Teachers for a Changing World* (pp. 275–326). San Francisco: Jossey-Bass.

Sun Lee, J. and Ginsburg, H. P. (2009) Early childhood teachers' misconceptions about mathematics education for young children in the United States. *Australasian Journal of Early Childhood, 34*(4), 37–45.

Thorndike, E. L. (1922) *The Psychology of Arithmetic.* New York: Macmillan.

Trundley, R. (2008) The value of two. *Mathematics Teaching, 211,* 17–21.

van Oers, B. (2003) Learning resources in the context of play: Promoting effective learning in early childhood. *European Early Childhood Education Research Journal, 11,* 7–25.

van Oers, B. (2010) Emergent mathematical thinking in the context of play. *Educational Studies in Mathematics, 74*(1), 23–37. doi: 10.1007/s10649-009-9225-x.

Vygotsky, L. S. (1935/1978) *Mind in Society: The Development of Higher Psychological Processes.* Cambridge, MA: Harvard University Press.

Wright, R. J. (2003) A mathematics recovery: Program of intervention in early number learning. *Australian Journal of Learning Disabilities, 8*(4), 6–11.

29

YOUNG CHILDREN THINKING AND LEARNING WITH AND ABOUT DIGITAL TECHNOLOGIES

Christine Stephen

Introduction

The consequences of children's engagement with digital technologies in educational settings and at home has become a source of intense and often polarised debate. The purpose of this chapter is not to 'take sides' or evaluate the outcomes of play with technologies but to consider the nature of the evidence available about the kind of thinking and learning supported when young children play with digital technologies and the contextual features that make a difference to these experiences. The chapter begins by considering the educational potential claimed for incorporating technologies into young children's play, then moves on to consider the kind of thinking and learning afforded by play with digital technologies. This is followed by a discussion of the support from adults that children need to sustain positive encounters with technology, and finally a review of the children's perspectives on playing with technologies.

The term 'digital technology' is used here to cover a wide range of digital and interactive resources. Digital technology is typically taken to mean desk-top computers and laptops, but young children are increasingly interacting with tablet computers, mobile phones and e-readers. As well as keyboard and mouse or touch-screen interfaces there are motion-sensitive technologies such as the Wii and games consoles manipulated through a range of hand-held controls. Digital cameras and leisure technologies such as television and DVDs are commonplace features of educational and home settings, along with toys that simulate appliances such as cash registers and microwaves. By the time they begin formal education children may already have experienced conversations with distant family members via Skype, been helped to compose emails or to shop on-line and own devices such as responsive globes and toy lap-tops marketed as educational resources. Although our evidence suggests that playing with technologies and technological toys does not dominate the lives of young children in the ways in which those who express concerns about the negative implications fear (Plowman *et al.*, 2010a) these resources are an everyday and popular reality in the homes, classrooms and playrooms of children in the developed world. As Kalaš (2010, p. 16) suggests, 'it is not necessary any more to prove that ICT matters in early childhood education. New digital technologies have entered every aspect of our reality, including families and lives of young people.'

Children's engagement with computer-mediated activities in particular (and other forms of technology in general) is typically referred to by practitioners and parents as 'playing with the computer'. But defining play or digital play is difficult (Stephen and Plowman, 2014) and claims about children learning as they play often fail to take account of the players' perspectives on the playfulness or otherwise of the activity. In this chapter the focus is on 'what is played', what is learned and the social circumstances that influence children's encounters with technologies. I will draw on the international academic literature and especially on a series of studies carried out and published jointly with colleagues at the University of Stirling over a period of ten years. Our work focused on the technological play experiences of children aged 3–5 years which we researched in their preschool settings and in their homes. Our methods and analysis were framed by our socio-cultural understanding of learning and an eco-cultural perspective which was concerned with the practices of technological play and the ways in which context shapes experience. We began by looking at encounters with technology in the preschool playroom (*Interplay* and other studies, Stephen and Plowman, 2008; Plowman *et al.*, 2010b) then extended our interest to children's everyday experiences with digital technologies at home through two projects *Entering e-Society: Young children's development of e-literacy* and *Young Children Learning with Toys and Technology at Home* (e.g. Plowman *et al.*, 2010b, 2012).

Educational possibilities and playing with technologies

Children are typically introduced to educational technologies because their parents or educational practitioners are keen that they should develop early familiarity with the ways of interacting with information which will be a feature of their educational and work experience or because the adults consider that the technologies offer ways of adding fun, speeding up or ensuring learning. Marketing materials suggest that resources such as the LeapPad reading scheme support children to become enthusiastic readers and the integrated television and on-line shows and games provided by media companies such as CBeebies are 'sold' as educational and entertaining. However, there is little developed understanding about how such digital experiences can and do support children's learning.

The gap between claims about the promise for educational development that technologies can bring and evidence of positive outcomes and change in educational practices has become an enduring feature of the debate over the introduction of new technologies at home and in schools. Writing in 1980, Papert saw computers as offering the potential to extend thinking and generate new knowledge, but 13 years later Cuban (1993) commented on the lack of change in the ways in which technologies are employed to support learning. Into the twenty-first century, Yelland *et al.* (2008)

were arguing for a shift to new pedagogic practices to capitalise on the ways in which technologies allow adults and children to engage with and share multi-modal ways of knowing. But, as Bolstad (2004, p. 71) concluded, 'literature about the *potential* of ICT in early childhood education is more common than research which evaluates its *role* in early childhood education' (original italics). Furthermore, reviewing the nature of the technological games and resources on offer and the research evidence that does exist about the outcomes for young children's learning of play with technologies leads away from clear expectations of positive outcomes to a more conditional and nuanced evaluation of potential.

The tentative nature of our understanding about young children's encounters with digital resources is evident in recent evaluation studies. For instance, Couse and Chen (2010) concluded that while tablet computers were a 'viable tool' for those aged 3 to 6 to use in an early childhood setting it was the way in which teachers employed the technology that was important. Spurred on by the proliferation of computer games, the associations claimed between playing computer games and the development of higher cognitive processes in adults and claims that computer play is a qualitatively different form of play, Verenikina *et al.* (2010) explored the affordances and limitations evident when children aged from 5 to 8 years old played computer games at home and in their classroom. They argue that that the influence of play with digital technologies can be found in on- and off-screen activities but that key design attributes must be present if the games are to support higher order thinking and enhance development. Bergen *et al.* (2010) carried out one of the few studies of children aged under 36 months engaging with technologically enhanced toys. They suggest that there is some evidence that these toys can facilitate exploration, practice and social play and expressions of humour.

Others such as Burnett (2010) and Zevenbergen (2007) make a case for educational research to take account of the influence of children's technological experiences beyond their classrooms and playrooms. There is evidence too that children's social interactions with peers in the playroom influence their engagement with technologies. Ljung-Djarf (2008) has demonstrated that specific roles and relationships emerge as children engage with each other and technological resources and Arnott (2013) has extended this analysis to show how children's social status and role influence their agency during play with technologies in preschool. In these circumstances it would seem naïve to seek a direct relationship between children's play with digital technologies, whether games on a computer or using an interactive toy cash register and scanner, and specific impacts on cognitive development.

Thinking with digital technologies

Engaging with digital technologies involves children in many of the same cognitive operations that they encounter with traditional toys at home and in their educational settings. They match, sort, categorise and count. They practise phonics skills and other literacy competencies as they navigate menus and screen displays, watch films and listen to audio-stories. While taking photographs with digital cameras can be part of a larger activity involving communication and reminiscence, and toys that simulate technologies can be incorporated into imaginative play, computer games are more likely to focus on comparing quantities, sequencing and identifying shapes and rhymes. Although these activities are presented in a playful way with accompanying animations, most rely on children applying and rehearsing knowledge and concepts already within their repertoire.

Few of the technological games are open-ended. Most reward the right answer with praise and congratulatory animations but incorrect responses are usually met not with a diagnostic response but with the giving of the correct answer without explanation after several failed attempts. So while access to digital technologies at home and in educational settings does extend the range of options available to children, when considered in terms of the cognitive nature of 'what is played' the scene appears little different from that of a learning environment without technologies. In addition, the closed design of many technological games seems to be at odds with contemporary curricular goals such as creativity and collaborative working and, as Vangsnes *et al.* (2012) have pointed out, there is sometimes conflict between the powerful gaming orientation of some computer activities and the educator's desire to promote higher-order thinking and problem-solving through discussion and cognitive challenge. Roberts-Holmes (2013) found evidence that playing computer games in an educational setting was more likely to be associated with behaviour indicating joint attention than shared cognitive challenge.

In our playroom-based study the creative use of technologies was restricted to the use of drawing packages, some of which were nearer to traditional 'colouring in' activities developing fine motor skills, than a medium for novel creation and self-expression. However, Marsh (2010) points to the growing numbers of examples of children in early years settings being involved in digital media projects such as making 'documentaries' or animated films. She suggests that such activities give young children opportunities to develop transferable skills such as problem-solving, negotiation and risk-taking. Edwards (2011) has written about the way in which children's cultural interpretations blend aspects of their experience of virtual and real world play at home. There was limited evidence of children's play incorporating technological and traditional forms in the homes included in our studies. For instance, we observed Larry using the internet to find and print images of characters which he then used as he acted out narratives, and we noted Jasmine building imaginative scenarios with her technological puppy. On the other hand, Kelly preferred to have her similarly interactive puppy switched off when it was included in her pretend play. However, Marsh (2010) has reported examples of slightly older children (5 to 7 years) playing with characters, negotiating plots and enjoying games with rules during on-line play in virtual worlds, just as they did in traditional play.

Learning with technologies

In the course of *Interplay* (Stephen and Plowman, 2008), the practitioners reported evidence of three kinds of developmental change associated with engaging with technologies. First, they observed that children became competent users of technological resources, reflecting both cognitive development and growing physical skill.

The second area of development was in curricular knowledge and understanding; requiring the effective storage, integration and categorising of new knowledge and practising the application of newly developed understandings and skills to varied circumstances. There were also examples of children acquiring specific knowledge or using newly acquired understanding across the curriculum areas: for instance, adding an understanding of the conventions of interviewing when using a video camera to their developing language and communication skills, developing their competence with matching and sorting across a variety of dimensions and enhancing their capacity to link spoken and written language and act upon aspects of a narrative. The third area of change, by far the most frequently noted, was the development of positive learning dispositions. Children grew in confidence, independence, and willingness to persist in the face of initial challenge. The dominance of references to children developing positive learning dispositions may in part be a reflection of the practitioners' goals. Nevertheless, these changes were an unexpected and welcome outcome of playing with technologies, suggesting that play with technological resources engaged children's emotional and social subjectivities, as well as the more obvious elements of mathematical and language learning typically present in the design of the resources.

When we studied children's engagement with technologies at home we found the same mix of possible learning outcomes as in educational settings (Plowman *et al.*, 2010a). Children developed operational skills, becoming competent with manual on-screen controls, acquired early e-literacy skills, such as the use of menus, icons and scrolling through pages, in parallel with traditional literacy capacities. Many of the games that children had access to at home on a games console, toy lap-top or 'real' computer were ostensibly targeted at developing literacy and numeracy (indeed this was often the reason why parents purchased the resources) but at home there were also enhanced opportunities to extend knowledge in specific areas of enduring interest, such as athletics for one boy with a keen interest in sport and the natural history of a favourite animal kept as a pet by another child's family. However, there was an additional area of new knowledge which was possible at home. Here children learned to take part in local cultural practices concerned with sustaining family relationships (for instance, reviewing and exchanging digital photographs, interacting via Skype and webcams) and family leisure and purchasing practices such as playing games with siblings on the Wii, watching DVDs, making choices during on-line shopping.

Sustaining play with technologies

The power of technologies, and of screen-based resources in particular, to engage children in a wide range of activities designed to support development is oft cited and on occasions in our research we observed children intensely engaged with digital technologies: for instance, exploring 'what if' or 'what next' options with a practitioner through a programme to explore space science, competing enthusiastically to gain points or collect targets, advising peers to choose particular responses and viewing peer-produced photographs and videos with friends. However, a closer look at children's play with technologies in educational settings suggested that children often became frustrated when they could not achieve their goals or reach the end point of a game with only the technological feedback supplied by the programme (Plowman and Stephen, 2005, Stephen and Plowman, 2008). We observed children abandoning the computer for other traditional activities in their richly resourced playrooms because they could not understand or comply with the instructions for the game, became 'lost' in layers of choices, were unable to cope with the cognitive demands of the tasks, lacked operational skills or were distracted by peers. These encounters with computers and other digital resources appeared unsatisfactory rather than motivating and unlikely to promote the kind of intense engagement which Kalantzis *et al.* (2005) describe as critical for learning.

The evidence we gathered during *Interplay* made it clear that, while the design and affordances of the material resource and individual children's interests and willingness to explore or take risks were important mediating factors, it was sensitive and responsive interactions with practitioners that made a critical difference to sustaining children's engagement with technologies and thus to the play, thinking and learning associated with the activity. We identified a range of practitioner actions that were a necessary addition to the interactions with technologies if children were to engage in ways that were positive and rewarding. We conceptualised these pedagogic actions as *guided interaction*, a repertoire of proximal and distal scaffolding activities that make a difference to children's thinking and learning with technologies (Stephen and Plowman, 2008). In the distal domain the activities that practitioners plan for groups and individuals, the resources they offer, the ways in which activities are presented in the playroom and the manner in which staff are deployed in order to facilitate interaction with children all make a difference to engagement with technologies and to the thinking and learning facilitated. Proximal guided interaction happens in direct interactions with the children. Effective proximal pedagogic support is multi-modal, enacted through gesture, expression and touch as well as the spoken word. It happens when adults are able to observe children as they encounter digital technologies, diagnose their difficulties or note the opportunities for extending play and then act in a finely tuned way to sustain the kind of interest and engagement that is associated with learning in action.

In their own homes children's encounters with technology are supported by distal and proximal guided interaction, as they are in educational settings. The evidence gathered in our study *Toys and Technology* (Stephen *et al.*, 2013) suggested that parents offered proximal support which mirrored the range of interactions observed in playroom practices. Like the preschool practitioners their actions were multi-modal. The children's encounters were sustained by verbal instructions and gestures, physical guidance for hands and larger movements, praise, explanations and monitoring. Only one form of guided interaction was noted more often at home than in educational settings; when playing competitive games with resources such as the Wii or a games console young children needed more support at home than in preschool to cope with negative emotions arising as they compete with others. Yet, despite the common repertoire of proximal guided interactions enacted by parents, the data suggested that children's everyday experience of playing with technologies was different in each family context. We identified four dimensions of this distal family context that make a difference to children's engagement with digital technologies (Stephen *et al.*, 2013):

- family perspectives on technology as an effective educational tool, influencing children's access to technologies and encouragement to engage with particular kinds of resources
- parental perspectives on appropriate ways of supporting learning, making a difference to children's opportunities to explore and their understanding of the potential and affordances of resources
- family interactions and practices, sibling interactions and demands on parents' time, defining when children engage with technologies, who shares in these activities and the alternatives on offer at home
- children's preferences and characteristics, influencing what play activity is chosen and the style of interaction with technologies.

Thinking about technologies: preferences and judgements

The children's preferences, interests and judgements about play with the technologies at their disposal made a crucial difference to their experiences, particularly at home where there was more scope for following individual likes and dislikes and less concern for 'balance' across activities, although it should be noted that all of the families in our studies were keen to ensure that their children played indoors and out of doors and experienced a variety of types of play. In the literature and in interviews with parents the impression is given that children are happy to engage with any technology and readily become competent users. However, when we explored the children's perspectives directly through structured activities and conversations and analysis of video observations a more differentiated picture emerged (Stephen *et al.*, 2008).

We found no evidence of play with technologies dominating the lives of children aged 3 to 5 (Stephen, 2011) and, although there was a gender difference between the kinds of technological resources that girls and boys favoured or were given, there was no difference in the proportion of the abundance of toys owned by girls or boys that were technological. Typically children said that they enjoyed traditional activities, particularly swimming, playing in the garden and riding bikes, and were happy to watch television and DVDs and play games on the computer or games console. While many children achieved a balance between traditional and technological play, some had no interest in gaining operational skills and were content to rely on parents and older siblings while a few were not interested in engaging at all with new technologies, despite the enthusiasm of family members and ample resources at home.

For some children particular technological resources, especially those owned by older siblings, were high status items which they were keen to play with even if their level of operational skills and conceptual understanding limited their participation. However, in general children were discriminating users of technology who knew what they liked to use and what they were good at and who made more selective evaluations of resources than their parents recognised. Children differentiated between games they found frustrating and failed to succeed at and those they enjoyed and with which they were successful. The young players talked about some activities being boring, too hard or too long or simply not having interesting content. Although we have no way of assessing the accuracy of their judgement it was interesting to find that

351

children could identify games they were good at and resources they could use alone and others with which they struggled. The 3- to 5-year-olds had readily articulated expectations about age-appropriate games and resources. They were more likely to suggest that another child would need help with operational features of a resource than to draw attention to ways of engaging with the substantive activity. For instance, we saw Arden seek help with operating the controls on a games console although later he seemed unaware of the goal of the game he was involved with and unsure about the meaning of the scores given. It is also possible that in some cases young children found it easier to complete an activity by dragging and clicking using a cursor and mouse than to control a pencil or manipulate small tools or objects such as jigsaw pieces, and touch-screen interfaces offer enhanced ways of interacting with technologies that afford a degree of manoeuvrability not necessarily available in 'concrete' objects. These findings about the ways in which children discriminate between technological play activities suggest that adult characterisations of preschool children as 'digital natives' may overstate the children's feelings of competence and overlook the differences in the ways in which individuals experience particular technologies or interfaces.

Concluding summary

Contrary to the popular rhetoric about the educational promise of play with technologies the research evidence suggests a more conditional and nuanced picture. It is clear that not all technological play resources offer the same opportunities for learning and that some kinds of thinking and aspects of development are more likely to be promoted by play with technologies than others. Nevertheless, play with technologies can support the development of operational skills, extend knowledge and understanding and enhance dispositions positively associated with learning. But if children are to have the kind of sustained encounters with technologies that are likely to support thinking and learning they need more than interactions with the hardware and software: they need scaffolding interactions with the adults who educate and care for them. And the contexts for play with technologies which families and educators create, coupled with the preferences and interests of individuals, make a difference to children's experience and expectations of digital media. In the light of this multiplicity of conditions the outcomes of play with technologies are inevitably uncertain.

References

Arnott, L. (2013) Are we allowed to blink? Young children's leadership and ownership while mediating interactions around technologies. *International Journal of Early Years Education*, 21(1), 97–115.

Bergen, D., Hutchinson, K., Nolan, J. T. and Weber, D. (2010) Effects of infant–parent play with a technology-enhanced toy: Affordance-related actions and communicative interactions. *Journal of Research in Childhood Education*, 24(1), 1–17.

Bolstad, R. (2004) *The Role and Potential of ICT in Early Childhood Education: A Review of New Zealand and International Literature*. Wellington: New Zealand Council for Educational Research.

Burnett, C. (2010) Technology and literacy in early childhood educational settings: A review of research. *Journal of Early Childhood Literacy*, 10(3), 247–70.

Couse, L. J. and Chen, D. W. (2010) A tablet computer for young children? Exploring its viability for early childhood education. *Journal of Research on Technology in Education*, 43(1), 75–98.

Cuban, L. (1993) Computers meet classroom: Classroom wins. *Teachers College Record*, 95(2), 185–219.

Edwards, S. (2011) Lessons from 'a really useful engine'™: Using Thomas the Tank Engine™ to examine the relationship between play as a leading activity. Imagination and reality in children's contemporary play worlds. *Cambridge Journal of Education*, 41(2), 195–210.

Kalantzis, M., Cope, B. and the Learning by Design Project Group (2005) *Learning by Design*. Melbourne: Victorian Schools Innovation Commission.

Kalaš, I. (2010) *Recognizing the Potential of ICT in Early Childhood Education*. Moscow: UNESCO Institute for Information Technologies in Education.

Ljung-Djärf, A. (2008) The owner, the participant and the spectator: Positions and positioning in peer activity around the computer in pre-school. *Early Years: An International Journal of Research and Development*, 28(1), 61–72.

Marsh, J. (2010) Young children's play in online virtual worlds. *Journal of Early Childhood Research*, 8(1), 23–39.

Papert, S. (1980) *Mindstorms: Children, Computers and Powerful Ideas*. Brighton: Harvester.

Plowman, L. and Stephen, C. (2005) Children, play, and computers in pre-school education. *British Journal of Educational Technology*, 36(2), 145–57.

Plowman, L., McPake, J. and Stephen, C. (2010a) The technologisation of childhood? Young children and technology in the home. *Children and Society*, 24(1), 63–74.

Plowman, L., Stephen, C. and McPake, J. (2010b) *Growing Up With Technology: Young Children Learning in a Digital World*. London: Routledge.

Plowman, L., Stevenson, O., Stephen, C. and McPake, J. (2012) Preschool children's learning with technology at home. *Computers in Education*, 59, 30–7.

Roberts-Holmes, G. (2013) Playful and creative ICT pedagogical framing: A nursery school case study. *Early Child Development and Care*, published online at: www.tandfonline.com/doi/full/10.1080/03004430.2013.772991 (accessed July 2013).

Stephen, C. (2011) *Playing and Learning with Technologies: Research Briefing Two for Digital Childhoods*, Scottish Universities Insight Institute (May).

Stephen, C., and Plowman, L. (2008) Enhancing learning with ICT in preschool. *Early Child Development and Care*, 178(6), 637–54.

Stephen, C. and Plowman, L. (2014) Digital play. In L. Brooker, S. Edwards and M. Blaise (eds) *SAGE Handbook of Play and Learning in Early Childhood*.

Stephen, C., McPake, J., Plowman, L. and Berch-Heyman, S. (2008) Learning from the children: Exploring preschool children's encounters with ICT at home. *Journal of Early Childhood Research*, 6(2), 99–117.

Stephen, C., Stevenson, O. and Adey, C. (2013) Young children engaging with technologies at home: the influence of family context. *Journal of Early Childhood Research*, 11(2), 149–64.

Vangsnes, V., Økland, N. T. G. and Krumsvik, R. (2012) Computer games in pre-school settings: Didactical challenges when commercial computer games are implemented in kindergartens. *Computers and Education*, 58, 1138–48.

Verenikina, I., Herrington, J., Peterson, R. and Mantei, J. (2010) Computers and play in early childhood: Affordances and limitations. *Journal of Interactive Learning Research*, 21(1), 139–59.

Yelland, N., Lee, L., O'Rourke, M. and Harrison, C. (2008) *Rethinking Learning in Early Childhood Education*. Maidenhead: Open University Press.

Zevenbergen, R. (2007) Digital natives come to preschool: Implications for early childhood practice. *Contemporary Issues in Early Childhood*, 8(1), 19–29.

30

TECHNOLOGICAL DESIGN AND CHILDREN'S PERSPECTIVES

Cecilia Wallerstedt, Ingrid Pramling Samuelsson and Niklas Pramling

Introduction

In this chapter, we will focus on the issue of children's sense-making. We will look at this issue in relation to new technologies. Technologies are today frequent features of children's lives also in educational settings such as preschools and school. By their design, technologies imply a certain use. Despite this fact, how children make sense of such artifacts remains open to negotiation. We will illustrate and analyse how children's sense-making is discrepant to the intended use as built into a technology. The particular new technology that we will use as example is a technology for improvising and composing music.

A basic premise of children's learning and development is that children make sense. That is, they do not simply receive, register and retrieve information, but actively shape what they experience. Phrased differently, children (as do adults) do not simply perceive or understand something in ready-made form; rather they perceive and understand something *as* something. This means that their ways of seeing and understanding the world are informed by their experiences, intentions and interests. Children's sense-making – or as it is frequently referred to, the child's perspective – has been foundational to developmental and educational research since the pioneering work of Jean Piaget in the 1920s–1930s.

A basic premise of education is the intentional, active shaping of how learners come to perceive and understand the world. For example, in science education the learner is expected to develop the ability to see water not only as something to drink but also in terms of a hydraulic cycle; or to see a cat not only as a pet but also as a predator. Learning language, the child is perhaps expected to develop the ability to read a novel as representing a particular textual genre. Hence, education could be conceived as the active shaping of the learner's perception and understanding.

Considering these two premises – that the child makes sense and that education at heart is the intentional shaping of what sense the child makes – it is inevitable that these two features of children's learning at times will be conflictual. This provides the rationale for the present discussion. However, rather than a teaching sequence *per se*, we will illustrate and discuss this issue by looking at how children interact with technology. By its very nature, technology is the organisation of knowledge for practical purposes. Human experience and insight are built into artifacts that through their design afford and promote certain use. For example, a bucket is designed for storing and transporting something (e.g. water) that the individual can carry by the handle. But children may put the bucket to novel use, filling it with sand and tipping it over to build sandcastles, using it as a mould for building rather than as a container for transportation. Thus, there is no simple linearity from technological design to actual use. What use is made of an artifact is the result of how the individual, in our discussion the child, makes sense of it and the activity in which it is employed.

The MIROR technology

The examples we will use for our discussion in this chapter come from a research project examining children's use of two novel technologies called *MIROR Impro* and *MIROR Compo*. These technologies have been developed by Sony Computer Science Laboratory in Paris (Pachet, 2004) and are designed for children to learn to improvise and compose music. These technologies work with an instrument (typically a keyboard) connected to a computer. The main idea is that the software should 'learn the child's style of playing' (Pachet, 2003). When the child stops playing on the keyboard, resulting in a pause for which a threshold can be set (typically 400 ms.), the system plays back a musical answer that should be related to but not identical to the child's playing. Hence, the output from the computer is not a precise repetition of, but similar to, the child's input. This is briefly how the *MIROR Impro* technology is designed. It is constructed to afford the child the possibility of having a musical dialogue with the computer. The *MIROR Compo* technology is a development of *MIROR Impro*, providing the child with the opportunity to compose music on the basis of his or her previously improvised playing in *Impro*. Everything that the child plays in *MIROR Impro* is stored and the child may then choose parts from what has been played, using an interface showing visualisations of the music. However, the programme is suggested to result in children 'thinking in sound' (Addessi, 2013, p. 53) about their composition. The child can listen to it and then make a composition by combining parts from his or her own stored material. The child can also choose to let the software generate different kinds of variations to what he or she has played and add these to the composition.

Debating and researching educational technologies

When technology is incorporated in early childhood education, it is not always clear what the purpose is. Is technology considered necessary in order to make teaching effective; as amusements for children; or is the premise that since society at large is becoming increasingly digitalised, early childhood should not be an exception? On the one hand technologies are sometimes regarded as something generally good, and on the other hand generally detrimental to development or even dangerous (for different positions in this general debate, see e.g. House, 2012; Plowman *et al.*, 2012). These competing discourses are described by Anna Craft (2012) in terms of 'young people as vulnerable and at risk; or alternatively as capable and potent' (p. 173). Hence, as implied by this reasoning, how technology is viewed is intimately related to how children are viewed.

The technology we will use to illustrate our reasoning is a music technology. When it comes to music in young children's lives, they are surrounded by music (Lamont, 2008; Young and Gillen, 2007) and already from a very young age many children are used to managing technologies by themselves, including for consuming music through computer tablets, smart phones and computers. Against this background, as argued by Young (2006), the issue is not whether digitised technologies should be a part of early childhood music education, but rather how to relate education to children's experiences of such technologies; the experiences children already have and the ones they will need to participate in music–audio cultures.

In educational debates, there is a long tradition of computer–aided instruction, with a basic premise that computers will come to replace teachers (see Säljö, 2010, for a critical discussion). This claim is often grounded on a behaviouristic perspective on learning (Skinner, 1958; see also Cuban, 1986, for a critical review). In such accounts, learning is a matter of shaping behaviour or transmitting predetermined information. However, taking a different point of view, we consider children's sense-making foundational to what activities they engage in and consequently what they will learn through interacting with a technology. Hence, what sense children make of and with a technology as evident in what activities they engage in will be of primary importance to investigate.

Children making sense of and using new technology: examples from the MIROR project

In this section, we will illustrate and discuss two examples of children engaging with and making sense of new music technology.

Improvise, compose or reproduce – the child's perspective

In our studies on the MIROR technologies (Wallerstedt and Lagerlöf, 2011; Lagerlöf *et al.*, 2013), we have seen how the children's agendas when using *MIROR Impro* and *MIROR Compo* often differ from what they were designed for. We will provide two examples. In the first example, we will follow a focus child, Anna (8:0 years old) when she interacts with *MIROR Impro*, as well as how she speaks about this activity afterwards with a researcher. We will look at what plays out when Anna plays with the technology and talks about her experiences of playing with it.

The researcher has described for Anna the rationale behind the software and the idea of turn-taking with the system: that is, she is to play a bit and then stop and listen to the response from the computer; and then take her turn to respond again and so on. Anna then tests the system. Anna plays for six minutes with a 'musical dialogue' consisting of 26 turns (what we in this context refer to as 'a turn' consists of an input from Anna followed by an output from the system). We will look at all turns and describe what she plays.

In Anna's first two inputs, she plays a melody that she has earlier told the researcher that her mother has taught her. The melody is to a song called 'I ett hus vid skogens slut' [in English, 'In a house at the end of the forest'], which is a famous children's song often sung with accompanying movements in Swedish preschool. After Anna's first input, the program responds by single notes, and after the second phrase of the melody she plays the program responds with single notes and a cluster. From listening to the video recording of what is played, these two inputs can be interpreted as one phrase with just a short gap. The short answer from the system is hardly discernible. At this point Anna leaves the melody and in her third phrase she instead plays a glissando (a musical movement that is caused when one's hand strokes sideward over the keys). The program responds by playing a cluster. A graphic representation of these dialogues is shown in Figure 30.1.

In the fourth turn Anna once again plays a glissando while the program responds with clusters in an upward movement. Anna responds with a cluster and gets a cluster and a glissando in response from the program. Finally, in turn 6 the program gives a brief fragment of Anna's melody for 'In a house at the end of the forest' in the response. It is the final three notes in the first phrase of the melody. Anna now resumes playing the melody but is given clusters and glissando in response from the program. For the duration of the five following dialogues (8–12), despite receiving apparently arbitrary responses from the program, she plays the different phrases of the melody. In turns 13 to 15, Anna plays glissandos and big clusters. Then, in turns 16 to 20 she appears to experiment with the tonal range C, D and E. In turn 20, once again a fragment of the melody of the song 'In a house at the end of the forest' that Anna has played several times appears in the response from the program. She immediately (in turn 21) picks up on this response, returning to playing the melody.

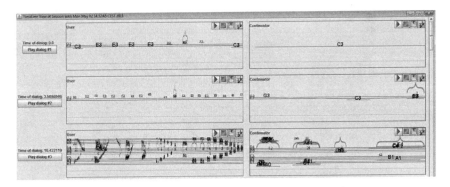

Figure 30.1   Musical dialogues 1–3; Anna plays the melody (which begins with the notes C, E and E). Then she plays an extra E, then D, E, F, but for the final E she accidentally touches an extra key). In dialogue 3, she first plays a glissando and then clusters with both hands that go from the edges into the centre of the keyboard.

In her response she indicates that she has discerned this feature of the response of the program. She continues playing the melody over turn 24, thereafter ending the session with two turns where she plays clusters.

Throughout Anna's session with the technology it is clear that she, as she does in the other sessions she has taken part in, is concerned with a particular melody that she is already familiar with, 'In a house at the end of the forest', but she also plays in other ways, such as glissandos, 'walking' with the fingers across the white keys, clusters (including sometimes banging on the keys with her hands) as well as playing with several fingers as in a more conventional piano style. It is not visible (or audible) that she picks up on the response from the program on these occasions. Her playing is contingent on the affordances of the keyboard as such, rather than the affordances of the program. In contrast, on both occasions that she resumes playing the melody, this has been preceded by the program having contained fragments of the melody in its output.

After her three sessions (of which we here have reported from one), Anna is interviewed by an adult, Cecilia. During the interview, which is conducted in the same room as the previous sessions, the keyboard and printouts from the program's interface are present. During the interview, which lasts approximately 30 minutes, we learn that Anna's parents play instruments and sing. Anna herself has a keyboard on which her mother has taped small notes to show the names of the keys. With this support, Anna has learnt to play different melodies. Like her parents, Anna is very interested in music. In the interview Anna speaks about how she has experienced playing with *MIROR Impro* in relation to the previous experience of playing the keyboard.

Excerpt 1: The difference between playing keyboard with and without *MIROR Impro*

40 CECILIA: But, how, did you think there was any difference when you played at home and when you played with this?

41 Anna: Not so much. It was more that here it answered.

42 CECILIA: Right. Did you think it was fun or boring or, kind of, or how did you think it was to have someone who answered, would you like to have that at home?

43 Anna: I don't think I'd want it 'cause it was rather annoying, but it was fun to play.

44 CECILIA: Yes, in what way was it annoying then?

45 Anna: That, at home I usually play the whole song, and then I think it's quite hard when it answered. But that I have books at home, I have five song books I think, and it's only with one song that I have both, 'cause we have like this (points at the keys) small (paper) notes, that mum has made, and then she has written both the tone and what it's called.

46 CECILIA: Yes.

47 Anna: And now I've learnt the tones and so, I've learnt to see which tones it is and I've only got one song, and it's the one that mum, 'cause mum has written down the whole 'Bä bä vita lamm' to me, so it's only that one that I have letters also.

As indicated already by the name of the technology, it is designed to facilitate musical improvisation. Through interplaying with the system, the child is expected to engage in an improvisational dialogue mediated by the system. However, as seen in Anna's explanations, she wants to play a familiar melody. Thus, the activity she engages in is fundamentally different to the premised one providing the rationale for the technology. As a consequence of this discrepancy between her intention and use of the technology on the one hand, and the in-built, presumed, use of the technology on the other, Anna simply finds the responses from the system to be 'rather annoying', finding it 'quite hard when it answered'. The design of the technology making it respond to the child's playing with a variation in order to facilitate the child's improvisation presumes that the child will engage in such an activity (i.e. identifying and being willing to improvise). But as seen in this example (and others in our data), playing music may primarily from the child's perspective have the sense of being able to reproduce a familiar and popular melody (song).

The multi-modal character of sense-making

Our second example of how a child engages with the MIROR technology and what this tells us about her perspective and how it relates to the design of the technology comes from a session conducted in a home setting. An adult (Cecilia) and a child, Suzy (8:6), interact with and around the technology *MIROR Compo* during a session that lasts about half an hour. After Suzy has put together ten parts into a composition (see above), the adult encourages her to see if they can also make a poem that 'fits' the song. The reason for this 'task' is to make the child consider the structure of her composition, rather than simply adding sections. Together they come up with the idea that when a musical part is repeated, there should also be a repetition of words. Therefore, they want to find out which musical parts of the ten are the same. At their disposal, they have the possibility of listening to the recorded parts and they have the visualisation of the composition on the screen as resources when comparing the different parts. Suzy is clearly oriented towards the visual aspect of the parts (i.e. what is shown in the visualisation), even after she has listened to how they sound.

Excerpt 2: 'The same' from an auditory perspective

309 CECILIA: Now let's listen to it. It sounded like that (see the first visualisation in Figure 30.2).
310 Suzy: Mm.
311 CECILIA: And we compare with that one, then (see the second visualisation in Figure 30.2).
312 Suzy: Yes, it will not sound the same. It will not, not sound the same (said with emphasis).
313 CECILIA: (Listens) No, it's not really the same. What's the difference then?
314 Suzy: But that, the one at the top, it was longer than that one (points at the two visualisations on the screen). And that one was shorter than that one up there.
315 CECILIA: Yes, precisely.

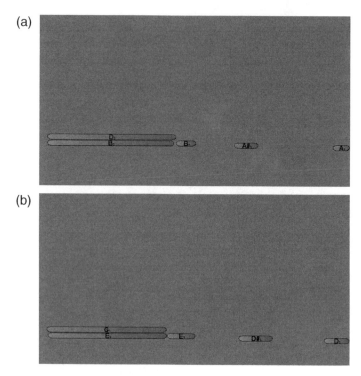

Figure 30.2 Notes (DB, B and A#) and notes (GE, E and D#); the rhythm is similar but the pitch differs; i.e. it looks similar but sounds different.

316 Suzy: And that one is much longer than that shorty.
317 CECILIA: Yes, mm, precisely. And if you listen to the sound, do you hear any difference in how they sound?
318 Suzy: Yes, that one sounds much darker than that one there.

When comparing the two parts, Suzy pays attention to the minute difference in length between the first two notes (turn 312). This represents a rhythmical difference that is hardly discernible to the ear. This difference is what she has discerned. The researcher's first question (turn 313) does not change Suzy's focus of attention, deictically referring to a visual aspect. But when rephrasing the question in terms of music (i.e. sound rather than vision, turn 317), Suzy aligns with this frame of reference and answers in terms of musically relevant distinctions (e.g. turns 316 and 318).

The visual representation appears to be dominant for Suzy (turn 314). What she discerns, supported by this representation, is a time-based one, through one of the two first notes in Figure 30.2 being somewhat longer than the other. She does not indicate that she has discerned that there is also a difference in height (representing differences in pitch). Through listening to the composition, this difference becomes more apparent, not only to the researcher but also to the child (turns 317–318).

The conversation between the adult and the child continues:

Excerpt 3: Account for 'the same'

321 CECILIA: (Nods) Precisely. But they were rather similar; in what way were they similar then?
322 Suzy: Eh, first it was long and then it was three 'duttar' [disperse in small amount] or what shall I say.
323 CECILIA: Yes, precisely, but dark and light (makes a gesture with her hand in two different heights).
324 Suzy: Mm.

Faced with the task of communicating about the music, Suzy uses onomatopoeia (turn 322): that is, she mimics the sound with her voice. She also uses a meta-marker (Goatly, 1997), indicating that she is clear that this is not the appropriate term, but a way for her to communicate her impression. The adult taking the role of a more experienced peer (Rogoff, 2003) confirms Suzy's suggestion and rephrases it in more conventional terms, 'yes, precisely, but dark and light' (turn 323), accompanied by a gestural metaphor. The technology *MIROR Compo* builds on the idea that children should be directed to musical structure (composition) through listening to and choosing pre-recorded snippets (see above, on *MIROR Impro*). However, in our work we have seen how children do not tend to engage in such a composition activity (which we have not illustrated here), but need to be introduced to this very idea by a more experienced peer such as a preschool teacher; and that rather than supporting children 'thinking in sound', Suzy as well as other children tend to make sense of the music in visual rather than auditory terms; again often requiring scaffolding by a more experienced peer to pay attention to the latter. Hence, the children – as with Suzy here – primarily make sense of the music in this kind of activity through how it looks on the screen, rather than in terms of how it sounds.

Discussion

As seen in the excerpts presented and analysed in this chapter, children do not necessarily make sense of technologies in the way that they were designed for. The children engage in other activities with these artefacts than as premised. In our first illustration, Anna, rather than improvising and thus creating new music, mainly struggled to play a familiar existing song, taking care not to vary the song. In our second illustration, we analysed a dialogue between an adult and a girl, Suzy, about her experiences of using *MIROR Compo*. The dialogue came to revolve around what was considered 'the same' in the music. In other accounts, the technology's ability to 'scaffold' the user 'thinking in sound' (Addessi, 2013, p. 53) has been emphasised. But as we illustrated, the child's sense-making is primarily based on the visual resources provided by the software. This should not be regarded as a fault in the technology, but as a reminder of the general multi-modal nature of sense-making. Children do not make sense of the world in only one modality (Kress, 2010); even when a technology is designed with the explicit purpose to get children to attend to one modality (here music as sound), they make sense of what they experience (also) in other modalities (here, how the music looks on the screen) and through onomatopoeia (a kind of musical language of the voice). In her scaffolding of the child's sense-making, the adult, as we saw, also used gesturing.

The design of a technology does not only imply a particular use (e.g. that it should be used for musical improvisation or composition), it also implies a notion of the user. With an interest in early childhood education and technologies, we may thus ask of a technology, who is the intended user, or, in other words, who is the implied child? A particular child is premised, having certain experiences, interests and knowledge of, in the present cases, music and how it may be improvised and composed. As we have briefly illustrated, it cannot be presumed that children in general will have such experiences, interests and intentions in using a technology. Consequently, children may make sense of a technology rather contrary to its intended use and thus engage in different kinds of activities. This implies the importance of basing debates on new technologies in empirical research on how children with different experiences actually engage (or not) with a technology: that is, what they actually do with and around it. This is not something we can make claims about on the basis of investigating technology alone. The child will always make sense of whatever he or she experiences; even with an artefact designed to afford and promote certain activities and perceptions, what sense children make of it and what activities they engage in will be open to negotiation. For educational practice, this further implies the important role of the teacher in mediating, that is, introducing children to new use of technologies (e.g. that we may also improvise and compose music, not only play familiar pre-existing music) and other cultural tools (e.g. musical distinctions and categories), and coordinating the child's perspective and the perspective in-built in the artefact (technology).

Acknowledgement

The work reported here is a part of a large-scale international research project on children's technology-transformed music learning entitled Musical Interaction Relying on Reflection (MIROR), financed by the European Union FP7-ICT (Grant 258338). The transnational project group is coordinated by Anna Rita Addessi (University of Bologna, Italy). The other partners and their national and technological project leaders are: Sony Computer Science Laboratory, Paris (Francois Pachet), University of Gothenburg, Sweden (Bengt Olsson), University of Exeter, UK (Susan Young), University of Genoa, Italy (Gualtiero Volpe), and University of Athens, Greece (Christina Anagnostopoilou).

References

Addessi, A. R. (2013) The reflexive interaction in (music) pedagogy. In *MIROR, Deliverable D5.2: Report on theoretical results related to the IRMS creative musical processes and cognition/ learning* (pp. 49–58). Available at: www.mirorproject.eu.

Addessi, A. R. and Pachet, F. (2005) Experiments with a musical machine: Musical style replication in 3 to 5 year old children. *British Journal of Music Education, 22*(1), 21–46.

Craft, A. (2012) Childhood in a digital age: Creative challengers for educational futures. *London Review of Education, 10*(2), 173–90.

Crow, B. (2006) Musical creativity and the new technology. *Music Education Research, 8*(1), 121–30.

Cuban, L (1986) *Teachers and Machines: The Classroom Use of Technology since 1920*. New York: Teachers College Press.

Goatly, A. (1997) *The Language of Metaphors*. London: Routledge.

House, R. (2012) The inappropriateness of ICT in early childhood: Arguments from philosophy, pedagogy, and developmental research. In S. Suggate and E. Reese (eds) *Contemporary Debates in Childhood Education and Development* (pp. 105–20). London: Routledge.

Kress, G. (2010) *Multimodality: A Social Semiotic Approach to Contemporary Communication*. London: Routledge.

Lagerlöf, P., Wallerstedt, C. and Pramling, N. (2013) Engaging children's participation in and around a new music technology through playful framing. *International Journal of Early Years Education, 21*(4), 325–35.

Lamont, A. (2008) Young children's musical worlds: Musical engagement in 3.5-year-olds. *Journal of Early Childhood Research, 6*(3), 247–61.

Pachet, F. (2003) The continuator: Musical interaction with style. *Journal of New Music Research, 32*(3), 333–41.

Pachet, F. (2004) Enhancing individual creativity with interactive musical reflective systems. In I. Deliège and G. Wiggins (eds) *Musical Creativity Research in Theory and Practice* (pp. 1–15). London: Psychology Press.

Plowman, L., McPake, J. and Stephen, C. (2012) Extending opportunities for learning: The role of digital media in early education. In S. Suggate and E. Reese (eds) *Contemporary Debates in Childhood Education and Development* (pp. 95–104). London: Routledge.

Rogoff, B. (2003) *The Cultural Nature of Human Development*. Oxford: Oxford University Press.

Säljö, R. (2010) Digital tools and challenges to institutional traditions of learning: Technologies, social memory and the performative nature of learning. *Journal of Computer Assisted Learning, 26*(1), 53–64.

Skinner, B. F. (1958) Teaching machines. *Science, 128*(3330), 969–77.

Wallerstedt, C. and Lagerlöf, P. (2011) Exploring turn-taking in children's interaction with a new music technology. *He Kupu, 2*(5), 20–31.

Young, S. (2006) Interactive music technologies in early childhood music education. In M. Baroni *et al.* (eds) *Proceedings of the 9th International Conference on Music Perception and Cognition* (ICMPC9) (pp. 1207–11). Bologna: Bononia University Press.

Young, S. and Gillen, J. (2007) Towards a revised understanding of young children's musical activities: Reflections from the 'Day in the Life' project. *Current Musicology, 84*, 79–99.

PART IV

Documenting and developing children's thinking

31

THE DEVELOPMENT OF LEARNING POWER

A new perspective on child development and early education

Guy Claxton

The goal of early education (and perhaps of all education) should not be seen as simply that of training brains whose basic potential is already determined. Rather, the goal is to provide rich environments in which to grow better brains.

(Clark, 2003)

Introduction

Children's development reflects an entwining of genetic endowment and experience. To understand development – and guide it successfully – we must understand the dispositions and capabilities with which babies come bundled, like the pre-installed software on a new laptop, into the world outside the womb. And we have to understand the way these potentialities are influenced by the world *in which* they find themselves, and the world *for which* their culture and their caretakers are preparing them. This mix of accidental and intentional influences moulds young minds in ways that leave their capacity for intelligent thriving either augmented and differentiated, or alternatively stymied and shrunk.

The story of child development can be told from many perspectives. The 'genetic epistemology' perspective made famous by Jean Piaget identifies a series of stages in the unfolding of a person's ability to handle abstract knowledge and logical reasoning (Piaget, 2001). The sociocultural perspective looks in more detail at the culturally mediated unfolding, and internalisation, of the child's abilities to think, imagine and remember (e.g. Vygotsky, 1978; Daniels *et al.*, 2011). The cognitive perspective uses the models and frameworks of cognitive psychology to chart the developmental trajectories of children's thinking (e.g. Gopnik *et al.*, 2011; Meadows, 2006). Moral perspectives, such as those of Kohlberg (Colby and Kohlberg, 2011) or Haidt (2012) look at the child's progressively more sophisticated understanding of 'right and wrong'. More recently, social and affective perspectives focus on the development of children's

367

interpersonal skill and the range of emotional expressions which their culture sanctions or prohibits (Schore, 1999; Siegel 2012).

In this chapter I want to offer a different perspective, that of the child's developing 'learning power', which draws on, and cuts across, many of the more familiar perspectives I have just mentioned. The need for this new perspective derives from the growing confluence of several streams of contemporary thinking: sociological, educational and psychological. One stream points to the increasing demands which the modern world places on people's psychological resources, especially on their ability to engage with complexity, uncertainty and change. Kegan (1995), for example, in a book tellingly entitled *In Over Our Heads: The Mental Demands of Modern Life*, points to the speed with which, for many children and their families, an 'automatic' is being replaced by a 'stick-shift' world. In an automatic car, as in a traditional culture, many decisions – like when to change gear, or what it means to be 'a girl' – are embodied in the functioning of the 'vehicle' (the car or the culture) and are not readily under the direct control of the 'driver'. In a stick-shift culture, deciding when to change gear, or what religion to follow, is the responsibility of the individual, and this is demanding and potentially stressful. That you *can* make so many decisions for yourself is liberating, but to the extent that you feel you *have to*, the responsibility can feel burdensome or even overwhelming (Gergen, 1991). For example, a survey of 3,500 young people's views on education as a preparation for their future commissioned by the Industrial Society (now the Work Foundation) concluded:

> Most young people fear that their world will generally become more challenging...
> [For many] their lives are riddled with insecurity; insecurity becomes an integral
> part of growing up ... Schools are seen as failing to equip young people with the
> ability to learn for life rather than exams.
>
> *(Industrial Society, 1997)*

Hence there is much current concern in the parenting literature about how best to help children prepare to flourish rather than flounder in such a world (e.g. Furedi, 2008; Palmer, 2007), and this is paralleled in educational research by a recognition of the importance of developing 'learning how to learn' (James *et al.*, 2007) or related 'twenty-first-century skills' (Istance *et al.*, 2002).

Another stream of thought concerns the academic conceptualisation of 'intelligence'. Instead of the traditional focus on intelligence as the discrete, unitary and relatively unchanging source of disembodied and disembedded rationality, recent work emphasises the extent to which intelligent behaviour, amid the complexities of real life, reflects a shifting and changeable composite of many resources and characteristics that include emotional and personality traits such as 'resilience' 'open-mindedness' or 'tolerance for uncertainty' (Lucas and Claxton, 2010). An early book in the field by co-founder of Harvard's influential Project Zero, David Perkins (1995), for example, was entitled *Outsmarting IQ: The Emerging Science of Learnable Intelligence*. Resnick (1999), another leader in the field, has defined intelligence as 'the sum total of one's habits of mind', thus emphasising both the composite and the malleable character of intelligence. And Piaget himself is often reported to have remarked that the essence of 'real-world intelligence' is 'knowing what to do when you don't know what to do'.[1] Some have even suggested that intelligence inherently involves processes that 'loop out' beyond the individual body to capitalise on material and social resources (Clark, 1997; Salomon, 1993). Thus social concern about young people's robustness in the face of difficulty is complemented by a renewed research focus on the psychological elements that underpin that robustness, and on the ways they can be developed.

The concept of 'learning power'(Claxton, 2002; Claxton *et al.*, 2011; Deakin-Crick, 2006) has emerged at the confluence of these streams of thought, and has excited educationalists' interest in the possibility of teaching children in a way that systematically prepares them for the rigours and responsibilities of lifelong learning.[2] However, learning power has so far lacked a developmental narrative that suggests how the genetic predisposition for learning, with which infants are so obviously endowed, unfolds through maturation in the early years; and how that maturational potential is cumulatively strengthened (or undermined) by cultural messages from the home and peers, as well as from the school. If we imagine that babies are biologically endowed with an entry-level Learning Operating System, let us call it LOS 1.0, we can ask how the power, the reach and the sophistication of that core psychological capability unfolds over the early years of life, and what kinds of experiences contribute to its development and differentiation.

What follows is an illustration of what such a narrative might look like. It is, in its current state, highly sketchy and schematic. Much of the detail, such as the exact progression or sequencing of developmental steps, and the ages at which they might normatively be expected to develop, is lacking. Nevertheless, it demonstrates, I hope, the value and validity of such a perspective. In brief, what I will suggest is that babies come bundled with a brain that is predisposed to learn, and also a built-in range of learning amplifiers that kick in during the early stages of development (provided all goes well biologically). Some of these on-board amplifiers set us to learn especially well from other people, and from the cultural products (language, digital media) with which they furnish the growing child's surroundings. Many of these culturally mediated tools are themselves powerful learning amplifiers. Thus one of the ways in which biology moulds cultural learning is (or can be) towards ever more sophisticated ways of approaching novelty, complexity and uncertainty both in school and beyond.

LOS 1.0: Natural born learners

Among the animal kingdom, human infants possess supremely malleable brains. Even before they are born, they are registering recurrent connections between aspects of their experience (Lyman, 2009). A tune 'heard' repeatedly *in utero* is preferred, by a newborn baby, to a novel tune, for example (Partenen *et al.*, 2013). In the first year, babies' brains experience a massive overproduction of dendrites which are 'whittled down' by experienced statistical regularities into well-worn circuitry. These 'cell assemblies' (Hebb, 1949; Pulvermuller, 2013) distil out of experience 'what precedes what', 'what goes with what' and 'what follows what', and, critically, 'how what I do alters the flow of events'. These regularities enable the child to stitch together connections between different states of the world, different interventions they can make, and the fluctuating array of needs which they have, and thus to begin to antici-pate and exert some control over the flow of events. 'If I smile, that might elicit a cuddle – but only if my mother's pupils are relatively dilated': that kind of thing. The inherent plasticity of the nervous system enables the child to gain an ever more sophisticated and reliable (though always open to surprise and correction) handle on the world. Exactly the same neural tune-ability underpins the adult's ability to learn to jive, play spin bowling or find their way around a new work-place. This basic sen-sorimotor learning capability has no developmental sell-by date. And the only fuel it needs to run on is an open sensibility to experience (Spitzer, 1999).

LOS 1.1: Attentional control

LOS 1.0 is exquisite, but it is passive, holistic, cumulative and slow (Clark, 2003). It can only track the patterns that come its way. It cannot take what it has learned to bits and improve just one part of it. But LOS 1.1 can, because it adds the abilities for top–down processing and attentional control. The ability to predict what might be coming up next, on the basis of cell assemblies that link what has just happened, or is happening, to what has ensued previously, can be used to speed up and refine the process of per-ception itself. Crudely, if I have just seen a cat's face heading to the left, through a slit in the fence, LOS 1.1 can quickly set itself to look for an up-coming cat's tail. We are able not just to *look at*, but *look for* things (see Clark, 2013). We can specifically attend to and adjust just those aspects of experience that *don't* match the prediction – the cat turns out to be Manx – and thus our learning capacity is sharpened and amplified.

So the ability to predict enables the child to begin to focus her attention. But to do this, she has to be able to inhibit other things she could be noticing, and other things she could be doing. And it is one of the main jobs of the rapidly maturing frontal lobes of her brain to do just that. Selective attention is the beginning of a much wider power: the capacity for self-control or self-regulation. As children develop this so-called 'executive function', they become able to prioritise and plan their activ-ities and therefore their learning. The kind of learning that Anders Ericsson (e.g. 1996) calls 'deliberate practice' – picking out the hard parts of a developing skill and working on them selectively and intensively – would be impossible without the brain's ability to keep reminding itself why it wants to excel so badly (or rather so well) that it can resist any kind of alluring distraction (Perkins, 2009).

The ability to control and focus attention also illustrates how the maturation of the brain enables the child to benefit from the social world of learning – how 'nature' and 'nurture' lock together to boost learning power. Towards the end of their first year, children master the tricky ability to know what someone else is looking at – and possibly talking about. By looking at the angles of their mother's head and eyes (helped, to begin with, often by a pointing finger), they can figure out the direction of her gaze, and – in their own mind's eye – look along this invisible line and find what she is attending to (Moore and Dunham, 1995). This is a hugely important learning amplifier: without it, it would be almost impossible to learn language. Once children have mastered the trick of joint attention, other people can begin to teach them their culture's ways of looking at and carving up the world. They can be taught (through what is called in the literature 'social referencing') what to notice for example, and also what to ignore – what to treat as trivial, disgusting or invisible (Dickstein *et al.*, 1984).

LOS 1.2: Exploration and prodding

Another way of enriching and focusing attention, and thus of amplifying learning, which also seems to be built in, is exploration. Babies do not just look at things; they soon learn to pick them up, stroke them, suck them, rattle them, drop them or throw them (to find out what kind of sound they make when they land – and what kind of sound *you* make when they break!). As soon as they can crawl they go looking for trouble, and they develop a useful set of basic tests that encourage new objects – a visitor, next door's dog – to reveal their properties. What does it tell me about itself if I smile at it, babble or pull its tail? As they grow up, the repertoire of such information-revealing, learning-enriching strategies will become more targeted and sophisticated. You don't just smile, you say, 'Hi, I don't think I've seen you here before …' Or, in a chemistry class, you will learn a specialised set of basic tests for getting an unknown compound to reveal something of itself. Does it dissolve in water? How hard is it? What happens if we put some dilute hydrochloric acid on it? And then you google the results.

Parents, caregivers and teachers of young children will spend time training and refining these world-revealing explorations and experiments, so they are informative but not life-threatening. But here we also have to introduce a new theme into the developmental story of learning power. Adults can inhibit learning as well as amplifying it. Bonawitz *et al.* (2011) demonstrated in young children what we all know: if someone tries to direct your learning too tightly, your curiosity can easily get turned off. Pre-schoolers who have the main function of a toy demonstrated to them subsequently played with it, and explored other things it could do, less than other children who were left to figure it out for themselves. The learning strategies of exploring and prodding can themselves be muted by the wrong kind of guidance and support.

LOS 2.0: Good guesses

Learning, to echo Piaget, is what you do when you don't know what to do. You find yourself in a situation that requires some kind of response – but you don't yet know what would fit the bill. When babies don't know what to do, they are designed to squirm and cry. From an evolutionary point of view, this is not a bad starter kit. We all still wriggle at night if uncomfortable, or to throw off a cover when hot; and we all ask for help when we are stuck (if not as loudly or urgently as the baby). But humans' success as a species depends on being able to invent and trial ever more targeted responses. (Just wriggling and yelling in the examination hall won't get you very far.) We need to be able to generate good guesses for what might work, and try them out. As children grow, they assemble a larger and more effective repertoire of ways of coming up with things to try. Their learning becomes more resourceful and creative.

LOS 2.1: Imitation

Babies are built to imitate (as are we all). There is little doubt now that the human (and primate) brain contains important circuits of 'mirror neurons' that predispose us towards interpersonal resonance and mimicry. When a person observes a significant other performing a meaningful action, their brain automatically primes them to execute the same (or a reciprocal) action (Glenberg and Gallese, 2012). This mimetic resonance with others is the foundation of empathy (Iacoboni, 2009), but it is also a powerful amplifier of learning. A learner who is stuck (on their maths or their painting, say) and stuck for an idea as to how to get unstuck, can look and see if there is anyone about who is making better progress, and try to copy what they are doing. Harris and Want (2005) have shown that young children are such inveterate copiers that they will faithfully mimic an adult's demonstration of how to solve a problem, even if it contains all kinds of superfluous gesturing (whereas chimpanzees seem to see through the irrelevancies and cut to the chase).

Imitation is one of the most important hinges that links biology and culture together. It is a built-in disposition that vastly accelerates the process of cultural learning in all its forms (Tomasello, 1999). Watching and copying others begins in early childhood, and remains a valuable learning strategy throughout life (whether the skill in question be high-jumping, violin-playing or telling jokes). Of course, there is no guarantee that what worked for them will work for you: there are all kinds of reasons why their 'solution' may not transfer lock, stock and barrel to you and your situation. But the attempt to imitate may get your own process of trial and error going again. And it is a learning tool that, like all the others, is capable of itself being sharpened through experience. Young children, for example, have already picked up that not all role models are equally reliable, and they pay greater attention to those whose modelling has proved the most helpful in the past (Harris *et al.*, 2013).

LOS 2.2: Imagination

Trial and error is a vital learning strategy, but when it is overt, out in the 'real world', it carries risks. Expensive materials might be ruined. Competitors might be engaging in a bit of 'industrial espionage'. So being able to run experiments in your own head is a great asset. Luckily, the human prefrontal cortex, through its ability to inhibit other areas of activity in the brain, confers just that advantage. Not only, as we have already seen, can inhibition keep us concentrated and on track; it also allows us to partially activate both developing skills and possible scenarios. It becomes possible to internalise 'pretend play', and thus inhabit a private laboratory for trying out fantasies and possibilities. Again, as children grow up, it is possible for imagination to become more targeted and sophisticated. We know that 'mental rehearsal', using the mind's eye to practise new levels of skill, is a powerful adjunct to actual physical practice (Beilock and Lyons, 2009). And when imitation and imagination work together, children become able to construct dynamic mental models of other people, and run simulations to explore 'what would Sophie do?' in a currently problematic situation, and thus generate 'good guesses' about possible courses of action for themselves.

LOS 2.3: Reverie

Putting yourself in someone else's shoes (to generate learning possibilities for oneself) or imagining oneself performing a skill to a higher level than one actually can, are learning amplifiers that require a high degree of cognitive control. They are quite deliberate, and children may need time and some informal coaching to master them. But ideas for action also occur to us when we are in more relaxed, less purposive frames of mind. The literature on creativity repeatedly attests to the value of interpolating periods of 'incubation' in between more focused and purposeful kinds of thought (e.g. Dijksterhuis, 2004). Children are natural day-dreamers, and need coaching if they are to develop the more disciplined kinds of thought. But in the process of developing the skills of deliberate, explicit rationality it is important that the learning potential of reverie is not neglected – indeed, is also cultivated. Highly creative learners, such as Nobel Science Laureates, know the value of being able to toggle between controlled and receptive modes of thought (Fensham and Marton, 1992), and there is no reason to deprive children of the same insight. The disciplined use of reverie can be learned, just as well as logic can (Claxton, 2006).

LOS 3.0: Language

With the advent of language, the Learning Operating System obviously receives a massive and highly intricate upgrade. There is no room here to do this proper justice: a few comments will have to suffice. Language enables parents and teachers to 'point' at interesting aspects of experience, and thus tune children's learning, much more accurately than they can through joint non-verbal attention by itself. Language can articulate experience not only in the sense of naming it, but also by being able to joint or segment ('articulate' as in 'articulated lorry') it more finely, and thus allow much more fine-grain learning. Language enables children to ask questions, ask for help, and communicate their learning difficulties. It will enable them to learn through all kinds of conversation, and in due time through reading and the mastery of a range of symbolic literacies (including mathematics).

Language enables children to 'fault-find' more precisely, and to generate (or apply) explanatory frameworks for puzzling or complicated phenomena that will, in their turn, generate fruitful ideas for action and experimentation. If you can give yourself an answer to the question 'Why?' – how come things behaved as they did – you are halfway to a new thought about what you might do to improve them. And language, of course, enables analysis and logical deduction, and thus boosts further the ability to come up with plausible, if not water-tight, lines of exploration and inquiry. (From the learning perspective, it is the capacity of language to support ever more intricate and interesting discovery that is key; not its ability to mount arguments, knock out small essays, or 'show your working' *per se*.)

Conclusion

Children grow with age in a variety of ways. They can become more logical, more sociable, more self-aware and more articulate, as well as stronger and taller. They can also become better at learning: more able to tolerate uncertainty and persist (sometimes for years) with really difficult problems; better at asking for help and learning with others; better at adopting different perspectives and deriving candidate solutions from well-informed explanations. As they grow, their capacity to learn itself grows. Or it could. But sometimes opportunities to strengthen children's learning power are missed. Adults do too much of the learning work for them, or imply that imaginative playfulness is merely an immature precursor to disciplined pages of writing or sums. In the worst cases, learning power is even undermined, as when parents or teachers inadvertently make children afraid of error or failure; or teach them (implicitly) that struggling with difficulty is a sign of lack of 'intelligence' (Dweck, 2000).

But intelligence is not a universal constant. What it takes to be smart depends on the world in which you find yourself. 'Intelligence' is a label that honours the constellation of habits of mind that a culture takes to be valuable. In a stable, traditional culture, it makes perfect sense to treat as 'intelligent' the ability to retell the myths of your tribe with accuracy and flair (Curran, 1988). In a turbulent, digital, globalised world, it makes more sense to honour the ability to engage confidently, calmly and capably with situations that are complex and fast-changing. In the world in which most of us live, it is smart to be a powerful learner. We need a perspective on child development that foregrounds the natural endowments, and the matured dispositions, that underpin this capacity for calm, intelligent presence of mind. We need to be able to chart the developmental trajectory along which children can travel, as their genetic potential guides the distillation of learning experiences into knowledge and skill, and also, crucially, into an ever-expanding competence in the face of uncertainty.

Notes

1 Though no one, to my knowledge, has yet come up with chapter and verse for this.
2 There is no claim that 'learning power' represents a unitary psychological capability. The term is merely a useful place-holder for a to-be-discovered constellation of strategies, skills, beliefs, dispositions, interests and values that have general utility in the face of difficulty or challenge.

References

Beilock, S. and Lyons, I. (2009) Expertise and the mental simulation of action. In K. D. Markham, W. Klein and L.A. Suhr (eds) *Handbook of Imagination and Mental Simulation*. New York: Psychology Press.

Bonawitz, E. B., Shafto, P., Gweon, H., Goodman, N., Spelke, E. and Schulz, L. E. (2011) The double-edged sword of pedagogy: Teaching limits children's spontaneous exploration and discovery. *Cognition, 120*(3), 322–30.

Clark, A. (1997) *Being There: Putting Brain, Body and World Together Again*. Cambridge, MA: MIT Press.

Clark, A. (2003) *Natural-Born Cyborgs*. Oxford: Oxford University Press.

Clark, A. (2013) Whatever next? Predictive brains, situated agents and the future of cognitive science. *Behavioral and Brain Sciences, 36*, 181–253.

Claxton, G. (2002) *Building Learning Power: Helping Young People Become Better Learners*. Bristol: TLO.

Claxton, G. (2006) Thinking at the edge: Developing soft creativity. *Cambridge Journal of Education, 36*(3), 351–62.

Claxton, G., Chambers, M., Powell, G. and Lucas, L. (2011) *The Learning Powered School: Pioneering 21st Century Education.* Bristol: TLO.

Colby, A. and Kohlberg, L. (2011) *The Measurement of Moral Judgment.* Cambridge: Cambridge University Press.

Curran, H. V. (1988) Relative universals: perspectives on culture and cognition. In G. L. Claxton (ed.) *Growth Points in Cognition.* London: Routledge.

Daniels, H., Lauder, H. and Porter, J. (2011) *Educational Theories, Culture and Learning.* London: Routledge Falmer.

Deakin-Crick, R. (2006) *Learning Power in Practice: A Guide for Teachers.* London: Sage.

Dickstein, S., Thompson, R., Estes, D., Malkin, C. and Lamb, M. (1984) Social referencing and the security of attachment. *Infant Development and Behavior, 7,* 507–16.

Dijksterhuis, A. (2004) Think different: The merits of unconscious thought in preference development and decision making. *Journal of Personality and Social Psychology, 87*(5), 586–98.

Dweck, C. S. (2000) *Self-theories: Their Role in Motivation, Personality, and Development.* Philadelphia, PA: Psychology Press.

Ericsson, K. A. (1996) *The Road to Excellence: The Acquisition of Expert Performance.* Mahwah, NJ: Erlbaum.

Fensham, P. and Marton, F. (1992) Whatever happened to intuition in science education? *Research in Science Education, 22,* 114–22.

Furedi, F. (2008), *Paranoid Parenting.* London: Continuum.

Gergen, K. J. (1991) *The Saturated Self: Dilemmas of Identity in Modern Life.* New York: Basic Books.

Glenberg, A. and Gallese, V. (2012) Action-based language: A theory of language acquisition, comprehension and production. *Cortex, 48*(7), 905–22.

Gopnik, A., Melzoff, A. and Kuhl, P. (2011) *The Scientist in the Crib: What Early Learning Tells Us about the Mind.* San Francisco: HarperPerennial.

Haidt, J. (2012) *The Righteous Mind.* London: Allen Lane.

Harris, P. L. and Want, S. (2005) On learning what not to do: The emergence of selective imitation in tool use by young children. In S. Hurley and N. Chater (eds) *Perspectives on Imitation: From Cognitive Neuroscience to Social Science,* Vol. 2 (pp. 149–62). Cambridge, MA: MIT Press.

Harris, P. L., Corriveau, K. H., Pasquini, E. S., Koenig, M. A. and Clement, F. (2013) Credulity and the development of selective trust in early childhood. In M. Beran, J. Brandl, J. Perner and J. Proust (eds) *Foundations of Metacognition.* New York: Oxford University Press.

Hebb, D. O. (1949) *The Organization of Behavior.* New York: Wiley.

Iacoboni, M. (2009) Imitation, empathy and mirror neurons. *Annual Review of Psychology, 60,* 653–70.

Industrial Society (1997) *Speaking Up, Speaking Out: The 2020 Vision Research Programme Report.* London: Industrial Society.

Istance, D., Scheutze, H. and Schuller, T. (2002) *International Perspectives on Lifelong Learning.* Buckingham: Open University Press.

James, M., McCormick, R., Black, P. *et al* (2007) *Improving Learning How to Learn: Classrooms, Schools and Networks.* London: Routledge.

Kegan, R. (1995) *In Over Our Heads: The Mental Demands of Modern Life.* Cambridge, MA: Harvard University Press.

Lucas, B. and Claxton, G. L. (2010) *New Kinds of Smart: How the Science of Learnable Intelligence Is Changing Education.* Maidenhead: Open University Press.

Lyman, B. (2009) *An Introduction to Prenatal Psychology.* Church Gate: New Providence.

Meadows, S. (2006) *The Child as Thinker: The Development and Acquisition of Cognition in Childhood.* London: Routledge Falmer.

Moore, C. and Dunham, P. (eds) (1995) *Joint Attention: Its Origins and Role in Development.* Mahwah, NJ: Erlbaum.

Palmer, S. (2007) *Toxic Childhood.* London: Orion.

Partanen, E., Kujala, T., Tervaniemi, M. and Huotilainen M. (2013) Prenatal music exposure induces long-term neural effects. *PLoS ONE, 8*(10), e78946. DOI: 10.1371/journal.pone.0078946.

Perkins, D. N. (1995) *Outsmarting IQ: The Emerging Science of Learnable Intelligence.* New York: Basic Books.

Perkins, D. N. (2009) *Making Learning Whole.* San Francisco: Jossey-Bass.

Piaget, J. (2001) *The Language and Thought of the Child.* London: Routledge.

Pulvermuller, F. (2013) How neurons make meaning: Brain mechanisms for embodied and abstract-symbolic semantics. *Trends in Cognitive Science,* in press.

Resnick, L. (1999) Making America smarter. *Education Week Century Series, 18*(40), 38–40.

Salomon, G. (ed.) (1993) *Distributed Cognitions: Psychological and Educational Considerations.* Cambridge: Cambridge University Press.

Schore, A. N. (1999) *Affect Regulation and the Origin of the Self.* Hillsdale, NJ: Erlbaum.

Siegel, D. (2012) *The Developing Mind: How Relationships and the Brain Interact to Shape Who We Are.* London: Guilford Press.

Spitzer, M. (1999) *The Mind Within the Net: Models of Learning, Thinking and Acting.* Cambridge, MA: Bradford/MIT Press.

Tomasello, M. (1999) *The Cultural Origins of Human Cognition.* Cambridge, MA: Harvard University Press.

Vygotsky, L. S. (1978) *Mind in Society: The Development of Higher Psychological Processes.* Cambridge, MA: Harvard University Press.

32

THINKING WITHIN THE WELLBEING WHEEL

Rosemary Roberts

Introduction

Babies' and young children's situations and early experiences make a profound and lasting impact on their thinking and wellbeing development, with important implications for practitioners working with young children and their families. Within the context of recent early years research, this chapter introduces a *wheel of wellbeing* that shows cognition to be a fundamental part of holistic wellbeing development, within an ecological framework. In *wellbeing play*, connections are made between key elements of agency in the wellbeing model, and the development of '*positive thinking dispositions*'. The processes involved in this holistic wellbeing development are termed '*companionable learning*'. In *four 'A's of wellbeing*, situations and experiences in early childhood education and care (ECEC) are explored that especially support babies' and young children's developing wellbeing and positive thinking dispositions. In *developing wellbeing together*, some implications for practice are identified, and the case is made for exploring ways to build collective wellbeing in families and communities.

Context

Since the end of the twentieth century, there has been a heightened awareness of the long-term impact of situations and experiences in the first three years of life. There is an ongoing debate about the policy and practice implications of these studies on the early development of the brain (Shonkoff and Levitt, 2010; Page *et al.*, 2013). Key findings informing this debate include the following factors: that relationships are found to be the key to brain development (Gerhardt, 2004; Sinclair, 2007); that there is a need, in our thinking, to integrate the cognitive and affective aspects of child development, and consequently to develop a more integrated range of services around children and their families (Roberts, 2010); and that a quality workforce is essential to quality services (Nutbrown and Page, 2008).

Underpinning these findings are concepts of interaction, companionship, collaboration, trust, caring and self-esteem (Roberts, 2006). Often the interplay between mother and baby reveals the natural sociability of infants which serves to motivate 'companionship', eliciting the intuitive parenting that is evident in so very many observations of mothers and infants (Trevarthen and Aitken, 2001). This idea of 'intersubjectivity' is a key concept (Stern, 1985).

An important element that has emerged in this context is the power of an ecological approach. Bronfenbrenner's work (1979, 2005) continues to break down barriers between the social sciences of psychology, sociology and anthropology by suggesting that human development is better analysed in terms of systems, rather than by reference to linear variables. He described the dyad, or two-person system, suggesting that if one member of the pair undergoes a process of development, the other does also. He argued that this relationship provides a key to understanding developmental changes not only in children but also in adults who serve as primary caregivers. The microsystem of a child's relationships can be seen to underpin the nature and development of wellbeing (Roberts, 2010). Bronfenbrenner shows how this idea extends through the ever-widening environmental contexts of our lives (see Figure 32.2: The wellbeing wheel).

The relationship between education and social policy has become both increasingly uncertain and increasingly relevant in the early years. This is in part because of the economic, cultural and social transformations of post-industrial societies. The issue of poverty and its impact on child health is dismayingly relevant (Spencer, 2000; Field, 2010). Concerns about citizenship rights, access to benefits and social inclusion have been matters for ongoing debate in the changing context of governments' shifting priorities.

The OECD thematic reviews (2001, 2006) of early childhood education and care highlighted ten policy areas for consideration. Three of these related to the child's social context; to wellbeing and learning; and to family and community involvement. Recommendations included attending to the social context of early childhood development; placing wellbeing, early development and learning at the core of ECEC work while respecting the child's agency and natural learning strategies; and encouraging family and community involvement in early childhood services. These are challenging recommendations for those now providing daycare for the very youngest children.

In a climate of reduced public funding, ECEC policy has been firmly linked with the need to raise family incomes through employment, with a perceived need for more women to be employed in the workforce. Consequently the availability (or lack) of childcare has been a key issue in ECEC policy development. It is concerning that this policy development appears to have been driven primarily by economic factors, rather than by the needs and the wellbeing of babies and young children. It is within this context that this consideration of wellbeing development, with its implications for practitioners and managers, is placed.

The wheel of wellbeing

In recent decades use of the term 'wellbeing' has become increasingly widespread. Definitions have varied considerably, as evidenced by various 'wheels of wellbeing' that have been developed. The research outcomes described here constitute one researcher's attempt to develop a theoretical model of wellbeing, bringing together her own evidence with recurring wellbeing themes in the literature (Roberts, 2010).

In order to attempt to make sense of these foundations of resilient wellbeing, a theoretical framework was developed that brings together the elements of cognition and affect in ways that reflect the daily lives of children.

The structure of child development with which we are so familiar has four main constructs – emotional, social, cognitive and physical. The tendency to think about each of these constructs in isolation has often led to a fragmentation of thinking about children's development, and about service delivery: public health, medicine, education and psychology have their separate identities, from local council services to university departments and career structures. However, now we are attempting to develop policies and services that reflect a more holistic approach, incorporating both separate aspects of children's development and a perception of children's everyday lives in which those various aspects are seen as fundamentally interdependent. In this more holistic and interdependent model, families, communities and physical environments are acknowledged as powerfully influential factors in everyday lives and development.

The holistic wellbeing structure now proposed also has four main constructs; but here, three of those constructs incorporate cognition and affect within them. The largely contextual 'physical wellbeing' is seen as a foundation construct for the other three: communication, belonging-and-boundaries, and agency.

The foundation construct of physical development is about the impact of the external and physical world on processes and states of wellbeing, including physical health. It is divided into two components: the first, health and development, contains such elements as eating, sleeping, motor control, health routines and managing ill health. The second component refers, more unusually in the context of children's physical development, to the physical *environment* of wellbeing, including family income, housing, and the local environment.

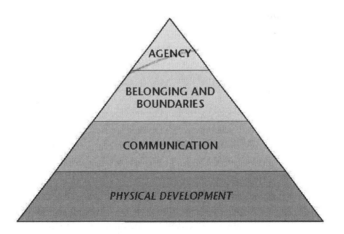

Figure 32.1 Wellbeing constructs

The next construct, of communication, is of a different order from the mainly contextual one of physical wellbeing. Communication is the *process* that, always in the cultural context, underpins all affective, social and ultimately cognitive functioning (Vygotsky, 1962). The construct of communication is about interactive *processes*. In this wellbeing framework, communication is structured into two components: received communication, using all the senses; and expressed communication, with such elements as body language, spoken language, visual representing, stories, music and moving.

This communication construct is not just about conversations between people but about all connections made with the world, using all the senses. It is about how we find out about things, by internally and externally formulating questions and interacting with the environment, including people, in order to discover. And it is about connecting with the awe and wonder of the natural world, and our impact upon it. Essentially, it encapsulates two-way processes of connection. This mutuality characterizes 'companionable learning', the process of wellbeing development described below. Companionable learning can also be termed 'diagogy' – a mutual, inter-subjective approach that incorporates the *processes* of wellbeing development.

The remaining two constructs, belonging-and-boundaries and agency, are proposed as *states* of wellbeing. The concept of 'belonging' used here is very closely associated with the theory of attachment (Bowlby, 1969; Rutter, 1972).

Elements of 'belonging' include a sense of identity in relation to others, the strength of attachment to 'companions', and a sense of belonging to place, as well as people. There is also an important association between the two components of 'belonging', and 'boundaries'. 'Boundaries' includes respect for people and places, awareness of expectations, familiarity with rules, understanding *reasons* for boundaries, and self regulation. These are all inevitable *consequences* of belonging.

In research, policy and service delivery, the separation of 'belonging' and 'boundaries' – in families, communities and societies – has not been helpful. Present-day challenges include the fragmentation of family life, a rise in behavioral problems in schools, and in youth offending (Rutter and Smith, 1995). We are used to the association of 'rights' with 'responsibilities'. This idea of 'belonging-and-boundaries' as two sides of the same coin with the one (boundaries) as a consequence of the other (belonging) is a related concept for early childhood.

A sense of belonging and its consequent boundaries delineates our external world, and underpins our interactions with people and environments; whereas the final wellbeing construct – a sense of agency – relates to the internal world that drives our thoughts and actions and the ways in which we communicate. This construct makes a fundamental impact on our wellbeing. Human agency can be described as the capacity of human beings to make choices, and to act on those choices in the world. It is about the ability and inclination to take initiative, to respond to challenges, to try to influence events – an individual's ability to act both alone and with others, to make a difference to their world. It is exemplified by the Reggio Emilia approach to early childhood education in northern Italy. Key components of this agency construct are the positive sense of self that is grounded in realistic self-esteem and achievement (Roberts, 2006); positive learning dispositions underpinning life-long learning (Carr, 2001); and 'influencing', containing internal locus of control, a sense of empowerment, and a caring disposition that encompasses caring both for the self, and for others (Bronfenbrenner, 2005).

The idea of making a difference collectively – together with others, rather than individually – generates the idea of *collective* wellbeing (Roberts, 2010). Right from the start, children need – in families, and in settings – to be enabled to take a measure of control, to develop a sense of 'influencing' as it is described here. The disposition to care and the ability to do so depend on a degree of confidence in the likelihood of success, underpinning the importance of children's development of a positive sense of self, and of realistic self-esteem.

The wellbeing wheel (Figure 32.2) shows the four wellbeing constructs of holistic child development as they operate across the spectrum of ecological interactions.

The four constructs of wellbeing are inextricably integrated and interdependent; and it is important to think about each one essentially in the context of the others. Here is an example of an incident where all four constructs were in evidence. Sasha, aged 19 months, is with her mother, Lara, and one of her brothers, Zeb.

> Sasha and Zeb are finishing their little bowls of ice-cream. Sasha is sitting on a gap in the floor between the piles of things, with her bowl on the floor between her knees, spooning melted ice-cream in with an adult dessertspoon and hardly spilling a drop. It is quiet in the room except for the click of spoons, and she is beaming at me between mouthfuls. After a while she looks round at her mother, who is sitting on the settee behind her, and they giggle.
>
> Now Sasha gets to her feet, clutching bowl and spoon carefully. 'OK then, don't spill it – do you want Mummy to do the last little bit?' Lara asks. 'I'll get the last little bit out for you … there we go, none left, is there? You going to put it in the kitchen then?' Sasha sets off across the floor, drops the spoon with a clatter, exclaims, and bends down to pick it up, grunting with effort and satisfaction as she stands up again. With her small shoulder she heaves open the door to the kitchen

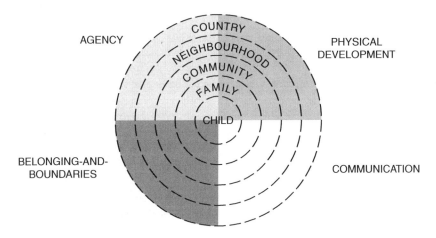

Figure 32.2 The wellbeing wheel

and giggles with satisfaction; but the baby gate across the kitchen area is closed. She tries to heave that too, but can't, and waits for Lara to come and open it.

In the kitchen the dishwasher is open, and we can see that there are dishes in it. Sasha glances at them and turns enquiringly to Lara, making questioning noises. 'No, that's clean in there, that needs emptying doesn't it? Put it up on the side then.' Turning back, Sasha stretches up as high as she can, making effortful sounds. She can just reach high enough to push the bowl and spoon up onto the counter next to the dishwasher. Then she turns and comes back through the baby gate, looking and sounding extremely pleased with herself.

This observation illustrates all four constructs of the wellbeing model. Sasha's motor control is evident in the way she manages the bowl and spoon; she and her mother communicate effectively with each other, and she learns from experience how the kitchen door and the baby gate work; her determination to put her bowl in the right place indicates her sense of being part of the family, together with the consequent awareness and acceptance of what is expected (no dirty bowls on top of the clean dishes, quite an achievement at 19 months); and her confidence, her eagerness to find out what to do, and her determination to help makes the whole episode a wonderful example of 19-month agency in everyday life.

Positive thinking dispositions

So where is *thinking* to be found within the wellbeing wheel? We know that the development of language and thought in early childhood is inextricably entangled (Vygotsky 1962). In addition to the development of language, the elements described above, of positive self concept and learning dispositions, are much discussed in the 'learning' literature. Our sense of self and the dispositions with which we struggle to make sense of the world, right from the start, are key factors in how we learn. But what is the purpose of our learning? Do young children think, and struggle to understand (processes very far from the acquisition of certain kinds of knowledge now often thought to be the main purpose of education) essentially for their own satisfaction of making sense of the world? Or is it also, in a most fundamental sense, in order to cause things to happen?

This seems to be the heart of the matter. What things need doing so much because they are at the core, cognitively, socially, physically and psychologically, of our survival drive, as individuals and in communities? This brief chapter cannot be the place to attempt to address such enormous 'meaning-of-life' questions. Yet the sometimes glib assertion that we need to be able to look after ourselves if we are to succeed in looking after each other is surely common sense. So what does it entail?

We need to develop – in ourselves and in children – the elements of agency, in order to think. The terms used earlier to describe the elements of agency were as follows: the positive sense of self that is grounded in realistic self-esteem and achievement; positive learning dispositions; and – for 'influencing' – an internal locus of control, a sense of empowerment, and a caring disposition that encompasses caring

POSITIVE THINKING DISPOSITIONS

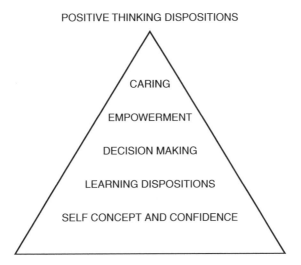

Figure 32.3 Positive thinking dispositions

both for the self, and for others. Our ability to think, to solve problems, and to look after ourselves and others, depends on our sense of agency. In Figure 32.3, these terms can be seen in a 'hierarchy' of positive thinking dispositions.

Thinking dispositions go further than learning dispositions. We think of positive *learning* dispositions as being about habits of mind such as watching, listening, exploring, persisting, learning from mistakes. Learning dispositions are perfectly formed at birth, and one of our tasks as companions of the youngest children is to maintain them. These are the ways in which babies, young children, and indeed adults, find out about the world and begin to acquire some sense of control. But we are not born with *thinking* dispositions – these have to be developed. The positive learning dispositions with which babies are born are like roots and branches that, when protected and nurtured, may ultimately flower into positive thinking dispositions. It is with these thinking dispositions that we develop the ability to discover and pursue new ideas, experiment, solve problems, make links and identify ways to do things.

This concept of positive thinking dispositions, derived from the components of agency, offers an answer to the question 'Where is thinking in the wellbeing wheel?' Thinking depends on having a sense of agency that enables us to understand, to influence, and to care; and nurturing such a sense of agency helps to develop thinking dispositions.

These ABC constructs and positive thinking dispositions are one half of the wellbeing model – the theoretical half. Now this chapter links the theory with the practical half of the model: to describe wellbeing play, companionable learning, and the four 'A's of everyday wellbeing. These are the rich situations and experiences in which wellbeing development, agency and positive thinking dispositions are most likely to occur.

Wellbeing play

Being clear about children's progression in play is one way to make sense of what they are doing. We can think of play as a continuum of three interlinked levels: first, watching and exploring; second, practising and representing; and third, playing creatively. This third level is wellbeing play.

Implicit in the first level is the question 'What is this?' At this stage children investigate and hypothesize; they are often on the move, and often new to the situation. They find out about the world and struggle to adjust to it. Struggle is a feature of this level. The second level is about acquiring new skills. Now the all-important question has progressed from 'What is it?' to 'How does it work? How can I control it?' Children practise new skills over and over again, often with amazing determination and persistence.

The third level is about playing – real playing. Now children use their experiences creatively, shaping their play through their own unique perceptions, and bringing together their skills and their previous experiences. Their question now is, 'How can I use my knowledge and skills to play *my* way?' Here, children are combining the rich texture of their observations, ideas, feelings and relationships; with the application of their competence and technical prowess. They have worked at exploration and achieving competence, and now they know about the things they have worked at so well that they can play with them. Athey (2007) explains struggle through practice to playfulness, and beyond competence to fun. She writes that if mere 'competence' is seen as an endpoint to knowledge, creativity and playfulness are lost.

Play at this third level can be thought of as 'real' play, often termed child-initiated or free-flow play (Bruce, 1987). Even the very youngest children may play at this level with certain people and things that they have come to know very well. This third level is what is meant by 'wellbeing play'.

What can wellbeing play tell us about how children develop the sense of agency that underpins positive thinking dispositions? The particular characteristics of the observed wellbeing play described below were rich in the development of agency:

> Lena had found an old shopping list of Mum's. 'This says "special cheese and Dinocrackers and apples",' she said to Jake. 'The shop's there,' she said, pointing to the store-cupboard that Mum was clearing out. 'Please can we have a pretend picnic, Mum?' she asked. She had seen their mum throwing away some small boxes, which had given her the idea. Mum said alright, so long as Jake didn't eat anything old out of the boxes and get a tummy ache.
>
> They went backwards and forwards between the store-cupboard and the yard with empty and half-full boxes, bags, trays and baskets. Jake soon got fed up with trailing backwards and forwards carrying things; he had a great time instead standing on the broken branch throwing things down into his truck.
>
> Lena brought out her dolls, and made them all sit up and eat their picnic under the tree; and then she told them a story about a magic rabbit that lived underneath the tree. When Mum saw the mess, she said she had sorted out all the boxes and things once and she wasn't going to do it all over again. She gave Lena a rubbish bag and said she could put all the boxes in, now the dolls had had their

picnic. Lena really liked putting everything in the bag – and then she said it was time the dolls had a rest in their cots. So off she went into the house, dragging the bag behind her and with the two dolls tucked one under each arm.

Lena's needs included anchored situations with human or imaginary companions; authority – importantly, her own; 'apprenticeship' materials that enabled her to base her play in her own daily experiences; and time and space to play. All the elements of wellbeing play are evident here. And in this kind of play, children's schemas (Nutbrown, 1999) can – as in this case – be given free rein, to children's deep satisfaction.

The positive thinking dispositions drawn from the elements of agency (see Figure 32.3), are clearly evident here: Lena's self-concept (the confidence with which she set up the pretend picnic), learning dispositions (she had watched her mother, listened to her, persisted with the long setting-up process), decision-making (she chose her own ways to do things), empowerment (she felt able to play this way, with her mother's blessing but not her mother's control, until the end), and her caring disposition (she involved her brother only as long as he wanted, and she took care of her hungry and tired dolls). This observation shows how Lena's developing thinking dispositions are being powerfully nurtured by her experience of wellbeing play. It illustrates why the provision of rich experiences of wellbeing play are so very important, in enabling children to learn to think.

Companionable learning

Research (Gerhardt, 2004) tells us that the most important underpinning element of all wellbeing development is the nature and style of the relationships the youngest children experience with their companions. Here, companions may be defined as children and adults who are together regularly and know each other well, and who are bound by love or affection; so for instance mothers, fathers, primary carers, peers and siblings, grandparents, extended family, neighbourhood people – the possibilities are extensive.

Companionable learning is a development mechanism for wellbeing, involving companionable engagement with such companions. It is about learning in the widest possible sense, i.e. all of a child's development that flows from active companionable engagement with the world and the people in it. The concept of companionable learning has a range of theoretical roots. 'Social capital' (Bourdieu, 1990; Giddens, 2006), a term frequently used in the literature and relevant here, refers to social relationships that generate positive benefits. Many neuroscientists (Shonkoff and Philips, 2000) have stressed the importance of early interactions, giving evidence that positive, emotionally charged interactions within secure relationships foster babies' learning and brain development. Social interaction and active styles of learning have long been known to be key factors in positive child development (Isaacs, 1954); and the work of other key proponents of social learning theory underpins this concept of companionable learning, for instance Vygotsky (1978), Bandura (1997), Wertsch *et al.* (1995) and Rogoff (1990).

At the micro level which is the main focus of this chapter, companionable learning describes the mutual intersubjectivity that involves the child and the adult (or sibling or peer) in a reciprocal dialogue. It involves a companionable shared preoccupation in which companions are learning together and sharing their thinking, in a process which is essentially interactive. But although they are learning together they are not, of course, learning the same things. For instance, an adult and a baby or young child are often simply learning about each other and what they both enjoy, in a companionable way. For both, this will constitute a great deal of important and often transferable learning.

Four 'A's of everyday wellbeing

Some aspects of everyday life are particularly rich in companionable wellbeing opportunities. These are described here as the four 'A's of everyday wellbeing. They are *companionable* anchored attention, *companionable* authority, *companionable* apprenticeship, and *companionably* allowing children the time and space they need.

Children's need for companionable 'anchored attention', and their delight in situations where they are 'anchored' with their companions, is evident to all who live and work with them. This process of anchored attention is at the heart of the 'belonging' half of the belonging-and-boundaries construct. Children (and companions) do not necessarily need to be physically anchored, as after a while anchoring can work as a mental process: for instance, knowing they are 'camped out' in their key person's mind (Elfer *et al.*, 2003). All those experiences in which, by definition, the adult is paying attention to the child and does not go away are often favourites of both the children and their companions: experiences such as bath time, book sharing, cooking together.

Companionable 'authority' can be seen to feed wellbeing development especially in the context of companionable attention. Companionable authority, an element of everyday wellbeing, is about a gentle yet firm style of authoritative companionship rather than a rigid, authoritarian approach. It can be especially helpful for children's sense of belonging-and-boundaries; the sense that underpins security. Here, authority is about companions being reliable, regular, consistent and predictable in their expectations. Underpinning companionable authority are the processes of establishing routines and rules; and gently but firmly sticking to them as long as they are appropriate.

'Apprenticeship' is about children's active companionable involvement in everyday tasks that they see adults doing. It is often referred to by children themselves as 'helping'. Clearly relevant to everyday life at home but also powerful in settings, this concept illustrates the strong potential of childminders (a UK term) providing family daycare in relation to wellbeing. Larger settings, too, can build up children's participation in this way; although apprenticeship activities – even when their importance is understood – are harder to organize in institutional daycare settings. Perhaps one of the reasons why apprenticeship is not, at present, seen as an important part of childhood in the UK is the insistent focus on children's *independent* achievements, rather than on their collaborative achievements with companions, for instance in helping to clear the table and wash up.

Time and space in childhood really matters. Children need time to process their experiences, and sometimes to relive them. And they need time and space for their play. Both at home and in settings, children also need 'somewhere to call their own' – even if only their own peg and shoe bag, or a particular area of the bedroom. Some children treat their buggy or car seat as their own space too. For them, being in these places offers the opportunity mentally to process what has been happening. They need time and space for reflection, an essential part of the learning process.

Certain situations and experiences in most children's everyday lives are rich in four 'A's opportunities. At these times the four 'A's described above are especially likely to occur, and children's sense of wellbeing is likely to flourish. The first set of situations and experiences relate to food: growing it, shopping, cooking and eating together, picnics and parties. The second set is about familiarity, or 'old friends': for instance people (companions), much-loved books, pets, childhood songs and rhymes, intensely familiar places. The third set involves going out on everyday expeditions and getting around outside the home, walking, or going by bus or train. All three sets offer multiple opportunities for anchored attention, companionable authority, apprentice-ship tasks, and even time and space. How effective these situations and experiences are is dependent not simply on providing them, but on how companionably the children experience them.

Implications for practice

The case for exploring ways to build a communal sense of wellbeing is very strong. During the wellbeing research (Roberts, 2007), in family discussions and in focus groups, collective wellbeing in communities, neighbourhoods and nations was seen as important. In some contexts, the idea that agency, belonging-and-boundaries, com-munication and physical wellbeing can apply collectively in families, communities, and societies can be liberating, particularly for mothers. In some Asian communities for instance, women are often uncomfortable with the essentially westernised concept of a child's or a mother's individual agency, but very positive about the prospect of helping to develop a collective sense of wellbeing in the family or community. Per-haps this offers new perspectives on the formulation of social policy in diverse communities.

In relation to thinking within the wellbeing wheel, are there implications for ECEC practice? What do babies and young children need for their wellbeing and for developing their ability to think, on a daily basis? First, babies and the youngest chil-dren need positive, responsive, respectful, consistent and sustained relationships. These relationships are the bedrock of child development, supporting a child's ability to cope with the many and varied transitions that are part of life in the early years. However, systems and structures in daycare can be unhelpful and even counter-pro-ductive in building such relationships. All too often, the very youngest children's experience of relationships in daycare is brief, fragmented, insignificant and inconsis-tent. While the use of a key person approach (Elfer *et al.*, 2003) that incorporates emotional relationships with organizational strategies is known to be vital, this approach has been open to misunderstanding and even neglect. There are many rea-sons for this, sometimes including a lack of managerial awareness, and reductions in service funding. In such cases the use of a companionable learning approach might go some way in helping to support the needs of the youngest children.

Second, a theoretical case has been made here for wellbeing play as the mechanism for developing positive thinking dispositions. These dispositions are surely the bedrock of education; and their development through daily experiences of wellbeing play should be explored as a priority.

Third, a crucial aspect of early childhood education and care is the importance of developing language, through communication, connection, and interaction. For the youngest children, the development of language begins with our universal first language of the senses: body language. In this broad definition of language, companionable learning is an essentially language-based way of sharing thinking and learning together. And while engagement in companionable learning is, by definition, about developing language, it is also a process that supports knowledge and understanding – of literacy, numeracy, environments and so on. Ways of building the processes of companionable learning into daily daycare will be ways of underpinning positive long-term outcomes for early education.

Finally, in relation to companionable learning, three other perspectives arise. First, young children long to be like the people they know and love best. Consequently it is important that children experience adults as companionable *learners* rather than as *knowers*. Second, as well as the need to belong, the youngest children need the security that comes from understanding boundaries as *a consequence* of belonging. And third, within their companionable relationships babies and young children need to begin to build a sense of their own agency. We can support them in doing this by deliberately helping them to develop their 'agency combination': confidence; positive learning dispositions; and learning how to influence their own wellbeing, and care for their companions.

Giving babies and young children the best possible start involves practice in ECEC that reflects what we now know. The training of practitioners at all levels needs to identify and value the many companionable things they already do; and it needs to support practitioners to understand the possibilities of companionable practice in building the life-long wellbeing of the youngest children.

As Bronfenbrenner wrote in 2005: 'No society can long sustain itself unless its members have learned the sensitivities, motivations, and skills involved in assisting and caring for other human beings.'

References

Athey, C. (2007) *Extending Thought in Young Children*, 2nd edn. London: Paul Chapman.
Bandura, A. (1997) *Self-Efficacy: The Exercise of Control*. New York: W. H. Freeman.
Bourdieu, P. (1990) *The Logic of Practice*. Cambridge: Polity Press.
Bowlby, J. (1969) *Attachment*, London: Penguin.
Bronfenbrenner, U. (1979) *The Ecology of Human Development: Experiments by Nature and Design*. London: Harvard University Press.
Bronfenbrenner, U. (ed.) (2005) *Making Human Beings HUMAN: Bioecological Perspectives on Human Development*. London: Sage.
Bruce, T. (1987) *Early Childhood Education*. London: Hodder and Stoughton.
Bruce, T. (1991) *Time to Play in Early Childhood*. London: Hodder and Stoughton.
Carr, M. (2001) *Assessment in Early Childhood Settings: Learning Stories*. London: Paul Chapman.
Elfer, P., Goldschmied, E., Selleck, D. (2003) *Key Persons in the Nursery*. London: David Fulton.

Field, F. (2010) *Independent Review on Poverty and Life Chances*. London: HM Government.

Gerhardt, S. (2004) *Why Love Matters: How Affection Shapes a Baby's Brain*. Hove: Routledge.

Giddens, A. (2006) *Sociology*. Cambridge: Polity Press.

Isaacs, S. (1954) *The Educational Value of the Nursery School*. London: British Association for Early Childhood Education.

Nutbrown, C. (1999) *Threads of Thinking: Young Children Thinking and the Role of Early Education*, 2nd edn. London: Paul Chapman.

Nutbrown, C. and Page, J. (2008) *Working with Babies and Children: From Birth to Three*. London: Sage.

OECD (Organisation for Economic Cooperation and Development) (2001) *Starting Strong: Early Childhood Education and Care*. Paris: OECD.

OECD (2006) *Starting Strong II: Early Childhood Education and Care*. Paris: OECD.

Page, J., Clare, A. and Nutbrown, C. (2013) *Working with Babies: From Birth to Three*. London: Sage.

Roberts, R. (2006) *Self Esteem and Early Learning*, 3rd edn. London: Sage.

Roberts, R. (2007) *Companionable Learning: The Development of Resilient Wellbeing From Birth to Three*, thesis submitted in partial fulfilment of the Degree of Doctor of Philosophy, University of Worcester in association with Coventry University. Available at: http://eprints.worc.ac.uk/511/1/Rosie_Roberts_complete_thesis.pdf.

Roberts, R. (2010) *Wellbeing from Birth*. London, Sage.

Rogoff, B. (1990) *Apprenticeship in Thinking: Cognitive Development in Social Context*. Oxford: Oxford University Press.

Rutter, M. (1972) *Maternal Deprivation Re-assessed*, Harmondsworth: Penguin.

Rutter, M. and Smith, D. (eds) (1995) *Psychosocial Disorders in Young People: Time Trends and Their Causes*. Chichester: John Wiley.

Sinclair, A. (2007) *0–5: How Small Children Make a Big Difference*. London: Work Foundation.

Shonkoff, J. and Phillips, D. (2000) *From Neurons to Neighborhoods: The Science of Early Childhood Development*. Washington, DC: National Academy Press.

Shonkoff, J. and Levitt, P. (2010) Neuroscience and the future of early childhood policy: Moving from why to what and how. *Neuron*, *67*(6), 9 September, 689–91.

Spencer, N. (2000) *Poverty and Child Health*. Oxford: Radcliffe Medical Press.

Stern, D. (1985) *The Interpersonal World of the Infant*. New York: Basic Books.

Trevarthen, C. and Aitken, K. (2001) Infant intersubjectivity: Research, theory, and clinical applications. *Journal of Child Psychology and Psychiatry*, *42*(1).

Vygotsky, L. S. (1962) *Thought and Language*. Cambridge, MA: MIT Press.

Vygotsky, L. S. (1978) *Mind in Society: The Development of Higher Psychological Processes*. Cambridge, MA: Harvard University Press.

Wertsch, J., Rio, P. D. and Alvarez, A. (eds) (1995) *Sociocultural Studies of Mind*. Cambridge: Cambridge University Press.

33

HOW YOUNG CHILDREN THINK AND LEARN THROUGH EXPLORING SCHEMAS

Cath Arnold

I paint objects as I think them, not as I see them.

Picasso

Introduction

After making many close observations of young children's spontaneous actions over many years, I cannot help but notice that children explore systematically and repeat patterns of action in their play. According to Piaget and Athey, the roots of learning are internal rather than external. What Picasso meant in the quote above was that 'he had this repertoire inside him' and this is what children develop through schemas (Athey, 2010).

In this chapter, I present:

- Schema theory as interpreted by Athey including definitions
- Ideas about 'content' and 'form'
- Ways of exploring schemas: through senses and action, functional dependency relationships, symbolic play, and thinking
- Their context and observations of two children to which I apply the theory
- Assimilation and accommodation

Note: throughout this chapter examples are drawn from Gabriella, aged 14 months and Nicole, aged 5 years 6 months (at the time of writing). They are my grandchildren so I have access to them regularly and to their parents' observations and views about their learning and their permissions to share these more widely. What distinguishes this as a study rather than an anecdotal account about my grandchildren are that the observations were recorded in note form, in photographs and/or on video at or near to the event being described and the video observations can be revisited. The observations are italicised.

Defining 'schemas'

Schemas are repeated patterns of action through which generalizations can be made. Young children try out the same action with different materials or objects in order to see what will happen. They then repeat those actions to establish reliability. Athey defines schemas as 'patterns of repeatable actions that lead to early categories and then to logical classifications. As a result of applying a range of action schemas to objects, infants arrive at the generalizations that objects are 'throwable', 'suckable' and 'bangable" (Athey, 2007, p. 49).

Piaget and Athey believed that our actions become our thinking, although this is difficult to test or to prove (Athey, 2007, p. 46). Through his detailed observations of his own three children from birth, Piaget demonstrated the small steps in progress made by each child over time (Piaget, 1954, 1962). Athey (2007) gathered over 5,000 observations of 20 children in a setting to show how sharing theory with parents and offering rich experiences to extend spontaneous actions enriched the educational experiences of the children and made the adults more aware of conceptual links between actions and thinking.

Piaget was not an educationalist but a genetic epistemologist with a background in biology. He believed that we adapt to the environment in which we find ourselves. Nature *and* nurture interact to enable children to construct higher levels of knowledge from elements contributed *both* by innate capacities and by environmental information (Das Gupta, 1994, p. 48).

During the 1970s Athey led the Froebel Project in London and observed 20 children, alongside their parents, over a period of two years (Athey, 2007). The project team were interested in what children aged 2–5 years *can* do. Athey was particularly interested in what each child 'brings to the learning situation' (their innate drive to explore and learn) (Athey, 2007, p. 44). There was a moment, during the project, when things became clearer to Athey and demonstrated that schemas could apply to 'static configurations' as well as to 'dynamic sequences of action' (Athey, 2007, p. 48). Chris Athey, as part of the research design, was observing a comparison group, a more privileged group of children. The teacher was telling a story, 'Madeleine in Paris'. There were three instances when the children would not let their teacher carry on with the story. Afterwards, Chris looked at the illustrations on those pages where the children wanted to linger. On the first was the Eiffel Tower. The second was a hammock ... then Chris looked at the children's drawings displayed on the classroom wall ... a window, a fence, a gate ... At that moment, Chris realised that many of the children were interested in the 'grid' shape and responded to the story partly because of the illustrations that matched their current cognitive concerns or schemas (Athey, 2010).

Content and form

Fundamental to understanding schemas is understanding the difference between 'content' and 'form'. Put very simply, the 'content' is what children are playing with, any objects or resources they are using. Before knowing about schemas, our clue as to what children's interests were was the 'content' they were using and what they were saying while using that content. 'Form' is what children are doing with what they are playing with. Understanding the 'form' they are exploring offers more scope for supporting and extending their play and can give deep insights into children's thinking. For example, Harry liked to use the train set ('content') at nursery but we discovered that he was also very interested in 'connecting' (the 'form' or schema). That meant we could offer a range of opportunities to 'connect' in different ways and using different resources, which expanded his knowledge of 'connecting' (Arnold, 2003). We noticed that he not only 'connected' in a physical way but seemed to use his 'disconnecting' and 'connecting' schema to work through his understanding of his parents separating (Arnold, 2010).

The importance of context

Although Piaget and Athey did not write a great deal about each child's context, I believe they almost took for granted that a rich learning environment both at home and in school helps children to learn more effectively. Athey talked frequently about 'offering worthwhile curriculum content' to help 'feed schemas' (Athey, 2003). My view is that we need to make connections with both the 'form' children are exploring and with their family experiences and context in order that each child fulfils their potential. Donaldson (1978) found that experiments and questions need to make 'human sense' to children and this human sense often comes from us, as adults, understanding the children's family experiences.

Nicole and Gabriella live in the Midlands. They are part of a reconstituted family. Nicole's mother, Evita, is from Latvia and her father is from Serbia. They met in England and separated when Nicole was a toddler. Nicole has sustained her relationship with her father and sees him every week. Nicole's mother married an Englishman, my son Paul, two years ago and Gabriella was born last year. Evita came to England eight years ago unable to speak a word of English and now speaks three languages fluently – Latvian, Russian and English – and although both girls are exposed to an English-speaking environment, Evita speaks to them in Latvian a bit each day so that they will develop the sounds necessary for both languages. Nicole attended nursery part time and has been at school a year. On a Saturday she attends dance classes, tap, ballet and stage, and a couple of months ago she was in a show at the local theatre. Nicole loves to draw and to paint. She is very physical and creative. Gabriella communicates well, is sociable, loves music, has just started walking and is good at letting you know what she wants and does not want.

The ways that children explore schemas

Although most writers on schemas clearly define the 'levels' at which children explore their schemas as 'sensori-motor', 'symbolic functioning', 'functional dependency relationships' and 'thought', I prefer to think about these as different 'ways' that human beings explore schemas (Athey, 2007, pp. 46–7). The difficulty I have with labelling them as 'levels' and also with clearly defined stages is that we tend to think of them as strict hierarchies when, in observations of human behaviour and actions, things seem to be much more fluid. As an adult, I frequently use my senses and actions to discover how something new works. I am also not convinced that babies do not think or use 'thought', although a baby obviously has less experience and physical prowess than a child or young adult and cannot yet communicate their thinking using language. So, in the spirit of thinking of these as ways of exploring schemas, I offer the following explanations and examples from observations of Nicole and Gabriella.

Senses and actions

Sensori–motor explorations are observed when a child is obviously exploring some-thing in order to see how it works or feels. This is when I am sometimes surprised and puzzled by their actions as I cannot always predict what they will do and it is difficult to set aside my adult experiences in order to see things from a child's perspective.

Example (Gabriella at 8 months 16 days)

I began to look after Gabriella two or three days a week when Evita went back to work. I knew about 'attachment theory' and that it was important to talk to her and to Nicole about their parents when they were at work. I made a book for Gabriella with photos of her, her mum, dad and sister. I knew her mum was keen to expose her to print so I labelled the pictures 'Gabriella', 'Mum', 'Dad' and 'Nicole'.

Figure 33.1 Gabriella's book

The first time I gave her the book she was 8 months 16 days. She liked it, opening and shutting it, looking at the pictures then putting the corner of the cover in her mouth. Then she noticed her name on the cover not fully stuck down – she seemed to be paying attention to detail and edges, labels etc. She managed to pull her name off. When she did, she ripped it in half and then ripped one bit in half again. Then she spent about 5 minutes trying to rip these small pieces in half. Finally she started to put them in her mouth. I took them off her at this point.

Analysis

I could see from this and other observations that Gabriella wanted to try and 'separate' or 'disconnect' things from each other. She did not know, at this stage, which was the whole and which were parts of that whole. I tried to think about what she was trying to do (her actions) and her motivation for those actions. In order that she could 'separate' her name and the other names from her book, I printed them again and laminated them and attached them to the book using Velcro. Gabriella found this extremely satisfying. She could rip all four names off the book and she practised this frequently, showing a real sense of satisfaction each time she successfully separated a name label from the book. It was months before she became interested in 'connecting' them to the book.

Example (Nicole at 5 years 6 months)

Nicole had been asking about going up to our attic so while Gabriella was asleep today, I told her we could go and have a look at the attic. I pulled down the

Figure 33.2   Gabriella looking at her book

ladder, climbed up and asked Nicole to follow, which she did although she was scared. At the top, I let her go ahead of me into the attic. Getting her to come down was really difficult. As she looked down, she was really scared. She shouted for Pop and the Fire Brigade to rescue her. I kept trying to encourage her to turn around to face the ladder but she couldn't do it. Eventually, she came down forwards with me in front of her.

Analysis

Nicole received feedback through her body and felt so afraid when she looked down that she did not think she could move. She had practised her 'up/down' trajectory movement for years and yet this was a new experience of going up and feeling higher than ever before.

Functional dependency relationships

We observe a child making functional dependency relationships when they 'observe the effects of action on objects or materials' (Athey, 1990, p. 70).

Example (Gabriella at 11 months 11 days)

Gabriella shuffled down the hallway carrying a ball in each hand. The hall was fairly dark. Gabriella dropped the balls and touched the nightlight so I switched it on. It lit up. Then I opened the bathroom door and the light went off. Gabriella looked a bit bewildered then touched the light with her index finger (left hand). She pointed and made an 'errh' sound. She moved nearer and tapped the light. It flickered on briefly. She repeated putting her left hand over the sensor three times and each time it came on. Then she covered the sensor with her right hand. It came on briefly. She repeated her action several more times with her left hand and less successfully with her right hand (possibly because of where she was sitting in relation to the light).

A few weeks later I noted that Gabriella (at 1 year 13 days)

> … went to the sensor light in hall and immediately covered the appropriate spot with her finger to make the light come on. She covered it with one finger and then her whole hand and both worked.

Analysis

I deduced from this that Gabriella had learned that the light coming on was functionally dependent on her 'covering' a particular area and that she must have remembered how that worked from one occasion to the next.

Example (Nicole at 5 years 3 months)

Nicole became very interested in the night light in our hall. She switched it on but it did not light up as it was daylight. Pop showed her how if you covered the small sensor at the front, it lit up. Then Nicole had the idea of closing all of the doors in the hall and as it became darker, the light came on. She made the light come on without covering the sensor.

Analysis

The light coming on was functionally dependent on the hall being dark and Nicole made it dark by closing all of the doors. There is clear evidence of her thinking about and understanding that she could 'envelop' the hall in darkness by closing the doors. She tried out her idea and it worked. This shows a more sophisticated understanding at 5 years than that of Gabriella at 11 months.

Symbolic functioning

We observe 'symbolic functioning' when a child or adult uses one object to stand for another. Piaget traced how very young children go from using the actual object in a way they have seen others do, to using objects that share some similarity with the real object in a similar way, to using objects that are manifestly different to the object being represented (Piaget, 1962, p. 120).

Example (Gabriella at 11 months 22 days)

Took all of the stuff out of my camera bag. When she took the remote control out, she pressed some buttons and then held it to her ear, saying something that sounded like 'Hello'. She then pointed the remote towards the TV screen twice.

Two days later (at 11 months 24 days)

Gabriella took all of my things out of the camera bag. She pressed the buttons and put the remote control against her ear, said 'Hello' and smiled at me twice and then held it towards the TV screen.

Analysis

The camera remote control, which is smaller than a TV remote control, has quite a bit in common with a mobile phone and, in this instance, the similarity to a mobile seemed to spark off Gabriella's actions of pressing the buttons, holding it close to her ear and pointing it towards the TV. She possibly thought it was a mobile phone although the mobiles she has seen recently are touchscreens. So although it was not the object itself, it was similar and her actions indicate that she recognised that similarity.

Athey (1990, p. 69) subdivided symbolic representation into:

1 Graphic representations of the static states of objects (configurational or iconic) (i.e. lining up or drawing)
2 Action representations of the dynamic aspects of objects and events (i.e. role play)
3 Speech representations of either the dynamic aspects of objects or events that accompanied representations of 1 and 2 (i.e. using language that relates to either the graphic representation or role play).

Example (Nicole at 5 years 2 months)

Nicole frequently engages in complex sequences of pretend play, which are 'action representations of objects and events', playing shops, hospitals and a favourite, often repeated, is birthdays:

> After making and decorating dough, Nicole went through the whole scenario of my birthday. Asked 'How old are you?' I said '66'. Nicole: 'We'll have 6 candles,' but actually used 4 candles and 2 candle holders. Sang 'Happy Birthday' and added an extra bit '6 claps 'cause you're 6' and then a pause and then 'one for luck'.

Analysis

Here Nicole was obviously re-presenting a whole scenario with which she was familiar. She may not have understood the concept of '66' but could certainly apply a concept of '6' to her actions, so the 'form' in this case was 'sixness' and she was using it to re-present my age as acknowledged and experienced during a birthday party. The whole scenario was a coordination of several schemas, including 'rotating' the dough to mix; producing a circular cake; placing 6 objects in the cake, in her mind, a 1:1 correspondence with my age; singing a set of words associated with birthdays and applied to me as she named me in the song.

Thought or thinking?

Although Athey has defined 'thought' as 'where a child gives a verbal account of an experience in the absence of any material or situational reminder of the original experience' (1990, p. 68), I am more inclined to consider 'thinking' and to seek evidence of young children developing their thinking. 'Thinking' can be thought of as an action that is developing and we can seek evidence of this, for example, when a child's body language suggests they are anticipating some event or recalling an event from the past. Currently Gabriella is interested in 'containing' objects inside other objects capable of containing them. One of her favourite actions is putting things in the bin, including recently, her mum's keys and her teddy, which she dearly loves. She really likes to put her wet or dirty nappy in the bin when she has been changed and cries if you do not allow her to do that.

Example (Gabriella at 14 months 23 days)

This morning we were in a completely different environment (a school and Children's Centre). We had had a look around and noticed a 'bin' in the foyer. Later on, Gabriella had a banana. When she had finished her banana, I said 'Go and put it in the bin' (which she would have done automatically at home). She went off from the area where we were, through an open doorway and found the bin we had seen earlier and put her banana skin into it …

Later on, in a different part of the Children's Centre, I located another bin for her and the second time she had some rubbish to put in, she, again, went to find the bin and put rubbish into it.

Analysis

At the least, Gabriella understands the symbols in spoken language that represent her actions. I would argue that memory is involved too and that she is able to generalise from her actions at home to other environments. We do not actually know whether she has an internalised image of her journey yet as she cannot yet articulate that but she must remember making those little journeys at home in order to make a connection with the words. Paul points out that she understands this instruction in both English and Latvian. One of Athey's findings was that offering language to articulate children's actions makes them consciously aware of their actions. Matthews (2003, p. 29) drew on brain research to demonstrate that language acts as a symbol and helps us recall all related experiences of particular actions. So the words 'put it in the bin' enable Gabriella to recall (in some way) her earlier actions and to repeat them in different contexts.

There are many examples of Nicole using 'thought'. This particular observation involves using a 'going through a boundary' schema to solve what she saw as a problem.

Example (Nicole at 5 years 4 months)

… Nicole seems fascinated with 'going through' – when I knock at their door, she shouts through the letterbox 'Who's there?' I say 'Mop' and she opens the door … Recently they had decking put down in the back garden and there was grass growing through. She overheard her mum telling her father about the grass growing through. He said it really needed plastic sheeting and small stones underneath. She said (thinking aloud), 'Mop and Pop have lots of stones' (in our garden). Next time she came to our house, she wanted to take some stones home but Pop said 'No'. Mop gave her some old stones, which she took home in an envelope. She immediately went out to the garden and dropped the stones through the gaps in the decking.

Analysis

Nicole was able to think about the need for stones, to locate them at our house (while she was at her home) and clearly understood that they could 'go through' the gaps in the decking.

Assimilation and accommodation

Assimilation 'is the fusion of a new object to an already existing schema' (Piaget, 1928, p. 175). The new object or experience is similar enough to be incorporated into and to expand slightly the child's current state of knowing.

Example (Gabriella at 12 months 22 days)

Gabriella had been playing with light plastic balls at home and at our house. Today she played ball using a small wooden ball (which is actually a puzzle). She throws it up and lets go – at one point she clonked her own head with it accidentally (did not cry). She threw it along the hall and went into the bathroom and dropped it on the tiled floor and then on the bathmat. She carried it as far as the front door and rubbed it on the doormat, which is very rough.

Analysis

Gabriella has learned some of the things she can do with small balls: throw them, drop them, 'transport' them and rub them against different surfaces. She assimilates this content (wooden ball) into the schemas she has been applying to the lighter plastic balls (and to other objects, e.g. pegs). They are different weights and the effect is different when she acts on them, for example, she can throw the light ball farther than the heavier wooden ball.

Accommodation occurs when the child's current state of knowledge changes. Sometimes this occurs when something different happens to what they were expecting or thinking and they take on that new learning. Athey (2007, p. 51) stated that: 'Probably the most important accommodations, or steps forward in knowledge, are where there is a new coordination between two separate aspects of knowing.'

Example (Gabriella at 8 months 14 days)

Evita told me she had given Gabriella a little box of blocks and she had tipped them out and put one block into the empty box and shook it, thereby coordinating 'containing' and 'trajectory'. Gabriella carried out the same actions several times while I was there and subsequently with other objects and containers.

Analysis

Although this is not as dramatic as some accommodations, it is significant in terms of combining two schemas to create a new set of actions and knowledge. Gabriella now knew she could put things inside and shake them up and down or side to side. She discovered that things often fall out when you do this.

Figure 33.3 Gabriella with her sister and friend in the garden

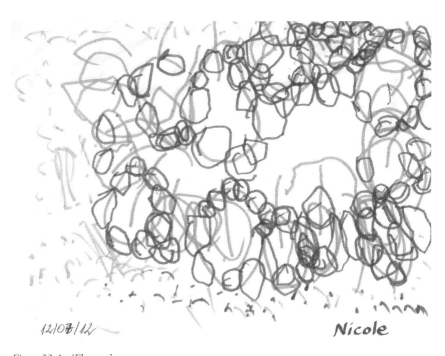

12/08/12   Nicole

Figure 33.4 'Flowers'

Actions to thinking

Gabriella

Gabriella is very sociable and her main interest seems to be in other people, especially babies.

What I have learned most from observing her these past few months is that she has been exploring a cluster of schemas from quite an early age. I can see some continuity in those explorations. For example, her parents have been saying the rhyme 'Round and round the garden ...' At my house she gets excited when she sees a windmill rotate in the garden and I say, 'It's going round and round'. She has begun to say 'Ra ra' which seems to mean 'Round and round'. One day recently (at 14 months) we went to a group and Gabriella noticed the water wheel rotating and immediately said 'Ra ra', recognising the similarity with other objects that go around.

Figure 33.5   Nicole with a bouquet of roses

Nicole

Nicole loves to draw. We have saved samples from she was 2 years 6 months. Typically, the marks she was making began with up/down and side to side movements. Then she drew 'round and round' before combining them. Just as I write to understand and communicate, Nicole seems to draw. Her mother points out that 'Nicole expresses her emotions through drawing'. A favourite of mine is the drawing which Nicole (at 4 years 5 months) named 'Flowers' (Figure 33.4).

The combination of 'enclosures' and 'lines' puts me in mind of a bouquet of roses, carried by Nicole at her mum's wedding 11 months earlier.

I am not suggesting that she was intentionally trying to represent the bouquet but that, like Picasso, she used her repertoire of schemas to draw, and when she had drawn, she saw what she had drawn and the drawing resonated with her earlier experience.

Conclusion

In this chapter I present some evidence of two young children's thinking, which I recognised through identifying their repeated patterns of action or schemas. Piaget firmly believed that our actions become our thinking and this is apparent in an observation of Nicole, aged 5 years 4 months, when she worked out (in her head) that she could 'transport' some stones from our garden to her family's garden in order to drop them 'through' the slats in the decking to stop the grass growing through. There is little doubt that Nicole had internalised those earlier actions of 'transporting' and 'going through' in order to come up with this idea.

References

Arnold, C. (2003) *Observing Harry: Child Development and Learning 0–5 Years*. Maidenhead: Open University Press.

Arnold, C. and the Pen Green Team (2010) *Understanding Schemas and Emotions in Early Childhood*. London: Sage.

Athey, C. (1990) *Extending Thought in Young Children: A Parent–Teacher Partnership*. London: Paul Chapman.

Athey, C. (2003) Personal communication.

Athey, C. (2007) *Extending Thought in Young Children: A Parent–Teacher Partnership*, 2nd edn. London: Paul Chapman.

Athey, C. (2010) DVD of Chris Athey talking about schemas, shown at a conference at the Pen Green Research Base, Corby, Northants (January).

Das Gupta, P. (1994) Images of childhood and theories of development. In J. Oates (ed.) *The Foundations of Child Development*. Oxford: Blackwell.

Donaldson, M. (1978) *Children's Minds*. London: Fontana.

Matthews, J. (2003) *Drawing and Painting: Children and Visual Representation*. London: Paul Chapman.

Piaget, J. (1928) *Judgement and Reasoning in the Child*. London: Routledge.

Piaget, J. (1954) *The Construction of Reality in the Child*. London: Routledge and Kegan Paul.

Piaget, J. (1962) *Play, Dreams and Imitation in Childhood*. London: Routledge and Kegan Paul.

34

THE ROLE OF SUSTAINED SHARED THINKING, PLAY AND METACOGNITION IN YOUNG CHILDREN'S LEARNING

Iram Siraj and Rehana Asani

Introduction

There has been a considerable resurgence in research on children's play in recent years, which provides clear guidelines as to the nature of provision for play, its purposes and the processes by which it influences children's development and learning (Broadhead *et al.*, 2010; Moyles, 2010; Whitebread, 2011). Powerful evidence has also emerged within developmental psychology as new research techniques using neuroscientific and other physiological measures have shown strong and consistent relationships between children's level of play and their cognitive and emotional development (Bornstein, 2006; Tamis–LeMonda and Bornstein, 1989).

Within the educational arena, play is widely recognized as a leading context for the child's acquisition of communication and collaboration skills and provides an important context for well-being, learning and development. The current Early Years Foundation Stage (EYFS) guidance (DfES, 2012) in England uses the role of play as 'an effective characteristic of learning', encouraging adults to use a rich range of experiences and resources through talk, modelling and joint-play activities.

The role of the 'adult' within joint activity is of particular interest here. The notion of *sustained shared thinking* (SST), referring to the sharing of thinking with an adult and to the sustained nature of some of the interactions identified in effective (in terms of child outcomes) preschool settings (Siraj-Blatchford *et al.*, 2002) is an area of current research development. As decades of research have shown, play begins first with solitary play and the child goes on to develop the capability to share, then to co-operate and finally to collaborate in their play (Siraj-Blatchford, 2008).

But solitary play, shared play, co-operative and collaborative play are not discrete 'stages' that the child works through. These experiences also support children in developing a greater awareness of their own development and learning, through building on their metacognitive abilities (i.e. processes whereby individuals become increasingly aware of and are able to control their own cognitive processes).

Thus, recent studies in the area of early childhood education (ECE) have examined the role of play in supporting children's development of 'metacognitive' and self-regulatory abilities (Whitebread and Pino-Pasternak, 2010; Robson, 2010). Studies ranging from experimental to ethnographic investigations have also examined how the field of play develops, how contextual factors support or impede its development and what its specific functions are. While much of the research has focused on early transformational abilities and how they enhance the development of a broad range of skills including literacy abilities (Pellegrini, 2009), the focus of this chapter is on how young children's play functions as a 'leading activity' (Vygotsky, 1933) and more specifically, how it might work in the child's development of metacognitive and self-regulation skills.

Until recently, it was thought that metacognitive skills did not emerge till later childhood (Veenman *et al.*, 2006). However, more developmentally appropriate methodologies now identify that children as young as 3 years old are able to demonstrate metacognitive behaviours including elementary forms of planning, orientation and reflection (Whitebread *et al.*, 2007, 2009) and early individual differences predict school achievement more robustly than other indicators such as IQ (Veenman *et al.*, 2004) and reading and maths skills (McClelland *et al.*, 2007).

The term metacognition was initially used by Flavell and by Brown in their early work in the 1970s to refer to knowledge about cognition and regulation of cognition. According to Flavell (1976), 'metacognition refers to one's knowledge concerning one's own cognitive processes and products or anything related to them' (p. 232).

Flavell (1977) recognized early on that the development of metacognition was a centrally significant cognitive-developmental hallmark of early childhood. Research based on Vygotsky's (1978) model of development showed how children's learning is a process of moving from other-regulation (performing a task supported by an adult or peer) to self-regulation (performing a task on one's own). Within this dominant Vygotskian framework, the role of an adult or educator supports children's learning, emphasizing the significance of mediation by an adult as 'sustained shared thinking' during such interactions. A range of studies have confirmed these theoretical interrelationships between metacognitive and self-regulatory performance by using child-initiated play (Berk *et al.*, 2006) where these higher order processes promote intentional learning in ECE.

The notion of SST as a pedagogical construct is thus defined as a vehicle for developing these latter strategies, first identified in a mixed method, educational effectiveness study (Siraj-Blatchford *et al.*, 2002). Pedagogic progression in the early years is then identified as an educational response to, *and an engagement with*, the most commonly observed, evidence-based developmental trajectories of young children as they learn through play.

The development of this chapter represents one stage in a continuing effort to develop a better understanding of SST as a pedagogic practice in ECE. We focus on the educational potential of shared playful activities within the context of metacognitive abilities.

Sustained shared thinking

To understand sustained shared thinking (SST) it is important to recognize firstly that it emerged as an analytic node or 'condensation symbol' in the process of qualitative research. These data were collected in the intensive case study analysis of 12 'effective' preschool drawn from the 141 settings involved in the Effective Provision of Pre-School Education (EPPE) longitudinal study. The term came to be defined as SST because research respondents and observers specifically referred to the 'sharing of thinking', and to the particularly sustained nature of some of the interactions identified in effective (in terms of child outcomes) preschool settings: sustained and meaningful to those sharing the interaction from just a few exchanges of conversation to much longer episodes.

What is novel and important about SST is its evidential basis in group settings, and as a useful concept for pedagogy. Arguably, many other researchers have adopted similar terms and have described similar pedagogic practices. In reviewing the literature for this chapter, the strongest theoretical resonances were found with Vygotsky (1978) who described a process where an educator supports children's learning within their 'zone of proximal development'. The zone of proximal development (ZPD) is primarily where children are given some support from an adult or experienced peer within the zone of effective learning. Forms of interaction underpin a support structure for the child to build on such as encouragement, simplifying the task, reminding the child of the goal, making suggestions and modelling answers. This temporary structure termed as 'scaffolding' enables the child to successfully carry out a particular task, building on their existing skills and understanding. The interaction has to be meaningful to the child and build on her interests.

But interactions of this sort have also been described as 'distributed cognitions' (Salomon, 1993), in terms of the pedagogy of 'guided participation' (Rogoff et al., 1993), and as 'scaffolding' (Wood et al., 1976). Similar examples of participation and interaction also characterize 'dialogic teaching' (Alexander, 2004), 'dialogic enquiry' (Wells, 1999), 'interthinking' (Mercer 2000), and 'mutualist and dialectical pedagogy' (Bruner, 1996, p. 57).

The research methods applied in the case studies to identify effective pedagogy in the EPPE project have been described fully elsewhere (Siraj-Blatchford et al., 2006). For the purposes of this chapter, it will be enough to explain that the research provided a qualitative extension to the (then) ten-year longitudinal EPPE study which has followed the progress of over 3,000 children in England.

EPPE controlled for the influence of family and child characteristics and was able to establish the 'effectiveness' of each of the preschool settings attended by the children in its sample. The qualitative case studies drew upon these findings to construct a stratified random sample of 'good' to 'excellent' settings for further in-depth qualitative data collection and analysis. EPPE was also able to provide data on the 'quality' of each of the settings as measured by the Early Childhood Environment Rating

Scale: Revised (ECERS-R: Harms *et al.*, 1998) and the Early Childhood Environment Rating Scale: Extended (ECERS-E: Sylva *et al.*, 2006).

Pedagogy was defined broadly in the qualitative analysis to include all of those processes and provisions that could be considered to initiate or maintain learning processes, and to achieve educational goals. Such a wide definition was considered important so that it would include the common practice of providing resources for exploration and (constructivist) 'discovery' learning environments (e.g. sand and water and play). The analytical process was initially 'grounded', as the process began with induction, and this was only followed later by stages of deduction and verification using the ECERS scores for quality. All of this initial work was also carried out blind in the sense that the researcher was unaware of the particular learning outcomes achieved by the settings and identified by EPPE.

In the identification of sustained shared thinking, the pedagogic 'instructional techniques' were at first coded with a multitude of subcategories that included 'Questioning', 'Demonstrating', 'Telling', and 'Dialogue'. The reclassification of some of the 'Dialogue' as 'Sustained Shared Thinking' (SST) with subcategories of 'Child-initiated SST' and 'Adult-initiated SST' initially took place after data such as the following were revealed:

CONTEXT: Children engaged in water play.
   Boy (4:1) (who has been watching various items floating on water), 'Look at the fir cone. There's bubbles of air coming out.'
   Nursery officer 'It's spinning round.'
   Boy (4:1) 'That's 'cos it's got air in it.'
   Nursery officer (picks up the fir cone and shows the *children* how the scales go round the fir cone in a spiral, turning the fir cone round with a winding action), 'When the air comes out in bubbles it makes the fir cone spin around.'
   Girl (4:9) (uses a plastic tube to blow into the water), 'Look bubbles.'
   Nursery officer 'What are you putting into the water to make bubbles? … What's coming out of the tube?'
   Girl (4:9) 'Air.'
   (Dialogue continued …)

The analytical process was continued further through theoretical sampling informed by an analysis of the EPPE multi-level outcomes data, and the centre quality ratings of the ECERS-R and ECERS-E environmental rating scales. Various positive correlations were found between child outcomes on, for example, Early Number outcomes with the ECERS-R interaction Sub-scale ($r=0.26$, $p<0.005$). Setting 421 (referred to above) was found to have achieved 'excellent' (95 per cent confidence level) practice in terms of the children's developmental progress according to their 'non-verbal' and 'number concepts' assessments. Performance in 'Language' was also found to be 'good' (above 68 per cent confidence level). Further analysis soon revealed a general pattern of high cognitive outcomes associated with sustained adult–child verbal interaction along with a paucity of such interactions in those settings achieving less well. SST thus came to be defined as an effective pedagogic interaction, where two or more individuals 'work together' in an intellectual way to solve a problem, clarify a concept, evaluate activities, or extend a narrative within meaningful contexts for the child. Thus, SST was subsequently found to occur most commonly in 1:1 adult–child interactions. An example is through questioning with instances of SST from the observations of practitioners:

> '… it is knowing your children, it's treating them as equal. It's asking questions of them, knowing that you really want to find out, not just because you want them to give you the right answer. It's entering into their thoughts …'
>
> *(421 interview with head, para 64)*

Play and pedagogic progression in the early years

Play is widely recognized as a leading context for the child's acquisition of communication and collaboration skills and provides an important context for learning and development, as Vygotsky (1933) put it: 'Only theories maintaining that a child does not have to satisfy the basic requirements of life, but can live in search of pleasure, could possibly suggest that a child's world is a play world' (p. 1). But: 'The child moves forward essentially through play activity. Only in this sense can play be termed a leading activity that determines the child's development' (p. 1).

In terms of empirical progression we know that play begins with solitary play and the child goes on to develop the capability to share, then to co-operate, and finally to collaborate in their play. We also know that these developments open up much wider opportunities for learning. However, there are no clear stages of 'solitary', 'shared', 'co-operative' or 'collaborative' play that the child works through. Even solitary play serves us well at times throughout our learning lives. In most theoretical accounts describing the ways in which these different forms of play open up the possibility of learning, the notion of emergent development is often implicit. For example, when describing play as a 'leading activity' (Leontiev, 1964; Oerter, 1993), it is only being suggested that it should be seen as a driving force in the child's development of new forms of motivation and action.

Activities that may all be considered examples of SST (Siraj-Blatchford, 2007) are considered by many neo-Vygotskian writers (Karpov, 2005) to mark the transition from learning activities that are characterized by 'emotional communication with caregivers' (Lisina, 1986), then to 'object-centred joint activity' (Elkonin, 1989) where the child begins object substitutions, and then on to socio-dramatic play (Leontiev, 1964), with finally activities that reflect the child's desire to learn more formally and embrace formal learning (or schooling) as the dominant learning activity.

Figure 34.1 summarizes these major developmental phases and identifies some of the major features of pedagogic progression. The figure follows the example of the English Early Years Foundation Stage (EYFS) Guidance (DfES, 2012) in referring to some of the most significant, overt and immediate learning that takes place throughout each phase as something for practitioners to 'Look, listen, and note', and to identify the potential developmental significance of this separately. In place of pedagogy

Playful activity	Sustained shared thinking	Pedagogy	Learning	Developmental potential
1. Emotional communication with caregivers	Communications with adults and peers involves the exchange of significant gestures	Adult models and leads (Treating all of the child's actions as 'communicative'). Scaffolding is then progressively reduced. 'Extensions' provided.	Object permanence 'Social smiles' and gestures, signs and symbols are increasingly recognised by the child as communicative acts	Towards the development of a conception of the 'self'.
2. Object-centred joint activity	Pretend role play and object substitution become internalised (as imagination) and as inner speech develops. Sharing play symbols and signs in pretend play with partners	Object substitution and 'pretend' modelled by adults and/or peers Scaffolding in the provision of props (e.g. dressing up clothes) and environments progressively reduced. Extension by encouraging more abstract symbolisation and open ended questioning.	Reciprocity in sharing peer relations Being an (object) other to oneself. Increasingly acknowledging other perspectives	Towards the co-ordination of 'self' to 'others'.
3. Socio-dramatic play	Collaborative involvement in improvised play with partners	Modelling by adults and peers. Progressively reduction of scaffolding in the provision of ideas and themes for play. Extend by encouraging play with more capable peers Introduction of games with more sophisticated rules.	Collaborative skills as socio-dramatic play becomes more as partners at first share symbols and then reciprocally negotiate roles Greater resilience	Towards a theory of mind and metacognition.
4. Transition to learning activity	Collaboration in increasingly structured activities and games with more complex rules	Encouragement of extended play (over days) to promote self regulation, planning and memory. Progressively reduction of scaffolding in planning. Scaffolding more disciplined collaborations, e.g. carrying out an 'investigation'.	Reflection upon the relationship between 'pretend' signs and 'real' meanings Orientation towards more formal learning and school Learning to learn	Towards learning to learn and the development of learning 'dispositions'.

Figure 34.1 Towards a model of pedagogic progression in play

we apply the more common phrase 'effective practice'. The first three developmental phases that are identified broadly correspond with Broadhead's (2001) empirical account of the 'social play continuum' levels for 'Associative Play', 'Social Play and Highly Social Play', and 'Co-operative Play'. There is no specification of the ages to which these apply and there is no particular problem with these being defined as broad and overlapping phases (as again applied in the EYFS). But arguably these processes do not end with play, or in school, or even in adult life. There is an essential continuity between the playful collaborations of the nursery and the more formal collaborations between peers, and between teachers and pupils in schools, in working partnerships, in the provision of apprenticeship and tutorial relationships and even professional mentors and collaborators at the academic and professional level. In terms of competence, progression goes from mastering the very informal and strongly improvised sustained and shared interactions to more highly structured and much more formal sustained and shared interactions in adult life.

Metacognitive development

The role of others

Researchers agree that social influences are central to metacognitive development. The dominant theoretical contribution is derived from Vygotsky's (1978) notion that children develop the capacity for self-regulation through interaction with more knowledgeable others. During episodes of true collaboration, the child moves from being 'other-regulated' to 'self-regulated' (Zimmerman and Schunk, 2001). Work within this approach has emphasized the significance of mediation by an adult who initially assumes responsibility for monitoring progress, setting goals, planning activities, etc.; however, over time, responsibility of these executive processes is given over to the child.

Findings from the Researching Effective Pedagogy in the Early Years (REPEY) study (Siraj-Blatchford *et al.*, 2002) have demonstrated the effective pedagogue orchestrates learning through the following adult–child interactions, for example:

- *Scaffolding* – to extend children's knowledge and understanding through the use of strategies such as open ended questioning;
- *Extending* – by making a suggestion that helps a child to see other possibilities;
- *Discussing* – which supports the interchange of information or ideas.
- *Modelling* – which includes the demonstration of activities and verbal commentary from the adult.

Such opportunities should be sensitive to the curriculum concept or skill being 'taught', which take into account the child's interests and ZPD (Vygotsky, 1978).

In principle, REPEY (Siraj-Blatchford *et al.*, 2002) established that the most effective (excellent) settings (for enhancing child development) achieved a balance between the opportunities provided for children to benefit from adult-initiated group work and in the provision of freely chosen, yet potentially instructive, play activities.

According to Whitebread *et al.* (2007), when adults are engaged in activities with children, they may tend to stimulate the children to reflect on and engage with what they know about their *own* learning more frequently.

Intervention research has also shown that children are able to benefit from pedagogical techniques to promote metacognitive development. Such instruction, particularly language (both oral and written), includes developing the students' awareness (encouraging talk about the strategies used and how they affect performance). Pramling (1988) argues that 'explicit talk' or 'metacognitive dialogues' between adult and child helps children become more consciously aware of their thinking, which ultimately supports their metacognitive development.

The role of peer-assisted learning has been well documented within the self-regulation literature. Evidence of metacognitive development has been found in playful contexts which involved another child or small groups with high levels of collaborative dialogues. Robson (2010) found extensive evidence of metacognitive and self-regulatory behaviours in preschool children's self-initiated play and shared talk. Opportunities for open-ended group-work, and child-initiated activities which encouraged children to articulate their ideas and explain their reasoning, were found to be significantly effective in stimulating metacognitive and self-regulatory behaviour (Whitebread *et al*, 2007).

The role of self-regulation

A number of studies have investigated 'the role of the child during play' and development of self-regulation (Berk *et al.*, 2006). Findings from these studies suggest that some types of play, i.e. social pretend play, can promote private speech (where children are observed to self-commentate) (Diaz and Berk, 1992).

Vygotsky (1962) initially proposed that private speech stems from social speech, which emerges from the guiding nature of children's parent–child interactions. Within his framework, he argued that higher mental functions develop through this internalization and transformation of mental processes. As adult and child participate in a linguistically mediated joint activity, a child creates a dialogue that can be internalized to form self-regulatory private speech (Fernyhough, 1996). As Fernyhough (2010) explains, words that were previously used by the child to regulate the thought and behaviour of others (or which others have used to regulate the child's thought and behaviour), become employed in regulating the thought and behaviour of the child.

Research has revealed interesting findings about the context of private speech occurrence in young children. Diaz and Berk's (1992) study shows that the use of private speech during goal-directed activities is firstly overt and is an important tool to guide attention and regulate behaviour during problem-solving tasks. It later undergoes a developmental transition where it becomes more internalized, fragmented and relevant over time (Winsler and Naglieri, 2003). Within the context of play in young children, studies examining private speech found a positive relationship between the development of self-regulation and make-believe play (Krafft and Berk, 1998). They found that the incidence of private speech was higher during open-ended activities, especially during fantasy play where children were involved in associative play with peers. In this view, the self-regulatory functions of speech have their origins in social exchange, and are not simple imitations of the adult's guiding speech (Berk and Spuhl, 1995).

The development of play

Let us now consider how SST develops over time in progressively more sophisticated contexts, as sustained and shared 'moments of activity' (Leontiev, 1978). We can begin by drawing upon George Herbert Mead's account of the processes that are involved in children's early 'emotional communications with caregivers' seeing these as gestural symbols that are at first recognized by babies as communicative acts.

To paraphrase Morris (1962): 'The "significant gesture", itself a part of a social process, internalizes and makes available to the [child] the means which have themselves emerged earlier, nonsignificant, stages of gestural communication' (p. xxii). 'Significant gestures' thus provide the means by which a baby is able to at first objectify the behaviour (or role) of the other, and control their own behaviour in response to these roles. It is also in this process that the child first develops a conscious awareness of the 'self'. The interactive contexts for these very early learning experiences usually involve the parent or primary carer playing 'peek-a-boo' or other baby games that involve taking turns. But the development of higher mental functions only 'emerges' following a multiplicity of these relatively simple interactions.

The pedagogy that might be considered implicit in these interactions follows a sequence where the adult at first repeatedly models a particular action or gesture (an early example may be a big smile following eye contact), or the adult provides a reward when the child responds and then as the child begins to initiate the game themselves, progressively reducing the scaffolding (in this case the adult initiation and rewards). The guided assumption here is that children at first cannot perform the leading activity independently without adult interaction. However, gradually children become full partners during these interactions, where 'playful activity' between parent and child operates within the child's zone of proximal development. Progressively, as the child continues to communicate with adults and other children, the meanings that they are constructing are mediated by all their previous historical moments of significant activity.

At this point conceptual knowledge and understanding of the 'other', and of the 'self', develop further and learning 'dispositions' become more significant (e.g. probably most clearly identified in studies of gender preference). The development of these sophisticated levels of abstraction (and meta-consciousness), commonly referred to as a theory of mind (ToM), also facilitates the development of metacognitive skills. The metacognition that is so important in learning-to-learn also develops as the child finds it necessary to describe, explain and justify their thinking about different aspects of the world to others.

Thus, from an early age, young children learn to separate objects and actions from their meaning in the real world and give them new meanings. This provides the basis for early representational thinking and in more advanced forms of representational thinking these 'props' are no longer required, so that problems may be solved entirely 'in the head'. With their play partners, communication is conducted, from their own historically constructed perspective, which includes their understanding of the perspective of themselves constructed by the other participant in the communication (or SST). This has important implications for development as 'the child's position towards the external world changes ... and the ability to co-ordinate his point of view with other possible points of view develops' (Elkonin, 1978, p. 282).

Forman and Cazdan's (1998) research suggests that children's problem-solving improves in collaboration, as the partners alternately provide scaffolding for each other within the partners' 'zone of proximal development' (ZPD). That is, the 'zone of capability' that extends beyond what the partner is capable of doing on their own to include those activities they may successfully do with the support of their peer.

This pedagogic sequence of *modelling – progressive reduction of scaffolding – extension* may continue to be employed in supporting children's learning in a wide range of play contexts throughout the early years.

As children develop, a range of particular (and increasingly unique) cultural, personal and situational factors will make some contexts more significant to the individual child than others. But in the child's first significant gestures, and later in many other communications, both positive and negative emotional influences are likely to motivate their learning, with the operation of interests, desires and impulses being applied on the one hand (perhaps dominating in the earliest years), and concerns about what Piaget referred to as 'disequilibrium' (and *cognitive dissonance or conflict*) being applied on the other.

For Van Oers (1998), the creative processes of learning that are involved can be characterized as a process of 'progressive continuous re-contextualization' (pcr-c), where it is considered that as soon as the individual recognizes the potential of achieving a recalled (and motivating) object (or outcome) they may choose to re-contextualize that object, transforming (or 'transferring') their (structure and meaning) of the activity to that end. The developmental significance of these first separations of meaning from objects is enormous: 'At that critical moment when a stick – i.e. an object – becomes a pivot for severing the meaning of horse from a real horse, one of the basic psychological structures determining the child's relationship to reality is radically altered' (Vygotsky, 1933, p. 1).

It is in this context that the power of play and pretence may be seen most clearly. Vygotsky (1933) argued that in the child's 'real' life, action always dominates over meaning. The evidence suggests that the crucial practice of *substituting a real object for a symbol* may occur spontaneously in play, but that this is also greatly facilitated in playful interaction with others.

Conclusions

This chapter has considered the role of SST as a form of pedagogy in the sense that it is something adults do to support and engage children's learning. SST is argued as a high order pedagogical concept as the adult has to sensitively tune into the child's interests and meaning making before extending it with them, and, as a common approach, has the potential to provide just this sort of continuity. Drawing upon broadly Vygotskian sources, the model presented suggests that learning can change the child's developmental level through ZPD to which adults can progressively introduce children to the cultural tools that they require to mediate cognitive development. Furthermore, through pretend play, the chapter has argued that symbolic construction and the role of language can be introduced as an appropriate pedagogic activity for young children to enhance both self-regulation and metacognitive abilities.

In discussing the transition from play to learning as 'a leading activity', Carpay and Van Oers (1993) argued that 'learning activity must be fostered as a new special form of play activity. As a new quality emerging from play activity, it can be argued that learning activity has to be conceived as a language game in which negotiation about meanings in a community of learners is the basic strategy for the acquisition of knowledge' (cited in Van Oers 1999, p. 273).

During the course of development, children experience more challenging SST in their play initially with adults, then in reciprocal peer play and later in sophisticated collaborative play. We can support this process in ECE by providing children with more challenging forms of SST and by initiating more sophisticated and abstract scaffolding props. The prime objective should be further opportunities for meaningful talk between adult and child, providing cognitive challenge that is manageable for the children.

References

Alexander, R. (2004) *Towards Dialogic Teaching: Rethinking Classroom Talk*. York: Dialogos.

Berk, L. E. and Spuhl, S. T. (1995) Maternal interaction, private speech, and task performance in preschool children. *Early Childhood Research Quarterly*, *10*, 145–69.

Berk, L. E., Mann, T. D. and Ogan, A. T. (2006) Make-believe play: Wellspring for development of self-regulation. In D. G. Singer, R. M. Golinkoff and K. Hirsh-Pasek (eds) *Play=Learning: How Play Motivates and Enhances Children's Cognitive and Social-Emotional Growth* (pp. 74 100). Oxford: Oxford University Press.

Bornstein, M. H. (2006) On the significance of social relationships in the development of children's earliest symbolic play: An ecological perspective. In A. Göncü and S. Gaskins (eds) *Play and Development: Evolutionary, Sociocultural and Functional Perspectives* (pp. 101–29). Mahwah, NJ: Erlbaum.

Broadhead, P. (2001) Investigating sociability and cooperation in four and five year olds in reception class settings. *International Journal of Early Years Education*, *9*(1).

Broadhead, P., Howard, J. and Wood, E. (eds) (2010) *Play and Learning in the Early Years*. London: Sage.

Bruner, J. (1996) *The Culture of Education*. Cambridge, MA: Harvard University Press.

Carpay, J. and Van Oers, B. (1993) Models for learning and the problem of classroom discourse. *Voprosy Psichologii*, *4*, 20–6.

DfES (Department for Education and Skills) (2012) *Practice Guidance for the Early Years Foundation Stage*. DfES Publications. Available at: www.foundationyears.org.uk/eyfs-2014/.

Diaz, R. M. and Berk, L. E. (eds) (1992) *Private Speech: From Social Interaction to Self Regulation*. Hillsdale, NJ: Erlbaum.

Elkonin, D. (1978) *Psychology of Play*. Moscow: Pedagogika.

Fernyhough, C. (1996) The dialogic mind: A dialogic approach to the higher mental functions. *New Ideas in Psychology*, *14*, 47–62.

Fernyhough, C. (2010) Inner speech. In *Encyclopaedia of the Mind*. Pashler: H. Sage.

Flavell, J. H. (1976) Metacognitive aspects of problem solving. In B. L. Resnick (ed.) *The Nature of Intelligence*. Hillsdale, NJ: Erlbaum.

Flavell, J. H. (1977) *Cognitive Development*. Englewood Cliffs, NJ: Prentice-Hall.

Forman, E. and Cazdan, C. (1998) Exploring Vygotskian perspectives in education. In D. Faulkner, K. Littleton and M. Woodhead (eds) *Learning Relationships in the Classroom*, pp. 189–206. London: Routledge and the Open University.

Harms, T., Clifford, R. and Cryer, D. (1998) *Early Childhood Environment Rating Scale – Revised*. North Carolina: Teacher's College Press.

Karpov, Y. (2005) *The Neo-Vygotskian Approach to Child Development*. Cambridge: Cambridge University Press.

Krafft, K. C. and Berk, L. E. (1998) Private speech in two preschools: Significance of open-ended activities and make-believe play for verbal regulation. *Early Childhood Research Quarterly, 13*, 637–58.

Leontiev, A. (1964) *Problems of Mental Development*. Washington: US Joint Publication Research Service.

Leontiev, A. (1978) *Activity, Consciousness, Personality*. Englewood Cliffs, NJ: Prentice Hall.

Lisina, A. (1986) *Problems of the Ontogenesis of Communication*. Moscow: Pedagogika.

McClelland, M. M., Cameron, C. E., Connor, C. M., Farris, C. L., Jewkes, A. M. and Morrison, F. J. (2007) Links between behavioral regulation and preschoolers' literacy, vocabulary, and math skills. *Developmental Psychology, 43*, 947–59.

Mercer, N. (2000) *Words and Minds*. London: Routledge.

Morris, C. (1962) Introduction. In G. H. Mead (ed.) *Mind, Self and Society* (pp. i–xii). Chicago: University of Chicago Press.

Moyles, J. (ed.) (2010) *The Excellence of Play*, 3rd edn. Maidenhead, UK: Open University Press.

Oerter, R. (1993) *The Psychology of Play: An Activity Oriented Approach*. Munich: Quintessenz.

Pellegrini, A. D. (2009) *The Role of Play in Human Development*. New York: Oxford University Press.

Pramling I. (1988) Developing children's thinking about their own learning. *British Journal of Educational Psychology, 58*, 266–78.

Robson, S. (2010) Self-regulation and metacognition in young children's self-initiated play and reflective dialogues. *International Journal of Early Years Education, 18*(3), 227–41.

Rogoff, B., Mistry, J., Göncü, A. and Mosier, C. (1993) Guided participation in cultural activity by toddlers and caregivers. *Monographs of the Society for Research in Child Development, 58* (7, Serial No. 236).

Salomon, G. (1993) *Distributed Cognitions: Psychological and Educational Considerations*. Cambridge: Cambridge University Press

Siraj-Blatchford, I. (2007) Creativity, communication and collaboration: The identification of pedagogic progression in SST. *Asia-Pacific Journal of Research in Early Childhood Education, 1*(2), 3–23.

Siraj-Blatchford, I. (2008) Understanding the relationship between curriculum, pedagogy and progression in learning in early childhood. *Hong Kong Journal of Early Childhood Education, 7*(2).

Siraj-Blatchford, I. (2009) Conceptualising progression in the pedagogy of play and sustained shared thinking in early childhood education: A Vygotskian perspective. *Educational and Child Psychological Society, 26*(2), 77–89.

Siraj-Blatchford, I., Sylva, K., Muttock, S., Gilden, R. and Bell, D. (2002) *Researching Effective Pedagogy in the Early Years*, DfES Research Report 356. London: DfES.

Siraj-Blatchford, I., Sammons, P., Sylva, K., Melhuish, E. and Taggart, B. (2006) Educational research and evidence based policy: The mixed method approach of the EPPE Project. *Evaluation and Research in Education, 19*(2), 63–82.

Sylva, K., Siraj-Blatchford, I. and Taggart, B. (2006) *Early Childhood Environmental Rating Scale – Extension (ECERS-E)*, 2nd edn. Stoke-on Trent: Trentham Books.

Tamis-LeMonda, C. S. and Bornstein, M. H. (1989) Habituation and maternal encouragement of attention in infancy as predictors of toddler language, play and representational competence. *Child Development, 60*, 738–51.

Van Oers, B. (1998) The fallacy of decontextualisation. *Mind, Culture and Activity*, 5(2), 135–42.

Van Oers, B. (1999) Teaching opportunities in play. In M. Hedegaard and J. Lompscher (eds) *Learning Activity and Development*, pp. 268–89. Aarhus: Aarhus University Press.

Veenman, M. V. J., Wilhelm, P. and Beishuizen, J. J. (2004) The relation between intellectual and metacognitive skills from a developmental perspective. *Learning and Instruction*, 14, 89–109.

Veenman, M. V. J. and Hout-Wolters, B. H. A. M. van and Afflerbach, P. (2006) Metacognition and learning: Conceptual and methodological considerations. *Metacognition and Learning*, 1(1), pp. 3–14.

Vygotsky, L. (1933) Play and its role in the mental development of the child. *Voprosy psikhologii*, 1966, No. 6, trans. C. Mulholland, *Psychology and Marxism Internet Archive 2002*. Available at: www.marxists.org/archive/vygotsky/works/1933/play.htm.

Vygotsky, L. S. (1962) *Thought and Language*. Cambridge, MA: MIT Press.

Vygotsky, L. S. (1978) *Mind in Society: The Development of Higher Psychological Processes*. Cambridge, MA: Harvard University Press.

Wells, G. (1999) *Dialogic Inquiry: Towards a Socio-cultural Practice and Theory of Education*. Cambridge: Cambridge University Press.

Whitebread, D. (2011) *Developmental Psychology and Early Childhood Education*. London: Sage.

Whitebread, D. and Pino-Pasternak, D. (2010) Metacognition, self-regulation and meta-knowing. In K. Littleton, C. Wood, and J. Kleine Staarman (eds) *International Handbook of Psychology in Education*. Bingley, UK: Emerald.

Whitebread, D., Bingham, S., Grau, V., Pino-Pasternak, D. and Sangster, C. (2007) Development of metacognition and self-regulated learning in young children: The role of collaborative and peer-assisted learning. *Journal of Cognitive Education and Psychology*, 6, 433–55.

Whitebread, D., Coltman, P., Pino-Pasternak, D., Sangster, C., Grau, V., Bingham, S., Almeqdad, Q. and Demetriou, D. (2009) The development of two observational tools for assessing metacognition and self-regulated learning in young children. *Metacognition and Learning*, 4(1), 63–85.

Winsler, A., and Naglieri, J. (2003) Overt and covert verbal problem-solving strategies: Developmental trends in use, awareness, and relations with task performance in children aged 5–17. *Child Development*, 74, 659–78.

Wood, D., Bruner, J. and Ross, G. (1976) The role of tutoring in problem solving. *Journal of Child Psychology and Psychiatry*, 17(2), 89–100.

Zimmerman, B. J. and Schunk, D. H. (eds) (2001) *Self-regulated Learning and Academic Achievement: Theoretical Perspectives*, 2nd edn. Mahwah, NJ: Erlbaum.

35

POSSIBILITY THINKING

From what is to what might be

Anna Craft

Summary

The transformation from what is to what might be, what I have come to understand as 'possibility thinking', seems to be inherent in human nature. This phenomenon, particularly as it applies to everyday contexts for children and their teachers, has been the focus of qualitative research in England for over a decade. It is now informing two European research studies which are concerned with how children, young people and adults working with them, engage in ethical social change. This chapter explores what the research tells us about the nature of possibility thinking and what nurtures it, and discusses future directions of the work.

Introduction: possibility thinking as the engine of 'little c' creativity

Human beings are inherently creative, transforming what is given to what might be in all aspects of their lives. We see this capacity in very young children as they first recognise and then explore ideas and resources: for example, finding that a flap on a toy reveals a mirror and then opening and closing it repeatedly, or holding up a stick and declaring it is an umbrella.

By asking 'what if?' the transition is made from 'what is' to 'what might be', or from 'what is this?' to 'what can I/we do with this?' This heart of creativity is what I call 'possibility thinking'. It is present at all ages and across life and can be seen as the engine that drives the shift from 'what is this?' to 'what can I do with this?' Such *what if* thinking can be seen in the toddler who makes mud and grass 'soup', in teenagers designing hyphotheses and fair tests in science and in adults taking a short cut in traffic or considering whether to introduce one friend to another.

As well as *what if* thinking, possibility thinking involves *as if* thinking: behaving as though one had a different identity and taking on another's perspective. This may be

416

intuitive, in the way young children take on other personae during role-play or in the way that older children may, for example, mimic behaviours of hero figures in, say, music or sport – or may be structured into learning experiences where students are encouraged to take on roles so as to play out a range of decision-making scenarios.

The term 'possibility thinking' (PT) was coined at the end of the twentieth century (Craft, 2000), embedded in exploration of the everyday creativity involved in successfully identifying and navigating life (Craft, 2001). It highlighted the value and nature of personal agency in the early twenty-first century as involving taking intentional action in relation to both finding and solving problems, using intuition as well as logic to cope with everyday challenges and as inherently innovative enabling forward motion in all aspects of life.

This everyday understanding of creativity was developed first theoretically and then through a mix of empirical and theoretical work to explore how it might reflect how young children in particular manifest their creative engagement (Craft, 2002). As with the account of PT in relation to adults, the account of PT in young children's lives foregrounds the everyday element of creativity. It is important to locate the work on PT in relation to the wider creativity research field, in relation to focus.

For, while creativity researchers are in agreement that creativity fundamentally involves novelty that is original and useful (has an impact), researchers also acknowledge a spectrum of originality and impact in relation to creativity.

At one end of the creativity spectrum, the creativity may be original to the maker but not necessarily more broadly, and so its impact too may be limited – this is sometimes referred to as everyday creativity, or 'little c' creativity. This is the end of the creativity spectrum at which possibility thinking has been researched. Boden (2004) refers to such novelty at a personal level as psychological, and the idea as P-creative. Craft (2001) refers to the same phenomenon as 'little c' or personal effectiveness and life-wide resourcefulness, while Kaufman and Beghetto (2009) distinguish mini-c creativity (personal meaning-making), from everyday creativity or little c (creativity shared with others). In the middle of the spectrum is what Kaufman and Beghetto (2009) call 'pro-c' (professional) creativity. And at the other end entirely, the continuum reflects high originality and impact, or 'big C' creativity (such as possessed by Gandhi or Einstein); this is what Boden calls 'H' creativity or 'historical' creativity, which changes the world, or generates novel ideas that transform paradigms.

It is argued that children's 'what if' thinking, and perspective-taking, or 'as if' engagement, are the engine of everyday creativity (Craft, 2001): the exploratory transition from 'what is' to 'what might be'. This chapter explores the concept of possibility thinking, discussing how the research has been undertaken and what has been learned from it.

What does the research tell us about possibility thinking?

Conceptual and empirical research on possibility thinking has been developed since the mid-1990s. Co-researching with teachers and practitioners in early years and primary classrooms using a qualitative research approach, we have sought to identify the nature of PT together with pedagogical strategies that seem to foster it. Carefully selected episodes of children's sustained, focused, playful activity (both in relation to imaginative play among younger children and in relation to more formal curriculum content among older learners), across the age range 2 to 11, have been analysed by university staff and teacher researchers. All the research has been undertaken in naturalistic settings in early years and primary classrooms in England, using observation, interview and video-stimulated review, enabling teachers and children to reflect on learning. Drawing material for analysis from immersive playful episodes, analysis has involved both inductive and later also deductive analysis.

Research focus 1: the nature of possibility thinking

The early empirical studies developed Craft's original conceptualisation and created a framework for identifying PT in a seminal study undertaken by Burnard *et al.*, 2006. The key features of PT were: question-posing, play, immersion, innovation, risk-taking, being imaginative and self-determination (Burnard *et al.*, 2006), as shown in Figure 35.1.

These features as seen in possibility thinking were defined as follows (Craft *et al*, 2008):

> **Posing questions**: children's questions, both verbal and non-verbal, frequently made visible through playful thinking in an 'as if' space.
> **Play**: children's serious, highly engaged, extended exploration, developing and combining ideas, imagining situations, generating and solving diverse problems.
> **Immersion**: children's deep involvement in a benign environment offering both high emotional support and high cognitive challenge.

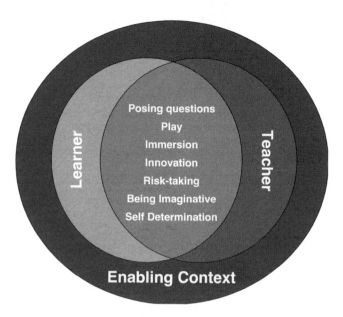

Figure 35.1 Key features of possibility thinking identified by Burnard *et al.*, 2006

Innovation: children's strong, playful connections between ideas, often supported, triggered and extended through well-chosen adult provocations.

Risk-taking: children moving into original spaces with courage.

Being imaginative: children engaging in what might be, inventing imaginary worlds as decision-makers and designers.

Self-determination: children exercising independence in decision-making and actions, their contributions valued by those around them as they generate and follow through ideas.

Beyond the seminal study by Burnard *et al.* (2006), four subsequent studies were undertaken. The first focused on children's questions, yielding a taxonomy of questioning in PT episodes (Chappell *et al.*, 2008). As shown in Figure 35.2, the analysis in this study illustrated how through immersive play environments, children's self-determined activity led them to generate and respond to their own questions with imagination and risk-taking, through innovative ideas and actions.

In this study, the analysis of how children engaged in such question-posing and question-responding to generate innovation brought out the vitally important role of the inherent breadth of possibility in any classroom activity, as well as relationships between question-posing and question-responding. It highlighted different kinds of questioning from 'leading questions', which frame the creative endeavour, to 'service questions', enabling enquiries to proceed, and 'follow-through' questions, often used

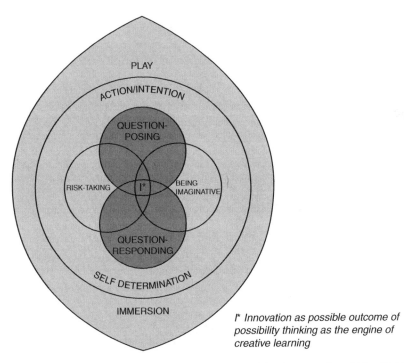

I* Innovation as possible outcome of possibility thinking as the engine of creative learning

Figure 35.2   Representation from Chappell *et al.* (2008) of the elements of possibility thinking

at a practical level. Questions were expressed verbally, and more frequently non-verbally, through enacted expression. The relationships between degrees of inherent possibility, question-posing and question-responding, and leading, service and follow-through questions are represented in Figure 35.3.

A second study beyond Burnard *et al.* (2006) drew back to a broader focus being concerned with the nature of possibility thinking in older primary children aged 9–11 (Craft *et al.*, 2012a). Episodes selected for analysis were again drawn from playful immersive contexts, this time from within science, art, and mathematics. The study further highlighted the role of the children's questioning stance, evidenced both verbally and non-verbally (through expression, gesture and body language). Most features of possibility thinking identified in the previous studies were evidenced strongly but risk-taking could not be discerned, which may perhaps reflect curriculum and assessment constraints affecting older learners. Significantly, the study identified peer collaboration as an emergent PT feature and documented integration in children's

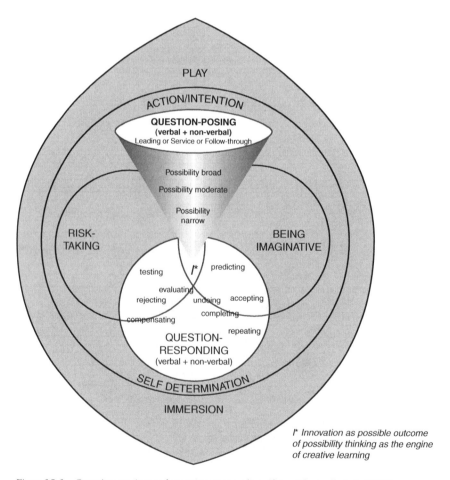

Figure 35.3 Question-posing and question-responding (from Chappell *et al.*, 2008)

engagement of imaginative and playful behaviour: particularly striking given the older age group.

A third study undertaken in parallel with the second focused on 4-year-olds in an early years setting (Craft *et al.*, 2012b) and explored possibility thinking as manifest in child-initiated play and adults' integral roles in this, not only in the provocation of play episodes but also in engaging within the playful episodes themselves. As shown in Figure 35.4, this study revealed blending of individual, collaborative and communal creativity inherent in the children's engagement, confirmed the role of risk-taking for these younger learners who were willing to pit their perspectives against those of others, including their teachers, and highlighted the framing role of the leading question. This study also identified five pedagogical strategies by which practitioners fostered possibility thinking in child-initiated play (discussed further below under 'Research focus 2'). The pedagogical strategies used were provoking possibilities, allowing time and space, being in the moment, making interventions, and mentoring in partnership. The first four of these blended child-initiated with adult-initiated impetus reflecting earlier work (e.g. Siraj-Blatchford *et al.*, 2002) exploring children's play.

A fourth study by Cremin *et al.* (2013) undertook a systematic re-analysis of all of the immersive, playful episodes involved in earlier studies, and investigated the role of narrative in each. This systematic re-analysis identified three different types of narrative (fantasy, everyday and historical) evident in children's playful episodes. As shown

Figure 35.4 Individual, collaborative and communal activity in child-initiated play (from Craft *et al.*, 2012b)

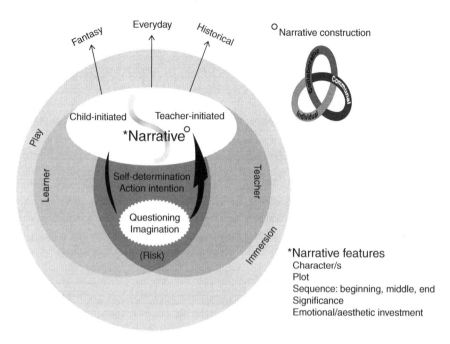

Figure 35.5 Overview of role of narrative in PT (Cremin *et al.*, 2013)

in Figure 35.5, analysis showed that all narrative episodes shared in common certain features: a sense of character, plot, sequence, significance and emotional investment.

This study of narrative showed how questioning and imagination each inherently involved narrative often shaped by children's questions and imagination, but also that reciprocally questions and imagination were fuelled by narratives developed during immersive playful episodes. While the parallel study by Craft *et al.* (2012b) discussed above had highlighted how children and adults frequently generate possibility thinking together, what the narrative-focused re-analysis revealed was that adult narrative was much less potent than children's own narratives in shaping their questions and imagination.

Taking the core features of PT together with the new narrative features, the research team is, as of 2014, adding a fifth study of the nature of possibility thinking by exploring the role of PT in social change in classrooms and schools. A small-scale study of PT was undertaken in England, in which the role of PT in creative social change in primary schools was investigated (Chappell and Craft, 2013; Craft and Chappell, in press). In this study, two large primary schools were studied for what they shared in common in terms of creative social change. The findings revealed each school demonstrated a strength of shared values that gave staff a sense of both direction and security, almost protection from other influences, for example from the wider policy environment. But while they shared this in common, the leadership styles of the head teachers were very different, one being closely focused on evidence within a clear hierarchical leadership with the vision for change initiated at the top, the other being much more organic with a flattened hierarchy of leadership with the vision for change emerging from the community.

In this fifth study, all core elements of PT were evident across the two schools. With the focus on adult leadership in this study, all elements were related to staff rather than pupils. In contrast to the classroom studies of PT where question-posing and responding belonged to the pupils, in this study question-posing and responding was driven by the head teachers. In both sites imagination was very strongly evidenced, as was self-determination although expressed differently. Each school expressed and evidenced action-intention, although to differing degrees. Both schools strongly evidenced innovation, adapting, developing and making connections between ideas to create new initiatives in schools. However, risk-taking was less evident. The study revealed the importance to staff in both schools of a sense of narrative, plot and sequence based in their core shared values. PT did seem to have a key role to play in making social change in each, with evidence of the life-wide dynamo at work in each.

In thinking about young children's creativity, PT helps us to understand how children inhabit the world of imagination that allows them to pose 'what if' questions as well as engaging in 'as if' behaviours. We see this at work in all aspects of their learning. A recent European study of creativity in science and mathematics in the early years across nine countries, Creative Little Scientists (www.creative-little-scientists.eu/content/deliverables), in which two of the core PT researchers have been involved, provided a great deal of evidence of children aged 3–8 engaged in PT.

For example, two 6-year-olds in England were investigating how a range of flat shapes might slot together to make a 3D shape. Their teacher had set them the challenge of making any 3D shape, but to use a rule in making it. Initially the children generated 'what if' questions, as the transcript of their talk shows:

> Girl: 'I've got an idea' [takes the hexagon flat shape] … 'We could make it irregular' [starts adding rectangles, Boy helps]
> Boy: 'We need more rectangles' [Extended dialogue]
> Boy: 'This is so hard … difficult'

As the children begin to struggle with the construction of their shape, they start to enter an 'as if' space:

> Girl: 'I'm going to walk inside … I'm going to break through the door … Open my house'
> Boy: [opens one the flap down] 'It's like a house, it's like a cylinder house'
> Girl: 'It's raining, I need to get into my house. It's raining, I need to get into my house' [laughter]

The children's laughter suggests that they know they are moving away from their mathematical investigation. However, their narrative then brings them back to the mathematics as they consider how to describe the shape that they have made. The girl highlights that the shape they have made is not a cylinder, having six sides, and so the two children name it a 'cylinca'. They inform their teacher, giving their justi-fication for it, demonstrating by touching the sides. Here we can see their 'what if' and 'as if' question-posing and question-responding, fuelled in an immersive, playful, emotionally enabling context, by imagination, self-determination, intentionality, and innovation. Their collaboration led to jointly generated and owned ideas.

What these studies of PT among children, adults and the interactions between children and adults have shown so far is how the consistent core features of PT are driven by question-posing and question-responding through individual, collaborative and communal engagement, driven by a shared narrative in an immersive context. The ownership of the questions is determined by the narrative that they form part of, whether the question-poser is a child or an adult. And while the ways in which the PT features are enacted through the different studies vary according to classroom and school culture, they are almost all (with the exception of risk, which is sometimes absent) always present in 'little c' creativity.

Research focus 2: pedagogy that enables possibility thinking

Alongside focus 1, which seeks to define and understand what PT is and how it drives everyday creativity for children and adults in learning contexts, is a second and inte-grated focus on *what pedagogical strategies enable PT*. Teaching for creativity, or enabling possibility thinking, demands classroom and school practices that encourage, nurture and celebrate 'what if' and 'as if' thinking in students. Research by the core team in early years and primary school settings in England over a number of years reveals that teaching for PT involves the development of an inclusive learning environment in which (1) children's experiences and ideas are highly valued; (2) dialogue between children and between children and teachers is encouraged; and (3) an ethos of respect is nurtured and children as well as teachers experience meaningful control, ownership, relevance and innovation in learning (Craft, 2007; Craft and Chappell, 2009; Craft and Jeffrey, 2004, 2009; Jeffrey and Craft, 2006).

An important aspect of pedagogy that fosters PT is how inherently 'possibility broad' or 'possibility narrow' any particular task is. Thus, the 7-year-olds who have learned about how to fold, bend, shape and fasten newspaper and who have been set the chal-lenge of designing a hat that will stay on their head and keep out the rain are able to engage in a much broader kind of possibility thinking than children of the same age given a range of hat templates to choose from in order to cut out, fasten and decorate one.

Being acutely aware of possibility breadth requires pedagogical sensitivity, as does another of the research findings documented alongside the original seminal PT study (Cremin *et al.*, 2006), which reveals how the features of PT are fostered by teacher–child interactions in an enabling context in which teachers offer children time and space to develop ideas, prioritise learner agency and 'stand back' in order to observe children's active engagement and to select when to intervene (Cremin *et al.*, 2006), as shown in Figure 35.6. This means that teachers recognise the dilemma of providing enough but not too much structure or intervention.

As indicated above, two later studies revealed the complexity of the relationship between children's and adults' thinking. In the first of these later studies, focusing on

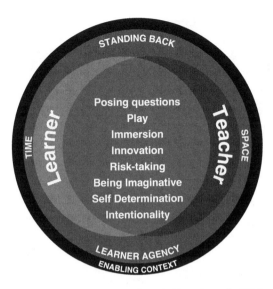

Figure 35.6 Pedagogy that nurtures PT, initial work (Cremin *et al.*, 2006)

4-year-olds, Craft *et al.* (2012b) explored PT manifest in child-initiated play and adults' roles in this. Analysis of this provocation-style approach to teaching and learning revealed an imaginative dynamic between practitioner and child; pedagogues 'stepped forward' and also 'stood back' as appropriate, encouraging, through use of provocation, which fuelled children's imaginative storying, as shown in Figure 35.7.

In the second of the later studies (Cremin *et al.*, 2013), we see that while questioning and imagination emerge from narrative, so narrative is built by children's questions and imagination within immersive playful episodes. While there is evidence among the 4-year-olds studied by Craft *et al.* (2012b) that PT is frequently generated by adults and children together, this wider study of episodes spanning the age range 3–11 showed that pedagogy that fosters such reciprocity between questioning imaginative engagement and narrative during playful episodes foregrounds the children's perspectives, which have far more potency than those of adults.

The potency of children's perspectives in relation to question-posing and narrative-building was evidenced in the European study Creative Little Scientists, exploring creativity in early science and mathematics. For example, in Belgium a class of children aged 4 to 6, working with two teachers, explored the story of Jack (Jacques) and the Beanstalk at their own request. This became the focus of science work prompted by teachers' questions but led by the children's own narrative, reflection, reasoning and evaluation. Although the questions are posed by the teachers, the episode below shows how the children's answers and ideas boost other children to interact.

> Teacher 1: 'What does Jacques have to do to escape?' [Several children are now reacting toward each other considering this question]
> Child 1: 'I know, maybe there is a key nearby to open the oven.'

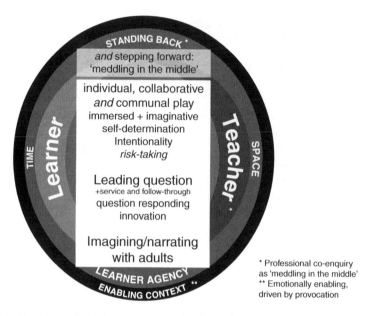

Figure 35.7   Adult and child engagement in play-focused PT (Craft *et al.*, 2012b)

Child 2: 'No, the giant has the key.'
Child 3: 'If the giant opens the oven and he sees the child.'
Teacher 2: 'Yes, what then?'
Child 4: 'Then the child has to go the between the legs of the giant. He has to loosen the goat and then the goat will attack the giant, who will fall.'
Teacher 1: 'But a goat against a giant. How large is the goat?' [One of the children, C, is showing how large a goat is, almost his own length.]
Teacher 1: 'Look at how large a goat is and C is a small child. C is maybe as large as Jacques.'
C: 'oepsie'

The children are keen and excited to bring in more ideas and solutions for Jacques. Children give their opinions. However, when there is too much commotion the teachers bring in another question, stimulating the children to reason and reflect. In this episode, after one child notices that in one of the pictures of the giant he has mushrooms growing in his armpits, the teachers stimulate inquiry and scientific understanding of children by reference to the children's own bodies. Investigations and observations are planned, evidence is gathered and communicated:

Teacher 2: 'Where is your armpit?' [The teacher asks this of all the children].
Teacher 1: 'Show me your armpit.' [Every child shows and points to their armpits].
Teacher 2: 'Yes, here is the hole under your arm.'

Teacher 1: 'Are there also mushrooms growing under your arms?' [The children are saying no and are also shaking their heads.]

Teacher 2: 'You know what, I'm going to check it by Child 2. We are going to see if there aren't any mushrooms growing in her armpits.' All the children are watching the teacher and Child 2. With the child's permission, the teacher rolls up the sleeve.

Teacher 1: 'Look at C2 her armpit. Are there any mushrooms growing there?' [The children are saying no].

Teacher 1: 'Why did it happen with the giant?'

Child: 'Because he is dirty.'

Teacher 2: 'Because he is dirty?'

Child: 'He has a pimple.'

Teacher 2: 'Yes and it looks dark at his nose and his ears.'

Child: 'Giants eat people.'

Teacher 1: 'What, do they eat people?'

Teacher 2: 'Do you get mushrooms if you eat people?'

Children: 'No' 'Yes' 'That is only with giants.'

What is striking about this example is the way the children and the teachers together enter both a 'what if' and an 'as if' space of imagination to seek to understand why the giant has mushrooms in his armpit and yet they do not themselves. The children's explanation is partially informed by their own fantasy narrative and partly by everyday narrative. The teachers step forward into the children's space but not so far that the children's agency is prevented.

This pattern of 'what if' and 'as if' engagement informed by narrative and where personal agency is foregrounded was evident too in the study of PT and social change in two English primary schools reported under Research focus 1 (Chappell and Craft, 2013). Further work is needed to explore the dynamics of what enables teachers' own PT; however, a very early study of this did highlight the delicate balance between individuals' creativity (Craft, 1996, 1998) revealing the dangers of a focus on teacher creativity without reference to the creativity of other teachers or of children and others.

From what is to what might be: PT generating social change

Since the earliest studies of PT, alongside the core research team's work PT has formed the focus of doctoral work mainly in the early years and primary age phase, at both the Open University and Exeter University and supervised by members of the core PT team (Anna Craft, Teresa Cremin and Kerry Chappell)[1]. Additional studies have also been undertaken, for example, PT in creative partnership among those aged 11–14 (Craft with Chappell and Rolfe, Exeter, 2008–10[2]). Perhaps the most significant direction of research, however, for PT is that which seeks to situate it in relation to how childhood and wider social change may connect.

The studies discussed in this chapter show that as children grow older, PT increasingly involves collaboration and 'sharing' (developing shared views), as well as 'shining' (having their own ideas). Older learners become increasingly absorbed in what emerges from their 'what if' and 'as if' thinking, in relation to taking action and doing something with ideas they have developed. The research on PT supports a perspective on childhood that sees children as capable and potent (as opposed to being vulnerable and at risk). These polarised perspectives on childhood are explored in some detail elsewhere (for example, Craft 2011, 2012) in relation to children's engagement in and responses to a marketised and globalised world.

The capacity to engage actively and responsibly in generating novelty that is valuable to the community as a whole is increasingly vital as pace and uncertainty in change at social, economic, technological and environmental levels demand creativity of young and old in framing present and future lives on the planet. Governments the world over recognise this and increasingly highlight the importance of developing creativity in the educational system. Recent research applications of PT led by the core team seek to explore its potency in enabling children to engage in such social change through two new European studies, which are both informed by the perspective that while children's lives are increasingly defined by and harnessed to the global marketplace, making them consumers and producers within a very narrow set of values (Craft, 2005, 2012, 2013, in press), educators and children can harness PT to challenge such assumptions and to generate ethically responsible creative change. The impetus to consider how PT can foster social change stems from discomfort with the increased marketisation of children's lives together with the increased agency afforded to children and young people by digital media (Craft, 2013).

The first of the European projects, which is looking at how PT can foster social change, C2Learn,[3] is working with learners aged 10 and above, to harness digital gameplaying and networking in learners' lives within school, college and university. Foregrounding the individual, collaborative and communal ethical dimensions inherent in creativity, and recognising the reciprocity involved in both making and being made (personal identity thus shaped alongside creative expression), this consortium from the United Kingdom, Austria, Denmark, Greece and Malta is applying the process of Wise Humanising Creativity (WHC) developed by Chappell and Craft (2011) within ethically demanding gameplaying scenarios. Fuelled by PT, the generative actions of learners are focused on 'quiet revolutions': in other words, social change valued by the community as a whole in which learners play a leading and emancipatory role. The study is exploring how a high trust and empowering digital gaming and networking environment facilitates children's 'what if' and 'as if' activity, enabling them to have ideas and see them through. Findings will start to be reported during 2014 through deliverables on the C2Learn website (www.c2learn. eu/?q=node/116) and journal articles.

In the second of the European projects, CREAT-IT[4] (www.creatit-project. eu/) the focus is on creative science education, and on teachers' professional development that encourages arts–infused creative science education with children aged 7 to 14, through science cafes, science theatre and 'write a science opera'. Spanning Belgium, England, Greece, Italy, Norway and Serbia, the consortium is using a pedagogical framework for the creative science education which has at its heart the trigger of PT. As in C2Learn, wise humanising creativity provides a lens and practical process through which children and their teachers and other partners working with them on creative projects consider the ethics and consequences of the creativity that is generated by PT. Informed by previous work on PT and wise humanising creativity, 12 pedagogical principles have been identified as a starting point in this study:

1 **Professional wisdom**: deeply contextualised knowledge often informed by intuition.
2 **Individual, collaborative and communal activities for change**: acknowledging shared identities, allowing for difference but with a shared creative process and purpose.
3 **Risk, immersion and play**: and recognising how pedagogy can assist in creating literal space as well as 'thinking' space for these to occur.
4 **Different ways of knowing**: knowing that (propositional knowledge), knowing how (practical knowledge), knowing this (aesthetic or felt knowledge), and embodied alongside the verbal.
5 **Dialogue**: between people, disciplines, creativity and identity, and ideas – recognising this can be embodied and that difference may mean conflict and irreconcilable difference.
6 **'Bottom up'/'top down'**: new ideas, knowledge, practices from 'bottom up' adult-learner activity are 'in conversation' with existing ideas, knowledge and practices.
7 **Interrelationship of different ways of thinking around a shared 'thread' or 'throughline'**: problem-finding, problem-solving, exploring, rationalising, reasoning, reflecting, questioning, experimenting.
8 **Discipline knowledge:** rigorous discipline knowledge of sciences and arts and creativity.
9 **Possibilities**: multiple possibilities thinking/spaces, knowing when to narrow or broaden.
10 **Ethics and trusteeship**: adult professionals and learners consider ethics of creative science, guided in decision-making by community priorities, 'trustees' of outcomes.
11 **Importance of materials**: material within which ideas are shaped is extremely important (e.g. their bodies, with props, with paper and pencil, with sculpting materials, with Bunsen burners and test tubes, with chemicals, with equations), contributing to defining the way ideas are thought through, as well as the form and content of ideas.
12 **Empowerment and agency**: through empowering pedagogies, children and adults gain a greater sense of their own agency and self-expression, applied to creative science.

At the time of writing (April 2014) the research outcomes for CREAT-IT and C2Learn are not yet available; however, it is expected that both European projects will lend insight into what is involved in PT triggering social change both in terms of its inherent processes and in terms of pedagogical strategies.

Conclusion

This chapter has discussed the body of qualitative research undertaken initially in England and mainly since the start of the twenty-first century on what PT is and how it is nurtured in classrooms and schools. Introducing more recent work, undertaken in a range of European countries and funded by the European Commission, on how PT fuels social change, it identifies the direction that this work is moving in. It traces the journey taken by the core researchers involved in this work from a focus on how children's idea-realisation is nurtured by adults, to an emphasis on how individual, collaborative and communal work between children and between children and adults, framed in a dialogic and ethical context, generates social change. Contexts that enable possibility thinking value all ideas, involve both collaboration and independence, value highly a stimulating learning environment and encourage reflection and acknowledge that those involved in making creative possibilities are trustees of ideas generated, both shaping and being shaped by them.

Work currently under way in the two European projects will, it is hoped, offer further insight into how children and adults can define, shape and transform their relationship with their social and cultural context. Such transformation, from what is to what might be, is right at the heart of the impetus of PT and it is hoped that this body of work offers not only insight into the transformative process but encouragement to challenge the performativity and marketisation that tends to define children's engagement with their learning.

Notes

1 Completed PhDs include PT in mathematics in upper primary education in England (Clack, Exeter), PT in drama in upper primary education in Taiwan (Lin, Exeter), PT and innovation education (Jonsdottir, Iceland), PT in secondary art in Taiwan (Ting, Exeter), PT in social exclusion (Greenwood, Exeter), PT in early years visual art in England (McConnon, Exeter). Three studies are in their final stages: PT in museum education in Cyprus (Gregoriou, Exeter), PT in piano tuition in Taiwan (Yeh, Exeter), and PT in creative partnership in Wales (Alderson, Open University). Each of these studies has confirmed the core features of PT identified in the Burnard *et al.* (2006) study and has added new perspectives to how PT can be understood in each particular context.
2 Dance Partners for Creativity (http://education.exeter.ac.uk/projects.php?id=339) was funded by AHRC grant AH/F010168/1 from 2008 to 2011. It generated many articles and a book, *Close Encounters: Dance Partners for Creativity* (Chappell *et al.*, 2011).
3 The C2Learn project is supported by the European Commission through the Seventh Framework Programme (FP7), under grant agreement no. 318480 (November 2012–October 2015).
4 CREAT-IT is funded with support from the European Commission through the Comenius Programme under grant agreement 539818-LLP-1-2013-NO-COMENIUS-CMP (November 2013–October 2015).

References

Boden, M. (2004) In a nutshell. In M. Boden (ed.) *The Creative Mind: Myths and Mechanisms.* London: Routledge.

Burnard, P., Craft, A., Grainger, T. *et al.* (2006) Documenting 'possibility thinking': A journey of collaborative enquiry. *International Journal of Early Years Education, 143,* 243–62.

Chappell, K. and Craft, A. (2011) Creative learning conversations: producing living dialogic spaces. *Educational Research, 53*(3), 363–85.

Chappell, K. and Craft, A. (2013) Possibility thinking for social change in creative primary schools. Presentation on Research Study, for Open University Research Event (6 November), Centre for Education and Educational Technology, Milton Keynes, England.

Chappell, K., Craft, A., Burnard, P. and Cremin, T. (2008) Question-posing and question-responding: The heart of possibility thinking in the early years. *Early Years, 283,* 267–86.

Chappell, K., Rolfe, L.,Craft, A. and Jobbins, V. (2011) *Close Encounters: Dance Partners for Creativity.* Stoke-on-Trent: Trentham Books.

Craft, A. (1996) Nourishing educator creativity: A holistic approach to CPD. *British Journal of In-service Education, 22*(3), 309–22.

Craft, A. (1998) UK educator perspectives on creativity. *Journal of Creative Behavior, 32*(4), 244–57.

Craft, A. (2000) *Creativity Across the Primary Curriculum.* London: Routledge.

Craft, A. (2001) Little c creativity. In A. Craft, B. Jeffrey and M. Leibling (eds) *Creativity in Education* (pp. 45–61). London: Continuum.

Craft, A. (2002) *Creativity and Early Years Education.* London: Continuum.

Craft, A. (2005) *Creativity in Schools: Tensions and Dilemmas.* Abingdon: Routledge.

Craft, A. (2007) Possibility thinking in the early years and primary classroom. In A. G. Tan (ed.) *Singapore Handbook of Creativity* (invited chapter). Singapore: World Scientific Publishing.

Craft, A. (2011) *Creativity and Education Futures: Learning in a Digital Age.* Stoke on Trent. Trentham Books.

Craft, A. (2012) Childhood in a digital age: Creative challenges for educational futures. *London Review of Education, 10*(2), 173–90.

Craft, A. (2013) Childhood, possibility thinking and education futures. *International Journal of Educational Research, 61,* 126–34.

Craft, A. (in press) Wise, humanising creativity: A goal for inclusive education, *Revista de Educación (Inclusive Education Journal).*

Craft, A. and Chappell, K. (2009) Fostering possibility through co-researching creative movement with 7–11 year olds. In S. Blenkinsop (ed.) *The Imagination in Education: Extending the Boundaries of Theory and Practice.* Cambridge: Scholars Publishing.

Craft, A. and Chappell, K. (in press) Possibility Thinking and Social Change in Primary Schools. Education 3–13.

Craft, A. and Jeffrey, B. (2004) Creative practice and practice which fosters creativity. In L. Miller and J. Devereux (eds) *Supporting Children's Learning in the Early Years* (pp. 105–12). London: David Fulton.

Craft, A. and Jeffrey, B. (2009) Creative practice and practice which fosters creativity. In L. Miller, C. Cable and G. Goodliff (eds) *Supporting Children's Learning in the Early Years,* 2nd edn. London: David Fulton.

Craft, A., Cremin, T., Burnard, P. and Chappell, K. (2008) Possibility thinking. In A. Craft, T. Cremin and P. Burnard (eds) *Creative Learning 3–11 and How We Document It.* Stoke-on-Trent: Trentham Books.

Craft, A., Cremin, T., Burnard, P., Dragovic, T. and Chappell, K. (2012a) Possibility thinking: Culminative studies of an evidence-based concept driving creativity? *Education, 3–13.* http://dx.doi.org/10.1080/03004279.2012.656671.

Craft, A., McConnon, L. and Matthews, A. (2012b) Creativity and child-initiated play. *Thinking Skills and Creativity, 71,* 48–61.

Cremin, T., Burnard, P. and Craft, A. (2006) Pedagogy and possibility thinking in the early years. *Thinking Skills and Creativity, 12,* 108–19.

Cremin, T., Chappell, K. and Craft, A. (2013) Reciprocity between narrative, questioning and imagination in the early and primary years: Examining the role of narrative in possibility thinking. *Thinking Skills and Creativity, 9,* 126–34.

Jeffrey, B. and Craft, A. (2006) Creative learning and possibility thinking. In B. Jeffrey (ed.) *Creative Learning Practices: European Experiences.* London: Tufnell Press.

Kaufman, J. C. and Beghetto, R. A. (2009) Beyond big and little: The four c model of creativity. *Review of General Psychology, 131,* 1–12.

Siraj-Blatchford, I., Sylva, K., Muttock, S., Gilden, R. and Bell, D. (2002) *Researching Effective Pedagogy in the Early Years (REPEY),* DfES research report 356. London: DfES, HMSO.

36

WHOSE ACTIVITY IS IT?

The role of child- and adult-initiated activity in young children's creative thinking

Sue Robson

Introduction

There is increasing recognition of the importance of supporting creativity and creative thinking for children of all ages (Siraj–Blatchford, 2007).This chapter looks at young children's creative thinking, as observed in their everyday behaviour while they engage in child-initiated, adult-directed and adult-led activities, and at the roles of adults in supporting and developing young children's creative thinking.

Creative thinking and creativity

In recent years the idea that creativity is a 'universal capability' (Siraj–Blatchford, 2007, p. 7), and thus that everyone has creative potential (Runco, 2003), has become more prevalent at all phases of education, including in early childhood. Looked at in this way, creativity can be seen as an everyday event (Richards, 2006), visible across the broadest range of contexts in daily life. Often referred to as 'little c' creativity (Craft, 2003; Kaufmann, 2003), this approach views creativity as 'a capacity of human intelligence, rather than a subject or event' (Prentice, 2000, p. 150).

What, though, might be meant by 'creative thinking', and what is its relationship to creativity? The National Advisory Committee on Creative and Cultural Education (NACCCE) defines creativity as 'imaginative activity fashioned so as to produce outcomes that are both original and of value' (1999, p. 29), while Sternberg defines creative thinking as 'thinking that is novel and that produces ideas that are of value' (2003, pp. 325–6). They share ideas of imagination, and originality or novelty – features of most standard definitions of creativity (Kaufmann, 2003) – but differ chiefly in outcomes, with the NACCCE focusing on something tangible, and Sternberg identifying ideas. Sternberg's use of 'novelty' highlights that, to count as creative, someone's idea does not have to embody thinking that has never occurred before in anyone. Rather, creative thinking is thinking that is new for *that individual*. Looked at in this way, while identifying whether any particular idea or act of a child is new for them will always be a challenge, it at least affords the possibility of recognising children's originality.

The second key idea in the definitions of both Sternberg (2003) and the NACCCE (1999) is the notion of value. This has two implications. First, it implies that creativity is inherently social. Amabile suggests that 'A product or response is creative to the extent that appropriate observers independently agree it is creative' (1996, p. 33). The second implication links creative thinking to so-called critical thinking. Choices and critical evaluations are made by both participants and observers as part of any creative process. The NACCCE suggest that 'creative thinking always involves some critical thinking' (1999, p. 31).

Sternberg identifies some key 'decisions', expressed in children's behaviour, that he believes underlie creative thinking, including redefining problems, analysing ideas, taking sensible risks, tolerating ambiguity, and allowing time and mistakes, *inter alia* (Sternberg, 2003, pp. 333–5). These 'decisions' may be useful indicators of creative thinking. Similarly, in her analysis of creative thinkers, Meadows (2006) identifies some characteristic attributes. Among these are choosing challenges rather than avoiding them, tolerating risk, enjoying complexity, and the ability to confront uncertainty. These attributes imply a role for qualities such as self-efficacy and self-esteem. Hypothesising, and making leaps of the imagination, require confidence on the thinker's part, and a willingness to take risks, suggesting a key role for motivation, particularly intrinsic motivation (Amabile, 1996).

Child-initiated and adult-initiated activity

The relationship between child-initiated and adult-initiated activity in early childhood settings, and the potential of both for affording children opportunities to learn, is a subject of long-standing debate. There is general acceptance that both child-initiated and adult-directed activities contribute to young children's development (Wood, 2007; Sylva *et al.*, 2010).

Child-initiated play may afford opportunities for children to develop their creativity and creative thinking, particularly in the generation and analysis of ideas and communicating these with others (Craft *et al.*, 2012). There is also evidence that child-initiated activity may support the development of young children's problem-solving (Ramani, 2012), metacognitive regulation (Whitebread *et al.*, 2007), motivation and self-concept (Graue *et al.*, 2004), persistence (Howard, 2010), prosocial behaviour (Vitiello *et al.*, 2012) and social communication skills (Maynard and Chicken, 2010).

At the same time, Sylva *et al.* conclude that 'children's cognitive outcomes appeared to be directly related to the quantity and quality of the teacher/adult planned and initiated focused group work for supporting children's learning' (2010, p. 161). Wolters (2011) asserts that direct instruction can foster the development of children's knowledge and ability to monitor and use self-regulation strategies, along with their motivation regulation. Vitiello *et al.* (2012) also found that adult-directed activities supported more positive engagements between children and adults.

The choice in practice is not, of course, one of 'either/or', but of the balance between adult-directed/led and child-initiated activity. Sylva *et al.* (2010) suggest that the 'excellent' settings in their study 'provided both teacher-initiated group work and freely chosen yet potentially instructive play activities' (2010, p. 161). This view is supported by Fuligni *et al.* (2012), who conclude that 'children can experience important opportunities for learning across a range of participation structures … which typically involve varying levels of didactic instruction and teacher scaffolding' (2012, p. 200).

The project

The research reported in this chapter took place in a Centre for Children and Families in London. The Centre had identified children's creative thinking as a priority for development. Participants were 30 children aged 3–4 years, teachers and nursery officers and other professionals, including a speech, language and communication therapist, music, play and movement therapists, an artist, family workers and two researchers.

Over a period of five months, episodes of child-initiated and adult-directed or adult-led play activities were video recorded in all areas and analysed and coded using the Analysing Children's Creative Thinking (ACCT) Framework (Fumoto *et al.*, 2012), set out in Figure 36.1. This framework, which draws particularly on the work of Sternberg (2003), Claxton (1999) Craft (2003), Meadows (2006) and NACCCE (1999), is underpinned by the view that young children's creative thinking can be inferred by observing a range of aspects of their everyday behaviour, as they engage in activities that have meaning and purpose for them (for information on its development see Robson, 2014). The episodes were event-driven, in an effort to capture more of the development of creative thinking by observing complete events. The time period of data collection included a Creative Week, during which the Centre was visited by various creative artists who led the children in a range of art, craft and music activities.

Data analysis and discussion

A total of 52 recordings were analysed and coded, using the ACCT Framework (Fumoto *et al.*, 2012; Robson, 2014). The recorded episodes ranged in length between 1 minute 30 seconds and 43 minutes, with an average length of between 7 and 8 minutes.

Episodes were categorised as child-initiated (activity wholly initiated by the child); adult-directed (child directed to activity by an adult, but adult may not be present); or adult-led (child directed to activity at which adult is present). The relative balance of activities, including whether occurring indoors or outside, is shown in Table 36.1. The predominance of child-initiated activity reflects the Centre's emphasis on promoting children's opportunities for choice and self-direction.

All participant children displayed evidence of creative thinking. The frequency of examples (an action, gesture, or talk of some kind) varied across the children from about every 11 seconds to every 72 seconds, across all activities. Throughout this chapter 'high' frequency of examples of creative thinking is defined as anything up to every 30 seconds, 'medium' is defined as frequencies of between every 31 and 50

CATEGORY	OPERATIONAL DEFINITION	EXAMPLE
E: EXPLORATION		
E1: Exploring	Child is keen to explore, and/or shows interest in the potential of a material or activity.	J is trying out buttons on the keyboard, causing a rhythm to play. He plays individual notes with alternate hands, smiling and watching carefully as he makes a note pattern.
E2: Engaging in new activity	Child is interested in becoming involved in an activity and taking an idea forward. The activity could be of his/her own choice or suggested by another child or adult.	A approaches a table covered in paint, where previous children have been working. She picks up a piece of paper from a pile and lays it on the table. Turning it over she spreads the paint that is now printed on it with her fingers.
E3: Knowing what you want to do	Child shows enjoyment or curiosity when choosing to engage in an activity.	K and adult A are standing at the woodwork bench. K has chosen a piece of wood, which he holds. He points to the back of the bench: 'In there.'
I: INVOLVEMENT AND ENJOYMENT		
I1: Trying out ideas	Child shows evidence of novel ways of looking and planning: uses prior knowledge or acquires new knowledge to imagine and/or hypothesise, or to show flexibility and originality in his/her thinking.	A is in the block area. She picks up 3 semi-circular blocks and lays two of them on the floor to form a circle, which she later calls a 'cheese'. She then puts one foot on each block and 'skates' across the carpet on them.
I2: Analysing ideas	Child shows either verbal or behavioural evidence of weighing up his/her idea, and deciding whether or not to pursue it.	R, N and K are building a tunnel from construction pieces. R watches as N and K build a cuboid, N puts a piece in front of the open end. R: 'No, they won't be able to get out.'
I3: Speculating	Child makes a speculative statement or asks a question of him/herself, or of other children or adults, relating to the activity.	H is outside, looking at herbs in the garden with adult J. H points to a herb and says 'Yes, but why is this spiky?'
I4: Involving others	Child engages with one or more children or adults to develop an idea or activity: may articulate an idea, seek to persuade others, or show receptivity to the ideas of others.	A, J and C are playing a 'Father Christmas' game in the block area. A: 'I'm Rudolph.' J: 'And he's Rudolph too … No, he … you can be …' C: (to A) 'You Comet, you be.' A: (to C) 'Why don't you be Comet?' C: 'No, I'm Donner.'
P: PERSISTENCE		
P1: Persisting	Child shows resilience, and maintains involvement in an activity in the face of difficulty, challenge or uncertainty. He/she tolerates ambiguity.	In the sandpit E has been filling a large tube with dry sand. He picks up the tube and goes to fill the hopper on a nearby toy lorry, but the sand runs out of the end of the tube. He looks up, smiles, but does not break his concentration, but instead uses his hands to fill the hopper.
P2: Risk taking	Child displays a willingness to take risks, and to learn from mistakes.	M is at the clay. She tries to fill a bottle by inverting it into a full cup of water, but this causes the water to flow out on to the table. She abandons this and pours water straight from the cup onto the clay.
P3: Completing challenges	Child shows a sense of self-efficacy, self-belief and pleasure in achievement: shows conscious awareness of his/her own thinking.	M has been at the mark-making table, using felt tip pens and paper. He finishes his drawing. M: 'I've finished' (smiling). Adult: Mm. M pats the paper and nods, then picks up the pen and makes a large 'M' in the bottom right corner. 'That's my Muh.' (He continues to write the other letter of his name.) 'I did it, I writ my name myself.'

Figure 36.1 The Analysing Children's Creative Thinking (ACCT) Framework

Table 36.1 Recorded episodes, divided into child-initiated, adult-directed and adult-led groups, and indoor/outdoor contexts

	Child-initiated	Adult-directed	Adult-led	Total
Indoors	26	8	6	40
Outdoors	8	3	1	12
Total	34	11	7	52

seconds, and 'low' frequency is defined as less than every 50 seconds. The data were considered from three perspectives, set out below.

Responsibility for choice of activity

The balance of child-initiated and adult-directed activity shown in Table 36.1 reflects the Centre's emphasis on child-initiated activity. However, the boundaries between these categories are often difficult to sustain. For example, in 11 of the 'child-initiated' activities, an adult was nearby at times, but in the role of co-player or companion, rather than providing input or instructions. This may also change in the course of an activity.

The total frequencies of examples, showing the relative distribution of creative thinking behaviour according to whether the activity was child-initiated, adult-directed or adult-led, appear in Table 36.2. Some behaviours fell into more than one category and were therefore coded more than once.

In order to investigate the extent to which the distribution of these activities might differ between child-initiated and adult-organised events, and since some of the frequencies in the second and third columns of Table 36.2 were quite small, the

Table 36.2 Observed behaviours in the three ACCT categories of Exploration, Involvement and Enjoyment and Persistence

	Child-initiated	Adult-directed	Adult-led	**TOTAL**
E1: Exploring	4	0	3	**7**
E2: Engaging in new activity	4	5	6	**15**
E3: Knowing what you want to do	17	9	7	**33**
I1: Trying out ideas	200	31	33	**264**
I2: Analysing ideas	66	13	14	**93**
I3: Speculating	15	6	5	**26**
I4: Involving others	106	43	17	**166**
P1: Persisting	34	5	3	**42**
P2: Risk taking	8	1	0	**9**
P3: Completing challenges	27	7	4	**38**
TOTAL	**481**	**120**	**92**	**693**

(34 child-initiated, 11 adult-directed and 7 adult-led activities)

frequencies in these two columns were aggregated and a 10 × 2 chi-square test was performed on the resulting overall frequency table. This showed a significant difference between the frequency distributions of the ten categories for the two types of activity (χ^2 = 34.21, df = 9, p < 0.05). Some aspects of creative thinking behaviour occur more frequently than others, in particular 'Trying out ideas', 'Analysing ideas' and 'Involving others'. These may also occur more frequently in child-initiated activities. Other aspects, such as 'Engaging in new activity', are associated more strongly with adult direction and involvement.

Type of activity

Given the free-flowing nature of young children's play, categorising activities can be challenging. Activities were categorised using the dominant form of activity in an episode. They comprised 2D activities such as mark-making and printing (11 episodes), 3D activities with clay, dough, paper construction and woodwork (8), construction (4), gardening (5), pretend play (8), sand and water (4), music (4) and mathematics, and a category of 'free play' (8), such as a group of boys exploring a box of magnets and toy cars.

The data here are too small to support a comparison of different types of activity for their creative potential, but it is interesting to note that activities often designated as 'creative' were no better at supporting and developing young children's creative thinking than other types of activity. Indeed, other types of activity were often more successful.

Overall about half of the 'creative' episodes led to the medium and higher frequencies of creative thinking. In the case of 'non-creative' activities, this figure rose to nearly three-quarters. Two possible factors accounting for this in this sample are that the 'creative' activities were often associated with adult direction (a number of them occurred during a Creative Week, including activities led by adults from outside the Centre), and more likely to take place indoors. In the case of the first factor, the data here endorse the view that child-initiated play may be more supportive of creative thinking (Craft *et al.*, 2008). In the case of the second factor, the differences between indoors and outdoors as contexts for creative thinking may be significant. The majority of outdoor play we recorded showed high levels of creative thinking behaviour in the participants, whether alone or with others, and regardless of adult presence or absence. Some of these episodes involved activities unique to outdoors – digging and gardening, for example, while others were activities that also occurred inside, such as mark-making and construction. It may be that outdoors affords children time and space to think creatively (Robson and Hargreaves, 2005), and facilitates a greater range of creative responses (Compton *et al.*, 2010).

One activity that may particularly afford young children opportunities for displaying and developing their creative thinking is pretend play, emphasised by Singer (1973) and Vygotsky (2004) as valuable for creative and flexible thinking. Pretend play, particularly socio-dramatic play, was the most likely activity to lead to high levels of creative thinking. A comparison of episodes of pretence and episodes of 'creative' activities showed similar frequencies of 'trying out ideas', particularly imagining and hypothesising, but activities involving shared pretence had much higher incidences of 'involving others', particularly in articulating ideas and persuading others, as in the following episode of Emma, Iliana and Amy as they play in the 'doctor's surgery' they have made:

Iliana: 'Give me a appointment.'
Amy looks at Emma, and holds out a card to her: 'Emma, you have this because you got a baby.'
Emma: 'No, I haven't got a baby!'
Amy smiles, gesturing at her tummy.
Emma: 'I have a baby, but it's a boy baby.'
Amy taps her on the arm.
Emma: 'A boy baby.' She seals the envelope with her papers in it and looks at Amy: 'I've got a *boy* baby in my tummy and this is my appointment card' (pointing to envelope).
Amy: 'And this is our card.' (pointing at papers on table).
Emma smiles.
Amy taps on the keyboard, looks at Emma: 'That's a hundred pounds.'
Emma: 'I haven't got a hundred pounds.'
Amy: 'You can go to the shop' (gesturing to another part of the nursery).

Much pretend play, particularly in this age group, is collaborative, providing a context for children to engage with others, hypothesising about their wishes and intentions, as they negotiate story lines, and imagine how co-players will feel, think and act. It is also generally child-initiated, and characterised by adult absence.

Types of creative thinking behaviour

Here the data are considered using the three ACCT categories of Exploration, Involvement and Enjoyment, and Persistence (See Figure 36.1 for categories and sub-categories).

Exploration

The nature of recording children's spontaneous involvement in activities meant that a child was sometimes already engaged in an activity before being noticed by a researcher, and recording started. This may have contributed to the relatively low number of behaviours in this category. At the same time, however, it was clear that children's exploratory play with materials and resources of all kinds was a very strong context for their creative thinking. For example, in a child-initiated activity, Ella spent much of one afternoon using a digital camera. She explored what the camera could do, pressing buttons and observing the lens extend, taking pictures and looking at them on the camera screen. She also focused on seeing what she could do with the camera, as she held it out in front of her, watching the image change on the screen as she walked across the nursery with it, or as she used it to 'see' underneath the climbing frame, pointing it upwards. She involved others as she took their photographs, and showed them the results on screen.

'Knowing what you want to do' (E3) was evident at different points throughout activities, both at the start, as in Mark's self-initiated play with magnets –

> Mark picks up a large horseshoe magnet in his left hand, and a smaller wand-shaped magnet in his right, he holds them against one another,

– and during an activity, as in Amayah's comments to Jodika. They have been printing with blocks. Removing a magnet that has been holding their paper to the easel, Amayah spots the only unpainted piece of paper:

> Amayah: 'Look! Let's do it! She picks up a block while Jodika holds the paper in place on the easel.

An interesting aspect of the data is the impact of adults on children's initial engagement and exploration. When talking about what they did, children often said they had chosen to engage in an activity for themselves, often citing the presence of friends as a reason. However, the data in Table 36.2 show that children's initial engagement in an activity was often the result of adult direction. 'Engaging in new activity' (E2) and 'Knowing what you want to do' (E3) are shown to be strongly associated with adult direction or leading. In the case of E2 this is particularly marked. The small size of the sample here means that such data are, at best, inconclusive, but indicates the value of further research on this aspect.

In addition, this evidence may be very important for practice. Exploration, having an interest in taking an idea forward, and knowing what you want to do are aspects of behaviour which, by their nature, often occur at the beginning of children's engagement in an activity. They serve as conditions, even as 'gatekeepers' for children's on-going involvement and persistence.

Involvement and enjoyment

This category was responsible for the majority of examples. 'Trying out ideas' (I1), 'Analysing ideas' (I2) and 'Involving others' (I4) between them accounted for just over 75 per cent of recorded examples. Child-initiated activities were much more likely to feature the highest levels of children's involvement. Laevers believes that a key factor of support for higher levels of involvement (seen by him as an indicator of children's 'intense mental activity') is the opportunities children have for choice: 'the more children can choose their own activities, the higher will be their level of involvement' (Laevers 2000, p. 26). Siraj-Blatchford *et al.* suggest that 'freely chosen play activities often provide the best opportunities to extend children's thinking' (2002, p. 12). In child-initiated activities, children were over twice as likely to try out ideas, and to display more flexibility and originality, imagining and hypothesising, and also significantly more likely to analyse ideas and to involve others. In I3 (speculating), the likelihood of creative thinking behaviour was roughly equal between child- and adult-initiated activity.

One factor of importance is the presence of play companions. High levels of involvement were observed in over three-quarters of the episodes of group play, and in about 60 per cent of episodes of pair play between friends, falling to approximately 50 per cent in episodes of solitary play. In discussion children often referred to the presence of friends as important, and friends have been shown to be more likely to succeed in problem solving activities than non-friends (Smith *et al.*, 2011).

Looking at I1 ('Trying out ideas' – using prior knowledge/gaining new knowledge), one interesting aspect of the data is the role of adults in supporting young children in developing their knowledge. All adults were skilful in encouraging children to make use of prior knowledge, such as reminding them of how to use resources, or ways of doing things. However, teachers, as a group, were most successful in supporting children in gaining new knowledge. While using prior knowledge is important, Vygotsky's famous statement, 'What a child can do with assistance today she will be able to do by herself tomorrow' (1978, p. 87), emphasises the value of the acquisition of new knowledge and insights, gained through joint thinking. This is reflected in the excerpts of adult-directed activity below, showing Teacher Anna and Artist Catherine, engaged in the same activity. While Anna models thinking, and engages in speculation and prediction with Jake, Catherine focuses on instruction and demonstration with Mimi:

Jake and Teacher Anna:
Jake is holding the hammer with the ball end facing the nail, not the flat end.
Anna: 'I wonder if it works on that side?'
Jake turns hammer over.

…

Jake hits the nail with the hammer, while Anna holds nail in position. Jake pulls Anna's hand away.
Anna (moving her hand away): 'Oh! If I let go it's going to fall over!'

Mimi and Artist Catherine:
Mimi picks up the hammer and goes to hit the nail with ball end.
Catherine (pointing to flat end of hammerhead): 'Bash it with this end' (turns hammerhead over) 'Bash the nail in there'.

…

Mimi is turning screwdriver anticlockwise on screw head.
Catherine: 'Turn it the other way, look, this way' (demonstrating).

It is interesting to speculate about why Anna and Mimi's interactions are so different. Sylva *et al.* (2010) concluded that adults with higher level qualifications, particularly Qualified Teacher Status (QTS) (DfE, 2011), were most likely to encourage young children to engage in activities with higher cognitive challenge. Supporting children in the acquisition of new knowledge embodies a higher level of cognitive challenge than asking them to recall or rehearse already acquired knowledge and skills. Sylva *et al.* (2010) also found that the adult's knowledge of subject matter and the curriculum was central. Requirements for QTS in England place considerable emphasis on trainees' subject knowledge and teaching of the statutory curriculum, more so than other early years qualifications such as the Level 3 Diploma for the Children and Young People's Workforce (CACHE 2012), and clearly more so than what may be required of other adults such as artists. As a result, teachers as a group (though not necessarily individually) may be more likely to be attuned to looking for potential opportunities to develop children's existing subject knowledge. It is, however, important to emphasise that it was only in this aspect, that of gaining new knowledge versus rehearsal of the known, that we found a difference in adult behaviours.

In 'Analysing ideas' (I2) the focus is on the ways in which a child might show some evidence of evaluating an idea to see if it works, as in this example of child-initiated block play:

> In the block area Fahida has built a tower-like structure of cuboids and places a triangular prism on top. She tries to balance a cylinder block on top of this, sees it will not work, and removes the prism. She places the cylinder on top instead.

'Speculating' (I3) was the least frequently observed area of Involvement and Enjoyment. During activities, adults were more successful at engaging children in speculative thinking than peers. This was often related to 'Involving others' (I4) in that children were expressing a view or posing a question and, while it might sometimes be self-talk, in these examples another child or adult was usually being addressed. Several of the behaviours coded in this category also fitted in I4, but Emma in the 'doctor's surgery' (see above also) seems to be speculating:

> Emma flicks over pages in the desk diary, roughly tears out two pages from it, and looks across the table: 'I think I need a big one. I need a big one. A big one so I can fold this …

'Involving others' (I4) contained a large set of observations, in which specific moves to involve others seemed to be driven by a range of intentions. All the coded behaviours in this category were further categorised, according to responsibility for choice of activity and intention, as shown in Table 36.3.

Categorising the data in this way reveals some interesting differences in children's behaviour. In child-initiated activities, the chief verbal contributions were aimed at making statements or suggestions which explained what was happening, often with the purpose of moving the game forward. Interactions between children supported thinking in that they were concerned with developing an idea, instructing another child, disagreeing/persuading others, defending an idea, or extending another child's idea. In such cases, children are obliged to both clarify their own thinking, and to try to 'get inside' the thinking of another person, in order to persuade them to go with your idea.

Attempts to attract attention or seek assistance were much more common in adult-directed/led activities than in child-initiated activities, and it was most frequently adult attention or assistance that was being sought. Such calls for help could be a simple gesture:

Table 36.3 Involving others: typical purposes of interactions

Involving others	Number of observations	Typical purposes of interaction, in approximate order of frequency
Child-initiated activities	106	• informing/instructing • developing the game • disagreeing/persuading someone round to their opinion/controlling • defending an idea • picking up another child's idea and extending it • enlisting others to join in • seeking attention or assistance
Adult-directed activities	43	• seeking attention or assistance • informing/instructing • defending an idea • picking up an adult's idea and extending it • picking up a peer's idea and extending it • enlisting others to join in • offering to help
Adult-led activities	17	• informing/describing a process • seeking attention or assistance • answering adult's question • asking permission • controlling adult input

Kyle is trying to use a drill to make a hole in a piece of wood; he looks at the adult and points to the top of the drill.

Adult: 'You want me to hold this bit, yes?'

Or they could be in the form of a more clearly articulated demand, or set of demands:

Amber folds her picture to make a card (picture on the inside) and tries to get practitioner Sally's attention: 'Sally, Sally, look.'

Sally: 'That's lovely, are you going to write your name on it?'

Amber: 'Yes'.

Sally continues to talk to various children.

Amber gets a pen and writes something in the very corner of her card: 'I can't do it.'

Sally: 'Do you want to get your name card to help you?'

Amber: 'Where is it?'

Interestingly, children were more likely to be receptive to other ideas, and for these to influence their thinking and action, when these came from an adult, rather than another child.

Persistence

Here the focus is on children's persistence and resilience, their ability to sustain their involvement in the face of challenge, and their willingness to take risks and learn from mistakes. These dispositions will influence children's sense of self-efficacy and pleasure in completing challenges, as well as supporting deeper understanding and more complex knowledge (Lambert 2000). The data in Table 36.2 show that the majority of examples here occurred in child-initiated activities. Of the ten observations with the highest levels of persistence in children, all were child-initiated, and in nine of them practitioners were absent. It may be that, in planning adult-directed activities that are skilfully matched to the children's competences, practitioners present the children with fewer problems or risks with which they must deal. In child-initiated activities where adults are not present, the interventions of peers can often result in challenges and problems which a child must overcome, without recourse to an outside arbitrator.

Persistence, of course, is not just a matter of how long a child remains involved in an activity. Children's persistence in the face of difficulty and challenge, and sense of self-efficacy, was present even in short activities. Again, this was most evident in child-initiated activities where practitioners were absent, as in this example of Orrin, during which he repeatedly rebuilt his construction:

> Orrin is kneeling on the floor, in front of a tall thin block construction. He stands up and carefully places a cuboid on top and stands back. The construction stays up, and he tells Jayvon nearby about it.
>
> He kneels down, stands a long cuboid on its end next to the tower, and puts another similar sized piece next to it. This falls back into his arms.
>
> Orrin: (self-talk) Ups, again. Go on, ups again.
>
> He moves the long cuboid further away from his tower, takes the second cuboid and puts this on top to create another tall tower, repeating the 'ups again' as he does so. He places another cuboid next to this, stands up and tries to rest another one on top to make a further tower. This is not stable, and it falls back towards him. In catching these he knocks the other tower, this topples forward and knocks over his original tower. He looks around, collapses on the floor and smiles at Jayvon behind him.

An important aspect of the data is the low incidence of risk-taking behaviour in the children. Craft *et al.* (2012) include risk-taking as one of the seven key features of 'possibility thinking', and Tovey (2007) identifies positive links between risk-taking and key areas of children's learning. These include the assessment and management of risk as a survival skill, a sense of mastery, and emotional well-being and resilience. The greater (though still low) frequency of risk-taking behaviour in child-initiated activities from which adults were absent may be because children support and encourage one another more in taking risks in their play, or, in the case of solitary play, because a child feels a greater sense of freedom from adult attention. Jake, for example, decided that a more interesting use for masking tape was both winding it round himself (involving much analysis of how long a piece of tape was needed, how this could be measured around your head when you cannot see the back of your head, and how to use scissors in such circumstances), and then around the legs and seat of his chair. It is children's sense of permission to use materials in different ways that may be important here, facilitated by adults' openness to children's thinking.

Conclusion

The data presented here show that children display their creative thinking in all types of activity and social context. Some aspects of creative thinking behaviour, particularly associated with child-initiated activity, seem to occur more frequently than others (in particular 'Trying out ideas', 'Analysing ideas' and 'Involving others'). Other aspects, such as 'Engaging in new activity', are associated more strongly with adult direction and involvement, and the observations point to the particularly important role of adults in supporting children's initial engagement in activities.

Children's exploratory play with materials and resources of all kinds proved a very strong context for their creative thinking. However, two particular contexts which may be supportive of creative thinking are outdoor play and pretence. Socio-dramatic play, in particular, was the activity most likely to lead to high levels of creative thinking.

Child-initiated activities were much more likely to feature the highest levels of children's involvement, particularly in comparison to activities led by adults, or even where adults were present but not directing the activity. One factor that seems to be important is the presence of play companions. What is also clear, however, is that interactions between adults and children influenced the ways in which children displayed their creative thinking. Children were more likely to be receptive to other ideas and for these to have an impact on their thinking and action when these came from an adult, rather than another child, and adults were more successful at engaging children in speculative thinking than peers. However, interactions between children more often supported higher level thinking than interactions between adults and children.

The majority of examples of persistence-associated behaviours occurred in child-initiated activities, although adult presence at such activities was often a powerful support for the children's persistence and completion of challenges. An important aspect of the data is the comparative absence of risk-taking behaviour in the children, and this is an aspect that is particularly worthy of further investigation.

Acknowledgements

The research discussed in this chapter is drawn from the Froebel Research Fellowship project, The Voice of the Child: Ownership and Autonomy in Early Learning, funded by The Froebel Trust.

References

Amabile, T. M. (1983) *The Social Psychology of Creativity.* New York: Springer Verlag.
Amabile, T. M. (1996) *Creativity in Context.* Boulder, CO: Westview Press.

CACHE (Council for Awards in Care, Health and Education) (2012) CACHE Qualification Specification: CACHE Level 3 Diploma for the Children and Young People's Workforce (QCF).

Claxton, G. (1999) *Wise Up: The Challenge of Life Long Learning*. London: Bloomsbury.

Compton, A., Johnston, J., Nahmad-Williams, L. and Taylor, K. (2010) *Creative Development*. London: Continuum.

Craft, A. (2003) Creative thinking in the early years of education. *Early Years*, 23(2), 143–54.

Craft, A., Cremin, T., Burnard, P. and Chappell, K. (2008) Possibility thinking with children in England aged 3–7. In A. Craft, T. Cremin and P. Burnard (eds) *Creative Learning 3–11 and How We Document it* (pp. 65–73). Stoke on Trent: Trentham Books.

Craft, A., McConnon, L. and Paige-Smith, A. (2012) Child-initiated play and professional creativity: Enabling four-year-olds' possibility thinking. *Thinking Skills and Creativity*, 7(1), 48–61.

DfE (Department for Education) (2011) *Teachers' Standards. Statutory Guidance for School Leaders, School Staff and Governing Bodies*. Available at: www.gov.uk/government/uploads/system/uploads/attachment_data/file/283198/Teachers__Standards.pdf (accessed 10 October 2013).

Fuligni, A. S., Howes, C., Huang, Y., Hong, S. S. and Lara-Cinismo, S. (2012) Activity settings and daily routines in preschool classrooms: Diverse experiences in early learning settings for low-income children. *Early Childhood Research Quarterly*, 27, 198–209.

Fumoto, H., Robson, S., Greenfield, S. and Hargreaves, D. J. (2012) *Young Children's Creative Thinking*. London: Sage.

Graue, E., Clements, M. A., Reynolds, A. J. and Niles, M. J. (2004) More than teacher directed or child initiated: Preschool curriculum type, parent involvement, and children's outcomes in the child–parent centers. *Education Policy Analysis Archives*, 12(72), 1–36.

Howard, J. (2010) Making the most of play in the early years: The importance of children's perceptions. In P. Broadhead, J. Howard and E. Wood (eds) *Play and Learning in the Early Years* (pp. 145–60). London: Sage.

Kaufmann, G. (2003) What to measure? A new look at the concept of creativity. *Scandinavian Journal of Educational Research*, 47(3), 235–51.

Laevers, F. (2000) Forward to Basics! Deep-level-learning and the experiential approach. *Early Years*, 20(2), 20–9.

Lambert, E. B. (2000) Problem-solving in the first years of school. *Australian Journal of Early Childhood*, 25(3), 32–8.

Maynard, T. and Chicken, S. (2012) Through a different lens: Exploring Reggio Emilia in a Welsh context. *Early Years*, 30(1), 29–39.

Meadows, S. (2006) *The Child as Thinker*. London: Routledge.

NACCCE (National Advisory Committee on Creative and Cultural Education) (1999) *All Our Futures: Creativity, Culture, and Education*. London: DfEE.

Prentice, R. (2000) Creativity: A reaffirmation of its place in early childhood education. *The Curriculum Journal*, 11(2), 145–58.

Ramani, G. B. (2012) Influence of a playful, child-directed context on preschool children's peer cooperation. *Merrill-Palmer Quarterly*, 58(2), 159–90.

Robson, S. (2014) The Analysing Children's Creative Thinking framework: Development of an observation led approach to identifying and analysing young children's creative thinking. *British Educational Research Journal*, 40(1), 121–34.

Robson, S. and Hargreaves, D. J. (2005) What do early childhood practitioners think about young children's thinking? *European Early Childhood Education Research Journal*, 13(1), 81–96.

Runco, M. A. (2003) Education for creative potential. *Scandinavian Journal of Educational Research*, 47(3), 317–24.

Singer, J. L. (1973) *The Child's World of Make-Believe: Experimental Studies of Imaginative Play*. New York: Academic Press.

Siraj-Blatchford, I. (2007) Creativity, communication and collaboration: The identification of pedagogic progression in sustained shared thinking. *Asia-Pacific Journal of Research in Early Childhood Education*, *1*(2), 3–23.

Siraj-Blatchford, I., Sylva, K., Muttock, S., Gilden, R. and Bell, D. (2002) *Researching Effective Pedagogy in the Early Years*, Research Report 356. London: DfES.

Smith, P. K., Cowie, H. and Blades, M. (2011) *Understanding Children's Development*, 5th edn. Oxford: Blackwell.

Sternberg, R. J. (2003) Creative thinking in the classroom. *Scandinavian Journal of Educational Research*, *47*(3), 325–38.

Sylva, K., Melhuish, E., Sammons, P., Siraj-Blatchford, I. and Taggart, B. (2010) *Early Childhood Matters: Evidence from the Effective Pre-school and Primary Education Project*. London: Routledge.

Tovey, H. (2007) *Playing Outdoors*. Maidenhead: Open University Press.

Vitiello, V. E., Booren, L. M., Downer, J. T. and Williford, A. P. (2012) Variation in children's classroom engagement throughout a day in preschool: Relations to classroom and child factors. *Early Childhood Research Quarterly*, *27*, 210–20.

Vygotsky, L. S. (1978) *Mind in Society*. Cambridge, MA: Harvard University Press.

Vygotsky, L. S. (2004) Imagination and creativity in childhood. *Journal of Russian and East European Psychology*, *42*(1), 7–97.

Whitebread, D., Bingham, S. Grau, V., Pino-Pasternak, D. and Sangster, C. (2007) The development of metacognition and self-regulated learning in young children: The role of collaborative and peer-assisted learning. *Journal of Cognitive Education and Psychology*, *6*(3), 433–55.

Wolters, C. A. (2011) Regulation of motivation: Contextual and social aspects. *Teachers College Record*, *113*(2), 265–83.

Wood, E. (2007) New directions in play: Consensus or collision? *Education 3–13*, *35*(4), 309–20.

37

YOUNG CHILDREN DRAWING

Providing a supportive environment

Kathy Ring

Introduction

Within this chapter I share findings from continuing analysis of a longitudinal research project, 'Supporting Young Children Drawing in Educational Settings'. The project builds upon the findings of previous research reported in *Making Sense of Children's Drawings* (Anning and Ring, 2004), where practitioners' perceived misunderstandings in relation to young children's use of drawing influenced their practice to the detriment of the child's experience. The key message of the chapter is the importance of early years practitioners developing a broader understanding of drawing, i.e. understanding it to be part of young children's multi-modal and physical engagement in the ongoing process of meaning-making. Within the project, it was by moving away from prioritizing detail and realism within drawing, or upon drawing's function being solely a lead-in to writing, and instead recognizing drawing as one tool within a symbolic continuum, that practitioners were able to better support children. As they engaged in the process of action research, practitioners focused upon providing an environment where all children could engage with drawing. This led to opportunities for practitioners to observe and reflect upon children's use of drawing as they, the children, gained confidence and fluency in its use as a tool for making sense of their new experience in the world.

Misunderstandings about drawing in early years settings

The analysis of seven young children's drawings, narratives, and contextual detail collected by Anning and Ring (2004) across their home, pre-school and school contexts, gave evidence of practitioners tending to prioritize conventional and formalized writing over drawing. Drawing lacked recognition and celebration by them as one of a range of tools used by young children to make meaning. Common difficulties for the children included not having constant access to paper and drawing tools; drawing being limited to a small 'mark-making' area where the young child was surrounded by letters and formats for writing; and over-direction from adults in relation to expected outcomes combined with lack of praise and recognition for creativity and originality.

Given the domination of literacy and numeracy across primary schooling in England and the narrow understanding of literacy as the reading and writing of words, drawing as 'mark-making' had become subsumed within preparation for writing in many of the educational settings. For many practitioners and children, replacing the term 'drawing' with 'mark-making' seemed to have separated it from play (Ring, 2003). This had a particularly strong influence upon boys. Boys were seen by the practitioners in the study to be generally uninterested in working in two dimensions and as having a preference for the larger-scale movements they were able to make in the open spaces of outdoors. The expectation that drawing would take place when seated at a table, on a small scale and with the support of the presence of an adult did not motivate the boys who sought action and adventure and identified with the powerful transformations of superheroes. As Howard (2002) recognizes, this kind of scenario is perceived as lacking the characteristics of play. In not encouraging boys to take a playful approach to drawing activity practitioners failed to harness intrinsic qualities such as motivation, enthusiasm, engagement and a willingness to take risks.

A case study of one child, drawing over a period of three years, gives evidence of practitioners within a Family Centre unsuccessfully attempting to impose drawing upon Luke at 3 and 4 years of age. His action drawing (Figure 37.1), validated by

Figure 37.1 Luke: Action drawing

Matthews (2003) as signifying movement rather than an object or person, was recognized by practitioners only as meaningless 'scribble' and given little value. Instead there was a concentrated effort made by his key worker to support him in drawing figures of people in order to tick the next box on the checklist of achievements used by the setting. Taking a didactic approach to drawing did little to encourage and value the kind of spontaneous and exuberant meaning-making Luke chose to do at home. It was only when transferred to the primary school, and supported by a confident and experienced early years teacher who recognized Luke's holistic needs, that he was given the time and freedom needed to explore his preoccupations through drawing. Figure 37.2, 'The bread making machine', is an example of Luke's use of drawing, when aged 5, to make a number of connections across his experiences: his friendship with another boy who loved to draw machines; his lead role in the about to be performed story of 'The Little Red Hen', where the hen grinds wheat to make bread; and his experience of baking bread alongside his grandmother, using her bread-making machine. At the beginning of the first year in school no pressure was exerted upon Luke to link drawing with writing, and drawing became part of his freely chosen playful activity and an important tool for supporting his thinking and making it visible.

At the time of this previous study, the impact of the social context upon young children's use of drawing was generally underplayed. When participants were asked about the theories of drawing that underpinned their understanding and decision-making, they all referred to the Draw-a-Man Test (Goodenough, 1926). This intelligence test, based on the notion of children developing in regular predictable patterns or stages (Burman, 2001; Edwards, 2004), had led to detail and realism in children's drawings of figures being commonly associated with a high score in intellectual maturity.

The research project

The aims of the current project were to support early years practitioners in developing greater understanding of how young children (aged between 3 and 5 years) use drawing as a tool for thinking and learning and re-evaluating their provisioning for drawing so that it could become a powerful tool for young children's thinking and learning.

Data collection took place between 2004 and 2010. A three-day course was designed for early years practitioners where training and action research were intertwined to address theoretical understanding and practical activity. The research approach and course programme was formulated around four principles of practice that have been validated through research:

- To work *with* practitioners to help them understand and engage with personal uncertainties about drawing and their role in supporting drawing. This would involve their participation in data collection, interpretation and analysis of findings, so that they could increase their impact upon practice (Noffke and Somekh, 2005).
- To *foreground visual methods*, for example, collecting digital images, videotape and booklets of annotated drawings alongside narrative in order to provide the teacher-researchers and the trainer/researcher (myself) with context-related images and narratives and rich data for joint analysis (Weber, 2008).

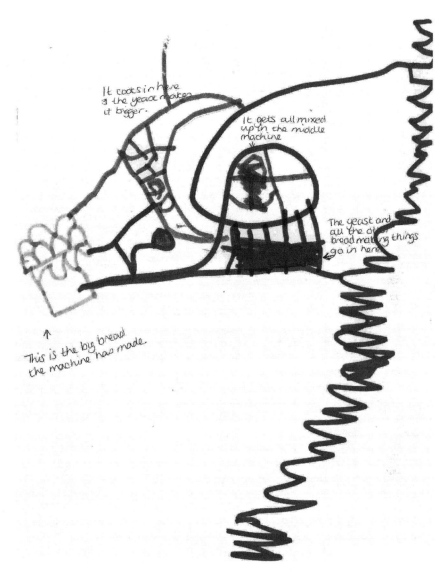

It cooks in here
& the yeast makes
it bigger.

It gets all mixed
up in the middle
machine

The yeast and
all the other
bread making things
go in here

This is the big bread
the machine has made.

Figure 37.2 Luke: The bread making machine

- To take a *longitudinal* approach with the initial action–research group forming the first phase of the project, followed by a second longer phase of in–depth study where I would be working more closely with a smaller number of interested practitioners;
- To take an *interpretive* approach, the primary goal being to understand the complexities involved in how practitioners develop and interpret their role in supporting young children's drawing in early years settings.

Stage 1	Initial and final questionnaires	Completed by individual practitioners as part of the training course and focusing upon their beliefs about drawing and the practices in their settings
20 participants	Notes of content of structured discussions in sessions	Completed by practitioners working in groups as part of training course
	Booklets of annotated children's drawings and digital prints of children's drawing in context	Completed by individual participants in own settings, recording evidence of change in practice and change in child drawing behaviours
Stage 2 10 self-selected participants	Digital images accompanied by practitioner and researcher narratives	Collected as the practitioner walked the trainer-researcher through their setting, pointing out evidence of change in provisioning or child behaviours in relation to drawing (described below)
	Semi-structured interviews	Completed by individual participants and trainer-researcher in practitioners' settings. Interviews structured by the annotated drawings and digital prints collected in the booklets and focused on change in practice and its impact within the setting
Stage 3 3 self-selected participants	Digital video evidence: Focus upon interaction around drawing activity	Completed by practitioner and researcher
	Notes of content of analysis of video	Completed by practitioner and researcher

Figure 37.3   Multi-method, staged approach to data collection

Over the six years of the project, 60 early years practitioners (three cohorts of 20), focused upon developing strategies for supporting and valuing drawing within their settings. Figure 37.3 shows the three-stage iterative approach taken to data collection.

The first cohort of practitioners comprised teachers working with children aged between 3 and 5 years in local authority settings. Project findings from this first cohort are reported in 'Supporting Young Children Drawing: Developing a role' (Ring, 2006). Cohorts two and three included both qualified teachers and early years practitioners. The majority of these participants were working with children aged between 3 and 5 but some 2-year-olds were also included.

Across the three days of the course my role was that of an empathetic and critical friend who began by exchanging theoretical knowledge for knowledge of everyday practice. I gradually became part of a collaborative team, as theory became embedded in participants' understanding of what they observed and interpreted. The project adopted a sociocultural approach to the study of young children drawing, moving beyond the limitations of the developmental psychological stance and giving greater recognition to the significance of the routines and rituals enacted within individual early years settings in terms of enabling or hindering children's use of drawing.

Supporting practitioners in gaining broader, more inclusive understandings of drawing

Taking a sociocultural approach means understanding young children's use of drawing to be part of their meaning-making (Wells, 1986). Children are understood to actively select and shape their own environments (Schaffer, 1996), and co-construct repertoires of ways of acting and behaving as they interpret the behaviour, demands and expectations of adults and other children (Dunn, 1988). Drawing is seen as arising out of young children's exploration of the world through their body movement and tool use and their growing recognition that they can leave their mark or impression upon the world (Matthews, 1999). In early years settings, the availability of materials, objects, language and actions carry a wide range of potential meanings. The child constructs or builds meaning within the boundaries that are set by everyday routines and rituals. With experience, children assimilate increasingly complex tools, allowing the child to work with ideas and information more fluently. Both drawing and writing emerge from children's exploratory behaviour, gesture, speech and social play. Young children's drawing is part of their playful, meaningful and multi-modal engagement with the world (Kress, 1997; Pahl, 1999).

Within the research project two diagrams were developed as part of the conceptual framework that supported practitioner thinking and provided a focus for discussion. The first, Figure 37.4, shows in diagrammatic form the mediating role of children's multi-modal meaning-making between their thinking as individuals and what is provided by culture. As played out in the pre-schools of Reggio Emilia, opportunities to make meaning across 2D and 3D forms allow children to: represent and communicate their ideas and feelings; develop fluency and flexibility in a range of symbolic languages; imagine, wonder, express and create; and think critically.

The second diagram, Figure 37.5, illustrates the complexity of the interrelationship between play and drawing and shows their development to be a cumulative process for the developing child. Dyson's (1993) understanding of the situated nature

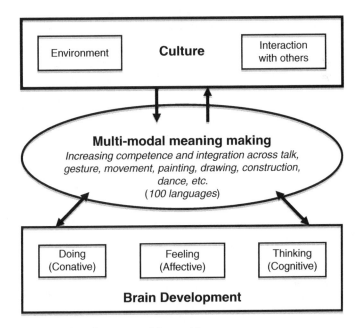

Figure 37.4 The child making sense of the world

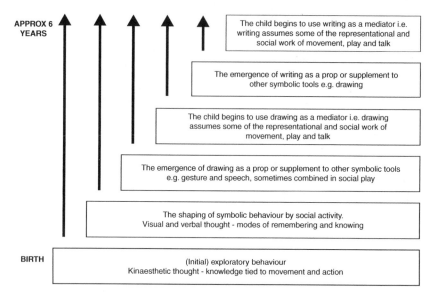

APPROX 6 YEARS

The child begins to use writing as a mediator i.e. writing assumes some of the representational and social work of movement, play and talk

The emergence of writing as a prop or supplement to other symbolic tools e.g. drawing

The child begins to use drawing as a mediator i.e. drawing assumes some of the representational and social work of movement, play and talk

The emergence of drawing as a prop or supplement to other symbolic tools e.g. gesture and speech, sometimes combined in social play

The shaping of symbolic behaviour by social activity. Visual and verbal thought - modes of remembering and knowing

BIRTH

(Initial) exploratory behaviour Kinaesthetic thought - knowledge tied to movement and action

Figure 37.5 The situated nature of drawing within a continuum of children's use of symbol systems (developed from Dyson, 1993)

of drawing within a continuum of symbol systems builds on Vygotsky's (1978) understanding of the close relationship between narrative, play and art and recognizes children as absorbing the forms of culturally significant symbol systems surrounding them at home and school. Importantly, children's development of symbol systems is not seen by her to be merely a hierarchical process. She highlights both the interrelationship of gesture, speech, play, drawing and writing for the young child and the positioning of drawing as a bridge between play and writing. Drawing is therefore emphasized as part of a sequential and cumulative process whereby it evolves from and is supported by exploration and play, and, in turn, supports the emergence of writing. It is through experience that children are seen to assimilate increasingly complex symbolic tools, allowing the child to work with ideas and information more fluently.

There are many examples in the work of Anning and Ring (2004) of children using drawing as part of what Dyson (1986) terms 'symbol weaving'. It can be seen that when drawing is recognized by practitioners as one of a range of meaning-making modes, it emerges as a self-chosen activity alongside play. In the case of 4-year-old Lianne, Dyson's understanding of the process of symbolic development within a continuum seemed to fit with the time available for Lianne to move across the continuum and become a successful, highly motivated user of writing within the multi-modality of her representation. Her visual representation of her version of a picture-book story called *We're Going on a Bear Hunt* (Oxenbury and Rosen, 1989) supported and was supported in turn not only by drawing but also by sounds and physical movement. The child was stimulated to make meaning by a whole class reconstruction of the journey of the bear, organized by her teacher (Figure 37.6). She modelled a problem-solving approach as she supported the children in her reception class in using a combination of three-dimensional found materials and two-dimensional drawing and this enabled them to enact the well-known story. Within this process, the children were able to use drawing and three-dimensional modelling as a means to 'order and understand their experience, shape ideas and communicate their thinking and feeling to others' (Adams, 2002, p. 222). Figure 37.7 shows Lianne's response to a letter sent to the class by the class teacher, ostensibly from a teddy bear in the stock cupboard, which was to reply to this communication using a combination of drawing and writing to reassure the bear that he would receive a warm welcome from the class.

Lianne developed fluency as a multi-modal meaning-maker through her access to time, space and key materials on an everyday basis. In her early years context she was able to maintain the sense of agency she had gained in her home context. She was confident in taking risks and in making meaning in her own way and had a strong sense of ownership in relation to both the process of self-motivated enquiry and the product. Through her playful use of drawing she was not merely recording what she had seen but was actively generating and developing thought.

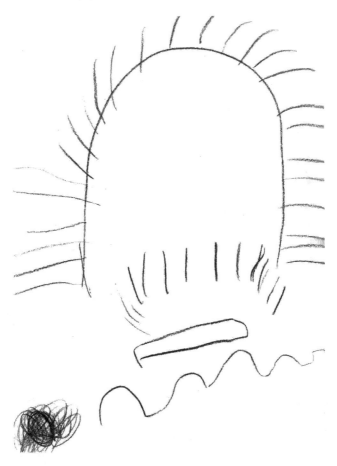

Figure 37.6   Lianne: The bear hunt

Figure 37.7 Lianne: Letter to bear in the stock cupboard

Findings: stage 1

The participant analysis shown in Figure 37.8 was completed at the beginning of the second day of the three-day course. It was the result of whole-group discussion and debate that followed on from participants' involvement in small group discussion and shared evaluation of ongoing provision for drawing within their individual settings. Responses from the whole group were listed, discussed, added to or modified.

An important aspect that helped practitioners to move their practice forward in relation to young children's playful use of drawing was their recognition of the domination of writing within their thinking and behaviours. They had become particularly aware of their previous acceptance that boys lacked involvement in drawing, and now saw this as unacceptable. The importance of practitioners' understanding of Matthew's concept of action drawing had become a starting point for recognizing the validity of boys' ways of making meaning. At the end of the first stage, participants appeared to be moving away from directing the content of children's drawing. The importance of the adult 'being there' and thereby giving value to drawing activity

Arrangement of space	Provision of materials	Interaction with children who are drawing
Importance of:	Importance of:	Importance of:
Provision of drawing space indoors and outdoors	Constant provision of materials	Adult understanding drawing's significance for the child as a 'child appropriate' tool for learning – not merely one of a range of art activities or 'colouring in'
Children having ownership – therefore freedom to move/ combine materials	Paper of various sizes/ shapes/ types/ quality/ colour	Modelling of drawing activity:
Comfort e.g. cushions, something to rest paper on	Size of paper – large paper leads to greater involvement, more collaboration – need big markers, pencils, charcoal/ pastels to make large, bold marks easily	• Children needing to see 'how to do it' – should adults draw when children are drawing? (Huge area of debate – problems with the child thinking this is the 'correct' way of drawing)
Large area of floor to accommodate children's access to larger pieces of paper –A1/A2	Drawing tools – pencils, crayons/ pencil crayons, felt tips – including metallic and fluorescent, chalks, pastels – wet and dry	• Positive impact of four year-olds modelling drawing behaviours in nursery settings
Resources being readily to hand where there is somewhere physical to be		Recognising the power of adult(s) and therefore difficulty of role e.g.
	Clip boards and pencil attached – A3 and A4	• How to know when and how to become involved – the child may not want to talk about drawing especially while drawing
Resources not neatly sorted on shelves – too distant	Having more clip boards available outside as it impacts upon boys' mark making	• Not interpreting and giving own meaning
Space to display – blu-tack so that children can display their own drawings	Whiteboards and dry markers, board cleaners	• Being interested but sensitive
		• Being non-threatening, giving time, not interrupting, watching with interest (being aware however that this could be intimidating)
Balance between tidiness and mess	Sticky tape, scissors, string, glue sticks – used particularly by sophisticated mark makers (reception class) for cutting out, tearing, folding, sticking and joining before mark making	Recognising that asking a child to name a drawing can be putting pressure on a child because:
Questions:		• They are not drawing a 'thing'
• Can too many things be over facing?		• They are in the process of making a decision
• Do children need fewer things easily to hand rather than neatly stored in one area?		• They know they will be asked and therefore cannot decide what to draw
		• They are drawing for an audience
• Is this dependent on age and/ or experience?		Adult seeing the process the child has gone through and therefore having greater understanding
		Knowing the child i.e. their interests and preoccupations
		The relationship the adult has with the child

Figure 37.8 Practitioner-researcher analysis of pedagogical framework for supporting young children drawing

came through strongly at this point and practitioners recognized this as a starting point for getting to know children as users of drawing.

Findings: stages 2 and 3

While all children continued to gain a sense of well-being through involvement in drawing activity, boys were particularly affected by the opportunities that had been made available to observe, draw alongside and collaborate with their male peers. Seeing boys engaged in drawing led to other boys recognizing it as something that boys did. With regular access to both the space and materials needed to enable them to draw on a large scale, they began to really explore drawing, make their own choices and become engrossed. Teachers' new understanding that boys often represented the movement of their own body or objects in space (Matthews, 1999) meant that they began to pay attention to the increasing confidence boys showed as they used drawing tools that moved fluently across the page or space or material and left a strong visible impact. Boys increasingly showed they were feeling secure enough within their environment to experiment and take risks with drawing, and build up their drawing skills and behaviours pleasurably within unpressurized conditions.

The provision of an environment where drawing on a large scale was part of continuous provision supported what Kress (2008, p. 95) would term transformative action, i.e. 'orderly change in one mode'. Gradually boys could be seen returning day after day to drawing activity, building upon previous expressive actions and showing increasing fluidity in their use of line (Figure 37.9). Being able to stretch out on the floor could be seen to allow them to create better controlled movements and engage in actively generating and developing thought. As recognized by Hope (2008, p. 45), 'creating, establishing, developing and communicating *meaning*' became the reason for drawing.

As children showed increasing confidence in their drawing activity, practitioners were developing confidence in their own less intrusive role. Alongside making continuous provision for drawing, they were allowing children to retain control of the drawing process and this included the content of their drawings. They articulated that 'Their drawings belong to them' and 'They need to tell their own story':

> It is nice to see the ones who wouldn't usually draw … people come that you wouldn't expect and join in which doesn't always happen, but give them a big piece of paper and for some reason they all get on with each other and everybody shares. Working on a larger scale is really good that way. (F2 Practitioner)

> The large board and also the large pieces of paper lend themselves to the group drawing. You know, I think in a way it's as much the fact that the children are together and that they've got the opportunity to discuss and develop ideas together as much as the drawing activity itself. It's completely open-ended so, you know, they're free to develop their ideas and their drawing in any way they want to. (F1 Practitioner)

Figure 37.9 Boy drawing, supported by lying on the floor

Sometimes they'll work together and they'll develop ideas together and their drawings will sort of be connected ... or if their drawings aren't connected, their ideas and discussion is connected. And then other times they might as well just have their own little piece of paper and it just happens to be their part of a larger piece. I just feel that this sort of group drawing gives those children that are not confident in their own drawing skills a bit more confidence to do it because they are working alongside others; they're sort of a bit more inconspicuous. It's not their own ... modelling by a child is something that's different to modelling from an adult ... there's no expectation. The other children don't particularly judge them. (F2 Practitioner)

A growing strength of many of the practitioners was their ability to listen (with all their senses) to what the child or groups of children were expressing and communicating, not just through their drawings but through what Rinaldi (2005) terms their

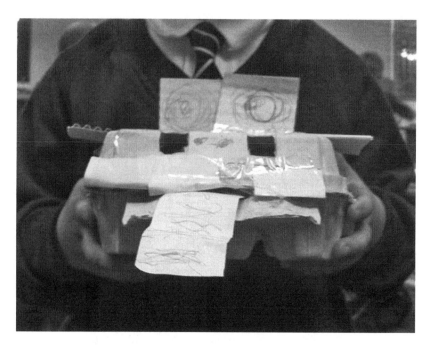

Figure 37.10   Making, marking, cutting, folding, sticking

Figure 37.11   The emergence of writing within drawing behaviours

'hundred languages'. As children were being given greater flexibility in terms of where, how and what they drew, they began to use materials for their own purposes, taking an increasingly playful, experimental and problem-solving approach and integrating drawing across two- and three-dimensional representation (Figure 37.10). For Kress (2008, p. 95) this movement across modes supports transduction, 'the drawing across from one mode to another', a process he sees as leading to profound changes in meaning and in patterns of thinking and behaviour.

When writing did gradually emerge it was integrated within draw and talk activity with peers, as part of children's playful and meaningful accumulation of cultural tools. While this kind of behaviour was seen most frequently in the work of the oldest girls, as they incorporated letters from their name into their drawings, in the case of boys it was more often numerals that were included and these held meaning in relation to the subject content of the drawing (Figure 37.11). Children's interest in both letters and numerals led to many children taking a greater notice of print in the environment.

Conclusion

Practitioners differed in their commitment to the project, both in the amount of time they could give to it and in their willingness to engage in reflection, particularly in making links between theory and practice. At first some were daunted by the explorative approach – the expectation that they construct rather than receive new knowledge. Those who volunteered to take part in stages 2 and 3 were particularly committed and came to recognize the power of first-hand observation in allowing them to access the unique nature of many children's responses to the changes made in both the physical environment and the impact of change upon the routines and rituals surrounding the use of materials. Where more than one participant from a setting took part in all stages of the project there proved to be greater risk-taking in relation to allowing children's agency and greater long-term change in practice.

A particular concern held by practitioners supporting children aged between 4 and 5 (F2) was the lack of opportunity their summer-born boys might have to continue their newfound practices on entry to the more formal curriculum of the Year One classroom. The danger for the youngest children was that a rush of formal processes and didactic interventions in relation to literacy, and particularly writing, would overtake the more natural and meaningful progression identified by Dyson (1993).

Importantly, the project gave practitioners the opportunity to see young children's ability to use drawing as a tool for generating, developing and reflecting upon their understanding of the world. As they reconsidered their provision for drawing and entered into a process of change and reflection upon change, many practitioners recognized the restrictions they had been placing upon children not only in terms of space, time and materials but also in relation to the messages, both implicit and explicit, they had given children that had limited the possibilities drawing held for them as a tool for learning.

References

Adams, E. (2002) Power drawing. *International Journal of Art and Design Education* (special drawing issue), *21*(3), 220–33.

Anning, A. and Ring, K. (2004) *Making Sense of Children's Drawings*. Maidenhead: Open University Press/McGraw-Hill.

Burman, E. (2001) Beyond the baby and the bathwater: Post-dualistic psychologies for diverse childhoods. *European Early Childhood Educational Research Journal, 9*, 5–22.

Dunn, J. (1988) *The Beginnings of Social Understanding*. Cambridge, MA: Harvard University Press.

Dyson, A. H. (1986) Transitions and tensions: Interrelationships between the drawing, talking, and dictating of young children. *Research in the Teaching of English, 20*(4), 379–409.

Dyson, A. H. (1993) From prop to mediator: The changing role of written language in children's symbolic repertoires. In B. Spodek and O. N. Saracho (eds) *Yearbook in Early Childhood Education: Language and Literacy in Early Childhood Education*, Vol. 4 (pp. 21–41). New York: Teachers College Press.

Edwards, A. (2004) Understanding context, understanding practice in early education. *European Early Childhood Education Research Journal, 12*(1), 85–101.

Goodenough, F. (1926) *Measurement of Intelligence by Drawings*. New York: Harcourt, Brace and World.

Hope, G. (2008) *Thinking and Learning Through Drawing*. London: Sage.

Howard, J. (2002) Eliciting children's perceptions of play using the Activity Apperception Story Procedure. *Early Child Development and Care, 172*(5), 489–502.

Kress, G. (1997) *Before Writing: Rethinking the Paths to Literacy*. London: Routledge.

Kress, G. (2008) 'Literacy' in a multimodal environment of communication. In J. Flood, S. Brice Heath, and D. Lapp (eds) *Handbook of Research on Teaching Literacy Through the Communicative and Visual Arts*, Vol. 2 (pp. 91–100). New York: Erlbaum.

Matthews, J. (1999) *The Art of Childhood and Adolescence: The Construction of Meaning*. London: Falmer Press.

Matthews, J. (2003) *Drawing and Painting: Children and Visual Representation*, 2nd edn. London: Paul Chapman.

Noffke, S. and Somekh, B. (2005) Action research. In B. Somekh and C. Lewin (eds) *Research Methods in the Social Sciences*. London: Sage.

Oxenbury, H. (illustrator) and Rosen, M. (author) (1989) *We're Going on a Bear Hunt*. London: Walker Books.

Pahl, K. (1999) *Transformations: Making Meaning in Nursery Education*. Stoke-on-Trent: Trentham Books.

Rinaldi, C. (2005) *In Dialogue with Reggio Emilia: Listening, Researching and Learning*. London: Routledge.

Ring, K. (2003) *Young Children Drawing at Home, Pre-school and School: The Influence of the Socio-cultural Context*. Unpublished doctoral dissertation, School of Education, University of Leeds.

Ring, K. (2006) What mothers do: Everyday routines and rituals and their impact upon young children's use of drawing for meaning making. *International Journal of Early Years Education, 14*(1), 63–84.

Schaffer, H. R. (1996) Joint involvement episodes as a context for development. In H. Daniels (ed.) *An Introduction to Vygotsky* (pp. 251–79). London: Routledge.

Vygotsky, L. S. (1978) *Mind in Society: The Development of Higher Psychological Processes* (ed. and trans. M. Cole, V. John-Steiner, S. Scribner and E. Souberman). Cambridge, MA: Harvard University Press.

Weber, S. (2008) Visual images in research. In J. G. Knowles and A. L Cole (eds) *Handbook of the Arts in Qualitative Research* (pp. 44–5). London/Los Angeles: Sage.

Wells, G. (1986) *The Meaning Makers*. Portsmouth, NH: Heinemann.

38

ALREADY EQUAL AND ABLE TO SPEAK

Practising philosophical enquiry with young children

Joanna Haynes

Introduction

Since the early 1980s theories of philosophy for and with children (P4C) have pro-liferated, along with widespread practice of its adopted pedagogy: the community of enquiry. Regardless of age or status, a principle of P4C is that all those taking part are valued equally in the collaborative dialogue and quests for truth. Philosophy in the mode of P4C is for children, but not only for children. The methods of enquiring and reasoning associated with P4C are widely adopted by people of all ages and in mixed age groups. Over the last 40 years, the community of philosophical enquiry, embodying ideals of democratic and poetic engagement, has grown in popularity across continents and various types of educational contexts.

The growing popularity of P4C over recent decades might be seen as an example of shifting attitudes to children's thinking. During this period, the landscape of per-spectives on childhood has become more varied, as both developmentalism and humanism have been critiqued and their dominance challenged.[1] Practical and schol-arly work in P4C has made an important contribution to a more detailed drawing and appreciation of this landscape. It has caused a stir, among educationalists and academic philosophers alike, through the generation of ideas about, for example, chil-dren being 'natural philosophers', the capacities and rights of young children to phi-losophise; the suitability of philosophical enquiry for young learners; the 'child as philosopher' and 'philosopher as child', as well as the encounter between childhood and philosophy. P4C brings a new figure of the child to the table where perspectives on childhood are unfolding.

This chapter is written from my standpoint as an experienced P4C practitioner and advocate; also as a parent/grandparent/family member and as a critical academic with a deep interest in philosophies of childhood. P4C has provided a kind of home for my educational thinking and practice for the last 20 years. I do not mean this in a sentimental way – after all, family life is often difficult – but in the sense of long-term involvement with a group of people with broadly similar aims; through collaboration and disagreement, reasoning and persistence: qualities that can allow a depth of practice and attention to detail to grow; qualities that generate new insights and theories.

In practice settings, children's opportunities to philosophise together are limited, unless adults are confident and happy to move in the sometimes new and unfamiliar spaces created by children's philosophical enquiries. The character of philosophical explorations that take place among adults and young children in the context of early education are often imaginative, playful and informal. Egan (1992, 2002) has commented on pre-literate children's capacity for metaphor and this often infuses their enquiries. Such philosophical novelty opens possibilities to challenge the sentimentality that sometimes distances adults from children. It paves the way for the deconstruction of adultism and childism. In his rich discussion of the adult–child relationship developing through experience of dialogues Kennedy suggests that it might result in 'an adult who is in touch with the child-dimension of her own subjectivity – its forms of feeling, intentionality, and cognitive style. Being more in touch with myself as a child means being more in touch with the child before me' (2006, p. 72). Kennedy lists skills and dispositions of careful listening, considering the perspective of the other, recognition of interconnectedness with the other, making decisions that take myself and the other into account equally, that comprise such an ethical re-orientation. He writes:

> The subject who recognises her shadow and withdraws its projection onto the other has entered into another, permanently transitional form of subjectivity, based on a value of world-openness that assumes an ontological potential for ongoing – and by implication social – transformation.
>
> *(Kennedy, 2006, p. 72)*

P4C presents itself as a transformative philosophy of childhood and education, one that entails a fundamental reconfiguration of adult–child relationships and school ethics. In everyday practice there are important choices to be made by practitioners working alongside young children and seeking to make philosophical conversations possible and pleasurable, through the pursuit of shared meaning-making. Experienced and willing practitioners can often see how to make possible what was previously believed to be out of reach to young children. Children's literature and story-based exploratory play in particular offer tangible and rich possibilities in this respect (Murris, 1992; Murris and Haynes, 2010; Stanley, 2011).

The chapter begins by looking back over some key moments in the development of P4C theory and practice and their contribution to the shifting landscapes of childhood and philosophy. I introduce the possibility of P4C being understood as emancipatory, even if in a transient and delicate way, bringing to bear the figure of the young child evoked by Jacques Rancière (1991) in my speculation about philosophising with children. Finally I offer brief examples of playful and imaginative approaches to P4C with younger children, working with children's literature and story-based exploratory play.

The emergence of philosophy 'for' and 'with' children

Philosophy for children was introduced in the late 1970s by US philosopher Matthew Lipman, who drew from Charles Sanders Peirce and John Dewey the notion of the 'community of inquiry' (Lipman 1993; Lipman *et al.*, 1980). The Philosophy *for* Children programme has the practical goal of establishing philosophy as part of the curriculum of public schools for children aged 6 upwards, and resources for children younger than 6 years were soon added to the mix by other early pioneers of the approach. As a professor of philosophy, Lipman felt his university students lacked the ability to question, think and reason with confidence. He believed that education should be based on thinking and reasoning and devoted his life to this project. Lipman argued that to affirm children's right to think philosophically is to assume an education into rationality, responsibility and personhood (Lipman, 1991). The work of the Institute for the Advancement of Philosophy for Children (IAPC) was first shown in the UK through the BBC's television screening of *Socrates for Six Year Olds* as part of a series about transformative approaches to education (The Transformers, 1990). The Philosophy *for* Children programme consists of a series of philosophical novels for children across the school age range, reflecting something of the history of western philosophy, particularly in logic, ethics and aesthetics, along with clear guidance for teachers using the material. These novels model a particular style of philosophical thinking and dialogue. Their narrative form is a key element of the pedagogy.

From the outset, philosophy for children was challenged by those who argued that younger children are incapable of the type of abstract and de-centred reasoning that they believe characterises philosophy. These discussions about whether or not children can do philosophy often concerned the capacities of children to behave as professional philosophers do and according to their rules (for example Kitchener, 1990). P4C scholars have engaged with such debates about the nature of philosophical reasoning and children's capacities for it (see, for example, Murris, 2000). P4C has added to knowledge in 'academic' philosophy while proposing a radical model of practical philosophy for all: collaborative philosophical enquiry. Philosophy for/with children practice worldwide is quite diverse. Teachers' choices, demonstrated in their classroom practice of P4C, express what Kennedy (2006, p. 155) has termed the 'psychic economy' of adult: internal dialogues about constructs of adult and child, adult–child relationships and the meeting between child and philosophy.

Teaching resources for philosophising with children have been created in different countries by practitioners seeking to respond to local contexts and experimenting with ideas. Murris (1992) proposed the use of already published picturebooks as an alternative to the purpose-written philosophy for children novels. Philosophical enquiry through picturebooks proved popular with teachers of younger age groups, as they were familiar and regarded as more 'child friendly'. Teachers could see how exploratory talk with children, sometimes of the kind associated with early literacy, could be extended through the sort of philosophical questions Murris included in her manual for teachers (1992). Such questions provided for exploratory dialogues, illustrated by transcripts from Murris' work with children and shaped by the children's questions about the things that puzzled them in picturebooks. These transcripts showed that much younger children enjoyed philosophising, when it was approached imaginatively, and when adults were prepared to take their thinking seriously (Murris, 1999).

Philosophy *with* children became associated in some quarters with the broader and growing ethical concern with listening to young children, and the recognition that a serious commitment to listening would require those who worked with children to review many aspects of their practice and assumed authority (Haynes, 2007, 2008; Haynes and Murris, 2013). *Picturebooks, Pedagogy and Philosophy* (Haynes and Murris, 2012) is a contribution to such a review and develops the association between philosophical themes in children's literature and the reconceptualisation and ethical sensitisation of adult–child relations in education. It suggests that certain picturebooks reflect these contemporary debates and are very likely to open up these questions of intergenerational relationships and attitudes to childhood.

P4C in the changing landscape of perspectives on children's thinking

Anecdotally, many adults, particularly those who spend a lot of time with young children, comment on the profound questions about the world that pre-school children in particular are prone to asking. As a father of young children in the 1960s, philosopher Gareth Matthews had noticed his 6-year-old daughter's capacities for philosophical thinking. The bedtime stories he read to his 3-year-old son raised philosophical issues that he was discussing with students in his university philosophy classes. Becoming more aware of the philosophical nature of some children's literature, Matthews used stories with his university classes to convince them of his view that philosophy is a natural, spontaneous and universal human activity. If philosophical questioning begins from a sense of puzzlement about the world, it is hardly surprising that many children are disposed to curiosity and wonder, by virtue of their recent arrival into the world. Arriving into the world disposes the infant towards such questioning and exploration. All being well, the linguistic and cognitive dispositions of the human mind enable such assertive curiosity to be apparent from a very early age (Egan, 2002). The construct of child as 'natural philosopher' highlights children's position as newcomers to the world, with an imaginative energy to bring to philosophical thinking.

Gareth Matthews' book *Philosophy and the Young Child* (1980) invited appreciation for children's sense of wonder and prepared the ground for the emergent field of philosophy of childhood, closing the gap between adult and child. He spoke of 'the need to rethink the child, not as an ignorant being, but as a rational agent who already has the capacity to reason philosophically' (1980, p. 172). His reflections on family life, his university teaching, his voyages of philosophical discovery with children in an Edinburgh school (1992) and his reading of conversations with young children such as those recorded over several years in a kindergarten setting by Vivian Gussin Paley,[2] were all a part of Matthews' reflexive research into human cognitive development. He was one of several thinkers of that period that were questioning the dominant preoccupations, strategies, methods and claims of developmental psychology and exploring neglected areas of children's thinking, such as the capacity to philosophise.

He understood the consequences of parents and teachers looking to developmental psychology for an expert view of what children *should* be like. He concluded:

> If there is no place in the developmentalist's story for the ability to enter into philosophical dialogue [...] then neither the adults nor the children will have any acquaintance with that wonderfully strange mode of inquiry in which grown-ups cannot control the outcome or rely on the advantage of age and experience to maintain their position.
>
> *(Matthews, 1992, p. 119)*

As with the universal description of any quality as 'childlike' there might be risks associated with suggesting a philosophical outlook is characteristic of all children everywhere. Many teachers and early years practitioners are drawn to P4C out of a desire to protect and nurture qualities they associate with 'being a child' and a wish to recreate this philosophical dimension in the classroom. Such claims do not have to be regarded as essentialist if we accept that such a sense of wonder can only flourish in certain social and cultural conditions, and that philosophical preoccupations permeate many forms of human culture and learning, regardless of age. However, recognition of children's sometimes superior disposition to ask philosophical questions points to the epistemic advantage of coming new into the world. In a world in which children are frequently marginalised such recognition seems to signal an ethical moment: greater openness by interested adults who find themselves moved to listen more attentively to children's thinking.

Early work in the field of P4C around the philosophy of childhood connected with wider debates about the ways in which schooling can result in the diminishing of some of young children's capacities of mind. Egan (2002) has argued that a hierarchical and integrative perspective on human development tends to ignore the losses that occur as other forms of thinking and learning are promoted. Taking the example of learning literacy, he suggests that it often results in a reduction in the powers of oral memory and creation of visual imagery. Both Matthews and Egan are among those who invite us to move away from the idea that children's thinking is merely an embryonic version of adult thinking. Egan suggests that looking at the child's mind *only* in relation to the adult mind parallels the way that literate cultures tend to view oral cultures (1991, 2002). Egan rejects a curriculum based on movement from simple to complex, familiar to unfamiliar, concrete to abstract and empirical to rational. Instead he proposes that teaching itself should adopt a narrative framework in order to capitalise on young children's particular capacities for metaphorical and imaginative thinking (Egan, 1988, 1991). Many P4C advocates and practitioners are sympathetic to Egan's ideas on imagination in teaching and curriculum design (see, for example, Lyle, 2009).

P4C's invitation to children at school to engage in collaborative thinking and reasoning is a well-informed one. By writing material that portrayed young children as thinkers and demonstrating the capacities of children as young as 6 to engage in abstract thought and philosophical deliberation, P4C challenged dominant discourses regarding the development of children's thinking. Widely held beliefs that children, below a certain age, cannot engage in abstract thought, cannot distinguish reality and fantasy, or are egocentric, have been contradicted by many classroom enquiries (Haynes, 2007). Research has suggested that the ability to articulate abstract ideas and reason with others, taking into account alternative perspectives, has more to do with children's opportunities than it has to do with the age of the children or young people involved. From a psychological perspective Doherr's research (Doherr, 2000; Doherr *et al.*, 2005) found that young children's experience of reasoning with others in philosophical enquiry encouraged cognitive flexibility and recognition of the standpoint of others at a level normally associated with much older children.

The early work of Lipman, Matthews, and others prepared the ground to challenge received wisdom about the aims of education, children's capacities for rationality and agency in their lives and for relations between child and adult, both in the classroom and beyond (Vansieleghem and Kennedy, 2011). Today's debates are less focused on whether or not children are capable of philosophising and more concerned with whether or not, and how, philosophy should feature in the school curriculum and, if so, how it might be justified (Hand and Winstanley, 2008; Stanley, 2011; White, 2012). In some settings, P4C has 'spilled out' beyond separate sessions of philosophical enquiry and into other classroom activities, such as sharing stories or drama and role play. Modes of questioning and reasoning adopted in P4C have found their way into extra-curricular work and into other subject areas, such as English and literacy, social and religious education, citizenship and science. Teachers often report that children use the rules and language of philosophical enquiry in their classroom conversations with one another (Haynes, 2008; SAPERE, 2006). Philosophers such as Phil Cam in Australia argue that philosophical thinking and reasoning have an important part to play across all the disciplines and subjects of the curriculum, and from the very beginning of schooling and education (Cam *et al.*, 2007).

In the context of international debates about the philosophy of childhood that might underpin the practice of P4C, forms of instrumentalism in both practice and articulation of its aims have been described and critiqued (see, for example, Biesta, 2011). Practitioners have sometimes promoted P4C by highlighting its benefits for improving children's language development, social skills, behaviour, self-esteem or academic success. In terms of its educational aims, Vansieleghem (2005), among others, has questioned its integrity, suggesting that it rests on limiting and potentially oppressive views of rationality, when its focus is on encouraging certain modes of abstract reasoning in children. Vansieleghem argues that an instrumental approach does not constitute an experience of freedom for children. She regards P4C's emphasis on autonomous, critical thinking as a repetition of an exclusionary discourse. The idea of reasonableness in interactions among adults and children has to be renegotiated if it is to escape its present limits and become inclusive. An expanded notion of rationality needs to develop in situated contexts of philosophical work with children. In a similar vein, Luce Irigeray's (1996) exploration of the question 'How am I to listen to you?' describes the ways in which relationships between adults and children have often assumed that 'the elder is supposed to know what the younger is and what he or she should become. The elder is supposed to know the younger and only listens to him or her within the parameters of an existing science or truth' (Irigeray, 1996, p. 116).

Cutting through narrow conceptions of the nature of philosophical thinking, Argentinian philosopher Walter Kohan describes philosophy as an unrepeatable experience arising from 'the encounter with what forces us to think, with what puts us into doubt, with what takes us out of our conformity, our naturality' (Kohan, 2002, p. 9). He proposes that it is an experience of encounter, both with philosophy *and* between adult and child. There are ethical implications when adults decide whether to join in more or less reciprocal dialogues with children (Kohan, 2002; Haynes and Murris, 2012). The effort to be made here is in conceptualising philosophy with children as valuable for its own sake and mutually educative, not as the giving of form to future, suitably skilled citizens. In this vein, educators involved in P4C over a long period of time often report the huge influences on their outlook. Through experiences of philosophising with children, adults are increasingly disposed to question the basis of conceptual distinctions and ethical relations between adult and child, drawing on a wider range of philosophical traditions.

We have begun to explore ways in which the nature of philosophy itself might be reconsidered when children become involved. We have looked at advantages that children might have when it comes to philosophical thinking and the notion of children being 'natural philosophers'. Gibbons (2007, p. 507) has suggested that the playfulness and creativity of the philosopher is a theme in the work of philosophers seeking to disturb the intellectualism of philosophy. He argues that 'the playful philosopher is then imagined as aspiring to be child-like, where child-like behaviour is that which has a genealogy at least as far back as Plato's child; a child who naturally plays and plays naturally'. However, Gibbons is concerned about the adult gaze on the thinking of young children, associated with practices like philosophy with children. Gregory and Granger (2012) have identified a turn to philosophical childlikeness in the work of those associated with P4C. In the introduction to an edited collection of writings on Dewey and the philosophy of childhood they suggest:

> Proponents of the figure of the Philosopher as Child see the practice of philosophy, ideally, as involving a turn toward childhood. They identify certain characteristics of childhood, such as impulsiveness, somatic awareness, and cultural naïveté, as important correctives to the personal and cultural habits of adulthood that impede growth as they become hardened and non-adaptive – especially as these habits have been manipulated by commercial, religious, and political forces.
> *(Gregory and Granger, 2012, p. 1)*

They explain that this is a critique of the fact that spontaneity, corporeality and naïveté tend to be associated almost exclusively with childhood, while habit, rationality, constraint and erudition are associated with adulthood. What P4C offers is the possibility of philosophical dialogue as a lenient (but not *laissez-faire*) space, and the notion of 'child' understood as the philosophical disposition and character upon which all may draw, rather than as a fixed temporal phase of human development, as in 'childhood'.

An exchange between Walter Kohan and North American philosopher David Kennedy (2008) focuses on the ontology of childhood through the lenses of temporality, power and language. As he discusses different conceptions of time, Kohan cites Heraclitus: 'Time is a child childing, its realm is one of a child.' Chronologically, child is at the beginning of the lifespan: when time is understood as the stretch between fixed points. Kohan suggests that the 'time' of childhood might be understood as another way of living time: a childlike way of being. Thus childhood is not only a period of time in early life, but also a particularly intense and forceful experience of being in time. Kohan adds: 'childhood is not [...] an absence of power but a singular mode of practising power' (Kennedy and Kohan, 2008, p. 8). Kennedy refers to childhood as an elusive condition of psychological immediacy, similar to forms of aesthetic experience such as the pleasure found in art or intimacy. We are all artists, philosophers and all childlike. Kennedy suggests: 'as much as the philosopher carries a childlike way of questioning into adulthood, the artist carries a childlike way of acting on the world into adulthood, and both of these act to transform the world' (p. 11). In this vein, child can shift from noun to verb. We can ask, what does it mean to talk of child as something I can do: to child?

A figure of the child – equally able to speak and philosophise

Many practitioners are drawn to Philosophy *with* Children because it strikes a chord with their experiences of conversations with children and because of its radical and emancipatory flavour: its democratic orientation towards listening to children. What is attractive about P4C is its playful approach to philosophy; an opportunity to be childlike and amateurish (in the sense of sharing love and enthusiasm for something). Quests for meaning and conceptual exploration at the heart of philosophy are an intrinsic part of the human relationship with the physical universe and of being in the social world with other human beings. P4C not only assumes the equal ability of all human beings to philosophise but also brings ability itself into question. Through this assumption P4C has created an exceptional space for listening to children and for being moved, politically, intellectually and emotionally, by dialogue with them.

Rancière's (1991) meditation on equality and emancipation is a social critique, not an alternative educational approach. We can put his figure of the child to work when considering questions of philosophy, equality, ability and childhood. His story does not tell us what to do but gives an opportunity to think about pedagogy and child-hood from a different place. It is not accidental that his work takes the form of a provocative story, a narrative form chosen to interrogate the explanatory authority of the pedagogue.

Rancière tells the story of an educational experiment which leads his protagonist Jacotot to reflect on students' use of their intelligence. Jacotot observes the way stu-dents proceed with a task just as they would have done to learn their mother tongue, 'the way children move, blindly, figuring out riddles' a 'true movement of intelligence taking possession of its own power' (1991, p. 10). This experiment had obliged stu-dents to use their own intelligence, an intelligence understood as universal, 'a power common to all reasonable beings' (p. 71). Through this story Rancière undermines the rarely challenged and subtle hierarchy of intelligence and shifts the paradigm of equality. Intelligence and equality are synonymous terms for Rancière. He argues that children and adults learn by themselves and this is explained by the equality of intelligence. Since we only ever know intelligence by its effects, and we cannot iso-late it from those effects and measure it, we cannot prove anything about it. Rancière suggests that the problem is not to prove the equality of intelligence but to see what can be done under that supposition. Rancière puts it succinctly: 'Equality must be seen as a point of departure, and not as a destination. We must assume that all intel-ligences are equal, and work under this assumption' (2000, p. 3). Arguably, the emancipatory power of a practice such as philosophy with children is realised when it is enacted with such an assumption of equality.

To endorse his case for the equality of intelligence Rancière invokes the figure of the child acquiring language, moving blindly through a forest of signs, without a translator or formal instructor, stepping into language. Equality is established on an assumption of what it means for a child to learn her/his mother tongue, a process described as the most difficult of apprenticeships, learning a foreign language that is 'for every child arriving in the world, called the mother tongue' (Rancière, 2002, cited by Biesta and Bingham, 2010, p. 54).

Biesta and Bingham (2010) have developed Rancière's figure of the child as depicted in *The Ignorant Schoolmaster* by recounting a detailed anecdote of a very young child beginning to utter her first few words, inventing and learning language and also becoming a political actor – as the two endeavours can be understood as one and the same (p. 49). The child in their anecdote is neither representative of all infants, nor unique. They argue that every child steps into the forest of signs in random, inter-esting, arbitrary and idiosyncratic ways. This chapter connects the figure of the child in mother tongue apprenticeship, with a discussion of its politics and Rancière's account of language itself. They assert that Rancière is not making a psychological observation but rather:

> while Rancière's figure of the child might seem at first glance to repeat the time-honoured tradition in educational thought of offering the figure of the child who is to be brought, by means of education and by means of psychological advances in education, into the realm of the political; instead, this child is already political even as she is acquiring her first language. That is, she is political even before she goes to school to become autonomous and emancipated.
>
> *(Bingham and Biesta, 2010, p. 57)*

At the moment when a child says a word not as a passive echo of something heard, but with intention, perhaps the parent will not understand what is meant, but the child will continue to speak until this is so. As Bingham and Biesta put it, from the outset the child must not only say something that stands as a sign, but 'gain the right to be counted as a speaker who can say what she needs to say within the community of speaking beings' (2010, p. 58). This is very much a political and not a psychological account of stepping into language, achieved through force of will onto another. They further argue that the child's 'insertion' into language is not only forceful and wilful but

> ambivalent insofar as it establishes a metaphorics of speakability at the same time that it communicates basic needs, desires and intentions ... This is important

because Rancière's child is not simply another conceit fabricated in order to stream-line how we bring children from a position of voicelessness to a position of voice.

(Bingham and Biesta, 2010, p. 63)

In our keynote presentation to the international conference on P4C in Cape Town (ICPIC 2013), Karin Murris and I made the case that the kind of play and explora-tion of concepts that we associate with philosophical enquiry are integral aspects of an infant's 'self-insertion' into language. This is evident from the very earliest interac-tions among young children and with their parents and carers. Moreover, such approximation and negotiation of concepts is an ongoing process that goes on throughout human life. From a pedagogical perspective, the question for adults is how to move with young children in this space, as Eulalia Bosch (2005) puts it, par-ticularly in the context of institutional settings.

Exploratory philosophical play and text talk: integrated approaches to P4C in the early years

In accordance with such political perspectives on philosophy and childhood, and seemingly responding to concerns about instrumentality, we can identify some expert practitioners that have finely tuned P4C to their teaching contexts. Highly experi-enced in working philosophically with younger children, Stanley has developed P4C in ways that are particularly suited to imaginative and playful curricula for the early years of education (Stanley, 2011). Stanley turns her classroom into a space of philo-sophical role play and adventure, listening to children's responses and developing philosophical conversations out of these moments. Building on the work of Egan discussed earlier in this chapter, Stanley's work draws on the binary oppositions that tend to shape fairy tales and legends such as good versus evil, or poverty versus wealth. Through the creation of what she terms 'story worlds' Stanley uses figures and pup-pets to develop enquiry within the story worlds she co-creates with children. She builds on the magical elements they contain, perhaps a key, a magic lamp or some gold coins and the fantasy characters that people the tales, such as giants and witches. She draws parents into these conversations through journals, photographs and invita-tions to talk at home with children about questions that have emerged in class. As well as drawing from fairy tales, like many early years practitioners in P4C, Stanley also works with contemporary picturebooks, creating philosophical enquiries inside the texts and between the text and children's talk. Stanley uses her close listening and tuning in to children's engagement with everyday concepts such as fairness or friend-ship, to open up enquiries in highly imaginative ways.

In terms of everyday practice on the ground in early education there are important connections to be made between early shared reading practices that foster 'inside-text' talk with children, and philosophical co-enquiry that extends thinking and talk outside and beyond the text. Young children welcome books that do not moralise or patronise, but communicate to them that they are taken seriously as thinkers by offering rich, complex and ambiguous pictures and texts. Picturebooks are life-like, but, at the same time, different enough to highlight certain aspects of 'reality'. Much of the power of picturebooks lies in what they omit: leaving out much of 'the real' serves to emphasise one particular dimension of experience in the world, making this all the more powerful and ripe to explore. With their multiple narratives, ambiguity and contradictions, picturebooks are emotionally and intellectually demanding texts for children and adults alike. The reader is pulled into different directions of meaning-making through the conjunction of images and/or text. A philosophical response begins with but goes beyond meaning-making within the text (Haynes and Murris, 2009a, 2012, 2013). A striking feature of many picturebooks is the way in which they assume the presence of both child and adult readers. The narratives often address an intergenerational audience, making them particularly powerful in terms of philosophising with children. The provocative nature of some picturebooks directly addresses relations between adult and child and often questions adult authority and control (Haynes and Murris, 2009b, 2012).

Concluding summary

This chapter has provided a flavour of the discussion about Philosophy for/with Children that has taken place over the last 40 years, both within and beyond the field. I have argued that both theorists and practitioners of P4C have enriched the wider landscape of childhood, helping to challenge the dominance of developmental and humanist perspectives. I have drawn attention to some criticisms of P4C being instrumentalist or overly focused on a given model of reasoning and democratic society. I have included brief examples of practice that seek to address such criticisms and to reflect the more integrated and flexible pedagogies preferred by many early years practitioners. I have suggested that Philosophy with Children has the potential to be emancipatory, to play with the social order, and to make an occasional site for what Masschelein and Simons call democratic moments (2010, p. 672).

Philosophy with Children creates the possibility of a move away from exclusive preoccupation with educational measurement and formation towards educational conversations with children that can reflect their uniqueness and their lived experiences, families and communities. To realise the possibilities, adults have to be ready to treat knowledge as contestable and to trust the perplexity expressed in children's questions when we think we already have the answers. Authentic listening in the classroom implies adopting a position of fallibility and challenging the assumption that being older means one is necessarily wiser. It entails accepting that children can easily draw our attention to something not yet considered or so far unspoken. P4C proposes a pedagogical framework to enable such a move, by positioning children as co-enquirers. We need to stay awake.

Notes

1 For critiques of developmentalist perspectives on childhood see, for example, Burman (2008) or Dalhberg and Moss (2005). For a critique of humanism see Braidotti (2013).
2 Such as, for example, *Wally's Stories*, published in 1981 and then in many subsequent publications. Further information about her ideas and books can be found at: www.naeyc.org/content/conversation-vivian-gussin-paley (accessed 18/02/2014).

References

Biesta, G. J. J. (2011) Philosophy, exposure and children: How to resist the instrumentalisation of philosophy in education. *Journal of Philosophy of Education*, *45*(2), 305–19.

Bingham, C. and Biesta, G. (2010) *Jacques Rancière: Education, Truth, Emancipation*. London: Continuum.

Bosch, E. (2005) *Education and Everyday Life: Short Stories with Long Endings, Philosophy for Children*. Moorabin, Victoria, Australia: Hawker Brownlow Education.

Burman, E. (2008) *Deconstructing Development Psychology*, 2nd edn. London: Routledge.

Braidotti, R. (2013) *The Posthuman*. London: Polity Press.

Cam, P., Fynes-Clinton, L., Harrison, K., Hinton, L., Scholl, R. and Vaseo, S. (2007) *Philosophy with Young Children: A Classroom Handbook*. Australian Curriculum Studies Association Inc.

Dahlberg, G. and Moss, P. (2005) *Ethics and Politics in Early Childhood Education*. London: Routledge.

Doherr, E. (2000) *The Demonstration of Cognitive Abilities Central to Cognitive Behavioural Therapy in Young People: Examining the Influence of Age and Teaching Method on Degree of Ability*. Unpublished clinical psychology doctoral dissertation, University of East Anglia.

Doherr, L., Reynolds, S., Wetherly, J. and Evans E. H. (2005) Young children's ability to engage in cognitive therapy tasks: Associations with age and educational experience. *Behavioural and Cognitive Psychotherapy*, *33*(2), 201–15.

Egan, K. (1988) *Teaching as Storytelling: An Alternative Approach to Teaching and the Curriculum*. London, Ontario: University of Western Ontario.

Egan, K. (1991) *Primary Understanding: Education in Early Childhood*. London: Routledge.

Egan, K. (2002) *Getting it Wrong from the Beginning: Our Progressivist Inheritance from Herbert Spencer, John Dewey, and Jean Piaget*. New Haven, CT: Yale University Press.

Gibbons, (2007) Philosophers as children: Playing with style in the philosophy of education. *Educational Philosophy and Theory*, *39*(5), 506–18.

Gregory, M. and Granger, D. (2012) Introduction: John Dewey on philosophy and childhood. *Education and Culture*, *28*(2), 1–25.

Hand, M. and Winstanley, C. (eds) (2008) *Philosophy in Schools*. New York: Continuum.

Haynes, J. (2007) *Listening as a Critical Practice: Learning Through Philosophy with Children*. PhD thesis, University of Exeter.

Haynes, J. (2008) *Children as Philosophers: Learning through Enquiry and Dialogue in the Primary School*, 2nd edn. London: Routledge.

Haynes, J. and Murris, K. (2009a) The wrong message: Risk, censorship and the struggle for democracy in the primary school. *Thinking*, *19*(1), 2–12.

Haynes, J. and Murris, K. (2009b) Opening the space for children's thinking. *Farhang, Journal of the Institute for Humanities and Cultural Studies, Tehran, Iran. Special Edition on Philosophy for Children*, *22*(69), 175–88, published in English and Farsi.

Haynes, J. and Murris, K. (2011) The provocation of an epistemological shift in teacher education through philosophy with children. *Journal of Philosophy of Education*, *45*(2), 285–303.

Haynes, J. and Murris, K. (2012) *Picturebooks, Pedagogy and Philosophy*. New York and London: Routledge.

Haynes, J. and Murris, K. (2013) The realm of meaning: Imagination, narrative and playfulness in philosophical exploration with young children. *Early Child Development and Care*, *183*(8), 1084–100.

ICPIC (2013) The 16th International Conference of International Council of Philosophical Inquiry with Children held at University of Cape Town, South Africa (August).

Irigeray, L. (1996) *i love to you: Sketch for a Felicity Within History* (trans. A. Martin). New York and London: Routledge.

Kennedy, D. (2006) *The Well of Being: Childhood, Subjectivity and Education*. State University of New York Press.

Kennedy, D. and Kohan, W. (2008) Aión, Kairós and Chrónos: Fragments of an endless conversation on childhood, philosophy and education. *Childhood & Philosophy*, Rio de Janeiro, 4(8), July. Available at: www.periodicos.proped.pro.br/index.php?journal=childhood&page=index.

Kohan, W. (2002) Education, philosophy and childhood: The need to think an encounter. *Thinking*, 16(1), 4–11.

Kitchener, R. (1990) Do children think philosophically? *Metaphilosophy*, 21(4), 427–38.

Lipman, M. (1991) *Thinking in Education*. Cambridge, MA: Cambridge University Press.

Lipman, M. (ed.) (1993) *Thinking, Children and Education*. Duboque, Iowa: Kendall/Hunt.

Lipman, M., Sharp, A. M. and Oscanyan, F. S. (1980) *Philosophy in the Classroom*;, 2nd edn. Philadelphia: Temple University Press.

Lyle, S. (2009) Imagination in education: The neglected dimension. The work of Kieran Egan. *Professional Development Today*, 12(3), 52–7.

Masschelein, J. and Simons, M. (2010) The hatred of public schooling: The school as the *mark* of democracy. *Educational Philosophy and Theory*, 42(5–6), 666–82.

Matthews, G. (1980) *Philosophy and the Young Child*. Cambridge, MA: Harvard University Press.

Matthews, G. (1992) *Dialogues with Children*. Cambridge, MA: Harvard University Press.

Matthews, G. (1994) *The Philosophy of Childhood*. Cambridge, MA: Harvard University Press.

Murris, K. (1992) *Teaching Philosophy with Picturebooks*. London: Infonet.

Murris, K. (1999) Philosophy with Preliterate Children. *Thinking*, 14(4), 23–34.

Murris, K. (2000) Can children do philosophy? *Journal of Philosophy of Education*, 34(2), 261–81.

Murris, K. and Haynes, J. (2010) *Storywise: Thinking through Stories*. International e-book version. Johannesburg: Infonet (www.infonet-publications.com).

Rancière, J. (1991) *The Ignorant Schoolmaster: Five Lessons in Emancipation* (trans. and introduction by K. Ross). London: Continuum.

Rancière, J. (2000) Interviewed by S. Guénoun and J. H. Kavanagh in Jacques Rancière: Literature, Politics, Aesthetics: Approaches to Democratic Disagreement by Jacques Rancière, S. Guénoun, J. H. Kavanagh, R. Lapidus. *SubStance*, 92 (29, 2), 3–24.

SAPERE (2006) *P4C Report for the Innovations Unit* (www.sapere.org.uk).

Stanley, S. (2011) *Why Think? Philosophical Play from 3–11*. London: Continuum.

The Transformers: Socrates for Six Year Olds (1990), first broadcast on BBC TV. *Communities of Enquiry*, DVD produced by SAPERE (www.sapere.org.uk).

Vansielghem, N. (2005) Philosophy for children as the wind of thinking. *Journal of Philosophy of Education*, 39(1), 19–37.

Vansieleghem, N. and Kennedy, D. (2011) Introduction: What is philosophy for children, what is philosophy with children – after Matthew Lipman? In N. Vansieleghem and D. Kennedy (eds) *Journal of Philosophy of Education, Special Issue Philosophy for Children in Transition: Problems and Prospects*, 45(2), 171–83.

White, J. (2012) Philosophy in primary schools. *Journal of Philosophy of Education*, 46(3), 449–60.

39

WHAT PRESCHOOL IS LIKE

Children's interviews, photographs, and picture selections from two different contexts

Darlene DeMarie, Jenna McLain, Laura Mockensturm and Colleen Stevenson

Introduction

Research on children's perspectives emerged when the United Nations Convention on the Rights of the Child, Article 12, declared that children had the right to express their views freely and to be heard (UN General Assembly, 1989). Consequently, researchers in Denmark, Iceland, New Zealand, and other countries made a paradigm shift in how children were understood (Einarsdóttir, 2005, 2007, 2010; Einarsdóttir *et al.*, 2009; Formosinho and Araújo, 2006; Peters and Kelly, 2011). According to a rights-based perspective, children are viewed as competent social actors who can express their opinions, views, and experiences (Einarsdóttir, 2010; Formosinho and Araújo, 2006; Harcourt and Einarsdóttir, 2011; Peters and Kelly, 2011).

As noted by Bronfenbrenner (1979), interactions among children and their proximal and distal environments impact development. Children are 'stakeholders' in early childhood education (Einarsdóttir, 2010). Kragh-Müller and Isbell (2011) said in order to promote development and learning, one must understand children's ideas about what represents positive experiences in school. Thus, it is important for teachers to understand children's views of their school experiences.

This chapter focuses on gaining insight into young children's thinking and understanding of their preschool experience. First, a review of the literature on several creative methods for capturing children's perspectives will be described. Next, we provide an overview of the present study, which incorporated three of these methods in order to provide a richer depiction of the children's views of their preschool. Through interview, autophotography (children take photographs to answer a question; see Ziller, 1990), and a picture selection task, children aged 3 to 6 years old from a rural area in Ohio and an urban area in Florida shared what they thought was important and representative of their preschool. Several differences from previous research, and why these and other differences occurred, are explored in this chapter. Finally, we hope to convey the importance of this research to educators as they strive to provide high-quality education for young children. Incorporating methods such as autophotography could provide them with a valuable tool for better understanding young children's thinking.

Methods for learning children's perspectives

Previous research demonstrated that children were capable of communicating their views when developmentally appropriate questions and methods were employed (Armstrong and Sugawara, 1989; Einarsdóttir, 2007, Formosinho and Araújo, 2006). Research in early childhood includes many different ways of acquiring and understanding children's perspectives (Einarsdóttir *et al.*, 2009; Peters and Kelly, 2011; Smith *et al.*, 2005). Three commonly employed methods are interviews, drawings, and photography. Other methods include picture selection (DeMarie, 2010; Smith *et al.*, 2005; Stephenson, 2009), questionnaires (Kershner and Pointon, 2000), puppet selection (Measelle *et al.*, 1998) and digital recording (Makin and Whiteman, 2006; Mantei and Kervin, 2010). Clark and others (e.g. Clark, 2005; Clark and Moss, 2001) developed the Mosaic approach, a method that uses a variety of methods to piece together children's individual as well as their collective understanding. Other researchers also typically include two or more methods, and doing so enhances what they learn (Einarsdóttir, 2005, 2009, 2010) about children's thinking. We will elaborate on the use of three of these methods: interviews, drawings, and photographs.

Interviews

When children are interviewed individually or in small group, adults hear their voice. Armstrong and Sugawara (1989) found that children's answers usually were understandable, appropriate, quick, and precise. However, there are several limitations of using interviews exclusively for data collection with young children. First, the findings may be filtered to align with the researcher's own perspective (Einarsdóttir *et al.*, 2009; Peters and Kelly, 2011; Smith *et al.*, 2005). Second, when researchers interview groups of children, the voices of the most vocal children may dominate the conversation (Einarsdóttir, 2010). Finally, very young children may not be able to articulate their thoughts fully in interviews alone. Drawings and photographs can be used as tools that help to scaffold children's communication (Bruner and Haste, 2010).

Drawings and photographs

There is agreement that the use of drawing and photography captures high levels of children's interest (Einarsdóttir *et al.*, 2009; Smith *et al.*, 2005). Einarsdóttir *et al.* (2009) found that drawings provided children with familiar contexts for engagement and allowed them to have more control. This meant that there was a more balanced relationship among researchers, teachers, and children, which allowed children additional avenues for conveying their thoughts. Drawing and talking allow children to construct and to convey meaning (Einarsdóttir *et al.*, 2009).

Many studies in educational research employ photography in the form of photo-narration (Keat *et al.*, 2009), photo-elicitation (see Harper, 2002), or autophotography (DeMarie and Ethridge, 2006). Photography is empowering because children choose the photographs they take (Ching *et al.*, 2010). Photography allows researchers to understand what children think is important (DeMarie, 2001; Einarsdóttir, 2005), and it provides an avenue for educators to understand the opinions, preferences, and thinking-processes of children (Kragh-Müller and Isbell, 2011; Sahimi, 2012; Einarsdóttir, 2005). For example, in research by Britsch (2010), Stephenson (2009), and Einarsdóttir (2005) young students led tours of their schools while taking pictures of their favorite places. In whatever way cameras are integrated into educational research, benefits include children's genuine interest in using cameras and in seeing pictures of themselves (Keat *et al.*, 2009).

Using autophotography with children of different ages, DeMarie (2001) captured both quantitative (i.e. number) and qualitative (i.e. type) differences in what children thought was important about a common experience they had. The children, who were aged 3 to 12, lived in rural Ohio and went on a field trip to a zoo that was in an urban location. They took pictures to show other children, who were not able to go to the zoo, what the zoo was like.

When adults think about going to the zoo, they most likely think about seeing animals. This certainly was what children who were 6–8 or 9–12 years old tended to photograph. More than 80 per cent of both of these groups' photographs included animals. However, both of these age groups' photographs differed significantly from the photographs of those aged 3–5. Only 56 per cent of the youngest group's photographs included animals.

In addition to the quantitative differences already noted, further analysis revealed qualitative differences among all three age groups. The children aged 9–12 photographed animals unique to the zoo environment. The children who were aged 6–8 photographed unusual examples of common animals from their home environment (e.g. an extra long green snake). The children aged 3–5 only photographed common examples of animals they already knew from home (e.g. goats) or from preschool (e.g. goldfish). Thus, the photographs captured additional information about what children thought was important about their zoo experience.

Despite all the virtues, several limitations of using photography must be recognized. First, using photography can be very time-consuming. Second, children may not take clear pictures of the objects, people, and places they like. The use of interviews along with photography helps to clarify children's intentions. Although one may wonder whether children's photography could be influenced by others, Sahimi (2012) found this was not the case. When the researcher gave a suggestion of something children might want to photograph, they stated they did not want to do so. Wiltz and Klein (2001) also noted that children did not exaggerate, echo, or conform to statements by their peers.

In the following section, we review research that investigated preschool children's perspectives about their preschool experiences. Many of these studies employed multiple methods of data collection.

Children's perspectives about their preschool experiences

Studies exploring young children's perspectives about their preschool experience often use visual aids to complement the interview procedure, and most report that children are happy with their experiences. Armstrong and Sugawara (1989) used a white board divided into six activity centers commonly represented in child care centers to capture children's perspectives of their experiences in them. The visual helped children to articulate their thoughts and feelings. Armstrong and Sugawara found the large majority of children preferred play activities (76 per cent) and had positive feelings about their center (88 per cent). Summers *et al.* (1991) reported a similar finding when they used the Children's Perception of Teacher Role and Importance Instrument. The instrument consisted of nine questions and a series of drawings to complement the questions. Summers *et al.* found that 92 per cent of children felt happy within their class and with their teachers.

Wiltz and Klein (2001) interviewed children attending four high quality and four low quality child care centers to determine if activities, events, experiences, and procedures were described differently from the children's point of view. The researchers used a combination of methods to gather children's perspectives: classroom observations, field notes, interviews, analytical descriptions, as well as children's drawings and children's conversations. Wiltz and Klein found that children were aware of the procedures and activities at the child care center, and children frequently verbalized this information dependably. They concluded it was important for children to choose and to influence their daily activities. One commonality for children in both high and low quality child care centers was the importance they placed on play. Einarsdóttir's (2005) research also found that play was important part of Icelandic children's preschool experiences.

Several other studies reported that children preferred play to more traditional academic activities (Einarsdóttir 2005; Kragh-Müller and Isbell, 2011; Wiltz and Klein, 2001). For example, in research by Einarsdóttir (2005) children led the researcher on a guided tour of the school while photographing aspects they thought were important, liked best, or where they felt good. The majority of photographs contained the outdoor playground or other children. Specific objects of play (e.g. Lego and computers) were also very popular subjects of photography. Of the 279 pictures, 141 were taken of play areas and playthings, 33 of other children, 23 of children's artwork, and 25 of classroom objects. Only six pictures were taken of the staff.

To see preschool from a child's perspective, Kragh-Müller and Isbell (2011) interviewed and collected drawings from children in the United States and Denmark. The different cultural contexts revealed both similarities and differences among relationships with peers and teachers and children's likes and dislikes about activities. Similarities they noted between the two contexts included unanimous agreement that play was the best thing about child care, the importance of children having influences and choices at child care, and the importance of positive care relationships. Children agreed one of the worst parts of child care was when a teacher was not nice.

Sahimi (2012) further investigated specific aspects of play that children favored. Photography and interview methods helped to compare preschoolers' preference for the outdoor or indoor environments. The study revealed that the children who were 4 years old focused their photography around objects and activities outside, while the children who were aged 5 favored indoor objects and activities for the majority of their pictures. Sahimi concluded that the outdoor environment was important to young children and should be incorporated into their play and learning for richer experiences. However, Sahimi later acknowledged that the proximity of the playground space also differed between the younger and older children, and this alone may have caused the observed differences in the photographs of the play space. Younger children, who were aged 4, had a classroom that was in closer proximity to the playground space than older children, aged 5.

To summarize, research findings revealed that children from different settings, different countries, and children in high or low quality child care all preferred play. Research also noted that children wanted to have influences and choices at preschool (Einarsdóttir, 2005; Kragh–Müller and Isbell, 2011). In Kragh–Müller and Isbell (2011) a comparison was made between children in Denmark and the United States. In Sahimi (2012) a comparison was made between children who were aged 4 and those aged 5. However, in order to make comparisons among groups, it is essential that procedures are standardized, and to the best of our knowledge, neither of these studies included standardized procedures.

In the present study, we employed both quantitative and qualitative methods of data analysis in order to get a fuller picture of children's experiences at preschool. We standardized the interview and photography questions and presented children with a standardized picture selection task. We were able to explore what was similar and what was unique for children who attended preschools in rather diverse contexts. The standardized procedure allowed us to make comparisons of the perspectives of children living in two completely different regions within the United States.

The children in Ohio attended a child care center that was located at a small private college in a rural region of the Midwestern United States. Their classroom was on the second floor of a large building, and they had to walk past two other buildings after leaving their building to get to their playground. The children in Florida attended a center that was located at a large public university in an urban region in the Southeastern United States. It had only one floor, and the play space was in close proximity to the children's classrooms. Although the climate in Florida made going outside year round possible, the climate in Ohio did not. Therefore, we wondered if we would find differences in how much play was represented in what the children said and photographed when showing others what preschool was like. The Ohio preschool classroom was mixed age with children aged 3 to 5 together, and the Florida preschool was separated by younger and older children, much like the classrooms in the Sahimi studies.

Despite large contextual differences, there were many commonalities between the two centers. First, both centers were considered high quality child care centers in their local context according to their Licensing Specialists. Second, until weeks before the study, both centers had long-term teachers who were hired by the universities. It is worth noting that these teachers both left their respective centers only weeks before the data were collected, so both centers had new teachers when children were interviewed. Third, both centers had fewer children per teacher (approximately six to eight children per teacher) than most other child care centers because college students in the early childhood programs completed internships for their early childhood certification within them. Fourth, both centers used a thematic curriculum.

The following questions were explored:

1   Are there commonalities in how children perceive preschool when they attend centers in diverse geographic contexts?
2   What differs in children's perspectives about their preschool experiences that probably is due to the uniqueness of the environment or the topics explored at a particular preschool?

The present study

The 51 children attended either a preschool in rural Ohio (n=20) or a preschool in urban Florida (n=31). All of the children were between the ages of 3 and 6 years. However, all children were together in one classroom in Ohio, but the children were in two separate classrooms (ages 3–4 and 4–5) in the Florida preschool.

Interviews with children

Each child was interviewed individually. The questions included: (1) Tell me about a day at preschool. (2) What is your favorite thing to do at preschool? (3) What does your teacher teach you? (4) What is your favorite thing to learn? (5) What is the most special thing about preschool? (6) Is there anything else you would like to tell me about preschool?

Autophotography

Under the context of making a book about their preschool, children took three photographs to show others what preschool was like. After children took each photograph, they returned to the original interview location to talk about it. As was done in Samuels' research (2004), we began with the general question: 'Tell me about the picture.' Next, they told why they took the picture, and finally, how that picture showed their preschool.

Picture selection

One week later, a different person administered the picture selection task. Each card had a labeled, representative photograph selected by teachers. Similar to the autophotography portion of the study, the picture selection task had minimal verbal demands and was standardized. Our goal was to determine the order in which children selected pictures to represent their preschool experience. Selecting pictures earlier was assumed to mean the picture was a better representation of preschool for children.

The researcher read each of the eight labeled cards and placed the cards on the table within a 4 × 2 card matrix. Children selected which picture they thought best showed what preschool was like. They explained why they selected that picture. This continued until all pictures were selected. Finally, the interviewer returned all photographs to the child and said, 'Now, of all of these, which is most important to you?' followed by, 'Why did you choose that picture?' Children answered two additional questions via picture selections: "Who do you look forward to seeing every day?" and "What do you look forward to doing every day?"

The findings

The findings are organized with sections representing each method employed in the study: interviews, autophotography, and picture selection. In general, both preschool contexts were quite similar quantitatively. However, there were interesting qualitative differences that are reported with quotes from individual children.

Interviews

All interviews were audio-recorded and typed. Individuals reviewed the typed interviews for themes found in previous research at elementary schools (see DeMarie, 2010). Unreported themes were eliminated, and new themes were added. There was consensus about the presence of 44 themes (the non-bold labels in Appendix A). Two independent coders reviewed children's responses to each question and tallied the number of times each theme (e.g. 'Teachers', 'Friends') was mentioned. Next, the non-bold theme statements were added together to obtain the total category percentage (i.e. the bold items in Appendix A). Finally, the percentage of statements for each category was calculated by dividing the total number of tallies for that category by the total number of coded statements in a child's interview, and then multiplying that result by 100.

The five most common themes/categories used for coding children's interviews were:

1 **Total Play category** (20 per cent of all coded statements).
2 **Total Special Activities category** (e.g. Art, Music, etc., the non-bold themes under 'Special Activities' in Appendix A, 12 per cent of all coded statements).
3 **Total Academics category** (11 per cent of all coded statements).
4 **Behavior Management** (12 per cent of all coded statements).
5 **Friends** ($M = 5$ per cent of all coded statements).

The fact that the category of 'Play' was the most commonly coded category was not surprising based on previous research. Analyses of Variance (ANOVAs) were computed on the percentage of statements coded for each of the categories (bold themes in Appendix A) with school as a between-subjects factor. The results of these ANOVAs revealed no statistically significant differences between the two contexts for any category (all $ps > .05$). However, because play was shown to be such an important part of children's day in other studies, we conducted follow-up analyses for each of the themes within the play category (see non-bold themes under the 'Play' category in Appendix A. The children in Florida talked significantly more [F (1, 49) = 5.49, p = .023] about play in general terms (e.g. 'We play'), and the children in Ohio talked significantly more [F (1, 49) = 8.12, p = .006] about the play equipment (e.g. 'You … go to the playground and swing at the playground'). How much children talked about outside games or inside play did not differ significantly between the two contexts (p > .05). Thus, despite the different contexts of these preschools, there were few quantitative differences in what children said when they described their preschool day, their teachers, or their learning at preschool.

Autophotography

Independent coders placed each photograph into one of the nine identified themes. Three of the children in Florida had autophotography data that could not be coded. If the photograph represented two or more themes, each theme received an equal part of the percentage. Of the 137 photographs the three most common themes were:

1) **Objects** (45 per cent of the photographs taken by all of the children). These objects included backpacks and lunch boxes at both places; play dough, crayons, and paper in Florida; and the flag and the new carpet in Ohio.
2) **Friends** (19 per cent of all photographs).
3) **Play** (15 per cent of all photographs).

The percentage of photographs coded into each of the seven other themes for all children was as follows: teachers (6 per cent), children's work (5 per cent), pets (4 per cent), classroom (3 per cent), other inside places (1 per cent), nature (1 per cent), and school building (1 per cent). ANOVAs were computed on the percentage of photographs each child took that were coded into each of the photography themes that were greater than 1 per cent. Each of these ANOVAs was computed on one of the themes with school as a between-subjects factor. There were significant differences by school for two of these themes: children's work, F (1, 46) = 5.23, p = .027; and play F (1, 46) = 9.60, p = .003. None of the children in Ohio took photographs that were coded as 'Children's Work' (0 per cent), but six children (21 per cent) in Florida did. Whereas, only one child (5 per cent) in Ohio took a photograph that represented 'Play', 13 of the children (46 per cent) in Florida did. Thus, the play theme was far more evident in the photographs than in the interviews for children in Florida.

Qualitative analyses

Although there were very few quantitative differences in the prevalence of interview and autophotography categories or themes, the qualitative analysis of what children said and photographed yielded interesting differences. In general, there was more consensus among children in Ohio than there was among children in Florida. The noteworthy topics for interviews and photographs in Ohio were historical facts and traditions, the pets Sammy and Gerby, and the new carpet. The noteworthy topic in Florida was artistic representation, while other topics were quite disparate from child to child.

Ohio preschool

Historical facts, symbols, and traditions common within the region and in the United States seemed to be important to the children in the Ohio context. Some of these were part of the children's preschool routine. Of the 20 children, eight (40 per cent)either mentioned or chose to take a photograph of the American flag. In one instance, the Interviewer said, 'What would you like to take a picture of first?' A child said, 'The American flag.' After taking that picture, he said, 'It's white. It's blue. It's red.' Later, the Interviewer asked, 'Why did you take that picture?' The child said, 'Because it's special.'

The changes in school routine from having a new teacher were noted by the children in Ohio. When asked his favorite things to do at preschool, one child said, 'Gym class and the Pledge of Allegiance, and we haven't been doing it for a while.' Saying the Pledge of Allegiance together had been a daily routine at the beginning of every preschool day when the former teacher was at the Ohio preschool, and the new teacher was not following this routine. When the interviewer asked what other photographs he would have liked to take, this same boy said, 'The American flag.' Another child who did photograph the flag explained the photograph by saying it 'shows America.'

Another example of learning that was common within this preschool in Ohio related to John Glenn, who was a hero for this particular region. In 1962 John Glenn was part of the first space mission with humans from the United States, and he orbited the earth three times. He later was a Senator in the United States' Senate, and he represented the State of Ohio. At the age of 77, he became the oldest person to go into space (see www.jsc.nasa.gov/Bios/htmlbios/glenn-j.html). When the Interviewer asked the children, 'What does your teacher teach you?' a child said, 'She teaches me about John Glenn.'

Sammy and Gerby were the names of pet gerbils in the Ohio preschool, and they were mentioned or photographed by seven of the 20 children (35 per cent). When asked his favorite thing to do at preschool, one boy said, 'Feed Gerby.' Later when asked his favorite thing to learn, he said, 'Feeding Gerby. Yeah, the teachers did teach me to feed Gerby.' Another child said, 'I love Sammy, and I love Gerby,' when she talked about the photograph she had taken. One child when taking the photograph of Sammy said, 'Say cheese, Sammy.'

Three of the children in Ohio (15 per cent) mentioned that they were learning Sign Language. When the interviewer asked, 'What have you learned in preschool this year?' a girl said, 'How you do Twinkle Little Star with your hands when you can't talk.'

Also in the Ohio preschool, four of the 20 children (20 per cent) mentioned the new carpet. This new carpet had a variety of pictures of people with different ethnicities and interests. After photographing the carpet, when answering the question, 'How does that photograph show your preschool?' a boy said, 'Because we got a new carpet and it's for everybody, and we sat on the people that looked like us.' Later, when asked what other pictures he would have liked to take, this same boy said, 'Probably the hockey player on the carpet … Because some kids look like that and they like hockey … That probably does look like me a bit.'

Florida preschool

The only theme consensus in Florida was artistic representation. For example, the top theme mentioned by five of the 31 children (16 per cent) in Florida was play dough. One girl not only talked about play dough in her interview, she also took a photograph of it. When asked to tell about that photograph she said, 'The rollers, there's stuff where we put the play dough to make spaghetti. The hammers bang stuff. They bang the play dough.'

Picture selection

Table 39.1 shows children's picture selection choices for all questions. Their first picture selection choice for 'Which picture best shows what preschool is like?' and 'Which picture shows what is most important to you?' are displayed for each preschool context separately, and for all children combined. It is important to note the

Table 39.1 Percentage of children who selected each picture as the one that "best showed" what their preschool was like or was "most important" to them by preschool

Picture Selection Card Captions	Which picture best shows what preschool is like?			Which picture shows what is most important to you?		
	Ohio	Florida	Total	Ohio	Florida	Total
Teachers	14%***	28%*	24%**	5%	31%*	17%***
Friends	23%*	28%*	26%*	14%**	14%	
Classroom	14%***	0%		9%***	3%	
Children's Work	5%	3%		5%	10%	
Play/Go Outside	9%	7%		23%*	17%***	20%**
Having Fun	18%**	10%***	13%***	14%**	3%	
Reading	9%	3%		9%***	0%	
Circle Time/Listening	9%	21%**		23%*	21%**	22%*

Picture Selection Card Captions	Who do you look forward to seeing every day?		What do you look forward to doing every day?	
	Ohio	Florida	Ohio	Florida
Teachers	**29%	*59%	---	---
Friends	*71%	**41%	---	---
Listening	---	---	**33%	**38%
Having Fun	---	---	*43%	***3%
Doing School Work	---	---	***24%	*59%

*1st Most Prevalent Theme
**2nd Most Prevalent Theme
***3rd Most Prevalent Theme

differences between the two contexts. Far more children in Ohio selected the picture that displayed 'My Classroom' than children in Florida when responding to both questions. More children in Ohio selected the pictures 'Reading' and 'Having Fun' than children in Florida. On the other hand, more children in Florida chose 'Circle Time/Listening to the Teacher' than children in Ohio for the question, 'Which picture best shows what preschool is like?' Florida children also chose the picture 'Teachers' as the aspect of school that was most important to them. However, that picture was not selected in the top three picture selections for Ohio children for that question.

Children did seem to interpret the questions, 'Which picture best shows what preschool is like?' and 'Which picture shows what is most important to you?' differently. In Florida, 35 per cent of the children picked the same picture for both questions, and in Ohio only 18 per cent of children picked the same picture for both questions. Of the children who picked the same picture, children picked 'Teachers' more frequently than other themes. This is not surprising since 'Teachers' was picked the majority of the time for each of the questions separately.

The meaning of the findings in light of previous research

Play was a dominant theme that was evident across all three methods of data collection. Play was the most commonly coded theme within children's interviews. It was the third most commonly coded theme for photographs, and it was the second most commonly selected picture to show what was 'most important' to preschool children. This finding was not surprising. Other researchers (Armstrong and Sugawara, 1989; Einarsdóttir, 2005; 2010; Einarsdóttir *et al.*, 2009; Kragh-Müller and Isbell, 2010; Wiltz and Klein, 2001) have noted the importance of play to children.

Although play was important to children, there were differences uncovered by each method of data collection. The children in Florida took more photographs that were coded into the theme of play than the children in Ohio. Nearly all these photographs were taken of the outdoor play space. One reason for the differences between Ohio and Florida may have been the proximity of the playground to the children's classrooms. Whereas getting to the outdoor play space in Ohio required a long walk, the outdoor play space in Florida was only steps outside the children's classroom. Perhaps for this reason, the children in Ohio equated play with play equipment. Going to play meant traveling to play equipment. We did not find any age differences within each of the two contexts with regards to the representation of play in the children's photographs. Instead, the contextual differences with regard to the proximity of the play space to children's classrooms probably were responsible for the observed differences.

Sahimi (2012) noted differences in children's photography, but these differences were attributed to age. In the discussion of the results Sahimi mentioned that an alternative explanation for these differences might also be attributed to the proximity of the play space to children's classrooms. In that study, the play space was reported to be very close to the younger children's classroom and much farther away from the older children's classroom. Our results support this latter explanation that proximity was responsible for the differences. With autophotography, it appears that children are more likely to capture events, people, and items that are in closer proximity to them.

One surprising difference between our findings and the findings reported in previous research (Einarsdóttir 2005; Kragh-Müller and Isbell, 2011; Wiltz and Klein, 2001) was the value these US children seemed to place on teacher-directed learning. When asked what they looked forward to doing each day, 97 per cent of the Florida children and 57 per cent of the Ohio children chose 'Listening' or 'Doing School Work' instead of 'Having Fun'. The themes 'Reading' and 'Social Science' were dominant themes noted in the interviews. 'Reading' and 'Circle Time/Listening' also were selected as pictures that showed what was most important to 23 per cent of Ohio children and 21 per cent of Florida children. Yet, there still was a discrepancy between the pictures they selected to 'best show' preschool and the picture selected for what was 'most important' to them. Play did have more importance in that latter case.

These findings both support and expand the findings from previous research (Einarsdóttir *et al.*, 2009; Wiltz and Klein, 2001). Children in previous research desired more influence over their preschool lives, but many children in the present study looked forward to 'listening' or 'doing school work'. Perhaps the current emphasis on early acquisition of academic skills in the United States is permeating the preschool culture and changing children's views about what preschool is like. Time will tell whether that emphasis has other long-term effects that were not assessed in the present study.

Conclusion

In conclusion, a child's perspective is challenging to obtain. However, researchers have developed a variety of methods to gather children's thoughts. In the present study interviews, autophotography, and picture selection were employed to understand children's views about their preschool classrooms in two different contexts in the United States, Ohio and Florida. The data revealed that contextual differences (e.g. pets, local historical figures, and forms of artistic representation) influenced what children understood to be important about preschool. The results supported the findings of previous research that used similar methods; children consider play to be the most important part of preschool. In addition, in the present research we found that the types of play differed between the two contexts, and that the proximity of the play space mattered in regards to children's representations of preschool obtained through autophotography. Although children selected the picture of play as being the 'most important' to them, few selected it as the one that 'best showed' what their preschool was like.

It appeared that children were able to give us a look into their authentic ways of thinking and understanding their preschool experiences. Though the task of assessing children's thinking, and understanding their perspectives has been challenging for researchers, these thoughts and opinions are important to know in order to create the best possible environments for stimulating children's learning. It is vital for children to feel safe and free to express their thoughts and creativity and for teachers to give children a voice in their early childhood educational experiences.

Appendix A

Theme Coding Sheet Used for Coding the Interviews for the Ohio and Florida Preschools

1. **Core Academics**
   Math
   Reading/Reading Books/ABCs
   Writing
   Social Studies/Science

2. **Classroom Objects**
   Markers/Pencils
   Books
   Flag
   Carpet
   Other Objects

3. **Special Activities**
   Field Trips
   Movies/ T.V.
   Gym
   Art/Drawing
   Music/Singing
   Computers
   Parties/Celebrations

4. **Play**
   Play (not specific)
   Outside (not specific)
   Outside Games Named (kickball)
   Inside Play with toys or games

5. **School Schedule**
   Schedule
   Centers/Center Time
   Circle Time/Carpet Time/
   Calendar
   Naps/Naptime

6. **Teachers**
   Teachers

7. **Friends**
   Friends

8. **Going Home/Coming to School**
   Going Home/Coming to School

9. **Places at School**
   Places at School

10. **Learn**
    Learn

11. **Fun**
    Fun

12. **Pets/ Animals**
    Pets/Animals

13. **Behavior Management**
    Rules
    Be quiet
    Consequences for Misbehavior
    Listen

14. **Implications of Education**
    Graduating
    Going to Kindergarten

15. **Food**
    Breakfast
    Lunch
    Snack

16. **Stuff**
    Stuff

17. **Positive Affect (Like)**
    Positive Affect (Like)

18. **Negative Affect (Dislike)**
    Negative Affect (Dislike)

19. **No Response/ I don't know**
    No Response/ I don't know

References

Armstrong, J. and Sugawara, A. I. (1989) Children's perceptions of their child care experiences. *Early Childhood Development and Care*, *49*, 1–15. doi: 10.1080/0300443890480101.

Britsch, S. (2010) Photo-booklets for English language learning: Incorporating visual communication into early childhood teacher preparation. *Early Childhood Education Journal*, *38*, 171–7. doi: 10.1007/s10643-010-0412-2.

Bronfenbrenner, U. (1979) Contexts of child rearing: Problems and prospects. *American Psychologist*, *34*, 844–50. doi: 10.1037/0003-066X.34.10.844.

Bruner, J. S. and Haste, H. (2010) *Making Sense: The Child's Construction of the World*. New York, NY: Methuen.

Ching, C. C., Wang, X. C., Shih, M. L. and Kedem, Y. (2010) Digital photography and journals in a kindergarten-first-grade classroom: Toward meaningful technology integration in early childhood education. *Early Education and Development*, *17*(3), 37–41. doi: 10.1207/s15566 935eed1703_3.

Clark, A. (2005) Ways of seeing: Using the Mosaic approach to listen to young children's perspectives. In A. Clark., A. T. Kjørholt and P. Moss (eds) *Beyond Listening: Children's Perspectives on Early Childhood Services* (pp. 29–49). Bristol: Policy Press.

Clark, A., and Moss, P. (2001) *Listening to Young Children: The Mosaic Approach*. London: National Children's Bureau for the Joseph Rowntree Foundation.

DeMarie, D. (2001) A trip to the zoo: Children's words and photographs. *Early Childhood Research and Practice 3(1)*. Available at: http://ecrp.uiuc.edu/v3n1/demarie.html.

DeMarie, D. (2010) 'Successful' versus 'unsuccessful' schools through the eyes of children: The use of interviews, autophotography, and picture selection. *Early Childhood Research and Practice*, *12*(2). Available at: http://ecrp.uiuc.edu/v12n2/demarie.html.

DeMarie, D. and Ethridge, E. A. (2006) Children's images of preschool: The power of photography. *Young Children*, *61*(1), 101–4.

Einarsdóttir, J. (2005) We can decide what to play! Children's perception of quality in an Icelandic playschool. *Early Education and Development*, *16*(4), 469–88. doi: 10.1207/s15566935eed1604_7.

Einarsdóttir, J. (2007) Research with children: Methodological and ethical challenges. *European Early Childhood Education Research Journal*, *15*(2), 197–211. doi: 10.1080/13502930701321477.

Einarsdóttir, J. (2010) Children's experiences of the first year of primary school. *European Early Childhood Education Research Journal*, *18*(2), 163–80. doi: 10.1080/13502931003784370.

Einarsdóttir, J., Dockett, S. and Perry, B. (2009) Making meaning: Children's perspectives expressed through drawings. *Early Child Development and Care*, *179*, 217–32. doi: 10.1080/03004430802666999.

Formosinho, J. and Araújo, S. B. (2006) Listening to children as a way to reconstruct knowledge about children: Some methodological implications. *European Early Childhood Education Research Journal*, *14*(1), 21–31. doi: 10.1080/13502930685209781.

Harcourt, D. and Einarsdóttir, J. (2011) Introducing children's perspectives and participation in research. *European Early Childhood Education Research Journal*, *19*, 301–7. doi: 10.1080/1350293X.2011.597962.

Harper, D. (2002) Talking about pictures: A case for photo elicitation. *Visual Studies*, *17*(1), 13–26. doi: 10.1080/14725860220137345.

Keat, J. B., Strickland, M. J. and Marinak, B. A. (2009) Child voice: How immigrant children enlightened their teachers with a camera. *Early Childhood Education Journal*, *37*, 13–21. doi: 10.1007/s10643-009-0324-1.

Kershner, R. and Pointon, P. (2000) Children's views of the primary classroom as an environment for working and learning. *Research in Education*, *64*, 64–77.

Kragh-Müller, G. and Isbell, R. (2011) Children's perspectives on their everyday lives in child care in two cultures: Denmark and the United States. *Early Childhood Education Journal*, *39*, 17–37. doi: 10.1007/s10643-010-0434-9.

Makin, L. and Whiteman, P. (2006) Young children as active participants in the investigation of teaching and learning. *European Early Childhood Education Research Journal*, *14*, 33–41. doi: 10.1080/13502930685209791.

Mantei, J. and Kervin, L. K. (2010) This is me! Empowering children to talk about their learning through digital story. *University of Wollongong*, 1–15. Available at: http://ro.uow.edu.au/edupapers/311/.

Measelle, J. R., Ablow, J. C., Cowan, P. A. and Cowan, C. P. (1998) Assessing young children's views of their academic, social, and emotional lives: An evaluation of the self-perception scales of the Berkeley puppet interview. *Child Development*, *69*, 1556–76. doi: 10.1111/j.1467-8624.1998.tb06177.x.

Peters, S. and Kelly, J. (2011) Exploring children's perspectives: Multiple ways of seeing and knowing the child. *Exploring Children's Perspectives*, *16*(3), 19–30. Available at: http://researchcommons.waikato.ac.nz/handle/10289/6111.

Sahimi, N. N. (2012) Preschool children preferences on their school environment. *Procedia-Social and Behavioral Sciences*, *42*, 55–62. doi: 10.1016/j.sbspro.2012.04.166.

Samuels, J. (2004) Breaking the ethnographer's frames: Reflections on the use of photo-elicitation in understanding Sri Lankan monastic culture. *American Behavioral Scientist*, *47*, 1528–50. doi: 10.1177/0002764204266238.

Smith, A., Duncan, J. and Marshall, K. (2005) Children's perspectives on their learning: exploring methods. *Early Child Development and Care*, *175*(6), 37–41. doi: 10.1080/0300 4430500131270.

Stephenson, A. (2009) Horses in the sandpit: Photography, prolonged involvement and 'stepping back' as strategies for listening to children's voices. *Early Child Development and Care*, *179*(2), 131–41. doi: 10.1080/03004430802667047.

Summers, M., Stroud, J. C., Stroud, J. E. and Heaston, A. (1991) Preschoolers' perceptions of teacher role and importance. *Early Child Development and Care*, *68*, 125–31. doi: 10.1080/0300443910680111.

UN General Assembly (1989) Convention on the Rights of the Child. Available at: www.cirp.org/library/ethics/UN-convention/.

Wiltz, N. and Klein, E. (2001) 'What do you do in child care?' Children's perceptions of high and low quality classrooms. *Early Childhood Research Quarterly*, *16*, 209–36. doi: 10.1016/S0885-2006(01)00099-0.

Ziller, R. C. (1990) *Photographing the Self: Methods for Observing Personal Orientations*. Newbury Park, CA: Sage.

INDEX

Added to a page number 'f' denotes a figure and 't' denotes a table.